Prison and Jail Administration

Practice and Theory

Peter M. Carlson, DPA

Judith Simon Garrett, JD

AN ASPEN PUBLICATION®
Aspen Publishers, Inc.
Gaithersburg, Maryland
1999

This publication is designed to provide accurate and authoritative information in regard to the Subject Matter covered. It is sold with the understanding that the publisher is not engaged in rendering legal, accounting, or other professional service. If legal advice or other expert assistance is required, the service of a competant professional person should be sought. (From a Declaration of Principles jointly adopted by a Committee of the American Bar Association and a Committee of Publishers and Associations.

Library of Congress Cataloging-in-Publication Data

Prison and jail administration: practice and theory / [edited by]
Peter M. Carlson, Judith Simon Garrett.
p. cm.
ISBN 0-8342-0867-9
1. Prisons—United States—History. 2. Prison administration—United States—History.
3. Punishment—United States—History. 4. Prisoners—United States—Social conditions.
5. Correctional personnel—United States. I. Carlson, Peter M. II. Garrett, Judith Simon.
HV9304.P725 1999
365'.973—dc21
98-44904
CIP

Orders: (800) 638-8437
Customer Service (800) 234-1660

About Aspen Publishers • For more than 35 years, Aspen has been a leading professional publisher in a variety of disciplines. Aspen's vast information resources are available in both print and electronic formats. We are committed to providing the highest quality information available in the most appropriate format for our customers. Visit Aspen's Internet site for more information resources, directories, articles, and a searchable version of Aspen's full catalog, including the most recent publications: **http://www.aspenpublishers.com**
Aspen Publishers, Inc. • The hallmark of quality in publishing
Member of the worldwide Wolters Kluwer group.

Editorial Services: Ruth Bloom
Library of Congress Catalog Card Number: 98-44904
ISBN: 0-8342-0867-9

Printed in the United States of America

1 2 3 4 5

For Charlotte and Julian, the lights of my life.
Judith Simon Garrett

To Rhonda, who supports and encourages me through all of my projects.
Peter M. Carlson

Table of Contents

Contributors

Editors

Peter M. Carlson, DPA
Regional Director
Western Region
Federal Bureau of Prisons
Danville, California

Judith Simon Garrett, JD
Executive Assistant
Information, Policy, and Public Affairs Division
Federal Bureau of Prisons
Washington, DC

Judy Anderson, MA
Chief
Institutional Operations
South Carolina Department
of Juvenile Justice
Columbia, South Carolina

Ron Angelone, MA
Director
Virginia Department of Corrections
Richmond, Virginia

Alan Appel, MEd
Director, Inmate Services Division
Philadelphia Prison System
Philadelphia, Pennsylvania

John J. Armstrong, MS
Commissioner
Connecticut Department of Correction
Wethersfield, Connecticut

James Austin, PhD
Executive Vice President
National Council on Crime and
Delinquency
Washington, DC

Herbert Bernsen, MSW
Assistant Director
St. Louis County Department of Justice
Services
St. Louis, Missouri

Jacob Bliek
Director of Operations
Pennsylvania Department of Corrections
Camp Hill, Pennsylvania

Julie A. Carlson
Account Executive
TMP Worldwide
Atlanta, Georgia

John Clark, MD, MPh
Chief Medical Officer
Los Angeles County Sheriff's Department
Los Angeles, California

Michael B. Cooksey, MA
Assistant Director
Federal Bureau of Prisons
Washington, DC

Clair A. Cripe, JD
General Counsel (retired)
Federal Bureau of Prisons
Former Professorial Lecturer
George Washington University
Washington, DC

Julius Debro, DCrim
Associate Dean, Graduate School
University of Washington
Seattle, Washington

John J. DiIulio, Jr., PhD
Professor
Politics and Public Affairs
Princeton University
Princeton, New Jersey

Tom Fewell, MA
Chaplain
Allen Correctional Center
Kinder, Louisiana

Mark S. Fleisher, PhD
Associate Professor of Criminal Justice
  Sciences
Illinois State University
Normal, Illinois

Lorraine Fowler, PhD
Director
Division of Resource and Information
  Management
South Carolina Department of Corrections
Columbia, South Carolina

Jeffrey W. Frazier, CJM
Superintendent
Northern Neck Regional Jail
Warsaw, Virginia

Robert S. George, FAIA
Architect
San Bruno, California

James A. Gondles, Jr.
Executive Director
American Correctional Association
Lanham, Maryland

Angela Gover, PhD cand.
Faculty Research Assistant
Department of Criminology and Criminal
  Justice
University of Maryland
College Park, Maryland

Marie L. Griffin, PhD
Assistant Professor
Administration of Justice
Arizona State University West
Phoenix, Arizona

Kenneth C. Haas, PhD
Professor of Sociology and Criminal Justice
Departments of Sociology and Criminal
  Justice
University of Delaware
Newark, Delaware

John R. Hepburn, PhD
Professor
School of Justice Studies
Arizona State University
Tempe, Arizona

James A. Inciardi, PhD
Director, Center for Drug and Alcohol Studies
Professor, Sociology and Criminal Justice
  Department
University of Delaware
Newark, Delaware

Gilbert L. Ingram, PhD
Criminal Justice Consultant
Adjunct Faculty
Department of Political Science and
  Criminal Justice
University of Southern Alabama
Mobile, Alabama

Michael H. Jaime, MPA
Chief, Labor Relations
California Department of Corrections
Sacramento, California

H. David Jenkins, PhD
Educational Liaison
Maryland Division of Correction
Baltimore, Maryland

Lavinia Johnson, CFP
Training Development Coordinator
Food Service Specialty
Academy for Staff Development
Virginia Department of Corrections
Crocier, Virginia

Sally C. Johnson, MD
Associate Warden, Health Services
Federal Bureau of Prisons
Butner, North Carolina

Harold L. Kahler, MEd
Instructor
Criminal Justice
Community College of Aurora
Aurora, Colorado

J.C. Keeney, MA
Warden
Arizona State Prisons
Phoenix West
Phoenix, Arizona

Ken Kerle, PhD
Managing Editor, *American Jails*
American Jail Association
Hagerstown, Maryland

Gothriel LaFleur, MA
Commissioner
Minnesota Department of Corrections
St. Paul, Minnesota

Robert B. Levinson, PhD
Special Project Manager
American Correctional Association
Lanham, Maryland

Jim Lyons
Assistant to the Warden
Minnesota Correctional Facility—Faribault
Minnesota Department of Corrections
Faribault, Minnesota

Doris MacKenzie, PhD
Professor
Director of Evaluation Research Group
Department of Criminology
  and Criminal Justice
University of Maryland
College Park, Maryland

Jess Maghan, PhD
Director, Center for Research
  in Law and Justice
University of Illinois
Chicago, Illinois

Paul McAlister, DMin
Professor of Theology, Missions,
  and Social Ethics
Minnesota Bible College
Rochester, Minnesota

Duane C. McBride, PhD
Professor and Chair
Behavioral Sciences Department
Administrative Director
Institute for the Prevention of Addictions
Andrews University
Barrien Springs, Michigan
Adjunct Professor
Department of Epidemiology and Public Health
University of Miami School of Medicine
Miami, Florida

Douglas C. McDonald, PhD
Senior Associate
ABT Associates, Inc.
Cambridge, Massachusettes

James A. Meko, MA
Instructor
Criminal Justice
Gannon University
Erie, Pennsylvania

Andora Moss, MSEd
Program Specialist
National Institute of Corrections
U.S. Justice Department
Washington, DC

Richard S. Peterson, MSW
Formerly, Assistant Director for
    Adult Correctional Institutions
Department of Corrections
State of Oregon
Manzanita, Oregon

Beverly Pierce
Associate Warden
Federal Bureau of Prisons
Terminal Island, California

J. Michael Quinlan, JD
Chief Executive Officer
Prison Realty Trust
Washington, DC

Richard H. Rison, DPA
Warden (retired)
Advisory Board Member
Center for Administration of Justice
University of Southern California
Los Angeles, California

James E. Rivers, PhD
Deputy Director
Comprehensive Drug Research Center
University of Miami School of Medicine
Research Associate Professor
Departments of Sociology amd Epidemiology
    and Public Health
University of Miami
Miami, Florida

Thomas P. Roth, MS
Warden
Sheridan Correctional Center
Sheridan, Illinois

Thomas V. Schade, PhD
Associate Professor
School of Justice Studies
Arizona State University
Tempe, Arizona

Steve Schwalb
Assistant Director
Industries, Education and Vocational Training
Federal Bureau of Prisons
Chief Operating Officer
Federal Prison Industries
Washington, DC

David Schwartz, DMin
Religious Services Administrator
Ohio Department of Rehabilitation and
    Correction
Columbus, Ohio

James F. Short, Jr., PhD
Professor Emeritus
Social and Economic Sciences Research Center
Washington State University
Pullman, Washington

Sam S. Souryal, PhD
Professor, Criminal Justice Ethics
The Criminal Justice Center
Sam Houston State University
Huntsville, Texas

Richard L. Stalder, MA
Secretary
Louisiana Department of Public Safety and
    Corrections
Baton Rouge, Louisiana

Louis Stender
Warden
Minnesota Correctional Facility—Faribault
Minnesota Department of Corrections
Faribault, Minnesota

Ernest A. Stepp
Warden
Federal Bureau of Prisons
Federal Correctional Complex
Coleman, Florida

Ronald J. Stupak, PhD
Principal and Executive Vice President
EMCO Group, LLC
Potomac, Maryland

Gaylene J. Styve, PhD cand.
Research Assistant
Department of Criminology and Criminal
　Justice
University of Maryland
College Park, Maryland

Anthony P. Travisono, MSW
Executive Director Emeritus
American Correctional Association
Lanham, Maryland
Instructor
Graduate Extension Education Program
Salve Regina University
Newport, Rhode Island

Tessa Unwin
Public Affairs Liaison
Ohio Department of Rehabilitation and
　Correction
Columbus, Ohio

Ashbel T. Wall, II, JD
Assistant Director of Administration
Rhode Island Department of Corrections
Cranston, Rhode Island

Arthur Wallenstein, MA
Director
Department of Adult Detention
King County
Seattle, Washington

David A. Ward, PhD
Professor
Department of Sociology
University of Minnesota
Minneapolis, Minnesota

Reginald A. Wilkinson, MA
Director
Ohio Department of Rehabilitation and
　Correction
Columbus, Ohio

Robert L. Wright, MA
Formerly, Superintendent
Callam Bay Corrections Center
Callam Bay, Oregon

Foreword

Prison and Jail Administration is more than its title implies. A wealth of information and a variety of perspectives and analytic strategies inform readers of important issues currently facing criminal justice—and, therefore, the entire society: the history of incarceration and of punishment, correctional models in the United States; prison and jail diversity and governance; functional organizational, management, and staff issues; special categories of inmates and programs designed for them; common (and not so common) emergencies and their handling; and a variety of legal and social issues related to correctional philosophy and practice. It is, overall, an impressive achievement, and it could not be more timely.

This country appears to regard incarceration as the most convenient answer for forms of objectionable conduct that many other countries treat in ways short of removing offenders from the community. Studies suggest that we have the highest rate of imprisonment of any modern nation, including those with far less democratic governments. By one estimate, about 3% of all adult residents in the U.S. are incarcerated in jails or prisons, or on some form of supervision by the criminal justice system.

This being the case, it is important that all citizens understand what goes on in prisons and jails, and that their operations meet high standards of professionalism, efficiency, and effectiveness. It is especially important that criminal justice students and corrections staff be in-

formed as to how best to achieve these objectives. The hands-on experience and the research that underlies and guides the contributing authors of this book is an essential tool toward that end.

Issues that on the surface appear to be straightforward and mundane often turn out to be critical to the efficient, safe, and humane administration of correctional institutions. Issues that appear complex and troublesome, tempting some administrators to ignore them or to suppress their expression, may in fact be critical to our democratic way of life. The fact that nearly all of those who are incarcerated in even the most secure institutions will one day return to the communities from which they came, or in other communities throughout the land is a compelling reason—and there are many other reasons—for doing all we can to ensure that they will be equipped to function in the larger society, and that they will want to do so in a productive, law abiding manner.

Despite declining crime rates in most areas of the country, incarceration rates continue to be high and to add to the burden of already overcrowded correctional institutions. The corrections community has demonstrated its willingness to entertain new ideas and programs oriented toward breaking the cycles of poverty, crime, and imprisonment, especially among African-American and Hispanic populations in the United States, and the revolving door between poverty stricken communities and prison. These programs require careful assessment and evaluation, and readers will find evidence of some of this research in these pages. There are criminal justice issues of importance other than those addressed in this book, to be sure, but those that are addressed here will continue to be of vital importance in the forseeable future.

Whether we should continue to incarcerate so many of our citizens is one of those other issues. In all likelihood, however, there will always be a need to remove some offenders from participation in civil society. In any case, correctional institutions and personnel must cope with the many problems discussed in this volume. They will need all the help they can get.

Contributors to this book, and especially co-editors Peter M. Carlson and Judith Simon Garrett—who authored several chapters between them and coordinated the entire enterprise—are to be congratulated for a signal achievement.

James F. Short, Jr., PhD
Professor Emeritus
Social and Economic Sciences
Research Center
Washington State University
Pullman, Washington

Acknowledgments

The two of us have many to thank for their exceptional assistance as we took on this major project. This text has to be the granddaddy of contributed books, or at least it seems so from our limited perspective. The tasks of identifying authors and then coordinating their efforts have been monumental and we truly appreciate those associates who have helped us in this endeavor.

The outstanding professionals who have been invited to author these chapters deserve high honors for their work. These individuals are experts in the field of correctional administration and have taken critical time from their schedules to write about a subject that means a great deal to them. These individuals believe passionately in their work and have expressed themselves well in these chapters. They have had to put up with tight time lines and requests for immediate action that have taxed their good will and over-extended schedules. We are in their debt.

Both editors would like to thank Barbara Priest of Aspen Publishers for her excellent skill in correcting this lengthy document and for her upbeat perspective on the text.

Our families deserve kudos and sincere appreciation for putting up with the many hours we grumpily spent on manuscripts. Both of us have developed a computer pallor that will rival that of any author or editor in the business! Thanks to Rhonda, Ed, and Charlotte for their good humor and encouragement.

PART I

History of Confinement

Reviewing the evolution of punishment in the United States is an important prelude to understanding today's jail and prison institutions. As the great philosopher George Santayana stated, "Those who do not remember the past are condemned to repeat it." Correctional philosophies and operations tend to be created, utilized, and discarded after a period of time, and then resurrected, reutilized, and eventually again dropped from the repertoire of programs, functions, and attitudes. Knowing the history of corrections in the United States can help people understand these cycles.

Part I gives a brief overview of the history of societal sanctions and American institutions of punishment. Punishment has been part of human cultures throughout time; sanctions for negative behavior evolved as early social groups attempted to control their members.

All societies have justified their desire to sanction those who transgress the law or social mores. In the United States, correctional systems have embraced four primary goals: deterrence, incapacitation, retribution, and rehabilitation. Deterrence is intended to convince a violator not to reoffend and to deter others from offending (e.g., giving a harsh sentence to a tax violator so all others are reminded of the punishment for not paying one's taxes). Incapacitation helps ensure that a convicted individual is not able to reoffend (e.g., locking up rapists so they cannot harm other victims). Retribution, simply, is defined as

punishment and is often referred to as "just desserts." Finally, rehabilitation refers to the intent to habilitate or "repair" one who has violated the law.

In American correctional history, the theme of punishment, or retribution, may be found in all applications of judicial sanctions. Those who have violated the public order may be sentenced for the stated purpose of rehabilitation, for example, but the underlying goal is the punishment of the offender by the state on behalf of those who were victimized.

The attempt to control unacceptable conduct stems from Western civilization's belief that crime is a voluntary act. If criminal behavior is purposefully chosen, then it follows that the threat of punishment should deter those who consider such illegal conduct.

In the past, perpetrators of illegal acts often withstood varied physical and mental atrocities as punishment from individuals. As Western societies began to move away from the individual imposition of corporal punishment steeped in the desire for personal revenge, they began to impose punishments officially, on behalf of the community.

It is extremely important to view the range of sanctions used in twentieth-century America in the context of this historical panorama of punishment. Many forces have shaped contemporary corrections: religion, economics, and politics all interact to create tremendous forces of change that impinge upon those who are pretrial, those who have been sanctioned, and those who are responsible for accused and convicted offenders. These powerful forces affect the American judicial system every day.

Depending upon the attitudes of community leaders, the degree of enlightenment of correctional action has varied. Within the short span of 300 years in American history, court-sanctioned punishments have ranged all the way from bloody corporal discipline to mere fines or community service. While physical retribution is not condoned in modern society, capital punishment is becoming more and more common.

Imprisonment is a relatively new form of societal punishment. Earlier societies in Europe and the United States did not value human worth to the point of wishing to salvage the individual, and most simply could not afford to imprison large numbers of their citizens. Yet today, confinement is the most common sentence administered by courts. Part I highlights the history of confinement in the prisons and jails of the United States.

LEARNING OBJECTIVES

After studying this section, you should be able to answer the following questions:

1. What social forces and desires shaped the early history of punishment in the United States?
2. What role did religion play in the development of punishment?
3. How did religion impact early jails and prisons in America?
4. In what sense did economics change early correctional facilities?
5. What were the common forms of corporal punishment in early American history?
6. How did the reformatory era affect the history of punishment?
7. What have been the primary goals of corrections? How have they changed?
8. What is the medical model of imprisonment? Why is it significant?
9. What are the four primary goals of correctional sanctions?

DISCUSSION/REVIEW QUESTIONS

1. Why has the concept of punishment become such a major force in the American administration of justice?
2. What philosophy of sanctions for deviant behavior was taken from early England as American colonies were established?
3. What is the primary type of punishment utilized by American courts today?
4. What are the differences between the Pennsylvania and Auburn systems of confinement?
5. How has economics shaped penal operations in the United States?
6. How has politics impacted the operations of prison and jail facilities over the years in the United States?
7. How has prison and jail architecture changed in the last 50 years?
8. Do you believe the medical model of institution programming is valid?
9. What is the philosophy behind the development of the correctional institution?

CHAPTER 1

The Legacy of Punishment

Peter M. Carlson

Our American society believes in punishment. The concept of "just desserts" has its roots in the early history of the original colonies, and before that in British jurisprudence. When an individual violates another individual's person or property, Americans believe a penalty must be exacted.

When people band together as friends, families, societies, or nations, social rules are developed and applied to all members. This system requires submission to the accepted mores, and, in turn, demands a sanction if a person does not comply with expectations. Nonobedience has a price—punishment.

Punishment is defined by the *Pocket Oxford Dictionary* as the infliction of a penalty: "loss or suffering."[1] In our social world, punishment has a long history.[2] Various types of physical and mental castigation date back to the origins of mankind. As cultures have evolved, so have their preferred forms of punishment. The evolution of punishment has intertwined with that of religion and other forces.

Prisons and jails play a big part in punishment today; short of capital punishment, confinement is the most serious sanction utilized by American courts. Imprisonment as punishment is a concept that developed in the United States and

has subsequently been adopted throughout the world. The rate of incarceration in America (427 per 100,000 people, as of 1996) is believed to be the highest in the world, assuming that the reported statistics from other countries are credible. The nation's federal and state prison inmate population, as of 1997, stood at 1.2 million—nearly a 50 percent increase since 1990.[3] Furthermore, the U.S. criminal courts are heavy-handed; U.S. prisoners serve longer sentences than prisoners in other countries do.

SANCTIONS OF THE PAST

Jails and prisons were not always the linchpin of the administration of justice. Colonial America borrowed its judicial practices from England, where houses of confinement, or gaols, were used for short-term detention of law violators awaiting trial. In early England, confinement would have been considered too easy a punishment; the Anglo-Saxons sought revenge. Felons were killed, tortured, banished, transported away from their homeland, and publicly humiliated. Corporal punishment was widely imposed, and the sanctions were extremely severe. Offenders were buried alive, beheaded, drowned, burned at the stake, boiled, stoned, and otherwise mutilated in every imaginable way. All punishment was public, and even minor sanctions such as placement in the pillory were conducted in front of amused crowds. These sanctions were greatly valued and have contrib-

Opinions expressed in this chapter are those of the author and do not necessarily represent the opinions of the Federal Bureau of Prisons or the U.S. Department of Justice.

3

uted to the seeming bloodthirsty nature of revenge and retribution. Justice certainly has evolved, yet the American sense of justice remains rooted in the physical and aggressive punishments of early England. Americans seem to believe that punishment should have a significant impact upon an offender.

As mentioned above, houses of detention were originally used only to hold pretrial detainees. In the sixteenth century, the Church of England began to use the bishop's facility at St. Bridget's Well for confining and beating misdemeanants for crimes such as prostitution and begging. Such institutions became commonplace and were referred to as "bridewells."[4] As these facilities spread, they rapidly deteriorated and became known as "houses of darkness" because of the conditions of confinement. These British gaols were filthy, without natural light, and disease ridden. The English prison reformer John Howard noted that more prisoners died of sickness and disease than were executed by the very common practice of hanging.[5] Men and women, juveniles and adults, murderers and petty thieves, were all confined together in these houses of pestilence.

British justice often deported criminals from their homeland as punishment. Hundreds of thousands of lawbreakers were shipped to the American colonies, and later to Australia, where they were forced into servitude for a number of years. This generally involved taking the role of an indentured servant rather than a prisoner. Individuals served up to five years in this capacity. Once released, the former prisoners were often given land for a new start.

These practices were the cornerstone of justice administration in the American colonies. Criminal codes and sanctions were essentially the same, as the American immigrants brought them from England to the new world. Justice demanded harsh penalties, and an extraordinary number of offenses were subject to death, banishment, or various forms of corporal punishment. When jails were used for the detention of pretrial offenders, the conditions were often as bad as those described in the English gaols.

After the American Revolution, the new society began to turn away from many concepts and practices imported from England. As new ideas emerged in the fledgling states, the prison and jail reformers had a major influence on the nature of punishment. In Pennsylvania, the Quakers tried to correct the negative and deleterious aspects of jail conditions. As described in the next chapter, the earliest institutions designed for long-term confinement as punishment (except for the failed Simsbury Mine) evolved from the Walnut Street Jail in Philadelphia, PA.

The Walnut Street Jail and the subsequent Eastern Penitentiary were the earliest penitentiaries in the United States. The Quaker reformers intended this punishing confinement to encourage repentance in the incarcerated. Prisoners were isolated in individual cells. This forced solitude was designed to reform criminals; prayer and interpersonal reflection were believed to correct criminal behavior. Prisoners did not see or speak to each other because it was thought that they would contaminate each other.

This type of confinement was eventually challenged by another prison philosophy that became known as the Auburn model. Developed in the state of New York, the Auburn model also advocated silence but added the idea of congregate work; permitting prisoners to work greatly reduced prison operating costs. Individual cells were much smaller than those in Philadelphia, and the Auburn prison became known for its regime of harsh discipline. This prison design and operating philosophy became the standard for prisons built in the United States for years; several of those built prior to 1870 are still in operation today.

Economical operation, restricted interaction between convicts, congregate work, extreme discipline, and tight control were enduring principles of penal operation and punishment for years. Strict obedience to instructions given by prison employees was demanded, and corporal punishment was used to enforce institutional regulations. Chains, beatings, solitary confinement, and limited food became instruments of punishment and control within the American prison.

Punishment today has evolved from the tyranny of physical and mental abuse to much more civilized sanctions. Public displays of offender humiliation are rare; the conditions of confinement have improved greatly, particularly in the past 10 years; and the death penalty is exercised much less often than it was even one century ago.

TODAY'S SANCTIONS

Economic penalties, probation, and incarceration are the basic punishments used by the current U.S. criminal justice system.

Economic Penalties

Fines are monetary sanctions imposed by courts for offenses ranging from misdemeanor violations such as shoplifting up to and including felony offenses such as arson, murder, and rape. Fines may be the only sanction imposed by the court, or they may be combined with probation, restitution, or confinement. The laws and guidelines that authorize the use of fines vary widely across jurisdictions and tend to be applied very inconsistently.

Research has not confirmed whether fines are an effective punishment. Do they affect criminal behavior? Monetary loss may be insignificant to those with more than adequate resources but may crush individuals who are poor. Some jurisdictions have tried to compensate for this imbalance by using fines that are based on the defendants' offenses as well as their capacity to earn. The "day fine," based on the individual's income and assets, is considered a much more equitable method of assessing monetary sanctions.

McDonald notes that some courts use a two-step process to establish the amount of the fine.[6] Step one is the quantification of the offense for the formula; more serious offenses have higher values. Step two establishes the worth of the convicted defendant based on his or her economic circumstances. Clearly, the short-

fall to such a system lies in the problem of accurately determining the true assets of the offender.

Another monetary punishment is a requirement to make restitution to the victim or the community. Restitution is often required as a partial sanction and can be used as a condition of another punishment such as probation. This sanction involves paying an amount of money to the person damaged by a criminal act or repaying the local community by the performance of services.

Opting for a different economic punishment, many judges require offenders to pay for court costs or to forfeit certain assets that they may have. The owned property that must be forfeited is often associated with the crime. For example, in federal courts it is commonplace for an offender to forfeit an automobile or airplane if the vehicle was associated with criminal activity.

Probation

Over 3 million adults were under state or federal probation supervision in the United States as of the end of 1995.[7] Probation supervision allows the offender to remain in the community with special conditions and accountability requirements. Probation is generally associated with incarceration in the sentencing process; if individuals do not meet all conditions of probation, they have their probation revoked and serve their sentence in prison or jail.

Intensive probation is another form of this community supervision sanction. It is occasionally used when courts consider individuals to be high risk. In general, intensive probation means the supervising probation officer has a smaller caseload and, therefore, is able to spend more time supervising and assisting the offender. This variation of probation also demands more intense reporting requirements and often involves more structured accountability for the probationers' whereabouts and living and working conditions.

Incarceration

Incarceration is a criminal sanction that involves the sentencing of an offender to a term of confinement in a prison or jail. Courts impose this sanction when the offense or the individual's personal characteristics lead a judge to believe that society must be protected from possible further victimization by the criminal.

Today, confinement is the primary punishment of American society. It is almost the only sanction used to punish serious and repeat offenders. The incarceration of a convicted individual, the taking of one's liberty, is what people believe correction is all about. The placement of a criminal behind bars is believed to have the most significant effect on crime.

The evolution of U.S. prisons and jails has followed the shifting social forces at work in the country. Those who have advocated reform of these institutions believe that an individual's social deviance is a problem that can be addressed and corrected. They have argued that correctional institutions must provide a healthy environment and work toward the goal of reforming criminals.[8]

The two opposing forces, one advocating punishment and the other advocating rehabilitation, have driven the many changes that have beset the operation of American penitentiaries. Yet the primary focus of confinement has remained a custodial function. Citizens of the United States have always viewed imprisonment as the punishment of choice.[9] Table 1–1 shows the attitudes of people in different demographic groups about the purpose of sentencing adults.

CONCLUSION

This text examines major aspects of jail and prison operations as the United States nears the twenty-first century. Punishment today—characterized mainly by the incarceration of those who violate laws—is certainly worthy of our study.

NOTES

1. *The Pocket Oxford Dictionary* (Oxford, England: Clarendon Press, 1996), 728.

2. G. Newman, *The Punishment Response* (Albany, NY: Harrow and Heston Publishers, 1985).

3. D. Galhard and A. Beck, *Prisoners in 1997* (Washington, DC: Bureau of Justice Statistics, 1997).

4. H. Allen and C. Simonsen, *Corrections in America: An Introduction*, 8th ed. (New York: Macmillan Publishing Company, 1997), 12.

5. J. Howard, *The State of the Prisons* (Publisher Unknown, 1780), 10.

6. D. McDonald, "Introduction: The Day Fine as a Means of Expanding Judges' Sentencing Options," in *Day Fines in American Courts: The Staten Island and Milwaukee Experiments*, ed. D. McDonald (Washington, DC: U.S. Department of Justice, Office of Justice Programs, 1992).

7. Bureau of Justice Statistics, *Correctional Populations in the United States, 1995*, NCJ-163916 (Washington, DC: U.S. Department of Justice, 1997), Table 3.7, 38.

8. R. Johnson, *Hard Times: Understanding and Reforming the Prison* (Belmont, CA: Wadsworth, Inc., 1987), 19.

9. M. Sherman and G. Hawkins, *Imprisonment in America* (Chicago: The University of Chicago Press, 1981), 86.

Table 1–1   Attitudes toward Most Important Purpose in Sentencing Adults

	Discourage Others from Committing Crime (%)	Separate Offenders from Society (%)	Train, Educate, and Counsel Offenders (%)	Give Offenders the Punishment They Deserve(%)
National	12.4	12.5	19.9	50.8
Sex				
Male	13.3	11.0	20.5	51.2
Female	11.5	13.8	19.4	50.5
Race				
White	13.2	13.6	17.3	51.4
Black	7.5	6.6	29.2	52.8
Hispanic	9.6	9.6	28.8	47.9
Age				
18 to 29 years	10.9	8.6	27.1	48.4
30 to 39 years	13.6	11.8	17.9	55.2
40 to 59 years	13.6	16.8	17.7	47.8
60 years and older	9.2	12.1	18.4	52.9
Education				
College graduate	12.5	20.0	21.8	42.5
Some college	17.2	11.6	19.3	48.1
High school graduate	10.2	9.5	19.1	56.6
Less than high school graduate	4.9	5.8	22.3	62.1
Income				
Over $60,000	12.8	16.6	25.7	42.8
Between $30,000 and $60,000	13.3	12.2	19.1	51.2
Between $15,000 and $29,999	10.9	14.2	15.5	57.3
Less than $15,000	11.9	6.8	25.4	50.8
Community				
Urban	9.7	18.1	14.8	49.7
Suburban	11.7	15.5	21.6	47.3
Small city	13.8	13.8	24.9	43.4
Rural/small town	12.6	8.1	18.6	58.0
Region				
Northeast	14.2	13.6	15.9	49.4
Midwest	8.5	11.0	26.7	48.7
South	11.7	10.9	16.6	57.6
West	15.8	15.4	21.2	44.4
Politics				
Republican	16.7	16.0	13.9	50.7
Democrat	8.9	10.7	23.8	53.7
Independent/other	11.7	12.2	22.6	47.3

Source: Reprinted from *Sourcebook of Criminal Justice Statistics—1996,* p. 153, Bureau of Justice Statistics, U.S. Department of Justice, 1997.

CHAPTER 2

American Corrections: From the Beginning to World War II

Thomas P. Roth

The history of American prisons has always been fascinating to most Americans. During childhood, many of us remember being captivated while watching Spencer Tracy as prisoner Tom Connors in *20,000 Years in Sing Sing* and Jimmy Cagney as Frank Ross in *Each Dawn I Die*. In fact, it's hard to imagine a time when there were no prisons in the United States. The massive fortresslike structures such as Leavenworth, Alcatraz, Joliet, Auburn, San Quentin, and Folsom hold years of history. They are fascinating embodiments of the changing philosophy of prison management.

What purposes have these prisons served over the last 200 years? Why do we confine those who violate our laws? This chapter will help to answer these important questions.

EARLY SANCTIONS

As our country was settled, American colonists tended to view crime as a sinful act, not a social problem.[1] Criminals were viewed as sinners, not as individuals who were led astray by imperfections in society.

Punishments imposed in colonial times resembled those used in England. Early America drew upon English law, and the colonists relied primarily on corporal and capital punishment. Punishments for violators were harsh; because they were enacted publicly, these punishments were also humiliating. Public whippings, brand-ing, the stocks, pillories, mutilations, and hangings were frequently used as visible reminders to the public of the consequences of violating the law.[2] The severity of punishment often depended upon whether the offender was a town resident. Colonists never considered the possibility of rehabilitation; their aim was to frighten the offender into law-abiding behavior. Imprisonment during this period was rare. Jails in America did exist but were primarily intended to detain those awaiting trial or sentencing, or those unable to pay their debts.

In the early 1680s, William Penn (1644–1718) arrived in the colony that would later bear the name Pennsylvania. Penn was the founder of Pennsylvania and the leader of the Quakers. In response to the harsh and humiliating punishment used throughout the colonies, Penn focused on reforming existing criminal sanctions and offered colonists a penal code known as the Great Law. This penal code retained the death penalty solely as punishment for homicide. The Great Law advocated imprisonment, hard labor, and fines, not humiliating and violent punishments.[3] Penn's code combined reform and rehabilitation with the existing philosophy of deterrence.

Following Penn's death in 1718, the Great Law was immediately dismissed. England's Anglican Code was reinstated, and Pennsylvania returned to using harsh corporal and capital penalties.

AMERICA'S FIRST PRISONS

As a result of early criminal justice reformers and the Quakers' significant influence, in 1790, the Pennsylvania legislature declared a wing of the Walnut Street Jail a penitentiary where convicted felons would be confined as punishment.

The Walnut Street Jail in Philadelphia was the first penitentiary in America. At that time, a penitentiary was a prison where the incarcerated were given the opportunity to repent for extended periods of time. There was an earlier attempt to develop a prison facility in an abandoned copper mine in Simsbury, CT, but this 1773 effort eventually failed because of chaos—management disorganization and institution riots. This poorly conceived underground penal facility, known as Newgate, was closed in the 1820s.[4]

The Walnut Street Jail enjoyed a popular following because of its humanitarian approach. It was heavily influenced by Dr. Benjamin Rush, who advocated single celling and the manufacturing of goods by prisoners to reduce operational costs. Rush believed that imprisonment could do more than just deter criminals; he believed that imprisonment could help control crime, protect society, and reform those imprisoned.

Helped by one of the first known prison societies, the Philadelphia Society for Alleviating the Miseries of Public Prisons, this jail introduced penal reform. The Society was active in establishing the jail as a state prison and, in effect, centralized certain aspects of political power. The advantages of being a state facility included consistent funding, and better leadership from appointed officials.[5] The jail eventually experienced problems such as overcrowding, prisoner idleness, limited control by institution staff over prisoners, and physical plant concerns. As a result, frequent disturbances and violence led to excessive staff turnover and the eventual closing of America's first penitentiary in 1835.

As losoph was co alternati work, sin portant lir rections in York State i ing the New and soon Kei New Hampshir ginia followed

10

.........tts, ...ont, and Virginia

AMERICAN PRISON PHILOSOPHY: PENNSYLVANIA VERSUS AUBURN SYSTEMS

In the 1820s, two prison models came to the forefront in the United States: the Pennsylvania system and the Auburn system.

The Auburn system, better known as the congregate system, was a harsh program where inmates were kept in solitary confinement during the evenings but worked together during the day. Throughout all activities, inmates were expected to maintain total silence. This program was implemented at New York State prisons at Auburn and Ossining, better known as Sing Sing.

Captain Elam Lynds was the disciplinarian who developed the Auburn system. He believed that all inmates should be treated equally, and he used a highly regimented schedule of inmate activities, including lockstep marching and extremely strict prison discipline. Inmates were dressed alike in black and white striped uniforms, worked and prayed during the day, received no visitors, could not send or receive mail, and, for those who could read, read only the Bible. Advocates of the Auburn system believed that the strict routine would transform violators into law-abiding citizens. Through hard work, isolation, religious instruction, penitence, and prison discipline, the offenders would change their ways and become productive members of society. This system was well received; it was cost-effective because of the inmates' work,

...rm order and control in the ...ting.

...nsylvania system was another model ...n management that was introduced in the ...20s. This model was initially established in Pittsburgh and later spread to Philadelphia.

In Pennsylvania's penal operations, proponents of the "silent system" advocated total silence and complete separation of each prisoner. Inmates were confined to their cells during their entire imprisonment; they ate, worked, and slept in their small cells. A walled exercise yard was located adjacent to each cell for the prisoner's use twice per day. The Pennsylvania system was based on the belief that prisoner interaction would hinder the reformation process. Rehabilitation was a goal that could be best achieved through isolation, contemplation, silence, and prayer. The pervasive idleness and isolation throughout these prisons in Pittsburgh and Philadelphia led many inmates to have emotional breakdowns. Given these problems and its high cost, the Pennsylvania system lost its wide public acceptance.

With its cost-effective congregate work, the Auburn system eventually emerged as the prison model adopted by most states. While the Auburn system prevailed, the Pennsylvania system's emphasis on reformation still affected the modern philosophy of prison management. This desire to resocialize prisoners, as well as the widespread conclusion that incarceration helped resolve social disorder, propelled the growth of U.S. prisons.

REGIONAL DIFFERENCES

Although the Auburn and Pennsylvania systems were popular, they were not universally accepted. Due to differing economic and social conditions in the South and West, the philosophy of managing inmates varied.

Southerners had no tradition of reliance on states to provide custody for criminals, and southern governments did not build prisons to rehabilitate violators of the law. The Southern economy was based on agriculture, and the plantation infrastructure was supported by slave labor. Southern states built road prisons to use inmate labor. They merged their familiar plantation philosophy with a leased labor program to serve the people of the South and to control those who had broken the law.[6]

As crime escalated in the West, settlers responded by establishing small local jails. As the need for additional space became more urgent, western territories contracted with other states and the federal government to house their prisoners. This concept, at the time, appeared ideal: western states were paying approximately 50 cents per day per prisoner for others to maintain custody of these law violators, and the states avoided the cost of building and maintaining large prisons.[7]

Over time, the western territories developed governments and, eventually, their own penal systems. Generally, the western states copied the design of the New York prisons but embraced a different philosophy: efficient operations and the interests of the state, not rehabilitation, were the focus.

DEVELOPMENT OF REFORMATORIES (1870–1910)

Prisons in the United States began to experience major problems in the mid-1850s. Overcrowding, poor management, and insufficient funding—when combined with the shifting of resources to the Civil War—led to the demise of the original models of prison management. Prison officials found the rule of silence difficult to enforce, and corporal punishment became more excessive and violent. Rehabilitation was overwhelmed by the increased focus on discipline and control, because wardens could not successfully achieve both competing goals. Eventually, the rehabilitation of inmates became secondary, and the custodial concerns of operating a prison became dominant throughout the country.

Despite, or perhaps because of, the wave of prison disturbances, public opinion seemed to favor improving how the government confined its citizens. This situation set the stage for the next attempt at penal reform, but experts still viewed prisons as ideal environments for reformation, not punishment.

To encourage positive change in institutions, the reformatory system was developed. Reformatories were to assist young adult offenders and emphasize educational and vocational programming.

In 1870, leaders in prison management and penology met in Cincinnati, OH, to plan the ideal prison system. This meeting was part of the National Prison Association, later known as the American Correctional Association. Some of the major concerns included corporal punishment, overcrowding, and the current physical conditions of prisons. These experts decided to replace prisons with reformatories.

During this meeting, the ideas and practices of a Scotsman, Captain Alexander Maconochie, and an Irishman, Sir Walter Crofton, were greatly discussed. Their philosophies undergirded the development of reformative rather than punitive services for prisoners in the United States. Maconochie believed that fixed sentences should be eliminated and replaced with a "mark system," in which a prisoner could earn freedom through the earning of marks

for industrial work and conformance with the institution's regulations. Maconochie also implemented a classification system in which an inmate could progress through various stages of increasing responsibility and gradually earn enough marks to qualify for release.[8]

Crofton's prison operational philosophy involved a series of stages of imprisonment, and progression through the stages moved an individual closer to release. The first stage included solitary confinement. After demonstrating positive adjustment, prisoners advanced through intermediate levels of privileges and incentives. In the final stage, prisoners worked within the free community. If prisoners found employment, they were allowed to live in the community under what is now referred to as parole.[9]

Maconochie's and Crofton's attitudes greatly influenced the penologists attending this meeting in Ohio as they conceived their new model of prison. The first reformatory was built in 1876 in Elmira, NY, and became the model most states followed. Zebulon Brockway was the first superintendent, and his remarkable effort with young inmates had a significant effect throughout corrections in the United States.

Sentencing was affected by this new system, and the indeterminate sentence was created. Ju-

---

Change within Prisons Is Slow To Occur

"In our view, the early branding in the public mind—that serious punishment means imprisonment—remains a powerful legacy. . . . If our view of history is correct, then the difficulty (to change punishments) was and remains very great, and past failures to achieve change are easily comprehensible. Except for their ambivalent and intermittent support of capital punishment, Americans have *always* given imprisonment a monopoly over other forms of punishment. It has always been the currency of American criminal justice. To acknowledge this is not a counsel of pessimism but of realism. All the traditions of imprisonment must be considered in any efforts to alter it. . . . This solid, balanced foundation goes far in explaining why later generations have found the superstructure so hard to change."

Source: Michael Sherman and Gordon Hawkins. *Imprisonment in America: Choosing the Future* (Chicago: The University of Chicago Press, 1981), 85–86.

dicial sentences were for an unspecified time with a maximum limit, allowing reformatory officials to decide when an inmate was ready to be released. Prisoners were to be released when they had made sufficient progress in education, either academic or vocational. Work performance and conduct played a significant role in the release decision as well. This early possibility of release also contributed the concept of parole to American justice.

While the concept of the reformatory was good, the program was not successful. The best intentions of the reformatory were canceled out by overcrowding, poorly trained staff, and the continuing emphasis on the importance of control of the prison. By 1890, Elmira had two times the number of prisoners it was designed to hold. Though Elmira was intended to house young first-time inmates, repeat offenders made up approximately one-third of the population.

Despite the failure of this model, the reformatory era gave U.S. corrections new models that included individual treatment, indeterminate sentencing, classification, parole, and a focus on education.

THE INDUSTRIAL PERIOD (EARLY 1900s)

As the populations of prisons and reformatories grew, work programs that kept prisoners busy and productive became major assets to institution administrators. The Auburn and reformatory models both had focused on congregate work, and the funds that could be earned with inmate labor were welcomed. Industrial programs, a natural extension of prison maintenance work assignments, offered a structured means of establishing a strong work ethic and trade training while offsetting some of the expense of institution operation. The public understood and generally supported this benefit.

There were several different prison industrial systems that developed during this time period.

• Contract system: Private businesses established industries within the prison by providing raw materials and contracting for the inmate labor.

• Lease system: Inmates were leased to private businesspeople who would transport the inmates to the work site, providing supervision and discipline. This usually included work in agriculture and mining.
• State use system: Products such as license plates, food, furniture, and clothing were manufactured by inmates but distributed only to other state agencies or nonprofit organizations. This system is the most popular today.
• Public works and ways system: Under supervision, prisoners worked outside the prison repairing, constructing, and maintaining public roads and buildings.

During this era, industrial prisons produced a wide range of finished products for military, civilian government, and private consumption. This congregate work led to the elimination of the silent system that was so vital in the initial Pennsylvania and Auburn systems. Industrial operations were and remain widely accepted because they employ inmates productively, lower operational costs, and create positive incentives for inmate management.

Industrial operations were eventually trimmed back as labor organizations began to complain about the competition they faced from inside the walls. As labor organizations became more powerful, and as examples of inmate abuse by the contract and lease systems became known, state and federal laws were enacted to control the use of prison labor. At the federal level, the Hawes-Cooper Act, passed in 1929, determined that prison-made goods would be subject to the laws of any state where the product would be sold. In 1935, the Ashurst-Summers Act was approved and prohibited interstate shipment where state laws did not approve of the interstate transportation of prison-made goods. It was amended in 1940 to fully prohibit the interstate transportation of prison-made goods.

THE PROGRESSIVE ERA

While some prison administrators stressed the industrial philosophy, others continued to pursue rehabilitation. In the attempt to find a system that worked, novel ideas were undertaken across the nation.

Reformers continued to view the ideal prison as an environment that closely replicated the free community. They proposed normalization of the institutional setting, developing programs similar to those available outside. Classification became very important as staff separated inmates by age, aggressivity of behavior, and program needs. Education and vocational training were reemphasized to promote literacy and prepare inmates to compete in the job market after their release.[10] Again, prison staff attempted to structure inmates' time to further the goal of rehabilitation.

TRANSITION AND GROWTH (1930–1945)

Congress created the Federal Bureau of Prisons in 1930, a significant decision that affected corrections in many ways. This new agency, led by Sanford Bates, pursued innovative programs and operations that were eventually adopted by state and local governments. This bureau developed a diagnostic and classification system that required the use of professional personnel, including psychiatrists and psychologists. New institutions were built for all security classifications, including a supermax prison for hard-core gangsters at the United States Penitentiary, Alcatraz Island, CA. Identified by professional classification procedures, the most hardened and dangerous convicts were sent to this remote island prison in the San Francisco Bay.

The Bureau of Prisons sought more humane treatment of prisoners and promulgated better living conditions in clean, well-managed institutions. Professionalism was a new goal established by many state and federal prison administrators.

CONCLUSION

The many and varied philosophies of prison management ebb and flow throughout the history of American penal institutions through World War II. It is clear that U.S. citizens had not clearly decided what was the preeminent purpose for confinement, and as a result, the wardens and superintendents struggled to embrace many responsibilities and roles. As societal views shifted, so did the specific missions emphasized within the justice administration ranks. Without a public mandate, and with little to help direct their efforts, correctional leaders have truly drifted.

NOTES

1. D. Rothman, *The Discovery of the Asylum: Social Order and Disorder in the New Republic* (Boston: Little, Brown and Company, 1990), 17.

2. Rothman, *The Discovery of the Asylum: Social Order and Disorder in the New Republic*.

3. H. Barnes and N. Teeters, *New Horizons in Criminology* (Englewood Cliffs, NJ: Prentice Hall, 1959), 326.

4. A. Durham, "Newgate in Connecticut: Origins and Early Days of an Early American Prison," *Justice Quarterly* 6, no. 1 (1989): 89–92.

5. P. Takagi, *Punishment and Penal Discipline: Essays on the Prison and Prisoners Movement* (San Francisco: Crime and Justice, 1980), 51.

6. B. McKelvey, *American Prisons: A History of Good Intentions* (Montclair, NJ: Patterson Smith Publishing, 1977), 228.

7. J. Conley, "Economics and the Social Reality of Prisons," *Journal of Criminal Justice* 10 (1982): 27.

8. S. Walker, *Popular Justice: A History of American Criminal Justice* (New York: Oxford University Press, 1980), 95.

9. H. Abadinsky, *Probation and Parole: Theory and Practice* (Englewood Cliffs, NJ: Prentice Hall, 1994), 144–146.

10. D. Rothman, *Conscience and Convenience: The Asylum and Its Alternatives in Progressive America* (Boston: Little, Brown and Company, 1980), 123–128.

SUGGESTED READINGS

Brockaway, Z. 1969. *Fifty years of prison service: An autobiography*. Montclair, NJ: Patterson Smith.

Clemons, D. 1940. *The prison community*. Boston: Christopher Press.

DiIulio, Jr., J. 1987. *Governing Prisons: A Contemporary Study of Correctional Management.* New York: The Free Press.

Keve, P. 1991. *Prisons and the American Conscience: A History of U.S. Federal Corrections.* Carbondale, IL: Southern Illinois University Press.

Teeters, N. 1955. *The Cradle of the Penitentiary: The Walnut Street Jail at Philadelphia.* Philadelphia: Temple University.

Toch, H. 1997. *Corrections: A Humanistic Approach.* Guilderland, NY: Harrow and Heston.

CHAPTER 3

American Corrections Since World War II

Anthony P. Travisono

Prisons in the United States have changed radically in the last 50 years. After an extensive and exhaustive war in which Americans fought between December 7, 1941, and August 15, 1945, on both sides of the world, people were eager to reinvent society. At the same time, a few were ready to revise how American prisons operated.

During World War II, the fairly new professional bodies of knowledge in psychiatry, psychology, and social work were used extensively to help treat the men and women who were traumatized by the war. These treatment programs were so successful that the newly appointed wardens, many of whom were military veterans, suggested that these treatment programs would also be helpful to inmates in federal, state, and local systems. In 1945, Garrett Heyns, Director of Corrections of Michigan, served as president of the American Prison Association (APA). In a presidential address entitled "Swords into Plowshares," he stated:

> Now we are in a transition between war and normal peacetime activity. We are beating swords into plowshares but we are not certain that we want those plowshares shaped exactly as they were before. The war found us sidetracking programs, postponing changes, accepting substitutes. Lack of proper personnel, the need of utilizing prison productive capacities, and similar considerations resulted in a less effective attack upon our problems. The time for transition is with us.[1]

President Heyns began the new rallying cry for more sensible and humanitarian programs.

During this transition period, prisoners were seen as individuals with social, intellectual, or emotional deficiencies; it was believed that they should be diagnosed carefully and that their problems should be clinically defined. Programs within the prisons were intended to help inmates return home and assume a productive, law-abiding role in the community. To achieve these goals, authorities believed it was important to require inmate participation in the treatment programs, to continue to humanize institutional living, to improve the educational level of line officers, and to increase the number of professional staff members responsible for treatment and training.

THE MEDICAL MODEL

This "medical model" of treatment was in vogue from the 1950s through the early 1980s. For approximately 35 years, correctional professionals were not only encouraged but also compelled—by public opinion and some legislators of state and federal governments—to adopt the model.

During the years immediately following the war, the medical model gained strength. The three components of the model—diagnosis, evaluation, and treatment—began to affect the everyday lives of staff and inmates.[2] Newly designed diagnostic centers were built in most state systems and within the Federal Bureau of Prisons. To ensure the success of the medical model, proper classification of offenders became important. (Although classification principles were developed in the 1930s, they did not really take hold until the early 1950s.) The designers of classification principles sincerely felt that these principles would become a useful tool in the rehabilitation and restoration process.[3]

Although classification was one of the greatest concepts invented during this period, it became at best a management process rather than a reliable tool to aid in rehabilitation. Classification, continually redefined, has been used extensively by all correctional professionals for the orderly management of institutions and the protection of staff and inmates.

Many leaders embraced this new correctional philosophy, but some wardens and politicians did not accept these novel ideas about "gentle" incarceration. Wardens have always been concerned about the methods of treatment to use regularly with inmates and staff. Up through the 1970s, the warden was considered the last vestige of absolute power within correctional institutions. The warden may have been thought of as a kind, gentle father figure or as a bestial throwback to the feudal period when the rule of law was "follow his law or else."

Wardens and superintendents had a difficult time accepting change. The concept of a department of corrections was just developing, and some wardens not only resented the new medical model but, more important, completely rejected the new control from "state house" agencies such as the board of control, department of social welfare, and department of corrections. In spite of the erosion of their power in the postwar period, wardens had to adapt, or they would face the wrath of the central authority attempting to gain a foothold in the new correctional leadership hierarchy.

STANDARDS DEVELOPMENT

In 1946, the APA published the very first *Manual of Suggested Standards for State Correctional Systems*. Those initial suggested standards drawn by professionals for professionals were not perceived as the forerunners of the accreditation movement, which began in the 1970s, but just as a reasonable way for prisons to be operated by reasonable men and women.

The pressure on administrators to maintain order increased again as prison crowding grew worse. Whenever the system is stressed, there are likely to be disturbances and serious rioting.[4] During the 1950s and early 1960s, major riots took place around the country (in California, Michigan, Pennsylvania, and Rhode Island). Correctional leaders pleaded with legislators to appropriate resources to alleviate the massive crowding, particularly in the most heavily populated states. Following a study by the APA, the correctional leaders concluded that the major deficiencies were lack of proper fiscal resources, enforced idleness (not enough jobs available in industry), continued lack of professional leadership, excessive crowding, appointment of staff by political figures, and, to some degree, improper sentencing practices.

The members of the APA were extremely disillusioned with the ignorance and neglect of the general public regarding prison matters. These professionals felt the out-of-sight, out-of-mind mentality was responsible for the major dilemmas of crowding and severe rioting in prisons across the country. So the APA passed a resolution to call vigorous attention to the results of community neglect and severely criticized what it considered poor television, movies, and radio programs. Media portrayals of prison life often highlighted violence, glamorized criminals, presented staff as corrupt and brutal, and generally presented false perspectives of penal operations.

It also condemned the lack of community supervision of leisure time activities for juveniles. Never before had professionals been so vociferous on these issues. Thus correctional professionals began a long and arduous journey to affect public attitudes and behaviors.

In 1951, APA leaders appointed a committee to reexamine the suggested standards of 1946. Even though these suggested standards were only five years old, the members tried hard to take another look at them. A committee, after reviewing the 15 chapters of the suggested standards, added another 12 chapters to cover new and essential correctional practices. Finally, in 1954, the *Manual of Correctional Standards* was published.

Professional correctional leaders, as represented by the restructured APA, wanted to broaden the scope of the APA from only prisons to the entire correctional system. The newly adopted standards were a significant move in that direction. The word "corrections" was being used more and more by professionals, politicians, and some newspapers, but it was still resisted by the APA because of the strong influence of wardens in the Association. But in 1954, after several years of debate, the Association changed its name from the APA to the American Correctional Association (ACA).[5] The correctional leaders also accepted the new medical model of rehabilitation and showed optimism about the future.

The standards were a new, valuable tool of practitioners. In 1959 and 1966, the ACA produced additional sets of standards. In 1974, the ACA established a separate not-for-profit agency, the Commission on Accreditation for Corrections (CAC), to create and revise measurable standards for all phases of adult and juvenile corrections and to adopt a workable accreditation process whereby correctional agencies could evaluate their progress.

Correctional leaders slowly began to accept the ideas of psychiatrists. Internationally renowned psychiatrist Sigmund Freud's theories on psychoanalytic treatment discussed the potential for "curing" criminal behavior. He almost singlehandedly accounted for the interest in a new approach that would begin to reduce the brutalization of inmates. Correctional leaders also considered the theory that inmates needed to stay in prison until they were cured. This was officially labeled the indeterminate sentencing concept. Along with it came a resurgence of the use of early release and supervision on parole.

Throughout the 1950s and 1960s, each system began to incorporate the new concepts. Laws were changed in most states, and, again, the new leaders used their powers of persuasion to try to recast ideas of rehabilitation.

Many of the new leaders authorized research to attempt to prove that the new programs had merit and reduced recidivism, but the data did not comply. California (which had a major research department within the department of corrections) and several other states spent millions of dollars to research many programs, and research studies during this time did not claim much success.

THE FEDERAL GOVERNMENT OFFERS HELP

Congress created a new federal agency to assist correctional agencies in their efforts to professionalize the field: the Law Enforcement Assistance Administration (LEAA) provided research grants to many colleges and universities to encourage students to enter the field of corrections and to help develop new programs for correctional institutions. However, LEAA offered little significant help. Professionals began to argue that there was never sufficient treatment staff to prove that programs could work, and many state and local systems provided only token acceptance for these programs.

The new medical model carried with it the idea that the public had some responsibility for what happened in criminal justice and corrections. The good intentions of the professional practitioner and the acceptance by the public were helpful for corrections, but, as after the

Civil War and World War I, the increase in crime and the resulting prison crowding thwarted the ideals of the forward-looking correctional leadership.

ARCHITECTURAL PROGRESS

One of the most fascinating aspects of the introduction of the medical model was the concept that new prison architecture had to be adopted. Prisons were supposed to include a school, college courses, an intensified vocational training program, more extensive health care, counseling, and significant work experience (prison industries), and the old-line fortress institution was no longer suitable. Because of the crowding and the new programs, the private architects began to invent a new correctional institution.

The first newly designed campus for a minimum security institution was opened in Vienna, IL, in 1965 by the Illinois Department of Corrections. The design was indeed revolutionary, compared with the institutions that were designed prior to the 1960s. In the new facilities, several prison features had been eliminated: gone was the cell house with five galleries, each holding 50 cells, on either side of the interior cell design; gone was the huge 500-seat dining hall; gone was the mass movement of inmates in a yard.

The old architecture, perhaps appropriate for the early 1900s, was no longer going to meet the needs of the new programs. Old institutions such as the Alcatraz Federal Prison in California, Jackson Prison in Michigan, Stateville Prison in Illinois, Attica Correctional Facility in New York, and other prisons in almost every state were now obsolete. The push to reduce usage of the maximum security institution was again in vogue, as it had been in the 1870s, over 100 years earlier.

THE EARLY 1970s

During the early 1970s, many minimum security institutions were designed and built, but nothing stopped the severe crowding that was taking place once again in the postwar Vietnam era. As time passed and the ideas of the 1960s began to have a positive effect on corrections, the medical model came under serious scrutiny in many systems and, in some, was found wanting. Young Americans had expressed anger at Americans' participation in a war that they considered useless and criminal. College students disrupted college activities. Drugs such as heroin, LSD, and marijuana were increasingly used by adults young and old. They marched on college campuses and in the urban areas, disrupting normal operations. Many of these young people were sentenced to prison; the conservative public was less than sympathetic to these "un-American" activities and wanted to toughen the system against irreverent youth. The words "mollycoddling" and "country club prisons" began to be used by the media, politicians, and the general public to describe some correctional approaches and facilities.[6]

It was becoming increasingly evident that the American youth and their adult sympathizers would question any military or civilian authority. The prison systems became caught up in the debates surrounding society's ability to punish as it had for so many years. Politicians were forced to take a new look at the communities for which they were responsible, especially the civil rights of minorities in the communities. People questioned discriminatory practices and lack of minority staff in prison systems. Prison systems were also being affected by constitutional issues of cruel and unusual punishment. The politicians were silent and refused to carry some of the responsibility, and correctional administrators were left to fend for themselves. Inmates, attorneys, and their friends who sought to destroy the prison system found a new ally in the federal court system. From the mid-1960s through the 1970s, thousands of lawsuits were filed. Because the courts now believed that inmates had complete access to and protection of the courts, inmates began to be treated very differently.

A sleeping giant began to cast a huge shadow over all civil and constitutional issues pertaining

**Comparative Attitudes
of the American Court System**

"It is well established in this circuit and in others, that but for exceptional circumstances, internal matters of a correctional system, such as administration and discipline are the sole concern of the states." *Adams v. Pate* 445 F. 2d 105 (1971)

"Liberty protected by the due process clause may indeed, must to some extent, coexist with legal custody pursuant to conviction. The deprivation of liberty following an adjudication of guilt is partial, not total. A residuum of constitutionally protected rights remained....The view once held that an inmate is a mere slave is now totally rejected....Liberty and custody are not mutually exclusive concepts." *Miller v. Twomey* 407 F. 2d 701 (1973)

to prison operation. This giant was the U.S. Supreme Court and the federal courts throughout the United States.[7] What was commonly called the "hands-off policy" of the federal court rapidly became a strong "hands-on" approach. Civil rights attorneys and inmates began using the courts to bring prison systems into compliance with the U.S. Constitution and the Bill of Rights.

The medical model, never wholly accepted, slowly began to change to a legal model of care. Chaos and confusion reigned during this period, particularly after the infamous riot of the New York State correctional facility in Attica in September 1971. There was no doubt that prison crowding was a major cause of the riot wars all over the country. Prisoners in Attica were able to take control of a major segment of the prison and held many officers hostage as they sought relief

from sordid conditions. It was perhaps the longest standoff and lengthiest negotiations that have ever taken place in correctional history. The state police finally attacked the prison, and a bloodbath ensued. Before the prison was under control, 20 prisoners and 10 correctional officers were killed. After this riot, corrections could never be the same; blame and costs were still being evaluated well into the 1980s.

PRIVATE FAMILY VISITING

Another major program that was to be a core component of the medical model was allowing inmates to be closer to their families. The furlough system and private family visits (conjugal visits) within the correctional institution resulted.

The furlough system caught on rather easily in the late 1960s and lasted through the 1970s and early 1980s. Thousands of inmates were awarded furloughs for educational programs in community colleges and weekends with relatives (particularly for married inmates). Furloughs were also granted to allow prisoners to pursue jobs. These furloughs were unescorted, and the rate of prisoner return without committing further crimes was 95 percent, if not higher. Occasionally, in a given state, an inmate would not return from or commit a crime during a furlough. When this happened, that state would be forced to reexamine and revise its eligibility criteria for furloughs.

The furlough program, which had been developing for 25 years, was seriously compromised and almost abandoned during the 1987 presidential campaign of Governor Michael Dukakis of Massachusetts and Vice President George Bush. One of the men granted several furloughs in Massachusetts was Willie Horton. During his last furlough, he attacked a young couple in Maryland, brutalizing and beating up the man, and raping the woman repeatedly. Vice President Bush saw an opportunity to embarrass Governor Dukakis and discussed what he considered the poor judgment of correctional officials in his campaign literature and television ads. Needless to say, the public was outraged, and legislatures began to cut back or eliminate furlough programs. Within two years, almost all furlough programs were dismantled. This aspect of the medical model had been abandoned due to a political campaign.

On the other hand, a program of family visiting, based upon the idea that spouses and children were vital to the effort to keep families together, began in the late 1970s. In Mississippi, the family visiting program had been in effect for many years. Several states such as California, Connecticut, Minnesota, South Carolina, and Washington adopted the practice of allowing families to have a private visit for 24 or 48 hours, usually in an area separated from the general prison population. For a period of time in the late 1970s, nine states allowed some form of private family visits. But because of conservative correctional administrators and other people who believed sex and private visits should not be a part of a punishment program, the idea never completely took hold.

DEMISE OF THE MEDICAL MODEL

The medical model lasted for a relatively short time in correctional history. It began to influence corrections in the early 1950s, and by the late 1970s, its hold on corrections had practically vanished. Many of the early proponents lost faith in the ability of the model to function properly in a prison setting, and many inmates and staff could not accept the permissive aspects of the model.

A major blow to the medical model was a rather infamous negative report produced in the early 1970s by a researcher studying rehabilitation programs across the country. In 1974, Robert Martinson produced a report about what was commonly called the "nothing works" syndrome.[8] Correctional professionals believed the report was based on erroneous facts regarding the new programs. Considering recidivism a major factor in assessing the success of rehabilitation program, the report attempted to show there

was no significant difference in the recidivism rate for those who were in rehabilitation programs and those who were not. Although correctional professionals were distraught about this study, the report intrigued politicians and the public. There was no doubt that this "nothing works" report helped bring down the evolving rehabilitation programs. All these programs (individual therapy, group therapy, and social work and psychology intervention) were considered "soft" on crime and criminals, and it became difficult to continue to sell these new ideas to a society that was increasingly becoming more punitive.

The medical model was never given an opportunity to function properly in a prison. Many prisons employed one psychiatrist for the entire prison population of sometimes more than 1,000 inmates. Few psychologists were on hand. Occasionally, there were three or four lay counselors in a prison. The test to prove the efficacy of the medical model just was not good enough and when it began to fail, the cynics rallied by saying, "I told you so."

But not all was lost. Treatment programs, or vestiges of them, have continued to be part of corrections in the 1980s and 1990s. Sound educational programs and psychiatric and psychological counseling, including group therapy, continue, but in limited scope. Perhaps the most important program to be enhanced was medical treatment. It has been vastly improved since the 1970s, mostly because the courts have mandated adequate care as a constitutional right afforded to each offender.

CONCLUSION

Prisons, jails, and other correctional environments have gone through many changes since World War II, as has American society in general. As the world outside is remodeled by the American public, our correctional facilities adopt new attitudes and philosophies. But as this period in U.S. correctional history has shown, neither extremely conservative nor extremely liberal approaches work very well.

NOTES

1. American Correctional Association, *The American Prison: From the Beginning...A Pictorial History* (College Park, MD: 1983), 193.

2. T.R. Clear and G.F. Cole, *History of Corrections in America* (Belmont, CA: Wadsworth Publishing Company, 1997), 69.

3. Clear and Cole, *History of Corrections in America,* 243.

4. J.W. Roberts, *Reform & Retribution* (Lanham, MD: American Correctional Association, 1997), 166.

5. A.P. Travisono and M.Q. Hawkes, *Building a Voice: 125 Years of History* (Lanham, MD: American Correctional Association, 1995), 86.

6. H.E. Allen and C.E. Simonsen, *Corrections in America,* 7th ed. (Englewood Cliffs, NJ: Prentice Hall, 1995), 80–81.

7. N. Morris and D.J. Rothman, *The Oxford History of the Prison: The Failure of Reform* (New York: Oxford University Press, 1995), 193.

8. R. Martinson, "What Works? Questions and Answers about Prison Reform," *The Public Interest* 35 (1974): 22–54.

PART II

Governing the Prison

Correctional systems in the United States are a mishmash of different hierarchies, personalities, policies, and jurisdictions. All 50 states, most counties, and many cities have their own correctional system. The federal government has a huge separate system, the Federal Bureau of Prisons. On top of the government-run penal operations, private for-profit correctional companies are rapidly becoming large entities in "the business." U.S. prison and jail systems range in size from the extremely large California Department of Corrections, with 33 huge institutions and over 155,000 inmates, to the North Dakota Department of Corrections and Rehabilitation, with two penal facilities and fewer than 1,000 adult felons. The management organizations that are required to support these operations vary widely.

Running prison and jail facilities is a complex task that requires exceptional skills. To handle the issues critical to the administration of justice, staff need intellect, experience, and the ability to think on their feet during rapidly unfolding events. Directors of agencies, wardens, superintendents, and sheriffs must have the expertise to manage staff. Some may oversee 20 deputies. Others may supervise a correctional staff of over 1,000 officers plus medical, food service, industrial, social service, business, and educational personnel. Penal chief executive officers (CEOs) have complete responsibility for multimillion-dollar budgets, deal with powerful and often challenging unions, and must be ex-tremely responsive to the public, the media, elected officials, and the judiciary. On top of these typical CEO tasks, a warden has the massive responsibility for controlling and safely managing prisoner populations that can range from small numbers in a county jail up to 7,000 inmates in some huge prison structures.

Today's institution leaders face dilemmas both within and outside the facilities. The public mood seems to become more conservative every day. At the same time, elected officials have a growing interest in micromanaging correctional facilities. Inmates seem to grow younger, less respectful of authority, and more violent each year, and the negative influences of gang affiliation expand exponentially. All constituencies demand immediate attention. Correctional leaders have as much job stress as CEOs of Fortune 500 companies.

Even great leaders cannot efficiently manage a correctional system or individual institution if the organizational structure is ineffective. The larger an agency or institution, the larger and more unwieldy the management hierarchy can become. If the hierarchical structure is too large, decision making can be very slow, and innovation may be crushed. Yet stability and consistency in leadership are critical to the organizational culture of any good company, private or public. A correctional agency must have a management structure that is strong enough to impart the necessary oversight and control, while being reasonably flexible and responsive to the many demands upon contemporary institution management.

This section examines the organizational structures typically found in today's correctional facilities, explains the importance of strong management accountability and oversight systems, and offers a challenge to the leaders of correctional agencies. Prison and jail governance requires individuals with exceptional talent. Their ability to lead determines whether prisons and jails will be only mediocre or truly great.

LEARNING OBJECTIVES

After studying this section, you should be able to answer the following questions:

1. What are the differences between a centralized and a decentralized model of correctional institution management?
2. Is it desirable to develop correctional leaders who can cross traditional lines between departments of penal facilities? Is "boundary spanning" good for the operation of a prison or jail?
3. Is managing a correctional facility different from managing a nonpenal business of comparable size in the private sector?
4. What aspects of prison or jail management do successful institution managers focus upon?
5. Should correctional administrators enter public debates about proposed new laws that affect the operation of penal institutions?
6. Do you believe there is a difference between a manager and a leader in the prison and jail environment?
7. How does one ensure that institutional staff are accountable for their actions and in compliance with agency policy when the facility operates 24 hours each day?

DISCUSSION/REVIEW QUESTIONS

1. What would be an example of decentralized prison management? How would it compare with a centralized model?
2. What are the principal goals of corrections, and are they in conflict with one another?
3. How would you define the basics of inmate care and custody?
4. Is performance-based management needed in the correctional environment?
5. Why are written policies and procedures necessary in prisons and jails?
6. What are four methods of ensuring management control (i.e., that staff are following established rules and regulations)?
7. Is there any benefit to outside or third-party review of institutional operations?

CHAPTER 4

The Organization of the Institution

Peter M. Carlson

U.S. prisons and jails are a strange, decentralized collection of systems. The federal government, each state, and most counties and cities operate individual correctional networks. The administration of justice in the United States is truly a potpourri of styles and management structures. Each system tends to operate independently with little or no linkage among agencies, even within a single city. This fragmentation has had a very negative impact on correctional institution management overall.

INSTITUTION OF OVERSIGHT AND EXTERNAL REGULATION

General oversight and control of correctional agencies varies throughout the United States. Some jurisdictions combine penal management with other social service organizations such as law enforcement or mental health departments. Other jurisdictions operate independent agencies ranging from very small city jails up to huge, centralized prison systems. An increasing number of state correctional organizations have evolved into separate departments with the chief executive officer selected by the state's governor. Today, 32 states have separate departments of correction reporting to the governor; 11 as de-

partments reporting to boards or commissions; 5 under a department of public safety umbrella; and 1 under a social services umbrella. Twenty-four of the separate departments have been organized in this manner since 1979.[1]

Clearly, vast differences within the field are created by these separate jurisdictions with different missions, types and amounts of funding, varying numbers of staff in roles as psychologists, counselors, case managers, teachers, etc., and types of inmate populations. But these agencies have one unifying characteristic: They each serve the people by confining individuals who have violated the law.

Criminal behavior is activity in violation of criminal law. Regardless of the indecent, coarse, immoral, or profane nature of an act, it is not a violation of a law unless it is declared one by the criminal laws of that community. The laws that govern conduct are established by the political authority of a specific community: a city, county, state, or federal jurisdiction. Accordingly, laws vary with boundaries, and each community has its own system of justice administration. Because of this one fact, there are many correctional agencies in America, each of which may have a different organizational structure.

This organizational fragmentation has evolved from the English legal system upon which this country was founded. The administration of justice is handled by many separate entities: police, courts, and corrections. Parole is usually directed by yet another distinct system.

Opinions expressed in this chapter are those of the author and do not necessarily represent the opinions of the Federal Bureau of Prisons or the U.S. Department of Justice.

Besides the obvious impediment to open communication created by system fragmentation within justice administration, this separation has greatly hindered each entity in the development of meaningful policy and interagency cooperation. For instance, many institution administration professionals have accepted that they simply have to receive and process what the police, prosecutors, and courts send their direction. And they are correct. The political process often precludes correctional experts from providing any meaningful input to the justice policy setting circles. Correctional professionals, as a result, have become very myopic, often unable to see beyond the boundaries of their own agency.

Correctional organization, or disorganization, in the various U.S. jurisdictions has created a disarray of services and programs. This complicates any concerted effort to systemically improve corrections. It is nearly impossible to shift financial or other resources among federal, state, and local jurisdictions; to establish common goals and coordinated policy; and to share exceptional procedures and programs between institutions in adjoining states or even among facilities within a single county or city. Simply put, agencies operate independently according to the philosophy of their jurisdiction's governing body—the sheriff, mayor, commissioner of corrections, governor, or federal government.

MULTIPLE MISSIONS IN CONFLICT

Prisons and jails are generally expected to accomplish several—often conflicting—goals in dealing with law violators. They are asked to punish, incapacitate, and rehabilitate offenders while at the same time deter others from violating society's rules and regulations. The organization and structure of a penal facility is significantly affected by these different goals; many people consider the conditions necessary to reform or rehabilitate an inmate to conflict with the conditions necessary to punish offenders.

As noted by James Q. Wilson, the critical task of an organization tends to define the actions of personnel. In a penal facility, the critical environmental problem is to maintain order "among numerically superior, temperamentally impulsive, and habitually aggressive inmates. The critical task [becomes] the elaboration and enforcement of rules sufficiently precise, understandable, and inflexible that inmates [will] not acquire the opportunity for independent or collective action."[2(p. 25)]

Wilson argues that the first priority of correctional facilities is to control and account for all inmates. Such organizations are "total institutions," as defined by Erving Goffman.[3] Goffman notes that these facilities exist predominantly to protect the public; custody is the way of life in a prison.

In a democratic society such as the United States, it is expected that institutions of social control will reflect citizens' expectations about what a correctional institution should be. Unfortunately, Americans are conflicted; some want correctional institutions to be harsh and cause suffering, while others want relaxed facilities designed to change antisocial behaviors.

Confronted by these contradictory pressures, correctional administrators often try to walk a fine line between opposing missions. "They are like repertory actors who must balance their performance according to the expectations of a moody and unpredictable public. By and large, they have attempted to resolve this problem by satisfying the more fundamental demands of security by means of concrete action and the demands for increased liberality by means of public statements."[4(p. 470)] But they do try to serve all masters, sometimes by having the parent agency designate different institutions for different purposes.

Criminologist Donald Cressey has said that correctional institutions may be placed on a continuum of organizational structures, ranging from a maximum security, old-line penitentiary surrounded by gun towers to a minimum security, program-oriented, unfenced facility.[5] At one extreme is the highly controlled, custody-oriented prison, and on the opposite end is the relaxed, unstructured institution focused on treatment and rehabilitation. However, most prisons and jails attempt to achieve both custody and resocialization goals.

ORGANIZATIONAL THEORY AND CORRECTIONAL MODELS OF MANAGEMENT

Organizational theory is a means of conceptualizing how authority is distributed within an organization and how it is used to accomplish the agency's mission and goals. A correctional setting's organization is extremely important to staff and inmates. Dwight Waldo said it best: "The welfare, happiness, and very lives of all of us rest in significant measure upon the performance of administrative mechanisms that surround and support us."[6](p. 70) Wilson, attempting to explain how and why bureaucracies work, said: "Organization matters, even in government agencies. The key difference between more and less successful bureaucracies. . .has less to do with finances, client populations or legal arrangements, than with organizational systems."[7](p. 23)

While all public organizations seem impersonal and monolithic, in reality each public entity is a complex mixture of people, personalities, programs, rules, and behaviors. Every organization is composed of people who act individually and collectively and create a culture. While a cursory glance at the staff of a public agency may lead an observer to believe the personnel are uninterested and uncaring functionaries, once one moves into an organization, it becomes apparent that staff members are each unique, with their own pressures and concerns. These individuals are impacted day after day by the organizational structure they work within, so the system of management and control of individual staffers is a key variable in work productivity, morale, and overall agency efficiency.

In the theory and practice of public organization, particularly in correctional administration, efficiency is the point around which everything turns. Many management experts have discussed how best to develop private business or government to produce the most efficient operations. In the early 1930s, business executives James Mooney and Alan Reiley noted important principles of organizational structure.[8] First, they noted the importance of coordination of work through unity of command. In corrections, this refers to the hierarchy of leaders: a single warden, several associate wardens, department heads, first-level supervisors, and line staff members. In this military-like structure, strong executive leadership was the goal, and every staff member would have only one supervisor. Second, Mooney and Reiley emphasized a "scalar principle," describing the vertical structure of an organization. In correctional agencies, this principle refers to the difference of responsibilities between the warden and a food service foreman. Third, they describe a functional principle as the separation among different divisions or departments; this refers to the differences between the role of a nurse in the institution's hospital and that of an electrician in the facility maintenance department, for example. Fourth and finally, these authors point to the relationship between line and staff roles. Line command flows through the direct chain of command, whereas related staff support offices (personnel, financial management) provide advice and assistance to the warden. This set of principles is an effective means of considering how a penal facility can and should be organized.

Within corrections, three different organizational models exist: an authoritarian model, a bureaucratic model, and a participative model.

The authoritarian paradigm is generally identified by the presence of a strong leader, very firm control of the prison environment, and harsh discipline of inmates (or staff) who do not acquiesce to the central authority. This style of institution was most in favor in the United States from colonial days through the mid-twentieth century.[9] This highly centralized style creates a regimented workplace with consistent application of rules for all. But the authoritarian model funnels all decision making to the central power figure, even though some decisions could be better made at a lower level. This model denies all other staff the experience of making decisions and can create an arbitrary and capricious system that may easily become corrupt.

The bureaucratic prototype also revolves around a strict hierarchical system but is not focused on one dominating personality. Organization control flows through the hierarchy with a strict chain of command and a formal process of communication. Rules and regulations for the correctional institution are written and specific. The facility has a clear set of standard operating procedures. People and personalities can change in the bureaucratic structure, but "the joint keeps on runnin'." The practical benefit of this model is that a correctional system or institution is not overly dependent upon one or two people and can easily promote or substitute personnel. Additionally, the policy parameters stressed in this management structure are clear for all parties, and staff can be held accountable if they do not comply with the written expectations. On the negative side, written rules do not guarantee consistent enforcement, and they are not helpful in every situation. Bureaucratic processes are slow to respond to change and do not encourage staff to demonstrate new initiative at any level of the organization.

The participative model of management is much more open and democratic than the first two models. This method allows and is dependent upon staff input about how the organization should be run. In a few experiments, inmates have given feedback as well. The assumption inherent in this model is that agency and correctional goals are more efficiently accomplished when all staff have participated in reaching a consensus on how to proceed. The participative style gives staff an increased sense of ownership in planning and operations, often resulting in better attitudes toward and support of routine events and new initiatives. Unfortunately, formal and open discussions and negotiations—collective participation in institutional operations—can be time-consuming.

The authoritarian and bureaucratic organizational structures are much more prevalent in cor-

rectional administration. These models, unfortunately, do not lend themselves to change; the built-in resistance to new ideas is self-defeating. Yet few successful administrators champion the looseness and lack of structure associated with participatory management.

Many successful agencies have adapted the bureaucratic model to include elements of the participatory style. These correctional leaders decentralize as much of the daily decision making as they can and seek participation from all staff in many avenues. The involvement of mid-level managers and line staff in specific work groups or in overall strategic planning can be extremely beneficial. Staff generally enjoy such activity and, as the individuals closest to the work arena, can make significant contributions. Such forms of representative democracy in the correctional workplace are considered quite effective.

INSTITUTION ORGANIZATIONAL STRUCTURE

As described in our discussion of organizational theory, the prevailing management structure in U.S. correctional facilities is hierarchical, centralized, and paramilitary (see Figure 4–1). The bureaucracy of institution management is very controlling and often inflexible, yet it is the most efficient and functional structure for the coordination and control of hundreds of staff members and thousands of prisoners. The critical and dangerous task of running prisons requires uniformity within each specific facility (fairness and equity—the perception that all inmates receive the same treatment) and precision of control. Prisoners must be closely regulated.

The individual responsible for the crucial, life-and-death responsibilities within the jail and prison is the chief executive officer; the working title of the post varies but is often warden, superintendent, or administrator. This individual is the senior staffer and the one held accountable for all aspects of institution life. The senior administrator establishes policy for the facility and is responsible for personnel, property, programs,

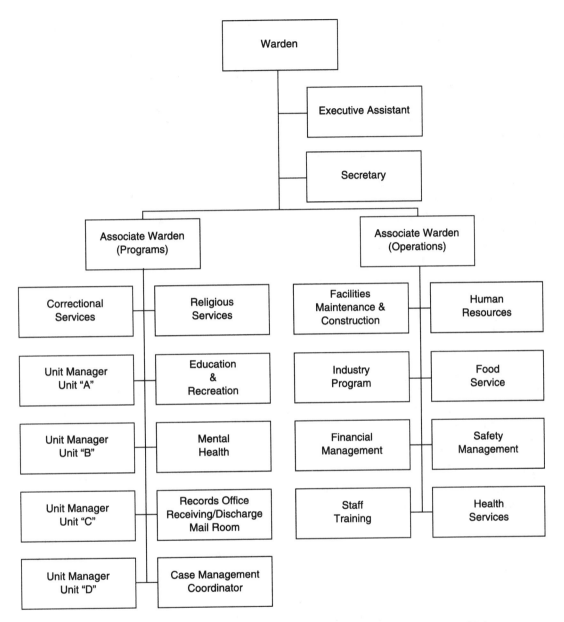

Figure 4–1 A Typical Adult Institution Organization Chart. Courtesy of the Federal Bureau of Prisons.

and activities. This staff member is also charged with handling the external world of the facility: the public, the media, the politicians, and the courts.

The chief executive officer must depend upon his or her senior staff, who serve as division heads within the institution. Several deputy or associate wardens (AWs) usually head the various organizational structures in large-scale institutions and report to the warden. Often, there is one AW who oversees custody, another supervises operations, and a third handles programs.

The custody AW is responsible for all security matters and supervises all correctional officers. The operations AW is accountable for all support services within the facility: food and medical service, facilities maintenance and construction, human resource management, and financial management. The programs AW usually heads classification, unit and case management, religious services, mental health programs, education/recreation, and records office/sentence computation functions. If a prison has a large industrial operation, there may also be an AW responsible for this production area.

Department heads are the next step in this hierarchy. These are generally veteran employees who are experienced in the tasks and skills required within each functional area of the institution. For example, department heads are assigned to areas such as health services, food services, correctional services, or the records office.

Other lower-level supervisors are below the department head. These may include assistant department heads or first-line supervisors. Finally, the line staff of the institution are the individuals who are responsible for the correctional facility on a day-to-day basis. These individuals, for example, correctional officers or case managers, have face-to-face contact with and are directly in charge of the inmates. These are the staff members who "make it happen" and are the heart and soul of the correctional system.

CENTRALIZED VERSUS DECENTRALIZED MANAGEMENT

The warden and AWs have traditionally held the power and accepted the associated responsibility within a prison or jail. The benefit of this authoritarian or bureaucratic style has been noted: Significant decisions within a centralized power structure are made by relatively few individuals, and these decisions are generally consistent and in accordance with the need to operate the penal institution in a safe and secure manner.

The negative aspects of fully centralized management is that department heads and line staff are not empowered and feel little ownership of any aspect of institution operations. Additionally, the very bureaucratic process of referring all decisions to senior staff can add great delays and high-level administrators may not be as familiar with a situation as lower-level staff are. If these decisions are not made locally (i.e., the authority rests in a headquarters office rather than the field facility), these negatives can be greatly magnified.

Decentralized management—the process of dividing and distributing authority and responsibility to administrative subpersonnel—is generally considered to enhance the effectiveness of administrative operations. When decision-making responsibilities are delegated among staff, the recipients of the authority gain greater expertise in and ownership of problems and their solutions.

Critics of decentralized management in the correctional setting believe dispersing authority and responsibility lessens accountability and does not promote consistent decisions. Decentralizing the process is often considered more expensive because the process involves training more staff about key issues.

One of the best examples of the successful decentralization of correctional management is unit management, which can be found in many state and all federal institutions. In this model, classification and inmate management authority is delegated to a team of staff members who work in close association with an assigned number of inmates. These staff members, representatives of case management, education, and psychology departments, have their offices in the inmate living units and are fully responsible for the day-to-day aspects of the inmates' lives. For example, the unit teams classify inmates for security level and custody needs, make work and program assignments, and handle disciplinary matters for their prisoner caseload. The staff members report to a department head, referred to as a unit manager, and are held accountable for the overall operation of the unit and the management of the inmates.

CONCLUSION

Prisons and jails throughout the United States operate under many organizational and management structures—some clearly more effective than others. The more progressive systems have integrated their operations into cohesive parts that work effectively to meet the societal goals of confining inmates and preparing them for their eventual and successful release back to their communities. In these few systems, the courts, corrections, parole, and probation staff seamlessly work with felons and then pass them from one stage of the correctional process to the next in a goal-focused manner.

Unfortunately, most systems do not operate this way. In these situations, the agencies work together as disparate parts and typically are involved with prisoners from their isolated perspective—and then pass felons on with little continuity of care and no ownership in the success, or failure, of the overall process. This is the disorganization that affects many correctional systems and is the biggest weakness in the system of justice administration in the United States.

NOTES

1. C. Riveland, "The Correctional Leader and Public Policy Skills," *Corrections Management Quarterly* 1, no. 3 (1997): 22–25.

2. J. Wilson, *Bureaucracy: What Government Agencies Do and Why They Do It* (New York: Basic Books, Inc., 1989), 25.

3. E. Goffman, *Asylums: Essays on the Social Situation of Mental Patients and Other Inmates* (New York: Doubleday, 1961), 1–124.

4. R. Korn and L. McCorkle, *Criminology and Penology* (New York: Holt, 1959), 470.

5. D. Cressey, "Prison Organizations," in *Handbook of Organizations,* ed. J. March (New York: Rand McNally, 1965).

6. D. Waldo, *The Study of Public Administration* (New York: Doubleday, 1955), 70.

7. Wilson, *Bureaucracy: What Government Agencies Do and Why They Do It,* 23.

8. J. Mooney and A. Reiley, *The Principles of Organization* (New York: Harper and Row, 1939).

9. I. Barak-Glantz, "Toward a Conceptual Scheme of Prison Management Styles," *The Prison Journal,* no. 61 (1986): 42–60.

CHAPTER 5

Leadership and Innovation in Correctional Institutions: New Challenges for Barbed-Wire Bureaucrats and Entrepreneurs

John J. DiIulio, Jr.

In 1987, over a decade ago, Jameson W. Doig and Erwin C. Hargrove broke new intellectual and polemical ground with the publication of their edited volume *Leadership and Innovation: A Biographical Perspective on Entrepreneurs in Government*. In their opening chapter, these authors challenged the conventional wisdom that government agencies in the United States had produced few, if any, remarkable federal, state, or local public executives and managers. Even in the nation's foremost public policy and public administration schools, they lamented, the pervasive and pessimistic message to "society's best potential leaders" was this: If you wish to use "your talents and energies to accomplish challenging tasks, government is not for you."[1]

Doig and Hargrove promoted the opposite message, offering as evidence and for inspiration a dozen highly readable essays covering the consequential careers of as many top-notch public sector officials. The annals of modern public policy and administration, they argued, were replete with examples of government executives and managers, including bureau chiefs, who had built, led, transformed, or sustained some of the most successful complex organizations to be found anywhere. "Entrepreneurs in govern-

ment," as they termed such public sector officials, often led and innovated successfully despite enormous political, legal, budgetary, and other obstacles.

Doig and Hargrove's can-do message about entrepreneurs in government was soon echoed by several more popular books. Most notably, in 1992, David Osborne and Ted Gaebler published *Reinventing Government*, a bestseller proclaiming that public sector executives and managers at all levels of government, and in areas ranging from local education to national defense, had caught the "entrepreneurial spirit."

Likewise, Doig and Hargrove's positive message about the potential for leadership and innovation in government was echoed by several much publicized blue-ribbon reports on the future of public service. For example, in 1989, the National Commission on the Public Service, chaired by Paul A. Volcker, issued *Leadership for America: Rebuilding the Public Service*. In 1993, the National Commission of the State and Local Public Service, chaired by William F. Winter, released *Hard Truths/Tough Choices: An Agenda for State and Local Reform*. Also in 1993, the National Performance Review, led by Vice President Albert Gore, produced *From Red*

Tape to Results: Creating a Government That Works Better and Costs Less.

But while duly respectful of what numerous government executives and managers had accomplished, and while opposed to "bureaucrat bashing" of any kind, neither the Volcker, Winter, and Gore reports, nor the major scholarly analyses that flanked and followed them—nor, in the first instance, Doig and Hargrove themselves—were Pollyannas when it came to presenting the difficulties of public sector leadership and innovation. All three blue-ribbon reports, for example, emphasized the need to reduce or eliminate perverse government personnel rules and inane government procurement regulations, and all three called for the development of more meaningful performance-based management and budgeting within government bureaucracies.

LEADING, INNOVATING, AND STICKING TO THE BASICS

The executives and managers of America's federal, state, and local "barbed-wire bureaucracies" are, for the most part, an extremely talented if largely unheralded lot. As highlighted in *Governing Prisons: A Comparative Study of Correctional Management,* what institution leaders do and how they do it greatly affects the quality of life behind bars, at least as measured by institutional order (rates of events that threaten the physical safety and well-being of inmates and staff), amenities (e.g., cleanliness, food quality), and service (education, drug treatment, and other programs intended to enhance inmates' prospects).[2]

Apart from such seemingly obvious (but, at least among many academic criminologists and sociologists, highly controversial) insights such as the need to organize maximum security facilities mainly around inmate–staff security and safety objectives, there are three basic conclusions about prison and jail administration.

First, other things being equal, correctional institutions work best when administrators stick to the basics of inmate care and custody, as ex-

emplified by wardens who, despite all the competing demands on their time and attention, and whatever pressures they may face (for example, extreme overcrowding), break free of "iron bars of paperwork" and follow the MBWA principle—"management by walking around."

Second, while sticking to the basics, the field's most successful executives and managers do not get stuck in the mud of "how we've always done things." Rather, they are open to both human resource and technical innovations, including such high-tech methods of sticking to the basics as the development (and use!) of computer-assisted management information systems.

Third, prison and jail leaders who last long enough to innovate are almost invariably individuals who, whatever their personality or ideology, operate as pragmatic professionals and political realists, not pseudointellectual reformers or public relations showboats (the "toughest no-frills warden in America," the "prison commissioner who opposes get-tough laws," and the like). Successful prison and jail administrators know from experience that they operate in the context of multiple and competing public objectives (punish, rehabilitate, deter, incapacitate), ever-shifting legislative priorities, small to sweeping judicial interventions, and always incomplete (and often crisis-driven) media renderings of their work. But they wisely seek neither to master nor to withdraw from external demands and pressures. Instead, they and their staffs are responsive to reasonable external demands and pressures, and they engage in the civic life of the surrounding community.

The overarching challenge facing contemporary prison and jail administrators is to remain focused on specific safety, program, and other operational goals and activities—the aspects of institutional life over which corrections executives and managers have more or less direct control, and for which they, regardless of how the legislative, judicial, community relations, or media winds blow, daily shoulder immediate legal, moral, fiscal, and administrative responsibility. Present-day institutional corrections leadership

The Basics of a Well-Run Prison

1. **Sanitation.** High standards of sanitation are an indication for inmates, staff, and visitors of a commitment to humane treatment and a pattern of excellent care. Good sanitation encourages civility throughout a prison.

2. **Inmate programs.** The orderly management of a prison depends upon effective programs for the inmate population. Programs that motivate, are well organized, and are at the interest and ability level of inmates support a climate of concern, productivity, and growth. They allow inmates to find meaning in their incarceration. Programs also give inmates hope and goals.

3. **Security.** Security is the responsibility of all staff and must be attended to with vigilance. Training is essential so that staff clearly understand all policies and procedures. All employees must be on the lookout for irregularities and must feel that they have a duty to communicate those problems to the appropriate individuals. Corrective action must be taken immediately. Security is an inter- and intradepartmental responsibility; communication must flow horizontally as well as vertically.

4. **Key control.** The security of an institution depends on effective key control; its compromise may pose a threat to the safety of inmates, staff, and the general public. Staff must be reminded of the importance of key control in departmental meetings. Problems must be reported immediately. Accountability must be maintained, and duplication of keys must be controlled.

5. **Tool control.** Tool control is equally important to the overall security of the prison. Effective control prevents the use of tools as weapons and in escape attempts. But tool control procedures also assist in overall institutional operations by improving the appearance of shop areas, keeping equipment in good repair, maintaining inventories, and teaching proper work habits to inmates.

6. **Visibility.** Visibility of staff throughout the institution helps prevent significant problems. Prison staff stay apprised of activities within the institution and develop a more complete image of the operation of the facility. Staff presence sends out several messages to the inmate population: that staff are interested, available, and responsive and that they are maintaining constant surveillance of the facility.

7. **Communication.** Communication is the lifeblood of any organization and is especially critical in a prison. Through constant and effective communication with inmates, staff stay informed and can react to problems before they escalate. Staff keep one another informed of what is happening within the institution through discussions and feedback. Members within a well-functioning prison communicate freely with one another without fear of reprisal. Because communication is so crucial in the prison setting, information must be conveyed accurately and in a professional manner.

8. **Responsiveness.** Attention to detail demands unequivocal observance of policy, procedures, and individual requests. Logs must be completed and

continues

monthly reports written on time. Inmate requests, phone calls, and requests for information from the public, the press, and members of the legislature must be answered in a professional and timely manner.

9. Staff training. Training is the key to the development of a professional prison staff. Training is not simply something that happens when an employee joins the organization but is an ongoing process of development. It must be an institutional priority, part of the organization's regular program.

10. Inmate accountability. The institution should have clearly articulated policies for acceptable inmate behavior that should be carefully explained to each new arrival. At all times during the day, inmates should have assigned areas and activities. With this system established, inmates should be held accountable for their actions and whereabouts.

11. Staff accountability. Staff also have duties to which they must be held accountable. They must perform their jobs as specified by policy and be responsible for the quality and timeliness of their performance. Supervisors must be held accountable for holding their people accountable.

12. Teamwork. Individual compliance with policy and procedures and subscription to high standards of professionalism alone will not produce a well-run prison. Much of the work of operating institutions involves common tasks—security, caring for the emotional health of inmates, scheduling, and programming. Teamwork (intra- and interdepartmental) is crucial. Staff throughout the facility must appreciate their mutual interdependence and realize that by pooling their talents, energies, and resources, they will be more effective.

13. Professionalism. Professional practice incorporates the character, spirit, and methods of sound and appropriate prison operations. It demands individual integrity, loyalty to the organization, honor, and trust. It includes attention to attire, mannerisms, and appropriate communications, as well as conscientious policy compliance and performance of one's duties.

14. Policy knowledge and compliance. The rule of law establishes that power be exercised within a set of explicitly and coherently stated regulations. Governance by the rule of law avoids capriciousness, uncertainty, and misunderstanding. Thorough and clearly articulated policy serves as the cornerstone of a rule of law within an organization.

15. Completed staff work. Staff should complete work that is assigned to them as fully as possible before passing it on to the next level.

Source: Reprinted with permission of Ronald Burkhart, Dathne, Alabama.

is neither an art nor a science but a craft, and the field of institutional corrections, for all its problems, for all its real or perceived failures, has been blessed with a truly extraordinary number and variety of superb craftspeople.

Still, have even the best prison and jail administrators kept pace with the best of the rest of public sector entrepreneurs in government? The field's present and aspiring leaders must answer this question for and among themselves with respect to at least three sets of issues: boundary spanning, performance management, and public communications.

BOUNDARY SPANNING IN INSTITUTIONAL CORRECTIONS

As Donald F. Kettl has definitively argued, most of contemporary governance and administrative politics involve "government by proxy," defined as public administration by taxpayer-supported bureaucracies that do their work in partnership with other government agencies (including agencies that operate at other levels of government), private firms, and nonprofit organizations.[3] For example, all major federal social and health programs enacted since 1945—Medicare, Medicaid, antipoverty programs, interstate highway construction, environmental protection, you name it—have been administered not by any one federal bureaucracy or public agency but via a complicated network of federal and state bureaucracies, private contractors, and nonprofit research and development or other organizations. And note: Most of the much publicized instances of waste, fraud, and abuse in government have occurred not within the confines of a particular public bureaucracy but in the often ill-managed or undermanaged interstices of such government-by-proxy networks. The rise of government by proxy has heightened public sector vulnerability to charges, fair and foul, of poor leadership, mismanagement, program failure, and outright corruption.

Even prison and jail administration, which some unknowing public management specialists still cite as the paradigm of traditional or "direct" public administration, has for decades now been very much a creature of government by proxy, with all its attendant administrative complications and possibilities. For example, prison and jail administrators interact constantly with the courts and other law enforcement agencies, including agencies representing other jurisdictions or levels of government. They deal with government safety or health inspectors. They hire for-profit and nonprofit consultants. In-

> "Every major policy initiative launched by the federal government since World War II—including Medicare and Medicaid, environmental cleanup and restoration, antipoverty programs and job training, interstate highways and sewage treatment plants—has been managed through public-private partnerships."
>
> Source: Donald F. Kettl, *Sharing Power. Public Governance and Private Markets* (Washington, DC: The Brookings Institution, 1993), 4.

creasingly, they contract for one or more basic or auxiliary services, from food services to physical plant maintenance.

If anything, in institutional corrections the list of daily and long-term planning functions performed as government by proxy is getting longer all the time. Thus, the work of contemporary prison and jail administrators, like that of most contemporary public sector executives and managers, of necessity involves what Kettl terms "boundary spanning," meaning essentially three things: (1) the capacity to work productively not only up and down a traditional bureaucratic hierarchy or "chain of command," but across functional divisions and units of a complex organization (some divisions or units of which may be, unlike the parent or umbrella bureaucracy, nonhierarchical, "flat," or "team managed"); (2) the capacity to establish constructive professional and administrative ties to other public sector organizations that can affect everything from the agency's daily internal operations to its vulnerability to legal action or its level of legislative support; and (3) the capacity to enter into cost-effective relationships or contracts with both nonprofit and for-profit service providers.

Unfortunately, my sense is that even the sharpest institutional corrections executives and managers have yet to "catch up," as it were, with the government-by-proxy nature of their work. Little of what still passes as top-flight leadership and management training or executive conferences in the field of corrections even acknowledges the realities of boundary spanning or the concomitant need to reengineer personnel administration and staff development programs. Not even the most highly regarded barbed-wire bureaucracies in the country have kept up with peer public sector organizations in fields ranging from environmental protection to health care finance.

Prison and jail administrators must begin to think strategically about organizational boundary spanning and to develop preservice and inservice training, and staff development programs that are bound to be more different from than similar to the standard training fare of the last 20 years.

Back in the 1980s, when computer-assisted management information systems first entered the prison gates, many veteran administrators tried to escape them, offering the all-purpose excuse that, as public functions go, "running prisons and jails is unique." Institutional corrections is uniquely challenging, and the field's best leaders and innovators lead and innovate while sticking to the care and custody basics. But, as hard as it sometimes seems for corrections professionals to accept, the "We're unique" truism also applies to government executives and managers who are responsible for running public sector occupational health and safety inspections, planning nuclear waste disposal schedules, institutionalizing quality-of-life community policing efforts, structuring or auditing intergovernmental pediatric medical care financing programs, and delivering the U.S. mail.

What are the first steps on the road to a field of institutional corrections that engages rather than evades the need for forward-looking human resource and technical innovations to enhance organizational boundary-spanning capacities? In many cases these steps are probably not very different from the first steps on the road to promoting rather than penalizing entrepreneurs in government, as outlined by Doig and Hargrove.

- Identify new missions and programs for the organization.
- Develop and nourish external constituencies to support the new goals and programs.
- Create internal constituencies that support the new goals through changes in recruitment systems and key appointments.
- Enhance the organization's technical expertise.
- Motivate and provide training for members of the organization that transcends standard or accepted training goals.
- Systematically scan organizational routines and points of internal and external pressure in order to identify areas of vulnerability to mismanagement, corruption, the loss of leaders' positions, and blows to organizational reputation.

Prison and jail systems that are led and managed by people who have already taken these preliminary steps should forge ahead with boundary-spanning retooling of their training and staff development programs. Prison and jail systems that are behind the entrepreneurs in government curve need to put first things first, most especially with respect to Doig and Hargrove's sixth suggestion—limiting vulnerability to mismanagement and corruption. This vulnerability grows exponentially as the number of staff and inmates increases and the interorganizational, government-by-proxy networks of institutional corrections become ever more intricate.

PERFORMANCE MANAGEMENT

In addition to overview essays on the strengths and limits of performance-based management approaches in criminal justice, the Bureau of Justice Statistics (BJS) handbook *Performance Measures for the Criminal Justice System* offers specific recommendations on measuring performance in community corrections, courts, prosecution and public defense, policing, and, last but not least, prisons.[4]

In his contribution to this handbook, James Q. Wilson, the country's leading expert on government bureaucracy and many aspects of crime policy, outlined a macro- and microlevel list of performance measures for police departments. Wilson's thinking on these subjects has inspired many leaders and innovators in criminal justice. One of the most notable, William Bratton, the former New York Police Department (NYPD) chief, adopted the "broken windows" thesis on effective policing first articulated by Wilson and George L. Kelling. New York City implemented, monitored, and tracked the effectiveness of new policing practices via the development of a computer-based performance-measurement management information system. The NYPD's efforts are widely credited with helping to drive 1993–1997 crime rates way down in the Big Apple.

But the NYPD's performance management success story is the exception to the organizational rule, not only in contemporary big-city policing, but in criminal justice more generally. There are, to be sure, other exceptions. For example, in the 1980s, the Federal Bureau of Prisons (BOP) pioneered the development of a key indicators/strategic support system (KI/SSS).

In a progress report circulated at BOP's 1988 annual wardens' conference, KI/SSS was described as an effort to help "translate" the agency's "broad goal" of "humane control of inmates . . . into more specific measures." By the mid-1990s, KI/SSS, though never problem free (no such system ever is), had developed into one of the most interesting and user-friendly computer-assisted management information systems of its kind to be found anywhere in institutional corrections, and, for that matter, anywhere in the federal service. And, by early 1997, several veteran wardens and other agency officials whom I had interviewed in the mid-1980s, and who had expressed reservations (to put it mildly) about the need for any such system—and deep doubts about the need for performance management itself—had the zeal of performance management converts.

Still, neither the BOP nor, to my knowledge, any other institutional corrections agency has yet witnessed or even thought through the full-dress development of performance-based management systems that are designed in ways that serve both internal administrative and external constituency-building needs. As Kettl has explained:

> The biggest difficulty in thinking through the problems of performance-based management is that reformers and managers far too often consider it simply as a problem of measurement. Committing the government to performance-based management, of course, requires that officials identify and measure results. The more fundamental question, however, is what to do with these measures. Performance-based management is most fundamentally about communication, not measurement. Moreover, this communication occurs within a broader political process, in which players have a wide array of different incentives. Performance based management will have meaning only to the degree to which it shapes and improves incentives. How does what (executives and managers) know about results shape decisions about what programs they adopt? And how does the process of measuring results affect the behavior of political institutions?[5]

Some institutional corrections agencies, like BOP, are already rather far down the path to performance-based management systems and need only to refine and elaborate existing systems, which they could do most profitably in the context of the sorts of boundary-spanning training and staff development programs discussed above.

Many institutional corrections agencies, however, have yet to begin even the measurement phase of performance-based management innovations. The aforementioned BJS volume on performance measures, most particularly Charles H. Logan's contribution on performance measures for prisons, would be very helpful for these organizations.

Logan's detailed, and not the least outdated, discussion covers 8 sets of performance criteria (security, safety, order, care, activity, justice, conditions, and management) and 50 specific performance measures. Data for and on all of these can be drawn from significant or critical incident logs, inmate employment records, education records, and other easy-to-access institutional sources. In all but a few respects, Logan's suggested performance measurement protocols for prisons are equally applicable to jails. Both prison and jail administrators who find themselves in the takeoff stage of performance-based management systems, and those who see the need for midcourse performance management corrections, should benefit from consulting his work.[6]

PUBLIC COMMUNICATIONS IN INSTITUTIONAL CORRECTIONS

Finally, any chance that prison and jail administrators will lead rather than lag behind the latest and best thinking and activity on improving government performance will be lost unless and until practitioners of the institutional corrections craft improve public communications about what they actually do and how, subject to legal and other constraints, they do it.

In particular, institutional corrections may be the only area of public sector life in which academics, analysts, activists, journalists, judges, lawyers, and lobbyists have turned the field's practitioners (corrections commissioners, veteran officers, or wardens) into little more than bit players in defining, for both elite policy making and mass public audiences,

- who their clients or customers are,
- what their incumbent budgetary and organizational needs and requirements are
- what the likely social costs and consequences of alternative ways of performing the public functions they now perform are

Prison and jail wardens and superintendents must actively enter these public debates; they are the practitioner experts in the field. Even fundamental factual matters such as what the criminal records and physical health, mental health, and employment histories of most prisoners look like—the stuff of "rap sheets," presentencing investigation reports, and reception and diagnostic admissions forms—are now largely defined by contending camps of nonpractitioner (or expractitioner) reformers and experts. The seeming lack of interest and involvement in these issues by our current correctional facility administrators is puzzling.

Presumably, prison and jail administrators know lots about the official criminal records and troubled life histories of the confined populations for whom they have daily responsibility. Presumably, they have an obvious organizational stake in sharing with the rest of us their best objective understanding of who their day-to-day clients are. Presumably, they have a keen sense of what this understanding implies about the demands and challenges that they as institution administrators face in providing care and custody to large, transient populations of troubled and troublesome persons. Presumably, they have ideas about which, if any, subpopulations of inmates (for example, recent admissions whose only criminal convictions or violations are for minor drug crimes, or, at the other end of the continuum, offenders with multiple convictions for violent crimes) should be sentenced or treated differently so as to better serve the public and its purse.

Presumably, but the poor state of public communications about the fundamentals of institutional corrections, the relative silence, is rather deafening. For the field's present and aspiring entrepreneurs in government, this silence is professionally and organizationally self-defeating and ought not to persist.

NOTES

1. J. Doig and E. Hargrove, *Leadership and Innovation: A Biographical Perspective on Entrepreneurs in Govern-*

ment (Baltimore: The Johns Hopkins University Press, 1987), 2.

2. J. DiIulio, Jr., *Governing Prisons: A Comparative Study of Correctional Management* (New York: The Free Press, 1987).

3. D. Kettl, *Government by Proxy: (Mis)Managing Federal Programs* (Washington, DC: Congressional Quarterly Press, 1988), 50.

4. J. Wilson, "The Problem of Defining Agency Success," in *Performance Measures for the Criminal Justice System,* ed. J. DiIulio, Jr. (Washington, DC: U.S. Bureau of Justice Statistics, October 1993), 157–165.

5. D. Kettl, "Building Lasting Reform," in *Inside the Reinvention Machine: Assessing Governmental Reform,* ed. J. DiIulio, Jr. and D. Kettl (Washington, DC: The Brookings Institution, 1994).

6. C. Logan, "Criminal Justice Performance Measures for Prisons," in *Performance Measures for the Criminal Justice System,* ed. J. DiIulio, Jr. (Washington, DC: U.S. Bureau of Justice Statistics, October 1993), 19–57.

CHAPTER 6

Management Accountability

Peter M. Carlson

The world of prison and jail management has long been unfairly considered a backwater of public administration, organizational theory, and management behavior. While the academic centers of the nation have been preparing future gurus of business; tomorrow's leaders of city, state, and federal government; and assorted other public administrative functions, no one has taken on the complex task of developing prison and jail administrators. This sector of public administration has truly been left to the rough and tumble school of hard knocks. Almost all of today's penal leaders have entered the field in an entry-level position and earned their way to top management roles.

Corrections is a demanding environment in which the leaders and managers of institutions must be fleet of foot, bright, and capable of governing thousands of staff and inmates. The challenges of prison and jail management have never been greater, with expanding inmate populations, legal complications, more aggressive and dangerous inmates, politicians that want to micromanage institutions, and staff issues that are complex and unending.

The need to effectively manage our correctional facilities—to focus staff on the basics of operating safe, secure, and humane institu-

tions—has never been more critical. Prison and jail professionals are responsible for the public safety, performing a public service of great significance. But other inside-the-institution management tasks are very important as well. A warden must constantly work to ensure staff safety, staff integrity, proper stewardship of government financial resources, and a safe environment for inmates. Corrections leaders are accountable to all constituents: the public, elected representatives, the judiciary, superiors in government, staff, and inmates. Management and leadership skills are very necessary.

This chapter outlines methods vital to the effective management of the correctional environment.

MANAGEMENT VERSUS LEADERSHIP—AN UNFAIR DICHOTOMY

Many exceptional researchers and authors distinguish between leadership and management. Warren Bennis describes the differences between leaders and managers as the differences between those who master the context and those who surrender to it.[1] He believes the manager focuses on systems and structure while the leader stresses the people in the business. Bennis believes managers are more "blue collar" and heavily involved in the nitty-gritty of organizational life. He paints leaders as being more en-

Opinions expressed in this chapter are those of the author and do not necessarily represent the opinions of the Federal Bureau of Prisons or the U.S. Department of Justice.

gaged in the loftier calling of organizational directing.

Tom Peters and Robert Waterman are a little kinder toward management, although they also stress that leaders go beyond the daily grind of basic decision making. Their stellar research reveals that successful people learn from their mistakes, think globally, encourage innovation, and master new knowledge.[2]

Other observers of leadership roles in prisons have softened the line between management and leadership. Kevin Wright has described a merger between the roles of managers and leaders.[3] While he describes many farsighted responsibilities of leaders, he puts them in the context of day-to-day management activities. A warden must watch the bottom line of the budget but be able to articulate the necessity of accomplishing longer-term goals.

Even if managers or leaders try to just watch the horizon and spend all day inspiring their staff, the reality of penal management will rapidly return their attention to the present. Prison and jail administration seems to require unique individuals with exceptional people skills. The craft of penology demands institution experience and the ability to lead others.

Chester Barnard puts it this way: "It is important to observe . . . that not all work done by persons who occupy executive positions is in connection with the executive functions."[4] If the warden or superintendent of an institution stops to listen to a complaint from an inmate or staff member, this is not expressly an executive task. As Barnard notes, nearly all high-ranking executives do a considerable amount of nonexecutive work, and this effort is sometimes more valuable than the executive function. The hands-on managerial tasks are generally associated with maintaining an organization and ensuring that systems of cooperative effort are emphasized and enforced.

It is critical for today's prison and jail chief executive officers to successfully combine the reality of management in the trenches with the ability to lead others toward the future. A warden must stay in close touch with the daily responsibilities of institution management yet set a tone that defines what the facility is and where it is headed. Separating management from leadership requires an artificial division that does not reflect the reality of organizational behavior. Hans Toch notes that penology deals with policy and administration, process, and procedures.[5] Daily oversight is necessary, and a warden's responsibilities are very much a hands-on experience.

The quality of prison administration is dependent upon many factors, but the most important is management practice. John DiIulio's exceptional study of institutions of confinement clearly shows that strong prison and jail governance is key to the attainment of effective and efficient operations.[6] But strong, involved management does not preclude the chief executive officer from exuding many intrinsic leadership qualities. On the contrary, the two roles must be merged. The effective, reality-driven manager must model other characteristics of a leader: empowering and delegating to capable staff and showing sensitivity to others, diplomacy, vision, and a willingness to take responsible risks.

THE CHALLENGE FOR INSTITUTIONAL LEADERSHIP

All wardens or senior-level leaders in any correctional environment want to be known for running a high-quality operation and getting positive results. But what are positive results in a prison or jail environment? An effective prison or jail operation is generally considered to be an institution that is safe, secure, clean, and responsive to the needs of its staff, inmates, and external constituencies. Yet if we gathered a group of correctional leaders and asked them to define these qualities, there would be some disagreement. Which factors are the most important? How do we operationally define successful attainment of each factor? How should staff go about trying to reach each goal, and how do we know when the goal has been attained?

It is critical that wardens and senior administrators establish a vision of a successful correc-

Failing to think through their objectives and to set priorities, government agencies and other public-service institutions tend to be ineffective. The cure is to seek the concurrence of staff at all levels of the organization and gain a reasonable level of agreement on clearly defined goals. Results-oriented management includes defining agency objectives by the outcome to be achieved, establishing priorities, generating performance targets, and using performance information to improve results.

Source: J. Wholey, *Evaluation and Effective Public Management* (Boston: Little, Brown and Company, 1983), 4.

tional operation. They must delineate institutional goals, train staff to ensure that all personnel are aware of the desired outcomes, implement the program, establish a system of feedback on progress toward the goals, and create a means of reinforcing successful accomplishment and good performance. Once this process is in place, accountability and tracking institutional operations become key.

DELEGATION

Management is often defined as the art of getting things done through other people. A leader must delegate the responsibility for specific tasks to qualified individuals while remaining ultimately responsible for these functions. Delegation is often referred to today as the act of empowering staff. The senior staff member must give the responsibility for the task as well as the authority and the resources for the recipient to accomplish the job. This can be a frightening concept in a prison or jail, where so many things can go wrong and some errors have extreme consequences. Yet delegation is necessary if a

major facility is going to operate effectively 24 hours a day.

Even driven, type-A personalities must allow their staff to take responsibility for work in the facility. Failure to delegate operational supervision to competent staff will guarantee personal burnout, damage the development of subordinate staff, reduce productivity, and harm the morale of all personnel.

If delegation is so essential to leadership and management, why is this such a difficult skill to develop? Richard Phillips and Charles McConnell believe there are three primary barriers to effective delegation: old habits, lack of faith in subordinates, and the perceived lack of adequate time to train staff.[7] Our traditional, comfortable work patterns can be difficult to change. To overcome this inertia, leaders must develop an awareness of this shortfall and practice new behaviors. Leaders must first surround themselves with a quality staff and then mentor them until the leaders become more confident in the staff's skills. All of these solutions require time; it's always easier for leaders to assume that the job will be done better if they do it themselves. Unfortunately, this assumption is not always true. Accordingly, true leaders invest time in training and supporting others for the sake of personal sanity and for the future of the organization.

Delegation is critical at all levels of correctional institutions. While the responsibilities of correctional management are more complex than those in many other lines of work, leadership and management in all organizations will require the sharing of responsibilities. Once leaders do delegate tasks, they must learn how to provide oversight and establish accountability.

IN SEARCH OF ACCOUNTABILITY— HOW TO MEASURE SUCCESS

Within the parameters of leadership and institution management, the most important factor in creating successful operations is the establishment of accountability. A superior manager creates high performance expectations, delegates the task, and follows up to evaluate results. Staff cannot and will not be able to comply with a superior's expectations if they are not clearly set forth. Senior managers and executives must share their ideas and concerns with staff. Once the information and desired expectations are placed on the table, it is important to set procedures in place to ensure compliance.

Paul Light highlights three primary avenues to accountability in a government agency.[8] First, *compliance accountability* is a method that seeks to measure conformity with written rules and regulations that are clearly defined. Auditing for compliance essentially seeks to find occurrences of non–policy compliance and correct the situation, if possible, after errors have been made. Staff who erred are corrected with negative sanctions. The second approach is *performance accountability;* in this model staff are prospectively encouraged to perform well through the use of incentive awards. This positive program seeks to encourage appropriate and voluntary compliance with policy at the inception of a task. The third approach, *capacity-based accountability,* requires the organization to place necessary resources in position that are required for a task: staff, money, and technology must be invested for the work to be accomplished in an effective manner.

While there is no clear best means of effecting accountability, in government the preferred method is compliance accountability. Auditing generally involves teams of personnel, internal or external to the agency, reviewing processes and procedures in order to compare actual performance with the expectations established by policy.

Historically, accountability in bureaucratic organizations has meant limiting staff discretion by utilizing carefully developed rules and regulations. Prison and jail employees in many situations and certain jurisdictions are treated as untrusted adolescents. The command and authority of large-scale organizations is generally very hierarchical, and every staff member's role and responsibility are clearly delineated. If all significant decisions are made by a limited number of senior executives, staff quit caring and pass all decisions up the ladder. Independence and creativity do not mesh well with this system. In this hidebound accountability structure, it is ironic that the mechanisms intended to ensure quality sometimes reduce quality. Innovative employee behavior and risk taking can be lost when administrative control is too tight.

Yet in corrections it is easy to understand the desire for tight administrative control. Prisoners of the state are not confined for conforming to laws. Many inmates are very willing to ignore a rule, policy, or general expectations of polite society. In short, they need external control. In order to ensure consistent application of institutional standards of behavior as well as develop a fair and standard way of operating, staff must know and follow correctional policy. How is this accomplished?

In prison and jail environments, the first step is to ensure that all staff clearly comprehend the agency's mission. The guiding vision must be established for all. If security and safety are to be primary goals, leaders must spell this out for staff. All personnel must grasp the purpose of the organization. Once this is established, the chief executive must establish the standards for operation that will support the organizational purpose.

There are important means of creating these standards and ensuring compliance with them.

Policy

All prison and jail facilities must have written policy and procedures. These documents should establish the philosophy of operation for each program area, identify the outcomes expected, and define what is required of staff and inmates. Policy must accurately reflect current expectation and be expressed in measurable terms. In the prison and jail setting, control of a facility is organized around rules, and consistency is maintained by ensuring that all staff enforce rules in an impartial manner. This requires extensive staff training so they understand policy requirements. Ongoing monitoring by first-line supervisors ensures that policies are applied correctly.

Training

It is not enough to plan, write, and publish policy in any business or government setting. All of those who will be expected to comply with rules and regulations, and those expected to enforce policy, must receive appropriate training in the process, program, or procedure. Inservice training is extremely important to ensure that all personnel are fully informed of the strategy, whether it is a new process or a change in the current practice. In general, staff at all levels of the correctional agency will fare better with policy if senior managers take the time to explain why it is important and seek staff input.

Compliance Audits

If policy is to mean anything, it is mandatory that the organizational leaders assess compliance with written directives; program audits are the best means of measuring staff operations. These routine reviews enable senior management to gauge program performance, determine the degree of risk, test the adequacy of internal control, and make midstream adjustments to operations to help achieve the desired results. It adds validity to the process if the reviewers know the program area but are organizationally independent.

Another aspect of auditing that can be very helpful is the requirement that program staff perform an internal review of their operations at scheduled intervals. Honest self-monitoring is truly the best means of keeping an organization on track and effective.

Benchmarking

It is always useful to compare one's operation to other similar programs. Key data points of institution management are easily identified: number of escapes, homicides, suicides, assaults, disciplinary reports, inmate grievances, and so on. Once this information is gathered, it is easy

to compare data for other periods of time at the same facility or for like periods of time at similar institutions. Such benchmarking can provide senior and middle managers with data points to analyze. For instance, is a positive "hit rate" of 13 percent of all urinalysis indicating an unusually high use of illegal and contraband substances? By comparing this percentage with the percentage at that institution one year earlier or with the percentage at another facility of similar security, leaders can better answer that question.

Accreditation

The American Correctional Association (ACA) has established standards for adult correctional institutions and separate standards for adult detention facilities. The ACA will, for an established fee, help correctional jurisdictions develop a local accreditation process and then provide a team of auditors to assess compliance with the nationwide standards on a preestablished schedule every three years. This excellent system provides external oversight of local implementation of nationally recognized standards. Such feedback can be very helpful in assessing institution operations, defending against legal challenges, and providing ongoing comparisons of significant aspects of facility management for line staff and senior managers.

Identification of Corruption

All correctional jurisdictions must have an internal affairs office to ensure that agency resources are used in a way that is consistent with the mission and that government resources are protected from waste, fraud, and abuse. Staff and inmates must be accountable for their behavior and should clearly understand the expected standard of conduct. A crucial piece of management accountability is the obligation to ensure that institution operations are conducted with integrity and in compliance with the law. Inmate and staff allegations of impropriety must be investigated promptly and all individuals held accountable for their actions. Federal agencies are subject to the Inspector General Act and the

Chief Financial Officers Act; state and local jurisdictions generally have similar watchdog legislation that puts teeth into management control.

Strategic Planning

Prisons and jails, or any organizations, cannot bounce from pillar to post as they move to meet new challenges. The management of change is one of the critical tasks of being a leader; it is imperative that correctional organizations have a living, breathing plan of advancing smoothly into the future. A warden must have a well-developed and -publicized vision of what an organization is and what it is striving to become.

Effective leadership does not require a sheriff, warden, or senior administrator who is charismatic and friendly, feared or revered. Indeed, some of the great leaders in the private world of business avoid the limelight, focus on creating an organization that handles basic functions well, and keep their eyes on goals, to which staff are deeply committed.[9] Core values are critical to an organization, and they are firmly rooted in the mission of the agency.

Staff at all levels must be involved in this process of preparing the institution for tomorrow's trials and tribulations. Once a strategic plan is developed, it should serve as a guideline for moving the facility through the issues that develop. Management accountability depends partly on the chief executive's ability to select appropriate organizational responses to new challenges and to ensure that staff stay on track with well-conceived goals.

LARGE-SCALE MANAGEMENT STRUCTURES ARE NOT REQUIRED

As identified by Vice President Al Gore, governments often have huge bureaucracies to ensure that personnel do what they are paid to do. In the past, this has meant many people watching other people perform routine tasks in a mediocre manner. Gore's effort to "reinvent government" has led to some recognition that less can be more.[10] It is important to create an atmosphere where staff believe in what they are doing, have input to how the work is structured, and are permitted to exercise judgment in day-to-day tasks. While some prison and jail managers would argue that more top-down management is better management, this is not necessarily true. And these opposing philosophies are not incompatible.

While it is critical to have policy that establishes broad parameters and requires ethical enforcement, it is not necessary to require mindless compliance with little room for individual innovation. Vice President Gore is absolutely correct in his quest to put common sense back into government and to encourage individual enthusiasm. Too much emphasis on policy compliance can drive all innovative thoughts out of an organization; a sense of reasonableness is important. The establishment of management accountability is the heart and soul of being a high-quality leader—and a manager—within the fast-paced correctional environment.

NOTES

1. W. Bennis, *On Becoming a Leader* (New York: Addison-Wesley Publishing, 1989), 37.
2. T. Peters and R. Waterman, *In Search of Excellence: Lessons from America's Best-Run Companies* (New York: Warner Books, 1982), 118.
3. K. Wright, *Effective Prison Leadership* (Binghampton, NY: William Neil Publishing, 1994), 3.
4. C. Barnard, "The Executive Functions," in *Classic Readings in Organizational Behavior,* ed. J. Ott (Belmont, CA: Wadsworth Publishing Company, 1989), 265–275.
5. H. Toch, *Corrections: A Humanistic Approach* (Guilderland, NY: Harrow and Heston Publishers, 1997), xiv.
6. J. DiIulio, Jr., *Governing Prisons: A Comparative Study of Correctional Management* (New York: The Free Press, 1987), 6, 7.
7. R. Phillips and C. McConnell, *The Effective Corrections Manager* (Gaithersburg, MD: Aspen Publishers, Inc., 1996), 60.
8. P. Light, *Monitoring Government: Inspectors General and the Search for Accountability* (Washington, DC: The Brookings Institution, 1992), 3.
9. J. Collins and J. Porras, *Built To Last: Successful Habits of Visionary Companies* (New York: HarperCollins Publishers, 1997), 8.
10. A. Gore, *The Best-Kept Secrets in Government* (Washington, DC: U.S. Government Printing Office, 1996), 15, 16.

PART III

The American Jail

The American jail is a familiar structure to most of us. We have learned about jails from movies, books, songs, and stories. We recognize the exteriors of our hometown jails. And some of us have even spent time in jail.

Jails are detention facilities that come in all shapes and sizes. They usually are used for short-term detention and for confinement and service of sentences of one year or less. But not always. Jails detain accused individuals awaiting trial and house sentenced offenders awaiting transfer to prison. But some jail facilities hold prisoners for longer terms—up to five years. Some jurisdictions have an inmate population so small that you can count it on two hands, and most jail operations house fewer than 50 prisoners; other regional jails are so large that they dwarf many prison facilities. For example, the average count during midyear 1997 in the New York City jail system on Rikers Island was well over 19,000 prisoners. According to the Bureau of Justice Statistics, at midyear 1997 an estimated 567,000 persons were held in local jails in the entire United States.

Many people mistakenly think of jails simply as small prisons. In fact, they differ in many ways. But size is not the distinguishing feature: The largest jail systems have a much greater capacity than nearly all correctional institutions.

Jails are complex facilities that house a wide variety of offenders. In many cases, the facility personnel know nothing about the inmates' background other than the offense for which they were arrested, the prior arrest record that matches their fingerprints, and whatever the newly confined individuals wish to admit during the booking process.

Jails hold overnight arrestees, pretrial offenders, those who have been sentenced to short-term confinement, and prisoners who are awaiting transfer to a prison. Jail populations include the inebriated and those high on drugs, individuals threatening suicide or mentally ill, and sophisticated prisoners who are extremely dangerous or likely to escape. Jails process and separately house males and females; they must book and detain senior citizens as well as juveniles. The diversity of those in a city, county, or regional jail is breathtaking.

The English gaol was the genesis of jail operations that developed in colonial America. In England, the gaol actually goes back to the medieval period. One of the earliest detention facilities was the Tower of London. In the twelfth century, King Henry II ordered gaols to be built in all British shires (counties). The "shire reeve" (from which the term "sheriff" derives) was the designated official for the detention of those accused of violating the king's law. These were strictly short-term detention facilities in which an individual was held until a court hearing was convened. In the sixteenth century, the concept of the workhouse evolved, and the sheriff became responsible for the confinement of those who were debtors and individuals charged with various misdeeds.

This was the jail system that the early settlers of the American colonies imported. Colonial jails were intended to detain law violators until they could stand trial, and also to house the vagrants and misfits creating problems for citizens. Jail terms were not used as a punishment; if the accused persons were found guilty in court, they received corporal punishment or were banished from local society.

As American society changed, so has the jail. Today, the local jail has multiple missions and an extremely wide variety of prisoners. Generally, jail operations have remained under local control and the supervision of the sheriff.

This section is intended to define the key responsibilities and functions of the personnel of American jails today and to identify key differences between jail and prison operations.

LEARNING OBJECTIVES

After studying this section, you should be able to answer the following questions:

1. What are the primary functions of jails? What are the main differences between jails and prisons?
2. Why is detoxification a greater issue in jails than in prisons?
3. What is the history of modern jail operations?
4. Why is the management of jail inmates, about whom staff have little background information, such a great challenge?
5. Why is medical screening for infectious diseases during the intake process extremely important in a jail facility?

DISCUSSION/REVIEW QUESTIONS

1. List six different reasons for which offenders are admitted to local jails.
2. Why do jail facilities admit and release large numbers of inmates?
3. Explain the difference between a prison, jail, and a lockup.
4. Provide three significant reasons for the extreme increase in the number of jail inmates within the last 20 years.
5. What is a jail matrix classification system and how does it affect overcrowding in jails?
6. Why do jails have an important effect on the public's perception of personal safety?
7. How did the closing of many state mental institutions affect jail populations?
8. Why is it critical for jail staff to maintain close operation linkages with the community?

CHAPTER 7

Intake and Release
in Evolving Jail Practice

Arthur Wallenstein

In the past, Americans have focused mainly on institutions housing sentenced offenders—large prisons—when discussing corrections. The over 3,000 U.S. jails were rarely mentioned in any serious discussion of criminal justice practice, and the role of the jail at the local level was ill-defined. Discussions about jails were always secondary to discussions about prisons.

This approach is now passé; jails must be and are central to any discussion of public safety and public policy. Interest in jails has grown as Americans have become more aware of domestic violence, drunk driving, mental illness and its relationship to public safety, victim's rights, increased levels of expenditures for public safety, and, above all, the staggering growth of jail population levels. This chapter focuses on the U.S. jail system and the many challenges that jail operations present.

LOCAL JAILS—THE SITE OF MOST CORRECTIONAL BUSINESS

According to recent data generated by the Bureau of Justice Statistics, federal, state, and local correctional facilities house over 1.7 million persons on a daily basis. Over 567,000 reside in local jails, suggesting that jails are a relatively minor part of the criminal justice structure that accounts for about one-third of our incarcerated population. But nothing could be further from the truth. Average daily population data, while instructive in some operational and policy dis-

cussions, do not adequately reflect the role of the jail and its vastly expanded importance in American criminal justice and public safety discussions. While over 567,000 persons occupy jail beds in this country on a daily basis, between 10 and 15 million persons pass through the jail systems during a calendar year.[1] This statistic suggests that jails handle at least 10 times the population of prisons and are in a position to impact public safety to a far greater degree than long-term sentenced facilities.[2] The people and policy issues incorporated in the practices of U.S. jails strongly affect community safety.

The public expects law enforcement to focus on crimes that the Federal Bureau of Investigation (FBI) refers to as indexed crime: murder, rape, armed robbery, aggravated assault, robbery, and burglary. While these crimes are extremely important, they are not the crimes that affect the largest number of persons in this country. Misdemeanor offenses involve public civility, domestic violence, substance abuse, and public safety (including the safety of streets and public places). They have an enormous impact on the public's perception of safety, more than the impact of prisons, where convicted and sentenced offenders are sent for increasingly long periods of incarceration. Most persons who are booked into jail remain for short periods of time ranging from hours to 12 months. The vast majority are returned to the immediate community, where they interact with citizens in communities all across this nation. The jail should not be an afterthought; any institution, public service, or support program that touches between 10 and 15 million persons per year should be a central component of any analysis of public safety.

Those who engage in domestic violence against wives and significant others and those who endanger citizens while driving automobiles while intoxicated have an enormous impact on street-level public safety considerations that far surpasses that of the FBI's indexed crimes. In their recent work on street-level civility issues and misdemeanant offenses and their impact on public safety in New York City, George Kelling and Catherine Coles argue that local jails should be seen as a focal point of correctional strategy and public safety policy, given the vast numbers of people who pass through jails.[3] Jails receive, house, treat, impact, and release hundreds of thousands of citizens who do not meet community standards. Substance abuse offenders, members of the sex industry, juveniles who are declined for youth prosecution, and persons who fail to appear for court hearings or trials or to complete required programs or conditions all go to local jails. A much smaller number of clearly serious and predatory offenders move through jails and eventually go to prison.

HEALTH CARE

One of the largest U.S. health care delivery system is in jails. This system is staggering in size and scope because virtually all persons entering American jails receive some form of health care—initial screening, evaluation, treatment, or community-based referral. This approach meets constitutional, risk avoidance, and professional growth standards and has at times conflicted with public concerns that prisoners receive better health care than others. The costs are enormous and account for large portions of correctional expenses in many jurisdictions.

People in jails have a magnitude of health care problems, some of which did not exist in the past.[4] Health care issues include the human immunodeficiency virus (HIV) and acquired immune deficiency syndrome (AIDS), several configurations of hepatitis, a range of sexually transmitted diseases, tuberculosis, numerous problems caused by years of alcoholism and substance abuse, disorders relating to an aging population and greater presence of heart disease and related problems, and a wide range of women's health care issues. Many people in jail have not had adequate care, preventive dental care, or knowledge of family planning and pregnancy issues. People often arrive in jail with pre-existing condition and little or no relationship to community health care programs. The jail must triage extant issues, secure emergency interventions, and provide referrals to community-based health care delivery programs when people are released.

Jails must also address homelessness, substance abuse combined with mental illness, and medication concerns. Health care staff simply cannot permit incoming prisoners to continue to take whatever medications they bring in. To avoid problems of drug abuse, improper medication, or related issues, physicians must review medications before a new inmate may be authorized to continue a pharmaceutical protocol.

Jails also receive persons seeking gender changes or in the middle of the gender change process. In these situations, jail staff must remain professionals, treating these people with respect. Difficulties often arise upon admission, and staff must make an appropriate gender classification decision.

Standards of Health Care Delivery

While public sentiment often reflects an ultra-conservative view that inmates do not deserve quality medical treatment, it is clear that if a county, city, or regional government intends to operate a jail, it must provide constitutional levels of health care. In the past 15 years, standards for health care in correctional operations have risen. Since the mid-1970s, health care delivery has been mandated through federal case law, and state and local guidelines establishing acceptable levels of medical treatment are a basic and almost irrevocable aspect of institutional patient care.

National health care accreditation has been the driving force in providing standards, guidance, discussion, and an evolving sense of what is right in jail practice.[5] Beginning in the 1970s with the dynamically creative accreditation program under the auspices of the American Medical Association (AMA) and now firmly established through the National Commission on Correctional Health Care (NCCHC) and the American Correctional Association (ACA) accreditation program, every jail in America—whether it seeks accreditation or not—has had a guide to a full range of health care standards that apply to jails. In many larger jurisdictions, NCCHC standards form the basis of health care delivery programs in jails, and regular national inspections help jails maintain proper levels of health care. This practice has worked well in programs of risk avoidance emphasizing proactive efforts to meet standards in the following areas: medication and pharmaceutical practices; intake screening; interviews; health assessments of longer-term jail prisoners; sick call procedures; emergency services; recordkeeping covering all aspects of health care delivery and referral; mental health evaluations, services, and treatment; and other protocols covering a full range of health care practices and treatment regimes.

Other critical issues include continuity of care, diet and exercise, special needs prisoners, suicide prevention, substance abuse protocols, restraint protocols, sexual assault issues, pregnancy, staffing standards and training requirements, and a broad range of essential data, confidentiality, and quality assurance requirements.

The standards of correctional health care have significantly improved medical decision making and have blended the security responsibilities of access to health care with the screening, evaluation, and treatment responsibilities of health care professionals. This blending of security and health care responsibilities and the demand for teamwork have been the greatest accomplishments of the standards movement, and enormous credit must be given initially to the AMA and

now to NCCHC for helping maintain the quality of health care delivery in jails. These standards have evolved during a period of negative political rhetoric regarding prisoners and lack of public support for quality health care in correctional facilities. Without a commitment to health care, local jurisdictions would have been subject to much legal intervention and potentially huge costs for negligence and failure to provide effective and constitutional health care. No area of detention practice is more important than health care, whether in the megajails of the largest jurisdictions or the smallest rural jails in the United States.

Mental Illness and Substance Abuse

It can be argued from the data that as outside community treatment as well as social and human service delivery systems are stretched thin, the jail systems increasingly become a human service provider of last resort. As medical assistance in other sectors of the community network cease to exist or are severely limited, the burden often shifts to correctional organizations. These cost shifts have been created by several important changes in social policy: closure of state mental hospitals and placement of large numbers of formal patients in the community, new approaches to health care delivery such as managed care and its relationship to the nature and extent of treatment, public civility ordinances and use of the jail for those who have numerous misdemeanor violations, homelessness and its relationship to mental illness and substance abuse, and a current political climate in which many in need of therapeutic intervention are not a high priority of our public policy process.[6,7] The growing use of jails for public health matters may not have been a conscious policy or the result of specifically targeted legislative efforts, but it has been a result of other policy decisions. Jails have faced the increased level of criminality that comes with housing more people with mental illness and substance abuse problems.

All across the country, local jurisdictions are reporting that more and more mentally ill per-

---

In Maine, Statewide Coordination Helps Local Jails

"The way Judith Regina sees it, there are two particularly unique aspects to the Maine Sheriff's Association Mental Health Initiative. First, it is statewide—all 16 sheriffs in Maine participate. Second, it was initiated by the criminal justice system, under the auspices of the Maine Sheriff's Association.

And the initiative, says Regina, who serves as the project's director, has been beneficial, both to the criminal justice systems in the state and to the people with mental illness who often end up in the jails there.

'A partnership exists here now—across the state and across the various service providers, including law enforcement, corrections, probation, shelters, mental health, and substance abuse providers,' says Regina. 'And many times the answer comes down to an information flow problem, sometimes because of a gap in our systems where the agencies don't work well together, or maybe it's because of a serious crime,' she explains. 'But because we have put together coordinating councils we can identify if gaps need to be addressed or if procedures need to be changed, or if funds should be shifted from one area to another. What has also developed is an understanding that jail is not a therapeutic environment and that the community has to have the capacity to be able to handle the mentally ill.'"

Source: Reprinted from *Corrections Alert,* Vol. 4, No. 17, p. 8, © 1997, Aspen Publishers, Inc.

---

sons are finding their way into the criminal justice system. Many prisoners have poor community relationships, a history of instability, and sporadic work records. Stays in jail occur more frequently and are of increasing duration. Studies have indicated that mentally ill prisoners may be held in jail longer than other prisoners who are booked for the same offense. Linkage to community-based mental health programs is difficult and often not a requirement of local and state funding contracts with community providers. In addition, there is a well-developed fear of what might happen in the community if a mentally ill person is released to the street without a place to go for treatment. Jails have never been intended as mental health treatment centers, and many people rightly fear that if jails provide longer-term treatment strategies, they will attract even more mentally ill offenders who will remain for longer periods of time. This reflects the logic of cost shifts as social policy is driven by changes in funding and efforts to reduce the cost of traditional mental health services in the community.[8]

Larger metropolitan jails have developed and expanded their mental health evaluation and housing capacities, in some instances providing all the facets of hospitalization. But few argue that jail is an appropriate mental health treatment environment. Community linkages must be decisively mandated so that a jail is seen as a clear extension of the community continuum of service; support should follow offenders into jail and remove them as quickly as possible as a service delivery requirement for community-based programs. Many mentally ill offenders are in jail for minor offenses, yet they require an enormous expenditure of resources for evaluation, monitoring, medication issues, short-term therapeutic intervention, special court provisions, and ongoing efforts at suicide prevention for those focused on self-destruction. Mental health courts have been developed in Broward County, FL, and in King County, WA, to seek alternative means of responding to the vast numbers of mentally ill people in jail who could best be served someplace else.[9] The walls of the jails must come down so that jails can collaborate with community-based treatment providers. This is one of the most important directions for corrections and detention at the local level. Across the nation, states have looked elsewhere rather than at the problem that state hospital closure has brought to local government.

Local governments are expressing more concern that state legislatures and executive branches often do not provide responsive fiscal impact statements on how mental health service reductions in state hospitals and community programs affect jail populations. The local governments are focused on the political reality of cost shifts that are often disguised as service or program improvements and as fiscal prudence. Movement of persons from the state hospital to the community to the jail is not an improvement—it simply ignores the issue of mental illness.

Jails are increasingly housing people with a wide range of substance abuse charges, including offenses associated with personal use of alcohol and drugs. Simply put, jails are filled with people who abuse substances. Their criminal behavior may not be a direct and irrevocable result of the consumption of alcohol and other drugs, but the relationship is clear. Jail populations would be dramatically reduced if levels of substance abuse diminished in the community. The increased criminalization of alcohol-related issues and much tougher sanctions for those involved in the drug trade result in billions of dollars in jail and prison construction and far greater operating expenses over the life cycle of such facilities. The paltry amount spent on intervention, treatment, and system linkages is an embarrassment given the industry that has developed around incarceration.

Jails offer little or no deterrence to those involved in the drug world; alcohol-related offenses often reflect a deep pathology in which relapse will occur until some treatment success can be realized. Public safety issues and political reality have driven legislative and executive ac-

tion to vastly expand jail population. But jails are poorly equipped to offer significant substance abuse treatment. Drug courts and Bureau of Justice Assistance funding of some institutional treatment reflect the data generated from the programs evaluating the extent of drug abuse among serious offenders entering a broad range of large metropolitan jail systems. Public policy must determine whether jails will provide significant substance abuse intervention, treatment, and referral—or simply function as custodial holding facilities.

Recent National Center on Addiction and Substance Abuse data from Illinois report that 80 percent of prisoners are involved in drugs or alcohol—the largest percentage reported to date.[10] Jails might as well be substance abuse intake centers. It is unclear why massive treatment intervention through proven modalities has not been suggested as an alternative to vastly expanded jail construction. There has been discussion, but little concerted action has taken place to challenge the traditional use of incarceration at the local jail level. If the jail is to be the response of choice to substance abuse, then direction should be provided to facilitate treatment programs and demand a fair split between enforcement and treatment to diminish the likelihood of criminal relapse. Jails can provide effective short-term substance abuse intervention and treatment if they are properly funded and there are requirements to refer people from jails to the local treatment system.[11] Drug overdose and alcohol-related medical crisis situations follow offenders into local jails throughout this country. Jail intake and booking units increasingly resemble hospital emergency rooms, with their focus on triage and emergency intervention.[12]

Co-Occurring Disorders

The number of people with a combination of mental illness, substance abuse, and antisocial personality disorders in jails is growing. Triage performed in jail intake and booking units has identified a growing population afflicted with co-occuring disorders, creating even greater need for more specialized services within local jails. As a facet of jail admissions and intake, this population represents in part an unintended aspect of deinstitutionalization. Given the disproportionate numbers of people with mental illness and substance abuse problems who find their way to local jails, a strong case can be made for the eradication of traditional boundaries separating elements of the treatment system. Staff must recognize that each element of disorders demand attention if assistance is to be provided and jail populations reduced when other environments and modalities are available.

The presence of persons with co-occurring disorders in jails does in part reflect the general focus of single-dimension treatment programs, which find it difficult to treat persons with multiple disorders. It has been suggested that "such persons may be arrested because they are too mad for substance abuse programs and too bad to be treated in mental health facilities."[13(p.1042)] This does not surprise jail practitioners, for the traditional "bad" and "mad" debate has placed many persons in jail who appear otherwise to be appropriate candidates for community-based treatment or inpatient treatment through involuntary commitment or self-imposed hospitalization.

Far too often, police are unable to find treatment options or referral programs that offer an alternative to jail. Given the propensity of persons with co-occurring disorders to come in conflict with some aspect of the criminal justice system, the local government will either deal appropriately with these critical cases or experience severe crisis situations that develop during the jail intake process.[14]

OCCUPATIONAL EXPOSURE AND COMMUNICABLE DISEASE SAFETY MEASURES

Staff are the single most valuable resource in jails, and they are finding that new issues are arising that did not exist in traditional jail correctional practice in the past. Fear gripped jail staff members over 10 years ago with the advent of HIV infection and a belief that occupational exposure would create personal risk for every person working in a local correctional facility. Information was scarce, but gradually, through the work of groups such as the Centers for Disease Control, the principles of universal precautions were understood and accepted. Jails that received thousands of persons potentially infected with HIV took control of their own environment through staff training. Staff education and the implementation of guidelines under both federal and state mandates have been essential. While HIV infection still concerns staff somewhat, even more threatening communicable diseases have now come into local jail facilities.

Bloodborne and airborne pathogens are now a routine part of jail operations. Communicable diseases found in jails include hepatitis A, hepatitis B, hepatitis C, HIV, tuberculosis, measles, rubella, and vancella. Federal and state regulations and guidelines generally demand an exposure control plan in all jails for bloodborne pathogens and tuberculosis to minimize and manage staff exposure. To ensure staff and inmate protection, jails must have a written exposure control plan (updated annually) with the following elements: engineering controls to isolate the pathogen; work practice controls such as universal precautions; personal protective equipment; staff training; hazard communication through proper labeling and identification of hazard items; availability of hepatitis B vaccine; a postexposure evaluation and follow-up; and detailed recordkeeping procedures for appropriate documentation of training, vaccinations, and postexposure care. Guidelines generally require written protocols for responding to spills, occupational exposures, and other possible means of transmission as well as confidential counseling and testing if an occupational exposure exists. Jurisdictions now have or are developing procedures to gain court orders to mandate testing after an exposure incident when the inmate is the source of the exposure and refuses testing.

For many years, jail staff understood the importance of following appropriate procedures in working with high-risk prisoners—those under the influence of alcohol or who were seriously mentally ill and potentially assaultive. Those were cases that usually could be easily identified. This new aspect of jail operations concerns dangers that cannot be seen or heard and that require a commitment and belief in training for universal precautions. Jail staff who have direct contact with thousands of newly admitted prisoners do face risks. But a decade of practice has clearly demonstrated that when safety measures are implemented, staff are trained to know the procedures, and proper equipment is provided, the potential for transmission is minimal. The materials of jails and admission practices (e.g., negative pressure cells, blood spill containment kits, ultraviolet lamps, and latex gloves) are changing as a function of community and public health issues and developments. In the past, "sharps" might have referred only to inmates' prison-made knives, but now it also applies to the searching of incoming prisoners who might have a syringe in their clothing. Concerns about jail security and the prevention of communicable diseases are integral to jail operations.

These staff safety issues also impact prisons, but less severely. Offenders sent to state prisons have almost always completed a period of pretrial incarceration or review and have been evaluated for obvious health care problems. The millions who pass through U.S. jails have not been evaluated, and many are gone long before any laboratory results could possibly be received.

VICTIM NOTIFICATION

Public policy has often been driven by the determined involvement of advocacy groups with special areas of focus such as domestic violence, violence toward women, and sexual violence. All across the nation, well-developed and knowledgeable victims' organizations have impacted not only legislative policy but jail practices. Historically, victims have never been a focus of jail operations. Jails held persons for very short periods of time and did not seek out the names and locations of victims in pretrial situations. The fact that a conviction might not have occurred, the large number of people in jail, and the brevity or uncertain duration of their stays in jail made such an effort to notify victims of an offender's status either very difficult or simply not part of local jail operations. Jails' approach to victims has changed dramatically with the high visibility of cases where persons accused of domestic violence have left jail prior to disposition of their cases and returned home or to the location of the initial violence and assaulted the victims again.

A nationwide movement has developed as victims' groups have demanded, with complete justification, the implementation of release policies that ensure a court hearing for most accused domestic violence perpetrators prior to pretrial release, and a program of victim notification at both the pretrial and completion of sentence stages of the jail corrections process. Information technology and traditional recordkeeping techniques now have made linkages with victims possible even in situations where thousands of prisoners are released annually from a jail. Jail practice is moving toward both policy and legal requirements that, given the relationship between crimes of domestic violence and the potential for repetition upon release, victim notification be part of the operations of any jail release process. In the near future, there will be no justification for even the smallest short-term jail to fail to provide victim notification for sentenced offenders and pretrial detainees upon their release on bail or through personal recognizance after a court hearing. Such operations conducted by local jails enhance the development of linkages with other groups, including local victims' organizations, victim–witness agencies, and the media. The names of those in custody or the designation of their crimes or alleged crimes are not kept confidential when the release of basic information would help victims stay safe.

INFORMATION TECHNOLOGY AND INTEGRATION

Historically, prisoners booked into jail often were released with additional charges pending and warrants outstanding because information systems were manual and subject to human error. Additionally, false names and incomplete basic data occasionally permitted persons with other serious charges pending to walk out of jail when the immediate charge was dismissed. Information technology and identification systems have vastly improved this situation through electronic imagery, swift fingerprint identification, sorting of names and other personal data and characteristics, and multiple systems to seek identity and related information.

Unfortunately, despite the vast technological growth that has impacted law enforcement, there has been very little systems integration among agencies. Most jurisdictions have proceeded on an individual basis with little or no real collaboration with other parts of the criminal justice system to facilitate real information sharing and joint information development. It is still not uncommon for data to be collected at numerous different points of access and to be entered separately into multiple systems—each of which has material about a particular person. Points of data entry might include the arresting police agency, jail booking unit, jail health care unit, pretrial release agency or unit, community supervision unit, numerous court elements, and community referral programs.[15] This in part explains the extent of incorrect information that systems collect and the vast amount of duplication. Duplication is costly, inefficient, and often the product of traditional bureaucratic processes.

Reengineering must occur within the jail field, or jails will drown under a sea of data that could legally and appropriately be shared on an ongoing basis with an array of system components and community-based stakeholders. Automation was an end in itself for the past 15 years; planners of work systems must now see automation as a method that will be no more valuable than hard copy recordkeeping unless true integration of systems occurs. Efficient labor utilization as well as data accuracy, timeliness, and completeness are compelling reasons to move toward true system integration. With the few exceptions of health care and substance abuse information, most correctional data can be shared; those judgmental notations and evaluative decisions of concern can be shielded through existing firewalls. Jail booking units are a critical data point in the criminal justice system, and jails must participate as advocates for true collaboration in information system integration.

MISDEMEANORS COUNT— THE HIDDEN JAIL POPULATION

Felons' criminal behavior drives the development of anticrime policies that focus on crimes of violence in the United States. State prisons have expanded enormously over the past 20 years in response to sentencing enhancements in nearly every state. The nature of misdemeanor offenses is less well understood. Many consider misdemeanor offenses to be somewhat insignificant criminal activity that is more of a nuisance than a threat to public safety. As mentioned above, this is one reason that local jails have not been seen as critical elements of the U.S. criminal justice system.

This logic has been challenged in recent years as a result of efforts to diminish criminal behaviors in large urban environments such as New York City. It has been learned through street experience that most public perceptions regarding street-level safety focus on misdemeanant behaviors. Experiences in New York City and now in other urban environments such as Seattle have demonstrated that when minor offenses are overlooked, felony behavior expands and felons are not apprehended. Public perceptions of personal safety are also diminished, and the urban environment is perceived as dangerous and not part of an open society. George Kelling, James Q. Wilson, and Catherine Coles have publicized these concepts over a period of years. Their argument about "fixing broken windows" emphasizes the importance of having policies that take misdemeanant offenses seriously and attack street-level behaviors.[16,17]

In many U.S. jails, thousands of misdemeanant bookings do not occur (either because of formal local practice or day-to-day decision making) as a result of insufficient jail space. Many communities and their elected officials are careful to avoid informing local citizens that police agencies may not bring many classes of misdemeanant offenders to jail and that hundreds of thousands of existing warrants are not served because of lack of jail space. These decisions, made without voter approval, challenge the efficacy of criminal justice and law enforcement at the local level. Jail populations may be artificially low because warrants are not served and citations are issued in cases where jail is the appropriate response. Site visits to cities where misdemeanant offenses and a vast array of warrants are not served or booked have shown offenders on street corners waiving citations in the air. This demolishes the morale of police officers in the field and speak poorly about a city's commitment to public safety and criminal justice.

This problem, which is far broader than generally understood, challenges many sheriffs. They are sworn to enforce the law yet must turn away prisoners because of lack of space and funds to provide adequate staffing for their jails. This is a partially hidden element of jail intake, but it reflects an evolving and growing practice in local jail operations when resources do not keep pace with need. Communities that do not restrict bookings or release prisoners early have often encountered sizeable financial costs—at the expense of popular recreation, social service, and health care programs. However, other communities have led the way in developing nonjail options and alternatives to traditional incarceration.[18,19] At the local level, these efforts include efficiency in court operations and all aspects of the pretrial process to maintain the integrity of the criminal justice system.

LANGUAGE, ETHNIC DIVERSITY, AND STAFF SELECTION AND DEVELOPMENT

Inmates processed in jail intake units reflect the cultural and linguistic diversity of this nation. Immigration patterns are shifting in response to political and social turmoil around the world. Jail intake units have a growing Latino/Hispanic component. Since the 1970s, the United States has been the immigration and refugee focal point for movement from Southeast Asia. Rekindled movements from Asia have been buttressed by movements from the former Soviet Union and throughout Eastern Europe, where there have been changes and turmoil. A portion of these population groups have entered our jail system, and the focus on ethnic and linguistic diversity has never been stronger.

Linguistic skills and cultural sensitivity are extremely important in the jail intake process, where language and cultural understanding may ensure the personal safety of staff or inmates or even facilitate critical life-sustaining decision. These concerns are changing staff development policies and broadening traditional bases of recruitment. One jail system recently sought special assistance in linking with a growing Russian community to recruit Russian-speaking and culturally knowledgeable corrections officers. This effort will be repeated throughout the country.

With large numbers of prisoners who are members of minority groups, jails must increase staff diversity. Jail administrators must develop a workforce that reflects our national community. Diverse populations mean even greater professional challenges for jail staff.

LINKAGES TO THE COMMUNITY— THE JAIL AS A FOCAL POINT OF SYSTEMS PARTNERSHIP

This chapter began with data about the millions of persons who are admitted to jails in this country. If those transactions are seen in part as opportunities for linkage with the community to which most jailed persons will be returning in a very short time frame, there will be enhancements to not only public safety but networks of people, service providers, and systems of assistance. Jails have a greater impact on public safety than prisons because jails release millions each year back to the community. These millions truly impact public perceptions of safety through their behavior. If our jails become part of expanding community-based service networks, then the jails will be seen as not simply a place where persons charged with serious offenses await disposition or a place where minor offenders spend a few hours or a few days. Local jails should be seen as an integral part of the community. Jails deal with their clientele in their home areas—where they grew up, reside, and will return to and where their families and associates continue to live.

Linkages are not defined just as calls to agencies about the release of a prisoner. Rather, they should be thought of as a collaboration with a service agency and information sharing between agencies from the time offenders arrive until they depart. Service delivery should be increasingly seamless. For years, co-occurring disorders have proved troublesome to treat for agencies focused on one dimension, which were unable to provide both mental health and substance abuse services overlaid with personality disorder considerations. In the same way, the jail was unable to access key services in the community (education, human service, social and family services, vocational training and referral, employment assistance, and health care in its broadest construction) because jails were seen as formidable physical plants without an interest in collaboration. Jails must serve as a broker of services or find broker-type information capabilities to assist persons leaving the jail, whether to secure a room for the night or to find people treatment for chronic mental health problems. With the expansion of information technology and the understanding of the relationships between many public safety and human and family service issues, the only option other than collaboration is isolation and a lost potential of great proportions. Public administrators and elected officials should seize the moment to understand the unique role of the jail and its potential in broader public safety considerations for the future.

NOTES

1. D. Gilliard and A. Beck, *Prison and Jail Inmates at Midyear 1997* (Washington, DC: Bureau of Justice Statistics, January 1998), 6.

2. M. O'Toole and A. Wallenstein, "Jail Crowding: Bringing the Issue to the Corrections' Center Stage," *Corrections Today,* December 1996, 76–81.

3. G. Kelling and C. Coles, *Fixing Broken Windows: Order and Reducing Crime in our Communities* (New York: The Free Press, 1996).

4. B. Anno, *Prison Health Care: Guidelines for the Management of an Adequate Delivery System* (Washington, DC: National Institute of Corrections/National Commission on Correctional Health Care, 1991), 5.

5. National Commission on Correctional Health Care, *Standards for Health Services in Jails* (Chicago: 1996), xi.

6. F. Butterfield, "Prisons Replace Hospitals for the Nation's Mentally Ill," *New York Times,* 5 March, 1998, 1.

7. "Jails Nationwide Trying To Cope with Increasing Numbers of Mentally Ill Offenders," *Corrections Alert,* 17 November, 1997, 1.

8. I. Miller, "Managed Care Is Harmful to Outpatient Mental Health Services: A Case for Accountability," *Professional Psychology: Research and Practice* 27, no. 4 (1996): 349–363.

9. Mental Health Court Task Force. "Recommendations for the King County Mental Health Court" (Seattle, WA: King County Government, 1998), 1–35.

10. National Center on Addiction and Substance Abuse. *Behind Bars: Substance Abuse and America's Prison Population* (New York: 1998).

11. T. Slyter, Jr., "Addicts in Our Jails—Do We Warehouse, Punish, or Treat Them?" *American Jails,* July/August 1998, 41–43.

12. National Institute of Corrections, "Survey of Mental Health Services in Large Jails and Jail Systems" (Longmont, CO: National Institute of Corrections Information Center, 1995), 1–15.

13. K. Abram and L. Teplin, "Co-Occurring Disorders among Mentally Ill Jail Detainees," *American Psychologist,* October 1991, 1042.

14. H. Steadman and B. Veysey, "Providing Services for Jail Inmates with Mental Disorders," *American Jails,* May/June 1997, 11–23.

15. SEARCH (The National Consortium for Justice Information Statistics), *System Integration: Issues Surrounding Integration of County-Level Justice Information Systems* (Washington, DC: Bureau of Justice Statistics, 1996).

16. J. Wilson and G. Kelling, "The Police and Neighborhood Safety," *The Atlantic,* March 1982, 29–38.

17. Kelling and Coles, *Fixing Broken Windows: Order and Reducing Crime in Our Communities.*

18. American Jail Association, *Jail Population Reduction Strategies: An Examination of Five Jurisdictions' Response to Jail Crowding* (Longmont, CO: National Institute of Corrections Information Center, 1997), 4.

19. P. McGarry and M. Carter, eds. *The Intermediate Sanctions Handbook: Experiences and Tools for Policymakers* (Washington, DC: Center for Effective Public Policy, 1993).

CHAPTER 8

Short-Term Institutions at the Local Level

Ken Kerle

Many people, even some who work in criminal justice, misunderstand the differences between (1) a jail and a prison and (2) a jail and a lockup. Much of this confusion can be directly attributed to members of the media, who use these words imprecisely. A news headline that reads "Accused Convicted and Receives a 400-Year Jail Sentence" indicates that the writer or perhaps the editors do not understand what differentiates various penal institutions.

Due to prison crowding, some states have mandated that local jails hold state inmates.[1,2] One must remember that jails admit 30 times as many persons as prisons do each year (if one compares jail admission with new court commitments to state and federal prisons).[3] From another perspective, according to the Bureau of Justice Statistics, more than 20 million people were booked in and out of the over 3,000 American jails in 1995.[4]

The Bureau of Justice Statistics defines different reasons jails admit people.

1. Jails receive individuals pending arraignment and hold them as they await trial, conviction, or sentencing.
2. Jails readmit probation, parole, and bail bond violators and absconders.
3. Jails temporarily detain juveniles pending transfer to juvenile authorities.
4. Jails hold mentally ill persons before they are moved to appropriate health facilities.
5. Jails hold individuals for the military, for contempt, as witnesses for the courts, and for protective custody.
6. Jails release convicted inmates to the community upon completion of sentence.
7. Jails house inmates for federal, state, or other authorities because of crowding of their facilities, and relinquish custody of temporary detainees to juvenile and medical authorities.
8. Jails sometimes operate community-based programs as alternatives to incarceration.
9. Jails hold inmates sentenced to short terms (generally under one year).[5]

Short-term jails in this chapter are defined as those that hold sentenced prisoners for no more than one year. An article published in *American Jails* illustrated the differences between jails and prisons by a representative model of two 1,000-bed facilities to show the admission disparities in a one-year period (see Table 8–1).

A jail is an institution (usually operated by the county and sometimes by a municipality) where both pretrial and sentenced prisoners are confined. A lockup is often a police-operated facility where arrested individuals are held from 24 to 72 hours, depending on the jurisdiction. After that period of time, the individual held in the lockup is transported to the local jail to be admitted (booked). Lockups are found frequently in larger cities where, for the convenience of the

Table 8–1   One Prison/Jail Comparison

	Jail	Prison
Rated capacity	1,000	1,000
Average daily population	1,000	1,000
Admissions	23,500	500
Total inmates	**24,500**	**1,500**

Source: Reprinted with permission from M. O'Toole, "Jails and Prisons: The Numbers Say They Are More Different Than Generally Assumed," *American Jails*, May/June, 1997, p. 28, © 1997, American Jail Association.

arresting officers, people are transported directly to the police precinct lockups, often found at the police stations or in city courts or other municipal buildings.

Nobody can give a precise figure as to how many lockups there are in operation. H. Hart did a national study in the 1930s and reported on 11,000 local police jails and lockups.[6] A text on United States corrections published in 1995 claimed there were more than 15,000 lockups in the country and around 3,400 jails.[7] In 1994, the American Jail Association listed 3,272 jails.[8] To my knowledge, there is no accurate published information about the exact number of lockups. Generally, states have done a poor job of keeping track of this data. In today's automated world, such information could be easily collected and disseminated.

Lockups are products of bygone eras. The fewer of them, the better. The International Association of Chiefs of Police (IACP) encourages police to get out of the lockup business, because often police departments lack staff to properly supervise people in these facilities. (Jerry Needle of the IACP provided this information in a comment at a November 12, 1986, meeting of the National Coalition on Jail Reform in Warrenton, VA.)

DIVERSITY AMONG JAILS

Not only are there differences among jail systems in the 50 states (6 states, Alaska, Connecti-

cut, Delaware, Hawaii, Rhode Island, and Vermont, for example, operate combined jail/prison systems), but there may be important distinctions within a state. West Virginia, which is moving toward a jail system of 10 regional jails operated by a state jail regional authority, is today a mix of regional jails and sheriff-run jails, a situation that will continue until sheriff-run jails are eliminated in the early part of the twenty-first century.[9]

Ohio, a state of 88 counties and hundreds of cities, classifies jails into four categories: full-service, five-day, eight-hour, and minimum security jails (see Exhibit 8–1). Ohio's minimum security jails are designed to detain sentenced adults for more than 120 hours for a misdemeanor or a felony of the fourth or fifth degree, provided the person has been classified as a minimum security risk by the jail administrator or designee.

Roughly 75 percent of jails in the United States are under the jurisdiction of an elected sheriff; the other 25 percent have an appointed jail administrator who answers to a county-elected or city board.[10]

THE BOOKING AREA AND ITS PROBLEMS

The most critical area in short-term or long-term jails is the admitting area—called the booking area. There are greater security risks in booking areas because so many people enter and exit the jail from this point. People arrested and brought into the booking area are often high on drugs, alcohol, or a combination thereof, which creates problems. The stress level of arrested suspects is apt to be high. Some are furious and ready to hit the first person who comes within striking distance. Perhaps not surprisingly, most jail fights occur in the booking area.

Jails also book in a substantial number of individuals who exhibit some form of mental disturbance, often in addition to their alcohol and drug problems. A 1992 survey of 1,391 city and county jail facilities discovered that more than 1 in 14 people in jail were seriously mentally ill.[11]

Exhibit 8–1   Ohio Jails

Category	Number
Full-service	94
Five-day	108
Eight-hour	50
Minimum security	15
Total	**267**

Note: In Ohio, the lockup is labeled an eight-hour jail.

Source: Reprinted with permission from G.A. Bucholtz and H.E. Hageman, "Examining Ohio's Jails: A Descriptive and Comparative Overview," *American Jails,* November/December, 1997 © 1997 American Jail Association.

A study by Linda Teplin estimated that from 6 to 8 percent of jail inmates suffer from a serious mental disorder.[12]

Ideally, the jail should have mental health personnel and substance abuse counselors on duty 24 hours a day to diagnose and manage these problems. Except in some larger jails, this frequently is not the case (especially in short-term jail facilities); then, the booking officer must identify unusual aspects of the inmate's behavior for senior staff. This quick diagnosis can be based on observations of sudden shifts in mood or personality, hallucinations, unrealistic physical complaints, intense anxiety, paranoia, delusion, and loss of memory.[13]

BOOKING FEMALE INMATES

In recent years, more females have been incarcerated in jail. From 1985 to June 30, 1997, the percentage of women in the average daily population in jails rose from 8 percent to 10.6 percent (over 19,000 in 1985 to almost 60,000 in midyear 1997).[14] Because women booked into the jail can stay from less than a day to more than a year in many jurisdictions, it is imperative that jail booking staff understand various aspects of female incarceration.

It is very helpful to have female employees. Bureau of Justice Statistics figures broke out the total jail payroll staff by sex and race for 1988 and 1993. The proportion of female jail officers increased from 22.6 percent in 1988 to 24.2 percent by 1993.[15] Thus, over three-quarters of jail staffs remain male. This means that often some jails, especially short-term facilities, lack female staff officers for the entire 24-hour shift.

Male officers assigned to intake operations need additional training to help them be sensitive to the different issues of women prisoners. For example, women prisoners often need information and reassurance about what will happen to their children.[16]

Jail booking forms in both short-term and long-term jails ought to be inclusive enough to contain questions about physical and sexual abuse, as a sign that jail managers recognize abuse as a major problem. It is also useful for staff to become more aware of the impact their own presence has on the jail environment—to know which of their actions may heighten the stress of new detainees or provoke violent responses.

FEMALE STAFF FACE CHALLENGES

As more women employees begin working in jails, some confront sexual harassment. Sexual harassment must be addressed by jails' top managers, with particular emphasis placed on good policies and procedures explained to the entire work force. The Rappahannock Security Center in Fredericksburg, VA, is atypical; 51 percent of the jail's general staff and 38 percent of its security staff are female. Top management at the institution recruited women because it considers this to be in the best long-term interest of the facility; they believe female staff to be more effective than male staff. Managers paid considerable attention to the harassment policies, because they believed that the successful implementation of these policies would be directly related to the successful integration of the female staff.[17] Unfortunately, small, short-term jail facilities often lack the wherewithal to see that proper training and policies are carried out.

A recent study, which examined the various problems stemming from sexism and sexual harassment in four county Colorado jails in the Denver area, makes the point that the organization of corrections work itself helps produce and reinforce workplace attitudes and behavior about sexism and sexual harassment.[18] To minimize this inappropriate behavior, administrators need to invest in the professional development of all employees, advance the ideals of professionalism, and establish closer linkages to line staff. The U.S. Supreme Court ruled in a pair of cases at the close of the 1998 spring term that employers will be held liable if they fail to publish policies and procedures on sexual harassment for employee guidance.[19]

LACK OF STANDARDS AND TRAINING

With a few notable exceptions, states generally have not paid enough attention to jail staff training. Training of jail staff started 50 years ago within the Federal Bureau of Prisons. This large agency, in conjunction with the U.S. Marshals Service, houses federal prisoners in a number of local jails. Formal training began when the federal agencies became concerned that states had defaulted on their responsibility to train jail staff. The Federal Bureau of Prisons established a weeklong training school for sheriffs and jailers back in 1948.[20]

Even in 1998, there were still 15 states that lacked both state jail inspections and training standards for local jails.[21] Since 1994, Kansas has completely eliminated all forms of jail inspection and Florida has abolished state jail inspection, replacing it with a system in which counties inspect other county facilities—which is equivalent to letting the fox guard the henhouse.

Absent formal training, some short-term jails have on-the-job training. If the "trainer" has had no formal training, the results are problematic at best. To the extent that the new hire has to learn by trial and error, the chance that jail litigation against the county will succeed is apt to rise sharply if there is a death or disaster. Small wonder that the International Association of Corrections Professionals (IACP) encourages police agencies to get out of the lockup and jail business.

JAIL SUICIDE

Short-term jails—more than any other government agencies—are places where people are likely to take their own lives. Apparently, the coming down off the high of substance abuse can contribute to a compulsion to self-destruct. In addition, some people who have been arrested for the first time cannot stand the thought of facing family and peers again. One study, *And Darkness Closes In,* documented that 143 out of 285 jail suicides occurred within 24 hours of admission. Jails should be preoccupied with preventing suicides.[22]

Most jail suicides occur because of hanging instead of gunfire or an overdose of pills.[23] This fact places short-term jail facilities, often understaffed, in vulnerable positions. Whereas drugs and firearms are not readily accessible in a confinement setting, inmates can hang themselves with sheets, towels, and articles of clothing.

Without suicide prevention training, it is difficult to defend the staff or agency against charges that it failed to protect the arrestee against his or her own darker side. In one short-term detention facility I visited in Saskatchewan, prisoners were recorded on video camera for their entire stay. If an incident took place, the recording could be produced to provide visual evidence as to what happened.

In the late 1970s and early 1980s, New York State had a significant number of jail suicides and made a diligent effort to see that the jail booking form got revamped to enable the booking officer to check off certain categories of behavior that would provide information about the prisoner's mental state. If a certain proportion of the inmate's characteristics fell into the negative column, the officer placed the individual on suicide watch. Jail suicide training also received emphasis. The *Trainer's Manual/Officer Handbook* told officers to trust their own judgment and not allow others to persuade them to ignore suicidal signals.[24] In a nine-year period, 1984–1993, New York jails had reduced the number of yearly suicides from 26 to 3.[25]

The Mobile County, AL, jail implemented a buddy system program where a select group of inmates would be trained to stay with other prisoners suspected of suicidal inclinations. The inmates were taught not to intervene but to report destructive behavior to the corrections officer. These inmate volunteers were screened and educated as to their duties. The sheriff organized a system to notify local judges about which inmates had completed an eight-hour suicide watch. A judge was not under any obligation to reduce a prisoner's sentence or award special privileges but was made aware of the inmate's contribution to the jail's suicide prevention program. After the Mobile County jail had implemented the program, it had no lawsuits initiated against it for successful suicide for two years.[26]

Training of jail staff in suicide prevention seems to have paid off. The Bureau of Justice Statistics' *Jails and Jail Inmates 1993–94* reveals a marked reduction in jail suicides from 129 in 1983 to 54 in 1993. The bulletin notes that the number of jail deaths from all causes were underreported by the small jails, which housed only 7 percent of the nation's jail population, but despite that the improvement in jail suicide reduction has been significant.[27]

Many of the smaller jails have little or no support from community mental health staff or other mental health professionals to deal with mentally disturbed prisoners and the possibility of suicide attempts. Local jails need to deal with suicide attempts and the mentally disturbed more competently, but considerably more support must be forthcoming from community agencies.

The joint report of the National Alliance for the Mentally Ill and the Public Citizen's Health Research Group made 12 recommendations to improve the situation.

1. States that have laws permitting jails to be used for emergency detention of mentally ill people not charged with any crime should immediately amend such laws to clearly prohibit this practice. Seventeen states had been identified that permitted this.

2. Jail diversion programs should be set up to minimize the number of individuals with serious mental illness who end up in jails.

3. All inmates with serious mental illness should be evaluated by a mental health professional within 24 hours of admission to jail. Ongoing psychiatric services, including medications if needed, should be available in the jails on a timely basis.

4. Inmates with serious mental illnesses in jail who need medication and have no insight into their illness should be medicated involuntarily if necessary to protect themselves and others.

5. In counties or states in which mental health authorities have failed to set up diversion programs and in which significant numbers of individuals with serious mental illnesses continued to be jailed on misdemeanor charges or without charges, the department of mental health should be required to transfer funds to the department of correction.

6. When inmates with serious mental illnesses are released from jails, follow-up psychiatric care as needed should be mandated by the courts as a condition of parole or probation. A specific individual under the local mental health agency should be held responsible for ensuring that such follow-up takes place.

7. Corrections officers who work in jails and police officers in the community should receive training on serious mental illnesses at the time they begin their employment and should receive annual continuing education.

8. All state or federally supported training programs for mental health professionals

should require trainees to spend a minimum of six hours training in jails.

9. Mental health professionals should be required to provide pro bono services for two hours per week to public mental health facilities, including jails, as a condition of licensure.

10. Increased resources under the Protection and Advocacy Act of 1986 should be devoted to assisting individuals with serious mental illnesses in jails.

11. Relevant federal and state statistical reporting systems should be modified to reflect the existence of seriously mentally ill people in jails.

12. For each jail in the United States, there should be a standing mental illness committee including a representative of the jail, the local department of mental health, the local public psychiatric inpatient unit, and the local chapter of the National Alliance for the Mentally Ill.[28]

CONCLUSION

In the twenty-first century, the short-term county and city correctional facilities could be improved if more emphasis were placed on integrating these institutions using cooperative arrangements with other community and criminal justice agencies (police, courts, prosecuting attorneys, probation, parole, education, vocational training, community mental health, public health, welfare, etc.) that handle many of the people who get arrested and end up in jail. Short-term jails would better serve their communities if more people placed in them were handled in community correctional alternative programs.

To improve the correctional system, jail staff need more education and training. County government leaders need to learn more about community correctional alternative programs, which can be cheaper and more effective for many individuals. Finally, the voters who elect these officials must also clearly comprehend the advantages to these new alternatives.

NOTES

1. R. van den Heuvel, "When Jails Become Prisons," *American Jails* 8, no. 5, November/December 1994, 11–15.

2. B. Harris-George et al., "State Jails—Texas Answer to Overcrowding," *American Jails* 8, no. 5, November/December 1994, 17–20.

3. United States Department of Justice, Press Release, March 6, 1997.

4. "Statistical Abstract of the United States 1996," in *The National Data Book* (Washington, DC: U.S. Department of Commerce, Economics and Statistics Administration, Bureau of the Census, October 1996).

5. D. Gilliard and A. Beck, *Prison and Jail at Midyear 1997*, NCJ-167247 (Washington, DC: Bureau of Justice Statistics, January 1998).

6. H. Hart, "A Special Report to the National Commission on Law Observance and Enforcement, Chairman of the Advisory Committee on Penal Institutions, Probation, and Parole," in *Report on Penal Institutions, Probation, and Parole,* no. 9 (Washington, DC: National Commission on Law Observance and Enforcement, 1931), 327–344.

7. M. Welch, *Corrections—A Critical Approach* (New York: McGraw-Hill Publishing, 1995), 179.

8. *Who's Who in Jail Management,* 2d ed. (Hagerstown, MD: American Jail Association, 1994), 2.

9. L. Parsons, "The Regionalization of West Virginia Jails," *American Jails,* July/August 1994, 51–54.

10. *Who's Who in Jail Management,* 2d ed.

11. E. Torrey et al., *Criminalizing the Seriously Mentally Ill—The Abuse of Jails as Mental Hospitals* (Washington, DC: National Alliance for the Mentally Ill and Public Citizen's Health Research Group, 1992), 14.

12. L. Teplin, "The Prevalence of Severe Mental Disorder among Male, Urban Jail Detainees: Comparison with the Epidemilogical Catchment Area Program," *American Journal of Public Health* 80, no. 6 (1990): 663–669.

13. B. Hill et al., "Working with Inmates with Mental Illness," *Jail Operations Bulletin* 4, no. 10 (1992): 1–6.

14. Gilliard and Beck, *Prison and Jail Inmates at Midyear 1997.*

15. C. Perkins et al., *Jails and Jail Inmates 1993–94,* NCJ-151651 (Washington, DC: Bureau of Justice Statistics, April 1995), 8.

16. B. Veysey et al., "Effective Management of Female Jail Detainees with Histories of Physical and Sexual Abuse," *American Jails,* May/June 1998, 50–54.

17. R. Friend and M. Leibowitz, "Sexual Harassment: An Issue for Women in Corrections," *American Jails,* May/June 1993, 11–14.

18. M. Pogrebin and E. Poole, "The Sexualized Work Environment: A Look at Women Jail Officers," *American Jails,* July/August 1997, 9–23.

19. J. Biskupic, "High Court Draws Line on Sexual Harassment," *The Washington Post,* 27 June, 1998, 1, 11.

20. "The County Jail Panel," *The National Sheriff,* May/June 1948, 5–7.

21. *Who's Who in Jail Management,* 2d ed., 648–651.

22. L. Hayes and B. Cajdan, *And Darkness Closes In— A National Study of Jail Suicides* (Mansfield, MA: National Center on Institutions and Alternatives, 1980).

23. W. Stone, "Means of the Cause of Death in Texas Jail Suicides," *American Jails,* May/June 1990, 50–53.

24. J. Rowan, "Beware the Halo Effect of Mental Health Personnel when They Say 'Not Suicidal.' Recommended: A National Policy Change," *American Jails,* January/February 1991, 24–27.

25. J. Rowan, "Suicide Prevention—Debunking the Experts," *American Jails,* November/December 1994, 21–28.

26. R. Manning, "A Suicide Prevention Program That Really Works," *American Jails,* Spring 1989, 18–22.

27. C. Perkins et al., *Jails and Jail Inmates 1993–94,* 5.

28. E. Torrey et al., *Criminalizing the Seriously Mentally Ill—The Abuse of Jails as Mental Hospitals,* 97–101.

CHAPTER 9

Jails as Long-Term Facilities

Ken Kerle

In the good old days, most jails in the United States kept only people with sentences of one year or less. Ocassionally, a person might be sentenced on two different counts that together could equal over a year in jail time. But anything over a year usually meant that individuals would serve their time in a state prison. These "rules" gradually disappeared in the 1980s and 1990s, when an increasing number of the larger jails found themselves housing more people serving longer periods of time.

Jail facilities have trouble dealing with long-term populations. Most jails are not designed for this purpose. They often lack program space, do not have staff devoted to education and training, and generally have extremely limited recreational facilities.

What has caused this surge in jail populations, and what can be done to deal with the problems presented by prisoners serving longer terms in facilities designed for short-term detention?

There are three broad reasons for the overall increase in the numbers of jail inmates, especially long-term cases.

1. More crime, more criminal arrests, less public tolerance for crime, and longer jail sentences have created larger numbers of typical jail inmates.
2. Many local and regional operations have been required to house prisoners who have been sentenced to state prisons, but the state facilities have been so over-crowded that they have been unable to accept the newly sentenced offenders.
3. Some local jurisdictions have attempted to "rent out" jail space to other jurisdictions. Such contractual agreements have created income for local authorities and an interest in seeking boarders from other jurisdictions—occasionally remote states.

U.S. jail populations nearly trebled from 1983 to midyear 1997, jumping from over 223,000 to over 637,000.[1] Two tables from the Bureau of Justice Statistics (Tables 9–1 and 9–2) show the growth in numbers of inmates held in jails from federal and state jurisdiction and from other local jurisdictions.

According to the *Sourcebook of Criminal Justice Statistics 1996,* 25 states had jails that held prisoners for other jurisdictions for whatever reasons—that is, whether coerced by state governments or trying to make money to pay off jail bond or put more dollars in the county treasuries (see Exhibit 9–1).[2(p. 514)]

In the November/December 1994 issue of *American Jails,* the editorial theme was "jails as prisons." In the BC (before crowding) days, most jails would hold a sentenced prisoner up to a year at most. Usually the only others were prisoners in transit—state inmates who had to appear in court the following day, parole or probation pickups, or people held in protective custody for other jurisdictions. When the crowding

Table 9–1 Inmates Held in Local Jails for State and Federal Authorities

	All Jail Inmates Held for Other Authorities		Jail Inmates Held Due to Crowding Elsewhere[a]	
Year	Number	Percent	Number	Percent
1983	17,281	7.7	6,470	2.9
1988	36,737	10.7	23,186	6.8
1993[b]	53,900	11.7	34,200	7.4

[a] Includes inmates held as a direct result of overcrowding in state or federal institutions.

[b] Because of nonresponse, all numbers for 1993 were estimated.

Source: Reprinted from Craig A. Perkins et al., *Jails and Jail Inmates 1993–1994,* Bureau of Justice Statistics Bulletin NCJ 151651.

Table 9–2 Inmates Held in Jails for Other Authorities, 1989 and 1996

Authority	1996	1989
Federal		
Federal Bureau of Prisons	9,181	7,111
U.S. Marshals Service	3,417	1,321
Immigration and Naturalization Service	1,877	2,299
State	28,882	22,729
Other local authorities	20,996	13,121
Unknown	2,207	925
Number	61,206	43,886
Percent of all jail inmates	12.2%	11.1%

Source: Reprinted from Carolyn W. Harlow, *Profile of Jail Inmates 1996,* Bureau of Justice Statistics Bulletin NCJ 164620, 1998.

Exhibit 9–1 States Housing Prisoners in Jails Because of Crowded State Facilities

Region	Number of States
Northeast	2
Midwest	4
South	12
West	7

Source: Reprinted from *Sourcebook of Criminal Justice Statistics 1996,* Hindelang Criminal Justice Research Center, Bureau of Justice Statistics, NCJ 165361.

LOCAL JAILS STUCK WITH STATE PRISONERS

Many of the excess jail prisoners in recent years have been legally the responsibility of various state penal institutions; more often than they like to admit, state prison authorities allowed these state inmates to be backed up in jails to relieve the crowding at the state prisons. Some jail administrators greatly resented being dumped on by state governments; invariably, local officials felt cheated by the sometimes-paltry amounts paid to house state inmates.

Probably the worst situation of this kind was found in the Texas prison system, in which thousands of state inmates were crammed into numerous county jails. Texas found itself in this contentious situation because of federal litigation, *Ruiz v. Estelle,* that had led the court to place the entire state prison system into receivership. Part of the hotly contested case was directly related to serious overpopulation of the state penal facilities operated by the Texas Department of Correction (TDC). The lawsuit resulted in population capacity limitations being imposed on the corrections department; over 21,000 state-sentenced individuals were left detained in Texas local jails, as the TDC was unable to accommodate new prisoners at the rate the state courts were sentencing them.

Many of the counties that were holding the surplus inmates were caught between a rock and

began, suddenly jails in some states began to hold sentenced inmates for two, three, four, or five years, or in some instances a life sentence.[3]

a hard place. Local governments were forced to build new jail facilities or expand existing operations. Because this was a very expensive problem for county leaders, the issue ultimately culminated in a lawsuit, *The County Nueces, Texas v. Texas Board of Corrections*. Nueces County was joined by many other counties in the litigation. The main charge, as one might surmise, was the failure of the state to meet its statutory obligation to receive state-convicted felons into its prison system. Local authorities prevailed; the state lost the contest in a lower court, appealed the decision, lost again, and eventually was required to pay the counties $20 per day for each convicted felon housed in local jails who should have been placed in the state prison system. For the period September 28, 1987, to February 28, 1990, the state owed the 12 counties $100.3 million for housing these state prisoners.[4]

The Middlesex County Jail in New Jersey found itself in an equally precarious situation. In 1994, there were over 16,000 inmates in New Jersey jails, and over 4,000 were serving state sentences. This county had held state inmates since the 1980s; the state did, however, work closely with the local jail system and avoided sending hardened prisoners to the jail.[5] The state allowed the local institution the option of sending those state prisoners who were troublemakers back to the state institutions.

Tennessee also had a similar problem. The Tennessee Department of Corrections lacked bed space and allowed its inmates to back up in local jails throughout the state. In a short period of time, local county jails—especially Davidson and Shelby (Tennessee's most populated counties)—began to feel the impact of this backup. At the Shelby County Correctional Center in Memphis, inmates sentenced to the Tennessee Department of Corrections arrived at the county facility; over a five-period (1992–1996), the daily count of state inmates averaged around 200.

In this situation, the Tennessee Department of Corrections worked with the local jails and attempted to limit inmates in jails to those considered less of a security risk; the state's diagnostic center took pains to see that those inmates left at Shelby County were classified as below maximum security. Restrictions were applied in the county jail system for these individuals. They were not permitted to work outside the correctional center, and they could not be housed at the adult offender center, designed for misdemeanant and low security felons, some of whom were on work release programs.[6] William E. Freeman, Jr., Director of Corrections, Shelby County—while participating in a panel discussion training seminar entitled "Jails with State Inmates" at the Fifteenth-Annual Training Conference and Jail Expo of the American Jail Association—noted that a state prisoner could be held for up to eight years in the Shelby County institution.

This situation had some positive results. Despite the crowding by this intrusion, some saw the practical side of keeping state inmates in their home county. These prisoners had much greater access to their families, and the telephone calls were not a major financial burden on their relatives; staff reported that these factors boosted inmate morale. The victims of crime also had easier access to parole hearings, should they wish to make an appearance.

Nevertheless, many jurisdictions simply could not accept the state prison system's inability to manage its responsibilities. In Arlington, VA, the sheriff and jail management staff noted that the jail was still not the place for state-ready inmates because it was a high-rise building with limited movement and minimal opportunities for family contact. Delays in the state moving out its state-ready inmates caused unacceptable and dangerous crowding problems.[7] Eventually, the Arlington County sheriff joined with two other sheriffs in Virginia and threatened court action to compel the state to remove its state inmates whose confinement in county facilities placed the state in violation of its own laws.[8] The state voluntarily removed its inmates and avoided possible protracted litigation.

The jail administrator in Albany County, NY, described the practice of crowding all New York county jail facilities with state inmates to the point that in the late 1980s the New York State Sheriff's Association sued the State Department of Correctional Services and won.[9] The New York Court of Appeals ruled that all state-ready inmates must be accepted by the State Department of Correctional Services within 10 days of notification of state readiness.[10]

JAIL BEDS FOR RENT—THE VACANCY SIGN IS OUT

By July 1994, state prison construction started to relieve the pressure on county facilities, many of which had been expanded. As the new state facilities accepted their prisoners, the inmate count at many county jails began to recede to normal and below-normal levels.

For example, in Texas many new jail facilities were underutilized. By mid-1995, the jail in Denton County held no more state inmates. The sheriff of Denton County described the dilemma: "I was faced with two choices—close part of the facility and lay off up to 50 employees, or seek a contract housing partner. I chose the latter option, as it made no sense to me to mothball a practically brand-new facility or lose trained personnel."[11]

The sheriff chose to establish a contract with Oregon and arranged to have three plane loads of Oregon prisoners flown to within 100 miles of Denton County. Transport vans were dispatched to drive the inmates to the jail facility. One stipulation of the contract was that all Oregon prisoners would have to return to Oregon for release and another was that the prisoners had to still have two years to serve on their sentences.[12] Eventually, the Oregon prisoners were returned home, and Denton County entered into a new contract to hold federal detainees/prisoners for the United States Immigration and Naturalization Service.

A similar, but less successful, situation developed in 1996 when Missouri contracted to house 400 prisoners in the county facility of Brazoria, TX; the government facility was contractually operated by a private corrections company. This business relationship was not of significant du-

ration. A tremendous public outcry arose nationally when a staff member of the private corrections company videotaped, apparently for a training class, a scene of officers utilizing police attack dogs on the inmates and inflicting kicks and punches on unresisting prisoners. Missouri quickly reclaimed its inmates.[13]

A saga of the Spokane County Jail in Washington State further illustrates the downside to this money-making approach. An article in *American Jails* opens with the following paragraph:

> In the early morning hours of December 15, 1988, 50 sentenced felons from the overcrowded Lorton Correctional Complex [Washington, DC] were shepherded aboard a chartered airplane at Dulles International airport and flown over 3,000 miles to their new home—the Spokane County Jail in Washington State. Their transfer came less than three weeks after the Spokane County Board of Commissioners signed a $1.4 million, one-year contract to house prisoners from the District of Columbia Department of Corrections in the county jail.[14]

Prior to this, the Spokane County facility had made extra money housing state inmates from Washington's state prison system, but an accelerated building program by the state emptied the beds, and the county found itself with a jail vacancy rate of about 25 percent. Ironically, the county had made up this revenue from other sources such as the U.S. Marshals Service and the City of Spokane, but the county board insisted that the sheriff and staff negotiate a deal with the District of Columbia (DC) government to house some of its prisoners.

The DC Department of Corrections had entered into a consent decree under federal court pressure to reduce the prisoner population or face $5,000 per day fines for holding more people that the court had decreed. Thus, the DC government was anxious to unload some of the excess prisoners on jurisdictions willing to accept DC inmates. The Spokane jail administrator, on directions from the sheriff, made the trip to the nation's capital in the fall of 1988 and met with DC officials. He indicated that Spokane County was prepared to handle only medium security prisoners who had no litigation or legal matters pending. But of the 50 African-American prisoners shipped, 23 had been convicted of murder or of multiple murders; as a group, they were responsible for killing 40 people.[15]

The DC inmates were not pleased by this transfer on such a short notice in the middle of the night. Three days after arrival in Spokane, they staged their first demonstration: burning clothes through their food slots in cell doors, clogging the cell toilets, causing minor flooding, and generally making the point that they did not want to be there. The correctional staff of the jail was not forewarned of the new arrival until a day before and were officially told that these prisoners were short-term inmates; the officers soon discovered that these offenders were doing long, hard time. Other factors added to the confusion: staff shortages, equipment inadequacies (their two-way radios and body alarms had not been operational for at least a year), and the lack of a trained emergency response team. All of this engendered a quick disenchantment with the county's money-making scheme. The question of the legality of this contract between Spokane County and the DC government never was settled because at the end of March 1989, the Spokane Board of County Commissioners voted to terminate the contract and by the end of April, the inmates had been further transferred to the authority of the Federal Bureau of Prisons.[16]

ISSUES TO BE RESOLVED IF COUNTY FACILITIES ARE COMMITTED TO OTHER JURISDICTIONS

As noted above, most traditional jails are ill-equipped for long-term prison inmates. Yet many large metropolitan facilities have been able to handle long termers well, and some smaller operations have successfully done so as well.

For many years, the Arlington County Detention Center, Arlington, VA—like many other jails—solely held pretrial detainees and sentenced misdemeanants. When longer-term inmates began to show up at the booking desk, it became clear that the old ways would no longer suffice. Arlington County went to direct supervision management and a new facility in 1994. They successfully developed new approaches to classification, academic and vocational education, substance abuse treatment, discipline, access to legal materials and counsel, maintenance of family ties, and reintegration into the community.

When prisoners are serving six years instead of six months, the orientation of the detention operation must shift accordingly. New Jersey staffer Richard van den Heuvel noted that program opportunities must be in place to help these prisoners survive lengthy jail stays in a productive manner. Additionally, security measures must be enhanced. For example, he suggested that staff rotation should be given significant emphasis; over an extended period of time, an officer might become too comfortable and too familiar with specific inmates.[17]

Few county officials think through the implications of renting out bed space to out-of-county prisoners. To most, it appears to be a simple dollars-and-cents proposition with the bottom line of increasing the revenue for the county treasury.

In New York, the Albany County jail administrator did assess the county's operations before seriously considering holding other jurisdictions' inmates. He contended that several questions had to be answered to determine if a money-making program would succeed for the county.

- Will my superiors want to take on this added work and responsibility?
- Will the legislative body [county] commit itself to the financial and political support?
- Will my staff work with me, not against me, to make it a success and not a failure?

- What type of reaction will surface from the community?
- Will the facility's physical plant provide the required services?
- Will personnel need to be increased and, if so, who will obtain them?[18]

Unlike the fiasco described earlier in Spokane County, New York's Albany County's efforts to recruit other agencies to rent its excess jail beds following its jail expansion have been successful. Since 1990, the Albany County Correctional Facility had generated more than $20 million in boarder revenues through the rental of vacant cells. This county worked hard to develop alternative programs to incarceration for local inmates to free up more jail cells for rent. The participants in the alternative program report to the correctional facility at 8 AM Monday through Friday and work until 4 PM at various not-for-profit agencies under the guidance and supervision of the corrections department. Services provided include basic labor, painting, landscaping, and general maintenance to the county and local governments and not-for-profit groups such as churches and food pantries.[19]

IF A JAIL IS OVERCROWDED, A MATRIX CLASSIFICATION SYSTEM CAN HELP

Large urban counties have found themselves under the gun in federal lawsuits over the past quarter of a century as expanding prisoner populations have increased the pressure to build more jail space. Local officials have responded by planning for the construction of new jail cells, which usually results in the issue being presented to voters in jail bond issues; voters sometimes refuse to approve such expenses. Such was the case of Multnomah County, Portland, Oregon. In 1986, the jail system had 732 beds and nearly 1,000 inmates. State voters had turned down four prison bond issues since 1980, and county voters had twice rejected local jail and inmate rehabilitation levies. The federal court

had placed the county facility under federal court order in 1983.

The county correctional officials developed a release matrix system to manage the crisis in overpopulation. In 1986, the federal court in Oregon empowered the sheriff to release inmates in order to maintain the established population limits set by the court.[20]

The matrix system was designed to release inmates early from the county institutions when the population exceeded capacity. The idea was to release the least dangerous people, as identified by the objective, computer-based scoring system, first. A person booked into the jail was scored on the basis of the nature of the crime committed, with additional points awarded for felony charges and failure to appear after having been served with a warrant. The matrix system was used to control the custody population without increasing the physical danger to the community. The system was designed to meet the following goals:

- It had to be objective.
- It had to consider all inmates equally.
- It had to allow for the input of additional information related to danger that could not be objectively measured.
- It had to be capable of being computerized.
- It had to have the capacity of generating a list of prioritized inmates at any time that releases may be necessary.
- It must seek to identify the physically dangerous inmates and limit their potential for release.[21]

Since the beginning of the matrix system in 1986, Multnomah County has released over 10,000 inmates to reduce crowding.

Los Angeles County, with the largest jail system in the United States, found itself under a court-ordered cap compelling the sheriff's department to change inmate sentences and length of stay. Release methods went beyond the scope of normal judicial setting and included such programs as citation releases, early release credits, and percentages releases (started in 1989 for inmates who had served 80 percent of their original sentences). A matrix system was also introduced.[22] The situation worsened when the state legislature passed a "three-strikes-and-you're-out" law when a number of inmates were put on the streets, sentences uncompleted, to comply with the court-ordered cap. "Three strikers" found plea bargaining no longer feasible and decided to remain in jail for a jury trial. This further exacerbated the overcrowding of the county jail system.

Combined with the difficulties of housing long-term prisoners in jails, overcrowding in jails is a more complex problem than overcrowding in America's prisons. As noted, most jails are not designed for detention and lack the programs and staff that are critical to the successful confinement of long-term offenders.

CONCLUSION

The current mania in the United States for locking everybody up has forced local jails to hold more prisoners for more jurisdictions at all levels of government. At one time, most jails held their own sentenced prisoners for less than a year, today, at least 25 states have jails that hold prisoners for other jurisdictions and jails. It is an unhealthy trend.

NOTES

1. K. Maguire et al., *Sourcebook of Criminal Justice Statistics 1996*, NCJ-165361 (Albany, NY: The Hindelang Criminal Justice Research Center, U.S. Department of Justice, Bureau of Justice Statistics, 1997), 512.

2. Maguire et al., *Sourcebook of Criminal Justice Statistics 1996*, 514.

3. K. Kerle, "Jails at the Crossroads," *American Jails*, November/December 1994, 5.

4. D. Gutierrez, "Texas Jails," *American Jails*, September/October 1993, 11–14.

5. R. van den Heuvel, "When Jails Become Prisons," *American Jails* 8, no. 5, November/December 1994, 11–15.

6. G. Schellman, "Housing State Offenders in a County Correction Center: The Shelby County Experience," *American Jails*, May/June 1996, 27–31.

7. D. Bogard, "State-Ready Inmates in Local Jails: Are You in Jeopardy?" *American Jails*, January/February 1995, 75–78.

8. S. Hsu, "3 Sheriffs Suspend Suit in Jail Crowding," *The Washington Post*, 9 June, 1995, D-6.

9. E. Szostak, "Jails and the Management of Other Agencies' Prisoners," *American Jails*, May/June 1996, 22–24.

10. 72 N.Y.2d 346, 533 N.Y.S.2d 849, 1988.

11. W. Lucas, "Out-of-State Contract Prisoners: A Success Story in Denton County, Texas," *American Jails*, May/June 1996, 9–14.

12. Lucas "Out-of-State Contract Prisoners: A Success Story in Denton County, Texas," 12.

13. K. Bell, "Texas County Jail Criticized for Allegedly Abusing Prisoners," *Milwaukee Sentinel*, 19 August, 1997, 3A.

14. L. Zupan, "The Jail for Rent—The Anatomy of a Deal Too Good To Be True," *American Jails*, January/February 1993, 22–32.

15. Zupan, "The Jail for Rent—The Anatomy of a Deal Too Good To Be True," 27.

16. Zupan, "The Jail for Rent—The Anatomy of a Deal Too Good To Be True," 32.

17. van den Heuvel, "When Jails Become Prisons," 11–15.

18. Szotak, "Jails and the Management of Other Agencies' Prisoners," 22–24.

19. Szostak, "Jails and the Management of Other Agencies' Prisoners," 22–24.

20. W. Wood, "Multnomah County Sheriff's Office Population Release Matrix System," *American Jails*, March/April 1991, 52–54.

21. Wood, "Multnomah County Sheriff's Office Population Release Matrix System," 54.

22. P. Myron, "Inmate Population Management," *American Jails*, January/February 1994, 69–73.

PART IV

Institutional Departmental Responsibilities

The supervision of today's correctional institutions, both prisons and jails, is a complex task in a turbulent and multifaceted environment. A warden or jail administrator and middle management staff must provide leadership and management for employees, ensure the safety and welfare of a large number of inmates, and be responsive to the daily administrative mandates that are unique to the prison setting.

Contemporary corrections officials face a dynamic world within a facility. Governance of a prison or jail is more an art than a science, often an act of juggling many tasks. Wardens, associate wardens, and department heads fulfill critical roles in the provision of services and programs in an extremely difficult environment.

Department heads are the senior managers of specific institutional operations. This part provides an overview of all functional operations in a typical prison or jail facility. While various correctional facilities may give them different names, these operations are integral to humane, safe, and secure detention activities.

The chapters in this part outline the basic roles played by specific departments. Most penal facilities organize these responsibilities into two management divisions often referred to as programs and operations. Program departments provide social service, supervision, and rehabilitative opportunities for the inmate population (e.g., security, case management, education, and mental health programs). Operations departments provide support services to the facility or to the inmates (e.g., personnel, food services, and financial management). These divisions are generally headed by assistant wardens or associate wardens who provide oversight and supervision to the department heads.

The security of a prison or jail has to be the foremost responsibility of correctional staff. Chapter 10 outlines the basic requirements of a sound correctional services department and establishes the simple fact that a correctional institution cannot perform any punishment, rehabilitation, or other function if prisoners are not safely and securely maintained in custody. By expecting all staff members to be responsible for custody and accountability, managers convey the message that each individual is a *correctional worker first*. Whether plumbers, vocational training instructors, or physicians, all employees should comprehend that the security of the institution is paramount and their *first* responsibility.

All departments in the correctional environment are designed to provide specific support or direction to the staff and inmates, and all must work together as a whole. For instance, it is critical that information about an impending fight between two inmate groups be passed on from a teacher in the education department to the correctional services department. If staff are not sensitive to the fact that they are in a penal environment and must share information and resources, the operation will be placed in serious jeopardy. Successful senior leaders and middle managers are committed to training staff to look out for one another and blending all departments into a single, cohesive operation.

With chapters covering topics that range from case management to medical operations, Part IV reviews the "bread and butter" of operations in a penal institution. As the various authors outline the significant responsibilities inherent in the day-to-day work of prison and jail facilities, it will become clear that wardens and associate wardens must demonstrate knowledge of and proficiency in many different areas.

LEARNING OBJECTIVES

After studying this section, you should be able to answer the following questions:

1. What is the basic division of departmental responsibilities within a prison or jail facility? How are the two divisions different?
2. Why do successful operations depend on all departments working cooperatively?
3. Should all staff be responsible for responding to a fight in the institution?
4. What is classification? Why is it important to a well-run facility?
5. Is it appropriate to provide education and vocational training, and other program opportunities for inmates at the taxpayers' expense?
6. Why are recreation and leisure activities provided for inmates?
7. List and describe the issues inherent in the provision of mental health care. Can treatment be required for an inmate in need?
8. Why is the provision of meals such a sensitive issue in a prison or jail?
9. How difficult is it to identify and control infectious diseases in the correctional setting? Can a prisoner be forced to submit to testing?
10. What do you believe is the most difficult task to achieve in the provision of programs or services for inmates?

DISCUSSION/REVIEW QUESTIONS

1. What is the concept of "correctional worker first"?
2. What are the critical elements of the inmate classification process?
3. What is contraband? Why is it such a management concern in a secure setting?
4. How can community resources be assimilated into a prison educational or religious program?
5. Why are weight lifting and bodybuilding controversial in a correctional institution?
6. Should human immunodeficiency virus (HIV) or aquired immune deficiency syndrome (AIDS) patients be allowed to enter the general population of a facility?
7. What are the significant issues associated with the provision of medical or mental health care in the institutional environment?
8. How has the Religious Freedom Restoration Act (RFRA) affected correctional programs?
9. Are institutional staff required to provide special religious diets for any inmate?
10. Why does institutional budget management represent a potential public relations nightmare?

CHAPTER 10

Custody and Security

Michael B. Cooksey

Most inmates prefer a quiet, clean, and orderly prison where they can serve their time in a safe environment. A well-run institution has a certain feel about it: The quiet rumble of daily activities with no loud noises, clean and shining hallways, and lack of clutter in inmate cells signify that the staff are in charge and running the prison. Few inmates benefit from disrupting daily activities. Proper security can ensure inmate safety and provide staff with good working conditions.

SECURITY BEGINS WITH INMATE CLASSIFICATION

It is difficult to begin a discussion on institution security without first discussing proper classification of facilities and inmates. Institutions must be designed to house a certain type of offender. Violent, aggressive, and escape-prone inmates require more physical security features and staff resources.

Classification can best be defined as the systematic grouping of inmates into categories based on shared characteristics and behavioral patterns. Using the inmate's history, staff can make fairly accurate predictions about the

inmate's future behavior and adjustment to incarceration. Inmates with similar characteristics living together in an appropriately designed facility are much easier to manage. Likewise, a strong inmate among a weaker population can wreak havoc. Escapes, assaults, and drug dealing very seldom occur in areas where the inmates are deliberately stratified.

But inmates may find ways to manipulate the system so that they can be in areas of the institution where there is little staff supervision. A few years ago, a federal prison suffered an escape of two inmates. Although not assigned to work on the food service rear dock, over time, these inmates were able to gradually manipulate staff to allow them to smoke or take breaks on the food service rear dock area virtually unsupervised. These two inmates made good their escape, with outside assistance, when they were able to hide in a false compartment of a vegetable delivery truck.

ACCOUNTABILITY IS KEY

Knowing where inmates are at all times is a must in secure facilities. A system of callouts, passes, and controlled movement at prescribed times greatly assists staff with inmate accountability. Housing unit officers should know which inmates are in the unit and the destination of inmates leaving the housing unit. When inmates are given assignments outside the unit,

Opinions expressed in this chapter are those of the author and do not necessarily represent the opinions of the Federal Bureau of Prisons or the U.S. Department of Justice.

75

such as work or educational programs, the work supervisor, education staff member, or some other staff person should be responsible for the inmate. A formal call-out system will greatly improve inmate accountability when an inmate is needed at a certain place for a short period of time such as medical appointments, counseling sessions, and so on.

In addition to formal counts at prescribed times, random census counts should be taken. During such counts, all institution activity stops and inmates are counted in place to quickly determine whether inmates are where they should be. If census counts are not practical, supervisory correctional staff can periodically check various work details, classrooms, or housing units to ensure that inmates are in their assigned areas.

Inmates should be informed of their responsibility to be in their authorized area. Disciplinary procedures should be established to deter inmates from being in unauthorized areas. Of equal if not greater importance are procedures that account for all staff and their approximate locations in the institution. Accounting for staff is difficult, as staff usually have more mobility than inmates within the institution. During emergencies, accounting for staff should be top priority. Determining if staff have been taken hostage has a tremendous impact on how the warden plans to resolve demonstrations, riots, or other emergencies.

PREPARING FOR CRISIS

Even in the best-run prison, emergencies occur. At the very least, plans dealing with escapes, riots, work or food strikes, hostage situations, outside demonstrations, natural disasters, bomb threats, and evacuations are necessary to ensure that staff are properly prepared to deal with emergencies. Prison administrators should identify those areas that most concern them and prepare detailed plans to address these issues. If the prison is close to major roadways, shipping lanes, or railways, plans should be developed in case of toxic or chemical spills. In areas susceptible to natural disasters such as wildfires, hurricanes, or earthquakes, evacuation may be necessary to save lives.

Emergency plans should be easy to read and informative. Although brief, they should set out specific responsibilities. The plans should be updated periodically as situations change. Emergency plans are only as good as the preparation to implement them. All staff should be fully familiar with emergency plans. At least yearly, staff should read and be given an opportunity to discuss the plans with peers and supervisors. Periodic mock exercises improve staff knowledge and make them more comfortable with their role in emergencies. Developing memoranda of understanding and involving sister agencies and law enforcement in mock exercises will not only improve the outside agencies' knowledge of the correctional facility but foster good relationships.

UNACCEPTABLE INMATE POSSESSIONS

Controlling contraband should be a top priority in all correctional institutions regardless of security level. Contraband is any item or article that an inmate is forbidden to possess. All correctional facilities provide inmates with medical care, room and board, clothing, and basic hygiene items. Most facilities allow inmates to purchase items in the commissary or receive items through other authorized channels. Anything else that the inmate possesses is contraband.

Weapons, escape materials, or excess property that add fuel during fires are all equally dangerous in the right circumstances. Most staff are acutely aware of the havoc that these items, as well as drugs and alcohol, can cause and the resultant danger for staff and inmates. Other items such as materials to make dummies, either homemade rope or buffer cords, maps, and unauthorized clothing pose a danger by facilitating inmate escapes. Gambling paraphernalia lead to inmate assaults to collect debts.

Institutions should have regulations that restrict the amount of personal property that an inmate may possess. Cluttered cells and excess personal property are excellent hiding places for more serious contraband. In addition, these areas are much more difficult to search, tying up valuable staff time. Excess property can fuel fires and pose health-related hazards as breeding grounds for bacteria. Institution regulations should specify the amount of newspapers, magazines, pants, shirts, and even underwear an inmate may possess. Medications should be tightly controlled. Legal property provides great hiding places for contraband, as staff are reluctant to properly search legal items. The amount of legal property that an inmate can possess should be specified and tightly controlled. It is important to properly document seizure, confiscation, and disposition of contraband in case of civil lawsuits.

Staff must know what items enter and exit the prison. Incoming boxes and packages should be X-rayed before entering the correctional institution and searched prior to being given to inmates. Visitors should pass through a metal detector. Because most serious contraband such as drugs is introduced by inmate visitors, visitors who behave suspiciously should be subject to a more thorough search prior to visiting. Thoroughly searching inmates following visits also will deter the introduction of contraband. All vehicles should be thoroughly checked, and trash receptacles should sit in the sally port through at least one count before being removed from the institution.

Random frequent searches of inmate living areas can greatly reduce contraband. Inmates who have a history of hiding unauthorized items on their person or in their living area should be identified and searched more frequently. Common areas in the housing unit should be searched daily in a systematic manner to ensure all areas are covered.

Likewise, inmate work areas should be searched daily not only to check for contraband but to make sure all equipment and fixtures are complete with no missing parts. Bars, windows, frames, and doors should be checked frequently to detect cuts and determine if the locking de-

vices have been tampered with. It is imperative that staff account for all tools in the institution. Only authorized tools should be utilized by staff and inmates. Staff should never bring personal tools into the institution. Should a tool be lost, all activity in the area should cease until a thorough search is conducted and the tool found. Limiting access to computers will protect the sensitive information they contain; two inmates at a federal penitentiary were able to obtain architectural drawings through a computer and make good their escape through a utility tunnel.

Drugs and alcohol are highly disruptive to the daily activities in a prison. Regular urinalysis and Breathalyzer tests of suspected users and random tests of the entire population will determine the scope of use and deter abuse. During the holidays, inmates are more lonely and susceptible to temptation, and accordingly searches should be made even more frequently to control fruit, sugar, and other items that may lead to a disruption.

WHEN COMMUNICATION FAILS

Occasionally it may be necessary to use physical force to gain an inmate's compliance. Naturally, the preferred scenario is for the inmate to comply with a verbal command, but in emotional and tense situations this does not always occur.

Having a written use of force policy greatly increases the probability of gaining the inmate's compliance without injury to staff or inmate. The policy should explicitly state when it is permissible to use physical force and describe (in detail) responsibilities of staff, from supervisors to those actually restraining the inmate. It is always best to videotape the use of force to prevent abuse and protect staff in case of a civil lawsuit.

Immediate use of force occurs when an inmate acts out with little or no warning and staff are required to physically restrain the inmate. These are highly charged, emotional incidents for both staff and inmate. Proper training allows staff to gain control of the situation, while controlling their own emotions and preventing inmate abuse. These incidents should be well documented (e.g., in witness statements) by those involved.

A calculated use of force occurs when inmates are confined in an area and do not present an immediate threat to themselves or others, yet are refusing to comply with staff orders. Staff should talk with these inmates to gain their voluntary compliance and allow time for staff to fully assess the situation. Staff should determine if the inmate has weapons and whether it is necessary to use gas, other less-than-lethal munitions, or a well-trained extraction team to move the inmate to the desired location. If more than one inmate is involved, the use of disturbance control or other tactical teams may be required.

Proper use of force has a great influence on staff and inmate morale. A highly professional attitude concerning use of force by administrative and supervisory staff will be modeled by line staff, prevent inmate abuse, and enhance inmate compliance with rules and regulations. Unfortunately, the history of corrections is marred by instances of staff physically abusing inmates. In many of these incidents, higher echelon staff have projected a cavalier or macho image that was imitated by line staff.

HANDS-ON MANAGEMENT

Accurate and reliable information about staff, inmates, the political landscape, and the local community is essential to running a well-organized and secure prison. The administrator who sits in the office waiting for information to arrive through the hierarchical organizational structure is doomed to be woefully uninformed.

Administrative staff should tour the prison often to assess firsthand the atmosphere of the institution. Some inmates are chronic complainers, but others go about their daily activities in an orderly fashion while being respectful to staff and other inmates. When this latter group of inmates is unhappy, administrators should take heed and address the problems. Staff at all levels need to talk and, more important, to listen to inmates. If staff listen, inmates will tell them what is happening in the prison. Staff who supervise inmate work details, teachers, counselors, and correctional officers working in the housing units are often trusted by the inmates and are excellent sources of intelligence. A mechanism that allows these staff to submit confidential reports of conversations and observations of inmates is critical to gathering accurate intelligence. Once collected, this information can be analyzed and evaluated by specially trained intelligence staff. These informed judgments allow administrators to manage institution security and forecast future security needs. Long-range strategic planning based upon accurate information allows the proper allocation of security assets.

SCANNING OUTSIDE THE PRISON

Prisons do not operate in a vacuum but are integral parts of communities and larger correctional systems. Reading daily newspapers and professional magazines and maintaining good relationships with elected officials will keep prison administrators abreast of public sentiment and possible changes directed by politicians. Not too long ago, prisons were forgotten places to the public and political arena. Today, correctional institutions are major employers and very visible to local communities.

Prison and jail walls and fences are very permeable in the sense that the external world has a strong influence on these institutions. Televisions, radios, newspapers, telephone calls, visits, interaction with staff, and newly arriving inmates all carry information from the outside community into the correctional environment. It is critical that penal administrators stay tuned to events outside that may influence the attitudes and beliefs of those that are confined. Some issues move inside the facility rapidly, and others take longer to affect the population. Staff must constantly be alert to changes within and outside their institution.

Sentencing Laws Cause Disturbances

A series of major and minor institution disturbances in federal prisons began on October 19, 1995, and continued through October 26. Fifteen separate incidents, ranging from full-scale riots to small episodes of inmates refusing to return to their cells, taxed the resources of the Federal Bureau of Prisons and, considered together, constituted the most serious nationwide period of disruption in the agency's history.

These disturbances were primarily related to inmates' extreme dissatisfaction with federal sentencing laws and specifically the disparity between penalties for crack cocaine and powder cocaine. This generalized perception of racial unfairness (crack violators were predominantly African American and crack cocaine penalties were much higher than powder cocaine penalties) created major tension. In this environment, any significant event might galvanize inmates to action. Just such a spark occurred after Congress voted on October 19 not to reconcile the cocaine sentencing disparities. That evening, there was the initial major riot at the Federal Correctional Institution in Talladega, AL.

Inmate perceptions of unfairness in the federal criminal justice system—external to the federal prisons—were based on changes designed to toughen penalties against law violators. Lengthy mandatory minimum sentences, the crack cocaine sentencing disparity issue, and loss of federal funding for selected inmate programs created significant resentment in many federal prisons. External issues fueled the tension, and an external event— the congressional vote that was taken that day—ignited the response.

On top of these external issues, the media reporting of the first disturbance meant that prisoners in other federal institutions quickly learned of the event. There were reactions in 14 other federal facilities in the next week. The Federal Bureau of Prisons took the unprecedented step of imposing a nationwide precautionary lockdown of its 92 prisons and focused all tactical resources on the critical locations as events developed. The crisis management response to this event was exceptional and led to the resolution of all situations with no serious injuries to staff or inmates.

PROTECTING INMATE VICTIMS

Certain inmates present unique challenges to prison administrators. Running prisons would be easy if all inmates were similar, serving their time and leaving when they completed their sentence. Good classification can ensure that similar inmates are in the same prison, but changing situations in inmate lives plus loopholes in the classification system can sometimes place in-

mates in the wrong prison. One category of inmates that has always caused problems can best be described as the "weaker" inmate. Weaker inmates typically have committed an especially heinous crime and have received a long sentence that requires them to serve their sentence in a higher security level institution. Once in prison they become prey for other inmates after the other inmates learn of their crime. Child sex offenders find it especially difficult to serve their sentence in the general population once other inmates learn of their offense. Weaker inmates usually spend great portions of their sentence in special housing units for protective custody. The weaker inmates are frequently transferred between prisons, as they are unable to cope in the general population. Weaker inmates may act out against staff, as they know that staff are prohibited from physically punishing them. In addition, weaker inmates are often very litigious, filing institutional appeals and court documents complaining about their conditions of confinement. Staff at all levels need to be properly trained in working with weaker inmates, as most cases of proven staff abuse occur in this area.

DANGEROUS INMATES—THE ASSAULTIVE, THE MANIPULATIVE, AND THE EAGER TO LEAVE

In many ways, the aggressive inmate is easier to manage than the weaker inmate. The highly assaultive, combative inmate lives best in a prison with other aggressive inmates. Aggressors seldom prey on aggressors. Many states and the federal system have developed super maximum penitentiaries to house aggressive inmates. Because the criteria for transfer to "super maxes" are usually behavior based, many staff and other inmates are the target of these inmates' aggressions before their placement in the super max. In systems that operate without a super maximum prison, aggressive inmates spend much of their sentences in special housing units. Policies and guidelines for handling aggressive inmates should be specific and followed by all staff. Ensuring staff safety is paramount when dealing with aggressive and combative inmates.

Sophisticated or manipulative inmates target staff, other inmates, and the political system to gain items or favors that are otherwise prohibited. They often have tremendous resources in the community—including finances and support groups. The media may follow their incarceration and show continued interest in their plight.

These inmates may be leaders or quietly give advice and counsel to inmate leaders. They are experts at detecting and exploiting staff insecurities and procedural weaknesses.

There are also inmates whose every waking moment is filled with fantasies of escape. These inmates tend to be smarter and more adept at recognizing weaknesses in physical structures and procedures. These inmates may take months and even years to closely observe staff for any habits or consistent failures to follow policy that these inmates may exploit. Many successful escapes involve the inmate simply walking out the front or rear entrance to the institution following visiting times or at shift changes. One notorious prisoner who had a history of escape was able to obtain what appeared to be civilian clothing and was actually escorted out of a correctional institution by staff who assumed he was a parole examiner. Other stories entail the inmate working for months hoarding escape paraphernalia in order to breach physical structures to make good an escape. Almost every investigative report following an attempted or successful escape reveals poor security procedures or staff's failure to follow proper procedures.

SECURITY THREAT GROUPS

Gang activity is increasing in major cities, rural communities, and prisons. Gangs are responsible for the majority of homicides and assaults in prison. Well-organized, highly structured prison gangs have been around for decades. These gangs have strong leaders and exert pressure on other inmates through violence or the threat of violence. They are interested only in providing illicit drugs, alcohol, and contraband to other prisoners, and prison programs mean little to them.

In recent years, more street gang members have been incarcerated. Additionally, more inmates have sought membership in groups from a certain city or geographical area. These gangs are unpredictable, less structured, and, in many ways, more difficult to manage than the tradi-

Gang and Race Divisions Create Chaos
Racial fighting between white and black inmates at the maximum security High Desert State Prison in California was blamed for a serious disturbance that erupted there on December 26, 1997. Correctional officers trying to quell the disturbance fired several warning shots, but the fighting continued. According to California Department of Corrections officials, one inmate was killed when a bullet from an officer's rifle struck him; four other inmates received bullet or bullet fragment wounds. Another prisoner suffered stab wounds from inmates using homemade knives in the fight. The incident was the second since October 1997 that was blamed on racial tensions. High Desert State Prison, which is located just outside Susanville, CA, has an inmate population of 4,000. *Source:* Reprinted from *Corrections Alert*, Vol. 4, No. 19, p.4, © 1998, Aspen Publishers, Inc.

CONCLUSION

An institution's security staff perform heroic and often dangerous duty, 24 hours a day, each and every day of the year. Maintaining control of a correctional environment is a daunting task, given the noncooperative nature of many of the inmates and the challenges they present to the staff. The key to a prison or jail security system's success is a well-trained staff that is held accountable for detail and required to be alert to the inmate population. Positive accountability of inmates and an appropriate sense of order and discipline are mandatory. A prison or jail must develop a culture that treats prisoners with respect, always reinforces positive communication between staff and inmates, and offers inmates a humane, safe, and sanitary institutional program. Good security is a product of good leadership and results from a high-quality staff that believe their work makes a difference. And indeed it does. Those who work "inside" and contribute to the daily supervision of inmates are public servants in the finest sense of the term.

SUGGESTED READINGS

Bowker, L. 1980. *Prison victimization*. New York: Elsevier.

Crouch, B. 1980. *The keepers: Prison guards and contemporary corrections*. Springfield, IL: Charles C Thomas Publishers.

Fleisher, M. 1989. *Warehousing violence*. Newbury Park, CA: Sage Publications.

Fox, J. 1982. *Organizational and racial conflict in maximum security prisons*. Lexington, MA: Lexington Books.

Haas K., and G. Alpert. 1995. *The dilemmas of corrections*. Prospect Heights, IL: Waveland Press, Inc.

Jankowski, M. 1991. *Islands in the street: Gangs and American urban society*. Berkeley, CA: University of California Press.

tional prison gangs. Several state prison systems have developed strategies to deal with gangs. Some correctional systems just deny the existence of gangs. In still other systems, the problem is so complex that it defies solution. Controlling gangs and their disruptive activities will haunt many prison administrators until solutions are found.

CHAPTER 11

Case Management/ Unit Management

Peter M. Carlson

"What's my release date?" "When will my girlfriend be added to my visiting list?" "Can you tell me when I will be eligible for transfer closer to home?" "When can I get my custody level reduced?" "How much time can I get in a halfway house?" "Am I going to get time off for participating in the drug treatment program?" These questions, and thousands more, are directed to staff every day within the jails and prisons of the United States. Most institutional staff respond by telling prisoners to see their case workers for help.

The case management staff of a correctional facility are responsible for a significant part of an institution's operation. Case managers are a primary communication link between inmates and other staff, as well as an important connection to the individual's future life in the outside community.

A case manager has different titles in various jurisdictions. Some agencies refer to this staff member as a case worker, social worker, criminologist, classification officer, or counselor. Whatever their working title, case managers' general responsibilities include inmate classification, social service support, institution program planning, and release preparation. Most

correctional professionals believe these tasks are critical to today's prison and jail operations.

CLASSIFICATION IS KEY TO SUCCESSFUL INSTITUTIONAL OPERATIONS

Most penal facilities offer social service staff to provide classification services for their inmate populations; this may be a small department of overworked case workers, or a large, organized network of social work and case management staff. The classification process is one of the preeminent responsibilities in a correctional facility. This categorization of offenders involves assessing an individual's social and criminal background and current programming needs and assigning him or her to an appropriately secure institution, housing area, work assignment, and program. How classification is organized and conducted varies a great deal by jurisdiction, type of facility, and institutional staffing levels.

In earlier years, all decisions about an inmate's security and prison assignments for work and housing were generally made by one senior management official designated by the warden, often the deputy warden.[1] This individual controlled all aspects of life inside the institution and made unilateral decisions based strictly on his or her often limited knowledge of inmates and their deportment and attitude. Although this was an effective method of establishing consistent governance in a very punitive en-

Opinions expressed in this chapter are those of the author and do not necessarily represent the opinions of the Federal Bureau of Prisons or the U.S. Department of Justice.

vironment, little attention was directed to inter-action with the prisoners, and virtually no emphasis was given to the goal of positively influencing an inmate's life.

As this process evolved, this responsibility shifted from the deputy warden to a classification committee. In most correctional facilities, classification committees are large groups of subject matter experts who gather regularly to evaluate new inmates or to reclassify inmates for custody, housing, and work and program assignments. The committee is often chaired by a senior management official such as an associate warden and comprises the heads of institution departments such as the captain of security, the chief of classification, the supervisor of education, and the inmate's case manager. Many classification committees require the attendance of the inmate being reviewed.

In the last 25 years, many correctional systems have adopted a unit management approach to classification. Unit management involves dividing a large prison or jail population into smaller groups, often separated by housing unit. Classification and other social service functions are provided in the unit by a team of staff who consistently work with these inmates: a unit manager, a case manager, a counselor, an education representative, a psychologist, and a secretary.[2]

A valid, objective system of classification allows staff to establish a logical, systematic, and orderly means of sorting large numbers of inmates. In earlier times, this classification process was often based on the subjective perceptions or whims of institutional staff; this seat-of-the-pants process was less than precise and often less than fair.

Objective, fact-based classification facilitates agencywide consistency that may be rationally defended and is perceived as equitable by all those involved in the process, including the inmates. Facts that most correctional systems have found to be important in the process are an inmate's prior record, the severity of the current offense, the history and recency of violence against others, the history and recency of escape from custody, institutional adjustment/behavior, and the amount of time remaining to be served. Once the classification system has been validated, all of these inmate personal characteristics can be quantified, and each inmate can be accurately scored. Further, the system can facilitate rescoring based on an offender's progress while incarcerated.

CASE MANAGEMENT

The provision of social support programs to an inmate population is a critical responsibility. Case management staffers maintain the official classification documents for each inmate and provide basic case management for all. In many jurisdictions, these staff members are not only responsible for determining the prisoner's custody and security needs but charged with helping the inmates plan their institution-based work and program assignments, representing the inmate with the parole board, offering counseling services, providing connections to the community, and handling release planning. Case managers perform myriad tasks that pertain to inmates' day-to-day life and guide inmates' activities with the ultimate goal of helping them make a successful transition back to their home community after release.

From the time an inmate arrives in a correctional setting, he or she will be dependent upon a case manager or counselor. Initial social screening of new arrivals is generally accomplished by these social service staff members, who ask new prisoners about their special needs. Interviewers will ask whether the inmate needs protection from others that he or she may have testified against and try to identify other potential enemies within the institution's general population. Screening questions also seek information about the offender's physical and mental health and other pressing management issues.

Case management staff gather background information about new inmates in pre- or post-sentence reports (prepared for the sentencing courts by probation and parole officers) and seek other basic information about individuals. This attempt to gather information about the inmate is a direct result of a philosophical change in contemporary corrections. As Americans began to expect prisons and jails to do more than simply "warehouse" offenders, most correctional agencies began during the early 1960s to implement programs to rehabilitate prisoners. This approach became known as the "medical model" in corrections, as it implies that an inmate is sick and his or her social deviance can be cured by program involvement during confinement.[3] Accordingly, this emphasis on treatment has required that staff focus on the criminal rather than the crime committed.

Once the case manager has complete information about the individual's prior arrest record and adjustment to earlier periods of incarceration, and social data about his or her family and friends, a classification study report is prepared in most jurisdictions. This document identifies the prisoner, mentions social factors that may have led to his or her life of crime, and recommends institutional programs that may help prepare the individual for eventual release. This report serves as the base information document. Details about the inmates' program participation, or lack of progress, are added to the case management central file throughout their confinement.

In many correctional systems, the initial assessment is completed at a reception and diagnostic center over a period of four to eight weeks. In the jurisdictions that utilize these centers, the newly arrived prisoner is put through an extensive evaluation that often includes a complete personality assessment, intelligence and psychometric testing, review of past work habits and lifestyle, observation of how he or she interacts with staff and inmates, and identification of those factors that may have led the individual to crime. In other jurisdictions that do not have reception and diagnostic centers, inmates are committed directly to an institution and go through a similar classification process.

Once the background classification report is prepared, the inmate is then formally evaluated at a classification meeting. This meeting entails the development of an integrated work assignment, permanent housing, and educational, vocational, and social improvement programs for the offender.

Classification is the backbone of the security program of any prison or jail. It is imperative that staff know the background of each inmate and the threat each presents to the effective custodial management of the facility (see Exhibit 11–1). If a realistic assessment is accomplished by case management staff, the inmate can be placed in housing with appropriate security and all other aspects of institution management will follow accordingly. It is important that inmates be placed in the least restrictive facility that is able to meet their security needs.

Once they classify and assign inmates, case managers track inmates throughout their confinement (see Exhibit 11–2). Classification is not a one-time event but an ongoing procedure. The case manager serves as the offender's liaison to the classification committee for any

Exhibit 11–1 Classifying Inmates: Basic Information about the Individual Is Necessary

1. Age and sex
2. Social history
3. Criminal sophistication: arrest and conviction history and current offense, with an emphasis on violence against others and the recency of this behavior
4. Special needs: medical or mental issues, educational and vocational deficits
5. Potential challenges to institution security: gang membership, separation requirements, known escape history
6. Special management factors: judicial recommendation, racial balance within the institution(s), program availability
7. Institutional capacity, space availability, and security (this factor requires that each prison or jail be classified by security level, type of prisoner housed, and availability of programs)

Exhibit 11–2 Typical Responsibilities of a Case Manager

1. Intake screening of new admissions
2. Classification of inmates by security/custody level, work and housing assignment
3. Assistance with supervision of inmates
4. Participation in inmate discipline hearings
5. Ongoing needs assessment of inmates for program assignment
6. Tracking of progress for inmate reclassification
7. Approval of an inmate's visitors
8. Counseling support
9. Release preparation

changes in his or her program that are desired. Program modifications could include changes in work assignment, approvals for program participation, requests for transfer, consideration for custody reduction, or different housing.

Case management staff are also usually responsible for release planning. This actually begins at the time of initial classification. The appropriate goals of all institutional classification and programming should be ensuring the safety and security of the inmate and institution and preparing the offender for successful transition back to free society.[4] Staff, during all interactions with offenders, should encourage individuals to increase their education, improve their job skills, strengthen their self-sufficiency, and take full responsibility for their lives.

UNIT MANAGEMENT

Functional unit management is, simply put, the decentralization of case management services to a diverse eclectic group of staff from different departments of the institution. The concept behind unit management was to subdivide the larger prison or jail into smaller groups of inmates, generally with their own housing unit, with staff offices within the unit. A set of staff members are assigned to the unit on a permanent basis; as noted above, this generally includes a unit manager, a case manager, a counselor, an education representative, a part-time psychologist, and a secretary.

Correctional officers are assigned to the unit on a rotating basis. They are accountable to the institution's head of security and the unit manager of their assigned unit.

Inmate classification decisions are made by this unit management team. General policy establishes operational guidelines for these separate teams, and these staff members are empowered to make classification, program, and inmate housing decisions.

There are benefits to choosing the unit management model instead of the centralized case management model outlined above. First and foremost, this decentralized management model permits decisions about inmates to be made by the staff who know the inmates best. Clearly, when staff offices are next to inmate housing, staff can better supervise and get to know inmates. Positive, professional relationships are more likely to develop between inmates and staff. Daily interaction is helpful.

Relationships between staff members are often greatly improved by unit management. Interdisciplinary staff of various departments who are assigned to a specific unit develop close working relationships that facilitate a productive working environment.

In general, research has demonstrated that staff and inmate morale is improved with unit management. Inmates are much more pleased with responsive staff who know them, and staff are glad to have the authority to make program decisions.[5]

But there are some negative aspects to the decentralization of prison management. It is much more difficult to maintain consistency in classification decision making when multiple teams are involved in inmate management determinations. It is critical that senior management establish overarching policy to guide the unit teams in their decision making.

It is also important that penal institutions with unit management have open and effective lines of communication for staff and inmates. If unit staff are aware of inmate unrest or brewing tensions, they must share this knowledge with senior staff members.

Levinson and Gerard describe three functions of unit management: correction, care, and control of the inmate.[6] Correction refers to the rehabilitation function of prisons and jails; care is used to describe the assistance, resources, and support given to an inmate; and control describes the level of required custodial supervision. All of these missions are crucial to the administration of justice and successful prison or jail management. Unit management offers an efficient means of achieving these goals.

CONCLUSION

The demands of managing today's prison or jail facility—immense numbers of prisoners, inmate violence, unending litigation, and increasing legislative oversight—can be formidable to any correctional leader. It is imperative for the chief executive officers of our penal facilities to establish an environment of confinement that is safe and secure for staff and inmates alike. Staff must impose a sense of order, and case managers must organize and oversee the inmate population.

Successful correctional leaders accomplish their important public safety mission every day by relying upon exceptional staff who are well trained, attention to daily facility operations, and the appropriate organization of and provision of services to inmates. Case management is one of the cornerstones of effective and efficient institutional operations.

NOTES

1. R. Levinson, "The Development of Classification and Programming," in *Escaping Prison Myths: Selected Topics in the History of Federal Corrections* (Lanham, MD: University Publishing Associates, Inc., 1994).

2. P. Keve, *Prisons and the American Conscience: A History of U.S. Federal Corrections* (Carbondale, IL: Southern Illinois University Press, 1991), 234.

3. R. Balch, "The Medical Model of Delinquency: Theoretical, Practical, and Ethical Implications," *Crime and Delinquency* 21 (1975): 116–129.

4. D. Glaser, *The Effectiveness of a Prison and Parole System* (Indianapolis, IN: Bobbs-Merrill Company, Inc., 1964).

5. H. Toch, *Corrections. A Humanistic Approach* (Guilderland, NY: Harrow and Heston, Publishers, 1997), 30–34.

6. R. Levinson and R. Gerard, "Functional Units: A Different Correctional Approach," *Federal Probation,* no. 37 (1973):15.

CHAPTER 12

Education and Vocational Training

H. David Jenkins

The National Adult Literacy Survey (NALS) provides important data on the educational performance of the ever-increasing prison population in the United States. For most persons working in corrections or correctional education, the data confirm what they already knew—that incarcerated persons are among the most educationally disadvantaged groups in the nation.

In the NALS, approximately one in three inmates performed at the lowest level of literacy and would have difficulty reading a short newspaper article, completing an employment application, or locating a piece of information in a document. They may not be illiterate in the popular usage of the word—unable to read or write—but they will have difficulty functioning in today's increasingly technological society.

Despite the sobering statistics on the educational level of most inmates, recent research suggests that effective programs can significantly improve inmates' educational performance and that inmates who complete education and training programs exhibit improved institutional behavior and are more successful when released. Research on the impact of education and training programs is far from uniform and exhibits various data collection and analysis problems. Data on the postrelease experiences of inmates who participated in correctional education programs have been difficult to collect and frequently available for only a small percentage of releasees. Despite these problems, an increasing body of research from federal, state, and local

authorities indicates that a positive relationship exists between institutional education programs and a number of indicators of success.

A review of 97 studies on the relationship between correctional education and recidivism determined that 85 percent of the studies reported a positive relationship between correctional education participation and recidivism.[1] Similarly, results from a large-scale study of Federal Bureau of Prisons releasees determined that inmates with training and/or work experience while imprisoned had better institutional adjustments, were less likely to relapse into crime, and were more likely to obtain employment upon release.[2]

Although the results of this body of accumulating studies are not uniform, there is good reason to believe that the positive relationships between education and training and several positive outcomes are not simply because of chance. Educational attainment is a powerful indicator of income and employment for nonincarcerated persons, and it would be counterintuitive to assume that these variables are not positively related for incarcerated persons. Given this evidence, it seems beneficial to establish inmate education and training programs where they do not currently exist.

This chapter offers suggestions on needs assessment, program design, program operation, evaluation, and community resources. Of course, facilities and resources vary greatly from facility to facility and from jurisdiction to juris-

---

NALS Results

The NALS, funded by the National Center for Education Statistics within the U.S. Department of Education, and administered by the Educational Testing Service, profiles the English literacy of adults in the United States, including prison inmates. The survey consists of interviews with nearly 1,150 inmates from federal and state prisons and 26,000 adults aged 16 or older in households around the country.

The survey consists of individual interviews wherein the respondent is asked a series of questions regarding demographic characteristics, educational background, and reading practices. He or she is asked to perform a variety of literacy tasks. Each respondent is assigned a score on three scales to reflect skill in prose, document, and quantitative literacy.

The results of the NALS indicate that there are substantial differences between the performance of the prison population and the household population on the three literacy scales. These differences, however, may be entirely attributable to differences in demographic composition and education attainment; when these factors are held constant, the differences disappear.

Source: Data from Karl O. Haigler, et al., *Executive Summary of Literacy Behind Walls: Profiles of the Prison Population from the National Adult Literacy Survey,* U.S. Department of Education, 1996.

---

diction. Even with limited resources, however, significant results can be obtained. With correctional education programs well established in most state correctional systems, the following information is directed primarily to local detention centers, jails, and smaller state facilities such as prerelease units.

IDENTIFYING NEEDS

The development of a successful education program depends on an assessment of inmate needs, community resources for education, and the labor market. Some of the data regarding inmate needs may already be available from intake interviews and other sources. Despite the evidence that most inmates exhibit serious educational deficiencies, inmate populations differ significantly among and within institutions.

Intake interviews and presentence investigations frequently yield important data on

- educational attainment prior to incarceration
- functional performance
- prior skill training
- employment history
- prior specialized treatment including special education service

This data can yield a profile of the population as well as the number of inmates with particular needs. In addition to the education and training histories, data must be collected on key criminal justice issues. How long will the typical client be available for services? What other programs and services are potential clients to receive? Will the educational program be in a "head-to-head" competition with other programs for the same inmate? In most instances, the development of an effective correctional education program will also require objective test data to determine the needs of the persons to be serviced. The Test of

Adult Basic Education is frequently used to assess the performance of adult learners. These two test instruments are widely used in adult education and corrections education programs.

The potential students are frequently a good source of information. Unfortunately, because these adult students are incarcerated, their valuable input is often ignored. Adult education providers and community colleges actively solicit input from students and potential students to ensure that their institutions' educational offerings genuinely interest the student "customers." Correctional programs could benefit from this customer model. The students themselves may have valuable input on which programs would benefit them most.

Information on labor market conditions and trends in the community or communities to which inmates are to be released is vital to the development of any effective training program. Corrections is unfortunately the home to more than its share of programs that train inmates for jobs that no longer exist or that exist but, because of the nature of the work, are unlikely to be open to ex-offenders. Involvement of potential employers in the development phase is likely to pay off later. Employers can provide relevant information and advice to ensure training programs are current and valid.

A results-oriented and goal-specific program helps institutions focus on this community-based information, which may be readily available from U.S. Department of Labor publications and state or local planning agencies. Local or regional libraries can offer assistance in this area.

COMMUNITY AND PROFESSIONAL RESOURCES

Having established the need for educational programs, an institution must develop them. Resources may be limited, but linking with community organizations can help. A thorough needs assessment frequently is the key element in accessing these community resources; it shows potential partners that an institution is serious and outlines a problem about which others may only be vaguely aware.

Resources to support educational programs for incarcerated persons differ greatly from jurisdiction to jurisdiction. However, institutions frequently underestimate the available resources. At the national level is the Correctional Education Association (CEA), an affiliate member of the American Correctional Association. The CEA publishes a professional journal on the education of the incarcerated and has established standards for correction programs. These high standards provide a benchmark against which an institution can measure its activities and programs.

State correctional education organizations exist in every state, although their organizational structure varies. In most cases, the state correctional education programs are organized as a unit within the state correctional system headquarters, included in the state educational agency, or set up as a separate school district. Correctional education can be reasonably included in the mission of adult education departments. Inmates are among the most educationally disadvantaged groups in the United States today and the number of incarcerated persons (federal, state, and local) now exceeds 1.2 million and is growing.[3] There has been considerable discussion and some legal action on the responsibility of local educational agencies for students who are incarcerated in local jurisdictions.

Frequently, available community resources are not pursued by correctional institutions. Community organizations may be willing to help if asked or if their initial fears are addressed. Community organizations that may offer help include

- literacy organizations such as Literacy Volunteers of America and Lauback Literacy
- fraternal and religious organizations
- local colleges and universities (a source of technical advice and possibly student interns)

- labor and employee organizations
- senior and retiree organizations

Local libraries may have directories of various organizations as well as information on their interests and types of community involvement. Even organizations which may not be interested in educational programs for incarcerated persons in general may be quite interested in and supportive of a special program of family literacy involving incarcerated women and their children.

What type of support can community organizations provide?

- financial support to establish and operate an education program
- training of staff and inmates involved in educating inmates
- sponsorship of various educational activities such as a learning lab, a family literacy center, or another special project
- volunteers to serve as instructors, tutors, aides, and office support (volunteers could be student interns, senior citizens, or interested persons with valuable skills)
- sponsorship of a graduation for program completers or the loan of gowns for a graduation ceremony
- volunteers to mentor students on postrelease opportunities, services, and various employment readiness activities and to provide advice on evaluation methods from local colleges and universities

THE TECHNOLOGICAL CONTINUUM

New technologies are available to deliver education and training programs to incarcerated persons. These new technologies include networked computer-assisted instruction, CD-ROM reference systems, interactive video classrooms, satellite broadcasting, and Internet services. Research suggests that measurable academic gains can be accomplished in a matter of weeks using computer-assisted instruction.[4] In most cases, inmate users are positive about edu-

cation programs incorporating these high-tech systems.

Unfortunately, these newer technologies can be quite costly to install and may be expensive to maintain. If an institution lacks the financial resources or infrastructure for these new technologies, positive results can be achieved using less sophisticated (and less costly) solutions. Older but usable computer equipment may be donated. Institution leaders should be careful about what equipment they accept, however, because appropriate software may not be available for some older systems.

Although the educational benefits of new technologies are clear, more traditional approaches can be effective as well. Video general equivalency diploma (GED) lessons such as those produced by Kentucky Educational Television (KET), used in conjunction with workbooks, can provide quality instruction at a reasonable cost. The only equipment required would be a television and VCR, which many institutions already own. A part-time instructor or qualified volunteer could support the video lessons. The same series may be broadcast by a local public broadcasting station, although the prerecorded video lessons offer more flexibility in that they can be shown whenever it is convenient. The videotaped version can also be sequenced to fit the needs of inmates. KET also provides other video courses for basic math and reading in an attractive format.

Institutions with very limited budgets can base instruction programs on inexpensive (less than $15) workbooks produced by several publishers. These workbooks frequently include diagnostic tests and a practice GED examination. Another low-tech delivery system involves the help of trained and motivated inmate tutors. Local literacy organizations such as Literacy Volunteers of America or Lauback Literacy may be able to train selected inmates to tutor other inmates. One-on-one tutoring can be a very effective educational tool, especially at the lower academic levels. The use of inmate tutors has the added benefit of providing useful, productive work for inmates who may otherwise be idle or underemployed. Inmate tutors need supervision and ongoing training by a staff member willing to devote a significant amount of time to the activity.

In summary, effective education programs for inmates can be developed at various levels of technological sophistication (and costs). The more sophisticated technologies such as networked computer-assisted instruction excel at recordkeeping and reporting, and provide an attractive instructional format. But low-tech, less costly systems can produce satisfactory results as well. Program developers should review these various options and their costs.

INCENTIVES

Incentives for participation in education programs in state correctional systems are widespread. These incentives include good time (time off or early release), wages or stipends, parole considerations, priority transfers, extra visits, and telephone privileges. Although there may be resistance in some jurisdictions to rewarding inmates for joining programs, incentives are a reasonable way to encourage participation, especially when other prison assignments provide incentives as well. It is important to treat school participation as a regular "job" with the benefits of other institutional assignments. Research strongly suggests that the completion of a major educational milestone— GED or vocational training, for instance—significantly improves inmates' postrelease success.

CELEBRATING ACHIEVEMENTS

Inmates (and correctional institutions, for that matter) frequently have little to celebrate. Mention of prisons and detention centers in the media is usually associated with an escape, an act of violence, a disturbance, or some similarly sensational and thus "newsworthy" event. Educational achievement can provide justifiable reasons to celebrate both individual and institutional achievements. To the degree possible, major education achievements such as literacy program completions, high school diplomas, or vocational training certificates should be recognized with a graduation. Outside guest speakers are appreciated by incarcerated students, as they show that the community is interested. Including other nongraduating students can motivate those students. (Many inmate students doubt their ability to achieve major educational goals, but seeing their fellow inmates graduate helps them belive in themselves.) Including parents and other family members in graduations can give them a more positive view of an institution. For many inmates, an institutional graduation will be the first public recognition of any educational achievement in their lives.

DISTANCE LEARNING

Dramatic developments in computer and telecommunication technology in recent years have spawned a variety of education programs where students can earn college credits or vocational skills without attending classes. Distance learning relies on videotapes, satellite transmission, faxes, electronic and quick delivery mail, and cable television as well as other means to link students with instructors who may be hundreds or even thousands of miles away. These learning technologies hold considerable promise for overcoming the isolation of prisons and correctional institutions from the larger society and its education institutions.

Despite its potential, distance learning is currently limited by a number of factors, including (1) the tuition and fees charged by the institution for postsecondary education; (2) the cost of the technological infrastructure—satellite transmission receptors, computers, and so on; and (3) security issues that arise when inmates have access to computers linked to the community via modems. The advantages of individualized, self-paced, high-quality instruction are likely to overcome the shortcomings of the new technologies, especially because technologies tend to become less expensive over time.

ANTICIPATED RESULTS

What results can a warden or facility administrator reasonably expect from the participation of inmates in an education program? Research at correctional systems at different levels (federal, state, and local) indicates that inmates who participate in education programs (academic and vocational) generally exhibit improved institutional adjustment and postrelease success. Although dramatic results are sometimes reported, carefully done studies report reductions in recidivism of 10 percent to 25 percent.[5] Education is not an inoculation against further criminal involvement; rather, it is an improvement in the offenders' chances to obtain legitimate employment and stay clear of further criminal involvement.

Additionally, the consensus of the research is that positive results are correlated to the intensity and length of the education involvement as well as the achievement of a major educational milestone. Yet some inmates have deep psychological problems and addictions and may be only slightly helped by educational participation.

PROGRAM EVALUATION

Program evaluation may range from a relatively modest inhouse design to an expensive professional evaluation by an outside consultant or university-based organization. Regardless of the level of the evaluation effort, an assessment of program impact is essential. An evaluation that includes both process and outcomes gives a balanced picture.

The establishment of reasonable goals for institutional programs is critical. What should the impact on the inmate clients be, and how will it be measured? If improved institutional behavior is a goal, how will that goal be achieved, and how will the data on that goal be collected? What rate of student progress has been identified? How many inmates are expected to achieve an established goal (a certificate of literacy, a high school diploma/GED, a job within 90 days

of release, or a reduction in the rate at which they violate parole or return to prison)?

Operational data are equally important in a correctional setting, where a three-hour scheduled class can be cut in half by just a few minor operational glitches (e.g., the pass list did not get to the housing unit officer, the staff were held up entering the institution because a new officer was working the post, the meal was late because a popular item was on the menu and everyone showed up for dinner). Consistent and reliable data on the operation need to be generated and provided to program managers for review and action. Last week's releasees or disciplinary problems may leave classes operating at half capacity even though the price of instruction remains constant.

One of the most overlooked areas of program operation in correctional facilities is the impact of the services on the postrelease success of inmates. Many administrators are especially adverse to evaluation efforts that focus on postrelease success because of research difficulties and the fear of being held responsible for the inmates' performance in a community setting. Put directly, if correctional education programs cannot impact inmates' postrelease success (and if this success cannot be measured), why invest in these efforts at all? In an increasingly results-oriented environment, the impact of institutional programs on releasees' success is the "bottom line" for policy makers and others who hold the purse strings. Increasing pressures on public funding strongly suggest that programs without objective, verifiable measures of results are at risk, and research indicates that reasonable evaluations of postrelease success can be accomplished with limited resources.

NOTES

1. T.A. Ryan and B. Mauldin, *Correctional Education and Recidivism: An Historical Analysis* (1994).

2. M. Harer, "Recidivism among Federal Prisoners Released in 1987," *Journal of Correctional Education* 46 (1995): 98–128.

3. D. Gilliard and A. Beck, *Prisoners in 1997* (Washington, DC: Bureau of Justice Statistics, 1997).

4. S. Duquid et al., "Using Recidivism To Evaluate Effectiveness in Prison Education," *Journal of Correctional Education* 47 (1996): 74–85.

5. Harer, "Recidivism among Federal Prisoners Released in 1987," 98–128; K. Hull et al., "An Analysis of Recidivism Rates for Participants of the Academic/Vocational/Transitional Education Programs Offered by the Virginia Department of Correctional Education" (unpublished); D. Jenkins et al., "A Post Release Follow-Up of Correctional Education Program Completers Released in 1990–1991" (unpublished).

SUGGESTED READING

Barton, P., and R. Coley. 1998. *Captive students: Education and training in America's prisons*. Princeton, NJ: Educational Testing Services.

CHAPTER 13

Prison Recreation

Harold L. Kahler

Having a well-run recreation program is a vital goal of every prison or jail administrator. Yet current correction texts barely discuss recreational programs, focusing more on academic and vocational education programs and their contributions to inmate rehabilitation. The texts usually are silent about the contributions recreational programs make to the orderly management of institutions and the personal growth of inmates.

Perhaps this omission stems from an awareness that prison recreation programs are not generally favored by the public. Unless just awakened from a slumber as long as Rip Van Winkle's, people know that tolerance of crime is now low. There has been a return to the idea that the pain resulting from criminal activity must exceed the gain. That pain is now delivered through the imposition of longer sentences, determinate sentences, mandatory sentences, and three-strike provisions. These actions attempt to curb what is perceived as a crime rate soaring out of control. Within this context, recreation programs for inmates are perceived as frills that mitigate the pain of imprisonment and coddle inmates.

THE "GET TOUGH" POLICY AND PRISON RECREATION PROGRAMS

One current attempt to "get tough" on criminals and increase the pain of punishment for criminal activities focuses on prison recreation programs. Discussions in college classrooms, letters to the editor, and Congress regarding prison recreation programs indicate a widespread belief that only bare-bones prisons—not the so-called "country club" prisons of today—will help lower crime. The courts, it is argued, send criminals to prison for punishment. They are not sent there to make ceramic pottery, attend movies, watch television, or participate in sporting events or musical jam sessions! Voters have told their elected representatives that "enough is enough," and their representatives have heeded the message.

In response to this outpouring of public concern, several states and the federal government have begun curtailing prison recreation programs. States that have banned or are in the process of banning weight-lifting equipment and/or restricting other recreation activities, including television viewing, include Arizona, California, Georgia, Mississippi, North Carolina, Ohio, South Carolina, and Wisconsin.[1]

THE ZIMMER AMENDMENT AND RECREATION IN FEDERAL PRISONS

The Zimmer Amendment, an attachment to the fiscal year 1996 Department of Justice Appropriations Bill, was approved by the U.S. Congress in response to the public's perception that prison recreation programs coddle offenders, cost too much, and create consequences detrimental to public safety. Provisions of this "no-frills" bill that directly affect prison recreation activities prohibit the purchase and replacement of weight-lifting equipment and electric and/or electronic musical instruments. The showing of R-rated movies in federal correctional institutions is also prohibited.

The effect of the Zimmer Amendment will be felt by every inmate in the federal prison system. In a prison community, as in every community, the adage "it takes all kinds" aptly describes the variety of interests and abilities of the community members. Less active inmates spend their leisure time watching movies and reading magazines; more active inmates spend their leisure time in the weight room or participating in team sports; and musically inclined inmates spend their leisure time in the music room. Correctional personnel argue that this amendment adversely affects not only the inmates' use of leisure time but inmate management. Consider the following:

1. Inasmuch as the most commercially successful movies carry the R rating, this prohibition, if strictly followed, limits the selection of movies to be considered for inmate viewing. Rather than attending G or PG films, some inmates may opt to fill their idle time planning or pursuing activities not conducive to the orderly running of the institution.

2. This amendment negatively affects many active inmates by eventually eliminating all weight-lifting activities. The weight room is a popular recreation area in the institution, and many of the inmates whose leisure time is spent working out with weights are not interested in participating in other fitness activities. In a prison weight room, inmates act as "spotters" for others and encourage each other. Cooperation and esprit de corps are evident within the weight room. This recreation activity is supported by proponents because it fills idle time, reduces boredom, reduces tension, builds self-esteem, and teaches the necessity of cooperation.

3. The prohibition against providing electric or electronic musical instruments will reduce the positive use of idle time by those inmates who currently spend leisure time in the music room. This prohibition may contribute to the idleness of this group of inmates.

The American Correctional Association's (ACA's) *Standards for Adult Correctional Institutions* describe the provision of recreation and leisure time activities "comparable with those available in the community" as essential elements of a correctional operation. According to the ACA, the following facilities and equipment are essential: an outdoor recreation area, an auditorium, a music room, and weight-lifting equipment.[2]

The Zimmer Amendment rejects these ACA standards, but accurately reflects many Americans' opinion that amenities provided prison inmates through recreation programs are too costly, coddle inmates, and create dangerous consequences for the personal safety of law-abiding citizens. If these charges are true, prison recreation programs should be curtailed. However, these views are not held by most prison administrators and their staff, and therefore, they should be examined in more detail.

COST, CODDLING, AND CONSEQUENCES EXAMINED

Cost

The history of U.S. correctional institutions shows that the cost argument is short-sighted. Every student in Corrections 101 knows that the two major problems plaguing prisons since their inception have been overcrowding and idleness. The promises accompanying the development of the Walnut Street Jail in the eighteenth century, the Auburn and Eastern penitentiaries in the nineteenth century, and the "modern" prisons of today were all short-lived and unfulfilled primarily because of overcrowding and inmate idleness. Today's inmates are serving longer sentences in vastly overcrowded institutions. This combination constitutes a potentially volatile environment. If inmates are not provided opportunities for the constructive use of idle time, they will fill that time in their own way.

The President's Commission on Law Enforcement and Administration of Justice noted that as early as the 1800s prison administrators realized "mere restraint could not accomplish the purpose of corrections, and that many of the features of prison life actually intensified the problems of offenders."[3(p.163)] These prison officials also recognized that "recreation would ease institutional tensions and contribute to an atmosphere less detrimental to rehabilitation."[4(p.163)]

Custodial and treatment staff recognize that prison recreation programs greatly reduce the probability of violence within institutions. Therefore, the cost of prison recreation programs to the taxpayer is minuscule when compared with the cost of repairing damages from wanton acts of violence and destruction or providing additional staff to supervise inmates who have no constructive alternatives for the use of idle time.

Given these facts, the "we can't afford prison recreation programs" argument should become "we can't afford NOT to have prison recreation programs!"

Coddling

If prison recreation programs were solely for the benefit of inmates, it might be appropriate to question them. However, as noted above, most correctional managers support these programs and consider them management and rehabilitation tools benefitting not only the inmates, but the staff and, ultimately, the public.

The President's Commission on Law Enforcement and Administration of Justice recognized the negative impact of idleness in America's prisons when it concluded that "sometimes institutions foster conspicuously deleterious conditions—idleness . . . and moral deterioration."[5(p.172)] After listing a number of abuses found in American prisons, the commis-

sion declared "a more pervasive evil is idleness; [and] this is especially destructive where there are no industries, no educational programs, no recreational facilities—only aimless loitering in corridors or yards."[6(p.164)] A model institution was then described as one having classrooms, recreational facilities, day rooms and perhaps a shop and library."[7(p.173)]

This judgment is echoed by line staff who work in these institutions. As one correctional officer at a state prison remarked, "I feel that giving the inmates recreation time—time for weight lifting, jogging, basketball, and other activities—to release stress is good. It makes it safer for the staff, reduces inmate idleness, reduces tension, and contributes to the orderly running of the institution." And a correctional supervisor in a privatized prison recently commented that "recreation activities are the things that keep the lid on here."

Consequences

Many people fear that prison recreation programs diminish the deterrent effect of incarceration. Others fear that these programs—especially weight-lifting programs—encourage intimidation, robbery, or assault of innocent citizens by released offenders who have used prison recreation programs to develop themselves physically.

Most criminologists would argue, however, that deterrence is ineffective mainly because criminals do not expect to be caught. Correctional recreation specialists assert that there is no reliable research confirming that the bodybuilding efforts of incarcerated inmates lead to victimization of citizens when the inmates are released. These specialists suggest that individuals committing street crimes usually rely on weapons, not brute strength, to coerce their victims into submission.

Therefore, it is difficult to conclude that prison recreation programs diminish the deterrent effect of incarceration or that weight-lifting programs result in an increase of violence against law-abiding citizens. But it cannot be denied that current recidivism rates indicate that the prison experience of many released offenders has not deterred them from subsequent criminal activities—including assault upon innocent citizens.

THE NEED FOR PROGRAMS THAT ENCOURAGE THE LEARNING OF NEW BEHAVIOR

Various strategies to rehabilitate offenders have been adopted in America's prisons. These strategies have sought to provide insight into the inmate's criminal behavior, to facilitate change in that behavior, to increase the inmate's self-esteem, and to empower the inmate to become a law-abiding, productive citizen when released. In most correctional institutions, counseling is the main treatment strategy. However, if counseling is to be successful, it must include voluntary participation and active involvement that is open, honest, and free of any attempt to manipulate staff or other inmates. These conditions are rarely met. Many inmates, forced to attend counseling sessions, are reluctant participants whose presence jeopardizes the effectiveness of the program for those inmates who hope to benefit from it. Other inmates consider participation in these programs an opportunity to manipulate staff to obtain increased institution privileges. For these reasons, no program yet developed has been overwhelmingly successful, although a few have yielded positive results for some individuals.

RECREATION PROGRAMS: A TOOL FOR REHABILITATION

Many citizens believe that offenders should not be sent to prison to attend college classes. In fact, offenders are not sent to prison to improve their education. They are, however, sent to prison for the protection of society, and, if possible, to be changed (for the better). Criminals are not occupying prison cells because they lack college credits. There are many competing theories about why people commit crimes. But the

inability to deal with frustration, control anger, and overcome a poor self-image combined with misguided use of leisure time almost always contribute greatly to criminal activity.

If the recidivism rate of offenders and the victimization of the innocent are to be reduced, prison inmates who are determined to continue their criminal activities when released must become active participants in programs that enable them to experience situations in which their usual way of responding does not work. When behavior as usual does not produce the coveted payoff, offenders are encouraged to learn new behavior.

A properly administered institution recreation program—although not generally recognized as such—can be an effective tool for teaching and developing the social skills that are necessary for participation in free society. Inmates involved in recreation activities learn the value of teamwork, fair play, anger management, and amiable conflict resolution. These programs also provide opportunities for the constructive use of idle time, relieve the stress and tension of incarceration, and help increase self-esteem. Exhibit 13–1

Exhibit 13–1 Traditional Institution Recreation Programs

1. Organized outdoor group intermural activities: flag football, basketball, baseball, soccer, volleyball, and handball
2. Organized indoor group activities: card games, bingo
3. Individual activities: weight lifting, jogging, walking, playing musical instruments
4. Hobby shop and arts and crafts programs: leather work, ceramics, painting
5. Television, radio, and movies
6. Talent and drama shows
7. Outside volunteer entertainment/music festivals
8. Club activities: Jaycees, Toastmasters, Key Club

lists some traditional institution recreation programs.

With the possible exception of prison industries, no other institution-based program is as enthusiastically received by the inmates, and no other institution-based program is a more effective management tool. Threat of exclusion from participation in recreation programs is usually taken seriously by inmates, so they are encouraged to consider the consequences of their behavior before they act. The threat of exclusion from typical treatment programs may be ignored; if exclusion does occur, the inmates may consider themselves rewarded.

RECREATION PROGRAMS AND THE COMMUNITY

Prison recreation activities that involve the community provide the institution administrator the opportunity to achieve an important goal of community corrections: preparing the public and the inmate for the inmate's successful reintegration into the community. Examples of these activities include (1) community members entering the institution to teach inmates various skills such as chess, ceramics, and sewing; (2) community teams playing with the prison's athletic teams; and (3) arts and crafts fairs held in the community in which inmate arts and crafts are sold. These are all opportunities for positive interaction between the offender and the community. This interaction may result in an empathetic awareness that the similarities between inmate and community member outnumber the differences. Thus, the activities help facilitate the reintegration of the offender into the community. Although he may not have had offenders in mind as he spoke, a passage in President Clinton's second inaugural address—"Great rewards will come to those who can live together, learn together, work together, [and] forge new ties that bind together"—illustrates the importance of reintegrating offenders into communities. Failure to achieve this reintegration guarantees a continuing recidivism rate unacceptable to everyone.

RECREATION STAFF AND "TREATMENT" STAFF: AN EFFECTIVE PARTNERSHIP

Recreation staff are role models and often parental figures to inmates. Because they speak the inmates' language and are at the institution after hours and on holidays, many inmates turn to them when they experience problems. Recreation staff also serve as sounding boards, helping to relieve the anger and tension inmates experience when they feel that staff or other inmates have wronged them. In these interactions, recreation staff develop rapport with inmates that is seldom attained by professional therapists.

Unlike staff in other disciplines, who often see behavior designed to mask the inmates' real self, recreation staff have a unique opportunity to observe inmates as they really are. On the playing field intent on making a play, or in the craft shop striving to perfect a ceramic item, the inmates' defense mechanisms may be momentarily dropped in a spontaneous reaction to failure and frustration. This reaction provides recreation staff an accurate portrait of the inmates' ability to cope with these unwanted but common experiences.

Recreation staff and counselors observe inmates from different perspectives. Therefore, if input from recreation staff is sought and considered by the inmate's institution classification committee prior to initial classification and subsequent program reviews, more effective inmate rehabilitation programs are likely to be developed.

SIGNIFICANT IMPLICATIONS FOR THE PRISON OR JAIL ADMINISTRATOR

It is important that institution staff not treat recreation as an unimportant add-on to daily institution operations. Staff must recognize it as an important resource for maintaining a safe and secure institution. Management staff should support recreation programs by occasionally attending activities sponsored by the recreation department.

Senior managers must be selective while staffing a recreation department. Recreation programs are important to inmate rehabilitation and should be led by carefully chosen staff. In addition to a background in the management of leisure activities (e.g., field sports, arts and crafts), staff should have some knowledge of basic counseling.

Wardens and superintendents should highlight the recreation program and stress its value to the community, the institution, and the inmate when addressing public gatherings, groups of judges, and legislative bodies. They should emphasize the importance of balancing work and free time in correctional institutions.

CONCLUSION

Institution recreation programs are currently under siege by the public and the public's elected representatives. The public decries the cost of these programs, but the advantages far exceed the costs. In fact, if there is any truth in the correctional supervisor's statement that "recreation activities are the things that keep the lid on," they are a bargain at almost any price.

While some people believe that prison recreation programs coddle inmates and are frills that should be curtailed, professional corrections organizations and prison administrators support prison recreation programs because they reduce inmate idleness and the tensions produced by incarceration. Recreation is an effective management tool.

Team sports assist in the development of social skills as they teach the value of teamwork, anger management, and amiable conflict resolution. Developing skills in sports and arts and crafts activities increases the inmate's self-esteem.

Inmates whose leisure time is consumed in the arts and crafts room, in the multipurpose room, and on the field are more easily accounted for and have less time and energy to engage in prohibited activities. In short, recreation programs play an extremely important role in the professional management of today's correctional institutions.

NOTES

1. S. Clayton, "Weight Lifting in Corrections: Luxury or Necessity?" *On the Line* 20, no. 5 (1997): 1–3.
2. American Correctional Association, *Standards for Adult Correctional Institutions* (Washington, DC: 1981).
3. President's Commission on Law Enforcement and Administration of Justice (Washington, DC: 1967), 163.
4. President's Commission on Law Enforcement and Administration of Justice, 163.
5. President's Commission on Law Enforcement and Administration of Justice, 172.
6. President's Commission on Law Enforcement and Administration of Justice, 164.
7. President's Commission on Law Enforcement and Administration of Justice, 173.

CHAPTER 14

Providing Correctional Health Care Services

John Clark

One of the greatest challenges to any professional working in a correctional environment—whether as a correctional officer, correctional management staff member, or a provider of health care services—is ensuring that adequate medical, dental, and mental health services are provided to the inmate population in a timely manner consistent with federal, state, and local laws; correctional health care standards; and community medical standards. These tasks have become more difficult as the inmate population in jails and prisons has changed over the past 10 years. I frequently describe this change in our population as "VSOL," indicating that inmates today are more Violent, Sicker, and Older and stay Longer in our institutions.

The recent changes are numerous.

- Many prisoners now enter the system with well-documented histories of criminal violence.
- Street and institutional gangs are more prevalent and sophisticated.
- The resurgence of tuberculosis and the emergence of new diseases such as human immunodeficiency virus (HIV) disease have resulted in the population at greatest risk for serious illness being the same population in the criminal justice system, specifically in the custodial setting.
- Lifelong substance abuses mean that many inmates exhibit medical characteristics of individuals who are chronologically much older.
- The average length of stay for pretrial felons has increased because of "three strikes" charges and decisions to go to trial as opposed to plea bargaining.
- The population of inmates sentenced to death continues to increase, in spite of the increased rate of executions in some states.

THE JUDICIAL FOUNDATION

As we move into the twenty-first century and as the political philosophies regarding management of the 1.25 million people who are incarcerated in the United States evolve, questions of how and why we are required to provide medical, dental, and mental health services continue to be raised.[1] Some new correctional professionals have a limited historical perspective on why the incarcerated have a constitutional right to these services, so this chapter will offer some background information.

The Supreme Court decisions on the conditions of confinement have addressed medical, dental, and mental health care. There are several significant rulings that directly impact health care issues and set the basis for all that correctional professionals do.

- *Estelle v. Gamble*, 429 U.S. 97 (1976). In this case, the Supreme Court established the framework for evaluating medical care in the prison setting with this prohibition against "deliberate indifference" to the inmates' serious illness or injury. The court concluded that the incarcerated inmate must rely on prison authorities to treat his or her medical needs, and if authorities fail to do so, those medical needs will not be met. Under the Eighth Amendment, the deliberate indifference to medical needs constitutes the "unnecessary and wanton infliction of pain." Further, it matters not whether the indifference is perpetrated by the prison doctor (by his or her response to the medical needs) or by the correctional officers (by intentionally denying or delaying access to medical care or intentionally interfering with the treatment once recommended by the physician).[2]

- *Bell v. Wolfish*, 441 U.S. 520 (1979). With respect to pretrial detainees, this case set forth that the Eighth Amendment's cruel and unusual punishment prohibition is not applicable because pretrial detainees have not been convicted. However, the pretrial detainee has the right not to be punished without due process. Therefore, under the Fourteenth Amendment, the pretrial detainee cannot be punished without due process and must have access to medical care, just as the convicted inmate has access to this service.
- *Ramos v. Lamm*, 639 F. 2d 559, 576 (10th Cir., 1980). This case deals with the provision of dental services. This does not mean the provision of cosmetic care but does include adequate care such as extraction, fillings, and care essential to the process of effective mastication.
- *Bowring v. Godwin*, 551 F. 2d 44, 47 (4th Cir. 1977). This case established that the same principles that apply to medical services apply to mental health services.

The courts agree that adequate mental health services include a screening process to identify inmates with mental health problems and appropriate treatment for those problems by trained mental health professionals.

There are numerous other decisions of the court that address specific areas pertaining to medical, dental, and mental health problems.

- women's health care issues: *Batton v. State Government of North Carolina, Executive Branch*, 501 F. Supp. 1172 (E.D.N.C. 1980)
- communicable diseases and AIDS: *Lareau v. Manson*, 651 F. 2d 96, 109 (2d Cir. 1981) and *Smith v. Sullivan*, 553 F. 2d 373 (5th Cir. 1977)
- starvation: *Zant v. Prevette*, 248 Ga. 832, 286 S.E. 2d 715 (1982)

STANDARDS OF CARE

The principle that the incarcerated have a constitutional right to health services is well established in our judicial system. Correctional professionals must understand these principles in order to avoid the temptation to modify the health delivery system for the sake of financial reasons and management efficiency. Until the laws are changed, correctional professionals are mandated to provide adequate medical, dental, and mental health services. Moreover, as laws are changed (e.g., in the Prison Reform Act of 1996), it is imperative to ensure that the issues and modifications are clearly interpreted and understood.

In the early 1970s, the effort to improve health care delivered to the incarcerated included several organized movements to set standards that would ensure that the constitutional rights of the inmates would not be endangered. The National Sheriffs Association, the National Advisory Commission on Criminal Justice Standards and Goals, and the American Public Health Association established standards for general medical and health environments.[3] The first health care standards established specifically for correctional facilities were the product of the American Public Health Association. Since these early efforts, the National Commission on Correctional Health Care has emerged as the principal standard-setting and accrediting agency in the nation for correctional health care. This body is a nonprofit organization that grew out of an American Medical Association task force commissioned to establish standards in the late 1970s. Many of the professional organizations in corrections, such as the American Correctional Association, the American Jail Association, and the American Psychiatric Association, continue to contribute to the improvement of correctional health care by revising and updating standards or by providing input into the process.

In spite of the fact that a wide variety of entities have been involved in this process, there have emerged several areas that are considered absolutely essential to ensure that the constitutional rights of the incarcerated are preserved. I strongly recommend that correctional professionals review and keep for reference the full set of standards promulgated by the National Commission on Correctional Health Care, the American Correctional Association, and the American Public Health Association.

The widely accepted standards for correctional health care are derived from the basic rights of inmates established by case law.

- the right to access care
- the right to care that is ordered
- the right to a professional medical judgment

The following areas are generally considered key to ensuring that constitutional rights are not violated:

- receiving screening
- sick call
- health appraisal
- referral and follow-up
- continuity of care
- management of pharmaceuticals
- special medical needs
  1. chronic medical care
  2. pregnancy-related care
  3. communicable diseases
  4. mental health
  5. dental care

Both the correctional health literature and the vast experience of correctional health professionals clearly document that it is in the best medical interest of the incoming inmate, as well as the legal interest of the correctional facility, to provide adequate screening for health problems when inmates are initially booked or received at a facility. This process must include an evaluation for

- history of any medical problems
- history of taking legally prescribed medications
- signs and symptoms of obvious injuries or disabilities
- history or presence of mental illness or suicidal ideation
- presence of communicable diseases

A thorough receiving process benefits the entire facility—inmates and staff. Because each correctional institution is unique, each will have a slightly different intake screening process.

Experts agree on the issue of the availability of sick call and access to the physician and/or midlevel practitioner, which is based on facilities' average daily population. There is an agreement that the mechanism to access sick call must be clearly explained to inmates verbally and in writing in a language that they can understand and that the process must be documented (facilities must document both providing the access information to the inmates and timely and appropriate responses to the inmates' requests for sick call services).

A health appraisal is essential for those inmates who have been incarcerated for more than 14 days. The approval provides a more in-depth medical/mental evaluation to ascertain whether or not any health problems were missed at intake or have developed since the time of initial incarceration.

It is also important for the health care provider and the facility to ensure that there is a mechanism in place to facilitate access to the appropriate level of health care (referral and follow-up) for any problems that are identified and cannot be managed at the facility.

Equally essential is ensuring the continuity of health care—both managing patients on justifiable treatment regimens prior to incarceration, as well as ensuring that there is appropriate documentation forwarded to the patients' health care practitioner upon release.

One of the greatest challenges to correctional professionals is the management of prescription medications; medications can be expensive, and there is concern about abuse by inmates and overprescribing by well-meaning health practitioners. New treatment regimens for HIV disease (protease inhibitors) and mental illness (selective serotonin reuptake inhibitors) must be handled with well-thought-out policies and guidelines. To this end, facility administrators must rely on the advice of their local health authorities, correctional health professionals, and professional associations and agencies.

Special medical needs are important for correctional facilities to address. As indicated above, there is significant case law that is the basis for identifying these health problems as special needs. Prenatal services and chronic disease care are vital to meeting any of the correctional health care standards that are used in our industry. Likewise, much interest and concern has been raised regarding the issue of communicable diseases and the potential risks for inmates and correctional staff.

Correctional professionals must make every effort to implement these standards of care and make certain that they are met daily through ongoing monitoring facilitated by well-structured quality assurance programs.

THE CRITICAL ISSUES

On a daily basis, the correctional health professional faces many issues that must be addressed and resolved. While these involve all phases of correctional operations, several of the critical issues related to health care services include

- managed care
- communicable diseases
- mental health
- use of force
- in-custody deaths
- risk management

Managed Care

During the past three federal administrations, there have been proposals to reform the nation's health care system. These calls for change have been answered by managed care. Many correctional professionals have expressed concern about how managed care will affect the delivery of services in correctional institutions.

The key components of managed care (universal access, limited scope of service, limited choice of provider, minimal copayments, and contracting for specialized services) are already an essential part of our correctional health care delivery system. In fact, many in correctional health care have been practicing managed care for the past 15 years, in that inmates have universal access to care, the scope of services is limited, there is no choice of provider, inmate copayment fees are widely used, and contracting for health services has been commonplace in many correctional institutions across the country. So managed care will not significantly change the delivery of health care services in correctional facilities, and physicians in medical practice in the community can learn much from correctional health professionals about managed care.

There is the possibility that as the scope of service for the nation's health delivery system becomes more well defined, the correctional system will be less vulnerable to litigation based on the premises that the correctional system is not providing minimal community standard of care (e.g., cosmetic surgery, sex change surgery).

Communicable Diseases

For the past 10 years, much concern has been voiced about communicable diseases and health and safety in the workplace. With the emergence of HIV disease and the resurgence of tuberculosis, these concerns are certainly justified; however, there is no need to overreact. First and foremost, educating and communicating with inmates and staff are our most effective tools in dealing with anxiety and curtailing risky behaviors associated with transmission of communicable diseases. Second, institution staff must implement the required health and safety programs concerning air- and bloodborne pathogens and universal precautions. Finally, inmates should be screened for communicable diseases at booking/admission to a facility, and there should be annual examinations of correctional employees for communicable diseases.

The correctional management team, comprising custody and medical management, must make informed decisions about the numerous treatment approaches that are now available for HIV disease (such as protease inhibitors). These treatment regimens are very costly, on one hand. On the other hand, they have become a part of the minimal standard of practice in treating HIV disease, and, therefore, we are obligated by the correctional health care standards (continuity of care and special medical needs) to make these regimens available. However, some guidelines are needed to determine which protease inhibitors to stock and use in treatment initiated in the institution, and to develop effective communications with treating physicians on the outside to facilitate continuity.

Mental Health

The adequacy of mental health services concerns correctional health care practitioners in almost every jail and prison system in the United States. Most mental health services in the free community are woefully inadequate, and the burden placed on corrections is compounded by the significant numbers of individuals who have

---

The Cost of Inmate Health Care

The cost of medical care for prison inmates (per inmate, per day) varies substantially among jurisdictions, from a high of $14.25 in Alaska to a low of $1.51 in Oklahoma, with an average of $6.59. These costs have been increasing steadily since 1990, when the average was $4.68 per inmate per day. Many departments of corrections have attempted to control rising health care costs by requiring inmates to pay for such care; the maximum charge is no more than $5 per day. These fees partially offset the cost of care provided by the agencies, but more important, they serve as a deterrent to inmates who seek to abuse the health care system. Thirty-one states contract with private providers or state hospitals for at least a portion of their health care services, and some states contract for all health care services.

Source: Data from C. Camp and G. Camp, *Corrections Yearbook 1997*, pp. 74–75, © 1997, Criminal Justice Institute, Inc.

---

a dual diagnosis of both mental illness and substance abuse. Moreover, there are numerous inmates who have marginal mental health problems that are accentuated by incarceration and rapidly progress to a state of severe mental illness. It is mandatory to screen for mental health problems at intake and to identify any inmate who may be at risk for committing suicide; correctional professionals must make every effort to reduce the risk of inmate suicide. Staff must look not only at the suicide data with respect to the so-called "national profile" of the suicidal inmate, but at all the epidemiological data that are generated in correctional facilities over a period of several years. There is no doubt that mental health will continue to be a high-priority issue for the entire correctional community.

Use of Force

The use of force is constantly a concern for both the professional correctional staff and the professional correctional health staff. The correctional health professional must realize that force will and must be used at times. Medical staff must be knowledgeable about force techniques and the consequences of a particular force technology. On the other hand, the correctional professional must anticipate undesired outcomes, including death. To this end, professionals must develop clearly thought-out policies and procedures and receive adequate training to ensure that the health and safety of inmates and staff are protected as much as possible. Lastly, sufficient attention must be given to discussion of positional asphyxia and ensuring that correctional officers refrain from "hog-tying" or "bow-tying" or placing out-of-control inmates in the prone position for prolonged periods of time.

In-Custody Deaths

In addition to understanding the facts about suicides and deaths from positional asphyxia, correctional professionals must review and evaluate each death that occurs in the correctional environment. This review should examine all the aspects of health care, including the initial screening process, access to sick call, and follow-up and treatment for problems that were identified. Correctional professionals should also review the epidemiological aspects of all the deaths (i.e., events must be compared to try to find any patterns or trends).

Risk Management

Proactive risk management is an essential part of managing any health care delivery system. To this end, institutions should develop a formal continuous quality improvement (CQI) program. There should be a defined CQI plan, which includes a mechanism for internal and external peer review of health care provided. The meetings of the CQI committee should be documented, and corrective action plans for identified problems should be written. Responsibility for follow-up within a specified time period should be assigned. Proactive risk management includes the hiring of qualified providers, continuing medical education, and effective counseling and discipline.

THE PERILS AND PITFALLS

Every step of the path toward providing correctional health care services is surrounded by traps. Each trap can spell disaster for the correctional administrator and the correctional health professional. Listed below are 10 pitfalls to avoid.

1. Do not hire any health care professional without having a written duty statement that clearly details the expectations for that employee. Have the employee sign and date the duty statement.
2. Do not allow health care professionals (especially physicians) to record more hours on their time records than they actually worked (e.g., signing in for eight hours but working only two or three hours).
3. Resist the temptation to listen to only one side of the story and do your own investigations until you can identify staff that can do thorough investigations in an objective manner.
4. Do not disseminate inaccurate or incomplete information, select one spokesperson for the medical unit, and ensure that the spokesperson is well briefed on the facts.
5. Never ignore warning signs, such as an impending outbreak of a communicable disease, or an acutely ill patient with mar-

ginally normal physical findings and/or vital signs.

6. Beware of chronic substance abusers, often labeled as malingerers. They can go downhill suddenly.
7. Watch out for high-profile inmates and do not deviate from established policy and procedure. Be prepared for the media, and be familiar with the legal aspects of medical issues.
8. Do not enter into crisis decision making without having several strategies outlined for implementation in the event that the original plan does not work.
9. Never walk alone on the path of pitfalls. Pick up the phone and call a colleague or counterpart in another correctional facility. Better yet, go onto the Internet and get help from one of the many correctional professional organizations with Web sites.
10. Last but not least, when you encounter an irresolvable problem, do not be too proud to retreat and try again later.

In spite of the difficult issues surrounding the delivery of correctional health care services, the future promises to be exciting. There is great potential to employ the rapidly developing technology and the increasing ability to incorporate innovative thinking into the provision of health care services. The future may involve many exciting elements, including

- coeducational programming for male and female inmates, particularly in regard to outpatient and inpatient medical services
- inmate self-medication programs and over-the-counter medications available through the inmate commissary
- telemedicine (remote diagnosis of inmates using video conferencing technology)

CONCLUSION

The basic principles and practices detailed in this chapter and this book will assist the correctional professional in managing and designing health care delivery systems for the next millennium. If systems are designed well and meet all standards, the future of health care in correctional facilities will indeed be bright.

NOTES

1. D. Gilliard and A. Beck, *Prisoners in 1997* (Washington, DC: Bureau of Justice Statistics, 1998).
2. S. Kay, *The Constitutional Dimension of an Inmate's Right to Health Care* (Nashville, TN: Vanderbilt University School of Law, 1991).
3. B. Anno, *Prison Health Care: Guidelines for the Management of an Adequate Delivery System* (1991).

SUGGESTED READINGS

American Correctional Association. *Standards for adult local detention facilities* (Lanham, MD: American Correctional Association, 1991).

Clark, J. 1991. Correctional health care issues in the nineties: Forecast and recommendations. *American Jails.* September/October.

Clark, J. 1993. Managing tuberculosis in short-term correctional facilities: Strategies for guerrilla warfare. *American Jails.* March/April.

Clark, J. 1997. Meeting the challenges of jail health care. *Sheriff's Magazine.* January–February.

National Commission on Correctional Health Care. *Standards for health services in jails* (Chicago: National Commission on Correctional Health Care, 1996).

National Commission on Correctional Health Care. *Standards for health services in juvenile detention and confinement facilities* (Chicago: National Commission on Correctional Health Care, 1995).

National Commission on Correctional Health Care. *Standards for health services in prisons* (Chicago: National Commission on Correctional Health Care, 1997).

CHAPTER 15

Mental Health Services in a Correctional Setting

Sally C. Johnson

Provision of mental health services is a necessary but complex part of the correctional operation. Ten to 20 percent of individuals involved in any stage of the criminal justice process can be diagnosed as suffering from a mental disorder.[1] Many of these disturbed offenders are ultimately sentenced to a period of confinement and become the responsibility of jail and prison staff.

According to the *Diagnostic and Statistical Manual of Mental Disorders, Fourth Edition* (DSM- IV), a mental disorder is a "clinically significant behavioral or psychiatric syndrome or pattern in an individual associated with distress or disability."[2(p.xxi)] The symptom presentation and the level of intervention required by mental disorders vary over time. The symptoms do not fit neatly into the structured routine of the correctional setting and often present as a crisis. The demand for crisis intervention is replaced quickly by the need for adequate evaluation. Evaluation needs, in turn, are replaced by needs for ongoing treatment and follow-up.

Mental health care requires significant resource allocation as well as careful administrative planning and oversight. Unplanned for and unmet needs of mentally disordered offenders can cause significant disruption in the correctional environment and give rise to liability concerns and litigation. Well-organized and adequate mental health services can contribute greatly to the smooth running of a correctional operation.

INSTITUTION REQUIREMENTS FOR MENTALLY ILL OFFENDERS

Several legal cases in the late 1970s and early 1980s speak to the responsibility of the states and federal government to provide the jail and prison population with access to medical and mental health care.[3–5] Little differentiation exists between the right to assessment and treatment of medical problems and the right to assessment and treatment of psychiatric problems. The standard for services has been set very low. Provided that the correctional administration ensures that deliberate indifference is not shown toward the medical and mental health needs of the incarcerated population, the standard is met. Examples of deliberate indifference were summarized by Shanski in 1989 and include lack of access to care, failure to follow through with care, insufficient staff resources, and poor outcome due to negligent care.[6] From a practical standpoint, however, a significantly higher level of services must be established to ensure that the level of care does not fall below the minimum standard in any individual case.

As the courts drew attention to the medical and psychiatric needs of the incarcerated popu-

Opinions expressed in this chapter are those of the author and do not necessarily represent the opinions of the Federal Bureau of Prisons or the U.S. Department of Justice.

lation, several professional organizations attempted to establish minimum guidelines and standards for ensuring the care and treatment of this population. The American Public Health Association,[7] the American Correctional Association (ACA),[8] and the American Medical Association[9] made early and lasting efforts to establish standards. Standards were revised and utilized by other groups, including the American Psychiatric Association,[10] which established a task force on the issue, and the National Commission on Correctional Health Care[11] (NCCHC), which became a monitoring and accrediting body. The American Bar Association[12] and the Joint Commission on Accreditation of Healthcare Organizations (Joint Commission)[13] also contributed to the process. Currently, mental health service provision in jails and prisons can be formally reviewed by the ACA, the NCCHC, and the Joint Commission. The process involves review of policy and procedures, review of documentation of care, and site visiting.

Institution services are reviewed against the standards established by each organization. Although there is considerable overlap of intent in the standards, the degree of fit between standards and a particular program and the degree of detail addressed by the standards varies greatly. The ACA standards are the least specific of the three, and thus many mental health programs within correctional facilities choose to undergo accreditation review by the NCCHC or Joint Commission in addition to the ACA.

The importance of external review and accreditation should not be underestimated. In addition to providing concrete guidelines for establishing and maintaining programs, preparation for the accreditation process forces internal auditing and review. The accreditation visit and reports frequently identify existing or potential problems in service care delivery and in the quality or quantity of services, and mandate establishment of a time frame for correction of those deficiencies. Successful accreditation provides support for the correctional program when claims of inadequacy of care are presented. The accreditation process also allows integration of the health care staff into the larger health care community and, by this, provides staff support and gives guidance to the correctional health care mission.

ACCESS TO CARE

Correctional administrators must identify and implement an adequate health care delivery system that can ensure inmate access to health care and health care providers. This access must exist from the point of arrest to the point of discharge from correctional supervision or oversight. Staff and physical plant resource needs must be determined, and a plan must be developed and maintained. Administrators must ensure that adequate policies and procedures are established and utilized to provide a framework for care delivery. These policies and procedures then serve as standards against which individual episodes of care can be compared as part of continuous performance improvement efforts.

An adequate care delivery system for mental health services in a correctional environment must address a range of functions and needs within the environment. In the case of *Ruiz v. Estell*,[14] the court focused on six issues required to meet minimally adequate standards for mental health care in a correctional environment: (1) a system to ensure mental health screening for inmates, (2) provision of treatment while inmates are in segregation or special housing units, (3) use of the training of mental health staff to ensure individualized treatment planning, (4) an accurate and confidential medical record system, (5) a suicide prevention program, and (6) monitoring for appropriate use of psychotropic medication. All these issues are essential parts of health care programs. Together, they form a continuum of services to meet the demands of the correctional population.

SCREENING THE POPULATION

Mental health care services begin at the screening stage. Given the volume of patients entering the correctional environment and the fact that the presentation of these individuals is often unplanned for and outside of usual outside working hours, it is important that a good initial screening system is in place. Inmates should be screened immediately, before they are placed in a housing situation without direct staff observation. Screening should be done on an individual basis. Initial screening should be conducted by a health care provider who has been trained in detecting symptoms of potentially serious mental disorders and who has mastered good interviewing techniques. Individuals entering the criminal justice system are often angry, upset, frightened, anxious, or confused and may have difficulty providing information.

The goal of screening is to quickly identify emergency situations and inmates who might require more extensive intervention prior to placement in the population of their assigned housing areas. During screening, staff members should identify themselves and the purpose of their interview. They should assess the inmate's general hygiene and understanding of the situation. The staff member should provide correct orientation as to place, time, and situation, to reassure and educate the individual if necessary. The same questions should be routinely addressed to each inmate, with further exploration and data collection where indicated. The response to each question should be recorded on a screening intake form, and this form should then be placed in the inmate's correctional health record after any necessary referrals have been made. Proper mental health intake screening will determine the type and immediacy of need for other mental health services. A sample screening form is shown in Exhibit 15–1.

MENTAL HEALTH TREATMENT

Inmates requiring further assessment/evaluation should be housed in an area with staff availability and observation appropriate to their needs. The assessment/evaluation should be assigned to a specific staff member and service and includes interviews, record review, physical examination, laboratory studies, observation, and possibly psychological testing. A differential diagnosis should be established, recognizing that, over time, the diagnosis will become more clear.

Treatment within the correctional environment can occur in a variety of settings. Levels of treatment include outpatient (housed in general population and usually seen in medical clinic or on the unit), inpatient (housed in hospital facility within the correctional environment or transferred to the community), and transitional/intermediate (usually housed in one area of a general population housing unit or a separate housing unit). Inmates may move from one level of treatment to another. Outpatient services involve counseling, consultation, medication management, and ongoing screening to identify any change in treatment needs. Much of the counseling is supportive and provides a cost-effective mental health intervention that may prevent escalation to a higher level of care. The frequency of visits varies from weekly to every 90 days. Psychiatric inpatient services are often established on site in correctional facilities to avoid the need to discharge into community settings and to ensure adequate security measures are in place. Some systems, however, continue to use a community-based hospital system. Admission is voluntary or by civil commitment. Each potential patient must be reviewed for competency to consent to hospitalization and volunteer for admission.[15] Common admission criteria for inpatient hospitalization appear in Exhibit 15–2.

In recent years, in part due to limited resources, improved screening, and efforts to manage rising costs, the concept of transitional, intermediate, or habilitative care has developed.[16] Inmates who have known mental disorders, are prone to relapse, have significant behavioral problems, or are unable to be well integrated into the general prison populations often benefit from this intervention. The goal is to stabilize them during a three- to six-month period of less intensive treatment in a somewhat sheltered environment. Treatment focuses on learning to cope with chronic symptomatology and learning to adapt to the general prison environment. The

Exhibit 15–1 Intake Screening Form

Inmate name: _____   Identification #: _____

Date of birth: _____

Education level: _____ (in years)

Can read: _____ YES _____ NO

Fluent in English: _____ YES _____ NO

History of psychiatric problems or hospitalization: _____ YES* _____ NO

   *If yes, list place and dates _____

   _____

Current psychotropic medications (list with date of last dose): _____

Known medical problems: _____

Allergies: _____

Substance abuse (list with date of last use): _____

Hallucinations: _____ YES* _____ NO

   *Describe: _____

Delusions: _____ YES* _____ NO

   *Describe: _____

Anxiety: _____ YES _____ NO

Depression: _____ YES _____ NO

History of suicide attempts: _____ YES* _____ NO

   *Date/Type: _____

Current suicidal ideation: _____ YES* _____ NO

   *Describe: _____

Homicidal ideation: _____ YES _____ NO

Recommendations (check all appropriate):

   _____ Immediate referral to psychiatry/psychology

   _____ Suicide watch

   _____ Medication

   _____ Outpatient clinic appointment

   _____ Cleared for general population

COMPLETED BY: _____   DATE: _____

goal of treatment is eventual integration into a regular prison population.

CRISIS INTERVENTION

The need for crisis intervention or suicide prevention may arise with inmates at any level of treatment, as well as those not identified as in need of treatment. Crisis intervention can be defined as short-term care for acute mental distress.[17] The level of distress varies from acute anxiety or anger to that associated with psychotic decompensation. Often the crisis entails identification of suicidal ideation or a suicide attempt. The frequency of suicidal thinking or behavior presenting as a crisis requires that all cor-

Exhibit 15–2 Admission Criteria

1. Presence of significant psychiatric symptomatology
2. Inability to be handled in a less restrictive environment
3. Need for complex/comprehensive assessment services not available in an outpatient setting
4. Court-ordered inpatient evaluation
5. Imminent danger to self or others
6. Need for complex treatment services not available in less restrictive setting

---

Inmate Participation in Mental Health Programs

On January 1, 1997, there were nearly 42,000 inmates participating in mental health programs in 43 correctional departments around the country; this figure represents 4.2 percent of all inmates confined in such jurisdictions. The participation rates vary substantially from a high of 12.6 percent (Ohio) to a low of 0.01 percent (New Jersey, Rhode Island, and Wyoming), with an average of 2.9 percent of inmates in a jurisdiction participating.

Source: Data from C. Camp and G. Camp, *Corrections Yearbook 1997*, pp. 92–93, © 1997, Criminal Justice Institute, Inc.

---

rectional staff be familiar with suicide prevention. The administration must ensure that an adequate suicide prevention program is in place within the correctional environment. A suicide prevention program includes adequate training of staff in identification of signs and symptoms of potentially suicidal inmates, ensuring the availability of a safe environment in which a suicidal inmate can be housed, and ensuring that the suicidal inmate is kept under constant observation. The latter requirement is costly and time intensive. This has led some systems to try using inmate companions or peer watchers in conjunction with rapid access of staff to intervene. An inmate companion program has been used successfully as part of the suicide prevention program in a number of federal prison facilities.[18]

Because of the relapsing nature of many mental disorders and the chronicity of others, discharge planning and follow-up are crucial both when returning inmates to a general population facility and when releasing them to the community. Successful discharge planning must begin with sound diagnostic assessment. Adequate and cost-effective treatment must be accomplished. Education of inmates about their illness and treatment needs will help increase the likelihood that treatment will continue outside the hospital setting. Assessment of dangerousness to self and others must be reviewed to ensure that discharge is the correct decision. To complete the process, there should be sufficient exploration of follow-up resources to ensure that resources are adequate to meet the inmate's needs as well as communication, verbally and through records, with the follow-up care provider.

A WIDE RANGE OF PATHOLOGY

Given the trend toward longer sentences and determinate sentencing, inmates have more opportunity to present health care needs while in the criminal justice system. There are many different mental disorders that may present in the inmate population. Clinicians have developed various classification systems to describe and group these illnesses. The most widely used classification system for mental disorders is DSM-IV.[19] It defines and explains over 300 different diagnoses, most of which can become evident in inmates. The diagnoses, however, can be collapsed into seven categories that generally describe the breadth of illness coming to the attention of health care staff in a correctional environment. Table 15–1 outlines these categories, their typical presentation, suggested treatment, treatment settings, and provider needs. This grouping serves only as a simple template upon which to build a more detailed and specific understanding of psychopathology.

CONFINEMENT COMPLICATES MANY PROBLEMS

The types of mental health problems and the types of services needed to address these problems are similar throughout the phases of the criminal justice operation. Individuals may enter the system at any phase of an illness or may present new symptomatology once in custody. The stress of being involved in the criminal jus-

tice system can itself serve as a precipitant to or aggravating factor of the symptom picture. Stressors include the legal system, separation from any existing community support systems, peer-generated problems, and internal stressors associated with loss of control and individual decision making. Sleep and eating routines are disrupted. Access to anxiety-reducing activities such as television, exercise, socialization, and smoking may be severely limited. All of these are compounded by a general lack of familiarity with or understanding of the legal or criminal justice process and the forced position of dependence. A functioning mental health service is crucial to adequately address the impact of these issues as well as identify and manage the mental disorders of a correctional population.

Table 15–1   Generalized Classification of Mental Disorders

Category	Symptom Presentation	Treatment	Typical Settings	Provider

Psychosis	Hallucinations
	Delusions
	Bizarre behavior
		Medication
		Supportive
		  treatments
			Hospital
			Outpatient
			Transitional
			  care
				Physician
				Psychologist

Mood disorders	Increased or decreased
	  mood
	Sleep disturbances
	Appetite disturbances
		Medication
		counseling
			Outpatient
			Hospital
			Transitional
			  care
				Physician
				Psychologist

Situational
  problems
	Anxiety
	Mild depression
		Counseling
		Environmental
		  support
			Outpatient
			Transitional
			  care
			Hospital
				Physician
				Counselor
				Psychologist

Substance abuse	Drug-seeking behavior Sleep disturbances Anxiety	Education Relapse preven- tion	Outpatient	Social worker Counselor

Mental retardation
  organicity
	Adjustment difficulties
	Viewed as vulnerable
		Assisted living
		Supportive
		  counseling
			Transitional
			  care
				Physician
				Social worker
				Unit team

Sexual offenders	Sexual offense by
	  history
		Education
		Relapse preven-
		  tion
			Outpatient	Physician
				Psychologist
				Counselor

Personality
  disorders
	Problem behaviors	Counseling
		Environment
		  support
			Outpatient	Unit team
				Psychologist
				Physician

The success of any care delivery system for mental health services is integrally related to the adequacy of the general medical services available to the correctional population. It is not uncommon for medical illnesses to present with psychiatric symptoms. Anxiety, disorientation, confusion, and hallucinations can herald the onset or unmask the existence of physical illness or disease. Between 24 and 60 percent of psychiatric patients have been found to have concurrent medical illnesses.[20] Too often, patients are dealt with only at the first level of symptom review, which may be the presentation of disturbed behavior. Each inmate entering the prison system should have a complete physical exam and baseline laboratory studies. Each inpatient admission to a psychiatric hospital facility within the correctional environment requires a current physical exam and review of medical history. More extensive laboratory studies to rule out organic causes of the symptom picture should be conducted. These will also serve as a baseline against which potential side effects from medication treatment can be assessed. Screening for infectious diseases (including tuberculosis, human immunodeficiency virus, hepatitis, and syphilis) should be completed.

PSYCHIATRIC TREATMENT HAS LEGAL REQUIREMENTS

Hospitalization in a psychiatric facility is on a voluntary basis unless inmates are so impaired as to present a danger to themselves or others, or could clearly benefit from care in a hospital and are unable to function in a general population. Each state, and the federal government by statute,[21] directs how an individual can be civilly committed for involuntary hospitalization in a psychiatric facility. Civil commitment in a prison facility parallels the process for non-prisoners and involves due process, legal representation, and judicial decision making. Voluntary psychiatric hospital admission must be agreed upon by a competent inmate.[22] The hospital record should contain documentation of the informed consent to hospitalization

and assessment of competence to give consent.

Hospitalization, whether voluntary or involuntary, alone does not grant the care provider authority to treat.[23] All treatments, as well as the absence of treatment, carry varying degrees of risks and benefits. The inmate must give informed consent to any type of psychiatric treatment, except emergency treatment or treatment allowed involuntarily after adequate judicial or administrative review of a court-committed individual. Informed consent requires that the care provider give adequate, understandable information regarding the proposed treatment to a patient capable of understanding the information. It is required that the care provider discuss alternative treatments as well as no treatment as options. The risks and benefits of proposed treatment must be discussed thoroughly with the patient. Any common or severe side effects must be reviewed. Patients must be made aware that they may elect to discontinue the treatment at any time simply by withdrawing their consent.

INMATE ENTITLEMENT TO PRIVACY

Every day, correctional health care providers confront the issue of confidentiality. Patients in prison and outside of prison come to their health care providers with the expectation that information shared will be kept confidential. Medical and mental health information can be shared among health care providers only on a need-to-know basis. Records should be kept secure on the treatment units with access limited to health care providers involved in the patient's care. Internal policy should define the parameters of the health care team. Patients should be advised as to the limits of confidentiality that may apply in special situations such as court-ordered forensic evaluations or injury assessment exams. Likewise, patients have the right to access copies of their records and to review their health care records unless the health care provider deems such reviews could be detrimental to the patient. Clinical staff may, at times, feel caught between their roles as caretakers and as correctional officers. Explaining these roles to the patient population at the onset of each significant encounter can be helpful in eliminating instances where the health care provider feels conflict between these roles. Patients need to be advised that any information that affects the security of the institution; requires intervention to prevent harm to the patient, other inmates, or staff; or concerns situations where serious damage to property will occur, cannot be kept confidential.

INSTITUTION CONTROL OF NONCOPING OFFENDERS

The use of special treatment procedures such as seclusion or restraint requires close attention in the correctional environment. Both interventions may be used in correctional situations that are not considered clinical in nature. They may also be used as part of the spectrum of treatment interventions for acutely disturbed psychiatric patients. A closely monitored review system must be put into place to ensure that special treatment procedures are used only as necessary and that the inmates' physical and psychological needs are addressed on an ongoing basis during the time they are secluded or restrained. Monitoring should ensure that patients are kept in these more restrictive situations for the minimum amount of time. Guidelines for the psychiatric use of seclusion and restraint have been published to assist in this process.[24]

Limited reasons for the use of these special treatment procedures exist and are generally restricted to (1) imminent risk of harm to self or others and (2) and imminent likelihood of serious damage to property. Inmates in seclusion require enhanced monitoring to the point of continuous observation if risk of harm to self is an issue. Inmates in restraints must be assessed regularly to ensure that circulation has not been compromised and that toileting, meals, and repositioning are accomplished as necessary. Health care providers must guard against the inappropriate use of special treatment procedures.

CORRECTIONAL FACILITIES AND MEDICATIONS

Medication prescription is another high-risk area within a correctional environment. Appropriate use of psychotropic medication can be defined as using the right drugs at the right dosages for the right period of time. Pharmacotherapy is a mainstay of current mental health treatment. Unfortunately, medication use can also be problematic in a correctional environment. As in any population, there will be some medication-seeking clientele. Frequent presentations will be chronic pain patients, insomniacs, and substance abusers without access to their drug of choice. Several guidelines in this area may be useful.

- Medication prescription should be kept to a minimum. All prescriptions should be time limited, and the need for continuing a particular medication should be thoroughly assessed.
- Sleep medication should be avoided except in acute situations and limited to three days without further review. The cause of the sleep disturbance should be sought, taking care to uncover any underlying depression.
- Medication compliance should be closely followed. Noncompliance that persists should result in getting documentation of treatment refusal and discontinuing the prescription. Mouth checks and blood and urine screens should be used to determine compliance.
- Cost and ease of use as determined by route and dosing frequency may make a great deal of difference in whether the patient remains compliant after release.
- Guard against polypharmacy (use of multiple medications from the same class or from similar classes). Inmates are known to seek out multiple care providers, and correctional staffing patterns with frequent rotation of staff may worsen this problem.
- Pay close attention to side effects of the medications prescribed. Stay alert to poten-

tial drug interactions. Be aware of the potential to overdose or use drugs in nonconventional ways. Document any adverse reactions.

IS THE INMATE REALLY MENTALLY ILL?

In any correctional health care setting, the topic of antisocial personality disorder frequently arises. Antisocial personality disorder is diagnosed almost exclusively on the basis of historical information. Criteria to support the diagnosis include a pattern of disregard for others demonstrated by breaking the law and lying as well as impulsive, irresponsible, and aggressive behavior. Not every incarcerated individual carries this diagnosis, but inmates with other mental disorders may also meet the criteria for this personality disorder diagnosis. Antisocial personality disorder is extremely difficult to treat and has nothing to do with how sociable an individual is. Despite its inclusion in psychiatric classification systems, this diagnosis is often not viewed as a mental disease or defect for legal purposes.

Malingering is a behavior that involves an individual falsely claiming and consciously faking symptoms of an illness. People malinger to avoid the consequences of being held responsible for their behavior or because it will enhance their situation. Malingering may result in an inmate getting referred for mental health evaluation or treatment. Staff in correctional treatment settings should not be too quick to label a patient as malingering. Malingering is always a diagnosis of exclusion, and the diagnosis is made only after bona fide psychopathology is ruled out.

THE UNIQUENESS OF CORRECTIONS

Staffing the correctional health care setting can be a difficult task. Few clinicians and other providers are trained during their professional education to work in correctional environments. Most stumble into the field and ultimately come to view it as either a challenge or a curse. Provision of adequate care constantly competes with maintaining adequate security. Security demands often put limitations on how efficiently or effectively programs can be run. Salaries may lag behind community levels. Professionals may view the setting as less than desirable, and this, in turn, can create low morale and prevent successful recruiting.

Ironically, despite these barriers, clinicians are currently realizing that the correctional environment may be one of the last public strongholds for adequate care of the seriously ill and treatment-resistant mentally ill patient. The structure of the environment, the absence of third-party payers, and the impact of externally imposed motivation to change create a unique setting in which to provide mental health care. Old assumptions about clinician/patient relationships, adequate data collection, personal responsibility for behavior, and the roles of genetics, economics, and education in the onset of illness become ripe for review. The experience of the correctional health care provider has much to offer to the broader field of mental health care.

NOTES

1. H. Steadman et al., "A Survey of Mental Disability among State Prison Inmates," *Hospital and Community Psychiatry* 38 (1987): 10.
2. American Psychiatric Association, *Diagnostic and Statistical Manual of Mental Disorders,* 4th ed. (Washington, DC: 1994).
3. *Newman v. Alabama*, 349 F. Supp. 278, 284 (M.D. Ala. 1971).
4. *Estelle v. Gamble*, 429 U.S. 97 (1976).
5. *Bowring v. Godwin*, 551 F. 2d 44 (4th Cir. 1977).
6. R. Shanski, Identifying and Correcting Constitutional Violations in Correctional Settings: The Role of Physician Experts (Paper presented at the annual meeting of the American Public Health Association, Chicago, November 1989).
7. American Public Health Association, *Standards for Health Services in Correctional Institutions* (Washington, DC: 1976).

8. American Correctional Associations, *Standards for Adult Correctional Institutions,* 3rd ed. (Laurel, MD: 1990).

9. American Medical Association, *Standards for Health Services in Prisons* (Chicago: 1979).

10. American Psychiatric Association Taskforce, *Psychiatric Services in Jails and Prisons* (Washington, DC: 1989).

11. National Commission on Correctional Health Care, *Standards for Health Services in Prisons* (Chicago: 1987).

12. American Bar Association, *ABA Criminal Justice Mental Health Standards* (Washington, DC: 1989).

13. Joint Commission on Accreditation of Healthcare Organizations, *Comprehensive Accreditation Manual for Behavioral Health Care* (Oakbrook Terrace, IL: 1997–98).

14. *Ruiz v. Estell,* 53 F. Supp. 1265 (S.D. Texas 1980).

15. *Zinermon v. Burch,* no. 87–1965 (U.S., February 27, 1990).

16. W. Condelli et al., "Intermediate Care Programs for Inmates with Psychiatric Disorders," *Bulletin American Academy Psychiatry Law* 22, no. 1 (1994): 63–70.

17. B. Anno, *Prison Healthcare Guidelines for Management of an Adequate Delivery System* (1991).

18. Federal Bureau of Prisons, *Suicide Prevention Program/Inmate Companion Program.* Internal policy statement #5324.03.

19. American Psychiatric Association, *Diagnostic and Statistical Manual of Mental Disorders,* 4th ed.

20. H.I. Kaplan et al., *Synopsis of Psychiatry,* 7th ed. (Baltimore: Williams & Wilkins, 1994), 229.

21. 18 U.S.C.A. § 4245.

22. *Zinermon v. Burch.*

23. *Washington v. Harper,* 110 S. Ct. 1028 (1990).

24. American Psychiatric Association, *Task Force Report No. 22* (Washington, DC: 1985).

CHAPTER 16

Religious Programs

David Schwartz and Tom Fewell

Religion has played an important role in the life of prison inmates since the inception of prisons in this counrty. The earliest prison facilities in Pennsylvania were founded on the beliefs of the Quakers, and the correctional programs of these institutions were based on society's desire for offenders to meditate on their sinful ways. The Bible and spiritual counseling from local clergy helped inmates achieve the goal: penitance. But the role of religion in American corrections has changed over the years as the institutions themselves have evolved.

The First Amendment to the United States Constitution guarantees inmates the right to hold whatever religious beliefs they choose. Prison administrators, however, can and do regulate religious practices within an institution. The U.S. Supreme Court has found such restrictions to be appropriate so long as they are necessary to further legitimate penological objectives. (This standard was established by the Supreme Court in the landmark decisions *O'Lone v. Shabazz* and *Turner v. Safley*.)[1,2]

The Constitution and laws of this country as well as professional standards such as those established by the American Correctional Association (ACA) require quality religious programs in prisons and jails. Prison administrators must strike the right balance between providing sufficient and appropriate religious programs and restricting religious practices for the sake of inmate security. Religious programs must be developed based on a clear understanding of the needs of both the inmates and the institution; staff should facilitate individual religious practices as long as they are not inconsistent with the security, safety, and orderly operation of the institution. Inmates may be encouraged to participate in religous programs as one means of preparing for reintegration into the community following release from prison. Administrators and other staff should also respect the beliefs of inmates who decline to participate in religious programs. Inmates should not be required or coerced into participating in religious activities of any kind. Religion must not be used as a tool for manipulation by either the staff or the inmates.

CHAPLAINS WEAR MANY HATS

The chaplaincy or religious services department should be headed by a professional chaplain. The chaplain is responsible for working with inmates of all faith groups, administering services and programs in a consistent manner, and supervising all contract and volunteer religious service personnel. Chaplains or religious coordinators are expected to perform a variety of functions in addition to providing the opportunity for inmates to practice their religions through congregate services. Specifically, chaplains administer special rites; provide religious education and counseling; assist with the development and provision of religious diets; respond to specific requests for objects, apparel, and literature; and coordinate observance of religious

Religious Freedom Legislation

In 1994, Congress passed the *Religious Freedom Restoration Act (RFRA;* Title 42 of the United States Code, Section 2000bb), intended to enhance citizens' freedom to exercise their religious practices. This law prohibited governments from interfering with individuals' religious observances unless the interference was the least restrictive means of furthering a compelling government interest. Nearly all departments of corrections around the country opposed this legislation, fearing it would require them to succumb to all sort of religious requests by inmates, stretching staff and budgetary resources, as well as threatening institution security. Of particular concern were requests from radical and/or militant organizations whose beliefs and practices are greatly offensive to other inmates.

In 1997, the Supreme Court ruled that the RFRA violated the United States Constitution (see *Boerne v. Texas,* 117 S. Ct. 2157 [1997]). As a result, state departments of corrections were free to return to applying the previous standard in determining whether to permit various inmate religious practices (pursuant to the Supreme Court's decisions in *O'Lone v. Shabazz,* 482 U.S. 342 [1987], and *Turner v. Safley,* 482 U.S. 78 [1987], prison regulations that interfered with inmates' religious practices were valid so long as they were reasonably related to legitimate penological objectives).

Recently, in response to the Supreme Court's ruling that the RFRA was unconstitutional, many states have enacted laws intended to protect their citizens from encroachments by state and local governments upon religious observances. The newly proposed and enacted state laws around the country require governments to meet the RFRA standard in justifying laws and actions that interfere with individual religious practices.

The new laws (and in at least one case [Alabama] a proposed constitutional amendment) are widely supported by various religious organizations that believe that additional protections are necessary to ensure religious practices are permitted, including Muslim students wearing head scarves to school despite a "no hats" policy and permitting Seventh Day Adventists and Jews to be assigned work shifts that don't conflict with their Saturday worship. Many corrections officials oppose these legislative initiatives for the same reasons they opposed RFRA: They are concerned that inmates will file lawsuits (and prevail) requesting a variety of religious accommodations that will threaten institution security as well as place substantial demands on staff and budgetary resources. Supporters of the proposed legislation argue that in many states the number of lawsuits filed by inmates did not increase following passage of RFRA; however, in some states the number of inmate grievances increased dramatically. Moreover, many departments of corrections counter that suits were not filed because the departments felt compelled to grant requests (that would have been denied but for passage of RFRA) based on advice from their counsel. Religious organizations argue that the protection of religious freedom provided by RFRA or similar state legislation is necessary to prevent corrections officials from denying legitimate, important religious requests, particularly because of the reputed connections between religious belief/observance and inmates' successful reintegration into society.[3]

holidays. Generally, chaplains must have a bachelor's degree, a master's of divinity or equivalent, clinical pastoral education or clinical pastoral training, and two years' experience in the ministry. In the past, a pastor with strong preaching and teaching skills was used to "do church" in the correctional setting. Therapeutic and administrative skills were secondary. But penological institutions have changed, and now it is essential for the chaplain to have strong administrative and counseling skills as well. This is particularly true where chaplains are part of the prison treatment staff along with social workers, substance abuse counselors, case workers, psychologists, teachers, and medical personnel. Accordingly, clinical training and certification are desirable qualifications for prison chaplains.

Religious issues or questions raised by inmates whose religious beliefs are outside the chaplain's expertise, training, and/or ecclesiastical endorsement should be referred to qualified spiritual leaders in the community.

Using contract chaplains is a reasonable alternative in small jails and prisons where a second chaplain is needed on a part-time basis. Contract chaplains are also used as spiritual leaders for particular groups of inmates. For example, in many institutions, a Catholic priest is contracted to provide Mass, religious education, and guidance to the Catholic inmates, and an Islamic Imam is contracted to serve as a spiritual leader for the Muslim inmates. These chaplains do not function as religious coordinators but as church pastors. Accordingly, they need only be recognized by the denominations or faith groups they represent. The role and function of the contract chaplains need to be stated in the prison policy, which should also specify the education, training, and other necessary qualifications they must have.

CONGREGATE SERVICES

Congregate services—the meeting of several people to worship, study, or pray—should be provided at all correctional institutions unless specific security issues present a legitimate management concern. In these cases, arrangements should be made to provide inmates with alternative means of practicing their religion. These services are not only expected by professional standards but also reflect sensible correctional practice. True spirituality is often discovered and developed through religion and may help prepare inmates for returning to the community. Inmates who discover God and become involved in religious programs have an improved attitude and a support group (a church) when they leave prison. After inmates are released, churches and religious groups frequently assist inmates and their families with jobs, clothes, housing, training, and other practical needs.

Many correctional institutions must provide a variety of worship services due to the broad spectrum of religions of their inmates. This problem can be ameliorated somewhat if congregate services are designed to appeal to the widest range of persons who share the basic tenets and beliefs of a particular religion. Congregate services should be led by a person with proper credentials. For example, a priest recognized by the Roman Catholic Church should conduct Mass for Roman Catholic inmates. When there are only a few inmates from a particular religious persuasion, a spiritual advisor can provide assistance. If the group is large, then the services of a local minister are often used, generally once a week.

RELIGIOUS EDUCATION AND PROGRAMS

The religious coordinator or chaplain should develop a religious program that includes more than weekly worship services. There should be study groups and religious education classes. Music education and choir provide variety and an opportunity for the inmates to express themselves creatively. Development of individual talents should be one objective of the religious program. Special events—including outside choir groups, entertainers, and evangelists—usually attract large groups and provide a needed emotional and spiritual outlet for the inmates.

RELIGIOUS DIETS AND HOLY DAYS

Inmates of many faiths may request special diets mandated by their religion. Inmates may be asked to document that the requested diet is a basic requirement or tenet of the faith group, and they also may be asked to prove their membership in the group. The institution should not be expected to accommodate dietary requests based solely on personal preferences so long as nutritionally adequate meals are provided that do not violate the inmates' religious dietary requirements. However, legitimate requests based on sound religious principles must be accommodated. For this reason, most correctional institutions offer a vegetarian or at least pork-free menu.

Some religious observances (i.e., Passover) require consumption of particular foods, and some observances require consumption of food at particular times (i.e., Ramadan, during which Muslim inmates must fast during daylight hours). Special accommodations should be made for both occasions. In some instances, particular religious observances include congregate ceremonial meals and work proscriptions that can generally be accommodated as long as the prison staff is given sufficient notice to make arrangements. The chaplain or spiritual leader is often called upon to explain to staff the significance of the religious observance and the specific accommodations that are required (for example, completion of all work before sundown of a Jewish holiday).

RELIGIOUS OBJECTS, APPAREL, AND LITERATURE

Inmates should have access to religious literature, including the holy book or scripture of their religion. Security, safety, and sanitation concerns may limit the amount of literature inmates may possess within their living areas, but the inmate library or chapel should contain religious literature and make it available to inmates.

Religious clothing and headgear may be permitted as long as it is consistent with the security

---

Denial of Religious Diet Not Unconstitutional

Providing meals that satisfy inmates' religious dietary needs has long been a difficult task for correctional administrators, particularly in jurisdictions that have inmates with many varied religious backgrounds. The United States Court of Appeals for the Fourth Circuit recently granted Maryland relief by upholding the state's decision not to provide kosher food to Jewish inmates. The court was convinced by arguments advanced by the correctional administrators that it was neither economically nor administratively feasible to provide special dietary requests to the small number of requesting inmates; that the inmates had available to them other means of practicing their religion; and that there were no ready alternatives due to the budgetary and administrative limitations. (See *Cooper v. Lanham*, No. 97-7183, May 7, 1998.)

Source: Adapted from *Corrections Alert,* Vol. 5, No. 3, p. 3, © June 1998, Aspen Publishers, Inc.

---

and good order of the prison. In some correctional facilities, inmates are permitted to wear the religious garb or accessories only while in the chapel and participating in religious worship. Religious items such as a medallion may pose minimal security concerns as long as they are inexpensive and small.

RELIGIOUS COUNSELING

Inmates may be provided religious or spiritual counseling from the institution chaplain, from a community volunteer, or by the inmate's religious leader from the community. Through institution visits, phone calls, and correspondence, religious representatives from the community often minister to inmates who were a part of their church or other religious organization prior to incarceration.

SPECIAL RITES

Special rites are formal religious ceremonies of initiation, such as baptism, confession, or individual communion. Special rites should be performed by the appropriate religious leader with proper credentials. The institution should approve special objects or supplies necessary to conduct such rites.

RELIGIOUS VOLUNTEERS

A corps of specially selected, trained, and supervised volunteers can greatly enhance the effectiveness of a chaplain. On the other hand, it is important to remember that volunteers generally have their own agenda, and volunteers may not have the clinical skills to counsel inmates. While volunteers should not be the source of all institution religious programs, they often represent a vital and necessary part of the overall ministry.

The role of the volunteer should be made clear from the beginning. Faith groups that are represented in the inmate population will often provide pastors who are interested in working with inmates from their faith. This will be especially true of smaller groups and nontraditional faiths. For example, Muslim volunteers will work with Muslim inmates, Jehovah's Witness volunteers will work with Jehovah's Witness inmates, and so forth. Volunteers need to understand that they are prohibited from recruiting converts to their faith. They can, however, work with those who seek them out. Volunteers must understand their role, and the chaplain must ensure that the volunteers operate within appropriate boundaries.

Community religious resources are the best sources of volunteers. The chaplain should establish and maintain a good relationship with religious leaders in the community, such as

through a community advisory board. Additionally, most states have prison ministry groups and representatives from national groups such as Prison International, Prison Fellowship, and Pious.

Training and orientation of volunteers (including an institution tour and orientation) are mandated by ACA standards and sound correctional practice. The volunteer should be given materials, including a handbook about the institution, its policy on religious practice and confidentiality, inmate characteristics and needs, a list of what makes volunteers successful, and a list of "dos and don'ts."

UNIQUE REQUESTS FOR RECOGNITION AND/OR ACCOMMODATION

Processing religious requests is a particularly important aspect of the chaplain's job. An institution religious request review board and a community advisory board can be very helpful. The institution board could include the chaplain, a social worker, the food service director, the legal advisor, a security officer, and one of the assistant wardens. The board should consider (1) whether the requested accommodation is a basic tenet and required of all of the religion's members, (2) whether the inmate meets the religion's requirements for this practice, and (3) whether the inmate shows good faith in the discussion of a solution and accommodation.

Additionally, it may be helpful to learn what other correctional institutions are doing as well as what is being done in the community to accommodate certain practices. Occasionally, prison administrators are requested to make special provisions for inmates who claim to belong to religions or faiths previously unknown, or to make unusual provisions for inmates who adhere to well-known religions (i.e., special dietary requirements for Protestant inmates). Generally it is best to rely on the classic definition of religion: an activity that concerns a person's relationship to God, to other people, and to him- or herself. That said, not all requests made in the name of religion will be accommodated. Behavior that threatens or harms others cannot be permitted. Of particular concern within a correctional institution is the creation of a religious organization that includes a hierarchy, which would give some inmates authority over others (e.g., one inmate appointing himself the leader, spiritual or otherwise, of a new religion). Also of concern are religions that espouse intolerance or even hatred of persons of particular races or ethnicities, and religions that proclaim the superiority of a particular group. To maintain the security and good order of the correctional institution, such organizations cannot be permitted to practice.

CONCLUSION

The religious programs in correctional institutions should be tailored to the mission and resources of the institutions. Small prisons and those with limited staff and resources may be able to provide only the basic elements, but larger facilities may have the ability to provide well-rounded programs that can affect large numbers of prisoners. Regardless of the extent of religious programming, such programs should be administered in a fair and consistent manner and provide inmates an adequate opportunity to prepare themselves for return to the community. The chaplain should look to the community for contract chaplains, volunteers, consultation, and support of the inmates' individual faith development.

The responsibilities of institution chaplains have grown over the years, and correctional clergy today are significant members of the management and program team of prisons and jails. The work is important, the opportunities are many, and the challenges are immense.

NOTES

1. *O'Lone v. Shabazz,* 482 U.S. 342 (1987).
2. *Turner v. Safley,* 482 U.S. 78 (1987).
3. M. Hollis, "Religious Freedom Law Spurs Statewide Debate. A New Measure is Needed, Some Say, But Others Say It Opens the Door for Controversy," *Sarasota Herald Tribune.*

CHAPTER 17

Receiving and Discharge, Mail, and Records Management

Jeffery W. Frazier

The initial receiving of prisoners into an institution, whether it is a jail or prison, is a critical process that individuals will remember throughout their confinement. The process begins as the citizen becomes a prisoner and is thrust into a new environment. Previous roles (e.g., father, husband, mother, wife, or pillar of the community) are all but eliminated. This identity change affects both the tangible and intangible. The citizen, now prisoner, is relieved of personal possessions (e.g., clothes, jewelry, and footwear) as well as personal routines and activities. He or she is now told what to wear; when to get up in the morning; when to eat breakfast, lunch, and dinner; and when to use the telephone or watch television. While some jails and prisons have policies that allow prisoners to keep their personal belongings, which may reduce the humiliation of incarceration somewhat, such policies will do little to ameliorate the substantial impact incarceration has on an individual's life.

PROCESSING IN

Staff who work in intake and booking should be mature, well-trained personnel who are skilled in interpersonal communication. Furthermore, these staff should be thoroughly familiar with the institution's policies and procedures, committal documents, confinement orders, and other such documents to ensure there is a legal basis for confining the prisoner.

If not handled properly, the admission process can create undue humiliation and stress that can lead to disciplinary problems along with safety, security, legal, and health concerns. The basic process has three goals: the prevention and reduction of contraband, information gathering and orientation, and the promotion of personal cleanliness.

Conducting a search requires tact and diplomacy on the part of the searcher. Further, extreme caution should be exercised during any search due to the close proximity of the prisoner to the searching officer. Upset, aggressive, or agitated prisoners should be given an ample "cooling down" period before a search is conducted, unless doing so would create a greater safety or security concern. An initial search should be conducted immediately upon the arrival of a new prisoner, preferably in an area that prevents the introduction of contraband into the secure perimeter of the institution.

The complete search should be conducted in a private area. It should be performed by a member of the same sex as the person being searched. The searching officer should explain to the prisoner, in a calm and respectful manner, the purpose and procedure of the search. The search should be conducted slowly and methodically, with instructions given to the prisoner throughout the process. If a strip search is required or allowed by policy or law (strip searches may not be conducted on individuals charged with certain crimes), the same procedures should be followed. However, touching the prisoner during a strip search is not necessary and should be avoided. Under no circumstances should a strip search be conducted by a member of the opposite sex. Body cavity searches, if and when necessary, should be conducted only by trained medical personnel in an area that affords privacy. Under no circumstances should a body cavity search be conducted within the view of other inmates.

It is critical to gather personal information about each inmate, but staff should be cautious not to ask questions related directly to inmates' criminal charges. All of the data gathered will assist classification staff in determining at what custody level (minimum, medium, or maximum) the prisoner should be held. Further, the data will help in determining housing assignments. There are a number of prepared forms available through the National Institute of Corrections that an agency can obtain, free of charge, to assist in the intake and receiving process.

All prisoners should also be oriented at this time to the basic rules and regulations of the institution. The arrestee should be given a copy of those rules, and staff should carefully go over the rules, answering all questions that the prisoner may have. It is important that intake and booking staff verify that the prisoner can read and comprehend the rules and regulations before proceeding.

In a jail setting, intake and booking usually begin with a complete inventory of the prisoner's personal property. Each item should be carefully noted; the inventorying officer should not omit any items (e.g., nails, staples, washers, and gum wrappers) regardless of how trivial they may seem. All jewelry should be described by color, not type of precious metal or stone. Rings, necklaces, and bracelets should be described as gold or silver in color. A ring, for example, might be described as "one gold in color wedding band containing a single clear stone." All identifying inscriptions should also be recorded. All clothing should be described as thoroughly as possible using sizes, brand names, and any other identifiable markings (e.g., stains, rips, tears). All money should be counted in the presence of the prisoner.

After the inventory, the prisoner should be required to sign a property/money slip indicating that he or she agrees with the inventory list. This slip should then be signed by the inventorying officer. A copy of this inventory should be given to the inmate, a copy placed with the property, and a copy forwarded to the records department to be filed in the inmate's institutional file. A well-conducted inventory of all personal property will help to reduce or prevent false claims of damaged, lost, or destroyed property.

All prisoners should be asked several basic questions about their current health condition, history, and medications. Such screening helps correctional and medical personnel address the individuals' personal health needs and protect the health and well-being of others incarcerated within the jail. This screening should also involve questions related to the individuals' psychological health, including any history of suicide attempts. Questions should be asked in an area that affords maximum privacy so that other prisoners do not overhear.

Most health screening forms are divided into two categories: observations and questions. Observations are details that the officer may notice, such as obvious bleeding, open sores or lesions, vermin infestation, intoxication from alcohol or drug use, signs of drug or alcohol withdrawal, convulsions, or seizures. Personal observations can be as detailed as the agency may desire. Questions should be worded so that the prisoner may respond initially with a simple "yes" or "no" answer. All "yes" answers should be followed up with additional inquiries to determine the exact nature and extent of the problem.

> (Q) "Are you allergic to any medications?"
> (A) "Yes."

(Q) "What medications are you allergic to?"
(A) "Penicillin."

Responses should be documented. All screening forms should give the intake and booking officer specific directions on what to do with critical "yes" or "no" observations and answers. If an officer notes that an individual is bleeding, for instance, he or she would immediately notify the appropriate medical and supervisory personnel. If the prisoner describes a history of, or recently tested positive for, tuberculosis, the officer may be required to immediately notify medical personnel and medically isolate the individual from the rest of the population.

The importance of the health and psychological screening process cannot be overstated. The first 48 hours of a prisoner's initial incarceration are the most critical, because this is the period when most suicides occur. Once completed, this report should be placed in the individual prisoner's file. A thoroughly completed health screening form is a valuable tool in preventing frivolous litigation, especially if an individual arrives with multiple superficial cuts and bruises and later claims that he or she was assaulted by jail staff. Further, this form will help medical personnel during their initial medical evaluation of the prisoner.

Jails and prisons have different personal cleanliness standards and procedures. However, many jails and prisons require inmates to shower and change into jail or prison clothing. This reduces the likelihood of introducing body lice and other insects into the institution. The change from personal clothing to jail or prison clothing also reduces the possibility of theft, gambling, bartering, and the strong-arming of inmates. Further, it reduces the problems that are associated with the laundering of personal clothing. During the showering and exchange of clothing process, the intake and booking staff should visually search for rashes, cuts, abrasions, scars, tattoos, and so forth, all of which should be documented. At the conclusion of this process,

inmates should be given clean linens, towels, and washcloths.

RELEASING AN INMATE

The process of discharge from jail or prison is very similar to the intake and booking process. Discharge is a major responsibility—probably one of the most critical assignments that an officer can undertake. It is of the utmost importance that the releasing officer verify the identity and sentence of the subject being released. Failure to do so could result in the wrong inmate being released or an inmate being released before the complete sentence is satisfied. Further, if a criminal background (i.e., wanted persons) check is not performed, a person who is wanted by a sister agency or state could be wrongfully released.

There are many reasons that an inmate may be released from custody.

- Personal recognizance. Release on personal recognizance is granted by a judge or other judicial officer based on the promise that the subject will appear in court on the scheduled date. Many factors are considered prior to releasing someone on personal recognizance, such as the nature of the crime, the subject's criminal history, and the subject's standing within the community.
- Bail. Bail is a specified amount of money, usually established by the court or other judicial officer, that must be presented before the inmate can be released. The money is held by the court to ensure that the subject appears in court when scheduled.
- Bond. A bond is something that is posted by a licensed bonding company or bondsman within a state. The subject is released into the custody of the bondsman, who will ensure that the subject appears in court on the scheduled date. If the subject fails to appear, the bonding company will be required

to pay the entire bond amount to the court. Most bondsmen charge at least a 10 percent fee (10 percent of the original bond amount) for taking the chance that the subject might not appear in court.

- Court order. An inmate may be released by the court for reasons such as time served, sentence reduction, dismissal of charges, or a temporary release so that the subject can attend the funeral of a loved one. When this occurs, the releasing officer should verify that a copy of such order has been obtained prior to release.
- Time served. The subject has satisfied the conditions of the original sentence and now can be released.
- Release to other law enforcement personnel. The subject is released into the custody of other law enforcement personnel who may have pending charges against the subject, or to another agency because the subject has already been tried and convicted of committing a crime and now must satisfy that sentence. When a prisoner is released to another agency, the transporting officer's identity should be verified and a receipt indicating that the transporting officer has accepted custody of the prisoner should be obtained.

Regardless of the reason for release, the releasing officer should verify that the release documents are in order and properly signed. If the subject is being released because of time served, the computation of his or her sentence should be verified. A "wanted persons" check should be made through the agency's computer system that is tied into the National Criminal Information Center network. Finally, the subject's identity should be verified to prevent the wrongful release of an offender. Release documents should contain, at a minimum, date of release; time of release; reason for release; if released to another agency, the name of the agency and to whom; the officer who released the subject; and a description of all personal property that was released with the subject.

The importance of record keeping and procedures surrounding the receiving and discharge of inmates is almost unparalleled in the correctional setting. The recent case of Billy Roy Pitts emphasizes this point.

Pitts was sought by Mississippi law enforcement authorities for the 1966 murder of Vernon Dahmer, a leader of the National Association for the Advancement of Colored People, who was killed when his house was hit with a firebomb. Pitts was convicted for the crime and sentenced to life in prison; such sentence was to be served following completion of a federal sentence for conspiracy. State law enforcement and corrections officials allege that the federal government failed to deliver Pitts to them following completion of his federal sentence and that federal officials erroneously released Pitts to the street. The federal officials counter that a thorough search of the records reveals that no request for custody (or "detainer") had been lodged against Pitts with the federal authorities, and thus they had no knowledge regarding the pending state sentence.

Following an intense campaign by Mississippi law enforcement authorities, Pitts surrendered so that a court might consider the propriety of returning him to prison to serve his outstanding state prison sentence.[1]

MAIL

The First Amendment to the United States Constitution gives inmates the right to send and receive mail. However, prisons and jails can place reasonable restrictions on these rights. The

Supreme Court established that a restriction on inmate mail is acceptable "If [the restriction] furthers an important or substantial governmental interest; and if the incidental restriction on alleged First Amendment freedoms is no greater than is essential to the furtherance of that interest."[2]

Thus, local regulations must show that a regulation that authorizes mail censorship furthers an important or substantial governmental interest such as security, order, or rehabilitation. In order to establish appropriate institution rules that comport with federal law, it is very helpful to delineate two types of inmate mail: legal and social.

Legal or official correspondence is an inmate's correspondence with police, probation and parole officers, judges and attorneys, and so forth. Official correspondence should be inspected, in front of the inmate, to ensure that contraband is not enclosed. But it must not be read; inmates have a right to confidentiality with their attorneys and other public officials. All official correspondence, both incoming and outgoing, should be documented in a logbook that records the name of the sender, address of the sender; date received, or if it is being mailed, the date mailed; name of the addressee; and a place for the inmate to sign that he or she received the official mail.

Social correspondence is the personal letters of a prisoner to and from family and friends. Personal correspondence can be inspected outside the presence of the inmate; however, as with official mail, it should not be read unless the legal tests of the previously cited Supreme Court decision can be met and staff follow the basic requirements outlined in that case.

Many institutions open all personal correspondence, inspect for contraband, and remove money orders so that the inmate's personal account can be credited. The mail is then forwarded to the inmate.

DOCUMENTATION

Today, it is important that each institution maintain accurate, up-to-date records on all inmates, from their reception into the institution until their departure or ultimate release. It is only through sound records management that a foundation can be created to protect the staff and agency from inmate litigation for alleged violations of constitutional rights.

While the courts, in recent years, have been willing to entertain inmate complaints, they are not always willing to interfere with the operations of an institution unless there are clear constitutional violations, such as living conditions that are extremely barbaric and inhumane.

There are a number of routine records that all institutions must maintain and others that will be determined by the institution's own needs or the statutory requirements of the locality and state. Mandatory records are as follows:

- admission and release records
- medical records
- disciplinary records
- inmate grievance records
- visitation records, both personal and professional
- criminal justice system records (e.g., court orders and time computation records)
- personal property records
- inspection records that reflect the conditions of the institution, both from a security standpoint and from a life, health, and safety standpoint
- logs that reflect all activities within the institution (e.g., meals served, recreation given, counts conducted, medication dispensed, mail delivered)

Documentation and records management provide administrators with data that can be used in making policy decisions, forecasting trends, performing staffing analyses, evaluating the climate of the institution, and projecting future budget needs. As the old saying goes, if it is not documented, it did not occur. Therefore, documentation is the first defense that must be taken to prevent litigation. Once litigation has been filed, proper, complete, and up-to-date records will greatly improve an institution's chance of prevailing in the courts.

CONCLUSION

The receiving and discharge of individuals is a critical process that requires the attention of responsible staff with excellent interpersonal communication skills and an eye for detail. It is the initial reception process that usually sets the tone of the prisoner's behavior during his or her stay at the institution and acts as the first physical barrier to contraband in the institution. The information-gathering phase of the receiving process gives the institution the ability to learn the personal history of the offender, which will be ultimately used to assist the classification department. Finally, through the promotion of cleanliness, institutions can better identify infectious disease and reduce the infestation of body lice.

During the discharge of individuals from confinement, the releasing officer must be extremely cautious to prevent the unlawful or wrongful release of prisoners. All release documents must be examined for authenticity. The releasing officer must indicate the date and time of release, the reason for the release, and a description of all property released. If a prisoner is released to an individual from another agency, the officer must indicate who that agency and individual are. Wanted persons checks must be performed to verify that the individual being released is not wanted by another agency.

Inmates have the right to send and receive mail, but the institution can place reasonable restrictions upon that right. Only official mail must be opened in front of the inmate. An institution can censor an inmate's mail if it can show that the censorship furthers an important or substantial government interest and meets certain established legal minimum standards.

Finally, it is through the maintenance of accurate records documenting all aspects of an inmate's stay that institutions are able to reduce the likelihood of litigation and increase their chance of prevailing in court if litigation is filed. Accurate records also provide managers with the necessary data to forecast trends, prepare budgets, and make policy decisions that affect an institution's entire operation.

NOTES

1. "Ex-Klansman Pitts Surrenders," *The Clarion-Ledger* (Jackson, Mississippi), 10 February, 1998.
2. *Procunier v. Martinez,* 416 U.S. 396, 94 S. Ct. 1800 (1974).

SUGGESTED READINGS

Cripe, C. 1997. *Legal aspects of corrections management.* Gaithersburg, MD: Aspen Publishers, Inc.

Jansen, F., and R. Johns. 1978. *Management and supervision of small jails.* Springfield, IL: Charles C Thomas.

Johnson, P. 1991. *Understanding prisons and jails: A corrections manual.* 2d ed. Jackson, MS: Correctional Consultants, Inc.

Johnson, R., and H. Toch. 1982. *The pains of imprisonment.* Beverly Hills, CA: Sage Publications.

Manville, D. 1992. *Prisoners' self-help litigation manual.* 2d ed. New York: Oceana Publications, Inc.

Miller, E. 1978. *Jail management.* Lexington, KY: Lexington Books.

National Institution of Corrections. 1989. *NIC jail resource manual.* 4th ed. Kents Hill, ME: Community Resource Services, Inc.

National Sheriffs' Association. 1980. *Jail officers' training manual.* Alexandria, VA: National Sheriffs' Association.

National Sheriffs' Association. 1989. *First/second line jail supervisors' training manual.* Alexandria, VA: National Sheriffs' Association.

Palmer, J. 1996. *Constitutional rights of prisoners.* 4th ed. Cincinnati, OH: Anderson Publishing Company.

Phillips, R., and C. McConnell. 1996. *The effective corrections manager.* Gaithersburg, MD: Aspen Publishers, Inc.

CHAPTER 18

Facilities Management

Jacob Bliek

The number of correctional facilities and institutions has been growing by leaps and bounds over the past 15 years due to the outcry for mandatory and longer sentences. While not much has been published regarding the maintenance, operation, and renovation of correctional facilities, the provision of effective facilities management is an essential aspect of prison and jail leadership.

Many correctional institutions are quite old, others have been substantially renovated and reconstructed and supplemented, and some are brand new. All institutions, regardless of their history, should have a well-balanced facilities program that includes preventative maintenance, corrective maintenance, as well as renovation and perhaps new construction; the program should not place undue emphasis on any one of the three elements to the exclusion of the others. An effective facility management program takes advantage of various diagnostic tools to minimize what are often substantial costs associated with maintenance and repair of correctional institutions. Timely and well-planned maintenance and repairs are cost-effective, while a reactionary and ad hoc approach is not. Some managers find that commercial computer software programs greatly assist in the use and control of the large amounts of information involved in facilities management. These programs help track incoming requests for facility maintenance work, schedule preventative maintenance, prepare budget estimates, and project maintenance requirements. Additionally, these software programs can effectively make use of and tie into other information systems such as those maintained by the business office.

PREVENTATIVE MAINTENANCE

Preventative maintenance can be a very effective tool to ensure that the equipment functions efficiently and without troublesome breakdowns, and to prevent substantial expenditures to repair equipment, or, worse yet, to replace equipment prior to the end of its expected life cycle. Maintaining a good records system (even as basic as equipment cards) can help maximize the life of pumps, fans, motors, and equipment. No maintenance department has a spare part for every piece of equipment in the facility, and no maintenance department can afford to discard equipment when it fails. Facility maintenance managers must learn to maximize the life of equipment and systems and minimize mechanical or electrical breakdowns. By following a good preventative maintenance program, maintenance managers can diagnose problems before failure or before high-cost repairs are necessary.

The most important aspect of a good preventative maintenance program in a correctional setting is limiting the failure of critical pieces of equipment that may cause security problems. It is always better to schedule a shutdown of lighting or security electronics systems than it is for them to go out when least expected.

Yet preventative maintenance can be expensive and may not always be the most cost-effective approach. There are a variety of both simple and sophisticated diagnostic or inspection tools that can be used to reduce the amount of unnecessary maintenance, while effectively predicting impending failure before it occurs and allowing scheduled maintenance at a convenient time. Employing a "predictive testing and inspection" approach using such tools will help institutions achieve the full expected equipment life, reduce maintenance costs, and ensure reliable operation of equipment.

PLANNING FOR NEW ADDITIONS AND RENOVATIONS

The time to consider creating the most reliable and efficient physical plants is the design phase of new prison or jail space. The quality of planning and design will directly impact whether financial resources will be spent during the construction or for repair and maintenance after the addition has been completed.

The importance of properly maintaining prisons and jails is made clear during crises. Broken heating or air conditioning systems can give rise to emergencies, including the release of prisoners before completion of their sentence. In Kentucky, a broken air conditioner in the middle of the summer resulted in several inmates being sent to the hospital from heat sickness and/or panic attacks and other inmates being released pursuant to a court order. The air conditioning system was broken for one week, and there was no certain date for completion of repairs. A total of 15 inmates were released as a result of the system's failure.[1]

The selection of building materials, equipment, and systems for correctional facilities is a challenge for design architects and correctional administrators. The equipment and systems selected should match the facility's desired security, safety, and supervision levels. The systems must withstand inmate abuse; be reliable and easy to maintain, repair, and operate; and be cost-effective over the useful life of the facility.

If reliable performance data are not available during the design/specification process, the operators risk costly future repairs or modifications and, therefore, maintenance costs are significantly increased. To perform as expected, equipment and systems must be properly installed, and the facility staff must be adequately trained to operate and maintain them.

If the design is limited due to funding, the architect and engineer must select materials that are cheaper. This will raise the maintenance costs beyond the expected 3 percent of total operational costs. Conversely, a building design that uses materials that are durable and can perform over the years raises construction costs but lowers maintenance costs.

It is important to select building materials and systems that have proven reliable and cost-effective to construct and operate. While designing space for a correctional facility, administrators must consider how long the facility is expected to last and then select appropriate construction materials and finishes for the building type. A warehouse, for example, would not need to be as durable as a housing unit. A housing unit is subjected to many more hours of activity and is expected to provide much more support than a warehouse building. Therefore, construction funds should be spent on the areas that are used the most in order to prevent premature failure of the building and its systems.

COST-EFFECTIVE CONSTRUCTION OF ADDITIONS/RENOVATIONS

Within the past 10 years, adult correctional facility construction costs have risen fairly slowly in some markets and substantially in others. One of the primary reasons for this has been the searching out of new ways to limit or reduce labor costs; a significant development has been the use of cells constructed off site. The industry has used precast panels, tilt-up walls, prefabricated steel cells, and precast concrete cells. The clear leader of these manufacturing processes is the precast concrete cell industry. By using off-site or shop-fabricated building components, the contractor can perform simultaneous construction activities. While the cells are being prefabricated and precast off site, the site is being graded, and underground utilities are being installed. As cells are being delivered to the job site, the foundation and floor slab are being poured.

The process is certainly not a new one. Since the 1950s, the construction industry has been producing components in steel-fabricating shops. These columns, beams, and joists are installed very quickly and early to accommodate the installation of the roof deck and roofing membranes. Producing components off site creates an additional benefit for the contractor and to the customer: time. By completing a construction project earlier, construction companies are free to bid other projects. Not all correctional systems have found that the prefabrication process is cost-effective and shortens the construction period. It might be advantageous in some situations, however, due to the reduced amount of time that the contractors spend inside the correctional institution, thereby limiting the opportunities for breaches of security and threats to safety.

For the customer, the ability to get occupancy of the space several weeks or months earlier is helpful. Major construction companies have realized that prisons and jails are big business and are trying to capture their share of this marketplace.

CONSTRUCTION MANAGEMENT

For administrators of correctional facilities, financing and design are two of the easiest aspects of the construction process. Few wardens are adept at the management of construction. When financially and administratively feasible, for new construction projects, a construction manager should be factored into the design costs. This provides the warden with a single person responsible for problems, changes, and construction coordination. Contractors building the prison should not act as construction managers because it would be a direct conflict. Construction management is less appropriate for renovations and additions to existing facilities because correctional staff would be required to escort the construction managers through the institution, causing a substantial drain on staff resources.

Whoever manages the construction activity should be knowledgeable about design, scheduling, and construction methodologies. An understanding of how a building is put together is invaluable in making decisions when changes occur or when construction problems threaten the budget and schedule. Correctional professionals are too busy managing the day-to-day operations of their existing overcrowded conditions to have time to deal with construction and renovation projects. Some of the issues that correctional agencies or local government should pay particular attention to are the detention hardware, fire/smoke alarm system, security electronics, and quality control. These four areas are typically responsible for construction delays and occupancy difficulties.

Another key factor is to include training for correctional staff as part of the contractor's or equipment supplier's responsibility. Too often, correctional staff are unfamiliar with new equipment and high-tech systems. If possible, correctional administrators should allow prospective staff to visit the construction site so that they may begin to formulate operational plans for occupancy. They should allow for a period of "shakedown" so that staff can become familiar with the space and systems.

Where possible, maintenance staff should have input into the mechanical, plumbing, and electrical system designs. They should review the specifications for equipment selection and be able to share concerns with the architect or engineer. Various elements can be added to the design to enhance the staff's ability to ensure the safety, security, and orderly operation of the prison. Examples include closed circuit television cameras, perimeter intrusion detection systems, duress alarms, fire/smoke alarms, and security electronics control panels.

SAFETY/SECURITY

Tool control is of paramount importance in a correctional facility. Some tools can be used as implements of escape, and many can be used as weapons. It is the facility's responsibility to write a policy that establishes procedures for the reception, disbursement, storage, control, and inventory of all tools. Tools may be defined as high, moderate, or low risk. The following are suggested guidelines for the classification of tools:

- High-risk tools. Tools that pose the highest risk of aiding an escape or being used as a lethal weapon. High-risk (HR) tools should be under the direct supervision of staff at all times. Kitchen knives are an exception and may be used by kitchen inmates without direct supervision when the inmate can be restricted or confined to an area within the kitchen while a knife is in use. Certain HR tools (e.g., bolt cutters, hacksaw blades, cutting torches) require enhanced security, handling, and storage procedures. These tools should be stored in areas that provide greater security and that are separate from storage areas in which other tools are stored.
- Moderate-risk tools. Tools that pose a moderate risk (MR) for injury or escape. These tools (e.g., hammers, wrenches, drill bits) may need to be modified to significantly increase the risk of escape or to be used as a lethal weapon. Depending on the nature of the work and the location within the institu-

tion, inmates using MR tools require close supervision.
- Low-risk tools. These tools (e.g., staple guns, levels, electric meters, chalk boxes) pose little risk of being used or modified for escape or for use as weapons. Low-risk (LR) tools require intermittent supervision, depending on the nature of the work and the location within the institution.

All tools should be stored, inventoried, marked, and disbursed so as not to compromise the security of the institution or subject staff and inmates to unreasonable risk of injury from tools. All tools should be identified by a distinctive marking indicating the department, shop, or area to which the tool belongs. Each tool should be inventoried and stored (as on a shadow board) to ensure easy and visible accountability. All tools should be kept in a locked storage area when not in use.

Contractors and repairpeople who bring tools into a facility should receive a security briefing. They should be required to submit a complete inventory of all tools in their possession or in their vehicles prior to entering the facility. All contractors or repairpeople should be escorted by a staff member while working in the institution and prior to leaving should have their tools checked against the inventory submitted upon their entrance.

AN INMATE WORKFORCE

Correctional facilities would not be able to operate without the use of inmate labor. Inmate work assignments vary from janitorial work, landscaping, and plumbing to installing high-voltage electric cabling. Contrary to what many people believe, most inmates are required to work and do not stay in their cells for extended periods of time (few inmates remain in their cells 24 hours per day, seven days per week). In many instances, institutions save thousands of dollars each year by using the expertise of their inmates and alleviating the need to pay outside plumbers, electricians, and others. Using inmate labor to maintain the institution is beneficial to all parties: the inmates, the staff, and the community.

Many people want inmates to provide some sort of restitution to the community, whether litter pickup, brush cutting, sidewalk construction, state or county beautification projects, or home repairs for the elderly. There is a growing trend to employ inmates in such community service projects as well as the more traditional institution maintenance and prison industry jobs. More than half of all states now allow private businesses to employ the incarcerated, doing everything from taking airline reservations to restoring vehicles.

Inmate job assignments assist in the habilitation of the inmates and are important to the operation of correctional institutions. But businesses, labor organizations, and civil rights groups have sometimes expressed concern about such programs. Supporters say employing inmates is good for the prisoners, the staff, and the community because it enhances prisoners' work skills and sometimes provides labor to organizations that may otherwise not be able to afford or complete those projects. In some instances, the opposition to inmate work programs stems from a concern for displacing civilian employees and reducing the market for some businesses, while in other cases it stems from a concern that inmates are being "exploited" by being paid low wages for substantial work, or that inmates will escape while in the community and harm persons or property.

While assigning inmate work crews to community projects does help the community, correctional administrators must weigh these positives against the direct and indirect costs to their facility. There is a substantial amount of money being saved by the use of inmate labor inside of prisons today, which is diminished when inmate laborers are sent outside the institution. The cost of operating facilities would virtually double if correctional agencies could not use inmate labor. The number-one employer in most institutions is food service, which is followed closely by either correctional industries or facility maintenance. These three areas account for nearly half of all employment of inmates in the facility. Inmate crews in the community are necessarily composed of the best-behaved, lowest-risk inmates—the most desirable employees for institution jobs as well. Even these inmates, however, must be supervised in the community, which takes correctional staff outside of the institution, where their services are also needed.

CONCLUSION

The operation and management of a correctional institution is certainly not an easy task. Administrators and staff alike are faced with serious and complex challenges every day. It is said that it takes a certain breed of people to work in a correctional facility. Truly, it does take dedication to hard work, resilience, and ingenuity to maintain a safe and secure environment for both incarcerated individuals and the staff responsible for their care and custody.

NOTE

1. "Heat Wave Assaults Danville Jail," *The Lexington Herald Leader* (Kentucky), June 1998.

SUGGESTED READINGS

Brown, D. 1996. *Facility maintenance: A manager's practical guide and handbook.* New York: Amarcon.

Krasnow, P. 1997. *Correctional facility design and detailing.* New York: McGraw-Hill.

Magee, G. 1988. *Facilities maintenance and management.* Kinston, MA: R.S. Means Co.

State and federal prisons: Factors that affect construction and operating costs. 1993. Upland, PA: Diane Publishing Company.

CHAPTER 19

Correctional Food Service

Lavinia Johnson

In no other setting do food service personnel face the demands and conditions found in American prisons and jails. The food service operation is no doubt the most personal service provided in a correctional setting. The kitchen is one of the key areas in the prison; if personnel do not do their jobs correctly and on time, negative reactions from the inmate population are likely to occur.

For the inmate, eating is a major diversion, and inmates look forward to their meals. Because of the major role food plays in the inmates' daily existence, the food service operation is subject to more scrutiny and publicity than any other aspect of the facility. Institutions' senior management and the public tend to hear about food service in correctional facilities only when there is a problem.

Private food service contractors operate the food service area in many prisons and jails. The private sector currently makes up 10 percent of the total market, and this percentage is increasing. But with or without a contract, the same standards apply for food service providers. The food service staff has to ensure that meals taste good, that meals meet appropriate nutritional requirements, that portions are appropriate, and that sanitary conditions are mantained.

Approximately 1.25 million people are incarcerated in this country today,[1] and that number is predicted to increase dramatically in the future. The food service for inmates nationwide totals approximately $2.1 billion each year.[2]

EXTENSIVE TRAINING REQUIREMENTS

The combination of external demands by legislators, law enforcement officials, and citizens' rights groups and internal demands of administrators and inmates have placed heavy pressure on corrections food service departments. Today, only the most highly trained professional can successfully direct an operation that meets these demands.

The Cost of Feeding Prisoners

As of January 1, 1997, the average daily cost to feed a prison inmate ranged from $1.22 to $7.43, depending upon the department of corrections. The average among all state departments of corrections was $3.65. Food service costs have remained relatively stable; in 1990, the average daily cost was $3.30.

Source: Data from C. Camp and G. Camp, *Corrections Yearbook 1997,* pp. 74–75, © 1997, Criminal Justice Institute, Inc.

The person responsible for this department must fully understand planning, preparing, and serving nutritious meals under sanitary, safe conditions. In addition, the food service manager and staff members must have highly developed interpersonal skills and the ability to act as role models for and trainers and supervisors of inmate workers. The effect of the food service staff on the correctional population is a dramatic one; effective management of this department positively influences the overall function of the institution. The alert food service professional is acutely aware of (1) the potential for explosive action from dissatisfied inmates and (2) the calming effect a good food program can have on both the inmates and the custodial force.

FEEDING IN INSTITUTIONS—EARLY AMERICAN INSTITUTIONS

Early in U.S. history, punishment did not rely upon confinement. Rather, there were many physical sanctions: flogging, death, slavery, and exile. Toward the end of the eighteenth century, the concept of confinement as punishment began to gain prominence; with incarceration came the problem of feeding prisoners. Early prisons in the United States were private, and, in some, inmates had to pay for their food, bedding, and water. In other prisons, inmates had to earn their way. Inmates were provided with the minimum food necessary to sustain life. Porridge, bread, and water; or beans, stew, and bitter coffees were typical menus. This attitude persisted even as state and local jurisdictions began to develop jails and prisons.

EVENTUAL CHANGE AND INSTITUTION FOOD STANDARDS

Although reform actually began in 1790, it was not until the major uprising and riot at the New York State Prison at Attica and subsequent disturbances across the country that the public interest in correctional facilities was aroused. As the courts started to abandon their previous hands-off policy, judges found that some correc-tional facilities did not meet basic standards for human decency. Inmates and concerned citizens groups took some institutions to court and won.

Lacking established professional standards to guide them, the courts attempted on a case-by-case basis to define inmates' rights and to impose standards for correctional institutions. Unfortunately, these standards were often inconsistent and unrealistic. To bring order out of chaos and to guide correctional administrators, the American Correctional Association (ACA) developed a set of standards in 1977.[3]

ACA standards provide a general picture of how a well-organized food service department operates. In almost all institutions, a full-time staff member who is experienced in food service management supervises the operation. This individual is given the resources, authority, and responsibility to manage the department effectively in terms of both labor and financial resources. The administrator of the food service department ordinarily supervises all the food service staff and others such as dietitians, bakers, and butchers. Depending on the system, a number of correctional officers may be assigned directly to the department also. More commonly, however, correctional staff are posted in the preparation and dining area but still work for correctional departments.

FOOD SERVICE FACILITIES AND EQUIPMENT

Food service facilities and equipment vary from institution to institution. Some facilities have state-of-the-art equipment. Other institutions have kitchens where the equipment and space are outdated. In some remote local jails, one still could find a live-in sheriff or deputy whose spouse cooks for the inmates from the same kitchen in which she prepares meals for her family.

The most common serving method in today's prison systems is the cafeteria system, where inmates are systematically fed three meals each day. Some of the facilities serve on open lines,

---

The American Correctional Foodservice Association

The American Correctional Food Service Association (ACFSA), formed in 1969, works to enhance, represent, and promote the correctional segment of the food service industry. The organization encourages standards of excellence and professionalism among its members to enhance food service operations in prisons. ACFSA provides education seminars, tours of correctional foodservice operations, written educational materials, and opportunities to discuss issues of common interest and establish a network among correctional foodservice professionals.

The ACFSA operates a certification program intended to raise the professional standards of foodservice personnel. Individuals who meet the rigorous standards for certification are designated Certified Foodservice Professionals, and may use this designation on letterhead, business cards, etc. The certification pertains to individuals only and not to institutions where the person may be affiliated.

Source: Reprinted with permission from American Correctional Foodservice Association Website: www.corrections.com/acfsa

---

some on blind lines where the inmates cannot see who is serving.

In many jail facilities and some prisons there are no cafeterias; meals are preplated in the kitchen and sent to the housing areas on plastic insulated trays, a hot/cold cart, or a system that utilizes rethermalization equipment. Retherm-

alization involves microwaving food platters to boost the temperature. This term also refers to new technology that involves quick-chilling cooked meals and then reheating the food in a special thermalization cart in the satellite feeding area.

MENU PREPARATION

ACA standards for prisons and jails require that there be some form of menu preparation in advance. For jails, one week of advance preparation is required. The jail standard is shorter than the prison standard because some jails have very limited storage and it becomes difficult to maintain on-hand supplies for scheduled meals. For prisons, the 28-day menu rotation cycle is the most commonly used, although the Federal Bureau of Prisons uses a 35-day cycle. The menus are more than likely planned by the food service manager and/or the dietitian.

If the dietitian does not actually plan the menu, then a registered dietitian should review it to ensure compliance with applicable nutritional standards.

All menus are planned according to the recommended dietary allowances of the National Research Council, National Academy of Sciences. This organization is a national authority that recommends a balance of specific food groups. Caloric requirements will vary with sex, age, and general activity level of the inmates. Daily caloric levels usually range from 2,600 to 3,000 within an institutional setting, with an average of 2,900 calories.

Menus should reflect the inmate population's cultural and ethnic preferences as well as provide for their medical and religious needs. Many jurisdictions actually ask their inmate population for their food preferences. These surveys are generally completed once each year.

FOOD SUPPLIES AND STORAGE

Food should be of the best quality possible within the institution's budget and of sufficient quantity to guarantee a wholesome diet. Available sources of food depend largely on the nature and location of the institution. Common sources are state purchasing warehouses, state contracts, local wholesale food distributors, and local vendors.

Some prison systems have food and farm operations that provide meat, vegetables, milk, grains, and other items for their institutions. Items such as cakes, pies, and breads can be purchased or prepared locally. Fresh vegetables and fruits are on a seasonal purchase, and availability is dependent on the region. All food should meet or exceed government standards. No longer are home canning or uninspected meat slaughtering acceptable.

The delivery and storage system should ensure that food supplies are fresh and delivered in a suitable condition. All incoming food not immediately used or processed in some way should be properly stored to prevent spoilage or waste. Proper storage should be available immediately for perishables such as meat, milk, eggs, and fresh vegetables and fruits. Semiperishable foods such as canned goods may be kept in temperature-controlled storage rooms.

Shelf goods should be stored at 45°F to 80°F, refrigerated foods at 35°F to 40°F, and frozen foods at 0°F or below. Each refrigerator or walk-in storage unit should have a thermometer on the door of the exterior wall so that staff can check these temperatures easily. Temperatures should be checked and recorded as required.

FOOD PREPARATION

Food is usually prepared according to a recipe system that the jail or prison adopts. This recipe system ensures that the quantity and quality of meals are uniform and that staff variables do not enter into the preparation. For this purpose, many institutions use the Armed Forces Recipe Cards as guides for food preparation.

Sanitation measures in the kitchen are absolutely critical. Each institution must have a daily cleaning and inspection system that ensures that the food preparation, storage, serving, and dining areas are sanitary. This is far more than a cosmetic issue. The health of every inmate and staff member in the institution hinges on the cleanliness of the food service area.

Each institution should consider having a hazard analysis critical control point system in place to ensure that proper food-handling procedures are being followed for receipt, storage, preparation, holding, and serving of foods. This is an optional program but may help ensure that good personal habits and cleanliness are a focus for all food service staff and inmate workers.

Adequate hand-washing facilities should be provided in the kitchen area. Clean uniforms and aprons should always be available, and food handlers should be required to wear head coverings, hairnets, and beard guards while cooking or serving food.

MEDICAL AND RELIGIOUS DIETS

Medical diets should be made available to inmates only based on medical authorization. Each prison system should know the medical diets that it will prepare: Diet orders should be specific and complete, furnished in writing to the food service manager. Medical diets should be planned so they are as close to the main menu as possible.

Prison and jail systems also have to deal with specific religious beliefs that require inmates to eat or not eat certain food. For example, Islamic and Jewish inmates are forbidden by their religion from consuming pork or pork products. Because of this, many institutions now have a pork-free menu. Religious diets are ordinarily approved by a chaplain. They should be specific and furnished in writing to a food service manager. In many systems, they are reviewed periodically. If a staff member observes an inmate approved for a religious diet eating from the regular bill of fare, the staff member should report this to the chaplain so that the religious diet status of the inmate can be reviewed.

A separate area in the kitchen under staff control may be used to store all diet trays, or they may be kept in a single hot cart behind the line for issue under staff direction. Many institutions use a diet card or pass system to ensure that only authorized inmates receive these meals.

MEAL SERVICE

When a new jail or prison is under construction, an important consideration is what type of serving system will be used. The degree of staff supervision required and the institution design will determine the system used for serving. Food can be served cafeteria style or preplated and carted to the inmates. Both systems have their own challenges.

Gathering a large number of inmates together in a cafeteria presents a security risk under any circumstances. The dining rooms create a potential site for serious disturbance and other incidents. As a result, in a cafeteria setting it is critical that correctional staff enforce an orderly system of food lines and seating as well as portion and utensil control.

To the extent possible, the dining rooms should be designed to enhance the attractiveness of the mealtime atmosphere. Meals assume a magnified importance in inmates' daily routine and are important to institutional personnel. Thus, the condition and cleanliness of the kitchen and dining area can influence an institution's entire atmosphere.

Food should be served as soon as possible after preparation and at appropriate temperatures. Temperatures are ordinarily maintained by keeping the food in warmers of some type, either cabinet or pan style. Direct service is usually from a steam table or some other type of cafeteria-style warming equipment. Food distribution should be supervised at all times. Frequently, inmates serving food will take advantage of an officer's temporary absence to take care of friends or to not give other inmates their entitled portions.

Selection of eating utensils should be dictated by the type of population confined in an institution. Many institutions now use highly durable, washable plastic utensils. Control of eating uten-

sils can be maintained by requiring inmates to dispose of them in a carefully positioned and supervised receptacle when inmates drop off their trays.

DINING ROOM ROUTINE

Inmates should be given enough time to wash before eating. Inmates working outside or in other active occupations should be allowed to change clothing before entering the dining room. Inmates must be fully clothed (in their issued uniforms) while in the dining room. Staff supervising the entrances should enforce the dress and smoking codes before inmates come into the area. Random inmate searches for weapons and contraband should be performed.

The dining rooms should provide normal group eating areas and permit conversation during dining hours. Whenever possible, there should be open dining hours to reduce the traditional waiting line. Many facilities have eliminated forced seating based on housing unit, shop assignment, and so on. Serving and dining schedules should offer a reasonable amount of time for inmates to eat. Tables and chairs should be arranged for good traffic flow and supervision.

Line cutting can become a problem in a crowded dining room. Close staff supervision can deter this activity and prevent major confrontations. The inmate dining room should not be used as a shortcut to other areas, and inmates should not be allowed to linger in the dining area.

UNIT DINING

This type of dining is used primarily in jails or regional adult detention centers or during prison lockdowns. The meals are preplated in the kitchen and sent to the housing areas. This can be done by using an insulated tray, hot/cold carts, or a rethermalization system (as described previously).

Specific correctional management principles apply to all types of unit dining.

- All food carts should be thoroughly searched by staff for contraband being sent into the unit from cooperating inmates in the main kitchen area.
- Inmates should not be used to serve food to other inmates in segregation status. This is a prime opportunity for inmates to try pressure and manipulate other inmates, tampering with the food of unpopular inmates, or passing contraband into the unit.
- Inmates must be required to give back all utensils and other items on the food tray; this is not only for the safety of the staff but also because keeping food in cells is likely to attract vermin and insects.
- Staff should ensure that all inmates' meals arrive at their cells at proper temperatures.
- Food service supervisory personnel should regularly tour the locked units during mealtime to ensure that inmates are properly served, with meals at proper temperatures: above 140°F for hot foods and below 41°F for cold foods.

COMMISSARY OPERATIONS

Home-cooked foods are not allowed in an institution. However, a commissary or inmate store is usually available in most locations for inmates to purchase a wide variety of discretionary food and other items.

Selecting the articles to be sold in a commissary requires careful study. Most commissaries limit the selection to snacks and light foods that are not in conflict with the regular food program.

SUPERVISION ISSUES

Traffic control in and out of the food service area is important. The unrestricted movement of inmates not only presents an accountability problem but also permits theft of food items and pilferage of other contraband from the kitchen; the more traffic there is, the harder it will be to detect these problems. For that reason, the kitchen area should be out of bounds for all non-

kitchen workers, and correctional staff should enforce that rule.

Also, controlling items coming into the kitchen through the loading dock is always a concern. The possibility of contraband coming in through regular food shipments from fixed sources of supply is quite high. Therefore, each institution should have a specific system for searching vehicles, loads, and drivers moving supplies into the compound

Trash control is another security issue that pertains particularly to escape attempts. Any trash truck or dumpster load should be kept locked in a sally port area through one or more counts, to be sure that inmates are not hidden inside. Probing and other search techniques may be used also. The same concerns and search techniques should be used for boxes or containers of food prepared inside and sent to satellite camps or other locations; inmates can be hidden in these containers also.

Trash compactors are another avenue for escape. Inmates have successfully (and at times unsuccessfully) fabricated skeletal frameworks of crushproof containers to hide in to escape via a dumpster. Using a sally port is the safest way to eliminate this avenue for escape attempts.

CONTROLLING KITCHEN TOOLS

Tool control in the kitchen consists primarily of knife control. However, in facilities with butcher shops, movement of saws and other tools will also need to be controlled. In most facilities, kitchen tools are stored in a locked cabinet in a secured area.

Inside the secure cabinet the tools are hung on hooks that are painted with shadow of each tool so that it is easy to see if any are missing. When an inmate or staff member checks the tool, a durable metal tag with that person's name or other identifier is placed on the hook so that it is clear who has the item. A written inventory of all items in the cabinet should be kept in it, and at each shift change the responsible staff member should check the inventory and initial the list. This inventory should also be jointly checked with a correctional staff member on a regular basis—not less than monthly.

Equipment should be constantly checked to make sure no parts are missing. Inmates are very innovative when it comes to making weapons.

YEAST, SUGAR, AND EXTRACT CONTROL

Yeast, sugar, and extract control is another major concern in an institution. Yeast and sugar can be used to make "home brew," also referred to as "mash" or "pruno." Also, extracts have alcohol in them, so inmates may drink these instead of alcoholic beverages. These items should be kept under lock and key with a strict inventory maintained.

Inmates with unusual amounts of sugar or fruits, or even small amounts of unbaked bread in their possession should be viewed with suspicion as potential brew makers. Even if the institution does not have a possession limit on these food items, an officer encountering them in large amounts should refer the matter to a supervisor for advice.

FOOD AS AN INCENTIVE

Using food as payment for work or as a special privilege should never be permitted, but when inmates work in outlying jobs or in odd shifts, it often is necessary to provide lunches or extra food to cover the shift portion of the day.

Some institutions take into account the fact that some work assignments are more physically demanding than others and provide extralarge rations.

CONCLUSION

Food service operations are very important to an institutional routine, and positive operations are contingent upon quality staff, effective training, and vigilant supervision. Nutritious and flavorful meals served in a pleasant and safe environment are not possible in a correctional setting without adequate resources and senior-level management support. The food service staff must ensure that proper nutrition, cost controls, security, and supervision practices are observed in the food preparation area. The distribution of food has to be fair, and teamwork is essential between food service staff and security staff in order to ensure a smooth operation. A well-run food operation will greatly enhance the morale, safety, and security of the prison or jail setting.

NOTES

1. D. Gilliard and A. Beck, *Prisoners in 1997* (Washington, DC: Bureau of Justice Statistics, 1998).

2. Gilliard and Beck, *Prisoners in 1997*.

3. American Correctional Association, *Foundation/Core Standards for Adult Correctional Institutions* (Washington, DC: St. Mary's Press, 1989).

CHAPTER 20

Institution Financial Operations

Richard S. Peterson and Beverly Pierce

Few correctional administrators have a professional background in the financial management of institutional operations. Traditionally, wardens and jail administrators have learned their craft through the apprenticeship system and earned incremental promotions up the ranks of the institution. Upon reaching senior management, most individuals are fiscally unskilled and totally unprepared for the significant responsibility of jail or prison financial decisions.

The cost of prison management is becoming a major issue in today's world of expanding institutional populations. As more and larger prisons and jails become necessary, these institutions garner more of the public and media attention. And as budgets take up an increasing amount of legislators' discretionary allotments, the issue of confinement can and will become the center of attention for influential third parties.

The budget is best explained in three phases: budget development, budget execution, and budget oversight. Budget development is the beginning of the cycle—the formulation of a funding request. Budget execution is the administration of those funds through expenditures and distribution. Budget oversight is the implementation of systems and internal controls that en-

sure that funds are used in a manner consistent with budgetary goals while protecting the integrity of the disbursements.

The dangers of making uneducated financial decisions can challenge the best-intentioned administrator; poorly thought-out decisions can lead to disastrous reactions from staff, the inmate population, the governor's office, and the state legislature. In private corrections, the bottom line is critical to the senior administrator's survival.

The following problems can result from badly made financial decisions:

- allowing expenditures that cannot sustain public scrutiny
- failing to manage program funds within funds allocated
- failing to understand the fundamentals of budgeting
- establishing insufficient internal controls to prevent fraud, waste, and abuse
- failing to provide adequate oversight for early detection of budgeting problems

Financial management of a multimillion-dollar institution budget requires specific knowledge and abilities such as understanding the budget concept, analyzing and comparing data, and differentiating between bona fide requirements and incidentals.

Mastering financial management means modifying many already-acquired management

Opinions expressed in this chapter are those of the authors and do not necessarily represent the opinions of the Federal Bureau of Prisons or the U.S. Department of Justice.

and administrative skills to apply to a financial arena. But nothing will serve the new administrator better than good old-fashioned common sense. Simply stated, do not spend more money than was allocated in the budget. Other lessons of survival are equally important in dealing with public perception of institutional management: A penal administrator should not spend money on programs that appear to provide inmates with a better quality of life than the general public has. Public administrators must also be cautious not to spend money to construct buildings and landscape that are so aesthetically pleasing that the correctional facility looks like a country club. Public stewardship also mandates that institution administrators not spend money for unapproved purposes other than what was appropriated. Every dollar spent should be able to sustain public scrutiny.

An administrator must have a planning staff—including both program and financial managers—that can analyze past expenditures and factor in adequate funding to future budget requests for necessary operations and projects in the out years (future fiscal years). Budget-tracking staff are critical to ensure money is spent as planned and appropriately conserved throughout the budget year. Anyone assigned budgeting and purchasing responsibilities should be required to participate in a financial training course, and program managers need to understand the financial network to maintain budget accountability. Clearly defined budgeting expectations and spending perimeters should be established in the agency operations policy. Finally, the chief executive officer of the facility must insist that common sense and good public stewardship are exercised by the staff given signature authority to expend funds.

PLANNING A BUDGET REQUEST— BUDGET DEVELOPMENT

In government budget cycles, handling strategic planning and properly preparing budget justifications are vital functions of the senior institution executive. Many state budget cycles actually require multiple-year lead time for budget submission, so anticipating and planning for future requirements is critically important. Per capita costs of inmate management (day-to-day costs associated with inmate housing, security, programs, and food and health expenses) must be factored into the daily cost projections and enhanced with necessary adjustments for anticipated inflation. Capital outlay (equipment, furniture, machinery) must be included, as well as capital improvement expenses (maintenance and new construction).

Poor planning and crisis management can attack and defeat a balanced budget. Urgent or emergency purchasing of goods and services results in sacrificing price for delivery time. All too often, a lack of planning translates into less value for the dollar. Because the financial resources for prison operations are precious, every effort must be made to allow the maximum time practical to permit shopping for the best value. Planning is critical in the budget development cycle and makes the difference between success and failure in managing the budget.

The most important and expensive part of the institution budget is human resources, the institutional staff. Salaries make up the greatest percentage of institution costs, and the number of staff members needed to efficiently, yet economically, operate each institutional department is not easily agreed upon. Line staff members and union officials always want to increase rosters. Senior administrators, consistently under pressure to reduce operating expenses, seek to do "more with less." Roster management of 24-hour, seven-day-per-week operations in the larger institution departments (such as the correctional security staff) can be a full-time job; supervisors must consider the need to cover all posts and to provide days off, sick leave, training time, and loaned staff for special projects. Inevitably, managers must use overtime hours to cover all critical areas of the jail or prison with reasonable supervision. Obviously, the payment of overtime requires budgetary expenditures that can destroy a carefully balanced financial plan.

Caution should be exercised when attempting to implement cost containment measures by reducing the correctional security personnel. These efforts can often be nothing more than smoke and mirrors. If staff rosters are reduced so drastically that overtime is the only alternative to handle special circumstances, staff have used the more expensive option. Overtime is a variable factor in budget planning and an expensive factor in budget administration.

Although employee salaries constitute the largest portion of a budget, they do not have to be difficult to project, provided the staffing pattern remains consistent. Usually, salary increases are negotiated or at least predictable prior to the budgeting cycle. Financial staff can provide reasonably accurate salary projections by taking the current work-year cost of each employee and adding a pay raise. (A work-year cost normally consists of 2,080 hours of paid employment—that is, 52 weeks times 40 hours.) A specific amount of funding to support overtime, incentive awards, and premium pay should be designated and included when the financial plan is developed. Once staff have figured out the salary projections, they have developed 60 to 70 percent of a budget.

A key element in the successful formulation of a good budget request is a clearly defined budgeting goal. Whether the goal is cost containment, enhancing programs, or renovation, staff need to know what they want to achieve. When staff have identified the budgeting objective, they are ready to build the foundation for the request.

A component of the foundation should be the establishment of a budget and planning committee comprising a financial manager, subject matter experts at the department head level, and the warden and administrators. The subject matter experts should provide input on the funding requirements needed to operate their programs and properly justify to the committee the need for increased funding levels. Conversely, they should be able to explain the reason for requesting less funding. In a zealous attempt to employ cost containment measures, staff may underestimate their requirements, harming the entire institution's budget. Compensating for shortfalls in underfunded areas can hinder budgetary goals.

The committee should serve in an advisory capacity to the chief executive officer and should meet periodically throughout the fiscal year. The committee should make recommendations to reprogram funds as needed to adjust surpluses and deficits.

Administrators must understand the political environment of their agency because it could impact their operation by requiring additional funding or changing the budget execution process. The budget should incorporate enough flexibility to allow staff to shift emphasis as missions change. Legislative changes such as sentencing guidelines, environmental issues, accessibility for persons with disabilities, and life safety issues can influence funding requirements.

There are more unknowns to consider when formulating the operations portion of the budget. However, prior year spending is still the best starting point for developing the operations budget. Financial staff can provide an estimate of anticipated increases based on historical data, and the consumer price index. After considering routine operations, staff must identify and add in any new requirements.

Multiyear formal contracting for purchasing goods and services can be a very useful budgeting instrument. Contracts ensure competitive pricing—the best value for the dollar—and can guarantee prices. Using contracts can increase the accuracy of the budgeting forecast, as it removes some of the guesswork.

Warranties and maintenance agreements for equipment can also be a good budgeting tool. They are a recognized cost and can reduce unanticipated expenditures.

The integrity of any proposed budget requires well-substantiated data, including a history of past obligations, new costs that are expected, and projections of a funding source for uncontrollable or unanticipated expenses (utility increases, institution emergencies, and catastrophic medical care events).

One of the greatest threats to the integrity of a budget request is the organization's own financial philosophy. Too often, staff believe that if they do not use all approved funding in one budget cycle, it will not be appropriated in future budgets. This belief perpetuates wasteful spending and discourages cost-containment initiatives.

MANAGING THE INSTITUTIONAL BUDGET

Laws, statutes, and administrative rule generally govern most financial matters for which the warden or superintendent is responsible. It is, therefore, critical that the senior administrator know the expenditure limits of the institution budget. This document is often a legislature-approved budget that has been certified by the corrections department. The individual with signature authority to expend jail or prison financial resources must know the limits of spending and the rules governing the transfer of discrete amounts of funds among fund categories (salaries, operations, capital outlay, and capital improvement) and ensure that all expenditures are reasonable and justified. Table 20–1 shows the fiscal year 1997 budgets for adult facilities throughout the United States.

The budgeting of planned expenditures is a dynamic process. The ebb and flow of jail and prison management requires some degree of flexibility in financial management, so it is critical that the senior administrator be prepared to shift funds between cost centers to the extent that the law or regulation will permit.

Additionally, senior administrators must ensure that there are internal controls that effectively prevent fraudulent or deficit spending. An easy checkpoint can be as simple as examining the percentage of the budget expended as a proportion of the full budget cycle. If staff have used 70 percent of the yearly budget and are only halfway through the budget cycle, there should be a reasonable explanation. Sometimes contracts are obligated for the entire cycle and can skew this checkpoint. However, department heads should be able to explain any departure from what appears logical.

Invalid obligations will distort the budget picture by overstating expenditures and underestimating available funds. Invalid obligations are funds that were overestimated for the purchase of goods or services and not deobligated in the accounting system after payment. This situation occurs when cost estimates exceed actual expenses. Often, accounting staff do not know when an order is complete and funds in excess of the requirement remain encumbered. This typically occurs with medical expenses. Frequently, the treatment or procedure is different than expected or even deemed unnecessary after the obligation has occurred. The opposite situation arises when funds are encumbered for a procedure that was more expensive than originally planned. This can cause deficit spending or an overstated budget balance.

Reducing the impact of these budget deceptions requires the input of subject matter experts. The program manager must review the open obligation records in the accounting system to verify the accuracy of encumbrances. When searching for explanations for budget shortfalls or surpluses, invalid obligations are a good place to start.

Early detection of disparities in the budget are critical to an administrator's ability to take corrective action. Identifying potential surpluses can be equally important if staff need to compensate for budgeting shortfalls or fund unforeseen expenditures.

While some correctional administrators may argue the point, most believe there are truly very few large-scale unforeseen expenses associated with prison and jail management. There are some obvious exceptions: natural disasters, inmate disturbances, and catastrophic medical care for inmates. Special funding must always be set aside for such contingencies to prevent such events from breaking the bank and an administrator's career.

Reserve funding can be accumulated by developing an equitable formula to sequester a percentage of the institution's budget from

Table 20–1 Adult Correctional Agency Budgets for Fiscal Year 1997

	Food	Operating Medical	Total	Capital	Grand Total	Percent of Jurisdiction's Budget
Alabama	$8,000,000	$22,278,881	$192,583,539	$1,050,000	$193,633,539	17.4%
Alaska	$5,088,000	$14,857,200	$138,745,500	$1,458,400	$140,203,900	6.0%
Arizona	$27,342,600	$56,381,900	$449,655,700		$149,655,700	8.2%
Arkansas	$6,589,154	$19,524,028	$170,239,828	$25,473,574	$195,713,402	4.5%
California	$233,790,000	$487,984,000	$3,636,079,000	$323,220,000	$3,946,299,000	7.4%
Colorado	$7,864,154	$23,675,129	$301,118,534	$28,297,217	$329,415,751	5.9%
Connecticut	$13,027,530	$50,875,859	$408,085,782		$408,085,782	4.3%
Delaware	$6,843,600	$9,395,000	$66,712,400		$66,712,400	3.7%
District of Columbia	$15,000,000	$25,807,000	$260,528,000	$4,894,000	$265,422,000	7.7%
Florida	$54,676,797	$198,877,642	$1,485,800,379	$28,607,286	$1,514,407,665	9.4%
Georgia	$51,277,577	$101,441,936	$695,760,881		$695,760,881	6.6%
Hawaii	$7,789,752	$8,287,745	$93,265,839	$1,816,000	$95,081,839	3.1%
Idaho	$3,062,900	$7,143,600	$71,310,000	$1,335,800	$72,645,800	2.4%
Illinois	$44,993,100	$52,479,400	$857,971,900	$38,691,000	$896,662,900	5.0%
Indiana	$18,600,000	$26,700,000	$373,900,000	$18,630,477	$392,530,477	
Iowa	$6,988,961	$8,629,521	$167,635,106	$14,719,116	$167,635,106	4.5%
Kansas		$18,240,155	$186,792,112		$201,511,228	2.6%
Kentucky	$7,500,000	$18,000,000	$226,832,300	$29,827,500	$256,659,800	4.1%
Louisiana	$10,250,279	$24,000,000	$222,321,228	$27,075,000	$249,396,228	3.2%
Maine	$1,525,213	$4,800,000	$65,610,941		$65,610,941	3.7%
Maryland			$432,502,029	$14,448,000	$446,950,029	
Massachusetts	$7,830,579	$12,504,884	$293,763,597		$293,763,597	2.0%
Michigan	$33,479,400	$93,493,500	$1,347,695,200	$82,500,000	$1,430,195,200	16.4%
Minnesota	$5,987,497	$10,574,767	$158,723,114	$89,000,000	$247,723,114	1.9%
Mississippi	$5,786,046	$15,594,520	$179,616,688	$3,946,558	$183,563,246	5.9%
Missouri	$15,388,648	$33,931,387	$348,590,712	$9,263,653	$357,854,365	2.5%
Montana	$2,300,000	$4,000,000	$62,700,000		$62,700,000	7.0%
Nebraska	$2,891,286	$6,765,097	$68,949,078	$400,000	$69,349,078	3.6%
Nevada	$7,573,836	$25,550,198	$118,219,889		$118,219,889	
New Hampshire	$2,246,975	$1,429,257	$49,380,869		$49,380,869	2.5%

continues

Table 20–1   continued

	Food	Operating Medical	Total	Capital	Grand Total	Percent of Jurisdiction's Budget
New Jersey	$25,360,000	$62,349,000	$596,671,000	$8,815,000	$605,486,000	6.4%
New Mexico	$7,748,700	$14,198,000	$145,565,900		$145,565,900	2.2%
New York	$44,700,000	$161,366,400	$1,455,277,000	$118,000,000	$1,573,277,000	
North Carolina	$28,650,751	$92,357,503	$884,753,830	$5,024,400	$948,123,134	1.0%
North Dakota	$658,600	$927,380	$15,900,000		$15,900,000	5.6%
Ohio	$81,878,324	$88,854,795	$1,162,858,503	$112,852,050	$1,275,710,553	6.0%
Oklahoma		$16,955,048	$285,108,433	$18,000,000	$303,108,433	6.0%
Oregon	$8,782,688	$17,382,768	$272,834,427	$411,147,814	$683,982,241	5.5%
Pennsylvania	$69,456,000	$124,640,000	$971,449,000	$342,461,000	$1,313,910,000	5.9%
Rhode Island	$4,850,100	$3,378,655	$114,234,639	$727,782	$114,962,421	6.6%
South Carolina	$9,800,000	$35,000,000	$301,658,034	$11,245,000	$312,903,034	6.0%
South Dakota	$3,053,655	$3,653,144	$19,003,926		$19,003,926	1.0%
Tennessee	$15,611,500	$35,237,300	$429,687,600	$8,300,000	$437,987,600	3.0%
Texas	$82,308,405	$256,712,312	$2,008,926,627	$380,374,244	$2,389,300,871	5.9%
Utah	$4,646,210	$4,015,940	$39,227,924	$3,381,513	$42,609,437	2.8%
Vermont	$1,712,000	$52,568,000	$42,800,000	$1,200,000	$44,000,000	6.0%
Virginia			$444,016,505		$444,016,505	3.0%
Washington	$11,168,468	$30,137,755	$390,145,266	$85,984,335	$476,129,601	2.8%
West Virginia	$2,300,000	$3,679,000	$41,506,688	$500,000	$42,006,688	2.0%
Wisconsin	$11,720,922	$18,439,265	$601,943,600	$54,492,500	$656,436,100	3.6%
Wyoming		$4,007,937	$35,841,890	$1,102,852	$36,944,742	0.1%
Federal	$197,800,000	$385,761,000	$2,713,054,000	$476,186,000	$3,189,240,000	0.002%
Total & Avg.	**$1,225,900,207**	**$2,747,843,808**	**$26,090,554,937**	**$2,784,448,071**	**$28,933,347,912**	**4.8%**

Blank spaces reflect that data are not available or not reported. *Source:* Reprinted with permission from C. Camp and G. Camp, *Corrections Yearbook 1997*, pp. 70–71, © 1997, Criminal Justice Institute, Inc.

each discipline. This should be done at the beginning of the cycle. The reserves can be used to correct budget problems or reappropriated to other projects. However, senior administrators must realize that using funds appropriated for inmate care for another purpose may draw criticism. For example, funding for medical, food, and inmate comfort items should remain in the salaries portion of the budget. The budget and planning committee should be able to identify personnel changes and salary variations in advance of catastrophe.

Accountability in any financial process is important, but in the budgetary environment it is mandatory. While it is acceptable, and generally desirable, to decentralize cost center management control to the department head level within the institution, it is critical that the overall budget manager assign specific tracking responsibility along with the authority to spend. Individuals with signature authority to spend must be required to justify expenditures in writing, account for all outlay of funds, and keep spending within preset limits.

Compliance monitoring or financial auditing is critical to the integrity of an agency's budgeting process. The parent organization probably has an official financial auditing system in place. However, an in-house review should be conducted periodically using specific financial auditing guidelines that focus on vital functions and prevent fraud. The facility's financial management operation should be able to sustain an audit from a private accounting firm or government accounting agency. This will require an internal auditing system to be used throughout the budgeting cycle.

Part of maintaining the integrity of a budget is being able to demonstrate the ability to protect and maximize the use of the financial resources entrusted to staff stewardship. This will require internal controls to prevent waste, fraud, and abuse. Internal requirements might include

- a system for accountability of property and equipment with a high acquisition value

- policies limiting or eliminating personal use of equipment
- a second level of procurement authority to ensure that contracts and small purchases are competitively priced and available to all eligible contractors and vendors
- documentation to support the destruction or removal of property that is no longer useful or in repairable condition

Jail or prison staff must be aware of special funds for which staff have stewardship responsibility. These funds may include inmate accounts, inmate wages, and canteen profit accounts designated by law or internal regulation for special institutional purposes. Inmates can be sensitive about these funds, which have often been the subject of inmate-originated lawsuits. Such accounts also receive, and deserve, close attention from outside auditors. It may be advisable to develop an inmate canteen committee that would allow inmates to have a voice in the use of canteen profits. At least a portion of these funds should be used to benefit the entire inmate population—purchasing recreation equipment or augmenting the children's area of the visiting room, for instance.

Senior institution staff must also pay particular attention to the expenditure of public money for employee travel and attendance at conferences or special training events. This type of activity can easily generate unwanted attention if such events are not reasonable and appropriate. Per diem expenses of staff on duty away from the institution offer great potential for abuse and subsequent negative publicity. It is important to exercise care in the approval process for training locations; if a conference is in a resort area, it can draw criticism from the public.

Public scrutiny must be an important consideration in all aspects of institution spending. The funding for a correctional facility, either government run or privately operated, is to a great extent linked to the tax dollar. Therefore, management of these resources must be logical, acceptable to the public conscience, and based on common sense. Institutional staff must develop a keen sensitivity to what people may consider inmate luxuries and avoid spending money on items that are not acceptable to the average citizen. In general, equipment and programs available to inmates should not be better than those available to the average free citizen.

CONCLUSION

Stewardship of the public's resources requires conservative decision making, a high sense of integrity, and the ability to apply administrative accountability to the overall process. Effective and efficient operations and programs require economical budget planning and execution.

SUGGESTED READING

Phillips, R., and C. McConnell. 1996. *The effective corrections manager*. Gaithersburg, MD: Aspen Publishers, Inc.

PART V

Staff Management Issues

The U.S. entertainment industry has typically portrayed the staff of correctional institutions as dullards and brutes who enjoy making inmates' lives miserable and are operating prisons and jails in a corrupt manner. Those in the profession of corrections tend to see themselves as heroes and protectors of the public safety. In truth, employees fitting both stereotypes have sometimes worked in American penal facilities, but the average correctional worker is rather like the classic next-door neighbor—an individual who works hard and is motivated by the same incentives that affect most other people: the desire to earn a living, the wish to succeed, the hope for recognition and promotion. Many have sought out the profession because they want to make a difference in the world and to positively affect those who have broken the law. Others simply enjoy working in the field of law enforcement and find value in the mission and challenge of operating penal facilities.

The staff members of local, state, and federal correctional institutions are real-life people who have to deal with the ordinary problems of life. Those who manage these personnel face the same challenges as any business or industry leader: motivating, correcting, creating ownership of new ideas, involving staff in planning for the future, and establishing a work environment that is safe, fair, and humane.

Everyone working in prisons or jails will agree that well-run institutions are orderly, free of violence, and clean; the food served is good;

health care is available; there is little idleness; and prisoners have access to programs that provide the opportunity for self-improvement. Staff must create and maintain all these aspects of an institution. But there are major impediments to the creation of these positive institutional characteristics, and interestingly, the shortfall is not necessarily the inmate population. Inmates generally do as they are told. Correctional staff must set a high standard for operations and enforce those standards.

Institutions that are well run are generally tightly controlled by staff at all levels. Wardens and other senior staff must train staff and then expect them to operate in a principled, fair, and firm manner. Chief executive officers must hold staff accountable for their daily performance, and staff, in turn, must require inmates to live within the preestablished boundaries.

Research and experience have clearly demonstrated that the strong management practice of line staff and their supervisors is the most important factor in creating high-quality prison operations. Prisons are manageable, and the key ingredient is a well-defined standard of operation.

Part V will highlight some of the prominent dilemmas of correctional management today. These chapters discuss the daily activities of a warden, dealing with and managing staff unions, facing corruption, training and developing new leaders, dealing with gender issues between prisoners and staff, and equal opportunity for women in the field of corrections. The last chapter in this section discusses the problem of inappropriate sexual conduct between staff and inmates.

To repeat an axiom mentioned earlier, inmates do not present the most difficult issues in institution management—the successful prison or jail leader must focus on his or her staff.

LEARNING OBJECTIVES

After studying this section, you should be able to answer the following questions:

1. How does the challenge of managing staff members of a correctional institution compare to the issues faced in the private sector of business?
2. What do you believe to be the most important management principle in the leadership of a prison or jail facility?
3. What is an "unfair labor practice" in labor–management relations?
4. Why is correctional institution staff corruption different from other types of public corruption?
5. Why is the continuous development of new leadership among the line staff of prisons and jails so important?
6. What are four important ways to mentor new staff and cultivate staff for supervisory roles?
7. Why have women had a difficult time being accepted in positions within male prison or jail facilities?
8. Can you explain why sexual misconduct between staff and inmates is more significant in a correctional setting than it is in other government or private industry settings?

DISCUSSION/REVIEW QUESTIONS

1. What leadership characteristics are associated with successful and efficient institution management?
2. Why is senior management required to deal with staff union representatives in matters that impact on inmate supervision? In what forum does this interaction generally take place?
3. How is staff corruption defined from sociological, legal, moral, and economic standpoints?
4. How can senior administrators and middle management staff systemically prevent staff corruption?
5. Why is it important to resolve labor-management problems at the lowest possible level?
6. What are five barriers that women employees have met with after taking a job in a men's prison?
7. How would you respond to this statement: "Good institution management begins and ends with the new staff hired for entry-level positions"?

CHAPTER 21

Governing—The Human Side of Personnel Management

Robert L. Wright

With most correctional facilities spending at least 80 percent of their appropriated funds on personnel services for staff salaries, and other payroll expenses, most prison administrators recognize that staff are the heart of their programs. Staff are involved in every aspect of a correctional setting. They serve as ambassadors, peace keepers, and role models. They lead, supervise, and control the activities of the men and women who serve time. Staff ensure that a facility is safe, humane, and efficient—a place where meaningful change may occur.

STAFF OPPORTUNITY AND MANAGEMENT CHALLENGE

People who have been recruited, screened, and trained to work in corrections are honest, hard working, and dependable. Their performance at previous jobs has been above average or better. They are valued members of their communities, participating in local organizations and helping to build strong, wholesome places to raise families. Corrections work provides an excellent career opportunity for people who have these distinguishing qualities.

In the 1990s, corrections is 1 of the 10 leading growth industries in the United States. And corrections continues to be a field where an employee may begin at the entry level—as a correctional officer, budget technician, teacher, recreation leader, or counselor, for example— and end up as a top-level administrator. With the growth in the industry, opportunities abound. The only limiting factors may be the employee's interest, education, and initiative. Many administrators recognize that the best wardens and superintendents have risen through the ranks and supplemented their correctional experience with criminal justice or human services education and specialized correctional education (offered by the American Correctional Association, the National Institute of Corrections, and local criminal justice academies).

As correctional leaders recruit, train, and promote new employees, they recognize that they are preparing the next generation of correctional leaders.

CORRECTIONAL STANDARDS

Correctional Standards for Adult Correctional Institutions, developed by the Commission of Accreditation for Corrections and published by the American Correctional Association, establishes expectations for correctional administration and personnel management in at least 10 areas of critical importance: written policy and procedures, staffing, affirmative action and diversity, selection, probation, physical fitness, compensation and benefits, ethics, personnel records, and employee counseling. Other standards address staff training and the minimum guidelines for adult correctional facilities.

The development of these correctional standards has been regarded by correctional professionals and the American Correctional Association to be the most significant accomplishment made during the twentieth century in corrections. Correctional administrators are encouraged to become fully conversant in these guidelines in their respective areas. Personnel and training are 2 of the 32 areas of correctional administration addressed by the 463 standards for adult correctional facilities.

THE LAW, RULE, COURTS

Correctional administrators must also understand the law and statutes of their area. There are statutes, administrative codes, executive orders, court decisions, and personnel and civil service merit system rules that are specific to each jurisdiction.

These laws, standards, court decisions, and personnel rules are not discussed further here, but not because they are unimportant. In fact, a working knowledge of these is central to enlightened, effective management. Legal counsel and personnel specialists guide correctional leaders. Their opinions are sought and respected.

WORKPLACE BEHAVIOR AND PROFESSIONALISM

There are other areas that corrections leaders must understand as well. Some wardens and superintendents recognize that the technical aspects of the business (such as shakedowns, searches, and counts) are often overshadowed by issues concerning workplace behavior and professionalism.

Simply stated, staff members may lose the opportunity to serve out their career if they do not pay attention to current expectations about workplace behavior and professionalism. Individual employees may be subject matter experts or other corrections specialists who have made significant contributions, but if they have lacked self-discipline, disregarded published departmental expectations, or neglected to treat fellow employees with dignity and respect, their corrections career may be short-lived.

Each correctional employee should be informed of the department's or agency's expectations. Employees at all levels should expect from each other and provide each other with

1. decent, civil speech, without profanity
2. common courtesy
3. respectful conduct
4. cooperation and teamwork

These four simple expectations are important. Where they are observed, all employees can expect a relatively pleasant, professional, and fair workplace. That workplace will be free from harassment, rude behavior, retaliation, disparate treatment, intimidation, and discrimination.

Illegal discrimination is based on age, sex, marital status, race, religious or political beliefs, creed, color, or national origin; the presence of any sensory, mental, or physical disability; or status as a disabled Vietnam-era veteran.

To encourage helpful, healthy working relationships, it is essential for correctional management to articulate these expectations about professionalism. And the agency managers, without exception, must not only talk about the desired behavior but model it in every interaction. These understandings should be included in an employee handbook that is presented to each employee, emphasized during recruitment and selection interviews, discussed and modeled in new employee orientation, and reviewed in annual inservice training.

Meeting the important objectives of professionalism and teamwork—with correctional employees conducting themselves in a manner that is courteous, respectful, and businesslike—is essential for the agency and its mission. These minimum expectations are also essential for ensuring that correctional employees meet their personal and career goals.

Correctional staff must manage the lives of others—individuals who, when left on their own, may be out of control. To achieve good results with others, correctional staff must first manage themselves. As agents of the city, county, state, or federal government, employees can expect that there will be inquiries about performance. Everything correctional staff do is subject to scrutiny. The correctional agency must have well-established procedures—published and available to all staff—that outline the agency's practices for conducting business and handling inquiries into allegations about staff performance and conduct. These reviews of employee conduct must ensure that staff have an opportunity to review allegations. The agency conducts an investigation, the results are shared with the employee, and the employee has a hearing and opportunity to respond.

When employees conduct their day-to-day business in accordance with agency policy, administrative codes, and the law, they have the full support of the agency and the attorney general and other jurisdictional legal counsel. When staff at any level operate outside the published agency guidelines, they are on their own, individually responsible for their behavior and decisions.

With respect to workplace behavior and professionalism, it is helpful to communicate the following understandings to employees:

- Be mindful. While at work, stick to business.
- Be polite. Work with others with courtesy and respect.
- Respect procedures and follow them.
- Respect honesty and deal factually with fellow employees and supervisors. Do not participate in negative gossip; staff have no business gossiping or passing on information that is not factual.
- Contribute to a healthy workplace.
- Understand that no one in public sector employment has any authority or license to participate in retaliation or intimidation—behavior intended to frighten, belittle, discourage, threaten, menace, harm, get even, or "pay back."
- Honor and expect the best of coworkers.
- Understand sexual harassment. Harassment is behavior that is unwelcomed by another;

it is not determined by the intentions of the teller but by the recipient.
- Respect the rights, feelings, and opinions of others (rude behavior is unacceptable).

All employees in the corrections agency need to understand that there is no higher priority than the workplace behavior of employees. Every employee must understand that each employee is responsible for the healthfulness of the corrections workplace, that fellow employees must be respected, and that concerns must be conveyed factually and with courtesy, never in a derogatory or mean-spirited way.

Correctional staff are challenged to be professional—to be honest, hard-working public servants dedicated to the public good. Correctional staff at all levels are constantly being evaluated by the public. The correctional employer and the agency should welcome inquiry and inspection.

Whenever correctional staff have disagreements, they should remember their role as peacemakers. Employees should go directly to the individual they have a concern with and discuss the issue, seeking resolution. If that fails to resolve the situation, they are encouraged to seek assistance from their supervisor.

There is enough negative activity in the corrections workplace that has been generated through the lives of the inmates serving time. It is simply destructive for corrections employees to be sidetracked or manipulated into negative behavior.

EMPLOYEE DEVELOPMENT— LEADERSHIP

Quality institutions with effective, determined, and inspired leaders that meet challenges effectively and professionally will foster many future leaders—unit supervisors, program managers, lieutenants, assistant superintendents, and superintendents.

Some of the most successful superintendents and wardens have learned from an effective, progressive leader. They have had the opportunity to observe the organization and the leader up close. Approaches and issues have been discussed, with the rationale for decisions examined and alternatives reviewed. Astute, attentive aspiring corrections executives are able to build on and apply the lessons they learn from their organization. Interaction with their peers provides opportunities for them to work together effectively. As these individuals participate in the business of the organization, modeling the behavior of the leaders, they are also providing opportunities for evaluation of their own leadership qualities and integrity.

Healthy and effective organizations will foster healthy and effective leaders. Correctional administrators should expect surprises among the talent pool in the effective and healthy organization and select leaders solely on the basis of merit. It is not beneficial to attempt to identify future leaders too early. Rather than expend special training resources on only selected individuals, it is best to create a rewarding and rich environment where excellence is the order of the day, performance is evaluated, competition is healthy, and the level of performance of all employees is raised. In the healthy organization, people understand that any entry-level employees may end up running the place. The only limit is their interest, their education and experience, and their ability to effectively apply their knowledge and work with others.

These views represent the opinions of wardens who have served in a healthy and effective organization run by an enlightened leader. Truly great leaders often credit their work in a vital organization as the key to their success.

There are few satisfactory substitutes for strong mentoring. However, many forums exist that are designed to assist and prepare future leaders. The American Correctional Association and National Institute of Corrections training, and professional corrections associations meetings certainly represent substantial opportunities for corrections practitioners to meet and share strategies and experiences. Also, the opportunity to read and study the accounts of correctional leaders can stimulate the insight, reflection, and assessments critical to the development of effective correctional leaders.

SETTING THE TONE AND CREATING THE CULTURE

It has been said that corrections management is an art, not a science. Some people have degrees and substantial credentials, but they can lack common sense and the ability to understand key issues and significantly influence the organization.

An effective corrections manager is never satisfied with the status quo. Goals and expectations are set and communicated, and the organization moves toward those goals. In large part, the effectiveness of the organization depends on the example that the leaders set. There is a direct correlation between the expectation of the leader and the results. When leaders or managers tolerate mediocrity, the result is mediocrity. When excellence and professionalism are the expectations, the momentum of the organization increases, and employees perceive the ways they may serve as helpful contributors.

Corrections is a people business. The staff of any correctional organization are common people; working together, they can achieve an exceptional result. Honest, hard working, and dependable, they follow instructions and treat others with dignity and respect. They show integrity and compassion, and they are effective team members. All staff must understand that they must follow agency guidelines and be consistent in performing their duties and enforcing rules. There is no room for free agents or mavericks; they create chaos and make the facility a dangerous place for others to work. When dealing with inmates, staff must remember to be firm, fair, and consistent; to do for one inmate only what they will do for all; and to hold inmates accountable for their actions. Staff in a healthy corrections organization are informed that one of the greatest opportunities they have is to serve as an example and influence the inmates in their care by their professionalism.

Staff at all levels are to be informed of the agency's position concerning rehabilitation. For example, they should be reminded that there is no quick fix for crime. While the agency provides opportunities for those in custody to make wholesome use of their time, there is recognition that if change occurs, it is from within the mind and heart of the individual. Change is possible, and many correctional employees are motivated by the hope that change will occur. A healthy institution is filled with hope, meaningful work and education opportunities, and significant self-help and leisure activities that challenge and motivate inmates.

Staff should understand that they set the tone in their facility. They establish the community and the quality of life. When staff understand their impact, facilities can offer life-enriching experiences for inmates serving time and a healthy and safe place for people to live, where staff are proud and honored to serve. Lives are positively impacted while the interests of the public are served.

CORRECTIVE/DISCIPLINARY ACTION

In a strong organization, staff are selected on the basis of merit, everyone is learning, and it is in the agency's best interest to provide the training and assistance to help all employees be successful—to help them handle the challenges of corrections. The agency has a duty to outline what each position requires, prepare staff for changing roles, develop operational procedures, and show employees how to follow those procedures. This means senior management must provide appropriate opportunities for staff to become informed and proficient.

As part of the training and orientation in a correctional institution, there must be an understanding that there are rules and regulations, not only for the inmates but also for the staff. Every organization must have discipline in order to achieve its objectives. Supervisors, to be effective, must know the rules and administer them fairly.

The communication between supervisor and subordinate is critical. Supervisors must be mindful that agencies must train and improve staff. Positive reinforcement helps develop personnel. But when an order or rule is disobeyed, supervisors cannot ignore it.

The most common method of correcting unacceptable behavior is a simple warning. A minor disciplinary action such as a warning must be instructional and constructive. It must help the employee understand the importance of and reason for the corrective procedure being followed, and the logic behind the facility's rules about how a task should be performed. Employees must understand that consistency, having all staff carry out their duties and procedures in a uniform manner, is essential for the institution.

Effective supervisors are thorough and thoughtful in addressing performance issues. When an event occurs, they find out what happened; who was involved; and where, when, and why it occurred. They address the issue with the employee privately in a calm and factual manner, without anger or debasing remarks. The warning should be appropriate for the individual and the situation, and present the facts to the staff member. It is often helpful to inquire about why the employee took the action in question: "I see you did it this way. Is there a reason for that?" This can help establish the motivation of the staff member. Once the employee realizes and admits to the error, and understands how to behave in the future, the warning process should gracefully be ended. It is generally not helpful to threaten a staff member about what would happen if future mistakes were made. It is important to be sure the employee understands that the "air is clear" and the situation is history.

There are few situations for a supervisor that require more tact, good judgment, common sense, and fairness than the handling of corrective action with a staff member. Every supervisor must understand that the objective of corrective action is to help the employee be successful. Often, the manner in which corrective action was taken matters more than what in particular was addressed. Exhibit 21–1 offers guidelines for disciplining a staff member.

Warnings, well intended as they may be, are not always enough. When repeated rule or procedural violations occur, a supervisor should follow up with the staff member. In these situations, the supervisor should follow the same guidelines as in preparing for a warning but also document the facts of the situation, the conversation with the employee, and the expectations for the staff member—in writing. It is helpful to have the employee sign this document to acknowledge that the facts are correct. This written document can be used in a memorandum of instruction or a letter of reprimand in the future. The document should be reviewed with and presented to the staff member in private, and a copy should be provided to the individual. If performance issues persist, it will become necessary to take progressive corrective or disciplinary action.

Normally, corrective or disciplinary action for successive infractions will follow a progression.

- verbal instruction
- verbal warning
- written memo of instruction
- letter of reprimand
- disciplinary reduction in pay
- disciplinary suspension without pay
- demotion
- discharge from employment

Exhibit 21–1 Guidelines for Disciplining a Staff Member

1. Is the action proposed by the supervisor based on fact? What are the nature and seriousness of the offense, and how did it relate to the employee's position and responsibilities?
2. Was the offense technical or inadvertent, or was it committed maliciously and for gain? Was the behavior repeated?
3. Was the employee's side of the story obtained and considered? Were there any mitigating circumstances such as unusual job tensions; personality problems; mental impairment; or bad faith, malice, or provocation on the part of others? Was the investigation thorough?
4. Is there a history of similar negative behavior by this staff member? Any other previous disciplinary action?
5. In taking a disciplinary action, did the supervisor consider the employee's past work record, including length of service, performance on the job, ability to get along with fellow workers, and dependability?
6. Did this offense affect the employee's ability to perform at a satisfactory level, and did it affect the supervisor's confidence in the employee's ability to perform assigned duties?
7. What action has the agency taken in similar cases?
8. Was the penalty used consistent with the applicable agency table of penalties?
9. Did the supervisor consider the notoriety of the offense or its impact on the reputation of the agency?
10. What was the clarity with which the employee was on notice of any rules that were violated in committing the offense, or had the individual been warned about the conduct in question?
11. What is the potential for the employee's rehabilitation?
12. Will the corrective action be seen as fair and appropriately dealing with the violation?
13. Did the supervisor consider the adequacy and effectiveness of alternative sanctions to deter such conduct in the future by the employee or others?

Information in part from the Federal Merit Systems Protection Board case of *Douglas v. Veteran Affairs,* 5 M.S.P.R. 280 (1981), often referred to as "The Douglas Factors." *Source:* Adapted with permission from P. Borida, *A Guide to Federal Labor Relations Authority Law and Practice,* pp. 610–611, © 1998, Dewey Publications, Inc.

Warnings and letters of reprimand are generally understood to be corrective action. Disciplinary action, on the other hand, is more severe and formal. Corrective action is usually taken by the supervisor, and disciplinary action is taken by the agency.

There are events or incidents that result in or require immediate separation from service and for which the principle of progressive discipline is not necessary: conviction in a civil court for domestic violence; crimes of moral turpitude (rape, child molestation); reporting to work under the influence of alcohol or drugs; trafficking in institutional contraband; sexual or inappropriate relationships with inmates; establishing personal relationships with families of inmates; or bringing weapons into the institution. These and similar offenses may be expected to result in the immediate suspension from duty of the employee, an investigation of the allegations, and a hearing as prescribed by the policy of the agency.

CONCLUSION

Creating a correctional facility where staff are recognized as the greatest asset, dignity and respect prevail, employees are valued and allowed to grow, and inmates and staff have a wholesome place to live and work is the challenge of the chief executive officer—the warden or jail administrator. These personnel management duties cannot be outsourced. They are the central business of the agency, and they require the personal direction of the agency's top administrator. Strong central leaders will positively influence the people who live and work in these prison communities.

SUGGESTED READINGS

Bennis, W. 1989. *On becoming a leader*. Menlo Park, CA: Addison-Wesley Publishing.

Block, P. 1987. *The empowered manager: Positive political skills at work*. San Francisco: Jossey-Bass.

Fisher, R. et al. 1991. Getting to yes: Negotiating agreement without giving in. 2d ed. Boston: Houghton Mifflin.

Keirsey, D., and M. Bates. 1978. *Please understand me: Character and temperament types*. Del Mar, CA: Prometheus Nemesis.

Wright, K. 1994. *Effective prison leadership*. Binghamton, NY: William Neil Publishing.

CHAPTER 22

A Day in the Life of the Warden

James A. Meko

There are few mundane workdays for a chief executive officer (CEO) of a jail or prison. Even on slow days, these CEOs must be ready for emergencies or unusual events. Accordingly, it is difficult to describe a typical day for senior administrators of today's jails and prisons.

A prison or jail CEO must be able to quickly respond to challenges that arise both inside and outside an institution. The best warden is proactive, anticipating and preparing for most crises. An institution leader who is reactive is often overwhelmed by circumstances and, therefore, slow to respond. Each day, strong leaders accomplish tasks that reflect their values and those of the people they serve.

A warden's day is not always limited to normal work hours, Monday through Friday. A proactive warden is available to staff at all hours, night and day. Such access to staff ensures that the CEO is always aware of important developments at the institution. The proactive warden ensures that communication moves along the chain of command in both directions. A lieutenant or department head should not hesitate to call senior staff on a question related to an important issue at any time, day or night.

Prior to arriving at the institution on a normal day, the warden should review the local newspaper and television and radio broadcasts in preparation for discussing with staff any significant events that could influence the institution. Examples of such events include legislation affecting staff or inmates, a local politician's negative remarks about the facility, or an incident at another lockup that could affect local operations.

Once in the institution, the CEO will start the day by reviewing the shift commanders' logs of the previous day's or weekend's activities. These logs typically summarize events in the institution and identify both the staff and inmates involved in any incident. The warden must be satisfied that these occurrences were handled appropriately. If they were not, immediate corrective action should be taken.

EARLY MORNING

A normal institution day often begins with a meeting involving the warden, the associate wardens, the warden's executive assistant, the head of institution security, and any other individual the CEO would like to have attend. Generally, the security chief reviews significant events that have occurred during the preceding day or weekend, and each participant is free to contribute new items or discuss plans for the day.

This meeting is important for several reasons. First, it keeps vital lines of communication open. Honest feedback, in both directions, ensures high-quality institutional operations. Such feedback also ensures that key players understand what is important to the warden and the agency, and empowers them to act accordingly. Second, the meeting enables the warden to give direction to one or all members of the group with the benefit that all hear the direction and are able to question the rationale for the direction. Such a system promotes mutual respect, shared values, and camaraderie.

For instance, to ensure a safe and sanitary institution, many wardens are proponents of the "broken windows" theory first put forth in 1982 by criminologists James Q. Wilson and George L. Kelling.[1] They argue that in community police work, minor violations create a disorderly environment and actually encourage more serious crime. If the authorities take care of small offenses like public urination, aggressive panhandling, and graffiti, there will be a decrease in more serious offenses. The same approach should be used in the prison community. If staff at all levels do not tolerate littering, defacing property, or having dirty, cluttered cells, they establish themselves as "in charge," the institution is clean and orderly, and inmates are less likely to engage in more offensive behavior. In short, everyone recognizes that there is a sense of orderliness within the facility.

The morning meetings with key staff enable the warden to share such strategies with decision makers at the institution and to ensure that all are "on board." These meetings should never be longer than one hour, because each principal is responsible for a vital area of institutional operations; they best serve the agency on the job and not in a meeting. At the close of the meeting, individual members should feel free to seek some private time with the CEO to discuss significant personnel issues not related to the group.

Wardens should never forget that discussions about sensitive issues such as discipline, personnel, tactics, and strategy should be discussed with staff on a "need-to-know" basis. This means that only individuals with a real need to know should be told specific information.

The departure of the group gives the warden time to review incoming mail, identify individuals to prepare responses, and establish suspense dates when the response is due. Staff who prepare mail responses must be aware of the importance of and pay special attention to particular individuals, such as those at the agency's head-

quarters, key legislators, judges, local officials, or local media representatives. The effective warden maintains a personal and continuing dialogue with all these individuals to keep them informed of noteworthy developments at the institution. This demonstrates respect for them and shows them that the leader is professional and responsive.

Mail reviewed or signed by the warden should be routed through the appropriate associate warden and department head for two reasons. First, it keeps them in the loop and ensures that they will feel a sense of ownership of the finished product. Second, it prepares each for positions of increased responsibility in the future.

MIDMORNING

Time must routinely be set aside to meet with key staff on important matters such as budget, personnel, facilities, industries, and strategic planning. It is important, however, that meetings not consume all of the CEO's time. The prison or jail administrator should establish guidelines for staff conducting meetings so that time is not wasted on extraneous, irrelevant issues. These guidelines should require a well-thought-out agenda shared with participants in advance and tied to articulated meeting objectives, specify the preparation required of participants, establish a time limit, state that discussion will be encouraged and dissent tolerated, require that data presented be accompanied by visual aids to facilitate the presentation, and state that no one will be permitted to monopolize the agenda. The individual chairing the meeting should ensure that each person's participation is monitored in a firm and dispassionately fair manner. These guidelines will ensure that the warden will have the time necessary to manage the institution by walking around.

Management by walking around, first identified by Tom Peters and Nancy Austin,[2] is a trait of administrators who are in touch with both staff and inmates. These senior managers know what is happening in their institutions. Such a philosophy encourages the warden to visit all ar-

"Prison executives face unprecedented challenges today. Inmate populations continue to soar, while state and Federal budgets face severe shortfalls. External scrutiny by the press, the courts, and legislative and executive budget analysts is increasingly intense. In some areas, unions are gaining strength and demanding different working conditions. The work force is changing. More women and minorities are entering prison service which, in itself is good, but creates a new set of organizational circumstances. . . . Within this morass of internal and external changes, prison executives must somehow attempt to maintain stable, coherent, and predictable institutions, where inmates and staff are relatively safe, conditions are humane, facilities are sanitary, and opportunities for meaningful work are available. The challenge is great. To meet these demands, contemporary prison leaders must be highly motivated to achieve excellence, excited about what they do, passionate about mastery of their craft, and sufficiently energetic to get the job done. Passive acceptance of responsibility will not lead to success. Rather, leaders must create an institutional vision of greatness and commit themselves to its accomplishment. They must give their hearts, not just their minds nor just their time. Prison leaders must commit that element of human character from whence fervor, inspiration, and dedication flow.

These are high sounding words—abstract and lofty. Few people working in prisons would argue with them, but when the Governor is calling, the inmates are threatening a food strike, and the safety supervisor has just informed you that the backup generator is insufficient should the facility experience a total power outage, you hardly have time for such lofty thoughts. Welcome to the world of prison administration!"

Source: Reprinted with permission from Kevin N. Wright, *Effective Prison Leadership,* pp. 1–2, © 1994, William Neil Publishing.

eas of the facility, ask questions, listen to answers, assess the morale of both staff and inmates, and identify problems to be resolved.

Successful prison leaders visit special housing units, the food preparation area, and the health services unit at least once a week to assess the quality of operations in each area, measure staff performance, and listen to inmate concerns. Other areas of the confinement facility should be visited on a regular basis, but not as frequently. Experience has shown that problems in these three underscored areas are good predictors of more serious difficulties.

While touring a jail or prison, administrators must really see what is happening. One must ensure that staff are communicating with inmates—not dictating to or haphazardly confronting inmates. If staff are permitted to aggressively deal with inmates routinely, they quickly develop a confrontation mentality when speaking with inmates. Frank and direct communication demonstrates respect and tolerance. A domination mentality begets fear, intimidation, and hostility. Truly exemplary staff members care and control, exerting both compassion and authority as needed.

A warden must insist that staff be responsive to legitimate inmate concerns and complaints. Showers without hot water, heating systems that do not work, stopped-up plumbing, and poorly prepared food are small nuisances for inmates. But if these little problems are ignored, they can quickly become the basis of negative, collective inmate activity. A warden who permits such inmate complaints to be ignored by staff will undoubtably face major problems.

While walking and talking, the prison administrator must ensure that agency policies are being followed and that, even more important, basic standards of propriety and decency are being respected by staff. With the growing numbers of young and inexperienced staff members, it is often the warden's responsibility to ensure that these staff members know what is expected of them as well as why something is being done. For example, security concerns dictate that inmates be strip searched upon arrival at a secure institution. However, an inmate's personal dignity can be respected in a search; the search should be performed in an area that protects an inmate's privacy.

Such tours also enable the warden to establish and maintain multiple lines of communication. In this way, the warden can take the pulse of the facility; firsthand knowledge of operations is an absolute necessity. It is a big mistake for a prison CEO to sit in his or her office and wait for subordinate staff to bring in news about what is happening. Too often, what the warden hears is what the reporting staff member thinks the warden wants to hear or what makes the staff member look good. Multiple lines of communication provide multiple sources of information to be analyzed and evaluated.

EARLY AFTERNOON

The afternoon begins with a daily stint "standing mainline" for the lunch meal. A proactive warden requires associate wardens and department heads to attend the serving of one meal each day. This provides additional opportunity to interact with the inmate population and staff; questions or concerns can be responded to, or written down and responded to later. This is yet another opportunity to assess the atmosphere of the correctional facility. Positive interaction between senior staff members and inmates in the dining room is a very visible way for senior

staff to demonstrate care, compassion, and fair management for inmates, as well as the importance of responsiveness to legitimate inmate concerns.

The CEO thus sends an important message to all inmates: Those who administer the institution are approachable and responsive. Never does the warden want to send the message that he or she talks to only certain inmate leaders or specific inmate groups; inmates must not be given the message that they must deal through other offenders to get things done.

It is equally important to ensure that all associate wardens and the warden are not in the dining room simultaneously. One of the senior staff members should always be outside the security envelope of the institution in the event of a hostage taking.

It is also good practice to regularly eat a meal in the inmate dining room. This allows senior administrators to evaluate the food, demonstrate concern for inmate welfare, and show confidence in the food service staff. Another good practice is to carry a food thermometer to test the temperature of food items on the serving line. This keeps staff "on their toes" and shows inmates that administrators care about what inmates are served.

After mainline, it is worthwhile to visit the staff dining room to relax, visit with staff, field questions, and assess morale.

MIDAFTERNOON

After returning to the office to check on and return phone calls, it is probably meeting time for the CEO. Meeting with various department heads enables the warden to monitor areas of facility operations. This can also be the time for "close outs" with agency auditors who have been in the institution assessing the quality of some specific operation (business office, personnel, case management, etc.). These should be looked upon as learning opportunities. When audit teams critique a department's operation, it is important that staff not be defensive or challenge an auditor's integrity. This is a perfect time to learn about necessary changes and evaluate the performance of individual staff members.

At this time of day, a CEO might also greet tour groups as they enter or leave the facility. These encounters provide the CEO with a great opportunity to personally offer insight into facility operations and present the agency in the best light possible. Such tour groups are often composed of college students, members of the media, or local citizens.

LATE AFTERNOON

Before calling it a day, a CEO must set aside time for staff development. The proactive leader sees staff development as a personal responsibility. This entails meeting with new employees to outline the agency's, as well as the warden's, standards for behavior and treatment of inmates. It is important to personally conduct annual refresher sessions on subjects such as staff integrity and career planning, and meet with employees at all-staff assemblies to present issues of the day and changes in operations that are anticipated. An institution leader must also meet with individual staff members who need career advice and seek mentoring from the warden.

It is important to "check out" with the associate wardens before leaving the institution to determine if there are any new developments that require the warden's attention. It is extremely beneficial to keep the associate wardens informed and to provide them with daily feedback about their performance. Administrators must carefully evaluate all the information staff provide in light of information received from personal observations and other sources.

Managing the senior leadership team of an institution is a subject that requires a volume unto itself. Suffice it to say that the CEO must never permit a situation to develop in which teamwork is adversely affected by unhealthy competition between associate wardens. Such an atmosphere is dangerous and debilitating. In a jail or prison setting, all associate wardens must

be capable of serving in the place of the warden for short periods of time. Given that requirement, each should be treated and informed with the knowledge that they may have to cover for the CEO tomorrow.

True leadership mandates that the institution warden give the associate wardens the necessary experiences and chances for personal development to assist them in achieving their career goals. This must include education, outside management courses, daily decision making, and agency training. In this manner, the leadership team at the institution builds on its strengths and overcomes its limitations.

On the way home, the warden should consider stopping by the gym and working out. Stresses of the day have less impact if one is able to exercise vigorously for a period of time. Once at home, the prison or jail administrator should try to forget the day's events and focus on loved ones. One should never let a job be all-consuming. Whenever possible, the warden should be involved in community activities such as youth groups, church groups, or civic organizations. This helps the administrator maintain a positive perspective and make contributions to the community outside of the job.

CONCLUSION

Correctional management is complex and demands a high level of energy, fairness, and integrity. Leadership of an institutional community requires a leader in the largest sense of the word; a warden really must be all things to all people. Wardens serve the staff and inmates of the institution and the people in the community. They must represent the facility.

The leader of a penal facility must be able to establish and maintain good relationships with people at all levels. Staff and inmates want neither a tyrant nor a pushover as their warden. They want a fair, firm, and consistent administrator who creates a positive interpersonal working environment. Everyone wants an individual who is friendly and cheerful, who listens more than he or she speaks, who keeps an open mind, and who is calm and considerate. A successful warden is one who praises as well as criticizes, who avoids discouraging comments and gossip, who is sensitive and considerate regarding others' shortcomings, and who holds others in high esteem.

To serve as a warden is indeed a high calling.

NOTES

1. J. Wilson and G. Kelling, "Broken Windows," in *Critical Issues in Policing,* ed. R. Dunham and G. Alpert (Prospect Heights, IL: Waveland Press, Inc., 1989), 208–218.

2. T. Peters and N. Austin, *A Passion for Excellence* (New York: Random House, 1985), 123.

CHAPTER 23

Labor Relations in Corrections

Michael H. Jaime

While many demands that prison and jail administrators face are inmate related, one of the most difficult aspects of institution supervision involves the interaction between management and labor organizations. This complex negotiation is referred to as labor–management relations (LMR).

All corrections administrators must become involved in the plethora of LMR activities. They must learn the vocabulary of LMR: grievance, unfair labor practice, job steward, collective bargaining agreement, mediation, arbitration, and so forth. But LMR need not be daunting. Every organization has a management professional that knows how to deal with LMR. Administrators should remain calm and handle any LMR matter professionally, not personally. If supervisors can avoid personalizing the process, they will minimize their chance of losing control.[1]

BRIEF HISTORY

In 1935, Congress adopted the Wagner Act, or the National Labor Relations Act (NLRA), which formally recognized employees' rights to form and join labor organizations and to participate in collective bargaining. The NLRA thrust upon the nation new rules that would be codified in later years—in whole and in part—by federal, state, and local jurisdictions. These rules provided rights to employees and labor organizations to organize, bargain collectively, and represent members before management and created definitions of unfair labor practices.

In 1947, Congress further amended the NLRA with the Taft-Hartley Act. The various amendments prohibited unions and labor organizations from engaging in certain activities. Further acts and amendments established other prohibitions and directions for labor and management.[2]

States adopted their own laws governing collective bargaining. For example, in 1967 New York State adopted the Taylor Law, which was used as a model by other states. This legislation granted employees the right to organize and to be represented by employee organizations of their choice, required public employers to negotiate and enter into agreements with public employee organizations regarding their employees' terms and conditions of employment, established impasse procedures for the resolution of collective bargaining disputes, defined and prohibited improper practices by public employers and public employee organizations, prohibited strikes by public employees, and established a state agency to administer the Taylor Law. The agency is called the Public Employment Relations Board (PERB).[3]

In 1977, California passed the State Employer Employee Relations Act, later to be called the Ralph C. Dills Act. The Dills Act is a comprehensive labor law that governs the collective bargaining process of California's state employees. The Dills Act, like New York's Taylor Law, provided employees the right to organize and be represented, required the governor or a designated representative to meet and confer in good faith on matters within the scope of representation, provided for a mediation process (impasse process) in the event the parties fail to reach agreement, defined unlawful practices for the state or an employee organization to engage in (unfair labor practices), and established a state agency, the PERB, which would be responsible for the administration of the Dills Act.[4]

Collective bargaining laws such as these empowered corrections employees to form and join the labor organization of their choice, via an election process, and to select the organization that would be their exclusive representative in labor matters before management (see Figure 23–1).

ISSUES THAT ARE DRIVEN BY THE UNION

Corrections administrators should research issues important to the labor organizations they are dealing with. These issues may vary from area to area; however, there are four basic vehicles used by the union to deliver messages to management.

1. master bargaining table issues or local bargaining issues
2. grievances
3. unfair labor practice charges
4. issues of importance that are discussed by the union with management on a regular basis

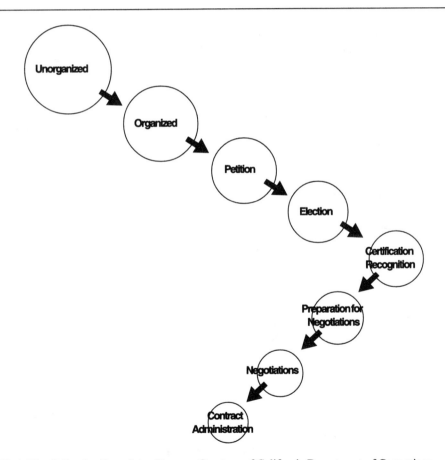

Figure 23–1 The Collective Bargaining Process. Courtesy of California Department of Corrections.

Bargaining Issues

The concept of meeting with recognized employee organizations is well established by law and routine practice in most state governments and the federal government. The basic and most important right in any collective bargaining law is the exclusive representative's ability to negotiate terms and conditions of employment on behalf of the rank and file. The term "meet and confer" is commonly used and essentially means to bargain. Both parties are obligated to personally meet and confer promptly, for a reasonable period of time, upon request by either side, to exchange information, opinions, and proposals, and to endeavor to reach agreement. Depending upon the provisions of each jurisdiction's bargaining law, items outside of the agreed-upon provisions of the master agreement may have to be negotiated with the employee organization. This commonly requires that a written notice be provided to the exclusive representative and that the employee organization, in turn, respond in writing stating its intention to negotiate the item that is subject to the change in policy or practice. Generally speaking, the impact of the change that is being made—not the decision to make the change—is subject to negotiations. However, depending upon each agency's collective bargaining law, in the absence of a master agreement, one may be obligated to bargain with the exclusive representative over the decision to make the change, not just the impact of the change.

Grievances

A grievance is a dispute between the employee organization and the employer, or a dispute of one or more employees against the employer involving the interpretation, application, or enforcement of the provisions of the master agreement. The grievance process, more than likely, will be specified within the collective bargaining agreement. Those jurisdictions that do not have such an agreement may have a grievance or a complaint process spelled out within some form of law. The exclusive representative will use the grievance process to challenge management's administration of the collective bargaining agreement. If not satisfied with management's response to the grievance, the union may ultimately elevate the grievance to a binding arbitration process (see Figure 23–2). It is at this step in the grievance process that management and the union must abide by the final decision made by the neutral third party, the arbitrator. Normally, only "contract grievances" have the potential to be arbitrated.[5] Once a grievance has been properly filed, management should review the practice that is creating the concern. A suggested process is contained in Exhibit 23–1.

Unfair Labor Practice Charges

Unfair labor practices (ULPs) are actions or decisions that directly or indirectly interfere with the organizational rights of employees or employee organizations. Actions or decisions that may be unlawful for the employer to engage

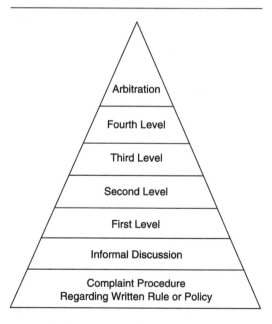

Figure 23–2 Grievance Procedure. Courtesy of California Department of Corrections.

Exhibit 23–1   Grievance Investigation Process

1. Identify the the problem.
2. Identify the violation (contract provision/policy).
   - What contract section or policy was violated?
   - Are other contract sections, policies, or regulations relevant to the issue?
3. Identify important facts.
   - List the facts that led to the grievance.
   - Visit the work area.
   - Question other employees, if appropriate.
   - Get the date, time, and place the problem occurred.
   - Identify the appropriate grievant.
4. Has the department been consistent in applying the contract provision, policy, or regulation?
5. Review grievance records for similar issues.
6. Know the grievant's personnel record, if applicable.
7. Obtain all relevant records.
8. What are the possible solutions to this grievance?
9. What is your decision?
   - Give your verbal answer to the grievant.
   - Explain your decision.
   - Make a record of what you did.
   - Follow through to determine if agreed-upon changes occurred.

Courtesy of California Department of Corrections.

in include imposing or threatening to impose reprisals on employees; discriminating or threatening to discriminate against employees; otherwise interfering with, restraining, or coercing employees because of the exercise of their guaranteed rights under a collective bargaining law; or refusing to meet and confer in good faith with a recognized employee organization.

Management may not dominate or interfere with the formation or administration of any employee organization, contribute financial or other support to it, or in any way encourage employees to join any organization instead of another; or refuse to participate in the mediation procedure.

Actions or decisions that may be unlawful for the union to engage in include causing or attempting to cause the employer to violate a collective bargaining law; imposing or threatening to impose reprisals on employees, discriminating or threatening to discriminate against employees, or otherwise interfering with, restraining, or coercing employees because of their guaranteed rights under a collective bargaining law; refusing or failing to meet and confer in good faith with the employer; or refusing to participate in the mediation process.[6] An unfair labor practice is adjudicated before the administrative body that is empowered by legislation to oversee the appropriate administration of the collective bargaining law. For instance, under the NLRA, unfair labor practice charges are brought before the National Labor Relations Board.

Issues of Importance

Employee organizations or their representatives frequently bring up other matters of concern to the organization and the membership within the context of other forums. These forums may include an informal or formal meeting with the agency director, warden, or other correctional administrator. Although the issue or item being referenced by the employee organization may currently be a topic in negotiations; may have been negotiated; or may be a topic of a grievance, arbitration, or unfair labor practice case, the union nonetheless may take every available opportunity to redirect its efforts in dealing with the issue. All management staff must be aware of what is important to the corrections organization. If the issue that is raised appears to be a significant item to the union, it would be very helpful for the manager to communicate this to the labor relations or employee relations office and the administration. It is best to coordinate a uniform response to the employee organization when dealing with matters of policy or significant practice that concern the employee organization.

As stated earlier, each organization generally has a professional or group of professionals who are trained in dealing with labor organizations and labor issues. Typically, in any prison or jail operation, this will be the employee relations or the labor relations office. In an effective corrections organization, the labor relations office provides resources to its departmental management staff. Investing administrative resources (time, staff, and training) will help create a coordinated program effort that will meet the challenges presented by the labor organization. Typically, a labor relations office or program within any governmental entity will be charged with representing management in all areas of LMR, including contract negotiations and administration, resolution of employee grievances and complaints, arbitration cases, unfair labor practice charges, and related court litigation.

Training is key to the success of an effective labor relations program. Training should be conducted in areas such as contract administration, grievance handling, supervisor conduct with the union, the bargaining process, and basic interaction with job stewards or union representatives. For example, within the California Department of Corrections, training in labor relations is offered to supervisors and managers in basic labor relations for supervisors and advanced labor relations for supervisors. There is also a management development training module on how to negotiate.

In basic labor relations for supervisors, first-line supervisors learn why the agency has collective bargaining with employee organizations, how to interact with the job steward, how to investigate and respond to a first-line grievance, how to identify the basic properties of an unfair labor practice, and how to avoid unfair labor practices. The advanced labor relations for supervisors training instructs second-line supervisors on the detailed background of and case law concerning the negotiation process. Second-line supervisors are given instructions on how to bargain, what makes a management bargaining team, the importance of note taking at a bargaining table, and how to implement a bargaining agreement. When second-line supervisors are promoted to the management ranks, they must attend a three-week management development training program. This includes a hands-on course on how to conduct local bargaining. Participants hear lectures on the negotiations process and become involved in a mock bargaining scenario. This training scenario allows the participants an opportunity to respond to hypothetical union proposals on staffing, health and safety issues, as well as other routine issues that regularly confront correctional managers.

Training sessions such as these will not make the average supervisor or manager a highly skilled labor relations professional. However, such training courses allow supervisory and management staff to become familiar with the labor relations area and help remove the mystique surrounding labor relations.

Working with the labor representative does not mean always reaching agreements and concessions. It does require treating the representative with integrity and respect. Agencies should refer to their own applicable laws or labor contract to be clear on what rights and responsibilities are conferred on both parties. Generally, exclusive representatives have the basic right to represent rank and file members in most matters involving terms and conditions of employment. It is always beneficial for management to resolve problems at the lowest level. Management, working with the representative as a problem-solving team, should make grievance handling a positive experience rather than one filled with conflict and hostility. Whether the representative becomes a link or a barrier between management and employees depends on the way management deals with day-to-day situations. "A steward can be a good ally, or a bad adversary, the choice is generally made by the supervisor."[7(p.32)]

Taking care of problems is key to effective relations with the labor organization. No matter how large or small, an issue can be equally as important to the union. A small, unattended problem can eventually blow up into a huge administrative nightmare. By dealing with issues professionally as they are brought forward, prison and jail administrators will be communicating a very important message to the union: Management is responsive and responsible. Administrators should not worry if the response they must provide is negative. "No" is a valid answer. Sometimes, management's response to the union will be affirmative. Management must know how to separate frivolous issues from bona fide ones.

Management's response should be deliberate and well thought out. It should initiate a course of action to take care of the problem. Stay away from the "you can trust me" approach; this will lead to the "you can't trust me at all" syndrome. If a management official loses credibility on one issue, it can affect all subsequent discussions about problems.

As mentioned earlier, grievances in a specific department should indicate the problem areas being encountered in the interpretation of the bargaining agreement. When in doubt about how to respond appropriately to any union concern or grievance, managers should contact the employee relations or labor relations office.

DEVELOPING THE MANAGEMENT TEAM

Communication helps keep the management team cohesive and effective. Corrections administrators should share the routine as well as the unusual occurrences involving the union with the department's labor relations staff. Administrators are not expected to know everything about LMR. If managers have questions, they should contact professionals who will be able to help.

The management team consists of all administrators, managers, and supervisors within the correctional facility or agency. Management staff involved in any specific issue may vary depending on the issue. For example, during master table negotiations, the management team will be led by the agency director, who is the deci-

sion maker. Wardens; other corrections administrators; and labor relations, personnel, and other administrative staff may participate as the main body of the negotiating team. It is not advisable to include top decision makers directly at the bargaining table. Similarly, at the local level, the warden or other senior administrator serves as the decision maker, and institution administrators and custody management and administrative staff will typically make up the main body of management's bargaining team that develops and researches proposals. Again, if the management team members have received appropriate training, their familiarity with the labor relations process will make them stronger management team members.

ETHICS AND LABOR RELATIONS

Ethics refers to standards of conduct—standards that indicate how one should behave based on moral duties and virtues, which themselves are derived from principles of right and wrong.[8] "Labor relations ethics" may initially appear to be an oxymoron. Take away the term "labor relations" and substitute the term "management decision making." The same principles used in evaluating all ethical behavior can be applied to ethics within the labor relations process. Ethical behavior in this process involves trustworthiness, loyalty, respect, responsibility, fairness, and caring.[9]

- Trustworthiness. When interacting with the union or employee organization, will the supervisor be looked upon as honest in communication and conduct? It is critical to be perceived as a reliable person who gets to the bottom of an issue and can interact in good faith with the union.
- Loyalty. This can be tricky. As a manager, being loyal to the corrections organization is the top priority. As long as a manager is straightforward with the union and not thought to be playing games, the union will respect his or her loyalty. The union representatives will argue a decision, but they will come back again and again if a supervi-

sor is perceived as fair to the union and loyal to the corrections organization.

- Respect. One can command the respect of others only if one gives others respect. While a union representative or job steward on the line may be a subordinate, when that representative is discussing labor relations issues with a manager, the representative should be treated as an equal. A manager should not be expected to take abuse from the representative. Civility, decency, and tolerance will promote a good relationship between both representatives.
- Responsibility. Being in charge of an institution, a housing unit, or other corrections area is a big responsibility that demands accountability, a pursuit of excellence, perseverance, and self-restraint.
- Fairness. Probably, the most important ethical characteristic that labor organizations expect from management is fairness. If a manager is resolving a grievance or an informal complaint, the job steward will always compare the manager's actions with actions taken in the past. Did management interpret the contract uniformly? Was any favoritism involved in the action? If a manager's actions are perceived to be unfair, the union will make life miserable for all concerned.
- Caring. Having a caring attitude doesn't mean one is giving everything away. If a manager is perceived as not having a caring attitude, the entire LMR relationship can be eroded. Consequently, instead of being considered an ethical corrections administrator, one may be perceived as being the opposite—one who lacks integrity.

CONCLUSION

Labor relations issues in any correctional environment are always affected by the percep-

tions of both parties. It is critical for management to deal with all LMR issues in a professional, honest, and straightforward manner. Emotions should never enter the arena; once an issue becomes personal, it will be extremely difficult to resolve. All prison and jail administrators have a network within the local agency and across jurisdictions. When a particularly tough issue arises, administrators should call other administrators or wardens and find out how they have handled similar issues. When in doubt, request assistance from labor relations staff.

While LMR can be contentious, both sides should remember that they are working for the same agency and share the goal of operating safe and effective correctional facilities.

NOTES

1. California Department of Corrections, *Basic Supervision Lesson Plan, Labor Relations.*
2. L. Kahn, "The Law of Labor Relations—An Overview," in *Primer of Labor Relations,* 25th ed. (Washington, DC: The Bureau of National Affairs, Inc.).
3. New York State, Governor's Office of Employee Relations, "NYS—Public Employees Fair Employment Act, The Taylor Law," http://www.goer.state.ny.us/About/taylor.html.
4. State of California Government Code, sec. 3512–3524.
5. *Agreement between the State of California and California Correctional Peace Officers Association, Bargaining Unit 6,* September 18, 1992 through June 30, 1995, article VI, Grievance and Arbitration Procedure, sec. 602, def. (a).
6. California Department of Corrections, *Basic Supervision Lesson Plan, Labor Relations.*
7. California Department of Corrections, *Basic Supervision Lesson Plan, Labor Relations,* 32.
8. M. Josephson, *Making Ethical Decisions,* 4th ed. (Marina del Rey, CA: Josephson Institute of Ethics, 1996), 2.
9. Josephson, *Making Ethical Decisions,* 9–17.

CHAPTER 24

Corruption of Prison Personnel

Sam S. Souryal

Corruption of prison personnel has traditionally been thought to be part of the broader spectrum of public corruption. Prison corruption and public corruption are similar: both are acts of betrayal committed by persons entrusted with preserving fundamental interests of society.

PUBLIC SERVICE CORRUPTION

When public officials display professionalism, they encourage trust. When they behave corruptly, they betray the public's trust. Corruption by public officials has been considered much more sinister than corruption by private sector employees, for several reasons. First, citizens have no choice but to use the available public services (e.g., to drive a car, to run a business, to pay taxes, to petition for a license), whereas they can choose among the services offered by different organizations. Second, public officials take an oath to faithfully execute the laws of the land and to serve society, making their failures, especially when unjustified, seem more "sinful." Third, because of their sovereignty, public agencies can inflict greater damage on unsuspecting citizens than can officials in the private sector. When corruption is discovered, citizens can lose faith in their political system, their elected officials, and themselves.

People, especially those in a democracy, expect their public servants to be efficient and civil (hence the term "civil service") and to consider their duties sacred obligations. While people should expect public officials to demonstrate a higher level of integrity than the average person, private officials and contractors must adhere to the rules and practice good faith management.

Alert and conscientious managers can fairly estimate the extent of corruption by monitoring several indicators, including (1) the formal and informal complaints filed against employees by dissatisfied customers, supervisors, or other employees; (2) the disciplinary actions taken against employees for violating agency rules and regulations; (3) the patterns of questionable behavior by workers such as involvement in alcoholism, drug use, or domestic violence, or patterns of depressive episodes; (4) the erratic behaviors by workers such as more out-of-town trips than are customary, radical changes in their lifestyle that might indicate the sudden acquisition or loss of wealth, or unexpected requests for reassignment or resignation; and (5) the graffiti on the walls and inside bathrooms. Based on these indicators, management should be able to determine when to intervene.

CORRUPTION WITHIN THE INSTITUTION

Prison and jail corruption differs from public corruption in general because of the uniqueness of the environment, function, occupational opportunities, and patterns of social relationships of correctional institutions.

First, not only do institution officials serve in environments that are relatively closed to public scrutiny (making it easier to carry out corrupt acts or to suppress evidence of such acts), they are also engaged in unusually stressful jobs for much longer periods of time. In most instances, they are given the difficult task of controlling a reluctant, resistant, and sometimes hostile inmate population whose welfare may seem better served by corruption than by honest compliance with prison rules and regulations. Second, because prisons and jails have played a major part in maintaining order in society, their operation has become a massive industry. More than 1.25 million Americans are now behind bars and another 5 million are under some sort of correctional supervision.[1] When huge numbers of inmates are confined to small spaces, prisonization increases. A culture of manipulation, violence, and—at times—barbarism may ensue. This can wear down the professional fiber of correctional officers, especially those assigned to highly stressful tasks. As a result, prison personnel may experience more resentment and cynicism than their counterparts in other public agencies.[2,3]

Third, prison and jail operations have become too complicated and expensive. This can increase the opportunity for economic corruption, especially if the workers are not quite professional and supervision is lax. As the complexity of the operation and the amount of capital involved grow, corruption tends to increase. California, for example, spends $3.6 billion per year on prison operations, and five states have a corrections budget of over $1 billion.

Fourth, the demographics of confined inmates today may be more conducive to another kind of corruption: racial cruelty and racial oppression. Prison and jail populations do not proportionately represent the general population of Americans. This disparity has grown more pronounced in the last 30 years. While African American males make up less than 7 percent of the U.S. population, they compose almost half of prison and jail populations, while the majority of their officers are Caucasian.[4] This composition of institution populations and the disparity between

the racial distribution among inmates and staff may give rise to staff violence against minorities.[5]

Fifth, correctional management has undergone a series of changes more radical than those confronted by any other public institution. In the last 20 years alone, an avalanche of new rules emerged concerning overcrowding, judicial review, parole conditions, acquired immune deficiency syndrome (AIDS), gang members, drug usage, the aging of inmates, and the use of tobacco products by inmates and correctional officers. These rapid changes can cause serious managerial problems, complicating the maintenance of discipline inside a correctional facility. As a result, officials—generally more attached to security issues than social issues—may feel hesitant to enforce the new rules, which they may consider vague, confusing, politically motivated, and possibly dangerous. The new rules, furthermore, have prompted the hiring of unprecedented numbers of correctional officers, creating yet another difficulty: inadequacies in screening and training. All in all, a state of institutional uncertainty seems to engulf prison operations, which, ironically, must be navigated every day by the least experienced personnel.

Sixth, given the relatively low pay of correctional officers, especially of those at the lower levels, the potential gains from corrupt behavior may be too attractive to resist. Correctional officers may, over time, become dependent on inmates for the completion of some tasks or the smooth management of the tier. In return, they may overlook inmate infractions and supervise with some favoritism.[6] Also, young and inexperienced personnel especially can justify accepting graft as "a lucrative albeit illicit way to supplement one's income—usually without significant risk."[7]

DEFINITION OF PRISON CORRUPTION

From a sociological standpoint, corruption in prisons and jails may be considered the arbitrary use of power, because the term denotes the use of power to achieve a purpose other than that for

"Corruption among correctional workers occurs at all levels and in many different forms. In some cases it is very limited in scope, such as results from a relationship between one inmate and one staff member. For example, a correctional officer in Texas recently resigned from her position which she had held for 2½ years after being arrested for smuggling a pound of marijuana into a Federal correctional institution. The officer gave the drugs to an inmate in exchange for $1000. Other corruption cases involve more elaborate schemes and involve substantially more money. The Kansas Supreme Court recently overturned the conviction of a county jail administrator who took money from an inmate account (an account holding inmates' personal funds, abandoned inmate funds and jail telephone commission profits) and put it into an interest bearing bank account. The transferred money was used to buy equipment for the jail and pay jail commissary bills; it was not used for the personal benefit of the administrator. The high court ruled that the transfer was improper, as it violated the terms of the trust by which the county held the money for the inmates and the administrator, as custodian, was responsible. However, because the money was neither county nor state property, the charge of 'misuse of public funds' was inappropriate; the more appropriate charge would have been theft."[8]

which it is granted. An officer might hire or promote a less qualified worker because he or she is a relative of a superior or because that is the warden's desire; treat inmates preferentially because the inmates serve as house trusties; or deny civil rights privileges to a group of inmates because of their faith or religion.

From a legal standpoint, corruption can involve the use of oppression or the use of extralegal methods to suppress the will of others. An officer might write up inmates for violations they did not commit because of their race or ethnicity; beef up charges against inmates (or other officers) because they are viewed as troublemakers; or permit physical abuses to be inflicted upon inmates (or other officers) because they are gay or lesbian.

From a moral standpoint, corruption may be the failure of staff to demonstrate compassion or to keep a promise; public officials are morally obligated to care for the needs of those in their custody or under their supervision. An officer might ignore an inmate's cries for medical attention believing that his or her shift is understaffed; trick an inmate into giving information regarding illicit or illegal activities of other inmates with the promise of better treatment that then is not rendered; or, in a parole hearing, withhold helpful testimony regarding the good behavior of an inmate because of his or her refusal to respond to the officer's sexual advances.

From an economic standpoint, corruption in the correctional environment could mean the abusing of authority for personal gain; public workers are forbidden to take bribes, kickbacks, or any unauthorized payments for discharging regular duties. An officer might write up a procurement contract that fits a specific vendor who had promised to pay a kickback if selected; exploit inmates by threatening to "make their lives miserable" unless their families pay a bribe; bring or sell contraband to inmates; or use prison equipment (e.g., a truck or a tractor) without authorization.

Prison corruption, regardless of how it is defined, inevitably falls into one of the following three categories:

1. Acts of misfeasance. These are deviant acts that an official is supposed to know

how to do legally (through education, expertise, and/or training) but are willingly committed illegally for personal gain. Misfeasance is most likely to be committed by high-ranking officials in the prison hierarchy or by others associated with the correctional facility through a political or a professional appointment. (One example would be a member of the oversight board who stretches the limits of his or her discretion, allowing for indiscretions by contractors that would undermine the public interest yet benefit the board member personally.)

2. Acts of malfeasance. These are basically criminal acts or acts of misconduct committed by institution officials in violation of the criminal laws of the state and/or agency regulations. Such violations are usually committed by officials at the lower or the middle management levels. (Examples include theft, embezzlement, trafficking in contraband, extortion, official oppression, or the exploitation of inmates or their families for money, goods, or services.)[9]

3. Acts of nonfeasance. These acts constitute failures to act in accordance with one's administrative responsibilities. They are basically acts of omission or avoidance by an official. Acts of nonfeasance are committed across the board, regardless of people's positions in the agency's hierarchy. Because of their subtle nature, acts of nonfeasance may be more responsible for corrupting correctional officers than acts of misfeasance or malfeasance.[10] Two types of acts are common in this category: (1) selectively ignoring inmate violations of institutional rules, such as looking the other way when marijuana or other drugs are smuggled into the facility by inmates or visitors in return for payment; and (2) failing to report another employee involved in misconduct out of loyalty or as a repayment for a previous favor.[11]

PREVENTION OF MISCONDUCT

Official corruption cannot be prevented; it can only be minimized. Because workers are not born professional and cannot be counted upon to police themselves—especially when faced with acute moral dilemmas—direction, guidance, and leadership must be provided. Ideally, a manager should serve as a role model, an arbitrator, a disciplinarian, and the conscience for all workers and inmates. However, this may be more easily said than done.

To have any chance at success, management must first be credible. Senior staff must create a work environment that is conducive to honesty, fidelity, and obligation. Honesty is telling the truth at all times unless concealment is justified for a higher good. Fidelity is keeping all promises made to workers, inmates, and to any other group associated with the prison enterprise. If management claims that it treats the officers fairly, fairness must be provided at each step of the officers' career, including assignments, promotion, demotion, and discipline. Obligation is treating each rule, policy, or directive seriously, and not acting in bad faith. Therefore, if management declares that it will enforce a rule by which every officer is to be searched at a point of entry, everyone, including the warden, must be faithfully searched.

Ethical institution leaders must also be consistent, reasonable, and sympathetic to the needs of officers and inmates. Their behavior—in public as well as in private—must be above reproach and their managerial decisions borne by moral reasoning, regardless of who is to win or lose. The use of manipulation and hidden agendas must be shunned, because it can substantially add to the resentment and cynicism of prison personnel.

The influence of management leadership should also be methodically exercised rather than casually discharged in occasional remarks at commencement ceremonies or staff meetings. If correctional officers note that their leaders do not truly care, they stop caring themselves, leading them to pursue personal interests that may be much more profitable.

To minimize prison corruption, management should articulate its position on corruption and corrupters, and develop and implement an anti-corruption policy. Management should first and foremost prepare a policy statement outlining its position regarding corruption and corrupters and distribute it to every official. The message must be perfectly clear: professionalism counts, corruption will not be tolerated, and all employees will be held accountable for absolute integrity in everything they do. By publicizing such a policy statement, workers are put on notice that a concentrated effort is being aimed at raising the consciousness of workers about the depravity of corruption, that management supports high ethical conduct, that the agency will identify and deal with policy violators, and that no one is exempt from compliance with the agency's professional standards.

Several approaches can be used in the agency's policy statement. An ideal policy statement, however, should:

1. Articulate the activities generally accepted as being corrupt by prison or jail officials, including criminal acts such as theft, assault, forgery, bringing in contraband, maintaining an illegal sexual relationship with an inmate or another officer, and falsification of evidence (by a member of internal affairs).
2. Specify the investigatory procedures and penalties to be meted out in each of the previous categories.

As a matter of policy, investigatory procedures should be conducted by the internal affairs division or an independent office and should not undermine the constitutional rights of the accused (e.g., the presumption of innocence, due process, and easy access to legal defense). Penalties should be fair and reasonable and may include suspension (with or without pay), termination, reassignment, payment of a fine, or in more serious cases, a judicial sentence to be imposed during a court trial.

After identifying and publicizing the agency's anticorruption policy, management must establish an anticorruption action program. Wardens may be reluctant to pursue an overtly aggressive anticorruption program because of concern about reactions from the correctional officers union, workers' morale, and an unfair or a vindictive media response.

Prison administrators should design their anticorruption programs to fit their specific function, culture, and resources. Regardless of how such programs are designed, four strategies should be included. First, upgrade the quality of correctional personnel. A natural place to begin developing agency defenses against corruption is the recruitment office door. There are two significant obstacles to pursuing this endeavor: low entry-level pay for correctional officers, resulting in relaxed educational requirements; and a higher turnover rate than in other public agencies (the national turnover rate among correctional officers in 1995 was 12.7 percent, and 20.1 percent of these people quit prior to completing the probationary period).

Managers of correctional institutions who are intent on fighting corruption should make every effort to ensure that their hiring standards keep out high-risk applicants. Careful attention should be given to conducting background investigations and reference checks during the screening process. Advanced psychological testing should be utilized to check the character of those who make the final cut, and a mandatory interview by a hiring board should be a routine procedure prior to appointment.

Second, establish quality-based supervisory techniques. Traditional supervision in correctional facilities focused on quantitative standards, such as the classification of X inmates or the preparation of X meals, should be replaced with a quality-based supervisory system that focuses on how well the tasks are performed (as well as quantity). Supervisors should be trained that trivial policy violations can—and should—be overlooked, but serious transgressions must be reported and aggressively investigated—regardless of who the corrupters might be. In this respect, well-trained and quality-oriented supervisors are expected to possess the professional wisdom to know which is which—without being told.

At the outset of the training initiative, management may have to face substantial employee resentment, and perhaps sabotage by some, but the eventual outcome should be worth the investment.

Third, strengthen fiscal controls. Most acts of official corruption involve the illegal acquisition of money. An effective tool to check corruption in correctional institutions is the proper design and administration of preaudit and postaudit controls within the agency.

Internal auditors can determine if bidding procedures have been followed, expenditure ceilings observed, and vouchers issued only for objects of expenditure. Toward that end, the American Institute of Certified Public Accountants has recently produced three volumes of comprehensive accounting and auditing standards, and the responsibility of internal auditors has been expanded to include the investigation of all aspects of fraud, waste, and abuse.

But controls by internal auditors are obviously not foolproof. They may be deceived when superior officials collect checks for services that are not rendered, bribes are paid for negotiated contracts, overtime pay is collected by workers who are on vacation, travel expenses are absurdly padded, and institution equipment in good working condition is sold as scrap metal.

Further, in corrupt agencies, it is possible that the auditors themselves are on the take. In such cases, the challenging question would be "who then watches the watchdogs?" To establish accountability in correctional facilities, the prison director, the regional director, or the warden must ensure that internal auditors are honest, are experts in the latest advances in the accounting field, and are willing to check out every business transaction, regardless of how small or complex. Internal auditors must also be autonomous in their decisions, save only for scrutiny by state auditors and members of the General Accounting Office. Advanced methods of control now include the establishment of a telephone hotline where whistleblowers can pass on tips about misconduct they may observe. This brings about another important observation: The tendency of correctional agencies to accept and appreciate the practice of whistleblowing (rather than frantically fighting it) confirms their eagerness to cultivate a healthy ethical culture. In professional agencies, employees should be encouraged, rather than discouraged, to report misconduct, and managers should not be disturbed by such practices because they should have nothing to hide.

Fourth, emphasize true ethical training. Correctional institutions have recently been involved in serious training at all levels—basic, managerial, professional, executive, and so forth. The American Correctional Association has been responsible for determining the minimum amount of training for all prison and jail systems, and the Commission on Accreditation for Corrections has been offering far more for the accredited institutions. Some of the more popular courses offered have been in cultural diversity, sexual harassment, stress reduction, classification techniques, and job satisfaction. Ironically, one of the least popular courses has been about ethics in corrections. While ethical training can make certain individuals feel guilty, it can make more people feel confident about themselves, their values, and the benevolence of their careers.

Leaders of professional institutions should make every effort to increase ethical training, both in-house and at national and regional conferences. They should be visible and active. They should subscribe to ethics journals and learn the arts of moral reasoning. They should participate in panel discussions debating what constitutes right and wrong behaviors, what distinguishes rational from irrational decisions, and how to promote a healthy ethical culture in their institutions. They should not shy away from facing their subordinates, engaging them in question and answer sessions, and guiding them in the pursuit of true professionalism. Anything short of this would defeat the purpose of establishing an anticorruption program.

CONCLUSION

Both professionalism and corruption are important concepts in institution management. Professionalism is an ideal toward which correctional personnel should strive, and corruption is a shameful reality they should rid themselves of. As long as corrections is part of the mandate to "establish justice and ensure domestic tranquility," correctional managers must redeem justice by stamping out corruption.

NOTES

1. D. Gilliard and A. Beck, *Prisoners in 1997* (Washington, DC: Bureau of Justice Statistics, 1998).

2. M. Braswell et al., *Justice, Crime, and Ethics* (Cincinnati, OH: Anderson Publishing Company, 1984).

3. J.M. Pollock, *Ethics in Crime and Justice: Dilemmas and Decisions,* 2d ed. (Belmont, CA: Wadsworth Publishing Company, 1994).

4. Donziger, *The Real War on Crime: The Report of the National Criminal Justice Commission.*

5. Pollock, *Ethics in Crime and Justice: Dilemmas and Decisions,* 2d ed.

6. Pollock, *Ethics in Crime and Justice: Dilemmas and Decisions,* 2d ed.

7. Braswell et al., *Justice, Crime, and Ethics.*

8. Beaumont/Pt. Arthur Texas Channel 4 Homepage (msnbc.com-kjac tv); "Panel Reverses Conviction of Ex-Wyandotte County Jail Administrator," *The Kansas City Star,* 16 June, 1998.

9. Braswell et al., *Justice, Crime, and Ethics.*

10. Braswell et al., *Justice, Crime, and Ethics.*

11. Braswell et al., *Justice, Crime, and Ethics.*

CHAPTER 25

Mentoring: Developing Tomorrow's Leadership

J. Michael Quinlan

One of the greatest weaknesses of many organizations—both in and out of corrections—is the inability to fully harness the power of the people who work in them. Although it is easy to assume that the best candidates naturally will rise to the top and fit into the leadership roles that are crucial to organizational success, it does not always happen that way. Indeed, the identification and development of future mid- and upper-level managers is a critical function that often is left to chance and the passage of time. In today's demanding correctional environment, that is a poor way to handle such an important task. A better approach is mentoring—a proven tool to harness the talent of any organization.

There are, of course, many ways to identify and develop managerial talent. From the smallest jail to the largest prison system in the nation, every agency has its own methods. And in some respects, the exact methods are not as important as an organized, effective approach overall. But to ensure the maximum amount of talent is being developed, an explicit effort has to be made by existing managers at every level to provide new and lower-level personnel with developmental opportunities—opportunities that will eventually produce future leaders. Of course, any in-house management development program starts with the premises that employees want the opportunity to grow professionally and that most up-and-coming staff have adopted learning as a lifelong priority. The rewards of that learning process ought to be recognition and job satisfaction, as well as a realistic opportunity to advance in the organization. When basic employee abilities are coupled with a genuine motivation to learn (which should be discerned early in the developmental process), then the agency should be ready to seize the opportunity to further develop that employee.

In many cases, that development will involve mentoring—a process in which a more senior employee personally teaches and guides the professional development of a junior staff member, with the intent of preparing the latter employee for more responsible positions in the future. For the balance of this chapter, the term "mentor" will be used to refer to the senior person in the mentoring relationship, and "mentoree" will refer to the junior employee who is being mentored.

While the mentoring process is usually thought of as facilitating the flow of managerial talent upward, it is worth noting that it can have other benefits as well. Mentoring can improve internal communications within the organization. It can be used to facilitate diversity goals. And it can very clearly be used to enrich and broaden the creative career experience of the mentors themselves, as they interact with employees who have younger, fresher ideas about the organization and its work. Exhibit 25–1 lists some ways that correctional mentors change others.

Exhibit 25–1 How Correctional Mentors Change Others

1. Role modeling
2. Teaching how the institution really operates (i.e., the politics within the walls and fences)
3. Sharing experience about prison or jail operations (more than war stories, real-life experiences are most helpful when they are true)
4. Shaping values and establishing the expectation of personal integrity
5. Understanding the real importance of interpersonal relationships—that tasks get accomplished because of the cooperation of groups of people
6. Developing maturity and appropriate behaviors in social situations
7. Helping create respect for staff from other departments, individuals in external agencies, and men and women of all races and backgrounds
8. Encouraging openness of expression and learning the benefit of seeking viewpoints of others with different opinions
9. Creating the expectation that inmates are not an interruption to correctional workers' business—they are the business
10. Instilling the importance of helping others who will be learning the business in the future

INFORMAL MENTORING PROGRAMS

Mentoring opportunities may be unstructured or structured. Indeed, unstructured developmental and mentoring activities exist in most organizations. In many cases, they moved today's managers to where they are now. The most basic example of mentoring in the jail and prison setting is the widely seen pattern of assigning a new correctional officer to a training post alongside an experienced senior officer. This provides the new staff member with the opportunity to learn the duties of the post. But at the same it usually is

a period of acculturation and indoctrination—deliberate or not—into the way the organization works. The employee learns about not only the formal organization but also the informal organization that he or she will work in and interact with over the coming years. And knowing those rules early in the game can greatly smooth career progression.

But many agencies also benefit from pairing (in normal assignment patterns) high-potential employees who are beyond the entry level with more senior staff in more advanced or demanding job settings. These inadvertent mentorees, as it were, can ask questions, observe how problems are addressed, and learn some of the nuances of how the mentor interfaces with the organization and its culture. These learning situations may or may not involve a significant personal investment on the part of the mentor. The mentoree may, in fact, often learn more by "osmosis" than by direct tutelage. Further interest by the mentor in the mentoree's later career may or may not be a part of the picture.

A variant on this theme is the more conscious (but still organizationally informal) effort that some managers make to personally identify high-potential staff and to take them "under their wing" as mentorees. Personal nurturing and guidance are part of the intended structure of this relationship. In such cases, the mentor often continues as an informal resource for the mentoree throughout his or her career. Likewise, the mentor can benefit from the future support of the mentoree as his or her career develops further.

Both of the above processes often include the mentor providing informal counseling and information regarding future jobs and career progression. Advancement in an organization depends on not only knowledge about the formal organization—what the agency does openly—but also the elements of organizational life that are less openly discussed or done. Knowing the why and the how of an agency's or institution's operation is critical for advancement. Mentors who have that knowledge can shorten the learning curve for their mentorees in that important area.

In some instances, the mentor may be able or willing to influence the organization, helping the mentoree to advance to positions for which he or she is qualified. This, of course, depends on the mentor's role in the organization and his or her inclination to assist a particular mentoree.

These are, of course, methods that are highly dependent on the nature and quality of the senior person's own experience and work habits. They can produce good managers or they can seriously impair the career development of an otherwise good employee.

FORMAL MENTORING PROGRAMS

To counter the possible negatives of the informal processes, many organizations have developed formal programs that combine mentoring principles with a more structured approach. As a starting point for these efforts, a jail may provide self-development and cross-training materials that employees can use to learn more about other aspects of the organization. Actual cross-training assignments (either short- or long-term) can offer high-potential employees the chance to interact personally with the people and issues of other specialties within the institution. Management and other related training courses provided by the correctional organization can offer (in a more compact manner) much of the same information that a single mentor could convey to a mentoree in an individual workplace setting. Agency-sponsored leadership forums and seminars can be used to provide mentorees with first-hand exposure to higher-order management issues and to meet and interact with top administrators. And of course, formal mentoring programs, assigning volunteer mentorees to preidentified mentors, have been established by numerous organizations.

At the entry level, some jail and prison systems use a formal "peer mentor" program that systematically pairs up newer correctional officers with more senior officers—a more rigid version of the informal inservice training system described above. While the application of this concept varies from institution to institution, the basic principle is that the new officer knows he or she is supposed to be learning from the senior person, and conversely, the senior officer also understands that he or she is to act as a mentor.

Formal mentoring programs for managerial candidates are widely accepted now. In the federal civil service, for instance, upper-level administrators who are being considered for the senior executive service (SES) have a specifically identified SES mentor. This arrangement is coupled with targeted developmental tasks and training intended to mesh with the mentoree's background, strengths, and weaknesses in order to prepare him or her for higher positions in the organization.

Other formal programs of this type at the state and local level vary greatly in scope and type, but generally involve several common features.

- Paradoxically, the first common element is that the mentoring process necessarily will be very highly individualized. It will differ for each mentor and for each mentoree (even those with the same mentor).

- Mentorees must indicate some level of interest in the program and must make a commitment to participate in its structured aspects. If the organization is going to invest time and effort in the mentoree, it is only reasonable to demand a minimum level of motivation.

- Mentors should be sufficiently knowledgeable about the organization and strongly identify with it and its culture. The last thing the organization wants to do is to sanction a mentoring situation where the manager is passing on incorrect information and inculcating dysfunctional views in the mentoree.

- The organization needs some method of evaluating the program, whether it is mentor and mentoree surveys, regular progress reporting, or statistical measures of the career progress of mentorees over time. This latter category probably is the most difficult, because it is longitudinal, but it also may be the best measure of what the program really does for the organization and its employees.

- Both informal and formal mentoring systems should provide an opportunity for employees to make decisions. This may best be done in an area where the mentor is particularly strong. Even if there is a risk that the task may take longer or that the outcome may be less than ideal, delegation of tasks and decision making is a vital step in the development of a mentoree. Mentorees must be allowed to be active participants in new and challenging experiences if they are to completely develop and be prepared for the next step in their careers. This inevitably requires something that is hard for any bureaucracy to do: allowing employees to test their judgment—even allowing them to make small mistakes—in the interest of improving their overall judgment and professional perspective. Actually, providing this latitude is good for both the organization and the individual staff member. It lets the agency see how well the individual is progressing and identify his or her remaining weak areas. It also provides a solid basis for employees to develop self-confidence as they make correct decisions.
- Of course, whether the informal or formal approach is taken, accurate, timely performance appraisal is a critical element in the success of any mentoring system. Mentorees must be given feedback on their performance, including frank discussions with their mentor regarding their strengths and weaknesses. In instances where the mentor is not the immediate supervisor (which often is the case in formal mentoring programs), a method must be developed to include the supervisor at some point in these discussions.

Mentoring programs, whether informal or formal, are important for more than just filling vacant management slots. They provide the junior employee with a feeling of value—the agency is taking the time and effort to improve my skills,

make my workday more satisfying, help me prepare for more advanced responsibilities. Investing the time in mentoring employees shows that an organization values their past contributions, believes they can make even more valuable contributions in the future, and, most important perhaps, respects and values them as people.

KEY LEADERSHIP ELEMENTS

There are key elements of leadership that should be impressed on all mentorees, regardless of what level in the organization they are in.

- The importance of integrity and honesty. These cannot be taken for granted and should be emphasized repeatedly.
- The need for quality performance. High standards are the hallmark of a successful organization and every aspiring administrator must understand the need to insist on adhering to them in every facet of their work and that of their subordinates.
- The critical role of effective communications, both up and down the chain of command. Critical communication skills can be enhanced in the mentoring process as the mentoree learns how the organization works from the inside.
- The value of having the respect of others and of giving respect to staff, inmates, and others. Jail and prison staff trade every day in the currencies of respect and its companion, credibility. In some instances, their lives and the lives of others depend on respect and credibility.
- The importance of making good, commonsense decisions. Developing and honing the ability to make solid, logical decisions is probably the most crucial of all leadership qualities that a mentor should learn.

CONCLUSION

Throughout the mid-1990s there has been an increasing emphasis on mentoring, and one may be tempted to assess this current surge of interest as a fad. But in fact, mentoring has been a time-honored technique that has resulted in the development of many, if not most, of today's leaders—both those who work inside and those who work outside of the jail and prison environment. In a time when we need more highly professional jail and prison administrators and when the demands of the correctional environment are increasingly difficult, mentoring is an effective way of developing tomorrow's correctional leaders.

SUGGESTED READINGS

Collins, J., and J. Porras. 1994. *Built to last: Successful habits of visionary companies.* New York: HarperCollins Publishers.

Lombardo, M. et al. 1988. *The lessons of experience: How successful executives develop on the job.* Lexington, MA: Lexington Books.

Schein, E., ed. 1978. *Career dynamics: Matching individual and organizational needs.* Reading, MA: Addison-Wesley Publishing.

CHAPTER 26

Correctional Officers Today: The Changing Face of the Workforce

Peter M. Carlson

Today's diverse group of prison and jail correctional officers—the "law and order" personnel of the correctional world—is very different from that of correctional officers decades ago; those officers were usually Caucasian men. Who are today's correctional officers, and what do they do?

Correctional officers generally make up over 60 percent of the staff of a penal facility and are charged with directly supervising prisoners. Officers oversee and control inmate housing, common areas throughout the institution, many work areas, and the dining room. These security staffers also are assigned to prisoner transportation for outside medical care or transfer to another facility, and to perimeter security. Officers are responsible for supervising inmates, maintaining order and discipline, and serving as informal counselors and mentors for those who they govern. These basic functions are key to the successful management of inmates 24 hours a day, seven days a week.

Staff often begin their careers in correctional institutions as correctional officers. Many state systems and the Federal Bureau of Prisons hire nearly all staff into this position for a period of time and subsequently promote them to other de-

partments and jobs. Correctional officers, also known as guards or "hacks," work various shifts in the facilities.

Salaries for these security positions have greatly improved in the last decade, and annual starting pay now ranges from a low of $14,000 to nearly $32,000.[1] The national average annual starting salary is approximately $21,000. The custodial department is almost always organized in a military, hierarchical manner. The department head is often a captain with subordinate ranks of lieutenants, sergeants, and officers. In some states, security staff that choose to stay in the correctional officer position can earn above $40,000; lieutenants and captains can earn up to $60,000.

In the past, prisons were in rural areas, and security staff were usually hired from the local area. But the demographics of U.S. correctional employees has changed drastically over the last 20 years, a shift that has paralleled the transformation that has occurred in other workplaces. Figure 26–1 illustrates the overall rise in the percentages of non-Caucasian and women correctional officers since 1985, and Figure 26–2 shows the overall growth in the numbers of correctional officers since 1990.

As Figure 26–1 shows, the numbers of non-Caucasian and women correctional officers have grown in the last eight years. Male minority staff made up 29.9 percent of this group in 1990; by 1997, their proportion had expanded to 32.2 percent.

Opinions expressed in this chapter are those of the author and do not necessarily represent the opinions of the Federal Bureau of Prisons or the U.S. Department of Justice.

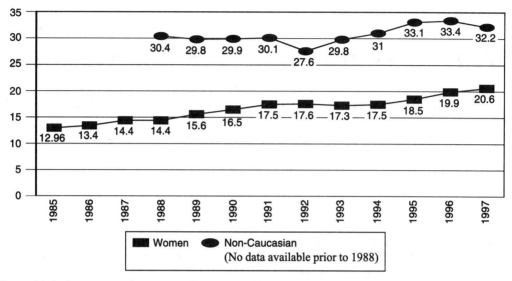

Figure 26–1 Percentage of Women and Non-Caucasian Correctional Officers on January 1 (1985–1997). *Source:* Reprinted with permission from C. Camp and G. Camp, *Corrections Yearbook 1997,* © 1997, Criminal Justice Institute, Inc.

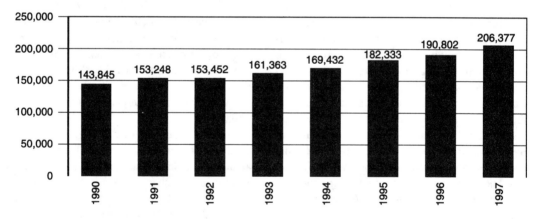

Figure 26–2 Total Correctional Officers on January 1 (1990–1997). *Source:* Reprinted with permission from C. Camp and G. Camp, *Corrections Yearbook 1997,* © 1997, Criminal Justice Institute, Inc.

As correctional officers became a more diverse group, the cohesiveness of this workforce seemed threatened. Many African American, Hispanic, and women staff reported that coworkers who were Caucasian men were very slow to accept them. Incidents of discrimination and racial abuse were reported by many. Some studies of the prison workforce found this nonacceptance to be rooted in a belief that non-Caucasians and women are too supportive of the prisoners and not trustworthy.[2] Change was indeed slow to be accepted.

CULTURAL DIVERSITY—A MANAGEMENT NECESSITY

Today, minorities and women are an integral part of the correctional workforce, as both correctional officers and senior managers. Administrators have tried to include people of all races and both genders and have become convinced that institutional management depends on the ability to relate to and communicate with jail or prison inmates. Positive control and accountability within a penal facility cannot be viewed as the ability to respond to negative behavior with force. A well-run institution is clearly one that has open communication between staff and prisoners—not tension.

Major riots and disturbances have often resulted from a lack of understanding and open communication. One of the most notorious rampages in correctional history was the riot at the New York State Correctional Facility in Attica, NY. The 1971 Attica prison revolt occurred because of many factors, but the commission that investigated the disturbance concluded that the predominantly Caucasian and rural correctional force could not understand or adequately relate to the African American and Puerto Rican inmates that were young and unwilling to accept the authoritarian attitude of the correctional staff.[3]

Attica and similar riots have provided some hard-learned insight into managing prisoners. Administrators have learned that fairness and reasonable treatment are critical factors in any well-operated prison or jail, and that staff members must be able to relate to the inmate population. The staff must "look like" the inmates; the ideal is to have the same proportions of Caucasians, African Americans, and Hispanics in staff and inmate ranks. This rule is a logical part of good institutional management. It makes sense to have a staff that can more easily relate to all inmates.

Additionally, women and minorities now make up a much larger share of new entrants into the American workforce. By the end of 1997, predictions about the shortage of workers in the year 2000 have already come true. With the major growth of inmate populations and the number of newly constructed correctional facilities, it has become critical for prisons and jails to adapt to the changes in the job market because they need more employees.

FEMALE CORRECTIONAL OFFICERS

Stereotyping of occupational roles by sex has deep roots in American culture. In every census year since 1900, most women have been concentrated in occupations that have historically been considered appropriate for women. Kanter has described this "sex-linked ethos" as specific occupational groupings being associated with one sex or the other.[4] The culture and ideologies surrounding the qualifications and pursuit of these employment roles tend to define both the qualified labor pool from which the occupations draw and the sought-after qualities and attributes of the people in that pool.

While the number of women in the general labor force has greatly expanded since World War II, women have not been fully assimilated into professional, technical, or management roles. This remains true despite the fact that women have performed extremely well in nearly all occupational areas.

On the "inside" of the criminal justice arena, the Joint Commission on Correctional Manpower and Training noted in 1969 that while women made up 40 percent of the general workforce, they accounted for only 12 percent of the correctional workforce. Women have been associated with prison work from its earliest days, but historically they have been employed for tasks associated with clerical duties, teaching roles, support services, or guarding female offenders. It was not until the 1970s that women correctional officers were placed in prisons with inmates who were men.[5]

While earlier data were not routinely compiled on a national basis, in 1985 approximately 13 percent of correctional officers in prisons were women (see Figure 26–1). In 1997, 12 years later, approximately 20 percent were women.[6] While this larger proportion is significant, it is still not as high as women's proportion in the American workforce in general. Correctional environments, like many other work settings, have long been the employment domain of Caucasian men.

The military has also demonstrated continuing bias against women. The U.S. armed forces have reluctantly mixed women into their ranks. This disparate treatment continues to this day with a general prohibition against women taking on combat roles.

Police rosters across the United States have reflected this same trend, and policemen's opposition to women officers has been widely documented. Since the hiring of the first sworn woman police officer in 1910, women have been selected by different employment standards than men and restricted to working with other women, children, and typewriters. The pace of change in policing has been dramatic since 1972, although many continue to believe that the sexual integration of the field has not kept up with changes in other occupations dominated by men.

WHY WOMEN ARE UNDERREPRESENTED

Explanations for the historical and contemporary employment bias in corrections cover a broad spectrum of arguments. It is clear that many men correctional staff have been displeased with the entry of women officers into their ranks. Many dispute the ability of women to maintain order and control in an adult men's prison environment. The conviction that prison tasks are "men's work" has been based in the belief that physical strength as well as bravery are requisites, and this belief presumes that women lack these qualities. Men have argued that the isolation and harsh working conditions of prison life are factors working against the entrance of women into corrections.[7] Others verbalize the concern that the use of female officers violates the right of privacy of offenders who are

men. Some believe that women create management problems by becoming romantically entangled with inmates or staff members.

Resistance to the employment of women as correctional officers goes beyond simple personal bias. This attitude is often embedded in the organizational structure and culture of the prison. As new employees are placed in the correctional environment, they must quickly accept the customs, traditions, values, and other criteria of conduct that are part of the institution's environment if they are to successfully assimilate into their new work culture.

Employees' expectations and internal belief systems often determine how much success they have at work. Kanter notes that both sexes behave differently in work organizations because men have more real power and greater promotional opportunity.[8] Individuals of both sexes, when placed in situations in which they are powerless and have limited promotion potential, respond by lowering their goals and develop differing patterns of behavior in comparison to those who see greater potential for opportunity and power. Sexual harassment, as defined by the victim, affects the workplace in very negative ways. (Harassing behavior can include swearing, touching, intimidation, or even inappropriate humor.) This type of conduct is often prevalent in work environments dominated by men and creates additional stress for women. In the prison and jail setting, men staff and inmates can present challenges even to the most competent women and establish an atmosphere that demeans and blocks women staff from achieving their potential. In its most favorable light, sexist and demeaning behavior creates an unpleasant work environment; at worst, such attitudes and behavior lead to high turnover rates and diminish the ranks of skilled women employees in the correctional facility.

Women in corrections report that even when they have the skills and commitment to the work, they are often at a major disadvantage. A glass ceiling, defined as an actual or perceived obstacle to organizational advancement for women or other minorities, is partially created by not including women employees in informal social circles, not providing mentoring assistance on the job, and holding women to a different standard of behavior. Paternalism or efforts to protect women often prevent them from working all posts in normal institution roster assignments; this places women at an experiential disadvantage and creates a competitive edge for others at the time of promotion consideration.

Numerous studies have reported great hostility and resistance from male staff when women have attempted to enter the correctional workforce as equals.[9] Criminal justice occupations have been often associated with machismo and masculinity, and the presence of women seems to throw doubt on this association. Some believe the jobs become devalued when women take them.

Researchers have found that women in law enforcement lack the aggressive social skills that men bring to the job. Women traditionally have had less experience with the aggressive behavior associated with organized sports and less experience with teamwork or asserting authority.[10] These skills have to be learned on the job and require new patterns of behavior and new body language, including facial expressions that project authority, not a pleasant demeanor or subservience.

Some men staff members fervently believe that women employees working as correctional officers jeopardize the safety of men officers by being more susceptible to rape. Men staff members believe this requires them to place themselves in danger by having to respond to such explosive situations.[11] This concern seems to confirm the belief that the security of the institution, and therefore men's safety, is placed at risk by the women's presence.

WOMEN'S PERFORMANCE AS CORRECTIONAL OFFICERS

Women in correctional uniform have performed very well in women's and men's facilities at all security levels. While women have had difficulty finding peer acceptance as correctional officers in prisons, they have adapted reasonably well to this work environment.

In the jail setting, studies have found mixed results. As predicted, women officers were perceived as being less effective in breaking up fighting inmates or controlling larger, more aggressive inmates. However, men staff members believe that women officers were very impressive in calming angry inmates and inmates who are mentally or emotionally disturbed.[12] Studies have found that inmates and men staff members have reacted positively to the presence of women personnel; men have controlled their language, acted more politely toward women officers, and exercised more care with their appearance.

Some evidence indicates that women working in male prisons conduct themselves differently as they perform the responsibilities of a correctional officer. Research has noted that some women adopt a more service-oriented demeanor than their male counterparts and take on a less confrontational style of dealing with offenders.[13] Many believe this style is an asset in the prison and jail setting.

A 1983 study of correctional officers in the California Department of Corrections found that men and women staff performed their jobs equally well. However, major differences were noted between the three job groups sampled: men officers, women officers, and men inmates. Both groups of men felt women were less effective in tasks requiring physical strength and in violent emergency situations. Women officers rated well in all other tasks evaluated, including supervisory performance evaluations, number of commendations and reprimands, and use of sick leave.[14] In general, women officers were found to have established a great deal of self-confidence on the job.

Women officers in the Federal Bureau of Prisons fared well in a more recent study.[15] Both studies of women correctional officers noted many reports of hostility from men staff and men inmates, and examples of sexual harassment of women staff. This study found no difference in job satisfaction between men and women officers.

Many men correctional officers in high-security U.S. penitentiaries expressed their surprise at how effective women officers have become at their jobs—particularly in the cellblocks. Men working in this environment highlight the women's ability to positively relate to men offenders; this skill becomes especially useful during tense situations, and many examples have been cited of women officers calming angry inmates. The majority of men staff, while initially opposed to hiring women officers in federal penitentiaries, changed their opinion after observing women in the job.[16]

Women have been successfully integrated into prisons and jails for men offenders in the last 20 years. While this public policy shift has not been easily accepted by the staff—mostly men—many institution administrators and line staff members believe women have helped increase the level of fairness and the quality of operations.

CONCLUSION

Equal employment opportunity and workplace diversity are important features of American society and institution administration. Correctional officers who are Caucasian men have had to adjust to the changing workforce. Many outstanding skills and abilities have been brought to the correctional environment by the new personnel, and institutional operations have benefited from this diversity. Minorities and women have become successful correctional officers, supervisors, and senior administrators in all areas of the American criminal justice system.

NOTES

1. C. Camp and G. Camp, *Corrections Yearbook 1997* (South Salem, NY: Criminal Justice Institute, Inc., 1997), 124–125.

2. J. Irwin, "The Changing Social Structure of the Men's Correctional Prison," in *Corrections and Punishment,* ed. D. Greenberg (Beverly Hills, CA: Sage Publications, 1977).

3. *Attica: The Official Report of the New York State Commission* (New York: Bantam Books, 1972).

4. R. Kanter, *Men and Women of the Corporation* (New York: Basic Books, 1977).

5. J. Pollock, *Sex and Supervision: Guarding Male and Female Inmates* (New York: Greenwood Press, 1986).

6. Camp and Camp, *The Corrections Yearbook,* 113.

7. C. Feinman, *Women in the Criminal Justice System* (New York: Praeger Publishing, 1986).

8. Kanter, *Men and Women of the Corporation.*

9. P. Carlson, "Assignment of Female Correctional Officers to United States Penitentiaries: Implementation in the Federal Bureau of Prisons" (DPA diss., University of Southern California, 1996), 12.

10. S. Martin, *Breaking and Entering: Policewomen on Patrol* (Berkeley, CA: University of California Press, 1980).

11. G. Ingram, "The Role of Women in Male Federal Correctional Institutions," in *Proceedings of the 110th Congress of Corrections* (San Diego, CA: American Correctional Association, 1981).

12. P. Kissel and J. Seidel, *The Management and Impact of Female Corrections Officers at Jail Facilities Housing Male Inmates* (Boulder, CO: National Institute of Corrections, 1980).

13. G. Alpert, "The Needs of the Judiciary and Misapplication of Social Research," *Criminology,* 3 November, 1984.

14. H. Holeman and B. Krepps-Hess, "Women Correctional Officers in the California Department of Corrections" (Sacramento, CA: January 1983, Research Unit, California Department of Corrections).

15. K. Wright and W. Saylor, "Male and Female Employees' Perceptions of Prison Work: Is There a Difference?" *Justice Quarterly* 8 (1991).

16. Carlson, "Assignment of Female Correctional Officers to United States Penitentiaries: Implementation in the Federal Bureau of Prisons," 162–163.

CHAPTER 27

Sexual Misconduct among Staff and Inmates

Andora Moss

The problem of sexual abuse of inmates by prison and jail staff has long concerned correctional administrators, but in the last decade the problem has become worse and gained greater attention from the public. It's one thing to say that offenders should be locked up for their misdeeds; it is another to say that inmates can be sexually abused while they are confined. It is clearly unacceptable to have correctional staff become inappropriately and personally involved with those in their care.

DEFINITION

Quite appropriately, legal definitions of sexual misconduct among staff and inmates and sexual harassment in the workplace overlap greatly in newly enacted state laws and policy. Title VII of the 1964 Civil Rights Act states that sexual harassment is a form of sex discrimination. Equal Employment Opportunity Commission policies state:

Unwelcome sexual advances, requests for sexual favors, and other verbal or physical conduct of a sexual nature constitute sexual harassment when (1) submission to such conduct is made

either explicitly or implicitly a term or condition of an individual's employment, (2) submission to, or rejection of such conduct by an individual is used as the basis of employment decisions affecting such individual, or (3) such conduct has the purpose or effect of unreasonably interfering with an individual's work performance or creating an intimidating, hostile, or offensive working environment.[1]

Though sexual harassment is clearly defined as sexual misconduct, the case and statutory law related to staff–inmate relationships acknowledges the additional factor of the abuse of power of persons in custody. Specifically, people in custody are not able to leave the presence of those who have authority over their day-to-day existence. Therefore, "welcomeness" is not an issue.

The inherent difference in power between staff and inmates has led many experts and legislators to take the position that there can be no consensual sex between staff and inmates. One policy regarding sexual misconduct of staff and inmates, developed under court order, defines sexual misconduct as "sexual behavior directed toward inmates, including sexual abuse, sexual assault, sexual harassment, physical conduct of a sexual nature, sexual obscenity, invasion of privacy, and conversations or correspondence of a romantic or intimate nature."[2(pp.2–3)] There exists

---

Opinions expressed in this chapter are those of the author and do not necessarily represent the opinions of the Federal Bureau of Prisons or the U.S. Department of Justice.

a range of definitions in state law and policy regarding sexual misconduct; for simplicity in this chapter, the term "sexual misconduct" will specifically refer to the relationships of staff and inmates, not the sexual involvement of staff with staff or inmate with inmate.

SCOPE OF THE ISSUE

There are several reasons why the prevalence of sexual misconduct in correctional settings is difficult to determine. First, data on investigations are usually documented in more general categories not specific to sexual misconduct, such as assault. Second, the degree to which sexual misconduct is reported may also parallel the historical underreporting of other forms of sexual assault. Because of fear of reprisal or fear that they will not be believed, or because relationships meet their needs in some ways, prisoners may not report sexual misconduct. Third, sexual misconduct is difficult to investigate, and investigative techniques that corroborate or add information beyond the word of the inmate are generally necessary to substantiate a claim. Even in states that have laws prohibiting sexual misconduct between staff and inmates, prosecution may not go forward if there is a lack of corroborating evidence.

The understanding of the frequency of sexual misconduct in institutions continues to grow with the enforcement of new laws and policies. Sexual harassment literature and experience caution that silence often speaks to the shame, pain, and lack of safety involved in "telling." Prison cultures breed silence, particularly if staff or inmates lack confidence that those reporting incidents will remain safe. In institutional settings, staff may feel they will be ostracized if they report a peer. The ingrained practice of silence among inmates and staff and the complexity of substantiating allegations limit the ability to define the prevalence of sexual harassment in correctional facilities, though there exists enough evidence through case studies that all institutional settings are vulnerable to incidents.

WHY NOW? CONTEMPORARY CORRECTIONAL MANAGEMENT RESPONDS TO SEXUAL MISCONDUCT

A careful reflection on the history of U.S. correctional institutions would yield many anecdotal and documented cases of staff and inmate sexual liaisons. The investigative files of all agencies would suggest that there have been a "few bad apples" among otherwise dedicated correctional staff. The evolution from general assumptions about sexual misconduct to current activities in law, policy, and management practice to define and combat staff–inmate sexual misconduct has occurred because of various factors both internal and external to the correctional environment.

Domestic Violence Awareness

In 1993, the first public education campaign against domestic violence was developed; publicizing the issue has produced ongoing and significant shifts in the attitudes of the public as well as law enforcement and criminal justice professionals about domestic violence. There are clear parallels between the growing awareness of domestic violence and the awareness of sexual misconduct, another form of abuse, within institutional settings.

Litigation in Women's Prisons

Just as very visible cases in the media highlighted domestic violence and brought the issue to the public, highly visible cases of sexual misconduct in women's prisons have spotlighted the issue in the 1990s. (A number of factors have contributed to the increase in this litigation, but that topic goes beyond the scope of this chapter.) The court orders and remedies in these cases have provided models of policy and practice that began to establish a correctional management framework for responding to an issue that impacts all institutions. The monetary awards resulting from individual inmate cases have also increased the concern of people, administrators, and advocates about prisoners' rights.

Though the highly publicized cases have been predominantly in women's prisons, sexual misconduct is not solely a women's prison issue. Sexual misconduct is a correctional concern for both men's and women's facilities, with documented cases involving all levels of staff of both genders.

GROWTH IN CORRECTIONS

According to a Department of Justice news release in January 1997, the prison population in this country grew from over 744,000 in midyear 1985 to over 1,630,000 in midyear 1996.[3] To the correctional practitioner, the reality of building new facilities, hiring large numbers of staff, and managing prisons during such extreme periods of growth has a tremendous impact on day-to-day institutional operations that has been somewhat difficult to document. However, several issues are especially important to understanding sexual misconduct within correctional facilities today.

- Premature promotions. With the growth of the offender population and prison operations, more supervisors have been needed to operate all aspects of prison facilities. Promotions have occurred sooner, with personnel spending far less time in positions along the way. Supervisors sometimes report that they are uncomfortable confronting sensitive issues such as sexual misconduct because they have worked as peers with the people they are supervising and were moved quickly to a supervisory position.
- Cultural collision within institutions. With the increase in the construction of correctional facilities, inmates are often far removed from their homes. The backgrounds of the staff and offenders may be very different. Also, the demographic profile of offender populations in some parts of the country has changed markedly. The Federal Bureau of Prisons reports that over 28 percent of its offenders are now foreign citizens. This cultural collision within the institution can often create difficulty in relationships among staff and offenders, both between and within groups. The diversity of staff continues to increase as well. Including more minorities and women in correctional staff rosters has sometimes resulted in communication problems and cultural clashes.
- Public's increased interest. With the growth of corrections, the budget required to meet the demands has skyrocketed to the point that most departments of corrections require a major portion of the taxpayer's dollar. Competing spending priorities include education, human services, and a myriad of local, state, and federal mandates. In the information age, corrections can be everybody's business, and there are many citizens who have a genuine interest in knowing the details of correctional practice in their communities. How resources are being allocated and the effectiveness of corrections are important to the public. Costly lawsuits combined with the general public's frustration with crime also contribute to an increased interest in corrections.
- Advocacy groups. Groups and individuals advocating for inmates' rights are particularly concerned that correctional leadership, law, and policy address abuse in institutional settings. In particular, the Women's Rights Project of the Human Rights Watch has focused attention on sexual misconduct in women's prisons.[4] Other national and state groups have served as watchdogs of prison officials. Some of these groups have also worked with officials from departments of corrections to develop remedies such as training inmates and staff to address sexual misconduct.
- Cross-gender supervision. When staff members of one sex supervise inmates of the opposite sex, it is called cross-gender supervision. The competing concerns of privacy for offenders and gender-neutral hiring prac-

tices have often collided. And the greater likelihood of staff and offenders engaging in sexual misconduct complicates staffing assignments (e.g., housing assignments and assignments of transportation officers). Court decisions in this area have been varied.[5] While Title VII of the Civil Rights Act of 1964 requires gender-neutral hiring, historically many women's prisons have had a much greater percentage of women as officers than they are currently employing. Likewise, women are gaining greater access to positions in men's institutions.

Case examples in state departments of corrections and the Federal Bureau of Prisons indicate that sexual misconduct is predominantly heterosexual. However, there are documented cases of same-sex misconduct as well. Though cross-gender supervision may affect the likelihood of sexual misconduct, it is important not to identify cross-gender supervision as the only reason sexual misconduct exists.

- Public policy. Public policy changes have sent ripples through correctional institutions. When the public demands a "get-tough" policy, then the "no frills prison" may need to be closely monitored for potential illegal trading of sex for prohibited items (e.g., cigarettes, cosmetics, electronics).
- Awareness of abuse of power. The media has publicized many examples of the abuse of authority and power by individuals charged to oversee, teach, or direct other individuals. Highly visible cases in the military, the academic community, churches, civic organizations, and the private and public sectors overall have raised the awareness of abuse of power in various settings.

DYNAMICS OF STAFF–INMATE SEXUAL MISCONDUCT

Highly publicized incidents of sexual misconduct have focused the attention of correctional administrators and those concerned with the criminal justice system on staff–inmate relations. There have been few studies of or publications about the dynamics of sexual misconduct. Many people wonder why staff do not understand the simple directive "Don't have sex with inmates." In fact, most staff do understand this directive and would never violate their professional duties. However, the boundaries between staff and inmate can become blurred. If, for example, staff members feel isolated or verbally abused themselves, then they may be vulnerable to overidentification with offenders. Similarly, prisoners do not leave their emotional needs or needs for the basic comforts of life in the courtroom. Whereas early training for clinical professionals such as psychologists, social workers, and clinical chaplains includes discussions of the critical boundaries between professionals and patients, training for correctional staff typically does not. Correctional staff are continually in close contact with those they supervise, but very few correctional training programs address the feelings and emotional dilemmas of officers or staff members when inmates become attached to or interested in them personally, or when the reverse is true. Some cases from the public record suggest that some correctional staff and inmates feel that they fall in love; some show that sex for favors may have been the primary motivation; and others are more coercive and violent. Each instance, however, is an abuse of power. Even cases in which staff member and offender enter into a willing relationship often involve abuse, particularly when the relationship ends.

Staff and inmate interactions must always be understood within the context of an environment that is a paramilitary structure with clear roles of custodian and inmate. If the culture of the institution does not support the objective reporting of and response to other nonsexual infractions, then the atmosphere for reporting staff sexual misconduct is greatly hampered. Correctional professionals should continue to examine the profile of prisoners in both men's and women's facilities along with staff profiles. For instance, understanding more about the effects of child-hood abuse and its impact on adult behavior pat-terns may be helpful in identifying ways to more effectively respond to day-to-day interactions between staff and inmates. There is growing evidence that male and female inmates have ex-perienced significant childhood abuse. Meda Chesney-Lind suggests that there are gender dif-ferences in the dynamics that follow an abused child into adulthood. She notes that girls are much more likely than boys to be victims of sexual abuse and that sexual abuse of girls often follows them into adulthood. This may suggest many women continue to be the "victim" as they enter institutions with more male inmates having a history of being the "aggressor." Strategies to address staff–offender relationships, particularly sexual misconduct, should consider these differ-ent dynamics.[6]

People often believe that sexual misconduct in prisons means only men officers with women inmates. But the cases of sexual misconduct have involved all levels of staff. Some prelimi-nary work has been done to develop a clinical profile of inmates and staff who become in-volved, but these samples are small. Case ex-amples used for training purposes demonstrate that even the staff members who might be thought least likely to become involved may sometimes cross the line. For example, a state deputy warden who had headed the depart-ment's internal affairs unit investigating sexual misconduct is now facing substantiated allega-tions for having inappropriate relations with an inmate.

MANAGEMENT RESPONSE

As correctional leaders throughout the coun-try continue to acknowledge the need to effec-tively address sexual misconduct, promising practices and management priorities have become more clear. Several remedies have emerged: state and federal law, agency policy, staff and offender training, objective investiga-tive techniques, effective inmate programs, and strong relations with the media and the commu-nity. Agency leadership must insist upon healthy institutional cultures that do not tolerate abuse. All allegations of sexual misconduct must be ap-propriately investigated. Staff may perceive this as an overreaction, and inmates who earnestly report inappropriate behavior may still face credibility problems because they are inmates. These challenges are complex and must be met with strong institution and agency leadership.

LAW AND POLICY

Many departments of corrections have ac-knowledged the need to develop policies that specifically name sexual misconduct as a viola-tion of the agency's professional code of con-duct. This is a clear shift away from policies with general language that, at best, makes vague allusions to sexual misconduct. Departmental policy may also give notice of separate criminal penalties for sexual misconduct when a state or jurisdiction has a law prohibiting that conduct. In November 1996, the National Women's Law Center (NWLC) published the results of a sur-vey of state laws on this issue: *Fifty State Survey of State Criminal Laws Prohibiting the Sexual Abuse of Prisoners*. The survey, which was up-dated in December 1997, found that 33 states, the District of Columbia, and the federal govern-ment had laws that prohibited staff from having sex with inmates or persons in custody.[7] This is a significant increase from 1992, when fewer than 10 states had such laws (then, attorneys in the Georgia class-action lawsuit *Cason v. Seckinger* did a similar survey). These laws vary widely in their definitions and sanctions. For instance, some laws implicitly and explicitly recognize consensual sexual relations between staff and inmates while many experts in the field specifi-cally refute the notion of "consent" in these rela-tionships. Brenda V. Smith, senior counsel at NWLC and author of sexual misconduct training materials, suggests that "good law," in order to succeed, in staff sexual misconduct requires ba-sic policy decisions to implement aggressive, visible enforcement of law and policy, including visible prosecutions.[8] There is a wide range of sanctions found in both laws regarding sexual misconduct of correctional staff and laws addressing sexual assault and sexual abuse in the community at large. On the federal level, the Civil Rights of Institutionalized Persons Act allows the federal government to initiate investigations when the U.S. Attorney has reason to believe the constitutional rights of institutionalized persons are being violated within state or federal institutions. Other federal statutes that provide for protection against staff sexual misconduct are (1) Title 18, U.S. Code, sections 2241 and 2246, which provide for criminal penalties.

In its 1996 publication *All Too Familiar: Sexual Abuse of Women in U.S. State Prisons,* Human Rights Watch digests these laws and the current practice related to the laws, with additional analysis of international human rights law. The development of law and policy regarding sexual misconduct has required a fine balance between the rights of inmates and the rights of staff. Concern for staff, often expressed by labor unions and administrators, against false allegations must be measured carefully with the reality that incidents of sexual misconduct do happen and corrections officials must take a strong management approach to the problem. Effective use of law and policy may provide all parties with critical structures and guidelines clarifying appropriate professional boundaries of staff and offenders. These structures will help institutions develop programs for training staff and for orientation and training of offenders.

TRAINING

Developing an understanding of agency policy and state and federal law through training is a fundamental management tool to introduce to new staff entering corrections. This training should center around events that create safe opportunities for discussion of professional roles and the anticipated dilemmas created in the correctional environment. A dynamic training approach should be based on the realities of institutional life for staff and offenders. This type of training not only sets a standard for the staff but helps them better understand the environment they are in and the personal commitment they must make to maintaining boundaries.

Beginning in October 1996, the National Institute of Corrections began a process of conducting focus groups in institutions that requested technical assistance in addressing the issues of sexual misconduct. As a part of the identification of training needs, staff and offenders in 12 institutions in all regions of the country have consistently acknowledged the need for training that honestly addresses the dilemmas related to the interaction of staff and offenders. Suggestions for effective training have included training designs that offer opportunities for small group discussion, role play, and case examples. The ability of the trainer to facilitate discussion and respond comfortably to sensitive questions from participants is critical. Credibility and concern on the part of the trainer for the topic area must be established in the beginning of the training experience and be demonstrated throughout the delivery of training.

OPERATIONAL AND MANAGEMENT PRACTICES

It is imperative that all correctional leaders understand the importance of maintaining work environments that value the morale of staff and the effective, humane treatment of offenders. For instance, if there is a staff shortage and staff must work too much overtime, they may be less able to maintain emotional boundaries. The structure of tasks and responsibilities can create an institutional environment that does not tolerate abuse. If these tasks are unclearly defined, poorly supervised, or outdated, then symptoms of poor inmate–staff relationships will likely appear. Rotation of staff assignments, awareness of facility design, careful training of investigators, clear reporting mechanisms, and strong relationships with volunteers and the community all promote a work environment where abuse is less probable.

RESPONSES OF STATE AND FEDERAL CORRECTIONAL AGENCIES

State and federal legislation regarding staff sexual misconduct involves a wide array of definitions and sanctions. Even so, correctional administrators have begun to emphasize zero tolerance for sexual misconduct. The National Institute of Corrections, for instance, has offered training to teams of administrators from federal, state, and local agencies.[9] These teams have developed agency action plans to implement or refine policy, law, and practice within their own jurisdictions. Some states without laws have studied states that have legislation and have started constructing them. Other states have expanded existing training or developed training and assessed operational practices in their facilities. Some states have increased dramatically the use of video cameras in institutions. Training events that reach commissioners of corrections, deputy commissioners, wardens, and correctional staff have focused on sexual misconduct of staff as a critical issue that demands their response. The issue has truly become a reality for correctional leaders.

CONCLUSION

Sexual misconduct among staff and inmates is an issue that has come to the forefront of agendas of correctional administrators and the criminal justice community within the last 10 years. Awareness of sexual misconduct has increased because of factors inside and outside the correctional environment. The relationships of correctional personnel on the front line with prisoners often create challenges for staff and offenders alike. An understanding of the importance of professional boundaries and the role of correctional staff in an often emotion-filled environment requires an understanding of inmate dynamics as well. An institutional culture is created and maintained by the example of leaders throughout the institution and the policies and practices adhered to daily.

State and federal laws provide a structural framework with consequences for inappropriate behavior. It is critical to the reputation of all justice agencies and important for the mission of corrections that the issue of sexual misconduct be openly discussed with staff and inmates, and that everyone understand and support the consequences of this behavior.

NOTES

1. M. Eskenazi and D. Gellen, *Sexual Harassment: Know Your Rights* (New York: Carol & Graf Publishers, Inc., 1992), 63.
2. Georgia Department of Corrections, *Standard Operating Procedure: Investigations of Allegations of Sexual Contact, Sexual Abuse and Sexual Harassment* (1995), 2–3.
3. U.S. Department of Justice, *Nation's Jail and Prison Incarceration Rate Almost Doubled during Last Decade*, Advance for Press Release, January 19, 1997, 1.
4. Human Rights Watch, Women's Rights Project, *All Too Familiar: Sexual Abuse of Women in U.S. State Prisons* (New York: Human Rights Watch, 1996), 1–15.
5. G. DeLand, "Cross-Gender Searches and Supervision: A Clash Between Female Employment Rights and Prisoner Privacy Interests," *Corrections Managers' Report* 2, no. 1 (1996): 1, 2.
6. M. Chesney-Lind, *The Female Offender* (Beverly Hills, CA: Sage Publications, 1997), 153.
7. B. Smith, *Fifty State Survey of State Criminal Laws Prohibiting Sexual Abuse of Prisoners* (Washington, DC: National Women's Law Center, 1996).
8. B. Smith, *The Making of a Good Law* (Washington, DC: National Institute of Corrections), 1.
9. U.S. Department of Justice, National Institute of Corrections, *NIC Service Plan for Fiscal Year 1998: Training, Technical Assistance, Information Services* (Washington, DC: National Institute of Corrections Service Plan, 1997), 9.

PART VI

Inmate Management Issues

The supervision of inmates and the operation of prison and jail facilities are difficult tasks even on the best days. Consider the target population or clientele: hundreds, maybe thousands, of men or women convicted of violating laws, deemed to represent too much of a threat to the public to be allowed to remain free, and placed in a closed penal environment where they are expected to conduct their lives among others who may have always solved problems violently or may believe other people are merely objects to be manipulated for their personal aggrandizement. Managing well-behaved inmates can be difficult; overseeing aggressive inmates who act violently is a tremendous challenge.

Dealing with prison and street gangs, managing racial violence, controlling sexual predators, cooking three good meals each day, offering satisfactory health care, preventing escapes, caring for geriatric prisoners with Alzheimer's disease, housing those sentenced to death, and protecting weak offenders are some of the responsibilities faced by institution staff every hour of every day. The issues and concerns presented by a population of incarcerated criminals are immense and unending.

Successful prison and jail management begins with the senior institution leaders recognizing that the staff who work with the inmate population every day are key to the establishment and maintenance of a professional institution environment. The management of prisoners, or for

that matter, any enterprise, is really about the positive and effective management of personnel. This premise is critical to understanding institutional operations.

Management of an inmate population requires that staff have the ability and knowledge to identify and work with a clientele that presents widely varying challenges. Correctional personnel must be sensitive to many different types of special needs offenders who may have learning disabilities, or visual or auditory impairments; be retarded or very old; be too weak or too scared to enter the general population; or have an infectious disease and require total separation from inmates and staff. Women and juvenile offenders must be housed in separate facilities and generally require different programming and care. The concept of "one size fits all" simply does not suffice in today's penal environment.

Part VI will address many of the issues faced by correctional leaders today. After a review of the types of inmates entering prisons and jails, various management programs that are deemed necessary to proactively operate an institution are presented in each chapter. Significant issues addressed by chapters include the need for a comprehensive discipline and control system, ways to work with various types of special needs offenders, the importance of a good inmate classification system, the need for ultrahigh security to protect staff and inmates from predatory prisoners, and the management benefit of having an inmate grievance system.

This part presents an overview of many basic correctional programs that are important aspects of working with those who are confined behind the walls and fences of U.S. correctional institutions.

LEARNING OBJECTIVES

After studying this section, you should be able to answer the following questions:

1. Why do critics refer to the burgeoning number of U.S. prisons and jails as a form of industry?
2. How has the type of offender being incarcerated changed in recent years?
3. What is the meaning of the term "special needs offender"?
4. Why is an effective inmate control and discipline system important?
5. Is there a true need for protective custody status in the correctional environment?
6. Why are prison gangs and security threat groups such a concern in the institutional setting?
7. Why are prisoners sentenced to death an unusual management problem for penal administrators?
8. Are administrative-maximum penitentiaries really necessary to effectively control inmates?
9. Why is an effective classification system an important part of a jail's or prison's security program?
10. Why are inmate grievance systems necessary?
11. Institution visiting programs are often a way that narcotics are introduced into the correctional setting. Should facility managers permit open visiting settings or utilize highly controlled visiting booths with no personal contact?

DISCUSSION/REVIEW QUESTIONS

1. How are today's inmates different from inmates confined 25 years ago?
2. What are three aspects of a good inmate discipline program?
3. What aspects of managing special needs offenders require special funding or unusual staffing resources?
4. What is "protective custody," and how do correctional facilities determine whether to assign a prisoner this status?
5. How do gangs in the prison or jail setting differ from those in the community?
6. What makes a sex offender program in an institution effective?
7. What are the ethical dilemmas associated with the administration of the death penalty?
8. Have authorities found a high rate of mental health problems in inmates confined in administrative-maximum prisons or in control units?
9. Why is inmate classification referred to as the cornerstone of corrections?
10. What are the benefits and drawbacks of confinement in a prison boot camp?
11. Why are conjugal visits so controversial?

CHAPTER 28

Corrections Countdown: Prisoners at the Cusp of the 21st Century

Jess Maghan

For the second consecutive decade, the United States is experiencing a deliberate and dramatic shift to using incarceration as the primary mode of dealing with lawbreakers. In January 1997, the Bureau of Justice Statistics announced that the incarceration rate in federal and state prisons and in local jails of the United States had almost doubled during the past decade alone. Between year-end 1985 and midyear 1996, the incarcerated population grew from about 744,000 to about about 1,631,000, an average growth rate of 7.8 percent per year.[1]

During this same period, the federal prison population increased by an average of 9.5 percent, state prisons by 8.1 percent, and jails by 6.9 percent.[2] The United States now incarcerates, at a per capita rate, more of our own citizens than any other country in the world; this is our legacy at the cusp of the twenty-first century. It is not surprising, therefore, that the Norwegian criminologist Nils Christie warned of rapidly approaching Western-style gulags as a form of industry.[3] Table 28–1 offers detailed information about the correctional population in recent years.

A matter of further concern is the racial component of these incarceration rates. The average percentage of nonwhite inmates in state adult correctional agencies rose by more than 2 percentage points in 1990, up from 46.8 percent to 49.1 percent. This percentage has since grown steadily over time, the average reached 50.7 percent in 1993 and approached 52 percent in 1996.[4] When interrupted time-series analysis is applied to these data, the levels after 1989 are significantly different at the $p < .01$ probability level. This analysis highlights the time frame and racial divide embodied in increased crack cocaine convictions. Projections by government and private sector researchers indicate that the numbers of minorities in the prison population will continue to grow in the future (see Figure 28–1).

Recidivism, a dilemma that continues to evade innovative efforts to stop it, has become a primary factor in incarceration rates. Recidivism has been characterized as a built-in feature of the criminal justice system: "Be it either offenders returning with past custodial sentences or while still on parole, the facts indicate that correctional services are increasingly admitting, processing, and managing past clients of the system."[5(p.3)] Conditional release returns in Canadian prisons have doubled in the past 20 years, and close to 25 percent of all admissions to prisons in Canada and the United States are returns to custody following the technical breach of release conditions.[6] For correctional administrators, overcrowding represents a barrier to meeting their professional mandates and to serving the public by processing and protecting inmates as stipulated by the courts.

TRENDS

Incarceration trends amplify the prison system's social and legal complexities. The

Table 28–1   Population of State or Federal Prisons or in Local Jails, 1985 and 1990–96

Year	Total Inmates in Custody	Prisoners in Custody Federal	Prisoners in Custody State	Inmates Held in Local Jails	Incarceration Rate
1985	744,208	35,781	451,812	256,615	313
1990	1,148,702	58,838	684,544	405,320	461
1991	1,219,014	63,930	728,605	426,479	483
1992	1,295,150	72,071	778,495	444,584	508
1993	1,369,185	80,815	828,566	459,804	531
1994	1,476,621	85,500	904,647	486,474	567
1995					
June 30	1,561,836	89,334	965,458	507,044	594
December 31	—	89,538	989,007	—	—
1996					
June 30	1,630,940	93,167	1,019,281	518,492	615
Percent change					
6/30/95–6/30/96	4.4%	4.3%	5.6%	2.3%	
Annual average increase					
12/31/85–6/30/96	7.8%	9.5%	8.1%	6.9%	
12/31/90–6/30/96	6.6%	8.7%	7.5%	4.6%	

Note: Jail counts are for midyear (June 30). Counts for 1994–96 exclude persons who were supervised outside of a jail facility.

State and federal prisoner counts for 1985 and 1990–94 are for December 31.

A dash indicates that information was not available.

The incarceration rate is the total number of persons in custody per 100,000 residents on July 1 of each reference year.

Source: Data from Bureau of Justice Statistics, 1997, NCJ-162843.

swift growth of the prison population is a result of many factors, including the nation's crime level, sentencing laws, and law enforcement policies (e.g., crack cocaine and related drug offense penalties). The primary factor producing these increases is the enactment of mandatory sentencing legislation in all 50 states, with Congress deeming incarceration the predominant approach to deter potential offenders and incapacitate convicted criminals, especially in "get tough" mandatory minimum sentences for repeat offenders. The very existence of *Overcrowded Times,* published as a compendium on crowding issues, indicates that there is an inordinate number of prisoners living in overcrowded conditions.[7] Concomitantly, the annual operating costs of incarceration at the state and federal level have swelled from $3.1 billion in fiscal year 1980 to about $17.7 billion in fiscal year 1994.

The dramatic reemergence of the private, for-profit incarceration industry has helped increase capacity. The private prison business has become one of the most rapidly growing new industries in the United States. While a wide range of problems associated with correctional privatization exists, new public–private partnerships are emerging.

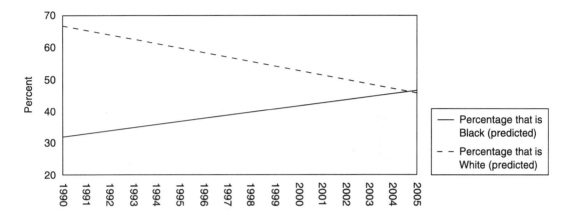

Figure 28–1 Projected Racial Profile: Federal Prisoners through 2005. *Note:* Least squares regression was applied to existing 1990s data on the racial breakdown in federal prisons in the Bureau of Justice Statistics, *Sourcebook of Criminal Justice Statistics—1995*, p. 574. The Black population percentage is growing, on average, at a rate of 1.16 percent per year; the White population percentage is falling at a rate of 1.31 percent per year. The graphical representation of the predicted values suggests that these statistically significant linear trends will intersect by the year 2005. *Source:* Data from *Sourcebook of Criminal Justice Statistics-1995*, Bureau of Justice Statistics.

INSTITUTIONAL IMPLICATIONS

Correctional agencies have minimal control over incarceration rates. As noncompetitive government agencies, correctional institutions do not vie for clients. Reporting in their respective jurisdictions to the executive branch of the government, and functioning downstream from other components of the criminal justice system, public sector jails and prisons are essentially residual agencies.

For many reasons, violence is on the rise in the nation's correctional facilities. Palermo et al. describe prison overcrowding as a situation that "breeds criminality by contiguity."[8(p.183)] *The Corrections Compendium* presented the findings of a national survey of institutional violence, noting that inmate incidents and assaults on staff are "occurring on a daily basis with sporadic outbursts of violence on the part of individuals and organized gangs."[9] Figure 28–2 illustrates the recent increase in violence in prisons.

NEW GENERATION OF INMATES

Quite simply, today's prisons and jails are more dangerous because of the unpredictability of the inmate population, which is composed of a new and highly distilled group of inmates. This new generation of inmates is younger, uneducated (illiterate or subliterate), unemployed, unemployable, and, as previously noted, increasingly members of minority groups. This population is also more alienated, more violent, less afraid of punishment, and more difficult to manage. These inmates are more likely to be substance abuse offenders and drug addicts. They are less healthy both physically and emotionally. DiIulio has termed this new generation of inmates as "super predators."[10] They tend to

• Be young
• Be members of minority groups
• Be tattooed

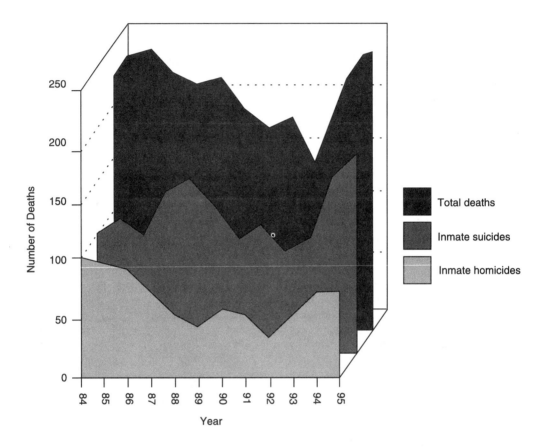

Figure 28–2 Prison Violence, 1984–1995. *Note:* "Inmates homicides" refers to inmates killed by the other inmates. "Total deaths" includes inmates killed by staff and staff killed by inmates. *Source:* Reprinted with permission from *Corrections Compendium,* Vol. 21, No. 6, © June 1996, CEGA Services.

- Not be healthy (10 years older than physical age)
- Have sexually transmitted diseases, the human immunodeficiency virus, or tuberculosis
- Have emotional/mental health problems
- Be emotional, spontaneous, and hedonistic
- Be violent predators
- Be gang affiliated
- Be children having children
- Not be married
- Be welfare clients
- Be products of single parent homes (usually headed by mothers)

PRISON GANGS

The infiltration of gangs into the prison environment is widespread. This gang culture has severely altered the traditional sense of security in correctional facilities, including juvenile facilities and adult women's prisons. Inmates are finding it harder to avoid gang involvement. These gangs are interracial networks organized around violence and criminal activity.

Antigang policies and procedures have moved to the forefront of institutional security priorities. Security officers refer to the prison gangs as security threat groups. The U.S. Bureau of Justice Assistance now provides information related to prison gangs, gang members, and prison gang activities through its Regional Information Sharing System. It also provides nationwide technical assistance and training to correctional agencies and allied law enforcement personnel. This network is beginning to reap success through the sharing of gang intelligence data and strategies. Connecticut and Michigan execute several of the more sophisticated strategies for gang control, including telephone call monitoring, canine teams, and increased collaboration with law enforcement agencies.

As Jacobs has noted, "Prison officials face two main problems—the threat of conflict among well-entrenched blacks, whites, and Hispanics and the threat of individual acts of predatory behavior by members of the strongest group against members of the weakest group."[11(p.82)] The new generation "convict code" is articulated along lines of racial and gang affiliation. A violence–threat paradigm is emerging that influences inmate–inmate and inmate–officer interactions. This situation is altering the viability

and style of traditional inmate–inmate and inmate–officer relations.

Correctional officers are also experiencing a growing sense of insecurity in their working environment. In this context, custodial control is not unlike the current initiatives to reinvent law enforcement through community policing programs that enable both officers and inmates to perceive the mutuality of their safety concerns. Interpersonal communication skills have become the lifeblood of effective correctional officer performance. This includes the capacity to understand the full range of inmate (verbal and nonverbal) modes of communication: the culture, the slang, the signals, the threat, and the fear that abounds. The fact that correctional officers are locked in and unarmed as they maintain daily custodial control is perceived only as an occupational responsibility. The simple fact that correctional officers cannot walk away from a confrontation or crisis within the institutional setting is often overlooked. The deployment of correctional officers, including the proper mix of new and seasoned officers, is of paramount importance. Figure 28–3 illus-

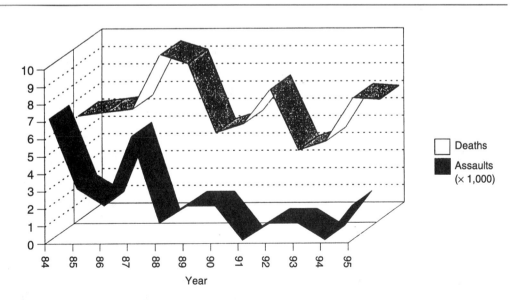

Figure 28–3   Violence against Staff at U.S. Institutions, 1984–1995. *Source:* Reprinted with permission from *Corrections Compendium,* Vol. 21, No. 6, © June 1996, CEGA Services.

trates the recent threats that correctional staff have faced.

CUSTODIAL CONTROL

Obviously, the environment that overcrowding has caused is considered unsafe. Accurate, aggressive, and highly flexible inmate classification is crucial to institutional safety and inmate welfare. According to the New York Department of Correctional Services guidelines, an inmate is classified as maximum security if he or she falls into one of the following categories:

- sophisticated level of crimes and criminal history
- pattern of impulsive, serious violence
- pattern of serious, callous violence
- history of violence against authority
- history of vicious, serious violence
- history of arson
- history of sex crimes
- group gang membership
- history of moving between cities and states
- history of aggressive homosexuality
- history of suicide attempts
- history of psychological instability[12]

These categories are generic and meet most state and federal prison parameters for maximum security classification.

MAXI-MAXI PRISONS

In the 1980s, several states determined that they needed prisons or units with super security. Consequently, "maxi-maxi" prisons have been constructed.

For budgetary reasons, most of these institutions were created by renovating existing prisons that did not have the architectural advantage of a prison designed for this purpose such as the U.S. penitentiaries in Marion, IL, and Florence, CO. On the other hand, new ultrasecure architectural models are also emerging. The trend is moving toward higher security with much more sophisticated technology and operating procedures. Despite security-conscious architecture and secure operating procedures, a great deal of violence occurs inside maximum security prisons in the United States. This is hardly surprising given the violent proclivities of offenders who are forced to live together in these crowded, restrictive conditions.

THE PHYSICAL PLANT

An aggressive retrofitting-construction industry that provides inflated sprung structures, tents, and trailers has emerged in response to the needs of the overcrowded prison market. Most of these structures meet only minimum standards for basic infrastructure security. These include retrofitted traditional security cellblocks changed into open dormitory housing. In some cases, these changes in physical plant usage obscure the appropriate security classification rationale for medium and maximum security risk inmates. Some correctional agencies are resorting to a wide range of jerry-built solutions (e.g., janitor closets converted to cells, and gymnasiums, public areas of cellblocks, and day rooms converted into dormitory housing). Overcrowding has also resulted in the redeployment and use of structures not designed to be prisons (e.g., hospitals, schools, and staff correctional academies). Efforts to accommodate overcrowding have also included the conversion of river barges, ferryboats, casino boats, and U.S. Coast Guard and Navy boats for use as correctional institutions.

WORKFORCE IMPLICATIONS

The deployment of the correctional officer workforce also has been directly affected by overcrowding. Traditional two-officer duty-post assignments are being altered to one-officer posts. Aggregate duty-post assignments are concentrated in these new congregate housing areas. Towers are being closed and new video surveillance and other security technology is being introduced to augment or replace archaic staffing models. While this new technology represents important innovations, it also precipitates a precarious process when it causes staff reductions in crucial support service areas. It is in these places—mess halls, corridors, chapels, recreation areas, classrooms, clinics and hospitals, transportation vans, shops, and work details—where violence has always been most prevalent. Research and documentation of current institutional violence indicate that incidents are more frequent, more violent, more severe, and more planned than previous violence in the last 50 years.[13]

ENVIRONMENTAL HEALTH

In the past, the occupational tools of the correctional officer consisted of keys, a belt, a flashlight, and a body alarm. Today, his or her occupational tools also include rubber gloves, plastic cuffs, and a CPR (cardiopulmonary resusitation) -lateral mask. The recurrence of tuberculosis and other contagious airborne diseases has made people think more about proper ventilation and sanitation in crowded quarters, including occupational health concerns regarding blood pathogens and hepatitis. These concerns have drawn attention to health risks associated with custody situations in closed holding cell areas and transportation vans.

Overcrowding also has increased the likelihood of enforced overtime duty for correctional officers. Excessive overtime or shift rotation necessitated by overtime potentially strains the physical and psychological well-being of staff and results in overindulgence in smoking and alcohol, poor diet, and the failure to exercise. Correctional officer divorce and suicide rates are inordinately high.[14] These situations easily can lead to a contagious pattern of deep cynicism.

PATTERNS OF INMATE VIOLENCE

Inmates define themselves, and are defined by, prison officials in terms of age, race, dangerousness, gang affiliation, and past incidents of institutional violence. Architecture, technology,

staffing, training, security, and operating procedures are geared toward preventing violence and, if that fails, toward identifying, punishing, and further incapacitating dangerous inmates. As previously noted, the areas of an institution prone to violence require custodial oversight. Inmate violence is multidimensional. It involves inmate-on-inmate attacks (including rape) and group conflict. Group conflict can erupt into large-scale incidents (intergang or interracial), or it can manifest itself in individual acts of violence by members of one group against members of another over an extended period of time. Idleness, found in most congregate institutional settings, contributes to acts of institutional violence.

The results of a study by Woolredge suggest that inmates who spend more time each week watching television are more likely to commit property crimes and to be victims of personal crimes: television watching is usually less directly supervised than "other forms of recreation."[15] Woolredge also found that inmates who do not receive regular visitors are significantly more likely to commit property crimes. Policies for reducing inmate victimization require a knowledge of inmates and their lifestyles (preinstitutional and institutional), which can influence their likelihood of both committing crime and being victimized during incarceration.

A PROBLEM STATED WELL IS A PROBLEM SOLVED

Unfortunately, many state and local correctional agencies have eliminated full-time internal operational planning and research functions. A viable research function guides an agency in examining both standard and nonstandard questions concerning operational integrity and effectiveness: What pressure does the larger criminal justice system place on corrections? What are the correctional policy variables over which public officials have some leverage? What goals underlie the competing theories of corrections? What are the common tensions and pressures affecting all states that make prisons today particularly vulnerable to violence? Do shared problems (such as the aforementioned gang oversight resources) point to shared, or at least generalizable, solutions?

These questions assist in identifying the potential general causes of, and solutions to, institutional violence. A standard set of variables and questions has emerged to help maintain effective custodial operations and control.

- Overcrowding. How have changes in sentencing practices changed populations? Are there demographic changes that make control of overcrowded prisons even more difficult?
- Idleness. What are the opportunities for inmates to occupy themselves (e.g., recreation, education, work) while incarcerated?
- Presence/absence of incentives for good behavior. How is order maintained? Does the prison management have a range of incentives to offer inmates? Can the management maintain control by adjusting those incentives?
- Inmate security. Do the inmates (and staff) feel reasonably safe and protected within the system? Can the management ensure the safety of those who feel threatened and minimize the opportunities for violence? Are inmates properly classified?
- Facility security. Are staffing levels adequate to maintain communication and backup? Is an emergency response plan in place? Are prison security procedures observed?

CONCLUSION

The fastest-growing segment of most state budgets is corrections. For the third consecutive year, corrections received more new state dollars than higher education. The racial composition of the U.S. prison population points to deep social problems, which correctional agencies increasingly are being asked to solve. Across the nation, state and federal penitentiaries exist as urban bubbles where city problems are custodially contained. If the city that feeds the prison has gangs on its streets, the prison has gangs on its blocks. If there is rampant drug use, drug dealing, and violence on the outside, these activities will also exist on the inside. Maintaining custody, security, and control in a humane and safe manner is becoming more difficult.

The magnitude of incarceration in the United States today casts a shadow on our larger social infrastructure. This situation raises important questions about the purpose and scope of incarceration: questions that can be answered only by social programs and other resources outside of prisons. The current trend is toward higher security with more sophisticated technology and procedures.[16] Current philosophies and techniques of unit management, direct supervision, and related operational methods for delivering services to inmates will assume even greater industrial proportion. As long as incarceration remains the primary mode of dealing with offenders, U.S. correctional agencies (federal, state, and local) will continue to do what they do best: provide care, custody, and control.

NOTES

1. Bureau of Justice Statistics, *Prison and Jail Inmates at Midyear 1996*, NCJ-162843 (Washington, DC: U.S. Department of Justice, 1997), 1–9.

2. Bureau of Justice Statistics, *Prison and Jail Inmates at Midyear 1996*, 2.

3. N. Christie, *Crime Control as Industry: Towards Gulags, Western Style?* (New York: Routledge, 1993).

4. G. Camp and C. Camp, *Criminal Justice Yearbook 1996* (South Salem, NY: Criminal Justice Institute, Inc., 1996), 8–9.

5. J. Austin, "Parole Outcome in California: The Consequences of Determinate Sentencing," *NCCD Journal* 3 (1989), 3.

6. A. Amoretti and P. Landreville, "Recycling Offenders: Reincarceration Trends in Quebec Federal Penitentiaries," *Critical Criminology, an International Journal* 7, no. 4 (1996).

7. M. Tonry, *Overcrowded Times* (New York: Edna McConnell Clark Foundation).

8. G. Palermo et al., "Death by Inmate: Multiple Murder in a Maximum Security Prison," *International Journal of Offender Therapy and Comparative Criminology* 40, no. 3 (1996): 181–191.

9. "Survey Summary: Violence on the Rise in U.S. Prisons," *Corrections Compendium* 21, no. 6 (1996).

10. J. DiIulio, "The Question of Black Crime," *Public Interest* 117 (1994): 3–32.

11. J. Jacobs, "The Limits of Racial Integration," *New Perspective on Prison and Imprisonment* (Ithaca, NY: Cornell University Press, 1983), 11.

12. New York Department of Correctional Services, *Security Classification Manual* 21 (New York Department of Correctional Services, 1988).

13. M. Silberman, *A World of Violence: Corrections in America* (Belmont, CA: Wadsworth Publishing, 1995).

14. J. Kamerman, "Correctional Officer Suicide," *The Keepers' Voice* 16, no. 3 (1996): 7–8.

15. J. Woolredge, "Inmate Crime and Victimization in a Southwestern Correctional Facility," *Journal of Criminal Justice* 22, no. 4 (1994): 367–381.

16. P. Carlson, "Correctional Trends for the Twenty-First Century: Our Future behind the Walls and Wire," *The Keepers' Voice* 17, no. 1 (1996): 5–8.

CHAPTER 29

Inmate Disciplinary Procedures

Clair A. Cripe

Social control of inmate behavior is critical to the successful governance of a correctional institution. To appropriately oversee inmates, positive discipline is necessary.

An inmate discipline policy establishes the institution program that regulates inmate conduct, attempting to keep that conduct within the limits of acceptable standards of institutional behavior. Good inmate behavior helps ensure the orderly and safe running of any prison or jail. A functional and well-implemented inmate disciplinary policy will instill respect for authority. It is hoped that the good behavior and respect for authority will persist after the offender's release.

THE IMPORTANCE OF INMATE DISCIPLINE

Those who have worked in prisons or jails accept without question that an inmate disciplinary process is essential. Those who are new to corrections may wonder why it is necessary to have additional discipline when these persons are already locked away from society. Perhaps those of us who work in corrections should ask ourselves a similar question, at least once in a while: What are we trying to achieve in our disciplinary procedures? Are the goals clear, and do our actions in disciplining inmates bring us closer to those goals?

Inmate discipline should achieve some agreed-upon goals: (1) making inmate conduct conform to a standard of behavior that ensures a safe, or-

derly, and respectful living environment; (2) instilling respect for authority; and (3) teaching values and respectful behavior (in a group of people who, by definition, have not displayed good values and behavior) that inmates may continue to use once transfered back to the outside community.

Society has adopted rules of behavior for its own protection and well-being. These rules are called criminal laws. They are enforced by law enforcement officers. From police officers' patrols and investigations, through prosecutions and criminal trials, into correctional facilities, which carry out the sentencing orders of the courts, the criminal justice system attempts to achieve the same kinds of goals that the inmate disciplinary system does within institutions: making behavior conform to accepted norms, protecting the safety and property of all, and instilling respect for authority.

Almost all people visiting a prison for the first time have the same reaction: "I am amazed at how much movement there is. At many times of the day, inmates appear to be moving in all directions. What is the purpose? How can all that activity be supervised and tolerated?" That reaction is nearly universal for two reasons.

1. Before we see (or work in) a real prison, our ideas have been formed by misleading sources: movies, television shows, images in textbooks, and media reports that portray prisons as closely regi-

mented, locked-down (i.e., with inmates in their cells all the time) facilities. Indeed, there *are* some locked-down, tightly regimented facilities, but there are only a few of them in the whole country.

2. Most corrections facilities emphasize free movement of inmates during daytime hours and evening activities. This free movement allows for various programs (work, education, self-improvement, recreation, and others) that are discussed by other authors in this book. In most administrators' minds and in those institutions where inmate conduct generally allows for it, inmate movement lessens tensions and normalizes day-to-day living, which benefit both inmates and staff.

But that movement of inmates—and the large variety of workplaces, programs, and activities—also increases the need for discipline. Most inmates appreciate the opportunity to join a variety of activities, and they adjust to the requirements of living in a prison environment. To assist those inmates in their good adjustment to prison life, and to help staff in their primary mission of maintaining a secure and safe institution, it is necessary to punish those who choose to break the rules. For those reasons, inmate disciplinary procedures are necessary.

ESSENTIALS OF INMATE DISCIPLINE

Keeping in mind the goals of disciplinary actions, there are three aspects of discipline in a good inmate disciplinary program.

1. There should be a written set of rules defining expected inmate behavior and the procedures for handling misconduct. Most institutions will have a misconduct code, a list of offenses that are subject to punishment in the prison or jail. An adjunct of that list of offenses should concern the types of sanctions that may be imposed for violations of the code.

2. The rules for discipline must be carefully and thoroughly communicated. First, all staff members must be taught how the inmate disciplinary program works, in general and specific terms. Every employee may be involved, as a witness or a reporting official or in some other capacity, in the disciplinary system. Second, inmates must be given the details of the system. They must know the kind of responsible behavior that is expected of them, and they should learn the penalties for misbehavior. All staff and inmates should be provided with a written statement of the policy and hear an oral presentation explaining how the policy works, with the opportunity to have their questions answered.

3. The disciplinary policy must clearly specify how inmates will be notified of suspected misconduct, how sanctions will be imposed, and what rights of appeal and rights to be heard they may have.

It is extremely important to have an inmate discipline program that is supported by written policy that specifies precise procedures. These procedures must be applied by staff who understand the importance of the disciplinary program and its procedural requirements. It is also important to apply the policy consistently to engender respect for the rules among staff as well as inmates.

It must be noted that informal handling of many kinds of misconduct occurs and is essential to the smooth running of any correctional system. Officers in correctional facilities are given authority to use their good judgment, and they will handle some misconduct informally. This does not mean that the inmate behavior is excused if it violates the rules. It means that there is official recognition that the goals of the disciplinary system (achieving a safer and more secure facility, and instilling respect for authority) may be achieved in many cases without processing misconduct through the official system.

Informal handling is usually used for less serious misconduct. For example, an inmate, especially one who has just arrived, may violate a rule without knowing that the conduct is considered misbehavior. In these cases, the officer's reaction is more instructional than punitive: Taking the inmate aside and explaining the proper way to do things communicates the expected behavior for the institution, and it also may open the way for good relations between the officer and the inmate. When to handle such an incident in this way will obviously be a matter of judgment: The officer must assess the likelihood that the inmate did not understand what was expected. The officer's assessment should always take into account other factors, such as the seriousness of the behavior, the sophistication level of the inmate, and the effect this handling of the incident will have on other inmates. Being "out of bounds," that is, in an unauthorized place at an unauthorized time, may be relatively innocent behavior for a naive new inmate, but it could be extremely serious behavior for a sophisticated inmate. If the misbehavior is related to an ongoing problem that must be cracked down on, informal resolution may not be acceptable, while at another time or in another part of the facility, it may be handled informally by the officer on the scene, with positive results.

As the behavior becomes more serious, or if an officer is not certain whether to have an informal discussion with the inmate or to write up charges (see Exhibit 29–1), the matter can be referred to a supervisor, who will make that decision. In addition to the officer on the scene, who may choose to refrain from filing certain charges, the correctional supervisor should be given authority to dispose of charges informally, rather than pursuing them in a formal disciplinary procedure. Again, these informal dispositions are to be used at the lower end of the spectrum (obviously, assaults, drug offenses, and escape attempts must be pursued with formal charges), but more than half of the offenses on the misconduct list can probably be handled informally in the right circumstances.

In a much more sensitive type of informal disposition, the staff member (officer or supervisor) is certain that the inmate has violated a rule, but a sanction is given without charges being filed. Sometimes, this is done by negotiating with the inmate (I will drop the charges, if you agree to do this). More often, and preferably, there are certain minor and agreed-upon sanctions that staff may use in these situations: extra work, restrictions in movement, or even changes in program (such as work assignments, recreation activities, or housing assignments). Taking account of the seriousness of the inmate's (current and past) behavior, these sanctions are imposed with a view to how they are used in each place and by each staff member. In other words, while there need not be a written code for informal sanctioning, it is good to apply sanctions consistently. To that end, facility management and supervisory correctional staff must specify how informal sanctions may be used. Supervisors should check that the power given to staff to punish inmates informally is not abused. When power is abused, inmates lose all respect for authority.

There are benefits of informal resolutions of inmate misconduct. The most obvious is that they "unclutter" the disciplinary process, reserving the procedural hearings for the more serious offenses. Inmates will have greater respect for staff who handle matters fairly but informally.

APPEALS

Appeals have not been required by the courts as a necessary component of inmate discipline procedures. For the more serious levels of misconduct, an appeal system is common, by administrative policy. There may be one or two levels of appeal of disciplinary action: In some systems, this would be from the disciplinary hearing officer or committee to the warden. In agencies with regional organization, there may be a level of appeal to the regional office. And many agencies do allow appeal to the headquarters level.

Exhibit 29–1   Example of an Incident Report

BP-S288.052 **INCIDENT REPORT** CDFRM
MAY 1994
U.S. DEPARTMENT OF JUSTICE
FEDERAL BUREAU OF PRISONS

1. NAME OF INSTITUTION:
   United States Penitentiary
   Lompoc, California

PART I—INCIDENT REPORT

2. NAME OF INMATE	3. REGISTER NUMBER	4. DATE OF INCIDENT	5. TIME
███████████	77700-386	3/28/98	7:10p.m.

6. PLACE OF INCIDENT		7. ASSIGNMENT	8. UNIT
L Unit Entrance		Plumbing Shop	M Unit

9. INCIDENT	10. CODE
Fighting	201

11. DESCRIPTION OF INCIDENT (Date: **3/21/98** Time: **7:10 p.m.** Staff became aware of incident)
While standing at the entrance to L Unit, I heard a commotion on the left side of the door. As I turned, I observed inmate ███████████, #77700-386, strike inmate ███████████, #98765-432, with his closed right fist on the left side of the face. ███████████ stumbled slightly and then responded by punching ███████████ in the stomach and chest areas numerous times with both fists. I activated my body alarm. Staff responding to the alarm had to physically separate both inmates. ███████████ and ███████████ were examined by medical staff. ███████████ sustained three bruises to his abdomen and redness to his chest. ███████████ received a laceration on his left cheek that required three sutures to repair.

12. SIGNATURE OF REPORTING EMPLOYEE	DATE AND TIME	13. NAME AND TITLE
███████████	3/21/98 8:25 p.m.	(Printed) ███████████

14. INCIDENT REPORT DELIVERED TO ABOVE INMATE BY ███████████	15. DATE INCIDENT REPORT DELIVERED **March 21, 1998**	16. TIME INCIDENT REPORT DELIVERED **9:18 p.m.**

PART II—COMMITTEE ACTION

17. COMMENTS OF INMATE TO COMMITTEE REGARDING ABOVE INCIDENT
I only hit him after he hit me. I don't even know this guy. He said something to me when he went by my unit. I followed him and asked him what he said. I was only defending myself after he jumped me. It's wrong to give me this ticket. You know I'm no trouble maker. This guy started the fight. Yes, I hit him.

continues

Exhibit 29–1 continued

18. A. IT IS THE FINDING OF THE COMMITTEE THAT YOU: _____ COMMITTED THE FOLLOWING PROHIBITED ACT. _____ DID NOT COMMIT A PROHIBITED ACT.	B. _X X_ THE COMMITTEE IS REFERRING THE CHARGE(S) TO THE DHO FOR FURTHER HEARING C. _____ THE COMMITTEE ADVISED THE INMATE OF ITS FINDINGS AND OF THE RIGHT TO FILE AN APPEAL WITHIN 15 CALENDAR DAYS

19. COMMITTEE DECISION IS BASED ON THE FOLLOWING INFORMATION

20. COMMITTEE ACTION AND/OR RECOMMENDATION IF REFERRED TO DHO (CONTINGENT UPON DHO FINDING INMATE COMMITTED PROHIBITED ACT)

Based on the seriousness of the incident, the UDC is referring it to the DHO for disposition. ▇▇▇▇▇'s actions warrant greater sanctions than are available at the UDC level if the DHO finds he committed the prohibited act. If the DHO finds he committed the act, recommend 30 days DS, loss of 27 days GCT, and a disciplinary transfer.

21. DATE AND TIME OF ACTION **3/24/98 3:20 PM** (THE UDC CHAIRMAN'S SIGNATURE NEXT TO HIS NAME CERTIFIES WHO SAT ON THE UDC AND THAT THE COMPLETED REPORT ACCURATELY REFLECTS THE UDC PROCEEDINGS)

▇▇▇▇▇▇▇▇▇▇▇▇▇▇   ▇▇▇▇▇▇▇▇▇▇▇▇▇   ▇▇▇▇▇▇▇▇▇▇▇▇▇

Chairman (Typed Name/Signature)   Member (Typed Name)   Member (Typed Name)

Record Copy—Central File Record; Copy—Inmate after UDC Action; Copy—Inmate within 24 hours of Part I preparation
(This form may be replaced via WP)
Replaces BP-288(52) of JAN 88

Page 2

PART III - INVESTIGATION	22. DATE AND TIME INVESTIGATION BEGAN 3/21/98 9:00 p.m.

23. INMATE ADVISED OF RIGHT TO REMAIN SILENT: YOU ARE ADVISED OF YOUR RIGHT TO REMAIN SILENT AT ALL STAGES OF THE DISCIPLINARY PROCESS BUT ARE INFORMED THAT YOUR SILENCE MAY BE USED TO DRAW AN ADVERSE INFERENCE AGAINST YOU AT ANY STAGE OF THE INSTITUTIONAL DISCIPLINARY PROCESS. YOU ARE ALSO INFORMED THAT YOUR SILENCE ALONE MAY NOT BE USED TO SUPPORT A FINDING THAT YOU HAVE COMMITTED A PROHIBITED ACT.   AT (DATE/TIME)
3/21/98 9:03 p.m.

THE INMATE WAS ADVISED OF THE ABOVE RIGHT BY

continues

Exhibit 29–1 continued

24. INMATE STATEMENT AND ATTITUDE

Inmate was advised of his right to remain silent and elected to waive that right. ████████ indicated that he does not know ██████████. He stated that ██████████ passed by his unit and said something to him. ██████████ claims he does not know what ██████████ said. When he followed ██████████ to ask him what he said, ██████████ stated ██████████ just hit him for no reason. He claims that he was only defending himself after he was attacked. ██████████ claims he has not had any trouble with ██████████ in the past.

25. OTHER FACTS ABOUT THE INCIDENT, STATEMENTS OF THOSE PERSONS PRESENT AT SCENE, DISPOSITION OF EVIDENCE, ETC.

There were no other witnesses to the incident.

I interviewed ██████████ and he stated ██████████ thinks he is a tough guy. ██████████ denied that he said anything to ██████████. When ██████████ approached him, ██████████ stated ██████████ was acting aggressively. He didn't know what ██████████ might do so he hit ██████████ to protect himself.

Injury assessment of both inmates revealed ██████████ had bruises to his abdomen and redness in his chest. ██████████ had a cut on his left cheek that had to be stitched. Injury forms for both inmates are included with the packet.

26. INVESTIGATOR'S COMMENTS AND CONCLUSIONS

██████████ and ██████████ both have histories of fighting. ██████████ has three incident reports in two years for this offense and ██████████ has seven incident reports for fighting or assault. Based on the officer's observation and medical assessment, which documents that both inmates sustained injuries consistent with being in a physical altercation, I conclude the incident report is warranted.

27. ACTION TAKEN

Both inmates were placed in the Special Housing Unit. The incident report is forwarded to the UDC for further disposition.

DATE AND TIME INVESTIGATION COMPLETED   3/21/98 9:45 p.m.

PRINTED NAME/SIGNATURE OF INVESTIGATOR ██████████

██████████	Lieutenant
SIGNATURE	TITLE

Because inmates are often unhappy with the results of the disciplinary proceedings, it is no surprise that disciplinary matters are frequently appealed. In some agencies, inmate disciplinary actions may be appealed through the inmate grievance system, in the same way other prison actions or conditions may be grieved. Many agencies do not allow disciplinary matters to be taken into the regular grievance system; in these agencies, there will be a separate procedure for review or appeal of inmate disciplinary actions. In those agencies where discipline appeals are grievable, it is common for appeals concerning discipline to account for the greatest number of inmate complaints. Similarly, when inmates go to court, disciplinary actions are, in most jurisdictions, the most frequent category of matters taken into court.

Review of disciplinary actions on appeal is typically limited to procedural review: The records (the discipline offense report, the investigation report, and the written report of the hearing officer or committee) are examined, to be sure that the procedures required by the agency's disciplinary policy have been followed. The facts of the case and the sanction imposed are summarily reviewed. There must be some evidence to support the finding of the disciplinary authority. The reviewer ensures that the sanction imposed is within the range of punishments authorized for that offense. There is a legal requirement that the hearing officer or committee record the evidence relied on to support the conclusion reached, and that the reasons for the sanction(s) imposed be given.

There are other significant legal requirements for inmate disciplinary proceedings, and corrections staff should be aware of them. As noted above, the inmate disciplinary program attempts to establish respect for authority. For the inmate disciplinary program to receive respect, it must be administered fairly and according to rules— what lawyers may call "due process." Apart from being the law, these rules are important for maintaining a fair and humane living environment in correctional facilities.

Legally, it is also essential that staff follow rules to avoid exposure to personal liability. In litigating inmate complaints over the last 30 years, the most frequently used legal action has been the *Civil Rights Act of 1871,* as codified in *U.S. Code,* Title 42, Sec. 1983. That federal statute provides:

> Every person who, under color of any statute, ordinance, regulation, custom, or usage, of any state or territory, subjects, or causes to be subject, any citizen of the United States or other person within the jurisdiction thereof to the deprivation of any rights, privileges, or immunities secured by the Constitution and laws, shall be liable to the party injured in an action at law, suit in equity, or other proper proceeding for redress.[1]

This law allows people who claim their constitutional rights have been abridged to go into federal court for legal relief.

Sec. 1983 has been popular for inmates to use for several reasons. In most states, and in the 1960s and 1970s especially, federal courts were seen as being more liberal and more receptive to inmate complaints than state courts. Legal rulings were obtained in one part of the country, which could be used as leverage to get favorable rulings in federal courts in another part of the country. Perhaps most important, Sec. 1983 could be used to obtain two kinds of relief. If constitutional violations were proved, the federal courts could give injunctive relief, and also monetary damages against the offending officials. Injunctive relief could require an agency to stop doing something it had been doing, to change its procedures, or to start doing something that was constitutionally required. Many changes were required, in response to court injunctive orders. More threatening to the individual official is the risk of being ordered to pay monetary damages because of constitutional violations.

A corrections worker may be held liable if he or she does not follow constitutional requirements that have been established by court rulings. Court rulings may be at different levels. For the individual worker, there may also be rulings in lower federal courts, or in state courts, which govern a particular type of activity covered by the Constitution (or statutes). It is the responsibility of lawyers for each correctional agency to make sure that employees are aware of any such local rulings and that agency policy reflects the constitutional requirements given in court rulings. Correctional staff then protect themselves by two major means: receiving staff training, which points out legal standards and constitutional requirements; and following agency policy, which must be most carefully done in those areas of possible constitutional liability where the courts have ruled.

INMATE DISCIPLINE: DUE PROCESS REQUIREMENTS

What are the legal requirements for inmate discipline, as established in constitutional rulings by the Supreme Court?

The constitutional provision that governs is called the Due Process Clause, found at two places in the Constitution. According to the Fourteenth Amendment, "nor shall any State deprive any person of life, liberty, or property, without due process of law."[2] This guarantees protections against actions by state officials or agencies. There is a similar provision, in the Fifth Amendment, that protects citizens against federal actions: No person shall "be deprived of life, liberty, or property without due process of law."[3]

Whenever a claim is made (for example, by inmates claiming violation of their rights because of disciplinary action), there are two inquiries to be made. First, there is the question of whether there has been any deprivation of life, liberty, or property. Not every type of government action that a person dislikes raises a due process question. Only if it is decided that there

has been a deprivation of life, liberty, or property, as guaranteed by the Constitution, is a second question asked: What process is due to the person who is being deprived? Generally, courts say that due process is a set of procedures that ensure that the action taken is fair, given the circumstances. Again, as a general rule, the more serious the action taken by the government, the more procedural protections (due process) will be required.

The Supreme Court, in 1995, gave new guidance as to the circumstances under which due process is required in prison actions, in the case of *Sandin v. Conner*. The Court greatly simplified the constitutional standard to be used to decide when prison action amounts to a deprivation of liberty that requires due process. The Court recognized in *Sandin v. Conner* that the purpose of prison disciplinary action is to effectuate good prison management and to achieve prisoner rehabilitative goals. As long as disciplinary action is in pursuit of those goals, and does not add on to the sentence already being served, or go beyond the conditions contemplated in the sentence being served, the disciplinary action does not create a liberty interest. The Court held that Conner's discipline in segregated confinement did not present the type of atypical, significant deprivation in which a state might conceivably create a liberty interest. . . . The regime to which he was subjected as a result of the misconduct hearing was within the range of confinement to be normally expected for one serving an indeterminate sentence of 30 years to life.[4]

Thus, the question is not whether the inmate is punished, or even punished severely. The question is whether the punishment is within the range of conditions, restrictions, and sanctions that are contemplated while serving the type and length of sentence that the inmate is serving. This substantially reduces the number of cases where due process protections are constitutionally required because the action taken by prison officials deprives inmates of liberty. Lower courts have been busy interpreting the scope of the *Sandin v. Conner* ruling. From the facts of the case and the Court's language, segregated confinement (or other housing restrictions or withdrawal of privileges) would not trigger due process requirements, but actions that might extend the time to be served (such as good time awards being taken away, or parole release being affected) would require a due process hearing. Some correctional agencies, as a matter of caution as well as fairness, continue to require certain procedural protections for any serious act of inmate misconduct.

WOLFF V. MCDONNELL, AND OTHERS

Wolff v. McDonnell is the leading case in the Supreme Court on inmate discipline. The Supreme Court recognized the special nature of prison disciplinary proceedings and specifically rejected claims for procedures (such as representation by lawyers) that would "encase the disciplinary procedures in an inflexible constitutional straitjacket that would necessarily call for adversary proceedings typical of the criminal trial."[5] In other words, prison hearings are "administrative" and call for much less procedural protection than court proceedings.

There are five minimum due process standards for a prison disciplinary hearing.

1. There must be advance written notice to the inmate of the claimed violation.
2. The hearing should be at least 24 hours after the notice, for the inmate to prepare for his or her appearance.
3. There should be an allowance to the inmate to call witnesses and to present documentary evidence, unless permitting him or her to do so would be unduly hazardous.
4. A representative (may be an inmate or a staff member) should be allowed to assist the inmate if the inmate is illiterate or if there are complex issues to prepare for.
5. There should be a statement by an impartial disciplinary committee of the evidence relied on to support the fact find-

ings, and the reasons for the disciplinary action taken.

Two requirements that had been strenuously sought for inmate hearings were specifically denied: There was no requirement for the inmate to be permitted to confront and cross-examine adverse witnesses (because of the special hazards those actions could present in a prison setting) and there was no requirement for allowing inmates to have counsel.

Other Supreme Court cases added some additional guidelines for prison disciplinary hearings. In *Baxter v. Pahnigiano,* 425 U.S. 308 (1976), the Court reiterated its ruling that inmates are not entitled to either retained or appointed counsel in disciplinary hearings. A new issue was the inmate's right to remain silent in the disciplinary proceeding. The Court said that it was permissible for officials to tell inmates that they could remain silent, but that their silence could be used against them (to draw an adverse inference) at their hearing. However, the inmates' silence by itself would be insufficient to support a decision of guilt by the disciplinary committee. (If the inmates were compelled [that is, ordered] to furnish evidence that might incriminate them later in a criminal proceeding, they would have to be given immunity as to use of that testimony in the criminal trial.)

In the case of *Superintendent v. Hill,* 472 U.S. 445 (1985), the Supreme Court ruled on the amount of evidence that was required, constitutionally, to support a prison board's findings. The Court said that due process required only that there be "some evidence" to support the findings of the disciplinary board—about the lowest standard of proof that could be devised.

USE OF INFORMANTS

There are some issues of inmate disciplinary proceedings that have not been addressed by the Supreme Court. One of the most troublesome is the use of evidence that comes from confidential informants, or that is developed as a result of the information given by such informants. Much in-

---

Due Process Rights Not Violated

In the case of *Miller v. Selsky,* F. 2d 3d7 (2d Cir. 1997), the Second Circuit decided that the Supreme Court's decision in *Sandin v. Conner* did not create an all-encompassing requirement that punishment in a prison setting in disciplinary confinement may never implicate a liberty interest.

An inmate at the Bare Hill Correctional Facility in New York, Vincent Miller, was charged with fighting. Miller was denied by New York State correctional authorities when he asked for access to confidential testimony. The informant's information was utilized to support a disciplinary hearing finding of guilty, and Miller was sentenced to 180 days in special housing, or disciplinary segregation, as well as a loss of good time credit.

Miller filed suit in federal court under the *Civil Rights Act of 1871,* as codified in *U.S.*

Code, vol. 42, sec. 1983, and alleged that his constitutional right to due process had been violated. The federal district court dismissed Miller's case, ruling under *Sandin v. Conner* that imposition of administrative segregation did not create an atypical and significant hardship.

The Second Circuit overturned the district court decision, and stated that *Sandin v. Conner* did not create a blanket rule in which disciplinary segregation would not ever create an "atypical and significant" hardship. Instead, district courts will be expected to consider specific circumstances of confinement that are unique to each case as they consider whether or not the conditions affect an inmate's liberty interest.

Source: Adapted from *Corrections Alert,* Vol. 4, No. 2, p. 3, © 1997, Aspen Publishers, Inc.

---

formation for the safer control of correctional facilities is supplied by inmate informants. Many correctional supervisors and officers rely on this information to keep track of the most sensitive inmate misconduct activities. In fact, many of them develop regular sources of such confidential information and even provide rewards to the informants. (Again, this practice has its counterparts in the community's law enforcement activities.)

In this chapter, discussing the necessity for maintaining prison security and safety, I concede the need to have such suppliers of information. But, to ensure the fairness of the disciplinary process (to have some due process in prison hearings), there must be protection against inmates fabricating information or providing false accusations, which they may do for

a variety of reasons. Although the Supreme Court has not addressed this issue, lower courts (and correctional officials and lawyers) have considered it and have concluded that there must be some way to ascertain the reliability of informants' stories. Informants, to protect their safety, cannot be called as a witness to a hearing. By the same token, their identity is also not revealed to the accused inmates. In the policy of most agencies, the disciplinary committee makes inquiry, away from the accused, as to the reliability of informant information that is present in the case. A conclusion that the informant is reliable is entered into the record. That conclusion may be based on the circumstances of the case, in which the informant's assertions have been corroborated by other facts; on a report from an investigating officer who gives reasons for believing the informant; on other situations where the informant gave reliable information; or on detailed information that could be known only by someone who was present to observe the facts that otherwise proved true.

Until the Supreme Court provides firm guidance in this area, correctional staff will have to look to any rulings that have been made by courts in their jurisdiction and follow those rulings. Staff responsible for drafting policy must make certain that the inmate disciplinary policy reflects any court rulings on use of informant information (and any other area where local courts may have special requirements, outside of or beyond those given by the Supreme Court). Line staff implementing the disciplinary policy must be able to rely on its accordance with any court rulings that apply in the local jurisdiction. With the Supreme Court's ruling in *Sandin v. Conner,* the exposure of staff to individual liability for constitutional violations in disciplinary proceedings has been greatly reduced—but not eliminated.

CONCLUSION

Disciplinary policy must be carefully written to ensure fairness and to guarantee basic due process standards. Staff must carefully follow that policy, to protect themselves from liability and, just as important, to maintain the integrity of the correctional environment.

NOTES

1. Civil Rights Act of 1871, *U.S. Code,* title 42, sec. 1983.
2. U.S. Constitution, amend. 14, sec. 1.
3. U.S. Constitution, amend. 5.
4. *Sandin v. Conner,* 515 U.S. 472 (1995).
5. *Wolff v. McDonnell,* 418 U.S. 539 (1974).

SUGGESTED READINGS

Camp, G., and C. Camp. 1996. *The Corrections Yearbook: 1996.* South Salem, NY: Criminal Justice Institute, Inc.

Blomberg, T., and S. Cohen. 1995. *Punishment and Social Control.* New York: Aldine De Gruyter.

CHAPTER 30

Special Needs Offenders

Judy Anderson

During the past 10 to 15 years, the term "special needs offenders" has become prevalent in the field of corrections. Practitioners have had to find ways of handling such offenders and have taken approaches ranging from complete lack of acknowledgment to provision of specialized services and units. Special needs can encompass many types of conditions and categories. For purposes of this chapter, special needs will be limited to men and women offenders who are older and those with disabilities, including physical impairments and chronic medical conditions; mental illness; and mental retardation (developmental disabilities).

CATEGORIES OF SPECIAL NEEDS

Older offenders are often referred to as being "geriatric," which denotes being 65 years of age or older. However, preventative health care dictates that an earlier age should be used as a guideline. In 1993, a national definition, that of age 50 or older, was developed for corrections and has been adopted by most correctional systems. The chronological age of 50 for defining older offenders was based on their socioeconomic status, including the access to medical care and lifestyle of most inmates.[1]

Inmates with disabilities have physical or mental impairments that substantially limit one or more major life activities, have a record of such an impairment, or are or have been re-

garded as having such an impairment. This definition from the Americans with Disabilities Act (ADA) passed by Congress in 1990 covers all persons, including inmates. Physical impairments are defined as severe mobility, visual, hearing, and speech limitations. People with mobility impairments include those who use wheelchairs or ambulate with assistive devices such as walkers, crutches, or canes. Chronic medical conditions include cardiovascular conditions, end-stage renal disease, respiratory conditions, seizure disorders, tuberculosis, and acquired immune deficiency syndrome.[2] These conditions will usually result in hospitalization and/or medical segregation.

Mental illness is any diagnosed disorder defined in the *Diagnostic and Statistical Manual of Mental Disorders,* published by the American Psychiatric Association. Mental illness causes severe disturbances in thought, emotions, and ability to cope with the demands of daily life. Mental illness, like other illnesses, can be acute, chronic, or under control and in remission. Mental health services can range from intake screening to crisis intervention to long-term therapy to outpatient treatment.

Mental retardation is defined as having less than normal intellectual competence, characterized by an intelligence quotient (IQ) of 70 or less. Retardation, or developmental disability, usually results in impairments in adoptive behavior such as personal independence and social responsibility.[3]

SEPARATE CARE OR GENERAL POPULATION PLACEMENT?

After acknowledging that special needs offenders may be in the prison population, the first major task is to decide how to handle these groups of inmates. Should they be segregated or mainstreamed?

Reasons cited for separating special needs offenders from the general population include

1. cost containment—more efficient use of funding if they are housed and treated as a group
2. managed care—more effective care can be focused on a specialized unit
3. concentration of resources (such as staff) in one location

But mainstreaming, the integration of a person with a disability into the "normal" prison population, is a basic premise of ADA; access to complete programs and services is a requirement. ADA allows correctional administrators to exclude or remove an offender with a disability from the general population if he or she is a direct threat to the health and safety of others.

Consequently, a combination of mainstreaming and segregation (with emphasis on the former) should provide services for inmates with disabilities as well as follow the law. This approach would also be consistent with the way persons with disabilities are handled outside correctional facilities. For example, a person with mental illness may be hospitalized (segregated) for a period of time but then go home or to a half-in, half-out program until he or she can return home. Another example would be an older person who no longer can live alone safely and may have a worker come to the home, move in with someone else, or move to an assisted living, intermediate, or long-term care facility. This will probably be a progression rather than a jump from independent living to long-term care and could involve movement back and forth among various levels of assistance. Again, the emphasis should be on mainstreaming, with segregation as

the last resort, except for the severely mentally ill and retarded. Even then, it is incumbent that services be provided so that persons with disabilities have an equal opportunity to benefit from programs.

PROTOCOLS FOR CARE

A second task is to develop written policies and procedures that are consistent with ADA. When evaluating services, it must be ascertained if there are policies, procedures, and practices that would prevent inmates with disabilities from participating. If there are, then reasonable modifications might be indicated to avoid discrimination. An example might be library or law books being brought to the wheelchair-bound inmate if the library is located in a building with a flight of stairs and no elevator or ramp. As noted earlier, ADA does provide for exclusion from a program if the inmate with a disability presents a direct threat to the health and safety of others. For instance, a mentally ill inmate who hears a voice telling him or her to kill another person would not be involved in general population activities.

ACCESS AND COMMUNICATION

A third area of concern is "program access," which usually refers to architectural or design barriers. Inaccessibility of facilities is not justification for denying programs, services, and activities. While ADA does require accessibility in new construction and alterations to existing buildings, it does not require that all existing facilities be modified to the new standard. Alternate methods of program delivery such as suggested in the library example above will suffice. The program, service, or activity can be brought to the offender, rather than the offender going to the program, service, or activity.

Universal design should be considered for all new construction so that ADA and other applicable standards for persons with disabilities will either be met immediately or be met with little modification. Examples of universal design include wider doors, ramps instead of stairs, higher commodes, flapper levers on sinks instead of knobs, and heavier building material (so that grab bars or railings might later be installed if needed). Universal design allows far greater flexibility in all aspects of programming now and in the future.

Communication is a factor in program access. Communications with inmates with disabilities should be as effective as it is with other inmates. This provision applies only to inmates with hearing, speech, or vision impairment. Examples of auxiliary aids for inmates who are deaf or have hearing impairments would include telecommunication devices for the deaf (TDDs), communication boards, and assistive listening devices. TDDs and communication boards could also be utilized for inmates with speech impairments. Written notes could also be effective for short or routine communications. Certified sign language interpreters should be accessible either on a volunteer or contract basis. Staff members could also be trained as interpreters. Tapes (played on battery- or manually powered players) and books in Braille are available for inmates with vision impairments. Signs in Braille throughout the facility would also enhance communications.

IDENTIFYING THOSE WITH UNUSUAL NEEDS

During intake, the process of evaluating inmates as they enter the correctional system, it is important that disabilities be identified as soon as possible in order to provide appropriate services, both during intake and throughout the period of incarceration. Intake is often conducted at a separate facility or unit, a reception and diagnostic center.

Within the first few hours of admittance, a medical examination or medical screening should be conducted. While a thorough medical examination is preferable, it may be impossible to provide if volume is too high. The medical screening, which serves as a minitriage, should identify medical and mental health concerns that may need immediate attention; these cases should be assessed immediately by medical staff.

HOUSING ACCOMMODATION

Special housing and programming will be indicated for special needs offenders. There should be wheelchair accessibility throughout the unit or an alternate plan for providing the various services. Inmates with mental illnesses or mental retardation, like those with acute medical concerns, may need to be admitted to a specialized unit and the intake process completed there or deferred until a later time.

Special needs inmates retained in intake should be housed on ground level near the officers' station or in a monitored observation cell, as would other inmates with presenting conditions. Some type of identification such as red reflective tape should be placed on the cell door at eye level and about a foot from the floor to denote "assistance required" should the facility need to be evacuated. Medical or human services staff should be assigned to the unit to monitor these inmates and to provide necessary services.

Alternate types of aids may need to be provided. For example, a "white cane" used by an inmate with a visual impairment is considered a weapon within a correctional facility and could be replaced with a collapsible one if it is consistent with the security level of the facility. For an inmate with a hearing impairment, communication boards and written notes can be used until more permanent arrangements can be made at the assigned institution.

CLASSIFICATION CONSIDERATIONS

During classification, the dangerousness and stability of inmates are evaluated, and persons with similar characteristics are sent to similar locations. Most classification systems consider risk factors such as prior convictions, current convictions, escapes or attempted escapes, length of sentence, and institutional adjustment.

Age, educational level, history of substance abuse, and history of violence may also be considered.

A provision for "override" allows staff to factor in information such as medical and mental health conditions and to change the custody and security of the inmate to accommodate these conditions. These override decisions should be made on a case-by-case basis and should place the inmate in the least restrictive custody possible. For example, inmates in wheelchairs would not automatically be placed in a medical unit but would be placed where they could best function, such as a regular housing unit on the ground floor with full access to all programs and services in the facility; this, of course, is mainstreaming. An inmate who is suicidal or psychotic should be placed in an appropriate specialized unit for treatment until it is determined that he or she can return to general population or step-down unit status. Again, an inmate with a disability who poses a direct threat to the safety of others may be excluded from a program or segregated. Classification decisions must not be made solely on the basis of the disability but must consider all factors.

PROGRAM AND ACTIVITY AVAILABILITY

Whether the inmate is assigned to a specialized unit or a modified living space in the general population, programs, services, and activities must be available. Again, the program, service, or activity may need to be brought to the inmate rather than the inmate going to the location. For instance, items might be folded or packaged for prison industries on the unit rather than at prison industries. If other inmates are offered work assignments involving pay or reduction of sentence, then the same must be available to inmates with disabilities. If boot camps and work release programs are offered, modified or alternate programs should be designed for inmates with disabilities. A work activities center that is a sheltered workshop would offer such opportunities. Contracts would be obtained from local businesses or government entities, and the inmates would perform the work. If the education area is inaccessible, then a tutor could come to the living unit. Staff must learn to "color outside the lines" and learn to think creatively, but with security foremost, in designing individualized programs. Specific inmates can also be involved in this process, as they would best know their own capabilities.

SPECIAL FACILITIES WILL BE IMPORTANT

As noted earlier, physical plant modifications will probably be necessary. Modifications (in addition to those noted above) include lowered storage lockers, booster seats on commodes, handheld shower heads, bath chairs, and middle-pedestal tables that allow a person in a wheelchair to roll close to the table. Blackboards can be hung vertically instead of horizontally to allow accessibility by wheelchair inmates. Of course, lowered telephones with volume controls, water coolers, bulletin boards, and door levers; specialized door closure systems or automatic doors; and roll-in showers also provide independence as well as accessibility. Air conditioning may also be needed, as many special needs inmates are on psychotropic medications, and overheating will cause medical complications.

Scheduling can also improve access. A separate meal shift can be established for inmates with disabilities who either need more time or assistance to eat or who need to be segregated from the rest of the population to prevent victimization. The same rationale should hold true for the amount of time allowed for moving from one location to another, such as living unit to work location or medical services, or for completing a task such as cleaning living areas.

SPECIAL SUPPORT MAY BE REQUIRED

Assistance may be required to complete activities of daily living or, in some instances, the task will have to be completed by other inmates or staff. Other inmates, either those with or those without disabilities, can work as caregivers or assistants. These jobs should have clear descriptions specifying that caregivers do not have authority over the inmates with disabilities. Caregivers should be as carefully chosen as staff. Training should be provided prior to beginning work with the individuals with disabilities and should be offered on a scheduled basis. All inmates who assist should be directed by staff and should consult with specified staff on a daily basis concerning job assignment.

SPECIAL HOUSING UNIT OPERATIONS

Lockup or segregation cells may also need modifications to handle special needs inmates. Cell doors may need to be widened, special markings outside the door may be used to indicate assistance needed for evacuations, and plumbing may require modifications. Prior to locking up a special needs inmate, medical staff should be consulted about what, if any, requirements must be met. These requirements may range from no restrictions to an order for no placement in a segregation unit. If no segregation is ordered, alternate arrangements such as placing a deadlock in the present cell should suffice.

PROGRAMS FOR THE MENTALLY ILL OR RETARDED

Mentally ill inmates, depending upon the severity of their illness, may require segregation in a specialized unit. Whether the unit is under the auspices of medical, psychiatric, or corrections professionals, there should be a liaison with the institution to ensure that sound correctional practices are followed. Frequently, there will be a medical or human services professional and a correctional staff member who will manage the unit together.

The major focus in such units is therapy, whether it be medical, psychological, or a combination of both. The emphasis is on returning the inmate to a state of mental wellness. As inmates progress, they may be returned to the general population either by participating in programs and work activities or by moving into a step-down unit that provides transitional care.

Mentally retarded or developmentally disabled inmates will probably also require placement in a specialized unit. Again, specialized staff will provide programming in concert with correctional staff. Because a major focus must be on the ability to function independently, daily living or survival skills will be central, resulting in activities that may seem out of place in a correctional environment. Such activities might include cooking, shopping, or doing laundry. Based upon their level of functioning, inmates might stay in specialized units until their release from the correctional system. As with all special needs offenders, continuity of services must be provided as the inmates move back into the community.

WOMEN OFFENDERS

Fewer in number, women offenders frequently have fewer options in the correctional system. For instance, many states have 1 or 2 institutions for women but 10 to 15 for men. Consequently, there may be fewer services available for women offenders. By law, women offenders must be provided parity of services. Parity does not mean sameness but does imply equality. Therefore, each correctional system will need to evaluate the special needs services for men and women and then rectify any inequalities. Because women more readily participate in programming and are usually considered less of a security threat, women's services may be provided either within the correctional system or in the community.

EDUCATION AND TRAINING

Education, training, and staff development are an integral part of corrections. The National Congress on Penitentiary and Reformatory Discipline—held in Cincinnati, OH in 1870—adopted a Declaration of Principles that proclaimed that "special training as well as high quality of head and heart, is required to make a good prison or reformatory officer."[4(p.1)] While pre-employment and annual training are required for correctional staff, little training focuses on working with special needs offenders. In order to effectively work with these groups, all involved staff should be provided with relevant training and development. Training components should include, but not be limited to, familiarization and/or sensitization, educational and medical information about special needs inmates, techniques and tips (see Exhibit 30–1), and strategies for managing special needs inmates more effectively. The professionally trained staff who work with special needs offenders, but particularly with the mentally ill and mentally retarded, have mandated training hours in order to maintain licensure and certification in addition to the agency, accreditation, and statutory requirements that all correctional staff must meet.

These professionally trained staff are a good source for providing training for the other correctional staff. The security staff should be able to learn techniques for managing special needs inmates, such as using belly chains instead of handcuffing behind the back for heart patients, transferring an inmate from a wheelchair to a bed, and communicating with inmates with hearing or sight impairments.

Other resources for training include state agencies, medical facilities, advocacy and special interest groups, and other providers of services. Additionally, training plans from other special needs correctional facilities might be available through the National Institute of Corrections' Resource Library or from the facilities themselves. Staff should be encouraged to participate in professional and special interest groups in the community for education and professional growth as well as for networking opportunities. The correctional staff should also inform the community about special needs inmates. Contacts and partnerships should be developed with the appropriate providers of services once the inmate leaves the correctional system to ensure that the needed information is provided to both the inmate and the service provider. Intake forms in corrections should be revised to collect the information that is required for the community service providers, especially those managed by state or federal agencies.

Exhibit 30–1 Tips for Working with Special Needs Offenders

- Move more slowly than normal. Sudden movements can frighten special needs inmates or make them think they are being attacked.
- Talk directly to the inmates. Those with hearing or speech disabilities may need to read lips.
- Address conversation to the inmates. Don't talk around them as though they are non-people.
- Talk at face level. If a longer conversation is indicated, either sit or stoop down to eye level with inmates in wheelchairs.
- Speak clearly, in a low tone. Do not talk loudly or in a shrill way.
- Use terms that the inmates can understand.
- Treat the inmates as adults. Do not speak to them as if they were children.
- Simplify instructions. Give one direction at a time to avoid confusion. Sometimes it helps to also put the instructions in writing.
- Establish and maintain a familiar routine. Do things in the same sequence—get up, straighten cell, have breakfast, go to pill line, and so on.
- Talk in positive terms. Talk about what can be done, not what cannot be done.
- Be patient. Allow extra time to complete tasks.
- Be flexible and creative when providing programs, services, and activities.
- Use large type or enlarge written memoranda so they will be easier to read.
- Utilize the public address system for announcing changes and to read memoranda concerning changes.
- Ensure inmates eat properly. Poor nutrition can lead to other problems.

CONCLUSION

Inmates with disabilities and ADA are having and will continue to have great impact on the correctional system. In addition to making physical plant modifications, correctional administrators will need to begin to lead their staff and facilities toward compliance with all provisions of ADA mandated federal and state laws and statutes and American Correctional Association standards. Policies, procedures, and practices may need to be altered to provide appropriate programs, services, and activities.

Resources are available through local, state, and federal organizations and agencies. Staff should partner with local providers so that necessary services can be offered to the inmate while incarcerated and upon release. Line staff must be selected carefully, as not everyone is suited for working with inmates with disabilities. These staff members must be provided the specialized training needed to provide the day-to-day leadership for the program. A successful correctional program for special needs inmates takes commitment from all levels—administrative, professional/program services, and security.

NOTES

1. J. Morton, ed., *An Administrative Overview of the Older Offender* (Washington, DC: National Institute of Corrections, 1992), 4.

2. B. Anno, *Prison Health Care: Guidelines for the Management of an Adequate Delivery System* (Washington, DC: National Institute of Corrections, 1991), 139–141.

3. P. Rubin and S. McCampbell, "The Americans with Disabilities Act and Criminal Justice: Mental Disabilities and Corrections," *Research in Action,* NCJ-155061 (Washington, DC: National Institute of Justice), 1–2.

4. American Correctional Association, *Declaration of Principles* (Lanham, MD: National Congress on Penitentiary and Reformatory Discipline), 1.

CHAPTER 31

Protective Custody Inmates

Ron Angelone

Practitioners and academics often disagree about the management of protective custody inmates. Many people who are unfamiliar with prison operations believe that any time inmates claim to need protection from other inmates, they should receive protection. On the other hand, professionals who have been in the field for some time assert that prison officials, rather than inmates, should decide which inmates should be separated for security reasons.

While other texts take a theoretical approach, this chapter will address protective custody from a practitioner's perspective.

PROTECTIVE CUSTODY—AN OVERVIEW

Protective custody is defined as specialized, segregated housing that may be used for many different types of inmates.

- those unable to pay off gambling or other debts
- those afraid of sexual predators
- those who are former law enforcement or correctional officers
- those reaching the end of their sentences who are trying to avoid disciplinary infractions
- institutional informants
- those with notorious criminal activities
- gang members or those participating in crimes motivated by racial or other types of discrimination who require protection from imprisoned members of the group they attacked
- those who have become government witnesses against codefendants, especially in capital and major drug cases
- those trying to manipulate the system
- some homosexuals
- those whose lives now may be in danger from those they formerly preyed upon

Protective custody is increasingly difficult to manage because of the different backgrounds and behavioral traits of those who seek it. In some institutions, it becomes necessary to impose some form of separation within the protective custody unit itself to protect protective custody cases from each other.

Protective custody inmates have been a significant portion of the prison population in the last 20 years. A 1990 survey conducted by consultant James Henderson found that 5.6 percent of all U.S. prison inmates are in one form of protective custody or another.[1] But according to the *Corrections Yearbook 1997,* from 1990 to 1997, the nation's prisons allocated an average of 1.6 percent of bed space for protective custody (see Table 31–1).[2]

Although estimates of the true number of such cases vary, it is clear that protective custody operations represent a significant cost to the correctional system. Protective custody units consist of expensive single cells and are labor-

Table 31–1   Inmates in Protective Custody on January 1, 1997

	Number of Inmates in Protective Custody	*Percentage of All Inmates*
Arizona*	310	1.4
Arkansas	230	2.4
California**	17	0.0
Colorado		
Connecticut	257	1.7
Florida	309	0.5
Idaho	10	0.3
Illinois***	970	2.5
Indiana	372	2.4
Iowa		
Kansas	34	0.4
Maine	16	1.1
Michigan	335	0.8
Minnesota	0	0.0
Mississippi	242	2.4
Missouri	797	3.8
Nebraska	112	3.5
Nevada	434	5.5
New Mexico	148	3.7
New York****	450	0.6
North Carolina	47	0.2
North Dakota	3	0.4
Ohio	268	0.6
Oklahoma	72	0.5
Oregon	0	0.0
Pennsylvania	16	0.0
Rhode Island	74	2.3
South Carolina	59	0.3
South Dakota	3	0.2
Tennessee	601	4.4
Texas	88	0.1
Vermont	0	0.0
Virginia	91	0.4
Washington	159	1.3
West Virginia	140	5.8
Wyoming	67	5.0
Total	6,731	
Average	198	1.6
Percentage of Total	0.8	

*Administrative and disciplinary segregation are treated as the same in this survey.

**Because not all administrative segregation units have a computer code, figure is undercounted.

***Figures are as of December 31, 1996.

****Figures are estimated.

Source: Reprinted with permission from C. Camp and G. Camp, *Corrections Yearbook 1997*, © 1997, Criminal Justice Institute, Inc.

intensive to manage because close supervision of all inmate activities is necessary.

As Henderson writes,

> Most veteran administrators in the correctional field do not recall protective custody being an issue until the past several decades. An investigation of the prison literature reveals no consistent mention of protective custody until the 1960s, and few actual numbers reflecting the extent of protective custody even then. Indeed, it was only in the 1970s that prisons began to routinely keep statistics on the protective custody population—an indication that it either was not a problem before then or that it was not previously considered important.[3]

Commentators cite various reasons for the growing use of protective custody, but the most common tends to be the greater threat of violence within prisons. Other factors include

- increased freedom of movement within institutions
- more contact between inmates
- modern practices of inmate classification and institution diversification, which result in greater concentration of hard-core inmates in certain institutions, thereby increasing the likelihood of violence in those institutions
- the fact that inmates currently incarcerated have histories of greater violence and more drug-related offenses than previous decades' inmates did
- increasing numbers of first-time young offenders arriving with little experience in how to "do time"
- the relative quiet and solitude of most protective custody units, which make them attractive to certain inmates, especially when an institution is crowded and has inmate gangs who prey on other gangs or weak inmates

In the 1970s, federal court decisions were handed down that increased the likelihood that inmates could successfully sue prison officials for failing to protect them. To avoid such suits, prison officials allowed protective custody placement with no more justification than an inmate's statement, "I want to lockup."

Moreover, in 1973 the National Advisory Commission on Criminal Justice Standards and Goals issued a standard, *Protection against Personal Abuse,* which declared, "Each correctional agency should establish immediately policies and procedures to fulfill the right of offenders to be free from personal abuse by ... other offenders."[4]

COURT CASES AND LEGAL ISSUES

From the 1970s through the 1990s, a series of court rulings have significantly contributed to the protective custody problem for correctional administrators.

In *Landman v. Royster,* 333 F. Supp. (E.D. Va. 1971), the court required the Virginia Department of Corrections to create procedures to ensure inmate protection. In *Woodhouse v. Virginia,* 487 F. 2d 889 (4th Cir. 1973), the Fourth Circuit Court of Appeals ruled that an inmate can sustain a lawsuit if he or she proves a pervasive risk of harm from other inmates to which officials failed to reasonably respond.

In yet another pivotal decision, the U.S. Supreme Court ruled in 1976 in *Estelle v. Gamble,* 429 U.S. 97 (1976), that deliberate indifference entails more than a lack of ordinary care or negligence. The court declared that "unnecessary and wanton" infliction of pain constitutes deliberate indifference that, in turn, violates the Eighth Amendment.

Further, many "failure to protect" lawsuits involve classification issues. In *Martin v. White,* 742 F. 2d 469 (8th Cir. 1984), the Eighth Circuit Court of Appeals considered allegations that the administration failed to provide inmates protection from the threat of rape. Included in their claims was a failure to classify inmates according to their violent histories. The appellate court reversed the trial court dismissal of the inmates' case, holding that a pervasive risk of harm was established.

In *Walsh v. Mellas,* 837 F. 2d 789 (7th Cir. 1988), an inmate was injured by a gang member assigned to his cell. The Seventh Circuit Court of Appeals concluded that there was sufficient evidence that officials failed to use reasonable screening procedures to protect the inmates from gang-related violence.

In addition to liability for the denial of a constitutional right, administrators face the possibility of being found liable under a state's personal injury law.

> Tort law requires correctional officials to use reasonable care to ensure the safety of inmates during incarceration including protecting them from other inmates. Unlike constitutional claims, ordinary negligence suffices in state tort cases, but plaintiffs usually must show that officials had actual or constructive notice of the danger, meaning they knew or had reason to know about a dangerous situation.[5]

Is it any wonder that prison administrators feel that they must provide protective custody if an inmate asks for it? A closer reading of court rulings, however, indicates that protective custody can be handled in a more controlled way. For example, the courts have also ruled that there are no guarantees of total safety, whether inmates are placed in special units or not. The significant issue in a protective custody decision is a prison or jail official's responsibility to take reasonable steps in response to an inmate's reported fears or actual need for safety. What is reasonable depends on the facts of each case.

In the past, legal activity in the protective custody area has centered on three issues: liability, due process, and programs. To prove liability, an inmate must establish that the injury was a result of deliberate indifference; the accepted standard is that an inmate should be protected from unnecessary harm and that reasonable care should

be exercised in the maintenance of an inmate's life and health.

Another legal pitfall concerns due process rights. The current legal thinking is that due process procedures are not necessary if the protective custody unit offers a genuinely equivalent program to that of the general population. Further, in *Sweet v. South Carolina Dept. of Corrections,* 529 F. 2d 854 (4th Cir. 1975), the court ruled that inmates who request protective custody are not entitled to due process protections.

Programs in protective custody areas must be equivalent to those available to the prison's general population, even if they have been organized in a certain way for legitimate security reasons. In *Williams v. Lane,* 851 F. 2d 867 (7th Cir. 1988), the court affirmed correctional administrators' responsibility to provide substantially equivalent programs in many areas to inmates in protective custody. In *Williams,* the court held that restrictions placed on protective custody inmates' ability to attend religious services, use the law library, and participate in vocational, educational, and recreational programs were unreasonable.

Most prison administrators can achieve equality of programming. Providing educational and counseling programs involves little more than altering staff schedules. While the programs may not be as effective as those in a traditional classroom or office, they will suffice. Recreation is more troublesome and staff intensive, as close supervision and recreation periods separate from those of other inmates are necessary to ensure safety.

INMATE CLASSIFICATION— TARGETING PROTECTIVE CUSTODY INMATES

Classification procedures—like legal issues—play a crucial role in protective custody management. Administrators are challenged by identification, prediction, and procedural issues that are part of classification.

In the last 15 years, new risk assessment instruments were developed, first by the Federal Bureau of Prisons and later by the National Institute of Corrections. In response to the court decisions referred to above, many states now have objective prison classification systems. These systems help make the best use of limited cell space and staff resources.

Classification is based primarily on objective measures of the inmate's offense severity, prior criminal history, family and social stability, and institutional conduct. These factors help administrators gauge the risk of assaultive behavior, escape, or other prison misconduct and assign classification levels such as maximum, close, medium, and minimum custody. Such designations are principally used to determine the inmate's facility assignment and level of freedom of movement in the facility.

Some prison systems are examining internal institutional classification in order to address housing and security needs such as protective custody. One of the best-known systems is Herb Quay's Adult Internal Management System (AIMS), in which Quay proposes a plan to separate inmates by personality types.[6] AIMS relies on two personality inventories to classify inmates. This produces three groups of inmates: heavy threat, moderate threat, and light threat. It is wise to house these groups separately to avoid the potential for victimization of inmates in the light-threat group.

A study involving separating inmate types was completed in the late 1970s at the Federal Correctional Institution in Tallahassee. Inmates were separated in four dormitory housing units. The study showed that this separation of inmates by typologies (derived from a combination of Minnesota Multiphasic Personality Inventory scores, the AIMS correctional adjustment checklist, and record reviews) significantly decreased the number of assaults on staff and other inmates that were reported.[7]

However, sophisticated statistical prediction methods cannot be relied upon to ensure accurate identification of protective custody inmates.

Additionally, such approaches are complex and costly to implement.

PROTECTIVE CUSTODY IN VIRGINIA— A MODEL FOR THE NATION

Does any facility have a protective custody program that conforms to court rulings, is simple and inexpensive to implement, and can separate valid protection needs from invalid ones? The Virginia Department of Corrections (VDOC) has a protective custody program that realistically approaches the problem of protective custody management.

Before 1994, the VDOC assumed a liberal, inmate advocacy position. Inmates would receive protective custody if they asked for it. In this manner, the VDOC believed it could protect the state from inmates' lawsuits regarding their safety.

While this approach may be theoretically desirable, it is not practical. Many inmates merely claimed enemies and locked up to obtain an individual cell or to manipulate a transfer. In addition, the wardens of the separate VDOC institutions did not have protective custody beds when they needed them for real protection cases.

With a change in VDOC leadership in 1994, the policy for handling protective custody requests changed, and staff members were given more discretion. As requests for protective custody were made, inmates were to be closely evaluated for safety needs. Today the VDOC has protective custody that is sometimes initiated by the staff and sometimes initiated by the inmates. Assignments to protective custody are made on a temporary or permanent basis. Inmates assigned to permanent protective custody must be reviewed by the Institutional Classification Committee and approved by the VDOC's chief of operations for classification and records.

This approach has worked well. Frivolous requests for protection have been denied, and the need for permanent protective custody cells has been reduced. Inmates may continue to request protection at any time, but these claims have to be investigated by the institutional investigator or the inmate's counselor and forwarded to the warden for final approval. If the warden believes that the protection claims are valid, he or she may request that the Central Classification Board transfer the inmate. The Central Classification Board's criterion is that the inmate has been physically harmed or there is a reasonable chance that serious harm may occur if the inmate is not moved. This conforms to the court cases cited above but is not an overcomplicated way of making decisions.

The issue of transfers is closely associated with protective custody. Inmates often claim enemies in order to be transferred from a location that they do not like. In Virginia, most of the inmates are from north and east of Richmond or Richmond itself. Yet most of the bed openings are in southwest Virginia, away from their families. In many cases, inmates will overload protective custody cells by claiming enemies, forcing administrators to transfer them.

Some unnecessary transfers may be avoided if conflict resolution strategies are required to be used before anyone is recommended for transfer based on claims of protective needs. Conflict resolution may be used to resolve protective custody transfers based on debts. Often, transfer to another cell or dormitory will resolve the problem, eliminating the need for lockup or transfer.

The Central Classification Board can investigate claims about enemies. During 1997, very few VDOC inmates who claimed enemies were moved; the Central Classification Board required comprehensive evaluation and validation of all enemies. Inmates were asked to name their enemies and explain the circumstances behind the problem. There were no murders of inmates, and inmate-on-inmate assaults did not significantly increase. By remaining in the general population, inmates continued to have access to regular education programs and recreation and were working, not being waited on by the correctional staff. The state lost no lawsuits as a result of this more realistic approach to protective custody management.

CONCLUSION

Protective custody is a challenging management issue, but with specific strategies, inmates claiming the need for protection can be handled efficiently and effectively. Administrators need not fear unreasonable court interference if they thoroughly document their processes, ensure equal access to programming, and observe due process if necessary. Further, cumbersome methods of statistical classification are not necessary. A common-sense approach that requires inmates to name their enemies and the circumstances surrounding the issues, as well as an evaluation of such claims by a central classification committee, will ensure uniformity and success in managing this difficult population.

NOTES

1. J. Henderson, *Protective Custody Management in Adult Correctional Facilities: A Discussion of Causes, Conditions, Attitudes, and Alternatives* (Washington, DC: National Institute of Corrections, 1990).

2. C. Camp and G. Camp, *Corrections Yearbook 1997* (South Salem, NY: Criminal Justice Institute, 1997).

3. Henderson, *Protective Custody Management in Adult Correctional Facilities: A Discussion of Causes, Conditions, Attitudes, and Alternatives.*

4. National Advisory Commission on Standards and Goals. *Corrections* (Washington, DC: U.S. Government Printing Office, 1973). Standard 2.4, p. 8.

5. B. Belbot and R. DelCarmen, "Legal Issues in Classification," in *Classification: A Tool for Managing Today's Offenders* (College Park, MD: American Correctional Association, 1993).

6. H. Quay, *Managing Adult Inmates: Classification for Housing and Program Assignments* (College Park, MD: American Correctional Association, 1984).

7. J. Austin, C. Baird, and D. Neuenfelt, "Classification for Internal Management Purposes: The Washington Experience," in *Classification: A Tool for Managing Today's Offenders* (College Park, MD: American Correctional Association, 1993).

CHAPTER 32

Gang Management in Corrections

Mark S. Fleisher and Richard H. Rison

Gang management in prisons and jails is an extremely difficult task. There are many types of correctional institutions, many types of gangs, and such a variety of management strategies at correctional facilities that proposing a single solution to gang control is infeasible and unrealistic.

There are a number of issues that influence how correctional administrators might approach gang management within their institution. Gang problems have no cures. But this chapter will offer some guidelines about developing and implementing a gang management program.

GANGS IN A CORRECTIONAL SETTING

When citizens demand that police do something about street crime, adolescents and young people are arrested for drug distribution, burglary, carjacking, firearms possession, and other offenses typically associated with gangs. These young people will go to prison. In many jurisdictions, gang crimes carry enhanced sentences, ensuring that gang members will pose problems for correctional managers for a long time. Correctional officials will be forced to cope with an ever-increasing population of gang-affiliated inmates, both men and women.

There are as many definitions for the term "gang" as there are gang specialists. While a rich scholarly literature on street gangs and street gang intervention is available,[1] there is little available on prison gangs, street gangs in prison,

and the control and management of prison and street gangs in correctional facilities.[2]

Generally speaking, the term "gang" has been applied to just about any group whose members commit crimes. Prison gangs and street gangs are distinguished from each other in a number of ways. Traditional prison gangs originated in state and federal correctional facilities in the 1960s and 1970s.[3] Prison gangs include, but are not limited to, the Aryan Brotherhood, Mexican Mafia, La Nuestra Familia, Black Guerrilla Family, Texas Syndicate, Dirty White Boys, and Mexikanemi.

City neighborhoods created street gangs. The National Institute of Justice reports that there are about 846,000 gang members.[4] The aggressive policing of street gangs' criminal activities has resulted in the imprisonment of tens of thousands of street gang members. Common street gangs found in prisons are Crips and Bloods. In the Chicago area, virtually all street gangs are aligned into either the Folks or People nation. Folks include well-known street gangs such as the Gangster Disciples, Satan Disciples, Latin Disciples, Black Disciples, and Two Sixers. People include Blackstone Rangers, El Rukns, Latin Counts, Mickey Counts, Latin Kings, and Vice Lords.[5]

Historically, the central differences between prison gangs and street gangs have been internal structure (the complexity of a gang's internal hierarchy—its bureaucracy) and leadership style (who gives orders and how these orders are enforced). Styles range from face-to-face coercion with reciprocity ("you do this for me, I'll do that for you") to sheer application of power ("you do this, or I'll have you killed"). Traditional prison

gangs of the 1960s and 1970s comprised adult criminals organized into complex hierarchies with rank differentiation among members and powerful, criminally sophisticated leaders. This

---

Puerto Rico's Prisons Being Terrorized by Gangs

"Puerto Rican officials say they will fight any attempt by the Federal government to take over operations of its 36 prisons. A recently released report by a team of Federal investigators concluded that a takeover may be the only solution to the commonwealth's problem with violent gangs. The investigators found that violent gangs virtually control the commonwealth's prisons, including all incoming mail, cellblock assignments, and access to educational and vocational programs, as well as job assignments.

The report was supervised by former Federal Court Monitor, Vincent Nathan, who recommended that the prisons be transferred to a Federal receivership. 'Long-standing conditions within Puerto Rico's prisons not only warrant, but demand, this extraordinary remedy,' Nathan said.

The report also stems from a class action lawsuit filed 18 years ago by prisoners against the corrections system. It was released in connection with a court hearing in August, 1997. Originally, the lawsuit centered on overcrowding, however, in recent years, it has focused on other areas—including inmates' health, rehabilitation, and prison security—all areas that are said to be affected by the dominance of gangs within the system. (Crowding is no longer a central issue, mainly because

the commonwealth constructed several new facilities during the 1990s.)

Gang activity is said to be so bad that inmate classifications as well as release dates often depend more upon gang affiliation than on the severity of their crimes. The investigators also said that gangs have control of all incoming mail, allowing contraband and drugs to flow into the facilities, virtually unchecked.

'The authority of the staff has been ceded to inmate domination to a degree which we have never before seen,' the report said.

Corrections Administrator Zoe Laboy has acknowledged that gangs are a major problem, but she also said that she's been working to strip them of their powers, since taking office [in March, 1997].

Inmates started a month-long strike in April, 1997 refusing to do prison chores, reportedly because Laboy refused to meet with leaders of the Netas, which is said to be the prison system's largest gang.

Since 1980, Puerto Rico has been fined some $130 million for violations of Federal court orders."

Source: Reprinted from *Corrections Alert,* Vol. 4, No. 11, p. 5, © 1997, Aspen Publishers, Inc.

meant that a prison gang was an efficient criminal organization that could smuggle drugs into prison and engage in other crime, including violence that supported that crime. In such groups, violence was used to further crime pursuits and was directed outward toward enemies and deadbeat inmates who did not pay drug and gambling debts. It could also be directed inward, toward a gang's own members. By comparison, street gangs in prison comprised younger inmates whose groups had relatively simple hierarchies, less status differentiation, and less defined leadership styles. Thus, these gangs were less effective criminal organizations.[6] A street gang and a prison gang were as different as a delinquent group of adolescents and an organized crime family.

Over the decades, these distinctions between prison gangs and street gangs have been lost. No longer do structure, leadership style, and age of members distinguish prison gangs from street gangs. Today, the Gangster Disciples and Latin Kings, classic examples of street gangs, are just as dangerous inside prisons as the Mexican Mafia and Texas Syndicate. To be sure, the prison-based Gangster Disciples, Latin Kings, and Mexican Mafia are often dangerous in urban neighborhoods.[7] To correctional administrators, how a gang originated 20 to 30 years ago is less important than its ability to disrupt cell houses today. Thus, the criteria that once distinguished a prison gang from a street gang in prison have become blurred as the correctional presence and criminal sophistication of street gangs have increased. Now, "inmate disruptive group" (IDG) is the name used for the inmate groups formerly called prison street gangs and prison gangs. An IDG is a group of inmates whose prison affiliation is based on race, ethnicity, geography, ideology, or a combination of these and other factors; who seek one another's protection; and who have an economic objective, such as drug distribution, that is often linked to violence and threats of violence.

The internal structure and leadership style of inmate disruptive groups differ. Therefore, it is essential for staff to understand these differ-

ences. This first step in comprehensive IDG management requires nonstop data collection and analysis.

IDGs are dangerous. For example, the Gangster Disciples or the Mexican Mafia are threats to institution security because they are well-organized crime organizations. The strength of an IDG depends on its structure and leadership style and also on the length of its membership roster. These groups lose members as old-timers are released, die, transfer, and "roll over" (inform) on former companions. Opportunities to obtain drugs, cash, and other property, as well as gain a sense of power and belonging, are compelling reasons for a young, uneducated, impulsive street criminal to join a gang when he or she enters prison. But an IDG with poor organization and dozens of members will not be strong. More members only make a disorganized group larger. Size alone does not enable a group to be a better crime organization.

STREET-TO-PRISON CONNECTIONS

Prison perimeters keep inmates inside, but these physical impediments are easily violated by the telephones, mail, and visiting rooms. To sustain prison drug and other crime activity, IDGs depend on street contacts—with girlfriends, wives, cousins, mothers, fathers, aunts, uncles, and neighborhood companions. Because those social tentacles are nearly impossible to eliminate, contraband will likely be smuggled into institutions, no matter how sophisticated their security procedures.

Street-level gang research shows that imprisoned gang members recruit companions still on the street to smuggle rock cocaine, marijuana, and other drugs into jail and prison visiting rooms.[8] Young women are especially vulnerable to recruitment. These women often were inmates' former lovers and had children fathered by them. Unemployed, these young women need money to pay rent and to buy drugs for their own use and for street-level distribution. Inside prison, these inmates may be pinched for drugs or cash to repay gambling and drug debts to

IDGs. Backed into a corner, these inmates may threaten the lives of young women who fail to work for them as drug "mules." Drugs inside a prison sell for prices 5 to 10 times higher than their street value. At those prices, smuggling contraband is worth the risk to inmates and visitors.

Gang management personnel must have listings of IDG members' visitors, monitor telephone calls and mail, and stay in touch with local police agencies. Smuggling contraband is a continuous activity. Visiting room staffers must be well trained by correctional personnel who know the techniques of smuggling contraband. Drugs can be passed between visitors and inmates in many ways, some of which look innocent to new staffers. Drugs can be passed casually during a kiss or spit into a cup of coffee purchased from a vending machine and then swallowed by an inmate. Conjugal visiting also facilitates the smuggling of drugs and other contraband.

A visiting room must be carefully monitored and visiting room staff well trained and supervised to ensure that these staffers have not fallen prey to corruption. Gangs control drugs; drugs equal money; money corrupts inmates and staffers.

GANG CONTROL

IDGs threaten prison security. But a greater, long-range threat is the willingness of inmates to organize themselves into these crime bureaucracies, despite institution sanctions against such activity. Inmates, particularly those who grew up in inner-city neighborhoods in large and medium-sized urban areas, know what happens when violent criminals (gang members or otherwise) terrorize a neighborhood. What happens in those neighborhoods also happens in prison.

IDG crime can to some degree be suppressed or controlled. But the key strategic management issues are how an institution's staff can prevent tomorrow's inmates from joining IDGs and how staff can encourage those who have joined IDGs to abide by institution policies.

Inmates, like everyone else, enjoy a comfortable environment. When given a choice between being locked down 24 hours a day, year after year, or enjoying good food, recreation, and other programs, most inmates choose a comfortable daily life. To be sure, hard-core gang members will not likely discard weapons or stop drug distribution in exchange for new recreation equipment and better food. However, research shows that a prison's social and physical environment does influence inmates' behavior.[9] This means that correctional administrators and managers can influence inmates' behavior through organizational development, strong management, and proactive planning.

This may seem counterintuitive to correctional personnel who believe that IDG members' rule infractions are best controlled by removing privileges and locking down group members and leaders for long periods of time in high-security institutions.[10] But withdrawing inmate incentives for good behavior and using lockdowns to control IDGs and other inmates is a dangerous gamble. If staffers lose the bet that inmates will behave well if they are punished harshly, they might also lose social control of their institution. This will lead to violence. Prisons, especially medium and high security institutions, are packed with criminals who have histories of violence, have shown years of disruptive behavior on the streets and in prison, and have been victims of harsh, often brutal treatment all their lives. These inmates have learned how to cope with and fight against harsh treatment in difficult environments. As prisons begin to house more of these hardened street criminals, the ability to control them through force will become increasingly difficult and expensive.

IDG control is inmate control. A fine balance must be achieved between institution security and inmate programs. Pressuring organized disruptive groups too hard with behavior control mechanisms, and offering inmates too few incentives to behave well, may congeal leadership structures and facilitate violence and other disruptive behavior. Ignoring gangs (standing back and not interfering in gang activities) may effect the same result. Somewhere between laying off and squeezing gangs is a strategy to fit each institution. Finding that point is the challenge of a successful IDG management program.

Examples show that squeezing gang-affiliated inmates does not accomplish long-term positive results.[11] Putting gang members together for housing or work re-creates street gangs' neighborhood geographic isolation (one area, one gang), reinforces the ties among gang-affiliated inmates, and creates animosities about which groups have the best cells or the best jobs. It is destructive to lay off—to allow gangs to run cell houses, "own" cells, and carve up territory on the yard that is off-limits even to staff. Administrators who negotiate deals with gang leaders to get peaceful cell houses and prison yards today may find calamitous consequences tomorrow.

IDGs are predatory; their leaders have insatiable appetites for money and power. Cutting deals with them will result in violence among inmates, discord between inmates and staffers, and staff corruption.

GANG MANAGEMENT

Prisons mirror the community. Citizens can feel secure and be physically safe as long as criminal activity is kept to a minimum. To keep gang crime to a minimum requires more than an IDG classification system; intelligence from local, state, and federal law enforcement agencies; and mounds of paperwork to classify inmates into one group or another. In today's and tomorrow's prisons there will be IDGs. The trick is to ensure that these affiliated prisoners do not violate institution rules to such a degree that sanctioned activity endangers the lives of inmates and staffers and engenders a feeling of insecurity in the institution.

James Q. Wilson's theory of broken windows, developed for problem-oriented policing, also applies to prisons.[12] Wilson argued that once an abandoned building has one broken window that is allowed to remain unrepaired, more windows will be broken, one by one, day by day, until all windows are shattered and the building disheveled. This observation also applies to the quality of life inside prisons. Cell house showers that do not drain well, toilets that do not operate properly, food that is badly prepared, recreation that is boring, inmate jobs that are menial, inmates who stop talking to staffers, and staffers who do not talk to inmates in a congenial way are a prison's "broken windows." Small repairs that are not attended to create an environment well suited for the development and expansion of inmate gangs. The responsibility of an institution's senior leadership is to control an institution's climate, oversee IDG management and other programs, and ensure that "windows" are always repaired.

The availability of inmate programs greatly affects the long-term management of inmate gang members. On the street and in prison, the most effective crime intervention is prevention. A gang management program should be one of a number of major programs in an institution's management plan, not an afterthought. The success of gang control plans is measured by management control data such as incident reports as well as the institution climate. If an institution does not have strong staff professionalism, high inmate and staff morale, open communication among staffers and between inmates and staffers, and, most important, an ample number of productive jobs for inmates, then IDG management alone may be insufficient to create a positive institution climate and control inmate gang crime.

The technical side of IDG management—the paperwork and procedures necessary to classify gang members, the strategies for investigating gang crimes—is straightforward. The human resource side of IDG management is more difficult. Generally speaking, the role of staff in this effort is equivalent to that of gang detectives on the street. They have a sensitive job with significant implications for institution safety. Thus, selecting qualified personnel is the single most important decision in establishing and maintaining a gang control program. Recall that IDGs have long social tentacles extending to the street. A careful screening of all potential applicants is essential. It should not surprise correctional officials to find that inmates' siblings, cousins, girlfriends, former wives, street companions, and lovers apply for employment as correctional staffers. Examining IDG members' presentence investigations may determine if relatives of gang members are already employed under different surnames.

Gang management, then, requires a comprehensive policy. This policy should clearly specify legal precedents, procedures, and guidelines for inmate IDG classification, verification of members, and so on. A strong policy does more than list procedures, however; it is a statement of an institution's philosophy on gang management. Such a policy should include an operational definition of an IDG, to establish the ground rules for gang investigations and prosecutions. The underclassification of inmates (identifying too few inmates as IDG members) can be dangerous, and overclassification can be just as harmful. Thus, creating a workable definition of an IDG that fits an institution's management plan is essential.

A well-planned management program does more than gang classification and intelligence gathering. It links IDG management to both institution security and inmate programs. This dual link should be emphasized. Removing from a general population those gang members who distribute drugs and engage in strong-arm activities may offer temporary control, but other inmates will replace those locked up, the network will persist, and the crime problems recur. A gang management program must be able to guide an institution with an increasing number of criminals with street gang ties. Other relevant strategic issues include but are not limited to identifying strategies to prevent newly committed inmates from participating in gang activities; allowing current, albeit marginal, gang members a way out of IDGs; and, more generally, developing an organizational culture that exhibits zero tolerance for gang activity while also encouraging inmates' participation in work and other programs.

These are difficult challenges, especially in higher security institutions. To achieve inmates' consensus means encouraging or at least slowing inmates' participation in systematic IDG-related criminal activity.

GANG MANAGEMENT DATA

IDG management personnel must display excellent data management and analysis skills. A key to comprehensive gang intelligence is having valid data that is continuously updated. Institution intelligence staffers must know the gangs and gang members operating in the local area, the region, and the nation. Gang members move from city to city and region to region, and staff should develop strong nationwide ties to gang units in police departments; participate in national correctional conferences on gang intelligence (the National Major Gang Taskforce, headquartered in Dallas, TX, convenes national conferences, attracting hundreds of gang experts); maintain collegial relations with fellow IDG management personnel in state and federal institutions; and establish contacts in police agencies and state's attorneys' offices. IDGs are expanding in number and membership, so the need for information about them increases daily.

The responsibility for collecting gang information should be spread across prison staff in all departments. A gang management program may have only a few specialists, but a prison has hundreds of employees. IDG management should be the job of all employees in a correctional facility. All staffers must be familiar with gang leaders and those inmates who are likely to do their bidding. Gangs are social groups; their members want face-to-face communication. They walk together, hang out in the yard, and sit together in the dining hall. Case managers, correctional counselors, leisure time activities specialists, food service employees, staffers who supervise industries and work details, and others must be familiar with gang tattoos, graffiti, and other symbols that demonstrate an inmate's affiliation. All staff should be trained at least in observational techniques of data collection, and institutions should have clear procedures for reporting information to the institution's intelligence personnel. Even more than staffers, inmates know gangs' destructive effect on a social environment. Reporting information about IDGs in safe and confidential ways should be an option for inmates, too.

Mounds of gang data are worthless if they are not well organized and carefully analyzed. Today's intelligence staff should be trained on databases and have the ability to create custom databases to accomplish specific tasks. An example of this would be linking visitors to inmate incidents reports for offenses such as the possession and use of drugs. If management personnel cannot write software for specific facility needs, then staff must know their specific programming needs and be able to describe those needs to someone who can accomplish these tasks.

At annual meetings convened by the U.S. Department of Justice, state correctional and police agencies, and local departments, correctional personnel can learn about technical aspects of gang management. Private vendors at such conferences display the latest hardware and software designed to ease the job of tallying gang rosters and make sophisticated analysis much easier than computer-averse staffers might expect.

CONCLUSION

Institutions should develop a gang management plan even before a problem exists. Prison IDGs, like gangs on the street, can dominate a prison community if that community is weakly organized against them. If staffers are co-opted by IDGs who offer them money and drugs or if gang members threaten the safety of staff family members, the quality of institution life will deteriorate for both inmates and employees.

A proactive defense against gang expansion will include the development of a comprehensive institution management system to encourage inmates' cooperation and participation in programs, including jobs with pay scales relative to inmates' skill and motivation level. Good inmate–staff rapport is essential, too. Inmates must trust staff to protect them from predatory inmates, whether or not these predatory inmates are gang members. In the end, the challenge of curbing IDG growth will best be met with modern crime intelligence techniques and good planning.

NOTES

1. A. Goldstein and C. Huff, *The Gang Intervention Handbook* (Champaign, IL: Research Press, 1992).
2. R. Fong, "The Organizational Structure of Prison Gangs: A Texas Case Study," *Federal Probation* 59, no. 1 (1990): 36–43.
3. M. Fleisher, *Warehousing Violence* (Newbury Park, CA: Sage Press, 1989), 70–72.
4. J. Howell, "Youth Gangs: An Overview," *Juvenile Justice Bulletin,* August 1998, 1. (U.S. Department of Justice Office of Juvenile Justice & Delinquency Prevention).
5. J. Jacobs, "Street Gangs behind Bars," *Social Problems* 21, no. 3 (1974): 395–409.
6. M. Fleisher, *Beggars and Thieves: Lives of Urban Street Criminals* (Madison, WI: University of Wisconsin Press, 1995), 146–156.
7. Chicago Crime Commission, *Public Enemy Number One* (Chicago: 1995), 17.
8. Fleisher, *Beggars and Thieves: Lives of Urban Street Criminals,* 169–172.
9. J. DiIulio, *Governing Prisons* (New York: The Free Press, 1987), 215.
10. G. Marx and C. Parsons, "Dangers of the Front Line," *Chicago Tribune,* 9 August, 1996, 1:8–9.
11. G. Lazarus, "Power Struggle," *Chicago Tribune,* 10 November, 1996, 1:12–13.
12. J. Wilson and G. Kelling, "Broken Windows," *Atlantic Monthly,* March 1982, 29–38.

CHAPTER 33

Sex Offenders

Gilbert L. Ingram

One of the most challenging responsibilities for corrections administrators is managing special needs offenders. Of all special needs offenders (including older persons, protected witnesses, and those with mental illness), sex offenders are thought (by many administrators) most likely to cause trouble during and after incarceration. Because of fear of failure, lack of resources, or lack of commitment, some managers have decided to avoid the issue by not officially acknowledging sex offenders as a group requiring special attention. This tactic is shortsighted, unprofessional, and even unethical. It should never be an option.

MAGNITUDE OF THE PROBLEM

Sex offenders have attracted tremendous negative publicity during the past few years. Highly visible sex crimes have always received an inordinate amount of public interest, but the recent intense media attention has created a public rage unprecedented in correctional history. Today, this already unpopular group of offenders has few people willing to fight for them. Because sex offenders have no visible supporters, politicians have leaped into action, calling for longer sentences and lifelong public identification after release from prison.

But how many sex offenders are there? It's not clear. Some people say that the problem is growing, but valid data are not available today. This lack of highly reliable studies can be attrib-

uted to many factors. Most offenders guilty of an act that is technically a violation in a particular jurisdiction are never arrested: Embarrassment, fear, or self-blame on the part of victims deter many from ever reporting these acts; and authorities, unless compelled to act or under unusual circumstances, frequently overlook sexual behavior that the public seems to condone. Some sexual acts are technical violations of the law, but are considered to be acceptable behavior when between consenting adults in private settings. Even if arrested, a large number of sex offenders are not legally convicted after arrest or plead guilty to a lesser charge. Only convicted sex offenders appear in sex crime statistics.

The collection of reliable data has been even more complicated in recent years. For example, the public spotlight on abuse by family members (fueled by claims of early memory recovery under hypnosis) and a generally more supportive environment for reporting victimization have encouraged more people to step forward. Additionally, the definition of sexual offenses remains a continuing problem; behavior deemed unacceptable in one state may be acceptable in another.

However, there are enough statistics available on commonly agreed-upon sex offenses to allow managers to conclude that the problem is fairly extensive. An estimated 250,000 sex offenders in our society today are being sought or have a past record, according to the Department of Justice. In 1993, there were 312,000 reported rapes

The Debate on Sexual Offenders—Hospitalize or Incarcerate?

Those who are convicted of heinous sex crimes against children stir up a significant moral debate in America: Should they be locked away in prison cells or placed in mental facilities for care and treatment? Most citizens respond to the question with cold anger and clearly want the transgressors punished and separated from society. These crimes are among the most terrible, and these offenders have a high rate of recidivism.

Twelve states and the District of Columbia have laws that permit the civil commitment of sex offenders. The number of states that permit this has declined in the last three decades, and there has been a trend to toughen the laws that regulate sentencing options.

In 1994, the State of Kansas created a Sexually Violent Predator Act that authorizes procedures to permit the state to indefinitely confine an individual who is diagnosed with a mental or personality disorder and who is likely to engage in predatory acts of sexual violence. This civil commitment statute can be utilized at the end of a prison sentence to keep a possibly violent sexual predator off the streets. The Supreme Court found this law to be constitutional in June 1997, in the case of Leroy Hendricks (*Hendricks v. Kansas,* 521 U.S. 346 [1997]). In affirming the statute, the Court approved of detaining sex criminals based on the standard of "mentally abnormal" rather than the more demanding standard of "mentally ill."
  Leroy Hendricks was an extreme example of a sexual miscreant. The 62-year-old was characterized by the Court as having "a chilling history of repeated child sexual molestation and abuse" beginning in 1955 and ending with his most recent plea-bargained sentence in 1984 for taking "indecent liberties" with two 13-year-old boys. He has stated that only death would guarantee a change in his behavior. After release from a 10-year prison term, Hendricks was committed to a mental hospital for an indefinite period of confinement and treatment.

As stated in a *New York Times* editorial, "it would be hard to imagine a less sympathetic defendant than a person who brought this legal challenge, Mr. Hendricks."* But it is a significant step to incarcerate an individual based on what egregious behavior he may engage in at a future time.

Should sexual predators be hospitalized or incarcerated? Is it morally right to lock someone away based on the government's view that the individual represents a threat to the community? With the recent Hendricks decision, many jurisdictions will undoubtedly create statutes similar to Kansas's. If such legislation is proper, might it be extended to crimes other than sex offenses?

Most U.S. citizens believe tougher sentencing is in order, and many support this recent Supreme Court decision.

*"The High Court's Mixed Record Wrong on Sex Offenders." Editorial. *The New York Times*, June 25, 1997, p. A26.

Source: Adapted with permission from S. Lally, "Steel Beds versus Iron Bars: New Laws Muddle How To Handle Sex Offenders," p. C–1, July 27, 1997, © *The Washington Post.*

and 173,000 other reported sexual assaults. Data generally indicate that sex offenders are more likely than other types of criminals to repeat their offenses. Federal studies confirm that rapists were 10.5 times more likely to be rearrested for rape than were other released prisoners. This is only a sampling of many generally accepted studies that confirm that deviant sex behavior is a large and continuing problem in this country.

It is easy to appreciate the reluctance of some public administrators to take responsibility for managing a very unpopular group whose aberrant behavior is extremely difficult to change. Even though successful treatment is possible,[1] many sex offenders do repeat their inappropriate behavior after release from custody. However, public administrators must keep in mind the greater public good that is sought. Many sex offenders may be deterred with proper intervention. Further, it is good management practice to involve all offenders in a meaningful activity to facilitate better control of the institution and to allow better use of public resources. If these reasons do not seem to suffice, managers have to remember that treating people humanely and trying to help them is the right thing to do. They should remember that most inmates, including sex offenders, will be someone's neighbor again in the future.

BASIC APPROACH TO SEX OFFENDER MANAGEMENT

Each correctional situation is different, and there is no single formula for successful management. Consequently, many programs producing good results in one institution have failed completely when someone tried to duplicate them elsewhere. Differences in administrator personalities and levels of motivation as well as insufficient resources have often made duplication difficult. However, certain basic management practices produce successful sex offender programs at local, state, and federal levels. In discussing these approaches, I will focus on men offenders because they are the largest concern for correctional officials. Nonetheless, it must be

kept in mind that instances of sex offenses by women have been increasing.

Correctly identifying sex offenders as soon after incarceration as possible is important. An efficient classification and designation process must be in place. During classification, there is no need to uncover the underlying psychological reasons for offenders' inappropriate sexual behavior; this information will be an integral part later, during the treatment program.

Immediately after classification, the offender should be separated from the general population as much as possible. At a minimum, a separate area for special treatment is necessary, and if possible, a separate housing area would minimize the many adjustment problems that sex offenders typically encounter. A special housing unit for sex offenders should be placed in an institution with a progressive, open-minded administration that can easily handle difficult cases. Inmate participation in other institution-wide activities outside the special unit seems to work well in this situation.

CLASSIFICATION

Early identification of sex offenders is not always an easy task. Sex criminals are usually reluctant to be candid about their activities, and they attempt to hide or alter facts in their favor. Official records are not necessarily the solution for classification purposes because details of the commitment offense are frequently affected by lengthy legal maneuvers and sometimes not available to classification staff when the records are needed. Also, many offenders are incarcerated for apparent nonsexual activities such as breaking and entering or assault when their intent may have been the sex offense of rape.

Classification staff need be sensitive to these possibilities and convince inmates that a complete reporting of their activities is in their best interests. This is a formidable task, but one attainable if interviewers are trained to deal with sex offenders. Offense details frequently help identify some of this target group, and self-reports from those already motivated to seek help also are useful. Ideally, made aware of the existence of a good sex offender treatment program in the correctional system, inmates who recognize their deviancy as a problem will cooperate during classification.

Classification staff should record the information they collect on a standard checklist or inventory.[2] Many checklists provide a structured format to ensure that all relevant areas of inquiry have been assessed. If the identification of sexually deviant behavior remains in doubt after the initial interview process, additional attempts to obtain background information should be made, and a follow-up interview should be scheduled. If they learn more about the treatment program or have more time to talk, reluctant inmates may be less guarded in their responses.

Trained staff should use their knowledge about typical sex offender profiles. For instance, they should remember that almost all sex offenders have engaged in many minor transgressions before the current incarceration and that their current offense is part of an unhealthy cycle of behavior.[3] To gain cooperation during the interviews, staff should tell inmates that many people have been involved in all sorts of sex acts as they matured and that they should not be concerned, because the interviewer has heard just about everything. Staff should not to condone such behavior but simply acknowledge its occurrence to elicit more information from the suspected sex offender.

Inmates who are sex offenders will not necessarily have histories of physical aggression or attacks. In fact, most sex offenses do not involve forceful acts, and most sex offenders do not fit the image of the dangerous psychopath. Many but not all appear to be psychologically or emotionally impaired, neurotic, psychotic, or even brain-damaged. A trained professional will be able to make these kinds of determinations.

Intelligence level, age, and income level are not very helpful in identification at this early stage of classification. Even though many sex offenders are young and have somewhat low intelligence, the same can be said of inmates in general. Similarly, most sex offenders started their inappropriate behavior at an early age and most come from poor family backgrounds, but the same can be said of other offenders.

STAFF ISSUES

After classification has been completed and transfer to the treatment unit has been accomplished, the offender will be handled almost exclusively by staff who specialize in dealing with sex offenders. The most essential step in developing and running a useful program for sex offenders is having trained staff who have the right attitude toward these inmates. Staff should not be people who view sex offenders as horrible persons who deserve the worst punishment that the institution can create for them. On the other hand, staff should also not be people who consider sex offenders to be victims of poorly conceived social laws, innocent byproducts of dysfunctional families, or youngsters guilty only of normal youthful experimentation.

Staff members should be realistic and mature. They should be people who view the sex offense as illegal and inappropriate but believe the offender is capable of changing with proper motivation and assistance. People who are uncomfortable with the topic of sex or show too much interest in the area may not be right for this job. It is best to hire professionally trained specialists. If this is not possible for all staff positions, additional personnel should be chosen carefully. There should be enough personnel that a great deal of individual attention can be given to each program participant. After staff are selected, they should be trained. They should learn about sex offenders in general, sexual behavior in all of its ramifications, and, of course, the particular treatment approach that will be followed. Staff should also be sensitized to the need for confidentiality, and to the possible negative feelings that other staff who work in other areas of the institution may exhibit.

Staff must work well as a team. Total communication and cooperation are needed to monitor progress and to make important decisions about readiness for additional programs, privileges, and, eventually, return to the community. Staff need to encourage positive behavior while also being able to react quickly, decisively, and appropriately to offender setbacks. Demonstrating acceptance but not approval of inmate transgressions is a very challenging balancing act, but it has been accomplished successfully in correctional environments.

Recruitment and financial limitations may make staff selection more difficult. The quality and quantity of professional treatment staff and resources available to administrators varies considerably in different locations. If professionals trained in sex offender treatment (usually psychologists and, less frequently, psychiatrists) cannot be hired, it may be best to defer implementation of the program. Attempting to run such a demanding program is difficult under the best of circumstances. If the right professionals are not present to train correctional staff or to provide specialized treatment, the program may fail. In most instances, a failing program is worse than no program and may cause significant legal liability.

However, too often administrators have used this rationale to justify not implementing programs when, in fact, they have not spent sufficient time or effort in seeking professional staff. The marketplace for suitable candidates is looking better as competition and cutbacks increase in the general medical area, and recent advances in treatment techniques for sex offenders produce more trained personnel interested in employment.

EVALUATING AND ADMITTING SEX OFFENDERS

After arrival at the special treatment unit, all sex offenders identified through classification or by the courts as suitable candidates for treatment should be given a full explanation of the program requirements. An excellent example of a comprehensive handout for sex offenders is used by the Federal Bureau of Prisons.[4] Candidates are told that they will need at least enough time to complete all program requirements before release, and that they should be within a reasonable period of time (two years maximum recommended) until their release date. (A natural progression from the special unit to a community facility would allow a more normal transition to free society.) After offenders understand everything they need to know about the program, particularly their responsibilities in it, they are asked to volunteer for participation. This willing acceptance is necessary because sex offenders often become resistive during treatment; they have had a great deal of immediate gratification from their sexual behavior. Because the program demands intensive work from offenders, successful treatment will not occur if they do not wish to take part.

In determining offender suitability for the program, staff must remember that full participation is not possible if severe mental illness or basic deficiencies in areas such as reading and writing are present. These needs should be addressed before the offender is formally admitted to the treatment unit. Those offenders who are seeking admission for reasons other than treatment of sexual deviancy should not be accepted; inmates hoping for a diversion from routine prison life or seeking an earlier release opportunity should be screened out.

The evaluation phase of the program continues after the offender is officially admitted. Because every sex offender has a unique set of problems that needs to be addressed, it is vital to program success that the offender complete very extensive questionnaires pertaining to family background, education, social history, and sexual behavior. This information will help staff develop a workable plan for treatment and release into the community.

Extensive psychological testing is also necessary at this stage. These tests may vary according to staff preferences, expertise, and availability, but a basic assessment of personality, cognitive abilities, social attitudes, and sexual thoughts is necessary. If competent staff are present, and the cooperation of all concerned has been obtained (including, for example, top management's commitment to support and defend the use of a potentially controversial treatment tool), an assessment of the participant's sexual response to deviant and nondeviant themes is conducted. This assessment is accomplished by use of penile plethysmography initially and at regular intervals during treatment. This widely accepted instrument consists of a small penile transducer, a circular gauge similar to a rubber band, that offenders attach to themselves in private. The information is not only useful in determining the proper course of treatment but is frequently used during the actual treatment to condition appropriate sexual responses.

All of the information gained during the evaluation period is used by staff to formulate an overall treatment plan for each offender. This plan may be modified at any time as more information becomes available.

TREATMENT PROGRAM

Teaching the offender to engage in meaningful social interactions, healthy recreation, and other self-improvement activities should be a high priority for staff. Like all inmates, sex offenders must be actively engaged in productive activities. Holding sex offenders accountable for their behavior, past and present, is equally important.

A comprehensive program for every sex offender includes specialized treatment activities in addition to the self-improvement and work activities assigned to all inmates. Full programming is as essential to good institutional management as it is to good treatment. Naturally, treatment takes priority initially, occupying most of the offender's time during the intensive part of the sex offender program.

Each participant is assigned a staff member who serves as the lead therapist, providing individual counseling and coordination of the total treatment plan. In addition to individual sessions at least once per week, various group therapy programs are essential. The basic premise of

treatment—which must be accepted by participants—is that there is no cure for their problem, but with their full participation and motivation, staff can teach sex offenders to control their deviant behavior.[5] Further, participants should accept that their sexual behavior is totally inappropriate and unjustified.

Individual therapy time is used to explore the dynamics of sex offenders' behavior, the difficulties they continue to have in relationships, and other issues raised in group therapies. As treatment progresses, discussions move to offenders' adjustment to the treatment program and finally to release planning.

Throughout the treatment program, offenders meet in group sessions aimed at resolving their long-standing difficulties and gaining understanding about their behavior. Regardless of the number of required therapy groups, one central group continues to focus on the basic deviant behavior, including a thorough discussion of inmates' offenses, victims, background, and present sexual thoughts and acts. The principal goal of this group is to examine how the offenders' behavior, feelings, and thought processes led to their inappropriate sexual activity. The individual sessions complement this group work and add to this intensive self-examination. Many offenders must deal with extremely sensitive issues in private sessions before they can explore them in the group setting.

Several other key groups are significant components of a complete treatment effort. One such group deals with abuse and its ramifications in the offenders' life. Most sex offenders were abused themselves as youngsters, frequently in a sexual way, but also physically or emotionally. In this group, offenders gain an understanding of how this abuse affected them and prepare for a later group that tries to develop in them the capacity for victim empathy. Other groups might address anger management, social skills, sex education, and substance abuse, areas that cause difficulty for many sex offenders and are frequently factors in their sexually deviant behavior.

The final mandatory part of group treatment is relapse prevention training. Offenders have to accept the fact that the probability of offending again is very high if proactive steps are not taken. This group teaches offenders to recognize risk factors associated with deviant sexual behavior, to anticipate and modify risky situations, and to cope successfully with their postrelease environment.

TRANSITION TO THE COMMUNITY

A comprehensive treatment program must include a plan for return to the community. Regardless of the offenders' level of program involvement, their success in completing the treatment goals, or the development of a realistic relapse prevention plan, staff must attend to another important task: ensuring offenders' successful transition back home. This home may be an offender's previous residence or a new location.

Presumably, after successful program completion, offenders can anticipate and know how to cope with the challenges of life outside the institution. Knowing that they will need help from many others to maintain a nondeviant lifestyle, offenders must seek out socially approved support groups, positive recreational activities, and other forms of community assistance. However, staff responsibility goes beyond helping offenders with these preparations and should include informing the relevant local authorities when and where the offenders will be released. Ensuring that all contacts required by law had been made was relatively simple until recently. Notifying the courts and probation authorities usually satisfied all concerned, but in the future, staff will need to contact local law enforcement.

Registering sex offenders nationally to ensure that local communities are aware of the offenders' presence has become a rallying cry for both political parties. Good communication and coordination are necessary between staff and not only the community but also the offender. Staff need to ensure that all sex offenders in their institutions are aware of this required registration and the anticipated increased public attention on them. The offenders need to be fully prepared for the hostile, perhaps even threatening, reaction they may receive in the community and taught how to deal with it. Staff should explain that facing this public reaction is part of being accountable for deviant behavior.

CONCLUSION

Although successful techniques for treating sex offenders continue to be developed, dealing with sexual deviance will remain problematic for both staff and offenders. The increased public attention will only exacerbate an already difficult task, in that no treatment program can promise that an offense will not recur. Fortunately, a realistic treatment effort can prepare the offenders to control their behavior and thereby better protect the community.

Sex offenders who take responsibility for their behavior, discuss their offense openly, understand why their deviant act was wrong, exhibit true remorseful feelings, and actively work in the treatment program to acquire relapse prevention skills will undoubtedly pose less of a danger to the community than they did before arrival at the institution.

NOTES

1. American Correctional Association, *A Directory of Programs That Work* (Washington, DC: 1996), 124–136.

2. R. Borum, "Improving the Clinical Practice of Violence Risk Assessment," *American Psychologist* 3, no. 1 (1996): 945–956.

3. L. Bays et al., *How Can I Stop? Breaking My Deviant Cycle* (Brandon, VT: Safer Society Press, 1990), 19–48.

4. Federal Bureau of Prisons, Federal Correctional Institution, Butner, *Program Participation Package* (Butner, NC: 1996), 1–36.

5. L. Bays and R. Freeman-Longo, *Why Did I Do It Again? Understanding My Cycle of Problem Behaviors* (Brandon, VT: Safer Society Press, 1989), 72.

CHAPTER 34

The Death Penalty in the United States

Julie A. Carlson

Capital punishment is one of the most highly debated topics of the century. Many questions arise in these emotional debates. Is the death penalty morally wrong, or is it just and fair? Does it deter criminals from wrong acts? Is it an effective punishment and worth continuing in America's judicial system? Finally, how should a correctional jurisdiction house inmates under a sentence of death?

HISTORY OF THE DEATH PENALTY

The history of capital punishment goes back to the earliest human cultures, when methods of executing the death penalty were extremely cruel. The goal of the punishment was to create a painful experience: stoning, whipping, and boiling were common. With the passage of time and the evolution of ideas, punishments have changed. Early in the twentieth century, death-sentenced American inmates were executed by hanging, electrocution, or firing squad. Now, 7 states use lethal gas, and 32 employ lethal injection as the method of execution. As of 1996, only 11 states continued to use the electric chair, 3 the firing squad, and 3 states allowed hanging as an option.[1] States that operate more than one method of execution allow sentenced inmates to choose their method of death.

The new execution methods allow the government to punish criminals in the most civilized and humane manner with the least amount of suffering. Particular problems noted with the electric chair have encouraged the development of new methods of executions. Several executions have been documented where the electricity administered was not enough to kill the condemned person. The most infamous example of this occurred in Alabama in 1983, during the execution of John Louis Evans. Three separate attempts of 1,900 volts of electricity were required to complete Evans's punishment. In Florida, during an electrocution on March 25, 1997, the electricity created flames that erupted from convicted murderer Pedro Medina's masked head during the execution. An international outcry resulted, causing Florida to suspend further executions pending a state court review of this method of execution.

States have handled the death penalty in different ways. Michigan, Rhode Island, Wisconsin, Minnesota, and Maine decided to abolish the death penalty in the early 1900s. And a few states abolished the death penalty and later reinstated it.[2] Most states, however, have maintained their capital punishment laws with little change, except for the court-required restrictions. After the Supreme Court articulated a new standard in the 1970s for the use of the death penalty, states returned to a greater use of the death penalty as their ultimate sanction.

From the 1930s through the early 1970s, the death penalty was handled most efficiently; those who were sentenced to die were executed fairly promptly. Nearly 4,000 men and women were executed during this time in the United States.

In the 1960s, executions slowed dramatically as courts became more and more involved in this arena and death row inmates took advantage of their right to exercise lengthy legal appeals. This trend culminated in the 1972 *Furman v. Georgia* court case, in which the Supreme Court ruled that capital punishment was cruel and unusual. This ruling held that the decision to execute as a punishment was not fairly applied to all defendants and resulted in the death penalty being annulled in 39 states.

These jurisdictions then embarked on an effort to rewrite their sentencing laws to deal with the issue of arbitrariness. In order to combat the Supreme Court's charges, state legislators mandated capital punishment for certain offenses and created specific guidelines for the judicial system to follow when deciding whether to implement the death penalty.

In 1976, the first test of the new laws appeared with the *Gregg v. Georgia* case. Although the Supreme Court ruled against mandating the death penalty for certain crimes, the guidelines for juries to follow were approved. Accordingly, the Georgia version of guidelines became the model for many other states.

ARGUMENTS AGAINST THE DEATH PENALTY

As the death penalty became more common within the United States, so, too, did controversy. The greatest argument against capital punishment seems to be that few individuals are actually executed. Currently, about 3,000 inmates are waiting for execution. The state with the most executions—Texas—has a current backlog exceeding 300 people.[3] In the U.S. only about 1 inmate of every 20 sentenced to die is actually executed. Despite these statistics, judges and juries continue to hand out death sentences at a rate of 200 a year, thus furthering the backlog of inmates on death row.

The haziness of who "qualifies" for the death penalty also seems to contribute to the problem. Federal and state prisons have an immense backlog of death row inmates simply because the laws addressing this controversial issue are nebulous. Although the goal of the moratorium imposed by the *Furman* decision was to reduce capricious sentencing, inmates today are able to find a myriad of loopholes within the laws to prolong their time on death row.

Determined lawyers manage to contest capital punishment rulings in creative ways, often because of the lack of consistent sentencing guidelines across state and federal jurisdictions. This inconsistency stems from ambiguous standards within the law.

Most death penalty sentencing guidelines are based on seven criteria.

1. murder committed in the commission of a felony (e.g., robbery, rape, or kidnapping)
2. multiple murder
3. murder of a police or correctional officer acting in the line of duty
4. especially cruel or heinous murder
5. murder for financial gain
6. murder by an offender having a prior conviction for a violent crime
7. causing or directing another to commit murder

The fact that these guidelines are loosely defined helps explain why interpretations are sometimes radically different within and among judges and juries in various state and federal jurisdictions. "Multiple" murders could refer to hundreds of deaths resulting from a bomb exploding in a large office building, or a street robbery of a couple in which both persons are shot. Another judge could believe that a single murder is particularly cruel. Judges and lawyers have difficulty deciphering the meaning of the laws. When the courtroom deliberation finally results in a decision on how to apply the law—a process that can be extremely lengthy—this decision becomes the basis of many appeals.

All three branches of government are concerned about the time delays and complexity of death penalty appeals. In May 1996, President Clinton signed the Anti-Terrorism Effective Death Penalty Act, intended to shorten the lengthy and cumbersome state and federal appeal process. It limits the appellate process for those under sentence of death to one federal appeal; if the individual seeks additional appeals, he or she must first receive approval from a three-judge panel.

With the current death penalty laws, an estimated 40 percent of capital punishment decisions are reversed.[4] The inmate is then resentenced. This starts a new cycle of retrying cases and appealing decisions. Taxpayers are left paying for keeping men and women in prison death rows for years while they await judicial review. Even if the current rate of execution were to double, it would take nearly half a century for this backlog of sentenced inmates to disappear.

Another major shortcoming of capital punishment is the immense cost. Many Americans support capital punishment because they believe it to be less expensive than a life sentence in prison without parole. Contrary to this conventional wisdom, capital punishment is the more costly option. Considering the average age of incarceration and typical life expectancy, the estimated cost ranges from $750,000 to $1 million per execution.[5] Some states even estimate the cost to be much higher. These costs are not affected by the method of execution but by the cost of extended legal review. Retaining attorneys, expert witnesses, and general investigation quickly creates significant expenses.

Even though the cost of a life sentence seems outrageously high, the cost of execution is higher. In Florida, the average cost of trying and executing one person is $3.2 million. This is almost three times the cost of a single inmate's imprisonment for 40 years in this state.[6]

The Roman Catholic Church has also weighed in against executions; the Vatican regularly criticizes death chambers in the United States. After a January 1997 controversial triple execution in Arkansas, Vatican Radio broadcast the following message: "After the Christmas holiday, American prisons have resumed their sad work and the rhythm seems like that of a macabre assembly line."[7] The Roman Catholic Church today believes the death penalty is legitimate only in the most exceptional circumstances, such as during wars. Pope John Paul has said such circumstances rarely exist today.

One cannot debate the death penalty without coming to the argument that the process discriminates against some races and ethnicities. Dr. David Baldus, professor of law at the University of Iowa, points out one disparity:

> About half of all the people who are murdered each year in the United States are black. Yet since 1977, the overwhelming majority of people who have been executed—85%—had killed a white person. Only 11% had killed a black person.[8]

Baldus has noted that the judicial system seems to value whites' lives most. Baldus also completed a study in Georgia that revealed that convicted offenders with white victims received the death penalty 4.3 times more often than those with black victims.

On death row, 50.6 percent are white, 39.1 percent are black, 7.3 percent are Hispanic, 1.8 percent are Native American, and 0.8 percent are Asian. If the statistics mirrored the U.S. population, only about 22 percent of the death row population would be black. Sociologist Michael Radelet has concluded from his studies that those of lower social class and poor economic status are also disproportionately given death sentences.[9]

In the study of capital punishment in Georgia, Baldus et al. determined that a mere 23 percent of death penalty–eligible criminals received that punishment.[10] The irregularity and inconsistency of dispensing the death penalty may be its greatest weakness. Many argue that the infrequency with which capital punishment is imposed can hardly be expected to deter others from crime.

The American Bar Association (ABA) voted in February 1997 to seek a halt to the death penalty. Its primary concern stems from the inconsistent quality of legal representation provided to criminal defendants facing the ultimate sanction. Some ABA attorneys argued that these critical judicial decisions turn not on the nature of the crime but on the quality of representation for the accused; they criticized lawyers as often inadequately paid or incompetent.

Opponents of the death penalty also argue that the possibility of killing an innocent human is a weakness of capital punishment. According to them, the chance that an innocent person may be wrongly killed is enough of a reason to ban the death penalty altogether.

SUPPORT FOR CAPITAL PUNISHMENT

Even with the negative publicity concerning its costs and delays, many people still favor the death penalty. It is supported by more than three-fourths of voters.[11]

Over the years, support for the death penalty has shifted. The *Gallup Report* from 1986 revealed that 70 percent of U.S. citizens support the death penalty when faced with the question "Are you in favor of the death penalty for persons convicted of murder?" But in 1966, only 42 percent supported capital punishment.

The argument about cost can be restructured as a defense of the death penalty, but only if capital trials are not extensive and prolonged and the appeals process is simplified. While every life should be valued and every American is guaranteed due process of law by the Fourteenth Amendment, this right does not confer the power to enjoy, as Raymond Paternoster calls it, "super due process."[12] While the Supreme Court has repeatedly claimed that the death sentence requires a more in-depth case study, the time-consuming appeals process has become extreme: A period of 10 or more years on death row is unacceptable to many people. Only when the judicial aspect of the death penalty is accelerated does capital punishment become a great deal more economical than life imprisonment.

Others contend that the death penalty is valid because it deters would-be criminals from committing violations. Because death is the ultimate sanction a court can deliver, it is believed that those criminals who consider the consequences of committing certain acts will certainly refrain rather than become a member of the death row population. Hundreds of studies have tried to determine whether a deterrent effect exists. Though these studies have been inconclusive, adherents to this argument hold that the death penalty has a significant deterrent effect. And polls find that 60 percent of people believe that capital punishment deters crime.

Yet deterrence and cost are not the most common justifications for the death penalty. The greatest reason people support the death penalty is that it offers merited punishment or just desserts. According to this argument, a person who takes the life of another has forfeited the right to his or her own existence and the moral fiber of a community is strengthened when it takes the life of a murderer because it can express its outrage. Even if little crime reduction or deterrence results from the death penalty, the public continues to embrace the deserved punishment theory. Walter Berns explains the argument easily.

> We surely don't expect to rehabilitate them, and it would be foolish to think that by punishing them we might thereby deter others. The answer is clear: We want to punish them in order *to pay them back*. We think that they must be made to pay for their crimes with their lives, and we think that we, the survivors of the world they violated, may legitimately exact that payment because we, too, are their victims.[13(p.152)]

Berns's argument allows the public the right to be angry with criminals—and to act on that anger.

The overwhelming amount of support the death penalty receives is rooted in the concept of retribution. A belief in justice, the creed of "an eye for an eye" (in this case, a life for a life), holds that retribution is the justification for capital punishment. People need absolute assurance that a convicted murderer will never again have the opportunity to become a repeat offender—and only the death penalty can offer this comfort.

Some people argue that the death penalty comforts the families of victims, giving them a sense of relief. Studies have been conducted of relatives of homicide victims across the country who have been through executions. These studies have revealed that while the execution did not diminish their sorrow, they did feel more peace of mind after it. Still, the long appeals process can be particularly frustrating to families of the victims. Most loved ones spend hours inside courtrooms, during repeated testimonies in the inmate's appeal process.

DEATH ROW OPERATIONS

Condemned inmates in U.S. penal facilities spend many years on death row. Operating institutions that house those sentenced to death is a unique challenge.

Each correctional system must consider how to house and treat these inmates. Prison administrators must decide if they will place these individuals in an open general population or operate a separate death row.

Several states, such as Delaware, have elected to mainstream their death-sentenced inmates and allow them to participate fully in general population work, education, recreation, and other program opportunities. These jurisdictions do not separate the inmate from others until the individual's date of execution is imminent.

Most state correctional agencies have developed separate death row operations. Generally, prison administrators (such as those in California) have chosen to run these cellblocks as segregation units, highly controlled custodial environments that offer a high degree of accountability for these inmates who are deemed to present the most extreme threat to society. These individuals spend the majority of their time in secure cells and are out solely for minimal periods for recreation and showers. For example, in Florida and California each condemned inmate is housed in a separate cell that is six feet by nine feet. Inmates do not have the opportunity to visit the dining room, chapel, education department, or work area. Most of the inmates' days are spent watching television in their cells, reading, or having conversations with their peers by yelling to other cells.

Other death row operations keep this group apart from general population inmates but permit relatively free interaction among the individuals under sentence of death. These units generally offer communal feeding, recreation, and work experiences. Religion, psychology, and education programs and other opportunities are often offered to these inmates within boundaries of the unit.

THE EMOTIONAL ORDEAL OF AN EXECUTION

Many correctional administrators who have been associated with carrying out the death penalty have expressed concern about the emotional toll it takes on the staff.[14] Despite the harsh rhetoric engaged in by proponents of capital punishment, even by correctional staff, it is extremely difficult to participate in an execution without experiencing personal trauma. Participating staff should be carefully selected.

Many wardens responsible for an execution personally pick the staff who will participate in the death watch during the two or three days prior to an execution and use only the most mature and experienced staff for the actual execution. This selection process often involves staff who volunteer for the task, with final selection made based on their experience and ability. Some agencies will not utilize staff that volunteer; instead they ask certain individuals if they would be willing to participate. Many institutions carefully protect the identities of staff who are involved.

The use of medical staff in an execution is another very sensitive matter. Many physicians will not participate in the actual execution and limit their involvement to the pronouncement of death. The American Medical Association sternly speaks out against physicians' participation and have stated it is a violation of their professional ethics and the Hippocratic oath. This can present a dilemma for those states who use lethal injection as the method of execution, because it is a medical procedure. Accordingly, most executioners are nurses or emergency medical technicians who are skilled at inserting a needle into an individual's arm. All jurisdictions offer complete anonymity for these individuals.

After an execution, it is important to debrief all those who participated. This emotional time is the most difficult for the execution team, and senior staff work very hard at providing necessary social services support.

CONCLUSION

For many reasons, the government-sanctioned taking of a life is a contentious and emotionally charged issue. Nearly every argument for or against capital punishment can be refuted by opponents. Whether one invokes economic, moral, social, or legal reasoning, it is not enough to convince the other side of the rightfulness or wrongfulness of the law. The debate over the death penalty has not been resolved by logic.

When over 70 percent of Americans ardently support capital punishment, an observer must look more closely at their societal beliefs. Clearly, emotional arguments are more significant and influential than arguments of reason. Most Americans accept the "just desserts" argument, and it seems clear that the death penalty will remain a viable force in criminal justice for years to come.

NOTES

1. L. Bartle, *Current Death Penalty Statistics* (Washington, DC: Death Penalty Information Center, 1996).
2. P. Keve, *Corrections* (New York: John Wiley and Sons, Inc., 1981), 468.
3. D. Von Drehle, "Why the Death Penalty Doesn't Work," *The Washington Post*, 5 February, 1995, 10.
4. L. Bartle, *Current Death Penalty Statistics*.
5. M. Costanzo and L. White, "An Overview of the Death Penalty and Capital Trials: History, Current Status, Legal Procedures, and Cost," *Journal of Social Issues* 50 (1994): 1–18.
6. Costanzo and White, "An Overview of the Death Penalty and Capital Trials: History, Current Status, Legal Procedures, and Cost," 10.
7. "Vatican Slams U.S. Triple Execution," *Reuters,* 9 January, 1997.
8. E. Eckholm, "Studies Find the Death Penalty Tied to Race of Victim," *The New York Times,* 23 February, 1995, 1.
9. M. Radelet, *Facing the Death Penalty* (Philadelphia: Temple University Press, 1989), 10.
10. Eckholm, "Studies Find the Death Penalty Tied to Race of Victim," 1–18, 1.
11. P. Ellsworth and S. Gross, "Hardening of the Attitudes: Americans' Views on the Death Penalty," *Journal of Social Issues* 50 (1994): 19–52.
12. R. Paternoster, *Capital Punishment in America* (New York: Lexington Books, 1991).
13. W. Berns, *For Capital Punishment: Crime and the Morality of the Death Penalty* (New York: Basic Books, 1979), 152.
14. Robert Watson, interview by author, Smyrna, DE, 13 October, 1994.

CHAPTER 35

Supermaximum Facilities

David A. Ward

Small penitentiaries with a large custodial staff exercising a very high degree of control over the most assaultive, escape-prone, and disruptive inmates in a prison system have existed in U.S. correctional systems for only slightly over 60 years. Most of these special penitentiaries have been part of the Federal Bureau of Prisons.

ALCATRAZ SETS THE STANDARD

The best known penitentiary in the world sits on a rocky little island in the San Francisco Bay. During the early 1930s, when gangsters appeared to operate freely in cities such as Chicago, Kansas City, and New York, while ransom kidnappers and bank robbers evaded local police and sheriffs, the attorney general of the United States, Homer E. Cummings, announced that the federal government was declaring war on the "public enemies." The Federal Bureau of Investigation was reorganized, and under new director J. Edgar Hoover, its agents worked under new federal statutes regarding bank robbery, kidnapping, and the interstate transfer of guns, stolen property, women (for "immoral purposes"), and fleeing felons. But there needed to be a greater punishment for those felons who survived the gun battles with fearless "G-Men." As historian Richard Powers put it, the government needed a superprison in which to lock up the supercriminals who were captured by the supercops.[1]

To achieve this end, Cummings approved the transfer of the former military prison on Alcatraz Island from the War Department to the Department of Justice and instructed Sanford Bates, the new director of a reorganized Federal Bureau of Prisons, to establish a special penitentiary for those criminals deemed to be very dangerous and irredeemable,[2] not at all likely to become law abiding citizens. Alcatraz was thus established as a prototype of the "last resort" penitentiary, with punishment, deterrence, and incapacitation as its goals. There was no pretense of rehabilitation; the prison stood as a symbol of the consequence for serious wrongdoing. In the new supermaximum penitentiary, with its high degree of control over prisoners who posed the most serious management problems in other prisons, prisoners were expected to be less disruptive. And without these troublemakers, it was hoped that other prisons could operate more openly, with the full range of work, recreational, religious, and educational programs.[3]

Alcatraz Becomes "the Rock"

The U.S. Penitentiary (USP) at Alcatraz Island, CA, opened for business in August 1934. Compared with other state and federal penitentiaries, its population was very small: 275 prisoners, supervised by a custodial force of 150. Chaplains came to the island periodically, but no teachers, vocational training instructors, social workers, or psychologists would ever appear on the prison's roster of employees. The Rock was a highly regimented institution.

- Direct commitments from courts would not be allowed. Even though judges might tell men regarded as hardened offenders "I'm sending you to Alcatraz," a trip to the Rock had to be earned by way of serious misconduct at other prisons.
- The only "program" on the island was work—a privilege that could quickly be taken away. A work assignment was a privilege because while no pay was provided, it allowed the inmate to be out of his cell during the day, and he could earn good time.
- As a maximum custody–minimum privilege regime, no commissary was established, no newspapers or telephone calls were allowed, and even listening to a radio station over a headset was not authorized until the late 1950s. Selected news magazines were circulated, but only after articles reporting anything related to crime or sex were removed. Correspondence with wives, children, and other blood relatives was limited to two handwritten sheets several times a month. Prisoners were allowed one visit each month conducted through a bulletproof window with communication over a telephone monitored by officers who had the authority to terminate the visit if the conversation strayed to crime, other prisoners, or prison "conditions."
- Punishment within the prison called for loss of the few privileges available; loss of good time earned and yet to be earned; and either days in a dark solitary confinement cell, on bread and water with a meal every third day, in the basement of the prison (until this form of punishment was stopped by Federal Bureau of Prisons headquarters); or confinement for months or years in a separate isolation wing in the main cell house—today called a "control unit."
- There were no due process proceedings in regard to judgments about prison rule viola-

tions or the transfer to or from Alcatraz, no law library, and paralegals to assist prisoners. No inmates could be paroled from the island; they could only provide a good enough record of obeying rules (the staff felt four to five years was generally needed) to earn a transfer to a standard penitentiary, where they could be considered for parole.
- Activities ended each day at 4:45 P.M., when each prisoner was locked in his cell, measuring five feet by seven feet by nine feet. Twenty-two counts during every 24-hour period assured that all the prisoners were in their places.

During its 30 years of service as a federal prison, no federal judge, no prisoner's rights group, no prison reform organization, no congressional committee, and no news reporter conducted an official inquiry into conditions at a prison that critics and prisoners labeled "America's Devil Island" and "Hellcatraz."

Controversial from the Start

The first supermaximum custody prison was controversial from its opening, despite the fact that it housed the federal system's most accomplished escape artists and riot leaders as well as prisoners who had assaulted or killed other inmates or staff. But while prisoners and staff knew those convicts who developed their reputations behind prison walls, the attention of the press and the public was drawn to the small number of prisoners on the island who had already earned national reputations by virtue of their criminal exploits: Al Capone, "Machine Gun" Kelly, "Doc" Barker, Alvin Karpis, John Paul Chase (partner of Babyface Nelson), and the leaders of Detroit's "Purple Gang." In later years, there were Morton Sobell, convicted with the Rosenbergs of selling secrets of the atomic bomb to the Soviet Union; Rafael Miranda, the Puerto Rican nationalist who shot up the House of Representatives; and 1950s and 1960s gangsters Mickey Cohen and Frankie Carbo. When these celebrity prisoners, along with the "worst of the worst" prison troublemakers, arrived at the Rock, which news reporters could see but not visit, the ingredients for high drama were in place. As the Federal Bureau of Prisons applied its policy of "no comment" and issued simple denials of the accuracy of every rumor, allegation, and even the sensational testimony of brutality and wretched conditions heard in several trials held in federal court in San Francisco over the years, only the critics of Alcatraz were heard.

News reporters, academic criminologists, mental health specialists, and even some prison administrators outside the federal system contemplated Alcatraz and imagined themselves in the place of the prisoners. Many concluded that the punishment was too severe, even for "public enemies" and riot leaders.

The reality of life on the island, however, was much less dramatic than the news headlines. During its three decades of operation, the prison did experience a number of escape attempts, some of them so sensational that Hollywood or television movies (e.g., *Escape from Alcatraz, Six against the Rock*) were made about them. In June 1962, three prisoners dug through the backs of their cells, climbed up and through a ventilation shaft in the roof, and disappeared in the cold waters of the bay. Then, in December 1962, another prisoner broke out of the cell house, drifted in the currents, and was pulled from the water near the southern base of the Golden Gate Bridge. None of the 1,550 or so men who were sent to the island successfully escaped.

But concerns in Washington, DC, about a regime that was depicted by the news media as so harsh that it made desperate men even more desperate increased during the 1950s with the emergence of the "medical model" in penology. This new view asserted that criminal activity was a product of bad parenting, negative social influences, lack of education and job skills, and faulty psychological development. It went on to assert that these deficiencies could be remedied, not by prison guards but by mental health professionals, educators, and other experts. Prison

employees began to call their work corrections, guards became officers, and prisons became institutions or facilities. As standard setters for the nation, administrators of the Federal Bureau of Prisons were uncomfortable with having one of their prisons thought of as representing a penal policy and practice considered outdated and pessimistic. In 1963, USP Alcatraz was closed. USP Marion, a replacement built in rural southern Illinois, opened with the full range of professional staff, programs, and privileges found in all federal penitentiaries; the strategy of concentrating all the troublemakers in one special maximum custody, minimum privilege penitentiary was discarded.

USP MARION BECOMES "THE NEW ALCATRAZ"

As Marion came on line, federal and state prisons across the country began to experience a dramatic increase in racial conflict and violence. Some black and Hispanic prisoners, reflecting the new attention to minority group rights expressed in the Civil Rights Movement, organized to advance their interests. They challenged traditional prison policies and specific staff actions they regarded as discriminatory and began to influence other prisoners. White prisoners in California, and then in the federal system, responded by organizing the Aryan Brotherhood to protect themselves and to advance their own prison enterprises. Hispanic prisoners were recruited as members of the Mexican Mafia, Nuestra Familia, or the Texas Syndicate; blacks as members of the Black Guerrilla Family, or later, the Mandingo Warriors. Drug trafficking and extortion became common in penitentiaries across the country. Violence became epidemic as the gangs settled scores; dealt with informers; attracted "wannabes" who were required to engage in violence to gain membership; and generally took an extremely confrontational position regarding policies and practices overruled by federal judges, who reacted with uncertainty about strategies to combat the growth of violence, escape attempts, and other disruptive activities in their prisons.

To meet this problem at the federal level, the Federal Bureau of Prisons established in 1973 a special close custody unit within USP Marion to house the system's most disruptive inmates. The purpose of the "control unit" was simply to separate, in a very restricted setting, the highly assaultive prisoners and gang leaders from the more law-abiding inmates. Violence continued to increase in federal prisons, however, and the Bureau next implemented a new inmate classification system that added a higher security rank to the five already in place. Under this system, USP Marion became in 1978 the Bureau's only "level 6" penitentiary, and the entire prison was designated as the home for some 450 gang leaders and members and sophisticated escape artists, as well as prisoners from some 36 states who could not be controlled or who had assaulted staff in state penitentiaries. Marion was not really identical to Alcatraz, though. Privileges and programs were still available, and the inmates had freedom to move throughout Marion. However, Marion did have one very special area referred to as the Director's unit (which housed a half-dozen spies, traitors, and other celebrity prisoners). Additionally at Marion, the Federal Bureau of Prisons had a very secure control unit, utilized to house very dangerous, assaultive, or escape-prone inmates who had disrupted other state or federal high security prisons throughout the United States. Despite these measures, between January 1978 and June 1979, federal prisons experienced 25 inmate homicides, 536 inmate-on-inmate assaults, and 344 assaults on staff. Even at USP Marion, violent incidents increased. Then, on October 22, 1983, in two separate incidents in the control unit, two officers were stabbed to death and four others were injured; four days later another prisoner, the twenty-fifth in Marion's history, was killed and three officers were attacked in the main corridor. A state of emergency was declared on October 28, 1983, and Federal Bureau

of Prisons Director Norman A. Carlson ordered that USP Marion be locked down.[4]

Indefinite Administrative Segregation

At Marion, federal prison officials established a regime that was even more rigid than that of Alcatraz. Inmates were locked in their cells for 23 hours each day, exiting only in handcuffs and leg chains under the escort of several officers for 1 hour of solitary recreation in the exercise cage within each unit, or in later months, for outdoor exercise in a yard that had been subdivided into smaller, caged areas. Exercise equipment was removed. All congregate activity ceased. Inmates were fed in their cells and work was no longer available because the industrial program had been disassembled and moved to other prisons as the result of several inmate work strikes. Inmates talked to case workers, psychologists, medical staffers, and chaplains through the bars of their cells. Visits with family members and other people (except attorneys) were conducted through a plexiglass window by telephone. All telephone calls and mail, except contact with attorneys, were monitored. Metal bed frames were replaced with concrete foundations and tamper-proof mattresses, and inmate clothing in the control unit and disciplinary segregation units was limited to jumpsuits and slippers.

Unlike Alcatraz inmates, however, USP Marion inmates could draw legal materials from basic law libraries set up in each unit. Other resources were available from the prison's main law library. And the Marion inmates (except those in disciplinary segregation) were allowed a five-inch black and white television set and up to three paperback books in their cells.

Getting in and out of Marion

Many people mistakenly believed that once inmates were sent to Alcatraz or Marion (promptly labeled after October 1983 by media representatives as "the New Alcatraz"), they would serve the rest of their long sentences there. But federal prison officials, with system-wide concerns, have always been aware that because space in Alcatraz (275 prisoners) or Marion (450 prisoners) was limited, prisoner turnover was required. Despite claims of hopelessness related to the policy of no parole from the island, inmates at Alcatraz spent an average of 55 months on the island before they were transferred back to USP Leavenworth, USP Atlanta, and other penitentiaries.

With a much larger inmate population in the 1980s, federal prison administrators established specific periods of time for inmates to be housed in the control unit and in the Marion general population. The upper limit for the most serious offenses, such as killing other prisoners or attempting to kill staff, was established as 48 months in the control unit. The key to moving through Marion was, of course, the prisoner's conduct, although in a lockdown regime the opportunities for dealing in contraband and assaulting other prisoners and staff were limited. To ease the transition from 23 hours per day of confinement to the open regimes of standard federal penitentiaries, Marion general population inmates who had clear conduct records for 12 months could move to an intermediate unit in which eating in the unit and exercising in small groups in the yard were allowed. Following another 12 months without serious misconduct, inmates moved to a "pretransfer" unit that allowed congregate activities such as eating together in the prison dining room; group television, recreation, and exercise; and a work assignment in an industries program. After completing 12 months in this unit without serious misconduct, inmates were then eligible for transfer to standard penitentiaries. The time spent at USP Marion averaged 52 months in the years immediately following the lockdown but dropped in recent years to 36 months; of the 373 prisoners who were at Marion when the indefinite segregation regime was established in October 1983, all but 22 had been transferred to other prisons by the end of 1990. Those who remained included prisoners convicted in the murders of the two officers in 1983, men regarded as the leaders of major

prison gangs, and several prisoners charged with plotting escapes.

This transfer policy has provided prisoners with a way out of an extreme confinement situation and ensured that space is always available for the newest group of troublemakers. Alcatraz held less than 1 percent of federal prisoners during its three decades, and even with a greatly expanded inmate population, Marion and its successor at Florence, CO (called "Alcatraz of the Rockies" by the media), have held less than one-half of 1 percent of federal prisoners. Confinement under supermaximum custody conditions, therefore, is reserved for only part of the sentences served by a very small percentage of federal prisoners.

IS CONFINEMENT UNDER SUPERMAXIMUM CUSTODY "CRUEL AND UNUSUAL" PUNISHMENT?

Alcatraz and Marion conjure up dramatic images of prison officials locked in a struggle for control with the most dangerous and sophisticated offenders in a penal system. Life under what is popularly called a lockdown is difficult to imagine for people who have never experienced a single night in jail or prison. And because these regimes and influential prisoners attract attention (from political organizations, inmate rights organizations, reporters, journalists, and some academics and mental health professionals) and provoke concern from prisoners' families, it is often asserted that this form of confinement damages prisoners' mental health, a claim that was made immediately after the lockdown in 1983 by a group of Marion inmates and several inmate rights groups.

More specifically, USP Marion was charged with implementing controls that constituted cruel and unusual psychological punishment. But after several weeks of testimony, the federal district court in southern Illinois rejected the arguments by the prisoners and their lawyers, and its decision in *Bruscino v. Carlson* was upheld by the Court of Appeals; Marion's indefinite ad-

Indiana's Supermax Facilities Spark Controversy

A watchdog group has condemned Indiana's supermax facilities as "excessively harsh" and has called on the state's legislature to review the treatment and conditions of inmates being confined there, especially those who are mentally ill.

In a report titled "Cold Storage: Super-Maximum Security Confinement in Indiana," Human Rights Watch concludes that confining mentally ill prisoners at the maximum control facility (MCF) and the special housing unit (SHU) of Wabash Valley Correctional Facility can cause great suffering as to "constitute torture" under international human rights law.

"The Indiana Department of Corrections (DOC) has the difficult job of securely housing disruptive or dangerous prisoners. But throwing them for years into the shocking conditions at the MCF and SHU is beyond the pale," said Jamie Fellner, associate counsel of Human Rights Watch.

In its report, Human Rights Watch noted that Indiana's use of supermax facilities to segregate and control its most dangerous prisoners is not unlike similar approaches in other states. Currently, 36 states and the Federal Bureau of Prisons have a total of at least 57 supermaximum security units, built either as annexes to existing prisons or as free-standing facilities.

Although conditions and policies vary somewhat from facility to facility, says the report, most follow the model established at the United States Penitentiary at Marion, IL—that is, lockdown between 22 and 23 hours per day.

According to Indiana DOC's Public Information Officer Pam Pattison, Commissioner of Corrections Edward Cohen believes that supermax isolation is a mechanism for ensuring the safety and security of the entire Indiana prison system. Pattison noted that those inmates sent to the supermax are the worst of the worst, prisoners who are predators. She stated that these inmates have engaged in assaultive behavior toward staff or offenders, including sexual assaults, and the behavior is repetitive.

Source: Reprinted from *Corrections Alert,* Vol. 4, No. 15, p. 8, © 1997, Aspen Publishers, Inc.

ministrative segregation regime had passed the test of constitutionality.

Nevertheless, the term "supermax" itself conveys images of harsh and punitive conditions, and prisoners reinforce these images when given the opportunity. In reality, fewer than 10 percent of the Alcatraz inmates manifested mental health problems as measured by clinical diagnoses, transfers to federal medical centers for psychiatric reasons, placement on psychotropic medication, or postrelease indications. The incidence of mental health problems for the inmates from the Rock was the same as that at USP Leavenworth, a standard federal prison, during the same era. At USP Marion, fewer than 3 percent of the inmates have been transferred to federal medical centers for psychiatric reasons or placed on psychotropic medications. (Data from the Alcatraz follow-up study were conducted under a grant from the National Institute of Justice and will be published in journal and book form in 1998. Data from the follow-up of Marion prisoners were gathered by Thomas Warlike, Research Analyst at USP Marion and its successor, USP ADD Florence, and I. These data will be published in journal form in 1998.) The Alcatraz and Marion inmates who did manifest symptoms of psychological disturbances may have brought those symptoms with them from other prisons. Those symptoms might have manifested themselves in any prison setting or even in what prisoners call "the free world."

The other important point to note about these exceptional prisons is that the prisoners, who prefer to call themselves "convicts," are also exceptional. Most have worked their way through the disciplinary segregation units of other penitentiaries until they finally reach supermaximum custody and are very experienced in doing big or hard time. They have learned to adjust to long periods of confinement in disciplinary segregation units of other prisons. These prisoners are leaders, they have strong personalities as well as physical prowess, and they are ready to challenge whatever punishment the federal government hands out to them.

Follow-up data indicate that the great majority of Alcatraz and Marion inmates did not so misbehave in the prisons to which they were transferred that they earned a return trip; fewer than 5 percent of the Alcatraz prisoners and only 16 percent of the Marion prisoners came back. Most inmates at these prisons were in their mid-thirties, and the aging process was beginning to influence them. Their desire to experience the better things of prison life instead of the deprived offerings of supermaximum custody became a factor. Inmates at Florence, CO, have shown the same tendencies.

Supermaximum custody institutions, as represented first by USP Alcatraz, and by USP Marion from 1983 to 1995, have served their purpose for correctional administrators; they have reduced the number of dead and seriously injured inmates and staff. Since October 1983, no officers at Marion have been killed or seriously injured. The rates of inmate murders in the more open units as well as inmate-on-inmate assaults have dropped since the lockdown began. And confinement in Alcatraz and Marion has not damaged prisoners' mental health and ability to adjust to other prisons.

THE STATES ADOPT THE "MARION MODEL"

As word spread among corrections officials in troubled state prisons across the country that the Federal Bureau of Prisons had found a management strategy by which control could be established over a prison system's most disruptive inmates, a strategy that had been satisfactorily tested in the federal courts, state commissioners and wardens began to visit USP Marion to learn more about what has come to be known as the "Marion Model."

By the mid-1990s, some 36 states had established supermaximum custody units within existing prisons or constructed new prisons for this purpose.[5] California, for example, after installing "adjustment centers" within four penitentiaries in the 1970s, moved next to a system in which the most serious management problems were sent to its well-known traditional prisons at San Quentin and Folsom. These two facilities established what were called special housing units (SHUs). When this strategy failed to control violence, a new SHU penitentiary was constructed at Pelican Bay in Northern California. The regime and various practices at the SHU have, however, been the subject of litigation, and the federal judge ruled against the state in a number of areas. In *Madrid v. Gomez,* the court determined that Pelican Bay authorities had hired an insufficient number of medical and mental health staff to serve inmate needs, that the staff on a number of occasions used excessive force in dealing with prisoners, and that the review procedures and supervision of employees using force were inadequate.[6]

The supermaximum security unit constructed within the Oklahoma State Penitentiary at McAlester has been condemned by Amnesty International on the grounds that prisoners are confined in windowless cells that do not allow natural light or natural air and that exercise facilities, psychiatric services, the quality of food, and procedures to review the prisoners' custody status were inadequate.[7] And the state of New York's "maxi-maxi" prison at Southport experienced an attempted inmate takeover attributed to an inadequate number of custodial staff and poor supervision of officers.[8]

The problems at Pelican Bay, McAlester, and Southport show how important it is for correctional system managers to pay attention to every aspect of confinement in these exceptional penal environments in which the government uses its maximum coercive authority. These units or prisons must provide the full range of medical, mental health, and religious services; ensure that prisoners have access to legal materials, their attorneys, and the courts; maintain acceptable (i.e., constitutional) conditions of daily living; and provide a system by which prisoners can move through these highly restrictive settings to standard penitentiaries. States that do not pay attention to these aspects of their supermaximum operations are likely to find that federal judges or their court-appointed, on-site experts (special masters) will determine staffing, programs, and policies for them.

CONCLUSION

Control units and supermaximum prisons will always attract attention, as they should, from the press, civil libertarians, mental health professionals, criminologists, and other correctional workers. The "Marion model" and the practices of some states (as they are examined, evaluated, and perhaps tested in federal courts) can provide examples of regimes that meet constitutional as well as organizational requirements and make prison life safer for inmates and employees.

NOTES

1. R. Powers, *G-Men: Hoover's FBI in Popular Culture* (Carbondale, IL: Southern Illinois University Press, 1983), 47.

2. R. Powers, *G-Men*, 44.

3. R. Powers, *G-Men*, 44. For further discussion, see P. Keve, *Prisons and the American Conscience: A History of U.S. Federal Corrections* (Carbondale, IL: Southern Illinois University Press, 1991), 173–202.

4. D. Ward and A. Breed, *U.S. Penitentiary Consultants Report* (Washington, DC: U.S. Government Printing Office, Serial #26, Oversight Hearing on June 26, 1985).

5. National Institute of Corrections, *Super-Max Housing: A Survey of Current Practice* (Washington, DC: forthcoming).

6. M. Grinfield, "Treatment of Mentally Ill in California's Pelican Bay Prison Ruled Unconstitutional," *Psychiatric Times*, April 1995, 5–6.

7. Amnesty International, "Conditions for Death Row Prisoners in H-Unit Oklahoma State Penitentiary" (London: Amnesty International Secretariat, 1994).

8. *Public Hearing into the Matter of Investigation of the May 1991 Incident at Southport Correctional Facility*, New York State Commission on Corrections, June 24, 1991.

CHAPTER 36

Classification:
The Cornerstone of Corrections

Robert B. Levinson

When practitioners in any field seek to better understand their subject matter, they sort their objects of study into categories. This process, known as classification, is important to corrections. For each new inmate committed by the courts to a department of corrections for a period of incarceration, the administrators of that system must make decisions about at least two issues: the inmate's level of physical restraint or "security level" and the inmate's level of supervision or "custody grade." Unfortunately, these two concepts are often confused. These two factors significantly impact a prisoner's housing and program assignments.

THE HISTORY OF CLASSIFICATION

It has taken many years for this contemporary classification process to evolve. In the early history of the United States, prisons or jails were essentially lockups. Prisons held offenders during trials and while they waited for punishment, from placement in the stocks to gruesome deaths. Incarceration in prisons was not a form of punishment.

Confinement in the United States closely paralleled the history of correctional practice in Europe. During the eighteenth and nineteenth centuries, all offenders—men and women, children and adults—were housed together. Then, officials began to separate broad groups of offenders (e.g., juveniles from adults, first offenders and debtors from "hardened" criminals, men from

women). Nevertheless, prisons were little more than warehouses, and corporal punishment was used to maintain control. There was also some rough classification based on social standing and the ability to pay for better accommodations.[1]

In the mid-1700s, Cesare Beccaria in Italy and John Howard in England suggested that inmates be segregated by sex and by severity of offense, sane and insane prisoners not be housed together, and young offenders be separated from adult prisoners. The British Parliament attempted to implement these reforms in the Hard Labour Act of 1779; however, the ideas met with resistance. It remained for the United States to test these new concepts.

The first true prison in the United States was Philadelphia's Walnut Street Jail, built in 1773. In 1790, shortly after the Revolutionary War, it became Pennsylvania's state prison. The Walnut Street Jail and New York's Newgate Prison are the prototypes of what later were known as the Pennsylvania (separate) system and the Auburn (congregate) system.

In the early 1800s, prisons were viewed as settings in which law violators were placed to read the Bible, contemplate their misdeeds, and become penitent—hence, the term "penitentiary." Because all prisoners were treated in the same way, classification had only a separation function. Prisoners were housed separately, in different cells.

By the mid-nineteenth century, the Irish prison system was considered the most enlightened. It combined religious, educational, and work programs with a graduated classification system through which an inmate had to progress before being released.

In the early twentieth century, criminologists, social scientists, social workers, and prison administrators began to study crime and punishment in order to create a more beneficial prison environment. The Wickersham Commission in the late 1920s urged better classification of inmates and progressive treatment to "reshape" prisoners. Classification was becoming focused on developing individualized treatment programs based on clinical data and each inmate's social and criminal history.

Despite the congressional act of 1930 that mandated classification of federal prisoners, not all correctional officials believed in classification at this time. One story tells of a new employee in the 1930s who, on his first day of work at the Atlanta Penitentiary in the 1930s, was greeted by the deputy warden. "So you're the new classification officer," the deputy warden said. "Come with me." They went down a number of corridors and through several grilles, then stopped at a closed door, which the deputy warden flung open. There stood an inmate with hands and feet shackled to the cell bars. "Now," said the deputy warden, "that's what we call classification in my institution!"

By the 1960s, a number of rehabilitative practices (e.g., group and individual psychotherapy, education up to a high school equivalency diploma, vocational training) had developed in prisons, particularly in facilities for juveniles. However, there were not enough "slots" to meet the needs of large numbers of prisoners. Classification was used to set priorities, and waiting lists proliferated. In effect, classification became the main tool for balancing a prisoner's right not to deteriorate while incarcerated and to be placed in the least restrictive housing against society's right to be protected from criminal behavior.

From classification as a single-person procedure—handled entirely by a senior administrator—the process has matured. The conviction

---

A Congressional Act, Approved May 27, 1930, Mandating Classification of Federal Prisoners

"It is hereby declared to be the policy of the Congress that the said institutions be so planned and limited in size as to facilitate the development of an integrated Federal penal and correctional system which will assure the proper classification and segregation of Federal prisoners according to their character, the nature of the crime they have committed, their mental condition, and such other factors as should be taken into consideration in providing an individualized system of discipline, care, and treatment of the persons committed to such institutions." (C. 339, sec. 7, 46 Stat. 390)

(supported by research) that group decision making is better than determinations made by one person led to the next step in the evolution of the classification process: the creation of a single, institutionwide classification committee. This group of 7 to 12 department heads initially was chaired by the warden, to ensure the group's decisions would have the warden's support.[2] The classification committee met on a weekly basis, and its major function was to decide prisoners' custody grades. That determined where the inmates could work and might affect where they lived. This committee also made recommendations to a parole board; thus, it could have a significant impact on when a prisoner was released. The difficulty with the one-committee approach was that important decisions were being made by personnel who had little or no contact with the people affected by the decision. The institution classification committee relied on second- and thirdhand information in the form of written reports. Also, as the size of institution populations continued to increase, it became more difficult for one committee to give careful consideration to each case while keeping pace with the demand for classification decisions.

This led to the next developmental step, classification teams. One classification committee in each institution was replaced by several classification teams, organized around a case worker's caseload. Inmates were assigned to a specific caseload on the basis of the last digit of their institutional identification number. While this is an equitable way of distributing the incoming population, it meant that every case worker had inmates in living quarters scattered throughout the facility. Nevertheless, it did allocate the demand for classification services among more personnel, thereby reducing the workload for any single staff member and making deadlines easier to meet.

The most recent development in this classification history has been unit management, in which a large prison population is subdivided into several mini-institutions analogous to a city and its neighborhoods. Each unit has specified decision-making authority (including authority in classification and reclassification decisions). The units are run by a staff of six (in addition to 24-hour correctional officer coverage), whose offices are on the living unit. Inmates are permanently assigned to a unit throughout their stay in the institution. Each unit consists of two caseloads, neither of which should exceed 150 inmates. In this arrangement, classification decisions are made by personnel who are in daily contact with their inmates and therefore know them fairly well. Additionally, information upon which decisions are based is more easily gathered, and decision making and feedback to inmates are more rapid and complete.

DIMENSIONS OF CLASSIFICATION

Corrections classifies newly committed offenders into different categories along four dimensions: security, custody, housing, and programs.

Security

New inmates are classified (designated) to a specific prison based on their security needs—the number and types of architectural barriers that must be placed between these individuals and the outside world to ensure that they will not escape and can be controlled. Most correctional systems have institutions at four security levels: supermax—highest, maximum—high, medium—low, and minimum—lowest.

Unfortunately, there are no universally accepted criteria to assign institutions to each level. For example, a level I inmate in system A, who gets transferred to a level I facility in system B, may move from an institution with one fence to a facility with no fence, a potentially worrisome situation. To deal with such a situation, Levinson and Gerard propose a method for classifying institutions that identifies specific criteria for each level.[3] Examples of these criteria are type of perimeter (fencing or walls), towers or mobile patrols, dormitory or cell housing, and number of staff members.

Custody

Each new arrival must also be assigned a specific custody grade, which determines the level of supervision and types of privileges an inmate will have. A basic concern here is whether the prisoner will be permitted to go outside the facility's secure perimeter. Many systems have adopted a fourfold array of custody grades—two inside the fence (one more restrictive than the other) and two outside the fence (one more closely supervised than the other). Different names have been used for these four grades, but it is most important that custody labels not duplicate those used for security. Some systems have named the grades close (i.e., maximum), medium, restricted, and out (i.e., minimum).

Housing

Every inmate must have a place to live while imprisoned. Traditionally, the basis used is "assign to the next empty bed." This is the least desirable bed assignment method. It can place the newly arrived, weak inmate in the same cell with the facility's most troublesome inmate—a very bad situation for both the new inmate and staff. A more sophisticated approach is known as "internal classification," in which inmates are assigned to live with prisoners who are similar to themselves.[4] These systems group inmates into three broad categories: heavy—victimizers, light—victims, and moderate—neither intimidated by the first group nor abusers of the second.

Programs

Using interview and testing data (obtained during the initial classification procedures), the newly arrived inmate is placed in work, training, and treatment programs. These programs are designed to help the prisoner make a successful return to society.

Reclassification

Once an inmate has completed a portion of his or her sentence, it is important that staff continue to review the initial classification decisions and gauge the individual's progress, or lack of progress, at the facility. As the original classification process established the prisoner's security and custody requirements, housing, and work assignments, each of these critical areas should be reviewed for current relevancy to the individual's present circumstances.

The overall classification process will be credible if staff and the affected inmate sit down together on a regular basis and document the individual's adjustment and progress within the institutional environment. Many jurisdictions conduct reclassification meetings at preestablished time intervals; some permit an inmate to request an earlier review if his or her circumstances have significantly changed, and if a staff member approves the request.

Reclassification reviews generally consider the four areas noted above, as well as program and educational progress, postrelease plans,

transfer requests for movement to another facility (e.g., closer to home), legal conditions (e.g., documentation of a detainer being filed by another jurisdiction for possible prosecution on other charges), and administrative concerns (e.g., racial balance of the institution population in all of the inmate's assigned work, housing, or program areas).

RATIONALE FOR CLASSIFICATION

Since 1969, the federal courts have become increasingly involved in prison conditions. In *Holt v. Sarver*, 300 F. Supp. 825 (1969), the plaintiffs alleged that confinement in the Arkansas prison system was cruel and unusual punishment. The court agreed that the totality of this system's prison conditions violated constitutional expectations. The first decision ordering that a classification system be designed and implemented was *Morris v. Travisono*, 310 F. Supp. 857 (1970). That decision, concerning the Rhode Island Department of Correction, stated that classification

contributes to a smoothly, efficiently-operated correctional program. . . . It furnishes an orderly method to the institution administrator by which the varied needs and requirements of each inmate may be followed through from commitment to discharge. . . . Classification not only contributes to the objective of rehabilitation, but also to custody, discipline, work assignments, officer and inmate morale, and the effective use of training opportunities. . . . It assists in long-range planning and development, both in the correctional system as a whole and in the individual institution. . . . Classification is essential to the operation of an orderly and safe prison. It is a prerequisite for the rational allocation of whatever program opportunities exist within the institution. It enables the institution to gauge the proper custody

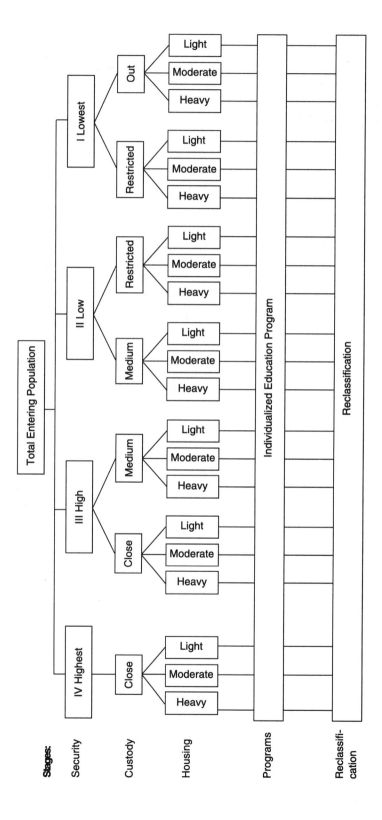

Figure 36–1 A Classification Process

level of an inmate, to identify the inmate's educational, vocational, and psychological needs, and to separate nonviolent inmates from the more predatory.[5]

No corrections system can meet constitutional requirements if it lacks a classification system.

TYPES OF CLASSIFICATION SYSTEMS

Subjective versus Objective

At one time, in most prison systems, a generally accepted understanding had developed among veteran staff about which type of inmates should be sent to which kind of institution. Age, length of sentence, offense severity, and criminal history were major points for consideration. Older inmates with long sentences for severe offenses and who had lengthy criminal records were sent to penitentiaries (high security facilities), while younger inmates with short sentences for minor offenses and who did not have lengthy criminal records went to minimum security institutions. Each facility then made its own custody grade assignments.

This type of ad hoc, clinical, intuitive, seat-of-the-pants approach is known as subjective classification. Such an approach to classification involved a review of records pertaining to an inmate's prior social and criminal history, school and work performance, test scores, and the impressions staff gained during an individual interview.

Some people argued that because subjective classification takes less time, is flexible, and requires fewer personnel, it is more economical. But the courts have found subjective classification approaches often fail to provide constitutionally mandated equal protection. Tonry defines this as one group systematically being treated differently because of race, gender, or other characteristics.[6] Thus, subjective placements may be unfairly discriminatory. Recommendations often tend to reflect the orientation of the caseworker rather than the needs of the offender. Further, it is also difficult for subjective systems to demonstrate that they are neither fixed and mechanical nor arbitrary and capricious (i.e., that they provide the offender with required due process protection). Most important, because of a high degree of inconsistency, it is virtually impossible to demonstrate the validity of a subjective classification system.

Subjective classification has been replaced in virtually all prison systems. Today's more rational, efficient, equitable approach is known as objective classification. The term implies that the factors used in making classification decisions are measurable and that the same criteria are applied to all inmates in the same way. An objective classification system

- uses classification instruments that have been validated on prison populations
- employs the same components and scoring approach for all offenders
- arrives at decisions through a rational, straightforward process, based only upon factors shown to be related to successful placement decisions
- assigns offenders to security levels consistent with their background
- promotes similar classification decisions on comparable offenders, while minimizing the use of overrides
- involves inmates in a process that is readily understandable to both staff and offenders
- is capable of systematic and efficient monitoring[7]

It is imperative that the items used on the classification form have demonstrated validity. That is, they must measure what they say they measure, predicting inmate behavior with an adequate degree of accuracy. Buchanan et al. report that the following seven items are the criteria most often used on initial classification forms: escape history, detainers, prior commitments, criminal history, prior institutional adjustment, history of violence in current offense, and length of sentence.[8]

Six of these constitute the Bureau of Prisons' (BOP) initial classification form; prior institutional adjustment is only considered in history of violence or escape. Kane and Saylor conducted a validation study based on a 10 percent random sample drawn from eight BOP institutions.[9] All six items on the BOP's classification form contribute significantly to the final determination ($N = 505$, $p < .0001$). No single item separates the inmates into security levels, and no age differences were found across security levels.

DECISION TREE VERSUS ADDITIVE

In decision tree classification systems, the response to one question determines the next question to be answered. In this approach, the decision-making process is clear and straightforward. The National Institute of Corrections cites two significant disadvantages to decision trees: If there is incorrect information at any stage, all subsequent responses may also be incorrect; and too much weight is given to single variables.[10]

In contrast, additive classification systems use a small number of well-defined factors. For each factor, points are assigned on the basis of documentation and individual interview information. These points are added, and the total places each offender into one of a limited number of security categories. Each security category contains a subset of the prison system's institutions that have security features appropriate for the inmate's needs. The inmate is sent to one of those institutions, based on such additional considerations as closeness to home and racial balance of population.

Additive classification has greatly improved the consistency of classification decisions. It also enables staff to clearly explain to inmates how their security level is determined. On the other hand, a disadvantage of this approach is that all decisions are made based on cutoff scores along one continuum.

THE ASSIGNMENT PROCESS

Once the classification form has been completed, each prison system follows a policy-driven procedure. Every new admission is assigned to a specific institution at the form-specified security level and is given a particular custody grade.

EVALUATING CLASSIFICATION

Having spent large amounts of time, money, and effort in developing, testing, and implementing a classification system, how will a correctional system know if it is working? In order to answer that question, some preliminary planning has to be done. Someone (usually the classification development task force, with the concurrence of the system's director) formulates some specific goals. What does the system want the new classification approach to accomplish?

For the BOP's security designation/custody classification system, different criteria of success were established. The new system demonstrated its utility by reducing overclassification—confining inmates in the least secure facilities for which they properly qualified (with no increase in escapes or assaults); balancing population—keeping facility populations more evenly balanced by overall numbers, race, and other specific administrative matters; reducing transfers—there were 2.5 times fewer interinstitutional transfers, particularly for an increase or decrease in custody; eliminating preferential transfers—new BOP policy indicated wardens no longer had transfer authority; and using resources better—for example, establishing consistent staffing patterns for all facilities of the same security level. Though the system failed to decrease protective custody (one of its goals), this was accomplished through internal classification. Internal classification is accomplished by assigning inmates to housing units based on their personal behavioral characteristics, e.g., aggressive inmates housed with other aggressive inmates.

Buchanan et al. reported that more than 50 percent of the agencies responding to a survey indicated that objective classification resulted in a "more balanced proportion of inmates at each security/custody level, improvements in risk assessment [and] amount of paperwork, and reduction in escapes/escape attempts."[11]

CONCLUSION

Several years ago, some federal wardens were asked to name their three major goals. They wanted to have no riots, to allow no escapes, and to stay within budget. They then added a fourth goal: to have no lawsuits. A sound, carefully developed, and valid classification system that is implemented with integrity by well-trained staff will help wardens meet these goals.

In U.S. correctional facilities today, all offenders are living in a more humane correctional environment. It is less physically and psychologically threatening than in the past. It offers inmates greater program opportunities, improving their chances for a successful return to the outside world. In all of these improvements, advances in the classification process have played an essential role.

NOTES

1. J. Roberts, *Reform and Retribution: An Illustrated History of American Prisons* (Lanham, MD: American Correctional Association, 1996), 5.

2. W. Megathlin et al., "Classification in Adult Male Correctional Institutions," *Criminal Justice Review* 2 no. 1 (1976): 107–112.

3. R. Levinson and R. Gerard, "Classifying Institutions," *Crime and Delinquency* 32 no. 3 (1986): 291–301.

4. H. Quay, *Managing Adult Inmates* (College Park, MD: American Correctional Association, 1984).

5. *Morris v. Travisono,* 310 F. Supp. 857 (1970).

6. M. Tonry, "Legal and Ethical Issues," in *Prediction and Classification: Criminal Justice Decision Making,* ed. D. Gottfredson and M. Tonry (Chicago: University of Chicago Press, 1987), 367–413.

7. R. Buchanan et al., "National Evaluation of Objective Prison Classification Systems: The Current State of the Art," *Crime and Delinquency* 32 no. 3 (1986): 272–290.

8. Buchanan et al., "National Evaluation of Objective Prison Classification Systems: The Current State of the Art," 281.

9. T. Kane and W. Saylor, "Security Designation: A Validation Study" (Washington, DC: Federal Bureau of Prisons, 1980).

10. National Institute of Corrections, *Prison Classification: A Model Systems Approach* (Washington, DC: U.S. Department of Justice, n.d.).

11. Buchanan et al., "National Evaluation of Objective Prison Classification Systems: The Current State of the Art," 285.

CHAPTER 37

Inmate Grievance Procedures

Ashbel T. Wall II

An inmate grievance procedure is a structured, standardized institutional process through which inmates can seek resolution of complaints and problems that arise as a result of their incarceration. It provides an avenue for inmates to pursue concerns that affect them personally and have not been successfully addressed through informal means. Grievance procedures are governed by a clear and straightforward set of written rules covering such elements as permissible subject matter, the manner in which a grievance is filed, responsibility for investigation and decision, time frames for reply, appeals, and recordkeeping.

REASONS FOR HAVING A GRIEVANCE PROCEDURE

Relief of institutional tension is a primary reason for a grievance process. Incarceration results in regulation and control over virtually every aspect of an inmate's life. Prison rules and regulations, the conduct of staff and other inmates, the provision of goods and services, and the facility's conditions have an overwhelming impact on inmates. However, an inmate's lack of independence sharply reduces the inmate's ability to address real or perceived problems in these areas. A grievance procedure presents an official mechanism through which inmates may seek redress for these issues. By providing an authoritative channel that assures inmates that their concerns will be heard, investigated, and answered, the procedure offers a safety valve for inmate frustrations. It reduces the risk that inmates will resort to measures that increase institutional tension and instability. When the process serves as the means to correct legitimate problems, it defuses unnecessary tension.

Enhanced communication with staff is another important reason to have a grievance procedure. A formal means of communicating concerns and responses reduces reliance on the institutional grapevine, with all its potential for rumor, inaccuracy, and distortion, as the accepted means of exchanging information. Inmates are afforded an approved pipeline to the administration, and the administration can convey information directly to a given inmate. In this sense, the procedure provides an uninterrupted avenue for explaining the administration's official position. Many grievances result from a misunderstanding of the agency's policies and procedures. As a result, an inmate may feel that he or she is being treated unfairly. Responses to these grievances "set the record straight," offering the administration an opportunity to restate the department's policy to inmates who believe they have been wronged.

Improved institutional management is a by-product of an administrative remedy program. The grievance process yields a wealth of information for the institutional manager. It helps to reveal systemic weaknesses that can then be targeted for resolution. If, for example, a spate of grievances arises regarding temperature control, the maintenance unit can be assigned to examine the air handling system. If inmates complain that they are not routinely receiving outdoor exercise, the policy, the schedule, or the activity of staff can be reviewed to determine whether a problem exists and which of these factors needs to be changed.

The information generated through grievances is also an invaluable resource for assessing the institutional climate. It can be used to identify problems with staff, inmates, policies, or procedures that may destabilize the facility. The administration can then make strategic decisions about how to maintain order and control.

Administrators may choose to aggregate and categorize grievances in order to spot trends over time. This type of analysis permits the manager to pinpoint persistent trouble spots, such as particular activities (food service, visiting procedures) or locations (particular shifts or housing units). This information should be circulated to managers and shift supervisors to heighten their awareness and solicit their perspectives. Similarly, the tracking of grievances at an agency's regional or central levels affords senior administrators at remote locations insight into issues arising at facilities that they may not be able to visit routinely.

Empowerment of staff is often a positive result of a grievance system. Line staff have a resource to use in managing the offenders they supervise. These personnel are responsible for working with the inmate population every day. However, correctional agencies are organized in hierarchical structures. The chain of command can be long and answers difficult to obtain quickly. Sometimes, as in the case of policy changes, the solution to a problem must come from the top. A grievance procedure permits the line officer to empathize with an inmate's predicament and offer a concrete avenue for easing the frustration. Thus, if an inmate is upset because a radio purchased from the store is not working, the staff member can respond, "I understand your problem, and we'll see if we can get you an answer." In this way, every employee

has the means for obtaining assistance from a higher level in the organization.

Another positive result of an administrative remedy process is often a reduction in litigation. The grievance process provides an alternative to judicial intervention. In fact, many courts require that inmates exhaust all existing administrative procedures prior to initiating a federal civil rights lawsuit pursuant to the *U.S. Code,* vol. 42, sec. 1983, relating to conditions of confinement.[1] If an agency has a grievance procedure, a prisoner must resort to it before the federal court will entertain a case of this nature. To the extent that a problem can be dealt with through administrative procedures, the expense, disruption, uncertainty, and possible liability associated with litigation can be avoided. Furthermore, even if a grievance is not successfully resolved through administrative channels, the documentation that the process yields provides a written record for the agency's use in defending against the claim.

CORE ELEMENTS OF A GRIEVANCE PROGRAM

While grievance procedures in various jurisdictions have different categories of grievable issues, levels of review, or time frames, virtually all of them share certain common characteristics. A number of the following core elements are contained in the *Code of Federal Regulations,* vol. 28, sec. 40.1–40.10 (Subpart A, minimum standards for Inmate Grievance Procedures), issued pursuant to the *U.S. Code,* vol. 42, sec. 1997.

Staff and Inmate Participation in Formulation and Review

Both staff and inmates should be afforded some opportunity to participate in the development of the grievance procedure policy. This approach enhances the credibility of the procedure that is ultimately promulgated and encourages the parties who are subject to its contents to feel a sense of investment in its provisions. This participation can take one or more forms: posting of notices on bulletin boards, solicitation of comments through newsletters, or meetings with such groups of representatives as union stewards or inmate law clerks. Reviews can occur on an annual basis or as changes are proposed.

Option of Informal Resolution

Notwithstanding the existence of a grievance procedure, inmates are encouraged to pursue resolution of their problems through informal means at the lowest possible level. Many institutions provide the inmate population with generic request slips that can be forwarded to the appropriate individual for action. No logging or tracking system is maintained, and no time frames are set. In other cases, the issue is resolved through conversations with staff. While utilization of informal channels is not a prerequisite to pursuit of the grievance process, it does represent a more efficient and less cumbersome option, and it is probably the most widely used means of settling minor issues. When this approach succeeds, the formal grievance process will be unnecessary.

Written Policy

The grievance process is governed by a written policy that is disseminated to all inmates and staff. The policy specifies which forms are used, how they are obtained, how they are completed, where they must be sent, what types of issues are grievable, the levels of review, time frames for response, and any specific limitations. For instance, the policy may exclude consideration of grievances that one inmate files on behalf of another or may set a limit on the number of days that can elapse before a complaint is deemed untimely. Each of these provisions may differ from system to system. Whatever their content, these details must be enshrined in policy in order to foster consistency and fairness.

Hierarchy of Review

While the number of levels of investigation and review will vary according to the size and complexity of a correctional system, a sound grievance procedure requires at least two. The lower level is that of the facility administrator, usually the warden. This rule is consistent with the philosophy that grievances should be dealt with at the lowest possible level. It reinforces the warden's authority and, because there is apt to be a greater familiarity with particular circumstances at the institutional level, permits a response that is more likely to suit the inmate's specific needs. The warden, in turn, designates an institutional grievance officer to investigate grievances and make recommendations for the warden's decision.

However, there must also be a higher level of review for inmates to pursue if they remain dissatisfied with the warden's response. This level must be situated outside the institution and be independent of the institution's administration. However many layers the external review process may have, it is likely to culminate in the agency's chief executive. In this model, the director employs a departmental level grievance coordinator as part of the central office staff. This individual reviews the appeals of grievances and, acting with delegated authority from the director, renders a final decision. Review by an authority independent of the institution alleviates the inmate's real or imagined fears about the fairness of the process. It enhances the system's integrity and increases the accountability of the institution's administration for its actions on grievances.

Two corollaries follow from the twin principles of authority and accountability. The first is that absent extraordinary circumstances, an inmate may not leapfrog over a prescribed level in the grievance procedure. If, for example, a departmental grievance coordinator receives a grievance without evidence that it was first filed at the lower level, it is returned to the inmate with instructions to follow the successive stages in the procedure. The second corollary, however, holds that the independent reviewer should be provided with copies of actions on all grievances, even if they were successfully resolved at lower levels and never appealed to a higher plane. This requirement facilitates monitoring of the grievance process as it operates in the institutions.

Fixed Time Limits

Clearly established time limits for decisions or grievances must be set forth in policy. If the grievance mechanism is to fulfill its purposes, timely action on inmate complaints is essential. Reasonable time frames for response must be created and failure to act within a given time frame should allow the inmate to pursue the grievance at the next level.

Emergency Provisions

If the grievance procedure is to relieve tension and promote trust, it must make allowances for cases in which strict observance of the normal time frames would be an injustice. There are occasions when resort to the customary process would deprive the grievant of meaningful action. The standard used by the federal government in the *Code of Federal Regulations* speaks to situations in which "disposition according to the regular time limits would subject the inmate to a substantial risk of personal injury, or cause other serious and irreparable harm to the inmate."[2] Such cases need not always involve physical danger. An allegation that a sentence expiration date has been improperly calculated and that the inmate is actually entitled to release within the next several days would suffice. In some systems, denial of a furlough to attend the wake of a parent, child, or spouse might be an appropriate subject of an emergency grievance.

In these cases, the rules permit immediate forwarding of the grievance to the level at which corrective action can be taken. Time frames for investigation and response are shortened to reflect the urgency of the request.

Written Requests and Responses

The process should be paper driven to ensure clarity, consistency, and accountability. The

inmate's grievance should be written on a departmental-issue form, with spaces provided for responses at various levels. Similarly, the investigators' reports should follow a standard format on a preprinted form. Each page should consist of multiple copies to permit circulation and filing of carbons.

Availability and Accessibility

The grievance process must be available and accessible to all inmates regardless of classification, security designation, custody location, and disciplinary status. In order to foster this accessibility, inmates ought to be able to resort to an array of options for transmittal: handing the grievance to any staff member or superior officer, placing it in locked boxes at such locations as the yard or the dining area, or sending it through the U.S. mail. If an inmate alleges that he or she did not use the standard forms because staff refused to provide them, the grievance should be accepted for investigation.

Safeguards To Avoid Retaliation

The integrity of the procedure is undermined if inmates fear that they will suffer adverse consequences for filing a grievance. The policy should make it clear that reprisals against inmates who lodge grievances are prohibited. Some systems do permit sanctions against an inmate for abuse of the process. Abuses may include the filing of excessive numbers of grievances, grievances intended to harass another person, or frivolous use of the process. The sanction may include restrictions on the number or subject matter of grievances for a set period of time. Emergency grievances remain an option even under these cases.

Consistent with the principles of availability and accessibility, the decision to impose limitations should not be made lightly. The disincentive that sanctions provide for a small number of inmates should be balanced against the credibility of the process among the inmate population when inmates know that their issues will receive attention.

Maintenance of Logs and Records

A log of all grievances—containing such summary information as the assigned grievance number, the inmate's name, the subject matter, the dates received and answered, and the disposition—should be maintained at the institution. Similar logs should be kept at each level in the process. In addition, the higher levels should be provided with updated copies of institutional logs for tracking and monitoring. Finally, hard copies of grievance packages, including the complaint, the investigation, and the response, should be maintained at the institution. Copies of the packages are forwarded to the upper level as well.

WHAT TYPES OF ISSUES ARE GRIEVABLE?

For the grievance procedure to be meaningful, it must be applicable to a broad spectrum of the inmate's institutional experience. The definition of a grievance procedure has been provided by the U.S. Department of Justice in the *Code of Federal Regulations:* "Grievance means a written complaint by an inmate on the inmate's own behalf regarding a policy applicable within an institution, a condition in an institution, an action involving an inmate of an institution, or an incident occurring within an institution. The term 'grievance' does not include a complaint about a parole decision."[3] As this definition illustrates, virtually all applications of policies, rules, and procedures; employee or inmate conduct; access to programs or services; and living conditions can be subject to grievance. Exhibit 37–1 offers an example of a grievance procedure.

Within these parameters, individual jurisdictions carve out their own exceptions to the body of grievable issues. One category of exemptions includes issues that are beyond the agency's scope of authority. State and federal laws and regulations, judicial decisions, and decisions of the parole board fall into this category.

Another set of exclusions involves situations in which the subject matter of the grievance is already governed by statutory or judicially credited procedures. In the Federal Bureau of Prisons, for example, requests for access to data or complaints about lost or damaged property are nongrievable issues. The first are handled under the provisions of the Freedom of Information Act and the second are covered by the Federal Tort Claims Act.[4] In Rhode Island, on the other hand, allegations of property loss or damage are subject to grievance. However, the decisions of discipline and classification boards are not, because they are covered by the provisions of a federal consent decree.[5]

States may establish other exceptions, such as security threat group designations or decisions by qualified medical personnel relating to an inmate's health. Some jurisdictions may make a distinction between failure to follow the provisions of a policy and the substantive decisions made pursuant to this same policy. Thus, for example, an inmate may be precluded from filing a grievance challenging a disciplinary board's finding of guilt. At the same time, the inmate may be permitted to grieve the fact that the board's decision was made outside the time limit prescribed by policy. Similarly, an adverse decision on an appeal may not be grievable, but failure to offer the appeal may be.

Whatever the distinctions among jurisdictions, it is critical that each agency issue a clear written description of those issues that are grievable and those that are not.

CONCLUSION

A properly functioning inmate grievance system in prison and jail settings can serve staff and inmates well. This type of program, although paper rich and time-intensive, allows prisoners the ability to air their concerns in a legitimate and above-board manner and permits staff to respond in a similar vein. If the process has credibility, it will reduce litigation and save staff a great deal of time that would be spent solving problems and avoiding court actions. An admin-

Exhibit 37–1 An Example of a Grievance Procedure

On 10/12/97, inmate E.L. lodged a grievance with the warden of his facility. He alleged that while he was being transferred to a new cell on 9/27/97, the officer told another inmate to carry his television because E.L. was already carrying several bags. E.L. stated that he did not give the inmate permission to touch his television. E.L. subsequently discovered that the T.V. was not working. The other inmate told E.L. that the television was dropped and broken during the transport. When E.L. spoke to the officer, the C.O. allegedly replied that it was not his problem. E.L. sought to have the television repaired or replaced at departmental expense. He used the Request for Resolution of Grievance Form 1 to state his complaint.

The grievance was received in the warden's office, where it was logged in, given a number, and assigned to the lieutenant who investigates grievances. He verified that the inmate in fact owned a television, that it was listed on his property record, and that he had changed cells on the date in question. However, the inmate had provided no information, such as the name of any officers or the inmate, with which to verify his claim. The lieutenant also noted that the grievance had not been filed within the time limit required by policy. The lieutenant completed his investigation on 10/21/97 and, the following day, the facility's deputy warden responded in writing to the inmate in the space provided on the Level 1 form. In denying the grievance, he cited the conclusions reached by the investigating staff member. A copy of all the paperwork was forwarded to the departmental grievance coordinator.

On 10/30/97, E.L. appealed to the next—and in this case, final—level: the director's office. He did so by filling out the Request for Resolution of Grievance Form 2—the form used for appeals. He gave it to the superior officer in his area, who acknowledged receiving it through a signature dated 11/4/97. This lieutenant conveyed the grievance to the institutional grievance coordinator, who logged in receipt on 11/5/97 and sent it to the director's office. It was received by the departmental grievance coordinator on 11/13/97.

In his appeal, the inmate explained that he was relatively new to the system and did not know the names of officers and inmates. However, he did produce a copy of the inmate property record on which his possessions were inventoried at the time of his transfer. E.L. wrote, "My block officer checked my newly bought T.V. and signed my property sheet. Once the officer took my T.V., he took responsibility for it and all my property. What he did to it (drop it, throw it) I don't know but once I got to [my new cell] my T.V. was not working. I can't read the names of the officers on my property sheets but I've enclosed copies of each. For more information refer to form #1."

The issue of E.L.'s untimely use of the grievance procedure was rendered moot when the departmental grievance coordinator ascertained that he had submitted an informal request for assistance with the problem immediately after the transfer. He filed his grievance only after the informal request did not result in the action he was seeking.

The departmental grievance coordinator communicated with the facility to determine the identity of the transport officer, whose signature on the inmate property record was illegible. During this time, the coordinator sent the inmate a letter explaining the delay and inviting him to forward the name of the inmate involved if he knew his identity.

Once the transport officer had been identified, he was contacted and provided a report concerning E.L.'s allegation. In his report, he wrote "Never in my six years have I ever let another inmate go with a transfer . . . nor is it a policy of the facility to do so. It is the responsibility of each inmate to move his own property wherever he goes. Therefore the claim made by inmate E.L. is totally untrue." Upon receipt of this report, the grievance coordinator summarized its contents and denied the grievance in a response to E.L. dated 12/19/97.

A subsequent letter from the inmate to the director's office was answered by making reference to the fact that the complaint had been properly investigated through the departmental grievance procedure and denied at both levels. As a result, the department considered the matter closed.

istrative remedy program establishes a win-win situation for all involved in the process.

NOTES

1. Civil Rights of Institutionalized Persons Act, U.S. Code, vol. 42, sec. 1997(e) (1980).

2. *Code of Federal Regulations,* vol. 28, sec. 40.8.

3. *Code of Federal Regulations,* vol. 28, sec. 40.1 (d).

4. Edward Crosley, telephone interview by author, January 28, 1997.

5. Rhode Island Department of Corrections, *Inmate Grievance Procedures,* Policy 13.10 (Cranston, RI: 1996).

CHAPTER 38

Boot Camps

Angela Gover, Gaylene Styve, and Doris MacKenzie

Boot camp prisons, often referred to as shock confinement, are designed to punish offenders in a short-term program that is generally quasi-military, similar to basic training in the military. Many states and the federal government have boot camp operations.

OVERVIEW

Boot camp prisons are increasingly being used as a sentencing option to instill order and discipline in the lives of young, nonviolent, first-time offenders. Many boot camp prisons provide an opportunity for offenders to shorten their sentences while, at the same time, they participate in therapeutic programs that would not have been available to them in a traditional prison. Typically, inmates follow a rigorous daily schedule of activities for 90 to 180 days in a program modeled after military basic training. Inmates must follow a strict set of program rules, such as requesting permission to speak or eating meals in silence. Minor rule violations are usually punished with physical exercise such as push-ups or running. Serious rule violations may result in removal from the program and return to a traditional prison. Offenders who successfully complete the program are released to community supervision and may participate in an after-care program that assists offenders with their transition from prison to the community. It is hoped that the regimented lifestyle of boot camp will help inmates lead better lives after they are released.

Programming within boot camp programs varies tremendously.[1-3] Some programs may devote nearly five hours per day to military activities such as drill and ceremony, marching, and physical labor. Other programs with more of a rehabilitative emphasis may devote more time to activities such as counseling, academic education, or drug treatment. Other differences among boot camp models include program capacities, program location, participant eligibility criteria and selection practices, program duration, populations served, and community after-care components. Because of all these differences, it is difficult to evaluate all boot camps using the same measures. Different programs have different goals.

POPULARITY

Since the inception of adult boot camps in Oklahoma and Georgia in 1983, the popularity of this intermediate correctional option for offenders has grown throughout the country. By the end of 1995, boot camp programs for men, women, and juveniles were operating in more than 55 states and jurisdictions. In 1995, the Department of Justice awarded $21 million in grants for jurisdictions to plan boot camp programs, renovate existing facilities for use as boot camps, and construct new boot camp facilities in

27 states and 3 territories. More than half of the awards were for juvenile facilities. In response to the rapidly growing boot camp phenomenon, the American Correctional Association developed accreditation standards for juvenile and adult boot camps.

Boot camp programs are considered to be an attractive sentencing option for several reasons. With assistance from the media, the public is learning to think of boot camps as an effective means to instill responsibility and respect for authority in criminal offenders. Many Americans have seen a story on the evening news featuring boot camps. These brief news clips usually project powerful visual images such as a platoon of inmates snapping to attention as their drill instructor approaches, inmates marching to a work site to participate in hard physical labor, or boot camp inmates performing community service such as cleaning state parks or highways. Such images capture the public's attention and support.

From the perspective of policy makers, boot camp participants are able to serve time and keep the public safe while saving tax dollars. Boot camp prisons were developed in a conservative political climate, with politicians supporting a "get tough on crime" attitude toward the allotment of criminal justice system funding. Correctional personnel believe that boot camps help alleviate prison overcrowding.

RESEARCH

While boot camp proponents argue that the programs are effective, research has not supported this conclusion. Studies examining the impact of programs emphasizing a military model have not found that they are effective in reducing recidivism.[4] Nor is there evidence that the programs successfully reduce prison crowding despite evidence that the programs have the potential to do so.[5] Most programs were either too small (relative to the prison population) or admitted individuals who would otherwise be on probation (and not using prison beds).

GOALS AND PHILOSOPHIES

In a 1991 survey, correctional administrators were asked to rate the importance of 11 different boot camp program goals.[6] Recidivism reduction, rehabilitation, and drug education were found to be "very important" program goals. Administrators rated reducing crowding, developing work skills, and providing a safe prison environment as "important" program goals. Goals deemed "somewhat important" were deterrence, education, and drug treatment. Punishment and vocational education were goals most often rated as "not important" or not even a goal.

A 1993 survey by the American Correctional Association found similar results.[7] The most important boot camp program goals were rehabilitation, reducing recidivism, and reducing prison crowding and costs. As in MacKenzie's survey, punishment was mentioned as a goal by only a few programs. Correctional administrators do not share politicians' attitude that punishment is a primary purpose of boot camps.

Boot Camps for Adult Criminal Offenders

As of January 1, 1997, there were 54 boot camp programs operating around the nation for confinement and treatment of adult criminal offenders. The first program opened in Oklahoma in 1984. The length of programs varies from three to six months, with an average duration of four months. The daily cost per inmate to operate the boot camps varies from a low of $21.44 to a high of $149.12, with an average of $56.77.

Source: Data from C. Camp and G. Camp, *Corrections Yearbook 1997,* pp. 98–99, © 1997, Criminal Justice Institute, Inc.

PROGRAMMING SIMILARITIES AND DIFFERENCES

As previously mentioned, boot camp programs allow many offenders to serve shorter sentences while incarcerated. Inmates are separated from traditional prison populations and participate in physical training, military drill and ceremony, and hard labor. Beyond these common similarities, boot camps differ in many regards.[8] First, adult program capacities range from a minimum of 42 offenders to a maximum of 1,500 offenders. Program size is often a factor in eligibility criteria and program dropout and expulsion rates. As a form of protection against liability, most programs require offenders to volunteer (in writing) for participation. Some offenders are directly sentenced to the program by judges. Other offenders may be sentenced to a department of corrections where program eligibility and suitability is determined. And other programs may rely on the discretion of the parole commission to identify participants. Most programs keep offenders between 90 and 120 days. However, some programs operate with a minimum of 30 days, while others may extend to 540 days.

Most boot camp programs operate as separate units within larger medium and maximum security correctional facilities. This gives the boot camp access to prison resources such as treatment, education, and vocational programs that may be too costly to implement in a smaller, independently located facility. In addition, the proximity of boot camp inmates to regular prison inmates may have a deterrent effect; boot camp inmates will see up close what traditional incarceration is like. However, the recent trend has been toward separate boot camp facilities, given the large amount of construction funding awarded to various jurisdictions.

Boot camp programs tend to have similar populations. Most programs restrict participation to inmates convicted of nonviolent offenses who have not been previously incarcerated for felony convictions, are open to men only, and house participants between the ages of 17 and 25. Additionally, offenders selected for boot camps are screened to ensure that they are physically and psychologically able to meet the strict physical requirements of the program.

Boot camps have increasingly focused on treatment. For example, most programs incorporate some drug education, drug treatment, or a combination of the two. Research shows that drug problems are prevalent among boot camp participants; some states are even developing programs to specifically target drug-related offenders. Often these programs are legislatively mandated to provide drug treatment to boot camp participants. As would be expected, drug education and treatment approaches vary tremendously. For example, programs spend from 12 to 180 days on these therapeutic activities.

BOOT CAMPS FOR WOMEN

Since the development of boot camp prisons, most participants have been men. Although many correctional systems have strived for gender equality in prison programming, research has shown that the specific needs of women offenders must be taken into account if they are to benefit from programs originally developed for men.[9]

Women who have participated in boot camp programs have reported difficulties keeping up with the physical demands and added emotional stress because most boot camp staff and inmates were men. The highly confrontational environments of boot camps triggered emotions associated with past mental and physical abuse. Women in programs designed for women only reported less emotional and physical stress.

Specific programming needs of women offenders include the following: employment or vocational training to prepare women to financially support themselves and their children; treatment for substance abuse; domestic violence and sexual assault counseling; and education and training on issues related to family obligations such as parenting, life skills, and community reintegration.[10–12] One advantage to boot camp programs for women is increased opportunities for drug treatment and parenting training in conjunction with community reintegration. Many women inmates have children for whom they will be financially responsible after leaving boot camp.

MILITARY MODEL DEBATE

The use of a military basic training model in corrections has faced strong opposition.[13] Although the boot camp concept has changed over the years, the relevance of basic training in boot camps is continually challenged. Opponents of the model assert that the military correctional philosophy is antithetical to treatment. They criticize the confrontational interactions between staff and inmates and the increased likelihood of injuries during physical labor and exercise as interfering with any treatment potential of the programs. The use of summary punishments combined with the authoritarian nature of the programs creates the potential for abuse of power by the staff. They argue that boot camps attract staff who are more susceptible to take advantage of the control they have over the inmates and get carried away when disciplining inmates. Also, opponents note that many standard boot camp practices associated with the military model (summary and immediate punishments, humiliating inmates, etc.) are not supported by national correctional practices.

Another perspective within the military model debate is a Machiavellian approach that is supported by many correctional administrators.[14] They view boot camps as a solution for two important problems: a lack of funding for therapeutic programming and limited prison space. They do not expect positive results from components of the military model per se (military drill, hard labor, etc.); however, Machiavellian supporters tolerate these program aspects as means to achieve desired ends. They recognize that a major source of boot camp popularity stems from the public's misguided perception that boot camps accomplish retribution, rehabilitation, and deterrence simultaneously due to the tough military environment emphasizing structure and discipline. The Machiavellian perspective takes advantage of the support generated by the military atmosphere to obtain increased funding for therapeutic programming and use it as a mechanism for early release, despite possible disadvantages associated with the model.

The third approach to the military model views it as an effective way to change criminal offenders.[15] The military model finds more support among practitioners who have worked in programs that emphasize strict rules, discipline, and confrontational situations, such as in the area of drug treatment. These proponents suggest that the military atmosphere actually creates an environment conducive to individual change.[16] The stressful environment in boot camps facilitates radical change in the inmates' lives, which makes them more accepting of the treatment programming both during and after the program. The military model is said to intensify the process of change by maintaining inmates' physical and mental health. Proponents reject the common criticism that discipline associated with the military model equates to abuse; with consistent boot camp policies, training of all staff, and continual monitoring of policies, abuse will be avoided, proponents say. Basic training programming that balances discipline and treatment while operating with committed, well-trained staff has great potential to make a difference in the lives of boot camp program inmates, proponents argue.

PROGRAMMING EFFECTIVENESS AND IMPACT OF THE ENVIRONMENT

Whether the military model has positive or negative effects on inmates leads to a larger question: Is it the military model that is making a difference, or is it other aspects of the boot camp environment, including control, activity, safety, care, structure, justice, and the quality of life within the facility. The mere classification of a program as a boot camp does not give a detailed enough description to enable us to identify the components that will produce desirable results. Research needs to address issues associated with the conditions of confinement and how these conditions affect program effectiveness. For example, there are questions about how individuals who are low academic achievers would do in educational programming in a boot camp environment. From one perspective, individuals may perform better in a highly structured environment if the educational program is high in quality. On the other hand, the confrontational nature of the program may create stress and reduce learning.

AFTER-CARE PROGRAMMING

First-generation boot camp programs developed during the early to mid-1980s did not have a heavy emphasis on after-care programming. As programming evolved through second-, third-, and even fourth-generation boot camps, the importance of continuity of services and supervision during the offenders' transition back to the community has become more recognized,[17] giving rise to a higher emphasis on community-based treatment, case management, and offender assessment and classification, not just increased levels of surveillance, as important elements of after-care. Some believe that the time spent in an after-care program should equal or be greater than the time spent incarcerated and that the treatment programming should be more intensive than the programming received in the boot camp.[18]

Intensive supervision programs may include employment counseling, drug counseling, and a continuation of the therapeutic services inmates received while incarcerated. Often, individual after-care treatment plans are determined by staff at the boot camp based on offenders' particular needs, and contact may be maintained between the boot camp and after-care participant. Offenders may be required to submit to random drug testing or comply with curfew requirements. The success of this model depends on formal links between community treatment providers, the boot camps, and the individual supervising the offender.

Some boot camp programs have developed innovative after-care models, such as transitional housing for boot camp graduates, often to graduates who do not have acceptable housing in the community. One program requires boot camp inmates to make renovations to the transitional housing residence to which they are released. Another program utilizes electronic monitoring as an aspect of after-care. These offenders are electronically supervised during their transition from incarceration to the community. Although postrelease programming varies, it is thought to be an important stage of offenders' successful transition back into the community.

CONCLUSION

In a recent review of treatment programs, MacKenzie reviewed correctional programs and their effectiveness as crime prevention techniques. Overall, there was no crime reduction effect for programs that focused on deterrence, physical challenge, the wilderness, or confrontation; used vague, nondirective, unstructured counseling; or increased surveillance (intensive supervision, house arrest, etc.) without providing services or treatment. On the other hand, programs that included appropriate rehabilitation did reduce future criminal activities. Effective rehabilitation programs were structured and focused, used multiple components, focused on developing skills, and used behavioral or cognitive–behavioral methods. They also provide substantial, meaningful contact between the participant and treatment personnel. Is the growth in correctional boot camps warranted? Because boot camps vary so greatly, there is no single answer to that question. Boot camps with philosophies and programs that have proven effective are clearly making positive contributions to corrections today.

NOTES

1. T. Castellano and S. Plant, "Boot Camp Aftercare Programming: Current Limits and Suggested Remedies," in

Juvenile and Adult Boot Camps (Laurel, MD: American Correctional Association, 1996).

2. D. MacKenzie and R. Brame, "Shock Incarceration and Positive Adjustment during Community Supervision," *Journal of Quantitative Criminology* 11 (1995): 111–142.

3. J. Zachariah, "An Overview of Boot Camp Goals, Components, and Results," in *Correctional Boot Camps: A Tough Intermediate Sanction,* ed. MacKenzie and Hebert (Washington, DC: National Institute of Justice, 1996).

4. F. Cullen et al., Control in the Community: The Limits of Reform? (Paper presented at the meeting of the International Association of Residential and Community Alternatives, Philadelphia, 1993).

5. D. MacKenzie and A. Piquero, "The Impact of Shock Incarceration Programs on Prison Crowding," *Crime and Delinquency* 40 (1994): 222–249.

6. D. MacKenzie, "Boot Camp Prisons in 1993," *Research in Action* (Washington, DC: National Institute of Justice, 1993).

7. Zachariah, "An Overview of Boot Camp Goals, Components, and Results."

8. D. MacKenzie, "Boot Camp Prisons," in *Introduction to Social Problems,* ed. Calhoun and Ritzer (New York: McGraw-Hill, 1995).

9. D. MacKenzie et al., "Boot Camps as an Alternative for Women," in *Correctional Boot Camps: A Tough Intermediate Sanction,* ed. MacKenzie and Hebert (Washington, DC: National Institute of Justice, 1996).

10. American Correctional Association, *Female Offenders: Meeting Needs of a Neglected Population* (Laurel, MD: 1983).

11. D. MacKenzie and H. Donaldson, "Boot Camp for Women Offenders," *Criminal Justice Review* 21 (1996): 21–43.

12. MacKenzie et al., "Boot Camps as an Alternative for Women."

13. M. Morash and L. Ruker, "A Critical Look at the Idea of Boot Camps as Correctional Reform," *Crime and Delinquency* 36 (1990): 204–222.

14. D. MacKenzie and C. Souryal, *A "Machiavellian" Perspective on the Development of Boot Camp Prisons: A Debate* (Chicago: University of Chicago Press, 1995).

15. E. Zamble and F. Porporino, "Coping, Imprisonment, and Rehabilitation: Some Data and Their Implications," *Criminal Justice and Behavior* 17 (1990): 53–64.

16. D. Andrews et al., "Does Correctional Treatment Work? A Clinically Relevant and Psychologically Informed Meta-Analysis," *Criminology* 28 (1990): 369–404.

17. L. Gransky et al., "Is There a 'Next Generation' of Shock Incarceration Facilities? The Evolving Nature of Goals, Program Components, and Drug Treatment Services," in *Intermediate Sanctions: Sentencing in the 90s,* ed. Smykla and Selke (Cincinnati, OH: Anderson Publishing, 1995).

18. Castellano and Plant, "Boot Camp Aftercare Programming: Current Limits and Suggested Remedies."

CHAPTER 39

Visiting in Prison

Reginald A. Wilkinson and Tessa Unwin

The operation of a visitation program is an integral element of any prison system. Hundreds of thousands of relatives and friends visit inmates in prison each year. Experienced correctional managers know that visitation improves the prison environment, so all institutions encourage visits from family and friends. Visits give inmates something to look forward to, an incentive to participate in rehabilitative programs, and a mechanism with which to cope with prison life. While there are challenges to the security of prisons and jails when visitors are allowed into the security envelope of an institution, and an elaborate system of rules and regulations governs the process, the benefits greatly outweigh the drawbacks.

BENEFITS

There are several reasons that visiting with family and friends is encouraged in the prison setting. The most important becomes evident after release. The prisoner who has maintained contact with supportive individuals such as family and friends has a "safety net" when he or she returns to the community. Family and friends provide a feeling of belonging to a group. They often help released offenders seek and find employment and conduct themselves in a positive, constructive manner after release. Dickinson and Seaman note that social role theory asserts that when the desirable social roles are not maintained during incarceration, newly released pris-

oners are more likely to see themselves and to be seen by others in one of the negative roles ascribed to former convicts. These ex-convict roles are more likely to lead inmates back to criminal behavior.[1] Visiting is also an incentive for good behavior, providing a powerful management tool. Prisoners are fully aware that the visiting environment for general population inmates is significantly freer than for those in disciplinary status.

DRAWBACKS

There is also a downside to allowing visits for a confined population. Visitors are a primary pipeline for the smuggling of drugs and other contraband into a facility. Significant numbers of alert staff are required, not only to carefully supervise visits but also to conduct background checks and search packages.

Some inmates schedule their visiting in order to get out of job assignments, while others become depressed because they have no visitors at all. Some prisoners use the visiting process to make contact with potential crime partners or gullible new friends whom they may later use to convey contraband into the prison. In many instances, prisoners first make contact with outsiders through pen pal organizations, then quickly exploit the friendship. Inmates also abuse the visiting privilege by convincing sympathetic visitors to bring them money or even participate in criminal activity requiring outside assistance.

Certain visitors may be partners in crime who help the inmate to continue running illegal street enterprises while incarcerated.

An interview with a former warden who served at several Ohio prisons brought numerous examples of inmate "scams" to light. For instance, an inmate at the Chillicothe Correctional Institution convinced a female friend to help him set up a phony charity. The plan was to solicit money from churches. When arrested, the woman was found in possession of an entire office setup, including an addressograph containing the names and addresses of churches. Another Chillicothe prisoner, a former male model, had one female visitor so enthralled that she cashed in her burial account in order to deposit funds in the inmate's prison commissary account. A young man incarcerated at the Southern Ohio Correctional Facility befriended an older couple who had read about his case in a local newspaper. The young man, accustomed to a comfortable upper-class existence, had killed his parents in a fit of anger. By the time his manipulation was discovered, the older couple had bribed an officer to take the prisoner money, sunglasses, and a fake employee identification card. The inmate had planned to simply walk out of the maximum security facility with other employees during a shift change.[2]

EMOTIONALLY CHARGED

A wise correctional manager knows that prison visiting is a sensitive and emotionally charged subject. Just as visiting provides a powerful incentive for good behavior, unfair treatment regarding visits, whether real or perceived, can create undesirable tensions. If a prisoner feels that his or her mother, spouse, or other family member has been unnecessarily hassled or in some way insulted, an outburst may result. Sensitivity training and professionalism are essential for staff involved in the visiting process.

Author Jess Maghan gives the following advice: "Correctional Officers must learn to be self-determining through personal and professional empowerment and a sense of dignity. They must realize that inmate rights improve the rights of officers and that everyone can benefit from change. Correctional Officers can take pride in their flexibility because it leads to the capacity to manage, control, and supervise the diverse group of inmates for whom they are responsible. . . . With this sense of empowerment, Correctional Officers truly appreciate the time-proven adage of 'accepting the things they cannot change, seeking the courage to change the things they can . . . and hoping for the wisdom to know the difference.'" [3(pp.59-60)] Lori B. Girshick provides quotes from women visiting the California State Prison at Soledad. The women's words graphically illustrate the many emotions involved in the visitation process.

> (Charlene) When I hit the visiting area . . . the first thing I do is pray that he's all right and that no unforeseen incident has occurred that would mess up our visit. Once I'm cleared . . . I block out the surroundings, the guards, prison clothes, etc. My attention is focused on the reuniting of our minds. It's a great feeling, and after the visit it's like I take on new strength even though I'm never sure of the exact day when I will visit again.

> (Carrie) I think we're being punished as much as they [inmates] are. I think the system is designed to make it as difficult on us as possible because it hurts them. It's awful to have to stand outside and freeze for three hours waiting to get in, when they're [staff] sitting in a warm office looking at you.

> (Cynthia) They're always threatening that if you don't settle your kids, you'll get a visit termination. What else can kids do but be kids? I feel bad that I have to tell [my daughter] you cannot run, you cannot do this, you cannot do that, you cannot, cannot, cannot.

(Vicky) There are things I get tired of, being there every week and telling them who I am. They can't find his file. They're rude. They humiliate you. It shouldn't be men doing this [searches] to women . . . it just shouldn't be, but it happens.[4(pp.59–60)]

THE COMMUNITY

Some community agencies and businesses are involved in the visiting process in various ways. Specialized bus companies offer regular charters to prisons from large cities, helping to alleviate the problems caused by long distances.

Local businesses such as motels, restaurants, and gas stations benefit from the visitors. But when protesting the siting of a new prison in their area, some people list the fear of prisoners' visitors disrupting their communities.

In many communities, volunteer visitors offer friendship to prisoners who have no other contacts on whom to rely. These mentors provide guidance and support while the individual is incarcerated and assistance with finding employment and a place to live after release.

CHILDREN IN THE PRISON ENVIRONMENT

Bringing families together is a laudable endeavor. Yet one must wonder about the lasting effects on children of seeing a parent in prison, especially when the parent confined is the mother. Authors Robert R. Ross and Elizabeth A. Fabiano have argued that the variety of prison visiting arrangements is a reflection of the complex social and moral issues involved in the question of whether children should be separated from their incarcerated mothers or exposed to prisons. The effects of such visits on the mother and child when the visit ends, the feelings of other inmate mothers who do not have contact with their children, the effects on the child of seeing the often frightening physical structure of prisons, and the possible long-term effects on the child of living in a prison for short or long periods of time are all significant issues. Ross and Fabiano also stress that there has not been research on the effects of separating children, particularly infants, from their mothers while they are in prison.[5]

Innovative programs are springing up nationwide to counter the deleterious effects of prison visits on children. For example, the Girl Scouts of America has formed partnerships with some women's prisons to pilot scout troops behind bars. Incarcerated women and their daughters work together on projects, earning merit badges and learning how to be successful teammates. In turn, the Ohio Department of Rehabilitation and Correction offers its training academy grounds and other resources to the Girl Scouts of America for use in outings and training.

In some women's prisons, overnight and weekend visits are granted as rewards for successful completion of parenting programs. This type of program, originating primarily in women's facilities, helps to "normalize" the prison visiting process. The Nebraska Center for Women has incorporated two unique incentive programs in its development of a family-friendly atmosphere. Its Mothering Offspring Life Development program offers longer, often overnight, visits for children of inmates who have met program requirements, including positive conduct. In 1994, this program was expanded to include an on-grounds nursery where expectant mothers can live and learn about childbirth and parenting while awaiting the birth of their own child. Infants born into the program may remain with their mothers for up to 18 months, provided the mother continues to meet work and conduct requirements. As a result of the level of accountability built into the program, there have been no reported incidents of any kind during its span of operation.[6]

NUTS AND BOLTS OF VISITS

Prison systems have myriad rules, regulations, and procedures regarding visits. Rules vary widely according to tradition, security needs, and the availability of staff and visiting space. Informing staff, visitors, and inmates of the rules and regulations ensures a smooth operation; perceived or actual inconsistency and arbitrariness add unnecessary tension to the process. A courteous, informed, and professional staff can make the visiting experience positive for everyone. Additionally, every effort should be made to inform visitors of restrictions or delays caused by special circumstances such as fog alerts, extra or extended counts, lockdowns, or disturbances.

Technology is also contributing to the prison visitation process. Various addresses on the Internet contain information and debate issues regarding prison visitation; some jurisdictions offer information on visiting rules, hours, and other information of interest to prison visitors.[7]

VISITING LIST

Most prisoners develop their visiting list while still in the reception process. Lists generally include family, friends, attorneys, and clergy. The list names the visitors, their address, their phone number, and their relationship to the inmate. After the individuals listed are screened and a background check is completed, some correctional systems actually interview visitors to determine their suitability for the prison setting. To avoid problems and conflict, prohibitions to visiting lists usually include known felons, former inmates, parolees and probationers, vendors, and prison volunteers.

GENERAL POPULATION VISITS

The number, frequency, and duration of visits are limited by space, personnel constraints, scheduling, and security considerations. Upon arriving at the prison, visitors are required to present photo identification and may need to submit to searches (see "Searches" below). Visitors are also informed of what constitutes contraband and the sanctions in place to punish those who attempt to convey contraband into the facility. Children must be accompanied by an adult guardian. Many visiting areas contain vending machines, diaper changing stations, and play areas set aside for children.

Some inmates are granted visits for unusual situations such as to accommodate someone traveling a long distance or to address a family crisis.

The *Standards for Adult Correctional Institutions,* published by the American Correctional Association (ACA), require that provisions be made to ensure attorney–client confidentiality.[8] Special arrangements for such communication encompass telephone communications, uncensored correspondence, and visits (ACA 3–4263). Whenever possible, separate visiting rooms are provided for inmates and their attorneys. This courtesy may also be extended to public officials and members of the media.

In the case of death row, administrative segregation, disciplinary detention, and protective custody inmates, security concerns outweigh concerns about family closeness. High-risk prisoners or those in disciplinary housing are often restricted to noncontact visits using screens, handcuffs, and leg irons at the discretion of the facility.

CONJUGAL VISITS

About half of America's prison inmates claim to be married, and six states allow conjugal visitation (see Exhibit 39–1).[9] In some jurisdictions, conjugal visits may be viewed as an unnecessary prisoner privilege and frowned upon by the general public and lawmakers. Jules Burstein compares this American conservatism to the more liberal attitudes in other countries and asserts that the acceptance of conjugal visiting outside the United States is generally attributable to two factors: a less puritanical and hypocritical attitude toward sex and a greater emphasis on the family as a primary and vital social unit. Many foreign cultures view such visits, along with home furloughs, as an individual's right.[10]

Exhibit 39–1   States That Permit Conjugal Visits as of January 1, 1997

California

Connecticut

Mississippi

New Mexico

New York

Washington

Source: Data from C. Camp and G. Camp, *Corrections Yearbook 1997*, p. 105, © 1997, Criminal Justice Institute, Inc.

CONTRABAND

Contraband is defined as anything not allowed into a particular facility and varies depending on the type and security level of that facility. Most systems divide contraband into two categories: major and minor. Major contraband consists of drugs and alcohol, tools, weapons, explosive ordnance, ammunition, currency, and the like, whereas minor contraband often consists of nuisance items such as excessive food. Without question, narcotics trafficking presents the largest dilemma to correctional staff.

Inmates and their visitors have devised many ingenious ways to attempt to smuggle drugs into jails and prisons. Drugs have been found in many types of food: resealed pudding cups, instant soup packets, jars of peanut butter, hollowed-out fruit pies, loaves of bread, and candy bars. Narcotics have been discovered in diaper linings, tennis shoe heels, tubes of shampoo and toothpaste, talcum powder, magic markers, stamps, greeting cards, and hollowed-out books. Illegal substances have been thrown over institution fences in tennis balls, taped to trash cans and toilets in the visiting room, sent in with packages of clothing, and left in a knapsack at an outside crew worksite.

SEARCHES

Searches are imposed to provide adequate safeguards against the introduction of contraband into correctional facilities. All searches should be conducted in a professional manner, without violating the legal rights of visitors and with due regard to human dignity. Searches may include a body cavity search, a strip search, a pat-down search, a metal detector search, or an X-ray. In most correctional jurisdictions, strip- and body cavity searches must be approved by the warden or designee and are performed only when there is a specific reason to suspect the visitor has contraband. In most states, only a medical professional is permitted to conduct an intrusive body cavity search. Anyone who refuses a search is usually prohibited from visiting on that day. Some systems also utilize drug-detecting canines at prison or jail sally ports.

High-tech drug detection devices such as ionizer systems are also being introduced into prison drug and explosive detection arsenals. More sophisticated technology is on the horizon.

VISIT TERMINATIONS

Violation of prison rules may result in a visit being terminated. The individual may also be suspended or removed from the approved visiting list. Violations include refusing to be searched, possessing contraband, attempting to convey contraband to an inmate, attempting to visit while intoxicated, falsifying identification, loaning identification to others, wearing inappropriate clothing, and engaging in prohibited physical contact, sex, or other behavior. If caught bringing illegal contraband into a prison, a visitor may be detained, arrested, and possibly prosecuted. Visitation may, obviously, also be curtailed or terminated in an emergency.

FACILITY DESIGN

Visiting areas should be designed to provide for adequate supervision and control. Visiting rooms should provide a comfortable visiting environment that is neat and clean, has adequate light and ventilation, allows good visual supervision by staff, and includes separate lavatory facilities for visitors and inmates. Today's visiting rooms must also be fully accessible for those with disabilities.

CONCLUSION

Correctional agencies, prisoners, visitors, and society in general can all benefit from an efficient, humane, and secure visiting program. Regular contact with visitors significantly enhances an inmate's quality of life and establishes a lifeline between the inmate and the free community. Ties with family members, friends, and other loved ones are critical to inmates' successful return to the community, and visiting helps maintain these relationships.

NOTES

1. G. Dickinson and T. Seaman, "Communication Policy Changes from 1971–1991 in State Correctional Facilities for Adult Males in the United States," *Prison Journal* 74, no. 3 (1994): 371–382.

2. Terry Morris, interview with author, December 17, 1996, Columbus, OH.

3. J. Maghan, "Styles of Control and Supervision," in *The Effective Correctional Officer* (Lanham, MD: American Correctional Association, 1992), 51–60.

4. L. Girshick, *Soledad Women* (New York: Praeger Publishing, 1996), 59–60.

5. R. Ross and E. Fabiano, *Female Offenders: Correctional Afterthoughts* (New York: McFarland and Company, 1986), 58.

6. Nebraska Department of Corrections, *1995 Annual Report* (Lincoln, NE: 1995).

7. http://www.wco.com/aerick/prison/html

8. American Correctional Association, *Standards for Adult Correctional Institutions*, 3rd ed. (Lanham, MD: 1990). Standard 3–4263.

9. Dickinson and Seaman, "Communication Policy Changes from 1970–1991 in State Correctional Facilities for Adult Males in the United States," 376.

10. J. Burstein, *Conjugal Visits in Prison* (New York: Lexington Books, 1977), 24.

CHAPTER 40

Rehabilitation: Reality or Myth?

James Austin

There is much debate regarding the potential of correctional treatment interventions to reduce crime in general and, in particular, among offenders who are under the control of the criminal justice system. But correctional treatment interventions do not operate in a vacuum. There are also factors other than correctional treatment interventions that influence criminal behavior. And the political climate will influence whether correctional administrators support rehabilitation and treatment programs, regardless of their efficacy. Given all these other factors, it can be difficult to determine whether rehabilitation programs—alone—reduce crime.

FACTORS RELATING TO CRIMINAL CAREERS

Criminologists have conducted considerable research that shows that criminal careers for both adults and juveniles do not follow predictable patterns. Many youths who are delinquent during their adolescent years cease their criminal activities by adulthood. And most adult offenders have not had juvenile crime careers (or at least not extensive careers) and are unlikely to continue their criminal behaviors indefinitely. There are many factors (other than treatment) that will influence patterns of criminal behavior.

The causal factors (affecting criminal activity) can be grouped into two categories. Structural factors are influences that are largely static

and cannot be modified. Situational factors are more dynamic and flexible.

Structural Factors—Gender and Age

Of all the factors that impact criminal behavior, sex and age are by far the most important. The vast majority of crimes are committed by young men. The highest rates of criminality are for men between the ages of 15 and 24.[1-3] Hereafter, the rate of offending declines dramatically, so that by age 30 (or sooner) many offenders have effectively "burnt out" and are no longer high-risk cases. There are, of course, exceptions to this generalization, but these exceptions tend to be adults with extensive juvenile and adult criminal histories who are unable or unwilling to pursue any other lifestyle.

The fact that most active criminals are young is especially relevant to the significant number of adult prisoners, probationers, and parolees. The average age of released prisoners is 31 years and is becoming higher. As expected, parolees are slightly older. Probationers are a couple of years younger but still well above the high crime rate years of 15 to 24. These age attributes suggest that many offenders who are under correctional supervision are well above their peak years of criminal behavior and can be expected to significantly reduce their recidivism rates due solely to maturation. With today's longer prison terms, increasing numbers of inmates will be in their late 30s, 40s, or early 50s when they become eligible for release. At these ages, the (former) inmates will be unlikely to recidivate, as people in these age groups have very low rates of criminality.

Several studies have shown that only a small proportion of the crimes committed each year can be attributed to released prisoners or parolees. The Bureau of Justice Statistics estimated that approximately 3 percent of all arrests for serious crimes could be attributed to released prisoners. Other research shows that 1 to 2 percent of all violent crimes in California can be linked to parolees. These data underscore that correctional treatment and punishment initiatives will have minimal, if any, impact on crime rates.

Situational Factors

Regular Employment

The ability of a former offender to maintain any form of stable employment (coupled with the aging process) will significantly reduce that person's criminal tendencies.[4–7] One important study in California found that providing even very modest economic assistance to released prisoners greatly reduced the rates of recidivism.

Stable Marriage

Another major factor that reduces offenders' probability of continuing their criminal behavior is maintaining a stable and supportive marriage.[8] A stable marriage helps ex-offenders maintain jobs and places to live as well as reduce drug and alcohol abuse.[9–11] But clearly there are also examples where less stable marriages have actually encouraged rather than diminished criminal behavior.

Societal and Economic Considerations

Criminologists also have examined the societal and economic influences on crime rates. Some factors produce social stress that in turn affects crime rates. States with high rates of the following social and economic factors tended to have high rates of violent crimes, mental illness, and suicide:

- business failures
- unemployment claims
- workers on strike
- personal bankruptcies
- mortgage foreclosures
- divorces
- abortions
- illegitimate births
- infant deaths
- fetal deaths
- disaster assistance
- state residency of less than five years
- new houses authorized
- new welfare cases
- high school dropout

It is also noteworthy that studies did not find an association between incarceration rates and crime rates. In fact, there is a well-established negative correlation (i.e., states with high incarceration rates tend to have high crime rates). Some experts believe that high rates of incarceration may contribute to high levels of social stress and thus increase crime rates.

THE ROLE OF INCARCERATION

There have been numerous studies of the relative effects of incarceration on crime rates in general and on individual offenders. In their pioneering study of 880 juveniles from adolescence through adulthood, Sampson and Laub found that both the number of incarcerations and the length of incarceration had no direct impact on a person's criminal career.[12]

They went on to note that incarcerations actually have a deleterious effect on recidivism, as they severely disrupt all efforts to maintain relationships with loved ones and to secure stable employment.

A review of numerous studies of the many early release programs that are now operating throughout the country found that neither moderate increases nor moderate decreases (3 to 6 months) in prison terms have an impact on either crime rates in general or an individual offender's rate of reoffending. Again, age is a dominant

---

Structured Punishment Work Detail

Over the past several years, many states have been experimenting with new prison programs hoping to better prepare inmates for a successful reintegration into society following release from prison. Some of these programs are based on the notion that if prisons are sufficiently uncomfortable inmates will be deterred from committing new crimes (deterrence), while other programs focus on providing inmates with skills to help them secure jobs and maintain family and other relationships following release from prison, hoping that these ties will preclude further criminal activity (rehabilitation).

The California Department of Corrections recently implemented an unusual new program that is based upon the deterrence principle frequently cited by states that have implemented chain gangs. This new two-year pilot program, Structured Punishment Work Detail (SPWD), requires inmates to perform intense manual labor with primitive hand tools. One assignment will involve inmates cleaning up an old sewer site, including breaking up granite and concrete by hand and hauling away the debris. In addition to the hard labor, inmates in the SPWD will not be paid for their labor, will have less recreation time, less opportunity to shop in the institution commissary, have no family visits, and not receive packages from home; phone calls will be limited to emergencies only.

California authorities are hoping that this new program will discourage inmates from committing new crimes, thereby reducing the rate of recidivism.

Source: Reprinted from *Corrections Alert,* Vol. 5, No. 5, © 1998, Aspen Publishers, Inc.

---

factor: Older inmates (age 35 and above) have by far the lowest rates of recidivism.

It also should be noted that there has been little evidence that adjustments in the use of incarceration have an independent impact on crime rates. For example, states with the highest crime rates have the highest incarceration rates, and states with the lowest incarceration rates have the lowest crime rates. But historical fluctuations in crime rates and incarceration rates reveal no clear relationship between incarceration rates and crime rates. The tripling of not only the prison population but also the probation, jail, and parole populations over the past 15 years, however, has had some impact on crime rates. At the same time, other developments such as an improving economy, reductions in unemployment and drug use, increases in deportation of illegal aliens, tighter gun control measures, and a growing number of prevention programs sponsored by private sector organizations have substantially reduced crime rates.

THE ROLE OF CORRECTIONAL TREATMENT

For years criminologists have debated whether correctional treatment helps juvenile and adult offenders. The debate began with the now-famous publication by the late Robert Martinson that left the unfortunate impression that "nothing works."[13] Martinson's publication was based on a review of existing evaluations of prison treatment programs by himself and his colleagues—one of the first meta-analyses that attempted to summarize the findings of numerous experimental and quasi-experimental studies of rehabilitation programs. This pioneering work has been followed by several other major meta-analyses that reach a different conclusion. These later studies conclude that under certain conditions, some treatment interventions can have a significant impact on recidivism rates. Put differently, many treatment programs fail, but a sizeable number succeed.[14-20]

Many have disagreed with these later findings. Put simply, they argue that the meta-analyses are suspect and overstate the merits of rehabilitation. In particular, the studies cited by these meta-analyses tend to have small sample sizes (under 250 cases for experimental and control groups). In many of the studies, the differences between the recidivism rates of control and experimental subjects were minimal (5 to 10 percentage points). Furthermore, the recommended conditions necessary for treatment to succeed are difficult to define and to replicate in other sites.

Well-designed and administered correctional treatment programs are the exception rather than the rule. Program integrity is often weak, which may explain the absence of strong treatment effects for many treatment programs. Correctional agencies are often ill-equipped to design and implement effective treatment programs. Most agencies do not themselves believe that effective treatment is possible or that it is part of their mission.[21] A survey showed that most prison wardens believe that only 25 percent of their inmates are amenable to treatment. The wardens also stated that involving inmates in rehabilitation programs was not a high priority for their organization. However, they do view such programs as having an important place in a prison setting.[22]

The Federal Bureau of Prisons has concluded, based on thorough research and analysis, that work experience and vocational training programs in federal correctional institutions have significant effects on offenders' ability to successfully reintegrate into the community following release from prison. Specifically, it found that prison programs can have a positive effect on postrelease employment and arrest in the short run, and on recommitment in the long run.

The research was based on data from more than 7,000 offenders who had been released from prison for 8 to 12 years. In the first 12 months following release, inmates who had worked in federal prison industries or participated in a vocational training program (the "study group") were more likely to be employed than inmates who had done neither (the "comparison group"). Additionally, the study group inmates were 35 percent less likely than the comparison group to recidivate during their first 12 months following release. Over the long term, the study group inmates were 24 percent less likely to recidivate than comparable inmates who had not worked in industries, and inmates who participated in vocational training or apprenticeship training were 33 percent less likely to recidivate than inmates who had not.[23]

The Federal Bureau of Prisons also has concluded that residential drug abuse treatment has a positive effect on inmates' propensity to recidivate. A recently completed study involving 1,800 offenders who had participated in intensive substance abuse therapy for either 9 or 12 months revealed that offenders who completed the program were 73 percent less likely than inmates who did not complete the program to be rearrested during the first 6 months back in the community. Similarly, graduates of the program were less likely to use drugs within the first 6 months. The large sample size (1,800 offenders), rigorous research design, and multisite sample make these findings particularly noteworthy.[24]

CONCLUSION

Among the various forms of rehabilitation programs, interventions (or treatment programs) that help equip an individual to secure meaningful employment in today's increasingly competitive economy will be the most successful. Unlikely to reduce recidivism are programs that are simply for drug treatment or cognitive learning–based interventions that do not enhance the offenders' ability to perform basic tasks essential for any form of employment. Further, the private and public sector must recognize the need to provide employment opportunities for this segment of the population.

Based on research to date, the following conclusions can be made regarding the impact of treatment and punishment on crime rates and individual offenders:

- The vast majority of crimes are not committed by persons released from prison. Consequently, prison-based treatment programs and punishment will have little impact on crime rates in general. There is also evidence from one study that crimes committed by probationers do not significantly contribute to a jurisdiction's crime rate.[25]
- Under certain circumstances, treating offenders can have positive results. These positive results are strongest for programs that provide for long-term aftercare and serve to increase the offender's ability to secure employment (part- or full-time).
- Under certain circumstances, punishing offenders can have positive results.
- Under certain circumstances, treating or punishing offenders can have negative results.
- Change (positive and negative) also can occur and often does occur based on other factors that have nothing to do with treatment (e.g., maturation, random events, etc.).
- The vast majority of correctional treatment programs have not been evaluated.
- Most correctional treatment programs are not well administered, target the wrong clientele, and are too small to have any impact on crime rates or public safety.
- It is extremely rare to find a well-administered treatment program that has been properly evaluated and has demonstrated dramatic treatment effects.
- Factors that will undoubtedly reduce the likelihood of maintaining a criminal lifestyle are age, no juvenile crime career, no history of violence, no evidence of drug use or abuse, the ability to secure employment, and the ability to maintain a meaningful marriage or relationship. Treatment and

punishment will have only moderate effects on crime rates.

Finally, one must take into account the current political climate. Although there is a considerable debate among criminologists and correctional administrators regarding the merits of rehabilitation, there is little if any support for such programs among many of our leading politicians. Rather than supporting the funding of more or different treatment programs, the current climate seems to encourage "truth in sentencing," three strikes laws, boot camps, chain gangs, lowering of the age for waiving juveniles into adult court, and austere prisons without programs and recreation.

Given this atmosphere, it will take more powerful evidence that treatment reduces rates of recidivism and increases public safety to persuade those who favor a more punitive approach. However, advocates of more and stronger forms of punishment have no conclusive scientific findings to justify their policies either. For this reason alone, the use of rehabilitation and treatment programs that help ensure a more humane and less costly correctional system is warranted and should be expanded. Most important, correctional agencies should become far more accountable (both fiscally and administratively) for such programs and engage in more studies of well-administered programs that better prepare offenders to secure and maintain meaningful employment.

NOTES

1. T. Hirschi and M. Gottfredson, "Age and the Explanation of Crime," *American Journal of Sociology* 89 (1987): 552–584.
2. Federal Bureau of Investigation, *Age-Specific Arrest Rates and Race-Specific Rates for Selected Offenses* (Washington, DC: U.S. Department of Justice, 1990).
3. T. Flannagan and K. Maguire, eds., *Sourcebook of Criminal Justice Statistics 1989* (Washington, DC: U.S. Government Printing Office, 1990).
4. J. Braithwaite, *Crime, Shame, and Reintegration* (Cambridge, England: Cambridge University Press, 1989).

5. R.D. Crutchfield, "Labor Stratification and Violent Crime," *Social Forces* 68 (1989): 489–512.

6. R.J. Sampson and J.H. Laub, *Crime in the Making: Pathways and Turning Points through Life* (Cambridge, MA: Harvard University Press, 1993).

7. N. Shover, *Aging Criminals* (Beverly Hills, CA: Sage Publications, 1985).

8. Sampson and Laub, *Crime in the Making: Pathways and Turning Points through Life.*

9. T.C.N. Gibbens, "Borstal Boys after 25 Years," *British Journal of Criminology* 24 (1987): 49–62.

10. B.J. Knight et al., "Early Marriage and Criminal Tendency in Males," *British Journal of Criminology* 17 (1977): 348–360.

11. A. Rand, "Transitional Life Events and Desistance from Delinquency and Crime," in *From Boy to Man: From Delinquency to Crime,* ed. M. Wolfgang et al. (Chicago: University of Chicago Press, 1987), 134–162.

12. Sampson and Laub, *Crime in the Making: Pathways and Turning Points through Life.*

13. R. Martinson, "What Works? Questions and Answers about Prison Reform," *The Public Interest* 35 (1974): 22–54.

14. D.A. Andrews et al., "Does Correctional Treatment Work? A Clinically Relevant and Psychologically Informed Meta-Analysis," *Criminology* 28 (1990): 369–404.

15. W.L. Davidson et al., *Interventions with Juvenile Delinquents: A Meta-Analysis of Treatment Efficacy* (Washington, DC: National Institute of Juvenile Justice and Delinquency Prevention, 1984).

16. C. Garrett, "Effects of Residential Treatment on Adjudicated Delinquents: A Metanalysis," *Journal of Research in Crime and Delinquency* 22 (1985): 287–308.

17. D. Gendreau and P. Ross, "Revivification of Rehabilitation: Evidence from the 1980s," *Justice Quarterly* 4 (1987): 349–407.

18. R. Gottschalk et al., "Community-Based Interventions," in *Handbook of Juvenile Delinquency,* ed. H. Quay (New York: Wiley and Sons, 1987).

19. Lipsey, The Efficacy of Intervention for Juvenile Delinquency (Paper presented at the meeting of the American Society of Criminology, Reno, NV, 1989).

20. T. Palmer, *The Re-Emergence of Correctional Intervention* (Newbury Park, CA: Sage Publications, 1992).

21. J. Austin, "Using Early Release To Relieve Prison Crowding: A Dilemma in Public Policy," *Crime and Delinquency* 32 (1990): 404–502.

22. F.T. Cullin et al., "The Correctional Orientation of Prison Wardens: Is the Rehabilitative Ideal Supported?" 31 (1993): 69–92.

23. W. Saylor and G. Gaes, "Training Inmates through Industrial Work Participation and Vocational and Apprenticeship Instruction," *Corrections Management Quarterly* 1, no. 2 (1997): 32–43.

24. *TRIAD Drug Treatment Evaluation Project: Six Month Interim Report* (Washington, DC: Federal Bureau of Prisons Office of Research and Evaluation, 1998).

25. M.R. Geerken and H.D. Hayes, "Probation and Parole: Public Risk and the Future of Incarceration Alternatives," *Criminology* 31 (1993): 549–564.

PART VII

Programming in Prison

Preparing inmates for a successful return to the free community—rehabilitation—is one of the primary goals of prisons and jails. Institutional programs, ranging from daily work assignments to drug treatment, are critical to any organized effort to offer offenders an opportunity to modify their behavior.

Rehabilitation, while not a new initiative, was greatly emphasized in the United States beginning in the 1950s. The post–World War II era was a time of regeneration. Prosperous and upbeat, people—including Presidents John Kennedy and Lyndon Johnson—sought ways to improve the lives of those less fortunate. This attitude filtered into our penal facilities, where many correctional leaders tried to enhance inmates' social, educational, and industrial skills as well as meet their facilities' custodial mission.

Prisons became correctional institutions, sentencing laws were modified from clearly defined sentences to indeterminate terms, and prisoners were released on parole after authorities determined that they were able to appropriately function within free society. The "medical model" was introduced to corrections; it was assumed that once an inmate's problems were identified, or diagnosed, institution programs would offer the key to successful change. Programs became the most important component of institutions.

Unfortunately, criminal behavior was not easily dealt with. It was (and is) extremely difficult to assess the reasons for an individual's shortcomings, and it was equally hard to design and operate the necessary programs to help an inmate—even one sincerely motivated to change. This dilemma was further complicated by inadequate funding for institutional programs, and the fact that few staffing resources were focused exclusively on program needs. And the need to control the inmate population within the confinement setting remained the primary role of the institution.

Research was conducted to determine how successful the rehabilitation effort was, and few studies found positive results. According to some studies, prisoners who had completed programs did not have lower rates of recidivism than those who had not.

Since Robert Martinson reported extremely poor results from those rehabilitative efforts he studied (the results were published in a 1974 article that became well known), many have written off institutional programming. Yet correctional administrators have continued to offer programs. Numerous authorities have subsequently presented excellent results from programs, although not all studies have found consistently productive results. It is clear, however, that no one program or combination of programs will rehabilitiate all inmates.

Some programs help normalize the institutional environment, some reinforce a work ethic in inmates, and some attempt to deal with addictive behaviors such as alcohol and drug abuse. Part VII examines prison and jail programs that have had some success.

LEARNING OBJECTIVES

After studying this section, you should be able to answer the following questions:

1. Do you believe rehabilitation works? How effective is correctional treatment today?
2. How do work assignments in the correctional setting help prepare an offender for release?
3. Should industrial programs teach marketable skills or focus on making a profit that eases the cost of confinement to taxpayers?
4. How do volunteers serve inmates in meaningful ways?
5. Can drug treatment be helpful to inmates who do not wish to be involved?

DISCUSSION/REVIEW QUESTIONS

1. How has rehabilitation been shaped by today's political forces?
2. How did Martinson's assessment of rehabilitation affect program offerings in the prisons and jails of America?
3. What are the management concerns associated with the assignment of inmates to work details in an institution?
4. What are the pros and cons of an industrial work program?
5. What are the basic components of a functional volunteer program for a correctional facility?
6. Are drug programs effective when operating inside a prison or jail?

CHAPTER 41

Inmate Maintenance Work Assignments

J.C. Keeney

During the 1990s, the public has taken a much larger interest in the inner workings of the nation's prisons. As crime rates have risen, many politicians and their constituents have advocated "getting tough on criminals" and blamed prisons for not rehabilitating inmates. They called for able-bodied inmates to be put to work, partly to pay for their incarceration. And they said that weight-lifting equipment, televisions, and college courses are amenities that should not be available to inmates.[1]

Prison administrators have long known the benefits of having inmates involved in meaningful work or program assignments, such as academic or vocational education. Institutions operate much better when most inmates are assigned to detailed work or a scheduled program and must report to an assignment each day.

Maintenance work assignments not only help create a healthy atmosphere in the institutional setting but reduce operating costs. In the past, inmates have been involved in preparing, serving, and cleaning up in the food service operations and have cleaned the housing areas. Obviously, it is easier to employ more inmates on maintenance assignments in lower custody level institutions than in close or maximum custody facilities. Close or maximum custody facilities house predatory individuals who are risks to staff and other inmates and usually pose security and escape risks, so the maintenance assignments in those facilities must be carefully evaluated. Inmates should be responsible for cleaning their own living areas. Common use areas such as aisles and toilets in dormitories, day rooms, and dining rooms should also be cleaned by inmates.

Staff should not have to clean up after inmates. It is degrading to the professional image of staff to have them sweep and mop floors that have been used by the incarcerated population. Staff should clean areas such as control rooms that are restricted from inmate access. Supervisory staff must be alert and observe these activities because, on occasion, staff will allow overly ambitious inmates into restricted areas to clean, thus relieving employees of this responsibility. This activity can seriously jeopardize the security of the facility. Supervisors need to be observant and tour inside the facility on all shifts so that they are aware of staff activity.

PHILOSOPHY

In prison and jail facilities, a written philosophy clearly defining the departmental policies concerning inmate employment must be in place. There also should be a written departmental policy that delegates to various facilities the authority to develop institutional policies and procedures covering the areas of inmate maintenance assignments.

Privately owned and operated facilities must have a written corporate philosophy concerning inmate work assignments that allows the individual facilities to develop policies and procedures. Private facilities contract with public entities for inmates. This contract must spell out the expectations of both parties concerning inmate work assignments. Privately operated facilities are usually contracted on a daily bed cost rate per inmate, and it makes economic sense and is good correctional practice to use inmates in as many maintenance assignments as is feasible from a security standpoint.

The commissioner or director of the agency must clearly define the agency's philosophical position relating to inmate labor. It is also his or her responsibility to put this position in the form of a departmental policy or directive. These policies must concur with those of the legislative body to whom he or she reports.

INSTITUTIONAL POLICY

The chief administrative officer of the facility must ensure that there are written institutional policies and procedures developed and made available to all staff and the incarcerated population. Policy helps establish the staff philosophy of inmate management, promote consistency of action by staff, and ensure that staff are operating within the scope of their responsibilities and the law. This written document must be based on the departmental philosophy statement and must be understood by all staff and inmates.[2]

A policy document that establishes an inmate work program should list

- the types of maintenance jobs available
- the skill levels required for each position
- the pay ranges of the individual positions (if there is an applicable inmate pay system)
- extra "good time" for work, if applicable, and any other items that merit defining

Staff and inmates must be aware of the procedure by which inmates will be assigned to work details. In some jurisdictions, inmate assignments are under the purview of classification. In some facilities, there are assignment officers who take inmate applications and assign inmates to the various job openings. The system must be consistent, and all must understand how it works.

Presentence investigations and inmate history sections in the inmate file will give some indication of work experience and employment history in and outside institutions. There are a variety of vocational interest and ability tests given during the reception process at the beginning of the incarceration period. Inmate talents and skills should be utilized as much as possible. It is normally the case worker's or counselor's responsibility to assess an inmate's skill level, vocational training accomplishments, educational level, and work history and make a recommendation as to the type of institutional assignment that would be most appropriate.

TYPES OF INMATE JOBS

The types of maintenance jobs will vary depending on the facility as previously mentioned, the security level. One of the largest users of inmate labor in a facility and, is the food service department. Within this department, there are a variety of positions, including entry-level porters, bakers, meat cutters, diet cooks, fry cooks, general cooks, servers, and janitors. There are many opportunities for inmates to start in food service in an entry-level, low-skill position and later advance to a higher skilled position.

Most facilities use inmates as housing unit porters who will work under the supervision of the housing unit officers. Detailed assignments must be given to inmate janitors so that they clearly understand their areas of responsibility. Staff must supervise housing unit janitors, and precautions need to be taken so that janitors are not able to access other inmates' personal property. In the event there is a problem of theft in the housing units, inmate janitors are instantly suspect. If the problem persists, the inmate janitors may be the victims of violence.

The maintenance department is another large employer of inmate workers. This is an area where skilled inmates may practice their trades. Frequently, there are plumbers, electricians, painters, welders, and heating and air conditioning specialists on the staff who will have a crew of inmate helpers. Obviously there are a great number of sinks, showers, and toilets, so there is always a need for plumbers, often during off hours and on weekends. Plumbing services can usually be provided by inmate maintenance plumbers working under the supervision of security staff who are on duty.

The warden or superintendent sets the standard for the facility's appearance and maintaining that standard provides many opportunities for inmate work assignments. These should include an ongoing painting program to cover any graffiti or worn paint areas. Inmates should be assigned to jobs maintaining lawns, shrubs, and the grounds in general. Clean, orderly, well-maintained facilities look much better and are an indication of how the entire institution operates.

There are a variety of other areas of the facility that will use inmate maintenance workers. The medical department as well as the administrative area of the facility will need inmate janitors. The motor pool can have inmates wash and service vehicles. The education department may use clerks, library aides, teacher aides, janitors, and one-on-one tutors.

It is important that the chief executive officer of the facility have a written policy stating that all work assignments should be filled by inmates of all races, in proportion to the racial makeup of the inmate population. Traditionally, there have been certain work assignments that inmates of certain races prefer. This should not be allowed. This theme of racial diversity should carry over to housing assignments and all other areas of the institution. There should not be any "one race" areas in the facility.

When the chief executive officer of the facility tours inside the institution, he or she should observe the racial diversity of the housing assignments and work crews and talk to staff and inmates to monitor the atmosphere of the facility. On these tours, the warden or superintendent must also ensure that the sanitation level and general appearance of the facility meet the standards that have been set. Wardens and su-

perintendents who are desk bound receive information only by memo or secondhand from subordinate staff who will offer their own opinions on how things are inside the institution.

PITFALLS

A well-rounded work and programs environment can greatly assist in maintaining a safe, secure, healthy institution. But there are several pitfalls to avoid.

As mentioned earlier, it is critical that staff not allow one race of inmates to dominate certain work assignments. Inmate gangs also attempt to control some work areas of an institution, so the intelligence staff must ensure that gang-affiliated prisoners are closely tracked.

Caution should be exercised to ensure that inmate clerks do not have access to computers. Inmates may create all sorts of mischief on a computer system, including illegally accessing staff databases. If inmates are given access to computers, the machines should not be networked, offer access to sensitive information, or have a modem or another way to contact other networks.

Inmates should not be assigned to the same job for an extended period of time. They become possessive, and there is danger of staff becoming overly friendly with and overly dependent on an inmate who has been on the same assignment for years. Rotating job assignments helps to avoid these problems.

An inmate should never be put in a position of authority over other inmates. Staff should handle all direction, instruction, and supervision. Prisons in the South especially have had problems when inmates were allowed to supervise other inmates. The use of inmate "building tenders" (inmates with authority over other inmates) that was made so popular in the Texas Department of Corrections (TDC) has been roundly criticized by the courts and others and created very negative results. Use of inmate supervisors was not well controlled, and prisoners became abusive in the use of their power. The system degenerated and staff lost control of many facilities throughout the TDC. John DiIulio argues that such a system requires strong control; once unleashed, inmates' authority over their peers quickly corrupts the system.[3]

Putting policies in writing is critical in all aspects of prison and jail administration. Not having written policy and procedures covering work assignments can give the inmate population the perception that the system can be manipulated and that favoritism is the norm. All aspects of the process (e.g., work applications, waiting lists for specific assignments) need to be spelled out in detail.

The quality of an inmate work program is often ignored or given little attention by managers. This can be a fatal mistake due to the sensitive nature of many of the inmate work assignments. Food service, in particular, needs to be monitored on a daily basis. In the history of corrections in this country, there probably have been more incidents and disturbances relating to inconsistent or poor quality of food preparation or serving than any other single issue. The food service department should never be the dumping ground for malcontents or problem inmates.

Oregon Mandates That Inmates Work Full Time

Declaring that "inmates who are confined in correctional institutions should work as hard as the taxpayers who provide for their upkeep," in November 1994 the voters of Oregon approved Ballot Measure 17, a constitutional amendment that requires inmates to work a 40-hour week. Vocational training programs also count toward the full-time workweek.

The new standard also impacts how inmates may be compensated for their work and requires the department to operate inmate work programs in a "business-like manner" that reduces the cost of government or generates a profit for the private sector.

This "get-tough-on-crime" initiative has been extremely difficult to implement in the Oregon Department of Corrections (DOC), a department that has expanded to over 9,000 inmates in the last three years. The DOC hopes to gradually implement this employment requirement, with full compliance scheduled to be achieved within the next several years. It is difficult to provide meaningful work for all prisoners in an institution, and many correctional jurisdictions have prisoners share half-day work assignments. In large facilities, idleness can be a significant management problem for staff. Measure 17 presents a challenge to the full utilization of inmate labor because there are conflicts between the amendment's requirements and federal laws governing interstate commerce. The new regulations restrict the use of inmate compensation, which has impinged upon the Oregon prison industry program for clothing manufacturing known as "Prison Blues," which is regulated by the national Prison Industries Enhancement (PIE) program.

The situation in Oregon is being scrutinized by other state and federal authorities, and they express concern that such statutory mandates could be forced on them.

Source: Reprinted from *Corrections Alert,* Vol. 4, No. 1, © 1997, Aspen Publishers, Inc.

Most correctional facilities require all able-bodied inmates to have a work assignment. This requirement can easily overload inmate crews. If it only takes 5 inmates to do a job and 10 are assigned, the extra inmates on the crew may make trouble. The facility would be better served working two 5-man crews for four hours each rather than having 10 men on a job doing little or nothing for eight hours.

CONCLUSION

The provision and maintenance of a sense of order in the correctional environment are critical to institution management. Staff must provide daily routines for prisoners that facilitate a normal, calm, and stable atmosphere. Work assignments contribute a great deal to this quality of life.

Inmates should be assigned to meaningful work or program assignments to enhance the operations of a correctional institution. Maintenance work assignments for inmates make an institution more cost-effective and contribute to other important aspects of corrections. For instance, work assignments can provide training for inmates that may assist them upon their return to their home communities. The act of going to work every day can help teach some individuals a work ethic.

It is important that supervisors and senior managers of an institution remain sensitive to all aspects of the work assignment and selection process, as well as the quality of work accomplished on a day-to-day basis. Supervisors should tour the facility each shift to observe and assist staff in this endeavor. Effective chief executive officers are inside the facility regularly to observe and talk to staff and inmates.[4] There is an old saying in corrections that's as true today as it was 50 years ago: "If you pay attention and take care of the small issues, the large ones will normally take care of themselves."

NOTES

1. P. Carlson, "Correctional Trends for the Twenty-First Century: Our Future behind the Walls and Fences," *The Keepers' Voice* 17, no. 1 (1996): 5–8.

2. M. Fleisher, *Warehousing Violence* (Newbury Park, CA: Sage Publications, 1989), 85.

3. J. DiIulio, *Governing Prisons: A Comparative Study of Correctional Management* (New York: Collier Macmillan Publishers, 1987), 39.

4. K. Wright, *Effective Prison Leadership* (Binghamton, NY: William Neil Publishing, 1994), 38–39.

CHAPTER 42

Prison Industries:
The History and the Debate

Steve Schwalb

There is much contentious debate about how prison industry programs should operate. Yet such programs continue to thrive because everyone agrees that convicts should work while incarcerated. For each person, the benefits of prison industry programs may be different: reducing the debilitating effects of idleness and boredom, improving the safe management of prisons, teaching inmates work skills, improving inmates' chances of success upon release, or just plain "making inmates' life hard."

Prison industries date back to the early history of corrections in the United States.[1] Yet the legal framework, the pros and cons of allowing industries to operate, and the conflicting prison industry mandates remain unresolved public policy questions today.

HISTORY

The idea of having prisoners work dates back to the early history of corrections. In England, reformers stated that "Labour, 'the only resource against ennui,' would be followed by immediate reward . . . Suitable rewards for efficiency, diligence, [and] orderly conduct might excite healthful emulation, and help form and maintain

good habits . . . after their liberation, they will have acquired some pecuniary and industrial resources."[2] In the early prison model, initiated by the Pennsylvania Quakers in the 1790s, the focus was on solitary confinement, Bible study, and penance. The lack of human contact seemed to cause many prisoners to deteriorate mentally. To reduce the debilitative effects of incarceration and to better prepare the inmate for employment upon release, inmates were allowed to work by themselves in their cells on shoemaking, tailoring, and other tasks. Thus began a focus on the economics of prison industry administration; the goal became generating revenue in excess of the cost of maintaining the prisoner.

In the early nineteenth century, New York State, an early leader in many corrections reforms, developed the congregate system, where inmates worked together in prison factories under very rigid discipline. This group production technique allowed the manufacture of items that could not be made efficiently by an inmate in a cell. Items produced included carpets, clothing, barrels, and furniture. Products were sold on the open market to American customers or exported, and the proceeds were used to reduce prison operation costs.

As the 1800s progressed, some other states (particularly those in the Midwest and South, where agricultural production was prominent) developed prison labor programs in which inmates were leased to private businesses. The

---

Opinions expressed in this chapter are those of the author and do not necessarily represent the opinions of the Federal Bureau of Prisons or the U.S. Department of Justice.

prisons benefited because the lease payments were used to reduce the cost of prison operations. The private businesses gained many long hours of virtually free labor. There were complaints, however, that inmates were abused by contractors. Despite these complaints, the prevalence of "convict lease" programs increased after the Civil War, as the southern states scrambled to partially replace slavery.

THE LEGAL FRAMEWORK

As might be expected, the open market sale of prisoner-made goods incited free labor and private business to unite to bring about legal restrictions on the sale of inmate products. They managed to eliminate certain prison industry operations. Several states passed laws that restricted inmate work and training programs. At the federal level, several statutes were passed, the most important of which was the Sumners-Ashurst Act. Passed in 1940, this law made it a federal crime to knowingly transport convict-made goods in interstate commerce for private use, regardless of what state law allowed. In 1979, at the urging of Senator Charles Percy, a Republican from Illinois, Congress passed the Justice Systems Improvement Act (commonly called the Percy Amendment), which permits waivers of the Sumners-Ashurst restrictions on the interstate sale of prison-made goods provided that inmates are paid the prevailing wage, with appropriate deductions for taxes, room and board, and court-ordered commitments such as restitution, child support, and alimony; that local labor union officials are consulted and approve; that free labor is determined to be unaffected; and that the goods are produced in an industry with no local unemployment. This amendment also created the Prison Industry Enhancement Certification program (commonly known as the PIE program), wherein the U.S. Justice Department certifies applicant programs for an exception from the Sumners-Ashurst restrictions. At the end of 1997, approximately 2,200 inmates nationwide were producing goods for interstate commerce under the PIE program.

Perhaps the most noteworthy development from the struggles between government and prison industry officials, private businesses, and labor leaders was the "state use" system. Also initiated in New York, this system precludes the sale of prison-made products to the public but promotes their purchase by the "state," that unit of government of which the prison industry is an integral part. Today, state use sales are, by far, the most common market for prison industry products across the country. Exhibit 42–1 explains the different types of prison labor systems.

PROS AND CONS

Prison industry programs have many virtues, some obvious and others well supported by high-quality research. The arguments against prison industries all center on their "adverse impact on the private sector." A more detailed review of the pros and cons can help put the debate in perspective.

Pro Arguments

First, prison industry programs save taxpayers money. Most prison industry programs are at least partially self-sustaining, generating their income from the sale of goods and services. To the extent that these programs can be self-sustaining, a work program can be provided to the inmates without appropriated funds. Thus, the cost to the taxpayers of operating prisons is reduced. Further, some of the wages paid to inmate workers are applied to restitution, fines, child support, and alimony. Inmates also send some of their earnings home to their families. These revenues can reduce outlays for public assistance of various types. In this era of fiscal conservatism, reducing the taxpayer burden is an important attribute of prison industries.

Second, prison industries contribute to the safe management of prisons. By providing productive work and reducing inmate idleness, the presence of prison industry programs reduces the likelihood of disruptions and other violent

Exhibit 42–1 Systems of Prison Labor in the United States, Past and Present

Contract system. Under this system, the state feeds, clothes, houses, and supervises the inmates. The state maintains the prisoners at the prison, and a contractor engages the state for the labor of the inmates, which is performed within or near the institution. The contractor pays the state a stipulated amount per capita for the services of the inmates, supplies the raw materials, and superintends the work.

Piece price system. This system differs from the contract system mainly in method of payment for the work of the inmates. The state maintains the institution and feeds, clothes, and supervises the prisoners. The contractor supplies the raw material and pays the state an agreed amount for the work done on each piece or article manufactured by the inmates. Supervision of the work is usually accomplished by prison officials. Institution staff maintain discipline and are responsible for the quality of the specified work product.

Public account system. As far as the inmate is concerned, this model is no different from the piece price system, but for the institution there are differences. In the piece price system, the contractor finances the business and assumes all chance of profit or loss. In the public account system, the state enters the field of manufacturing on its own account. It buys the raw material, manufactures and markets the product, and assumes all risk of doing business.

State use system. Under this system, the state conducts a business of manufacture or production as in the public account system, but the use or sale of the goods produced is limited to the same institution or other state institutions. This system is based on the principle that the products may be used for the state's own consumption only and may not compete with the business of manufacturers employing free labor.

Public works system. This system is very like the state use system. In this model, labor is applied not to the manufacture of articles of consumption but to the construction and repair of the prison or of other public buildings, roads, parks, breakwaters, and permanent public structures.

Lease system. Under this model, the state enters into a contract with the lessee, who agrees to receive the inmates; to feed, clothe, house, and supervise them; to keep them at work; and to pay the state a specified amount for their labor. The state reserves the right to make rules for the care of prisoners and to inspect their quarters and place of work.

All of these methods of employing prison labor are now found in the United States with the exception of the lease system. The contract system has declined steadily over the years. The public account system and state use system are prevalent today.

Source: Adapted from *United States Prison Service Study Course,* p. 10, 1934, Federal Bureau of Prisons, U.S. Department of Justice.

inmate behavior, so prisons become safer places for staff to work and inmates to live. A well-managed prison is also a better neighbor to the host community than a poorly managed prison.

Third, prison industry experience improves inmate success upon release. Several research projects have tracked inmates upon release. One of the more comprehensive was conducted by the Federal Bureau of Prisons; over 7,000 inmates with comparable characteristics were evaluated for as long as 12 years following release. The results indicated that inmates who worked in Federal Prison Industries (FPI) while in custody were 20 percent more likely, upon release, to be crime-free, employed, and earning higher wages.[3]

When former inmates are employed and not engaged in criminal behavior, the obvious additional benefits include reduction in crime, improved public safety, greater contributions to the gross domestic product, and increased tax revenues.

Fourth, prison industries create jobs for law-abiding citizens. Prison industrial operations require raw materials, supplies, services, and equipment, which are purchased from the private sector, creating jobs in various businesses. Supervision of inmate workers is provided by staff, whose salaries are normally paid from industrial revenues. Some of the monies paid inmates are spent in prison commissaries, which stock items procured from local private sector vendors.

The number of civilian jobs created by prison industry revenues is substantial. This is an important consideration in evaluating the impact of prison industries on the private sector.

Con Arguments

First, a provision commonly referred to as the "mandatory source" provides prison industries an unfair advantage. Because many of the prison industry programs are confined to state use sales, there are often statutes or regulations requiring that the government agencies buy first from the prison industry program. The private sector companies feel that this essentially locks them out of a percentage of the government market, which is unfair and has an adverse impact on their businesses. They advocate competition between prison industries and the private sector for all government business.

Second, low inmate wages provide an unfair advantage to prison industries. Opponents argue that this low wage structure gives an undue advantage to prison industries. They reject the assertion by prison industry officials that the constraints of prison work programs such as increased civilian supervision, tool control, pat searches, and unskilled workers substantially increase the total overhead costs. With the exception of the aforementioned PIE programs, inmates are paid a small amount, an average of less than $1 per hour.

Third, prison industries take too much work away from the community. The heart of this issue is how to fairly determine the share of the market that prison industries should have. There is no magic formula, and the current practice varies widely. On the one hand, for instance, there is essentially no commercial production of license plates in the country. They are virtually all made in prison industries. On the other hand, there are numerous products purchased by the government that prison industries will never make, including computers, aircraft, ships, and weapons systems. On more common items, however, such as office furniture, there is a balance needed between the percentage provided to the government by prison industries and that provided by the private sector. As the prison inmate populations rise, so will the need for more inmate jobs, increasing the probability of elevated market share for prison industries. This elevation will come at a time when many private sector firms are facing increased competition, both domestically and from imports, and when many of them will rely more heavily on sales to the government.

THE CONFLICTING MANDATES

So how does one balance the pros and cons? Compromise. Given the checkered history of and the wide spectrum of opposition to prison industries, it is no surprise that prison industries' success is judged by the extent to which they can be "the most things to the greatest number" of constituents. The FPI statute, for example, requires that FPI diversify production as much as possible so as to minimize impact on any one industry; employ as many inmates as practicable, performing work in a deliberately labor-intensive manner; be financially self-sustaining; sell only to the federal government, producing products that are comparable to those of the private sector in features, quality, and delivery and that do not exceed current market prices; produce no more than a reasonable share of the federal government purchases, so as to avoid an undue burden on private sector business and labor; and teach inmates a marketable skill.

Taken individually, almost everyone would agree with these mandates. Putting them together, however, creates what Warren Cikins, a criminal justice consultant and former senior staff member at the Brookings Institution, calls a "convergence of righteousness," describing the tension associated with simultaneously pursuing these competing demands in a balanced way.[4] Ultimately, the debate is not about whether prison industries should exist or whether prisoners should work. Rather, it is about the manner in which prisoners should work.

PRISON INDUSTRIES: THE PUBLIC POLICY QUESTIONS

There are many public policy questions associated with prison industries, and none of them have clear answers.

Should prison industry programs be required to be self-sustaining? Those who answer "yes" would argue that this requirement encourages prison industries to be more efficient and businesslike. It also reduces the burden on taxpayers, because if the prison industry program were not self-sustaining, more appropriated funds would be required for an alternative program. Those who answer "no" would suggest that the private sector businesses that compete with prison industries are bearing an unfair share of the burden. They would also suggest that if the manufacturing done by prison industries were turned over to the private sector, the additional taxes collected from the increased sales would offset much if not all of the increased appropriated funds required to fund replacement programs.

Should prison industries be labor-intensive? Idleness reduction is a critical contribution of prison industry programs. The less labor-intensive the programs are, the more idleness there will be. On the other hand, as the economy becomes less and less labor-intensive, the extent to which inmates are being provided market-based skills becomes questionable, yet this also argues that the effects of prison labor on private sector jobs wanes with each passing year. Those who support labor intensity in prison industries argue

that inmates are being taught a work ethic, which employers indicate is the most important skill they look for in new hires.

Should prison industries have a mandatory source? Those in favor of retaining this preference would suggest that when it was agreed to limit prison industry sales only to the government, there was consent between private industry and labor that a certain amount of the government's business would be reserved for prison industries. Opponents argue that having a mandatory source keeps the government from getting the most bang for its buck through full and open competition.

Should inmates be paid the minimum wage? There is no support for inmates being paid minimum or higher wages without deductions for room and board, taxes, and so on. If an employer had to pay minimum wage, the number of inmate jobs would reduce dramatically because the labor costs would be far too high to be competitive. This could affect the total number of inmates employed and increase idleness. An argument can also be made that when the government provides room and board, education, and medical care at no cost to the inmate, lower tax-free inmate wages can be paid and the net income for the inmate is virtually the same as minimum wage with deductions.

Should prison industries be able to sell their products to the private sector? Advocates of this approach (which would essentially constitute a repeal of the Sumners-Ashurst Act) argue that the United States imports products from foreign countries that pay their workers wages comparable to prison industry wages in this country. Some economists would argue that any value added in the economy, regardless of the source, is advantageous. Opponents envision a return to the abuses of the past. Trade experts would also question whether statutes and foreign trade treaties disallow the sale of prison-made goods in the domestic economy. Exhibit 42–2 discusses a recent development in the debate over privatizing prison labor.

To what extent should the private sector be allowed to operate prison industries? Some

Exhibit 42–2 Experts Call for Privatized Prison Labor

Congressional testimony was delivered on June 25, 1998, that stated "It's time to make wardens marketers of prison labor rather than the uncompetitive producers of shoddy prison-made goods."* Morgan Reynolds of the National Center for Policy Analysis (NCPA) testified before the House Judiciary Committee's subcommittee on crime and was extremely critical of the current federal laws that regulate the marketing of prison industry products. Reynolds's testimony proposes a rethinking of the old ways of using prison labor.

This testimony comes at a time when many are criticizing the use of inmates to produce goods that may compete with community businesses. This proposal seeks to encourage private sector firms to hire prisoners for work both inside and outside the correctional institution environment. Reynolds favors reinventing the current system so it would be more competitive and increase inmate productivity.

NCPA proposes that Congress
- Repeal the existing federal ban on the interstate transport of prisoner-made goods
- Gradually switch FPI to an open, private sector model
- Pay full wages to the productive inmates, subject to deduction, rather than paying a fee to the attorney general

*Reynolds presented his testimony in support of pending legislation proposed by Congressman Bill McCollum's [R-Florida] Free Market Prison Industries Reform Act of 1998.

would advocate granting greater access to inmate labor by private industry. Others would suggest that private companies should operate the current industrial programs run by the government, injecting the business principles at which the private sector is arguably more adept.

CONCLUSION

The issue of prison industries is very important to many people. Prison administrators understand the critical contributions prison industry programs make to the safe operation of their facilities. Legislators appreciate that prison industries may reduce costs and make prisons more manageable. The private sector is legitimately concerned that prison industry growth will come at their expense. There are no easy choices among the various options and competing interests. Successful industrial programs are the byproduct of good communication, quality production programs, and skill in juggling competing interests.

NOTES

1. J. Roberts, *Work, Education and Public Safety: A Brief History of Federal Prison Industries* (Washington, DC: Federal Prison Industries, 1996).
2. C. Phillipson, *Three Criminal Law Reformers: Beccaria, Bentram, Romilly* (Patterson, NJ: Smith, 1970), 212.
3. W. Saylor and G. Gaes, "Post-Release Employment Preparation Study Summary" (Washington, DC: Federal Bureau of Prisons, 1991, updated June, 1996), 4–8.
4. W. Cikins, Remarks before the Subcommittee on Crime, House Judiciary Committee, May 19, 1994.

SUGGESTED READINGS

DiIulio, J. 1991. *No escape: The future of American corrections.* New York: Basic Books.
Reynolds, M. 1996. *Factories behind bars.* Dallas, TX: National Center for Policy Analysis.

CHAPTER 43

Volunteering Inside

Richard L. Stalder

Today, administrators of correctional programs must make a declining or static resource base stretch to meet expanding service requirements. At the same time, the public is becoming more focused on resource allocation in corrections. The public demands that funds must first be expended to ensure an acceptable level of safety and protection. Then, legislative and judicial pressure demand that funds be devoted to organization, discipline, and stability. Priority must also be given to the provision of basic services, which includes an adequate and safe physical plant and food, clothing, and medical care. Only after this foundation is laid can an administrator focus on program elements that are directed toward initiating a process of change in inmates.

The resource base on a real dollar, per capita basis is shrinking. Yet long-run solutions to crime still demand attention to meaningful programs that provide an opportunity for change—an opportunity to develop inmates' basic skills and new ways of thinking.

What is the solution? The only answer is to marshal the help of volunteers to compensate for inadequate financial resources. In the future, volunteers will be the cornerstone of correctional programs that are able to fully meet the demands of society and the needs of the offender. No longer will volunteers be peripheral, related to only inmate enrichment. They will be essential to fulfilling the mission of correctional facilities.

TYPES OF VOLUNTEERS

There are two primary classifications of volunteers in a correctional program: direct service and indirect service volunteer providers.

Direct Service Volunteers

Direct service volunteers generally provide on-site service to the program, its staff, or offenders. The scope of services may range from infrequent brief participation with a large group of volunteers to daily or weekly involvement as individuals. This category of participation typically demands the greatest sacrifice of time from a participant and may involve additional risk, depending upon the area an individual is serving. Direct service volunteers are the core of most successful programs. They interact with staff and offenders and, in a properly administered volunteer initiative, can be very effective in contributing to the success of agency goals.

Indirect Service Volunteers

Indirect service volunteers are typically not involved on site and generally do not have contact with the primary receivers of service. They can, however, offer valuable assistance. Activities involving indirect service volunteers include, but are not limited, to fund raising; developing policy, procedure, and training manuals; offering technical assistance in the review of budgeting, accounting, and financial audit issues; and donating materials and supplies.

Many programs have come to rely on the fund-raising assistance of outside organizations to enable them to provide services that are not included in their core budget. Indirect service volunteers often provide or coordinate access to facility beautification funds, which are not otherwise available. Individuals who sacrifice their time to raise money are real volunteers who have a real impact.

Advice and assistance from professionals in administrative and training areas are important indirect services. Volunteers can contribute by developing or reviewing core policy documents and training curricula or manuals. Many professionals will donate time to assist correctional institutions in areas for which budgeted funds are not available.

Often overlooked are those volunteers who solicit and donate materials and supplies for various projects. Important elements of community restoration are often not possible without this type of involvement. In Louisiana, for example, appropriated monies were not available to provide supplies to an inmate artist who wanted to paint and donate pictures for patient rooms in a local hospital. Volunteers talked with individuals and organizations and were able to get materials donated. Other inmate groups were interested in making toys for needy families at Christmas. Again, budgeted funds were not available for wood, glue, tools, and the many other supplies needed to make the project a success. Volunteers came to the rescue and provided everything necessary to build thousands of toys.

SOURCES OF VOLUNTEERS

Sources of both direct and indirect volunteer services include individuals with particular skills known by key agency or facility staff, civic clubs, religious organizations and churches, fraternal organizations, and special purpose organizations.

Perhaps the best mechanism to meet a defined volunteer need is to identify and solicit, through key staff, individuals who can provide the specific service. All staff must help develop a resource bank of individuals who can be called upon and who will provide assistance. In an ideal world, citizenship through service would be a part of everyone's agenda and prison, jail, and field service staff would simply call upon individuals when they were needed. Regrettably, this ideal is rarely met. Therefore, the likelihood of securing individual participation may improve if potential volunteers are contacted by someone they know who is familiar with the program.

The support of civic, religious, fraternal, and special purpose organizations is critical to any volunteer initiative. Civic clubs such as Lions, Rotary, Optimist, Toastmasters, and the Jaycees consider service to their community one of their primary functions. They do not discriminate against corrections and are underutilized only when they are not called upon. Their service can be both direct and indirect. Many individuals from these organizations are community leaders. Their volunteer service helps them become better informed, more effective advocates for corrections.

Religious and fraternal organizations generally have outreach programs that are related to corrections initiatives. While the scope or type of service may be defined by the organization and not the agency, the ultimate goals typically coincide. Many mainstream religious denominations, as well as the Volunteers of America and the Salvation Army, have core service commitments to criminal justice. They provide strategic assistance to offenders and their families in areas where there would otherwise be a void.

Special purpose organizations also enable and enrich the delivery of critical services. Alcoholics Anonymous and Narcotics Anonymous best typify this category of organization. Broad-based programs of substance abuse education and counseling would simply not be available in many correctional institutions and work release centers or to probationers and parolees without these groups. There is little question of their importance; probably 80 percent of the 85,000 individuals under some form of correctional supervision in Louisiana have substance abuse experiences that relate to their criminality. Without Alcoholics Anonymous and Narcotics Anonymous, many inmates would not change their substance abuse behaviors and, therefore, would be less likely to succeed after release.

COMPONENTS OF AN EFFECTIVE VOLUNTEER PROGRAM

The components of an effective volunteer program include initial development and organization, recruitment, selection, training, and recognition. Exhibit 43–1 offers suggestions for starting and maintaining a volunteer program.

Exhibit 43–1 Suggestions for Starting and Maintaining a Volunteer Program

1. Evaluate the need. After determining what tasks are not getting done or are overextending staff, decide whether these tasks could be handled effectively by volunteers.

2. Develop goals and job descriptions. Write up the goals of the volunteer program, as well as job descriptions for volunteers, so that administrators, staff, and the volunteers themselves know what volunteer positions entail.

3. Involve staff. Be sure to include staff (especially staff who will work directly with volunteers) in all planning and implementation of volunteer programs. If their input is included, staff will have a greater desire for the program to succeed because they will share a sense of program ownership.

4. Actively recruit volunteers. There are many organizations one can contact to find volunteers. Churches, civic groups, retirement organizations, and colleges and universities are all good choices for volunteer recruitment.

5. Educate volunteers about inmates. Before inmate contact begins, caution volunteers on the pitfalls that await those who are not familiar with the inmate culture and who may be easy prey for manipulative inmates. This is necessary to protect volunteers from being used and to maintain the institution's security.

6. Explain security needs to volunteers. Instruct volunteers on the institution's security policies and procedures, and explain why they are needed. Otherwise, volunteers may resist institution security precautions simply because they don't understand their purpose.

7. Give volunteers the big picture. Teach volunteers about the institution's mission and services so they have a sense of how their contributions are a part of the facility's overall operations.

8. Evaluate program effectiveness. Once a volunteer program is in place, it is crucial to know how well it works. All volunteer activities must be carefully documented so program and volunteer effectiveness can be evaluated. Once the program has been established, it also should be formally evaluated by staff, inmates, and volunteers. With this information, one can make sure the program's purpose is being served.

9. Recognize the volunteer's contribution. Volunteers, like all of us, need to be recognized for their work and accomplishments. A pat on the back can go a long way, particularly in a demanding field like corrections. Recognizing volunteers for their contributions can help keep them motivated and involved.

Source: Reprinted with permission from Kevin R. Ogburn, "Volunteer Program Guide," *Corrections Today,* Vol. 55, No. 5, p. 66, © 1993, American Correctional Association, Lanham, Maryland.

The initial development and organization of the volunteer program in a correctional institution will help ensure its ultimate effectiveness. Initially, policies and procedures must be drafted and incorporated into the formal structure of the departmental program that utilizes the volunteers. This will minimize the possibility of disruption and provide consistency and direction to volunteers and staff alike. Inherent in this effort should be establishing clear lines of authority and appointing a volunteer coordinator. Whether full-time or part-time, this important position will improve communication among volunteers and staff and allow for the clear definition of expectations.

Recruitment strategies must be well defined. Failure to enlist the support of enough volunteers will endanger the program's success. Too many people can be overwhelming and result in chaos with reduced productivity. Recruitment strategies must aim for the right number of the right kind of volunteers. The volunteer coordinator must use the personal contacts of staff and the reputation of established organizations to ensure that recruitment is successful. If other well-known organizations have successfully integrated their volunteers to the institution, it will encourage others to do so.

Selection follows recruitment. Improper volunteer selection will weaken a program. Neither the agency nor the volunteer nor the community benefits from informal selection practices. Unfortunately, in volunteering, one size does not fit all. Senior citizens who were very successful in hospital programs may find that the stress of a foster grandparent assignment in a secure juvenile correctional facility renders them ineffective. Interviews, education about agency expectations, and discussion of what the potential volunteer wants to accomplish are essential elements of proper selection practices. Because there are so many areas in which volunteers participate, a motivated individual can almost always be utilized in some capacity. Background checks are important, especially in direct service. Current or recent clients of the criminal justice system are generally not the best candidates

for facility volunteer assignment. Anyone who visits an inmate in a secure facility must be restricted from participating as a volunteer. Relationships with offenders in direct volunteer service must be limited to the boundaries of the volunteer duties. Formal recruitment and selection procedures are the best first line of defense to ensure that the security of the facility is not jeopardized by the volunteer program. Programs involving juveniles must use extra scrutiny in volunteer selection.

Prior to beginning his or her duties, the volunteer should participate in a structured orientation program that covers at least the following topics:

- the basic mission and goals of the criminal justice system and the agency in which services will be provided
- the facility or field service area in which services will be provided and the specific division in which services will be provided
- basic security procedures as appropriate to the security level of the program (including definitions and control of contraband and the importance of maintaining professional relationships with offenders)
- safety and emergency procedures
- cultural diversity

It is often feasible to use existing staff to train volunteers. The curricula and the length of training will vary in accordance with the scope and frequency of services provided. Initial orientation training, including a system of registration and identification that will track the volunteer throughout the period of active service, should be completed before any volunteer activity begins.

Perhaps one of the most important elements of ensuring the long-run success of a volunteer program is the formal recognition of the contribution made by the volunteers. Appreciation banquets or similar functions can often be combined with short inservice training segments.

Plaques and letters of commendation become important mementos of service rendered. Goodwill and commitment are fostered by simple attention to saying "thank you."

POTENTIAL AREAS OF VOLUNTEER PARTICIPATION IN A CORRECTIONAL PROGRAM

The impact of a comprehensive program of volunteer services can be very positive. The result of volunteers' efforts may be seen in many areas, including religious services, recreation, education, staff training, social services, substance abuse treatment, and prerelease programs.

Perhaps the most traditional and largest area of volunteer service in a jail or prison is religious programming. As a result, the staff chaplain often handles the overall coordination of volunteers. Facilities typically are unable to provide assistance to all faith groups without the help of volunteers. Congress's recent enactment of the Religious Freedom Restoration Act, *U.S. Code,* vol. 42, sec. 2000bb, underscores the importance of volunteer service in this area. Although a 1997 Supreme Court ruling specifies that state agencies are not subject to this federal act, federal institutions are required to ensure access to often obscure religious programs. Volunteers may make the difference in whether compliance can be achieved and maintained.

Another important area of service is recreation. The community is an important ingredient in sports programming in a facility. Leadership and sportsmanship can be taught very effectively by volunteers who compete as individuals or teams, participate in training officials, or serve as coaches or even just as supporters. This is an organizational component of most institutions that is not supported by appropriation and therefore depends on volunteer involvement.

Staff training is an often overlooked area where volunteers can make a contribution. Many institutions do not have staff members to provide training in areas such as cultural diversity, employment law, management and supervision practices, and technical medical and mental health issues. The professional development of staff is a good opportunity to involve the community in the institution.

Offender education programs require volunteer support to provide service to any significant number of inmates who need to develop academic and vocational skills. Volunteers can work in literacy, adult basic education, and job skills development programs. The enhancement of educational skills is a cornerstone of any program to reduce recidivism by improving opportunities for legitimate employment after release. It also is an area with funding too low to meet the needs of all inmates. Therefore, education should be a primary focus of the volunteer initiative.

As previously mentioned, without volunteers, the ability of facilities to provide broad-based programs of substance abuse education would be severely diminished. Alcoholics Anonymous and Narcotics Anonymous have a long, widely heralded record of accomplishment in correctional institutions. The commitment of individual volunteers, many of whom have previously conquered substance abuse problems, is a significant factor in this success.

Prerelease and postrelease programs are further examples of critical areas that receive too little budgetary support, given their importance in meeting correctional goals. Volunteers fill this gap. They provide service, not just enrich that which is already provided. Community support to the released offender is frequently the only support available. Involvement begins at the institution with education in a prerelease setting about how to access services. The involvement continues after release, with volunteers serving as mentors and providing guidance and support.

These are only examples of areas in which volunteers can be used. Each institution will have unique needs and unique opportunities. For example, volunteers may also be used in institutional library settings, administrative support roles, legal service programs for staff and offenders, and health care.

CONCLUSION

Everyone is a winner in a properly organized and administered volunteer program. Inmates receive services they would otherwise not receive. This can only improve the odds for successful adjustment in and out of the institution. Staff receive the benefit of community expertise in sharpening their own skills and enhancing their ability to be effective in their jobs. The agency and facility are opened to the community, and traditional misconceptions about jails and prisons are erased as external support increases. The most important player, the volunteer, is also a winner. Citizenship through service is its own reward.

SUGGESTED READINGS

American Correctional Association. 1993. *Helping hands: A handbook for volunteers.* Laurel, MD.

Love, B. 1993. Volunteers make a big difference inside a maximum security prison. *Corrections Today* 55, no. 5: 76–79.

Prison Literacy Project. 1993. *Prison literacy project handbook.* Philadelphia.

Sigler, R., and K. Leenhouts. 1985. *Management of volunteer programs in criminal justice.* Denver, CO: Yellowfire Press.

Weston, P. 1977. *Volunteers in justice.* Washington, DC: National Association on Volunteers in Criminal Justice.

CHAPTER 44

Drug Treatment behind Bars

James A. Inciardi

A considerable body of literature describes and documents the effectiveness of five major modalities of substance abuse and addiction treatment: chemical detoxification, methadone maintenance, drug-free outpatient treatment, self-help groups, and residential therapeutic communities. Each modality has its own view of substance abuse and addiction, and each impacts the client in different ways. Moreover, each modality exists in one form or another in prisons and jails.

CHEMICAL DETOXIFICATION

Designed for persons dependent on narcotic drugs, chemical detoxification programs are typically situated in inpatient settings and last for 7 to 21 days. The rationale for using detoxification as a treatment approach is grounded in two basic principles. The first is a conception of "addiction" as drug craving accompanied by physical dependence that motivates continued usage, resulting in a tolerance to the drug's effects and a syndrome of identifiable physical and psychological symptoms when the drug is abruptly withdrawn. The second is that the negative aspects of the abstinence syndrome discourage many addicts from attempting withdrawal, and hence, make them more likely to continue using drugs. Given these principles, the aim of chemical detoxification is the elimination of physiological dependence through a medically supervised procedure.

Methadone, a synthetic narcotic, is the drug of choice for detoxification. Generally, a starting dose of the drug is gradually reduced in small increments until the body adjusts to the drug-free state. While many detoxification programs address only the addict's physical dependence, some provide individual or group counseling in an attempt to address the problems associated with drug abuse, while a few refer clients to other longer-term treatments. For drug-involved offenders in prisons and jails, the mechanism of detoxification varies by the client's major drug of addiction. For opiate users, methadone or clonidine is preferred.[1,2] For cocaine users, desipramine has been used to ameliorate withdrawal symptoms. Almost all narcotic addicts and many cocaine users have been in a chemical detoxification program at least once. Studies document, however, that in the absence of supportive psychotherapeutic services and community follow-up care, virtually all relapse.

In all detoxification programs, inmate success depends upon following established protocols for drug administration and withdrawal. In a recent assessment of research literature on the effectiveness of detoxification, there appear to be increasing rates of program completion.[3] Yet many clinicians feel that mere detoxification from a substance is not drug abuse "treatment" and does not help people stay off drugs.

From this perspective, for detoxification to be successful, it must be the initial step in a comprehensive treatment process.[4-6] Thus, detoxifi-

---

Substance Abuse Problems among Inmates

In January 1998, the National Center on Addiction and Substance Abuse (CASA) at Columbia University released "Behind Bars: Substance Abuse and America's Prison Population," a report of a three-year study demonstrating the powerful connection between substance abuse (drugs and alcohol) and the rate of incarceration in the United States. Perhaps the most significant finding is that 80 percent of the 1.4 million persons imprisoned in this country are seriously involved with drug and alcohol abuse. Included in the 80 percent are inmates who used an illegal drug at least weekly for a period of at least one month, have been incarcerated for selling or possession drugs or driving under the influence, were under the influence of drugs or alcohol when they committed their crime, committed their offense to get money for drugs, or have a history of alcohol abuse.

CASA reports that the tremendous increase in the prison population in this country (from 1990 to 1996, the population increased 239 percent, from about 502,000 to about 1,701,000) is largely attributable to substance abuse. Many of the offenders were convicted of violating drug laws (30 percent of the prison population increase from 1980 to 1995 is attributable to drug law violators), and others committed crimes while under the influence of drugs or alcohol or to facilitate their drug use. The problem is compounded by the fact that substance abuse is closely related to recidivism; inmates with prior convictions are significantly more likely than first-time offenders to be regular drug users.

As of January 1, 1997, there were over 96,000 prisoners enrolled in drug treatment programs in correctional institutions around the country. In addition to treatment programs, all states had drug testing programs intended to curb drug use inside prison; most states conducted random drug tests and tests based on suspicion. On average, just over 9 percent of the inmates tested were found positive for drug use. The cost of the tests range from $1.30 to $31.50 per test; the average cost was $6.65.

Source: Data from *Behind Bars: Substance Abuse and America's Prison Population,* © 1998, The National Center on Addiction and Substance Abuse, Columbia University; C. Camp and G. Camp, *1997 Corrections Yearbook,* © 1997, Criminal Justice Institute, Inc.

---

cation is a temporary regimen that gives addicts the opportunity to reduce their drug intake; for many, this means that the criminal activity associated with their drug taking and drug seeking is interrupted. Finally, given the association between injection drug use and the human immunodeficiency virus (HIV) and acquired immune deficiency syndrome (AIDS), detoxification also provides counseling to reduce AIDS-related risk behaviors.

METHADONE MAINTENANCE

Methadone was synthesized during World War II by German chemists when supply lines for morphine were interrupted. Although chemically unlike morphine or heroin, it produces many of the same effects. Methadone was introduced in the United States in 1947, and since the 1960s the drug has been in common use for the treatment of heroin addiction. Known as "methadone maintenance," the program takes advantage of methadone's unique properties as a narcotic. Like all narcotics, methadone is cross-dependent with heroin. As such, it is a substitute drug that prevents withdrawal. More important, however, methadone is orally effective, making intravenous use unnecessary. In addition, it is longer acting than heroin, with one oral dose lasting up to 24 hours. These properties have made methadone useful in the management of chronic narcotic addiction.[7]

During the first phase of methadone treatment, the patient is detoxified from heroin on dosages of methadone sufficient to prevent withdrawal without either euphoria or sedation. During the maintenance phase, the patient is stabilized on a dose of methadone high enough to eliminate the craving for heroin. Although this process would appear to substitute one narcotic for another, the rationale behind methadone maintenance is to stabilize the patient on a less debilitating drug and make counseling and other treatment services available.

Studies have demonstrated that while few methadone maintenance patients have remained drug-free after treatment, those who remain on methadone have favorable outcomes in a number of areas. More specifically, a number of investigations have found that patients continued to use high levels of such nonopiate drugs as cocaine and marijuana.[8] On the other hand, much of the research has concluded that those on methadone maintenance have been more likely to reduce their criminal activity, become employed, and generally improve in psychosocial functioning.[9] Well-designed programs, furthermore, tend to be integrated with other forms of treatment and social services.[10]

As such, methadone maintenance is effective for blocking heroin dependency. However, methadone is also a primary drug of abuse among some narcotic addicts, resulting in a small street market for the drug. Most illegal methadone is diverted from legitimate maintenance programs by methadone patients. Hence, illegal supplies of the drug are typically available only where such programs exist.

The role of methadone in prison settings is a bit complex, and the number of programs for incarcerated populations are few. The difficulties seem twofold. First, there is a major security concern. Prison officials are uncomfortable with the general distribution of methadone to potentially large numbers of their inmates. Moreover, many feel that treatment should be "drug-free" and that methadone simply continues drug dependence.

One of the few methadone maintenance programs in a jail is the Key Extended Entry Program (KEEP) at New York City's Rikers Island Penitentiary. KEEP's client population includes those awaiting trial as well as sentenced prisoners, with some 3,000 receiving treatment each year. The program meets all federal guidelines. An evaluation of KEEP found that those in the program were more likely to continue treatment after leaving jail than those in other types of drug treatment.[11]

Perhaps the major argument for methadone maintenance in a jail setting is that, unlike stays in state and federal prisons, jail stays tend to be short. In KEEP, for example, the treatment period is only 45 days. As such, a strong case can be made for offering methadone maintenance as a means for continuing or initiating treatment for those returning to the street community relatively soon.

DRUG-FREE OUTPATIENT TREATMENT

Drug-free outpatient treatment encompasses a variety of nonresidential programs that do not employ methadone or other pharmacotherapeutic agents. Most have a mental health perspective. Primary services include individual and group therapy, and some programs offer family therapy and relapse prevention support. An increasing number of drug-free outpatient treatment programs are including case management services as an adjunct to counseling. The basic case management approach is to assist clients in obtaining needed services in a timely and coordinated manner. The key components of the approach are assessing, planning, linking, monitoring, and advocating for clients within the existing nexus of treatment and social services.

Evaluating the effectiveness of drug-free outpatient treatment is difficult because programs vary widely—from drop-in "rap" centers to highly structured arrangements that offer counseling or psychotherapy. A number of studies have found that outpatient treatment has been moderately successful in reducing daily drug use and criminal activity. However, the approach appears to be inappropriate for the most troubled and the antisocial users.

The number of rigorously designed studies of corrections-based "outpatient" programs is quite small.[12,13] One of the few examples involves a relatively well-funded and designed program known as "Passages"—an 8 hours per day, 5 days per week, 12-week nonresidential program for women incarcerated in the Wisconsin correctional system.[14] Although the treatment staff and correctional administrators agreed that the program improved clients' self-esteem and their ability to deal with important issues, evidence of subsequent reduced drug use and criminal activity was not reported.

SELF-HELP GROUPS

Self-help groups, also known as 12-step programs, are composed of individuals who meet regularly to stabilize and facilitate their recovery from substance abuse. The best known is Alcoholics Anonymous (AA), in which sobriety is based on fellowship and adhering to the 12 steps of recovery. The 12 steps stress faith, confession of wrongdoing, and passivity in the hands of a "higher power." The steps move group members from a statement of powerlessness over drugs and alcohol to a resolution that they will carry the message of help to others and will practice the AA principles in all affairs. In addition to AA, other popular self-help 12-step groups are Narcotics Anonymous, Cocaine Anonymous, and Drugs Anonymous. All these organizations operate as stand-alone fellowship programs but are also used as adjuncts to other modalities. Al-

though few evaluation studies of self-help groups have been carried out, the weight of clinical and observational data suggest that they are crucial to recovery.

Research has failed to demonstrate that anonymous fellowship meetings by themselves are effective with heavy drug users.[15,16] Further, there are few known evaluations of prison-based self-help programs, for a variety of reasons: Prison administrators and treatment professionals tend to prefer other types of programs,[17] the model contains variables that are extremely difficult to operationalize and measure, members and leaders often view scientific studies of their groups as intrusive threats to anonymity and therapeutic processes, and evaluation research funding is more often available for innovative programming than for such well-established services.

Nevertheless, self-help programs are widespread in correctional settings. There is a widely shared belief that they work. The meetings are organized and run by volunteers at no cost to the prison authorities, and the meetings appear to help inmates make the transition from correctional to community-based settings.[18,19]

RESIDENTIAL THERAPEUTIC COMMUNITIES

The therapeutic community (TC), is a total treatment environment in which the primary clinical staff are typically former substance abusers—"recovering addicts"—who themselves were rehabilitated in therapeutic communities. The treatment perspective of the TC is that drug abuse is a disorder of the whole person—that the problem is the person and not the drug, that addiction is a symptom and not the essence of the disorder. In the TC's view of recovery, the primary goal is to change the negative patterns of behavior, thinking, and feeling that predispose a person to drug use. As such, the overall goal is a responsible, drug-free lifestyle. Recovery through the TC process depends on positive and negative pressures to change. This pressure is brought about through a self-help process in which relationships of mutual responsibility to every resident in the program are built. In addition to individual and group counseling, the TC process has a system of explicit rewards that reinforce the value of earned achievement. As such, privileges are earned. In addition, TCs have their own rules and regulations that guide the behavior of residents and the management of their facilities. Their purposes are to maintain the safety and health of the community and to train and teach residents through the use of discipline. There are numerous TC rules and regulations, the most conspicuous of which are total prohibitions against violence, theft, and drug use. Violation of these cardinal rules typically results in immediate expulsion from a TC. TCs have been in existence for decades, and their successes have been well documented.

A number of corrections-based TCs and other types of residential treatment programs have been evaluated and have been described in the literature: the Hillsborough County Sheriff's Office Substance Abuse Treatment Program in Tampa, FL; the Stay 'N Out TC in New York's Arthur Kill Correctional Facility; Oregon's Cornerstone Program; Delaware's KEY and CREST Outreach Center TCs; and the Federal Bureau of Prisons' Residential Drug Abuse Treatment Program.

The Hillsborough County jail program was established in 1988 to address the short-term treatment needs of pretrial jail inmates.[20] The program provides services for 60 inmates—48 males in a direct supervision pod, and 12 females housed in a unit with women who are not in treatment. In a treatment milieu emphasizing recovery, cooperation, and interdependence, treatment is provided in groups of 8 to 12 inmates using a cognitive–behavioral, skills-based approach that focuses on relapse prevention. The goals of the program are to encourage long-term abstinence and to involve participants in ongoing treatment services after release from jail. After-care is accomplished through linkages with the local programs.

The evaluation examined 535 admissions to the program from June 1988 through January 1991, and 422 untreated "controls" who requested treatment but were not admitted because either a lack of space or release from jail prior to treatment entry. At two months after release from jail, 16 percent in the treatment group and 33 percent in the control group had been rearrested; at six months, 46 percent in the treatment group and 58 percent in the control group had been rearrested. During the year after release, those in the treatment group had a mean elapsed duration of 221 days prior to rearrest, as compared with 180 days for those in the control group.

The Stay 'N Out TC in New York's Arthur Kill Correctional Facility was established in 1974 and follows the traditional TC model.[21] Treatment occurs in prison, and no after-care services are provided. In a follow-up study of several client samples (as well as a no treatment control group), the major outcome variables were arrest and parole outcome.[22] For both men and women, the lowest proportion arrested were those in the TC group.

Cornerstone, founded in 1976 on the grounds of Oregon State Hospital, is a prerelease TC program with a six-month after-care program. Clients are referred from the state's three prisons. In a three-year follow-up study, 144 Cornerstone residents who graduated between 1976 and 1979 were compared with three other groups—inmates who dropped out of Cornerstone within 30 days of entry, all Oregon parolees with a history of alcohol or drug abuse who were released during 1974, and a similar population released in Michigan at the same time.[23] The Cornerstone dropouts had the highest rates of recidivism, with 74 percent returning to prison within three years after release. The Michigan group had between 45 and 50 percent who returned, and the Oregon parolees, 37 percent. The Cornerstone graduates had the lowest rate of recidivism, with 29 percent returning to prison within three years after release.

Delaware's KEY/CREST program is a three-stage continuum of treatment that begins in the institution and extends to community-based after-care. Treatment begins in the KEY, a prison-based therapeutic community for male inmates established in 1988 and located at the Multi-Purpose Criminal Justice Facility in Wilmington, DE. During the closing months of 1990, CREST Outreach Center was established in Wilmington, DE, under a five-year National Institute on Drug Abuse (NIDA) treatment demonstrations grant as the nation's first work release TC. CREST is a transitional facility with a six-month residential program that continues the basic TC treatment approach combined with work release. After six months at CREST, clients proceed to community-based after-care.[24,25] Follow-up studies have demonstrated this treatment continuum to be highly effective in that those who have received the full continuum of treatment are three times more likely to be drug-free and almost twice as likely to be arrest-free 18 months after release than the no treatment controls.[26] What this suggests is that an integrated continuum of treatment may be a highly promising approach .

The Federal Bureau of Prisons' Residential Drug Abuse Treatment Program attempts to identify, confront, and alter the attitudes, values, and thought patterns that led to criminal behavior and drug or alcohol abuse. The program consists of three stages. First, there is a unit-based treatment within the confines of a prison where prisoners live together and undergo therapy for either 9 to 12 months. Second, following completion of the residential portion, inmates continue treatment for up to 12 months while in the general population of the prison, through monthly group meetings with the drug abuse program staff. Third, if transferred to community-based facilities prior to release from custody, inmates who completed the residential portion (and the institutional transition portion, if time allows) participate in regularly scheduled group, individual, and family counseling sessions.

The Federal Bureau of Prisons' recently completed interim evaluation (with funding and assistance from the NIDA), revealed that offenders who completed the program were 73 percent less likely to be rearrested during the first six months back in the community than inmates who did not complete the program. Similarly, graduates of the program were less likely to use drugs within the first six months than those who were not treated. The large sample size (1,800 offenders), rigorous research design, and multisite sample make these findings particularly noteworthy.[27]

Although TCs are the most visible drug abuse treatment programs in prison settings, there are numerous other types, many of which are grounded in individual and group counseling and 12-step approaches. However, there is limited information about these programs in the substance abuse literature.

CONCLUSION

A legacy of the 1980s and 1990s "war on drugs" has been a criminal justice system that is "drug driven" in many respects. In the legislative sector, new laws have been created to deter drug use and to increase penalties for drug-related crime. In the police sector, drug enforcement initiatives have been expanded, which, in turn, has increased the number of arrests for drug-related crimes. In the judicial sector, the increased flow of drug cases has resulted in overcrowded dockets and courtrooms and the creation of new drug courts, special dispositional alternatives for drug offenders, and higher conviction and incarceration rates. In the correctional sector, there has been the further crowding of already overpopulated jails and penitentiaries.

In response to this situation, criminal justice systems throughout the United States have been structuring and implementing treatment programs at every level—for arrestees, those released before trial, those on probation, jail and prison inmates, and parolees and those with other forms of postrelease surveillance. Although some highly visible programs have been highlighted in the literature, little is known about what is being accomplished in most jurisdictions.

More information is needed in a number of areas. For example, although it is generally agreed that criminal justice systems throughout the United States are overwhelmed with drug users, little is known about the actual health services and treatment needs of drug-involved offenders. Moreover, only minimal attention has been focused on the issue of comorbidity. As such, it is important that treatment needs assessments be conducted to determine what services and how many treatment slots are needed by criminal justice clients at all levels. Similarly, little is known about what services are available to drug-involved offenders, including those with dual diagnoses. As such, research is needed to determine the number and type of treatment services available to probation departments, diversion programs, and other criminal justice entities.

NOTES

1. D.R. Gerstein and H.J. Harwood, eds., *Treating Drug Problems.* Vol. 1 (Washington, DC: National Academy Press, 1990).
2. R.P. Mattick and W. Hall, "Are Detoxification Programmes Effective?" *The Lancet* 347 (1996): 97–100.
3. Mattick and Hall, Are Detoxification Programmes Effective? 97–120.
4. Gerstein and Harwood, eds., *Treating Drug Problems,* 174–176.
5. D.C. McBride and C. VanderWaal, "An Evaluation of a Day Reporting Center for Pre-Trial Drug-Using Offenders," *Journal of Drug Issues* 27 (1997): 377–397.
6. S. Magura et al., "The Effectiveness of In-Jail Methadone Maintenance," *Journal of Drug Issues* 93 (1993): 75–99.
7. V.P. Dole and M. Nyswander, "A Medical Treatment for Diacetylmorphine (Heroin) Addiction: A Clinical Trial with Methadone Hydrochloride," *Journal of the American Medical Association* 193 (1965): 80–84.
8. C.D. Chambers et al., "The Incidence of Cocaine Abuse among Methadone Maintenance Patients," *International Journal of the Addictions* 7 (1972): 427–441.
9. J.C. Ball and A. Ross, *The Effectiveness of Methadone Maintenance* (New York: Springer-Verlag, 1991), 202.
10. Ball and Ross, *The Effectiveness of Methadone Maintenance,* 162.
11. Magura et al., "The Effectiveness of In-Jail Methadone Maintenance," 75–99.
12. R.H. Peters, "Drug Treatment in Jails and Detention Settings," in *Drug Treatment and Criminal Justice,* ed. J.A. Inciardi (Newbury Park, CA: Sage Publications, 1993), 44–80.
13. J. Wellish et al., "Treatment Strategies for Drug-Abusing Women Offenders," in *Drug Treatment and Criminal Justice,* ed. J.A. Inciardi (Newbury Park, CA: Sage Publications, 1993), 5–29.
14. G.P. Falkin et al., *Treating Prisoners for Drug Abuse: An Implementation Study of Six Prison Programs,* (New York: Narcotic and Drug Research, Inc., 1991).
15. Falkin et al., *Treating Prisoners for Drug Abuse: An Implementation Study of Six Prison Programs.*
16. Wellish et al., "Treatment Strategies for Drug-Abusing Women Offenders," 6–9.
17. B.S. Brown, "Program Models," in *Drug Abuse Treatment in Prisons and Jails,* ed. C.G. Leukefeld and F.M. Tims, NIDA Research Monograph no. 118 (Rockville, MD: National Institute on Drug Abuse, 1992), 31–37.
18. Peters, "Drug Treatment in Jails and Detention Settings," 65.
19. Brown, "Program Models," 35.
20. Peters, "Drug Treatment in Jails and Detention Settings," 55.
21. H.K. Wexler and R. Williams, "The Stay 'N Out Therapeutic Community: Prison Treatment for Substance Abusers," *Journal of Psychoactive Drugs* 18 (1996): 221–229.
22. H.K. Wexler et al., "Outcome Evaluation of a Prison Therapeutic Community for Substance Abuse Treatment," *Criminal Justice and Behavior* 17 (1990): 71–92.
23. G. Field, "The Cornerstone Program: A Client Outcome Study," *Federal Probation,* June 1985, 50–55.
24. R.M. Hooper et al., "Treatment Techniques in Corrections-Based Therapeutic Communities," *The Prison Journal* 73 (1993): 290–306.
25. J.A. Inciardi, "Prison Therapeutic Communities," in *Examining the Justice Process,* ed. J.A. Inciardi (Fort Worth, TX: Harcourt Brace, 1996), 397–409.
26. J.A. Inciardi et al., "An Effective Model of Prison-Based Treatment for Drug-Involved Offenders," *Journal of Drug Issues* 27 (1997): 261–278.
27. *TRIAD Drug Treatment Evaluation Project: Six Month Interim Report* (Washington, DC: Federal Bureau of Prisons Office of Research and Evaluation, 1998).

PART VIII

Legal Oversight
and Prisoner Rights

Americans are consistently amazed when they learn that prisoners have many constitutional rights. Facing numerous lawsuits regarding inmate rights, correctional practitioners have long known that the wall and fences of correctional facilities do not separate inmates from their rights.

Private citizens, especially victims of crime, are generally exasperated at the thought of rapists, murderers, and other lawbreakers having the ability to sue public officials over alleged violations of the prisoners' sensibilities and lifestyle. The ability to bring a lawsuit while confined also greatly irritates institution staff because inmates often hold up the threat of litigation as a means of forcing a decision or response from their keepers.

Yet American citizens are protected by the Constitution, even if they are banished from society as a sanction for violating the rights of others. This country honors its laws, and the Supreme Court has ruled time and time again that prisoners of the state are not bereft of constitutional protections.

It has not always been so. In early Western civilization, those convicted of crimes were often punished with what was referred to as "civil death"; criminals were sanctioned with the loss of their citizenship, liberty, and property. Early legal opinions in the United States also held that convicted felons were virtually unable to gain any redress in the courts; this hands-off policy continued for many years and did not start to shift until the 1970s. As the Civil Rights movement flourished in this country, the prisoner rights movement took hold, and federal and state judges began to take great interest in prison issues. The conditions of confinement became the subject of many lawsuits.

Prisoners are able to gain access to the courts through a legal tool referred to as a writ of habeas corpus (a Latin term that means "produce the body"). This process permits inmates to challenge the lawfulness of their confinement. It is often used as a vehicle to sue the state over the conditions of incarceration. Further, habeas corpus is an action that requires swift response from the court, and these legal petitions are placed ahead of other civil actions. Relief in habeas corpus actions is release from custody.

State prisoners may also file legal complaints in federal court for allegations of violations of their constitutional rights under the Civil Rights Act of 1871, U.S. Code, title 42 sec. 1983, and federal inmates may pursue redress for similar constitutional complaints under *Bivens* case law. Section 1983 and *Bivens* lawsuits are the most commonly used means of challenging conditions of confinement.

It is fair to state that following a period of nearly 20 years of court activism and intervention in the management of local, state, and federal penal facilities, the legal system in the United States has adopted a more reasonable response to prisoner litigation. Decisions have been much more balanced, and both state and federal courts have taken a more measured stance in prison and jail judicial review. The courts seem to have struck a balance between an inmate's right to a humane, safe environment and a penal administrator's authority to operate a correctional facility. The rule of reasonableness seems to prevail.

Part VIII addresses the operational requirements of correctional administrators and their staff to comply with the Constitution and examines a prisoner's right to access the courts.

LEARNING OBJECTIVES

After studying this section, you should be able to answer the following questions:

1. Why are prisoners able to bring lawsuits against correctional officials after the prisoners have been sanctioned with a term of imprisonment for violating the rights of others?
2. How did the Civil Rights movement in the United States affect the rights of inmates?
3. What case law has significantly impacted an offender's ability to access the American court system?
4. Have the courts served as the primary source of change within the prisons and jails of the United States?
5. What does the term "deliberate indifference" mean? How does it relate to correctional litigation today?

DISCUSSION/REVIEW QUESTIONS

1. What are the specific constitutional rights generally enjoyed by prisoners? What are specific examples of violations of these rights?
2. What must be proven in a court of law when an inmate files a lawsuit alleging that an individual employee has violated the inmate's rights?
3. What twists and turns have American courts taken in response to inmate litigation over the last 200 years?
4. Is judicial intervention in the administration of prisons and jails a necessary component of the American justice system or not?

CHAPTER 45

Compliance with the Constitution

Judith Simon Garrett

The old adage that "a lawyer who represents him- [or her-]self has a fool for a client" is even more true for a nonlawyer who attempts to represent him- [or her-] self. Prison wardens and jail administrators should not assume that they can substitute their thorough and detailed understanding of correctional management for the legal training and knowledge of a lawyer. The prison or jail should employ an attorney to be available to consult with the warden or superintendent on an ongoing basis. If this is not possible, an attorney employed by the state, city, or county should be readily available for consultation. It is always preferable to discuss potential problems with the attorney before they arise rather than after the formal complaint has been filed in court. It is also helpful for the institution to have a formal grievance procedure in place to permit the administration, with advice from the attorney, to attempt to resolve issues thereby limiting the number of inmate lawsuits. (The facts compiled through the grievance process will facilitate the more expeditious dismissal or resolution of the suit.)

This chapter provides a general overview of the types of major legal issues that arise in the corrections setting and how the issues have been resolved by the courts. It would be impossible to

address every legal issue in this area, and thus specific legal questions should be referred to an attorney.

CORRECTIONS LAW

"Corrections law," as it has come to be known, emanates from several important Supreme Court decisions and federal statutes. A general description of the most important principles is provided below.

Inmates are not deprived of their constitutional rights. Indeed, they maintain many rights while in prison and are constrained from exercising other rights only to the extent that to do so would interfere with the safe and orderly operations of the prison. The rights most important to inmates emanate from the First, Fourth, Fifth, Sixth, and Eighth Amendments to the Constitution (note that for state inmates these rights are provided through the Fourteenth Amendment to the Constitution). There are also important rights created by federal statutes, including the Civil Rights Act of 1964 (specifically section 1983, which creates individual liability for state officials who interfere with prisoners' rights guaranteed by the Constitution or by federal statute). Some rights created by state statutes may also be significant.

Although the courts will scrutinize prison conditions when allegations of brutal or inhumane treatment are raised, they are less likely to become involved with prison management than

---

Opinions expressed in this chapter are those of the author and do not necessarily represent the opinions of the Federal Bureau of Prisons or the U.S. Department of Justice.

321

they were several decades ago. Recently, Congress has somewhat limited prisoners' rights (and to some extent, the judiciary has returned to the "hands off" attitude toward corrections that it had prior to the 1960s).

The Prison Litigation Reform Act of 1996 (PLRA) limits inmates' ability to file lawsuits, particularly by requiring inmates to exhaust all available administrative remedies prior to filing suit, requiring the payment of full filing fees, imposing harsh sanctions (including the loss of good time credits for filing frivolous and malicious lawsuits), and requiring that any damages awarded to inmates be used to satisfy pending restitution orders.[1] Additionally, the PLRA limits the scope of prospective relief that courts may order such that only changes necessary to correct the violation of law are permitted. Even then, courts must ensure that the relief is narrowly drawn, and the court must consider any potential adverse impact on public safety and prison operations that could result from the relief ordered. Courts are also substantially limited in their ability to grant prisoners early release. The PLRA provides the government with new means to modify or terminate relief that was previously ordered in prison condition cases.

The PLRA and similar sorts of legislation enacted in several states are not intended to inhibit prisoners from challenging prison conditions that fail to afford them basic rights and privileges protected by federal laws and the Constitution.

The First Amendment protects individuals' rights to express themselves. Historically, inmates have been primarily concerned with their right to receive publications (*Thornburgh v. Abbott*[2]), their right to correspond with friends and family (*Procunier v. Martinez*[3]), and their right to practice their religion freely (this subject is discussed in detail in Chapter 16).

The general rule on prisoners' First Amendment rights was articulated by the Supreme Court in *Turner v. Safley*[4] and *O'Lone v. Estate of Shabazz*,[5] in which the Court ruled that an inmate's constitutional rights may be restricted if the restriction is reasonably related to legitimate penological interests. This standard has

In 1996, there were over 31,000 lawsuits filed by inmates around the country against 46 departments of corrections and their staff. Additionally 36 percent of such jurisdictions were under a court order regarding conditions of confinement, 33 percent were operating under a court-ordered population cap, and 31 agencies' operations were overseen by a special monitor or special master. The number of lawsuits has remained relatively stable between 1993 and 1996, despite the substantial increase in prison population over these years.

Source: Data from C. Camp and G. Camp, *Corrections Yearbook 1997*, pp. 54–55, © 1997, Criminal Justice Institute, Inc.

proved to be quite easy for prison administrators to meet, as courts have defined a host of legitimate penological interests such as safety and security, rehabilitation, budgetary constraints, prison order, and equal opportunity. The courts have ruled repeatedly that the judgment of prison administrators should be given substantial deference, as they are best suited to determine security and safety needs in particular. Accordingly, as a general rule, inmates may not be denied all means of communicating with friends, family members, and others in the community. The prison may not suspend or eliminate phone calls, correspondence, and visits simultaneously and indefinitely, except in some very unusual and dangerous situations. However, the courts have permitted prisons to limit inmates' avenues of communication to correspondence and phone calls and prohibit visiting, or to permit visiting and not phone calls. Moreover, restrictions frequently limit the people with whom inmates may correspond or visit. For example, many states prohibit inmates from corresponding with one another and in few instances are former inmates permitted to return to visit those remaining in prison.

Inmates' rights to practice their religion were greatly enhanced through the Religious Freedom Restoration Act (RFRA),[6] which was intended to restore the level of religious freedom that preceded the Supreme Court's decision in *Employment Division v. Smith.*[7] Specifically, RFRA prohibited the government from "substantially burdening" an individual's religious exercise unless such burden was necessary to further a compelling government interest and the burden was the least restrictive alternative to further such interest. The law gave rise to a substantial number of lawsuits and resulted in substantial changes in the types of inmate religious activities permitted behind prison walls. However, on June 25, 1997, in *Boerne v. Flores,* the Court ruled that the RFRA was unconstitutional with respect to application of the law to state and local governments.[8] Presumably, the standard established in *O'Lone v. Estate of Shabazz* will again become the test for determining the constitutionality of prison rules and policies that allegedly interfere with inmates' religious practices in state and local correctional facilities.

The Eighth Amendment protects inmates from suffering "cruel and unusual" punishment. Prisoners rely upon this amendment to challenge "conditions of confinement" that include their basic human needs such as medical care, housing, food, clothing, safety, and exercise. The Supreme Court has held that in order for conditions of confinement to violate the Eighth Amendment, they must present an unreasonable risk of harm to the inmates,[9,10] and the prison administrators must be "deliberately indifferent" to these dangerous conditions. Most cases filed under the Eighth Amendment are found not to rise to the level of a constitutional violation. With respect to medical care, the Eighth Amendment prohibits medical care that is so inadequate as to show "deliberate indifference to a serious medical need."[11] While the federal government, many states, and some localities enjoy at least some immunity from civil actions seeking monetary damages and thus cannot be sued under a theory of medical malpractice, many prisons employ medical providers on a contract basis, and these providers could well be liable in cases of negligence or other wrongdoing.

Prisoners also rely on the Eighth Amendment to challenge instances where prison officials use force against them. In *Hudson v. McMillan,* the Supreme Court ruled that inmates need not suffer severe physical abuse in order to sustain an Eighth Amendment claim, so long as the force involved the "wanton and unnecessary infliction of pain" or force was used "maliciously or sadistically for the very purpose of causing pain."[12]

The Fourth Amendment prohibits unreasonable searches and seizures. In the community, this constitutional provision is often relied upon to challenge searches of people, their homes, or their cars, particularly in the absence of a search warrant. In prisons, the Fourth Amendment has limited applicability, due to the Supreme Court's repeated rulings that prisoners have a limited privacy interest in their cell[13,14] or in their person.[15] As a general rule, prison administrators are on sound legal ground in routinely searching inmate cells for contraband and requiring inmates to submit to shakedowns for the same purpose. Such searches would not be proper if conducted for another purpose (such as to harass the inmate) or in a discriminatory fashion (such as searching only Hispanic inmates). Prisoners of both genders have used the Fourth Amendment to challenge searches of their person by correctional officers of the opposite gender, but with little success, so long as the searches are conducted in a professional manner and with no sexual connotations or innuendos. The courts have urged prison administrators to make some effort to protect inmates' privacy as much as possible, such as permitting only limited viewing of the inmates in the shower or while dressing. Courts generally prohibit cross-gender strip searches except under exigent circumstances. (Note, however, that women inmates in Washington State prevailed in a cross-gender search case based on an Eighth Amendment claim of cruel and unusual punishment. The inmates, overwhelmingly, had extensive histories of sexual and physical abuse, and they successfully argued that the searches by men officers caused them substantial emotional trauma).[16]

The Fifth Amendment, in conjunction with the Fourteenth Amendment, prohibits the state from depriving any person of life, liberty, or property without affording the person due process. Due process is often raised in the context of inmate discipline, inmate classification, and inmate transfer decisions.

The recent Supreme Court decision in *Sandin v. Conner*[17] substantially altered the standard for determining the types of situations for which inmates must be granted due process. In *Sandin,* the Court ruled that "discipline in segregated confinement did not present the type of atypical, significant deprivation in which a state might conceivably create a liberty interest," and thus the inmate was not entitled to due process. Accordingly, after *Sandin,* to determine whether a liberty interest has been created (thus giving rise to a right to due process), one must ask whether the restraints on the prisoner "impose atypical and significant hardship on the inmate in relation to ordinary incidents of prison life." If they do not, prison administrators may take the action without providing due process.

Generally, correctional employees are protected from suits seeking personal liability so long as they act reasonably and within the scope of their employment. Those who behave recklessly or take actions outside the scope of their employment could be held personally liable for violating inmates' statutory or constitutional rights. However, the Supreme Court recently ruled that corrections officers in private firms are not entitled to the qualified immunity enjoyed by state employees in cases where inmates claim violations of their civil rights under Section 1983. In *Richardson v. McKnight,* the Court ruled that Section 1983 was intended to deter "state actors" from depriving persons of their rights, but that private corrections employees are not "state actors" and thus the deterrence argument does not apply.[18]

GRIEVANCE PROCESSES

A formal grievance process can be extremely helpful in avoiding lengthy and complicated legal proceedings. The formal grievance process provides an opportunity for prison administrators to create a clear record for the court of the facts in a particular case and to address a worthy complaint appropriately before litigation begins. Assuming that the prison administrators behave appropriately, the court should have little difficulty deciding the case based upon the materials presented through the grievance process documentation, thereby averting the expense of a hearing. Unfortunately, where no such documentation exists, it is much more difficult to establish the factual record. Then, the court must engage in fact finding to evaluate an inmate's claims of mistreatment.

Pursuant to the PLRA, administrative grievance procedures are no longer required to meet minimum standards or to be certified by the federal government; the PLRA effectively repealed inconsistent provisions in the Civil Rights of Institutionalized Persons Act of 1980.[19] However, in order for a "formal grievance process" to be viewed by the courts as credible, it must purport to document a statement of facts and an explanation for the action taken. The inmate grievance process of the Ohio Department of Rehabilitation and Corrections (DRC) may help other departments establish their own new grievance process.[20]

The Ohio DRC's grievance process encourages informal resolution of problems and inmate complaints. But inmates who are not satisfied with such efforts may use the formal grievance procedure to challenge any aspect of institutional life including policy, procedure, rule and application of the same, and may take issue with action of any staff member. However, the complaint must pertain specifically to the grieving inmate.

The formal complaint must be filed within 14 days of the inmate becoming aware of the action giving rise to the complaint. The remedies available through the grievance procedure include modification of policies, restitution/restoration of property, and disciplinary action against an employee if there has been a willful violation of a rule.

The DRC ensures that the grievance procedure is accessible to disabled inmates and that all inmates are informed of the process (in all languages that are spoken by a significant portion of inmates).

A locked mail box is available for inmates to mail their grievances ("kites") to the institution inspector; inmates may also contact the inspector and relay their grievance orally. An oral or written response is provided as soon as possible and in no more than five days. If, in the judgment of the inspector, the subject of the grievance is such that the inmate is in substantial risk of personal injury or serious, irreparable harm, the inspector should take immediate corrective action.

The inspector takes whatever action is necessary to resolve all grievances, and retains a written log of all complaints, and their resolution, as well as written records of all interviews, records researched, and other investigatory steps as well as the conclusion and any recommendations. Either the inmate or the inspector can require that details of the complaint be documented on a particular form, and the inmate may seek assistance from the inspector in completing the form. A copy of the form shall be given to the inmate.

Grieving inmates can request the participation of other inmates and/or staff in resolving the complaints. The inspector will solicit opinions from inmates and employees in investigating complaints challenging general policies and procedures.

If a complaint is not resolved within 10 days, the inmate must be notified, and if the matter is not resolved within 15 days the inmate can file a complaint with the chief inspector. Extensions beyond 30 days must be approved by the chief inspector. If the potential resolution exceeds the authority of the inspector, he or she must submit

recommendation to the managing officer for action within 10 working days.

Inmates may appeal resolutions within 5 days to the chief inspector who then has 20 days to respond. Extensions of up to 90 days may be taken, but the inmate must consent to any further extension.

The inspector may interview anyone, access any records, and generally inspect areas to ensure compliance with rules and regulations. He or she must submit a monthly report to the managing officer.

The inmate's inability to substantiate an allegation is not a basis for disciplinary action against him or her. However, if an inmate makes false accusations in a knowing, deliberate, and malicious attempt to cause injury to another, and if the potential for injury is substantiated, he or she may be subject to disciplinary action. Only the inspector can file a disciplinary report in such instances.

There is no reprisal for the good faith use or participation in the grievance procedure. No documentation related to grievances is placed in inmates' files that are made available to the parole board unless the document contains false accusations that could be the basis for disciplinary action (see above).

CONCLUSION

Constitutional and statutory provisions that apply to corrections are numerous and complex. However, by keeping in mind a few fundamental principles, administrators can avoid most serious problems. First, prisoners are human beings and should be treated with respect and dignity. Second, although deprived of their liberty, prisoners remain citizens of this country and are entitled to most of the rights to which other citizens are entitled. Third, inmates should be granted free access to the courts (as described in Chapter 46). Prison administrators should let the courts judge whether inmates' claims have merit, not try to prevent inmates from filing.

NOTES

1. P.L. 134, 104th Cong., 2d sess. (April 1996).
2. *Thornburgh v. Abbott,* 490 U.S. 401 (1989).
3. *Procunier v. Martinez,* 416 U.S. 396 (1974).
4. *Turner v. Safley,* 482 U.S. 78 (1987).
5. *O'Lone v. Estate of Shabazz,* 482 U.S. 342 (1987).
6. *Religious Freedom Restoration Act, U.S. Code,* vol. 42, sec. 2000bb (1993).
7. *Employment Division v. Smith,* 494 U.S. 872 (1990).
8. *Boerne v. Flores,* 117 Sup. Ct. 2157 (1997).
9. *Wilson v. Seiter,* 111 Sup. Ct. 2321 (1991).
10. *Helling v. McKinney,* 113 Sup. Ct. 2475 (1993).
11. *Estelle v. Gamble,* 429 U.S. 97 (1976).
12. *Hudson v. McMillan,* 112 Sup. Ct. 995 (1992).
13. *Hudson v. Palmer,* 468 U.S. 517 (1984).
14. *Block v. Rutherford,* 468 U.S. 576 (1984).
15. *Bell v. Wolfish,* 441 U.S. 520 (1979).
16. *Jordan v. Gardner,* 986 F. 2d 1521 (9th Cir. 1993).
17. *Sandin v. Conner,* 515 U.S. 472 (1995).
18. *Richardson v. McKnight,* 117 Sup. Ct. 2100 (1997).
19. *Civil Rights of Institutionalized Persons Act, U.S. Code,* vol. 42, sec. 1997–1997j (1980).
20. Ohio Department of Rehabilitation and Corrections, *Inmate Grievance Procedure,* Internal Policy #5120-9-3.

CHAPTER 46

Prisoners' Access to the Courts

Kenneth C. Haas

The Supreme Court has made many decisions on the subject of a prisoner's right of access to the courts, and these cases have greatly affected jail and prison administration. The right of access is the most important of all prisoners' rights because it is the right upon which all other rights turn. Without it, prisoners would have no way to appeal their convictions or to vindicate their rights in such areas of law as the First Amendment's protections of speech and religion, the Eighth Amendment's ban on cruel and unusual punishments, or the right to Fifth and Fourteenth Amendment due process in prison disciplinary proceedings. There have been significant cases that involved the constitutionality of various prison policies that allegedly interfere with inmate efforts to seek judicial relief.

THE PATH OF RIGHT-OF-ACCESS LAW: 1941 TO THE PRESENT

Prior to the 1960s, American courts generally followed a policy of declining jurisdiction in nearly all suits brought by prisoners. Known as the "hands-off doctrine," a term that originated in a document prepared for the Federal Bureau of Prisons,[1] this policy reflected the traditional view of the prisoner as a "slave of the state" without enforceable rights.[2] As a practical matter, the judiciary's reluctance to become involved in the internal operations of prisons made it extraordinarily difficult for prisoners to seek judicial relief from alleged mistreatment or harsh conditions of confinement.[3]

Generally, courts based refusals to review inmate petitions on one or more of the following rationales: (1) the argument that prison management is exclusively an executive branch function and that judicial intervention would violate the "separation of powers" doctrine, (2) the fear that judicial intervention would subvert prison discipline, (3) the claim that judges lack expertise in penology, (4) a concern that opening the courthouse doors to prisoners would lead to a flood of inmate litigation, and (5) the view that considerations of federalism and comity should compel federal courts to refrain from considering claims brought by state prisoners. The last of these rationales remained surprisingly strong until the Supreme Court's decisions in *Monroe v. Pape,* 365 U.S. 167 (1961) (holding that section 1983 of the Civil Rights Act of 1871 gives federal courts original jurisdiction over claims alleging violations of federal constitutional or statutory rights by state or local officials), and in *Cooper v. Pate,* 378 U.S. 546 (1964) (affirming that state prisoners could bypass the state courts and bring section 1983 suits against state correctional officials in federal courts). Until these holdings, the vast majority of state-prisoner lawsuits were brought under the federal habeas corpus statute, which, unlike section 1983, permits no monetary damages and requires petitioners to go through the time-consuming process of exhausting state judicial remedies.

A strict version of the hands-off doctrine prevailed among most courts until the early 1960s. Nevertheless, in 1941—while the hands-off doctrine remained strong—the Supreme Court first recognized that the due process clauses of the Fifth and Fourteenth Amendments guarantee all Americans—even prisoners—the right of access to the courts. In the case of *Ex Parte Hull*,[4] the Court struck down a Michigan prison regulation that required inmates to submit all their legal petitions to prison officials for approval. Whenever prison authorities felt that inmate petitions were frivolous, inaccurate, or poorly written, they would refuse to mail them to the courts. The Supreme Court held that this procedure amounted to an impermissible denial of the right of access to the courts. The justices told prison officials that "Whether a petition for a writ of habeas corpus addressed to a federal court is properly drawn and what allegations it must contain are questions for that court alone to determine."[5]

In the years following *Hull*, most courts remained reluctant to interfere with prison policies restricting inmate access to the courts. Many courts approved such prison practices as refusing to allow prisoners to purchase or receive law books, allowing the confiscation of an inmate's legal documents found in another inmate's cell, refusing to permit a prisoner to type his or her own legal papers, and censoring or withholding legal correspondence between prisoners and attorneys. Moreover, even when prison regulations were more accommodating to the right of access, other factors such as ignorance, illiteracy, and poverty kept prisoners from filing their complaints.[6]

Today's prisoners also are likely to find that legal barriers and personal handicaps can make court access difficult. The right to a state-supplied attorney does not extend to inmate actions attacking prison conditions or to discretionary appeals of a criminal conviction.[7] Most prisoners lack the money to hire attorneys, and only in the rarest cases would an attorney take an inmate's case without a fee or on a contingent fee basis. Consequently, most cases brought by prisoners originate from either the petitioning prisoner or from a "jail-house lawyer" or "writ writer"—a prisoner who claims to have expertise in law and prepares legal documents for fellow inmates. Thus, it is not surprising that the first major right-of-access case after *Hull* involved the limitations that prison officials could place on jail-house lawyers.

INMATES AS LAWYERS

In *Johnson v. Avery*,[8] decided in 1969, the Supreme Court invalidated prison regulations that prohibited jail-house lawyers from helping other prisoners with their legal problems. The Court acknowledged that jail-house lawyers may burden the courts with frivolous complaints and undermine prison discipline by establishing their own power structures and taking unfair advantage of gullible prisoners. These concerns, however, were outweighed by the importance of ensuring that prisoners have reasonable access to the courts. Because most prisoners possess neither the funds to hire attorneys nor the educational background to write their own appeals, their only recourse in most cases, reasoned the justices, was to seek the help of a fellow inmate. Accordingly, the Court concluded that prison officials could no longer enforce no-assistance rules unless the prison itself provided some type of legal services program that was reasonably effective in helping prisoners pursue their legal claims.

The *Johnson* decision, more than any other case, paved the way for more effective efforts by prisoners seeking access to the courts. Following this decision, it became increasingly difficult to escape the logic that if inmates have the right to the assistance of another inmate in the preparation of legal documents, they cannot be absolutely restrained from acquiring the requisite legal materials and due process protection needed to assist in the preparation of petitions or to acquire an attorney or some other type of competent assistance to help them seek an appropriate and speedy judicial remedy.

However, the *Johnson* decision lacked precision. It provided prison officials with only the basic parameters of the right of access. Since 1969, the Supreme Court has resolved several important issues left unsettled by this case. In 1971, the Court affirmed a lower court ruling that required prison officials to provide inmates with an "adequate" law library—one that contained enough books and materials to ensure that literate prisoners could do meaningful research in support of their petitions.[9] Three years later, the Court struck down a California prison policy that barred law students and legal paraprofessionals from working with prisoners.[10] Also in 1974, the justices invalidated a Nebraska regulation stating that prisoners could seek legal assistance only from a single "inmate legal advisor" who was appointed by the warden and who was permitted to provide assistance in preparing only habeas corpus petitions and not civil rights complaints brought under section 1983 of the Civil Rights Act of 1871.[11]

INMATE LAW LIBRARIES

Arguably the most important of the post-*Johnson* decisions was announced in 1977 in the case of *Bounds v. Smith*.[12] This court held that even when prison policies allow jail-house lawyers to operate, prison officials nevertheless must provide prisoners with either an adequate law library or adequate assistance from persons trained in the law. But like the *Johnson* opinion, the *Bounds* opinion was far from specific in explaining what it would take to provide "adequate" legal services and materials for prisoners. The *Bounds* majority simply noted:

> While adequate law libraries are one constitutionally acceptable method to assure meaningful access to the courts, our decision here . . . does not foreclose alternative means to achieve that goal. . . . Among the alternatives are the training of inmates as paralegal assistants to work under lawyers' supervision, the use of paraprofessionals and law students, either as volunteers or in formal clinical programs, the or-

ganization of volunteer attorneys through bar associations or other groups, the hiring of lawyers on a part-time consultant basis, and the use of full-time staff attorneys, working either in new prison legal assistance organizations or as part of public defender or legal services offices.[13]

Not surprisingly, there is still a great deal of confusion and continuing litigation about what prison officials must do to guarantee inmates meaningful access to the courts. Questions involving the adequacy of particular prison law libraries or legal services programs must be answered by the state and federal courts on a case-by-case basis. Most courts have held that *Bounds* is satisfied when states provide inmates with adequate law libraries and access to materials with some quasi-professional help.

However, in 1982, a federal district court in Florida held that the state's plan to provide prisoners with law libraries staffed by inmate law clerks and librarians was insufficient to guarantee prisoners access to the courts. The court ordered the Florida Department of Corrections to provide some form of attorney assistance as part of its legal services plan.[14] On appeal, this decision was reversed by the Eleventh Circuit Court of Appeals. The court of appeals held that the lower court had interpreted *Bounds* too broadly and that attorneys were not required.[15] In other words, a combination of law libraries and inmate law clerks will meet the *Bounds* mandate. The Ninth Circuit also approved the use of inmate law clerks rather than lawyers, but it added that the clerks must have received at least some sort of legal training.[16]

Implementing the right of access to the courts raises especially difficult problems—both for prison officials and for courts—when the prisoner has been placed in disciplinary segregation or some other type of administrative segregation designed for particularly disruptive or dangerous inmates. It would be quite costly to establish a full-fledged prison law library in every special housing unit in a prison, and releasing the prisoner from restrictive confinement for a visit to the prison's main law library may pose significant security and logistical problems. On the other hand, a prisoner placed in restrictive confinement does not lose his or her right of access to the courts.

In an important 1993 decision, a Third Circuit panel approved a Delaware prison policy that did not permit inmates in a special maximum security unit to go to the prison's main law library. Instead, the maximum security inmates were provided with three types of legal resources and services: (1) a very small satellite law library in the maximum security unit, (2) a paging system through which inmates could request photocopies of materials contained in the main law library, and (3) varying degrees of legal assistance provided by paralegals who had been trained by an attorney. Although a federal district court had found that this combination of services fell below the requirements established in *Bounds,*[17] the appellate court declared that prison officials had done all that was necessary to comply.

The parameters of *Bounds* remain unclear, but at a minimum, it appears that most courts will require both an adequate law library and assistance from persons who have some demonstrable understanding of the legal process.[18–20] When determining whether the inmates of a prison have the assistance necessary to prepare court documents with reasonable adequacy, courts will have to examine such factors as (1) the number of prisoners entitled to legal assistance, (2) the types of claims these inmates are entitled to bring, (3) the number of persons rendering assistance, and (4) the training and qualifications of those who render assistance.[21–23]

EXTENT OF ACCESS THAT MUST BE PROVIDED TO INMATES

Although *Bounds* remains substantially intact, a significant 1996 decision, *Lewis v. Casey,*[24] has narrowed the scope of the prisoner's right to court access in a way that may give prison officials more breathing room in establishing a constitutionally permissible system of providing legal assistance to prisoners. By a five-to-four margin, the *Lewis* Court held that an inmate alleging a violation of *Bounds* must show that shortcomings in the prison's library or assistance program caused him or her "actual injury"—that these shortcomings hindered or stymied his or her efforts to pursue a legitimate legal claim.

Writing for the majority, Justice Scalia argued that *Bounds* did not create "an abstract, freestanding right to a law library or legal assistance."[25] As Justice Scalia saw it, permitting an inmate to bring a right-of-access claim simply by demonstrating that his or her prison's library or legal services program is "sub-par in some theoretical sense"[26] would be just as pointless and wasteful of scarce resources as allowing a healthy inmate to bring an Eighth Amendment medical care claim because of the alleged inadequacies of the prison infirmary. Therefore, a prisoner asserting a *Bounds* violation must show not only that the prison library or legal assistance program is deficient but that the deficiencies obstructed his or her efforts to file a legal claim.

> He might show, for example, that a complaint he prepared was dismissed for failure to satisfy some technical requirement which, because of deficiencies in the prison's legal assistance facilities, he could not have known. Or that he had suffered arguably actionable harm that he wished to bring before the courts, but was so stymied by inadequacies of the law library that he was unable even to file a complaint.[27]

Justice Scalia added that an inmate could not satisfy the actual-injury requirement by pointing to "just any type of frustrated legal claim."[28] Prisoners are entitled to adequate legal assistance only when they bring a "nonfrivolous" or "arguable"[29] claim that either challenges the conditions of their confinement or attacks their sentences, directly or collaterally. The impairment of any other kind of legal action, Justice Scalia stressed, "is simply one of the incidental (and perfectly constitutional) consequences of conviction and incarceration."[30]

Many corrections officials, understandably, welcome the latter portion of the Court's holding. *Lewis* makes it clear that prison officials have no constitutional obligation to assist a prisoner in general civil matters. Accordingly, officials do not need to provide the extensive law libraries or elaborate legal services programs that would be necessary if *Bounds* were to be interpreted to entitle inmates to assistance in virtually all civil and criminal matters, including divorce proceedings, parental rights actions, workers' compensation claims, or small claims court matters. In Justice Scalia's words, *Bounds* was never intended to transform inmates into "litigating engines capable of filing everything from shareholder derivative actions to slip-and-fall claims."[31]

Other aspects of the *Lewis* decision, however, are not so clear, and lower courts may disagree about how to apply it in various right-of-access cases. One issue that is certain to provoke disagreement is whether this case should be read to limit the duration of the requirement for legal assistance to the preparation of initial pleadings. Justice Scalia's opinion states at one point that the *Bounds* right is "a right to *bring to court* [emphasis mine] a grievance that the inmate [wishes] to present."[32] One court has already held that prisoners are entitled to legal assistance only in preparing and filing court papers and not in submitting or responding to motions, pleadings, or discovery requests.[33] This appears to be an unjustifiably narrow reading of *Lewis,* however. A closer examination of the majority opinion indicates that Justice Scalia simply wanted to emphasize that *Bounds* was not meant to transform inmates into miniature law firms. The *Lewis* opinion also stresses that it is the role of courts "to provide relief to claimants, in individual or class actions, who have suffered, or will imminently suffer, actual harm."[34] Obviously, a court cannot provide relief based solely on a prisoner's initial complaint. A prisoner who brings a nonfrivolous claim to court will be required to defend the claim, respond to motions to

---

Prison Law Libraries

Historically, making legal materials and expertise available to inmates has been a substantial expense. Legal books are very expensive to purchase, and many require constant updating (such as compilations of state laws and reported judicial opinions), thereby demanding significant staff resources. Prisons can augment their legal resources through hiring or contracting with legal staff or making other arrangements to ensure legal professionals are available to assist the inmates. Recent technological developments are likely to bring the most substantial relief to prisons and jails that seek to ensure that inmates are provided all necessary and appropriate legal resources. (In most instances, an investment in personal computers for the inmate law library is a necessary first step.) For example, in many instances, state laws and judicial opinions are available on CD-ROMs, compatible with most personal computers and easy to use. Additionally, through the Internet there are a variety of services that can be accessed to learn of recent court decisions, statutory changes, and other forms of legal research. It should be noted that many prison and jail administrators are reluctant to grant inmates access to the Internet due to the potential for abuse (in the form of fraud or other criminal activity).

---

dismiss or for summary judgment, and to move the case toward judgment and ultimately trial. It makes no sense to interpret *Lewis* as giving prison administrators the power to hinder or thwart nonfrivolous suits as soon as they are filed.

Properly understood, *Lewis* should cast no doubts on the continuing validity of other well-established concomitants of the right of access to the courts. For example, it will still be illegal for prison staff to retaliate against prisoners for having exercised their right of access to the courts.[35–37] The long-standing consensus that prison officials cannot, without good cause, read or interfere with incoming or outgoing inmate–attorney mail does not seem to be undermined by *Lewis*.[38] (It is worth noting, however, that the Connecticut Supreme Court recently held that prison officials can place reasonable restrictions on inmates' telephone calls to attorneys so long as other viable means are provided to the inmates to pursue their legal claims.[39]) And *Lewis* does not overrule lower court decisions holding that out-of-state prisoners must be provided with such legal materials as statutes and relevant case law from the sending state.[40,41]

The *Lewis* holding, however, will have, and already is having, a major impact on prison administration. Since it was announced on June 24, 1996, federal and state courts have dismissed dozens of inmate right-of-access claims for failure to meet the actual-injury requirement.[42–45] Correctional officials have every reason to believe that *Lewis* will reduce both the number of frivolous lawsuits filed by prisoners and the costs of defending prisoner-filed litigation.

PRISON LITIGATION REFORM

Another recent development—the April 1995 passage of the Prison Litigation Reform Act—will almost certainly lead to a reduction in prisoner lawsuits.[46] This law requires, among other things, that before a prisoner can file a civil rights action in a federal court, he or she must exhaust all available administrative remedies including the prison's inmate grievance system. The act also generally prohibits a prisoner from filing an in forma pauperis petition (a petition to permit an indigent litigant to proceed with a case when the court determines that he or she lacks the funds to pay the full filing fee) if the prisoner has filed three or more federal petitions that

were dismissed as frivolous or malicious, or for failing to state a claim for which relief can be granted. Additionally, the act provides for sanctions to be imposed on federal prisoners whose petitions are dismissed because they were filed for malicious reasons or because the inmate presented false testimony or evidence.

CONCLUSION

The combined effects of the *Lewis v. Casey* decision and the Prison Reform Litigation Act will be significant. Important questions pertaining to the proper scope of the prisoner's right of court access are not directly addressed in *Lewis* or in the new law. Nevertheless, both of these developments unmistakably signal the end of an era in which prison officials' obligations to provide legal assistance to prisoners were gradually expanded. *Lewis* and the Prison Reform Litigation Act undoubtedly will result in differing and conflicting decisions among lower courts, but the pendulum clearly has swung in the favor of correctional officials. It is important to remember, however, that the line of Supreme Court decisions from *Ex Parte Hull* in 1941 through *Bounds v. Smith* in 1977 remains the law of the land, and prisoners have retained the right of access to the courts.

NOTES

1. Fritch, *Civil Rights of Federal Prison Inmates* (1961).
2. *Ruffin v. Commonwealth,* 62 Va. (21 Gratt.) 790, 796 (1871).
3. K. Haas, "Judicial Politics and Correctional Reform: An Analysis of the Decline of the 'Hands-Off' Doctrine," (1997).
4. *Ex Parte Hull,* 312 U.S. 546 (1941).
5. *Ex Parte Hull,* 549.
6. D. Edmonston, "The Expansion of a Prisoner's Right of Access to the Courts" *1 Capital University Law Review,* 192 (1972).
7. *Ross v. Moffitt,* 417 U.S. 600 (1974).
8. *Johnson v. Avery,* 393 U.S. 483 (1969).
9. *Younger v. Gilmore,* 404 U.S. 15 (1971).
10. *Procunier v. Martinez,* 416 U.S. 396, 419–422 (1974).

11. *Wolff v. McDonnell*, 418 U.S. 539, 577–580 (1974).

12. *Bounds v. Smith*, 430 U.S. 817 (1977).

13. *Bounds v. Smith*, 828.

14. *Hooks v. Wainwright*, 536 F. Supp. 1330 (M.D. Fla. 1982).

15. *Hooks v. Wainwright*, 775 F. 2d 1433 (11th Cir. 1985).

16. *Lindquist v. Idaho Board of Corrections*, 776 F. 2d 851 (9th Cir. 1985).

17. *Abdul-Akbar v. Watson*, 775 F. Supp. 735 (D. Del. 1991).

18. B. Kempinen, "Prisoner Access to Justice and Paralegals: The Fox Lake Paralegal Program," *New England Journal of Criminal and Civil Confinement* (1988): 67.

19. C.E. Smith, "Examining the Boundaries of *Bounds:* Prison Law Libraries and Access to the Courts," *Howard Law Journal*, 9 (1987): 27.

20. R. Ducey, "Survey of Prisoner Access to the Courts: Local Experimentation with *Bounds*," *New England Journal on Criminal and Civil Confinement*, 9 (1983): 47.

21. *Kelsey v. State of Minnesota*, 622 F. 2d 956 (8th Cir. 1980).

22. *Walters v. Thompson*, 615 F. Supp. 330 (N.D. Ill. 1985).

23. *Martin v. Phelps*, 380 So. 2d 164 (La. 1979).

24. *Lewis v. Casey*, 116 Sup. Ct. 2174 (1996).

25. *Lewis v. Casey*.

26. *Lewis v. Casey*.

27. *Lewis v. Casey*.

28. *Lewis v. Casey*.

29. *Lewis v. Casey*.

30. *Lewis v. Casey*.

31. *Lewis v. Casey*.

32. *Lewis v. Casey*, 2181.

33. *Carper v. DeLand*, 54 F. 3d 613 (10th Cir. 1995).

34. *Lewis v. Casey*, 2179.

35. *Woods v. Smith*, 60 F. 3d 1161 (5th Cir. 1995).

36. *Harris v. Fleming*, 839 F. 2d 1232 (7th Cir. 1988).

37. *Hall v. Sutton*, 755 F. 2d 786 (11th Cir. 1985).

38. *Muhammad v. Pitcher*, 35 F. 3d 1081 (6th Cir. 1994).

39. *Washington v. Meachum*, 680 A. 2d 262, 283–286 (Conn. 1996).

40. *Petrick v. Maynard*, 11 F. 3d 991 (10th Cir. 1993).

41. *Story v. Morgan*, 786 F. Supp. 523 (W.D. Pa.).

42. *Penrod v. Zavaras*, 94 F. 3d 1399 (10th Cir. 1996).

43. *Pilgrim v. Littlefield*, 92 F. 3d 413 (6th Cir. 1996).

44. *Stotts v. Salas*, 938 F. Supp. 663 (D. Hawaii 1996).

45. *Stumes v. Bloomberg*, 551 N.W. 2d 590 (South Dakota 1996).

46. Public Law 134, 104th Cong., 2d sess. (April, 1996).

SUGGESTED READINGS

Branham, L., and S. Krantz. 1997. *The law of sentencing, corrections, and prisoners' rights.* 5th ed.

Nahmod, S. et al. 1995. *Constitutional torts casebook.*

PART IX

American Prison Architecture

If it is true that form follows function, American prisons and jails have truly been built for the primary task of custodial confinement. And there are many of them. In 1998, there are over 1,500 U.S. adult long-term correctional facilities alone. Many of these are outmoded bastilles that state and federal jurisdictions would like to shut down, but the large numbers of new commitments demand that they stay open. Accordingly, correctional institution architecture today varies from gloomy concrete and steel behemoths to well-planned and secure penitentiaries with modern designs.

Although the history of long-term penal facilities in the United States began in 1773 with Newgate Prison, in an abandoned copper mine in Connecticut, the underground caverns made little contribution to the architecture of today's correctional institutions. Institution design in the United States started in 1790 with the construction of the Walnut Street Jail in Philadelphia, PA. This unique facility, designed by the Quakers, provided single cells with total isolation from other prisoners. The religious philosophy required total silence and no activities except meditation on one's sins. This approach evolved into the Pennsylvania system of confinement, which continued to emphasize silence so inmates did not infect one another with their criminal thinking. This emphasis on moral reformation meant that prisons were designed to de-emphasize group contact.

The competing model of confinement, known as the Auburn system, developed in 1819. It also emphasized the silent system, initially, but prisoners were expected to perform congregate work. This approach required an architectural design with facilities for inmates to eat, work, and worship together. The Auburn, NY, prison also was the first to use the tier system in the cell houses; the small cells were built on different levels, stacked on one another.

Because the Auburn system was much more cost-effective than the Pennsylvania system and the productivity of the inmates was considered a very positive aspect of the system, Auburn eventually became the model adopted throughout the United States. In fact, this prison design was hailed as an important American innovation internationally.

American correctional facilities have evolved into industrial prisons, especially in the North, and agriculture-based field prison camps in the South. The design of the institutions was specific to the region of the country and the type of work that the inmates were to accomplish. All prisons attempted to take full advantage of inmate labor to minimize the cost of confinement to the public.

Prison design is a separate, large industry today, and institutional architectural programs are extremely functional. New facilities are built to help staff supervise inmates, and the modern building structure reflects on appreciation for the importance of staff and inmate safety.

Newer institutions are much more open, and yet they are secure. The direct supervision model of prisoner control has been accepted as appropriate for all but the most dangerous inmates in supermax facilities. Rather than imposing steel bars and concrete between the supervising staff and the inmate population, direct supervision designs place staff close to the prisoners and encourage ongoing, personal contact and conversation. This improved communication enhances staff control of the area and improves the institution environment. Inmates are confined to their cells for fewer hours and have more time for leisure and program activities in the common areas of the housing units.

Part IX provides an overview of the types of adult correctional institutions found in the history of American corrections, offers information regarding accommodations that must be made for inmates with physical challenges, and offers advice for those enmeshed in the difficult process of designing a new adult detention center.

LEARNING OBJECTIVES

After studying this section, you should be able to answer the following questions:

1. What are the differences among the primary penal designs in the United States? What are the different architectural requirements of each design?
2. How have social, moral, and religious forces in American society affected prison and jail design?
3. What is the direct supervision model of institution management? Can it be used in older prison designs?
4. Is an open, campus-style prison compound a benefit to the staff and inmates of the facility? How does the public respond to such a design?
5. Is it appropriate and necessary to expend public funds to make old correctional facilities completely accessible for offenders with disabilities?
6. Should the staff who operate and manage a prison or jail be involved in the design and supervision of the construction of a new institution?
7. Does the architectural design of an institution affect the staff and inmates who work and live inside the structure?

DISCUSSION/REVIEW QUESTIONS

1. How are today's correctional institution designs affected by public opinion?
2. How did the use of prison labor shape the architecture of prisons throughout the United States?
3. What is the Americans with Disabilities Act (ADA), and how has it affected correctional institutions?
4. Do the ADA requirements affect the hiring of correctional personnel?
5. What is "fast track" construction, and how does it affect correctional systems?
6. Why should a correctional system building a new penal facility be directly involved in all aspects of design and construction?

CHAPTER 47

Prison Architecture

Robert S. George

To design a prison or jail facility, architects must consider many factors, including the characteristics and numbers of inmates, management philosophy, the funding available for construction, and staffing requirements. The defining element in the composition of a prison complex is the type of housing unit. Correctional institutions are communities unto themselves and require all the services of a small city: food service, medical support, maintenance, work and industrial areas, education facilities, and so on. But the inmate housing unit design tends to affect the design of all other aspects of prison or jail architecture.

HOUSING CONFIGURATIONS HAVE EVOLVED

The evolution of prison housing concepts corresponds closely to the evolution of correctional management practices over the centuries. Prison architecture is largely influenced by the operating agencies' policies and management styles. Societal attitudes toward incarcerated people affect decisions about the architectural details of a housing unit as well.

There have been few changes in housing unit design over the centuries, but most have been dramatic departures from their predecessors. Sometimes the changes reflect a swing toward more punitive attitudes. At other times, design changes reflect how much people believe that

the behavior of sentenced criminals can be improved.

The desire to separate criminals from society and punish them has been the most consistent influence on correctional architecture through the years. Architecture is a language of symbols. Some prison architecture conveys a message of extreme punishment. In recent years, architecture has changed as classification systems to assess inmate behavior and to forecast their needs while they are in custody have been introduced.

The history of prison architecture has been greatly influenced by specific facilities. This chapter will review the impact these facilities have had on correctional design.

THE BASTILLE

The Bastille was built around 1370 as part of the fortifications for the wall around Paris. During the seventeenth and eighteenth centuries, it was used to house political prisoners sent there at the whim of royalty. Citizens of every class and profession were arrested and sent to the Bastille indefinitely without accusation or trial. It was attacked and captured by a mob assisted by royal troops at the outbreak of the French Revolution in 1789, and the destruction of the hated stronghold began days later.

The physical characteristics of the Bastille, whose name stems from the French word for fortress, are clearly linked to the approach to punishment there. It was a stone masonry fortress four levels high contained within a thick, continuous wall. Its massive form derived from eight cylindrical towers joined together with straight-walled sections enclosing two interior courtyards. The walls had several windows on each level arranged directly over the ones beneath. Much like a medieval castle, it had a projected, crenelated parapet (a series of stone shields running along the top of the wall) to protect defenders against arrows and other flying projectiles. Also like a castle, it was accessible only by drawbridge. The Bastille's architectural features tell us that the primary (and probably the only) goal of its design was to contain people en masse and to resist attackers who might seek to force prisoners' release.

An example of Bastille-like design on the other side of the Atlantic, the Second Western Penitentiary of Pennsylvania, was built near Pittsburgh in the 1830s. Four levels high with thick walls and a crenelated parapet, its architectural proportions are different from its parent in Paris, but its origins are undeniable. Secure, punitive, and gloomy, it operated throughout most of the nineteenth century to warehouse people in a hopeless, degenerative environment.

CONVICT HULKS

Numerous wooden ships docked in harbors such as Portsmouth were widely used in England in the last half of the eighteenth century to confine convicted persons. These dirty surplus boats with crowded, disease-ridden, infested conditions, separated England's convicted from their freedom regardless of their offense. These hulks were probably unsupervised, and their wooden construction made them a perpetual fire hazard as well. The convict hulk had a long-term influence on prison design. English prison reformers felt compelled to come up with a more humane design.

PENNSYLVANIA

Once the United States had broken from England, the Quakers of Pennsylvania took advan-

tage of their new opportunity to express their horror at the corporal punishment practices that had prevailed in colonial America. The Pennsylvania constitution allowed for imprisonment with hard labor instead of public, corporal punishment for criminals, and prison design emerged as an important issue. To replace the open bay or congregate style of housing dozens of people that had prevailed in previous centuries, the Walnut Street Jail was erected in 1790 with small cells to house individual prisoners. A little later, the Eastern Penitentiary at Cherry Hill in Philadelphia, PA, was developed. It had cellular housing. Erected in 1829, Eastern became the parent institution in the United States for the Pennsylvania system. At opposite ends of the eighteenth century, cellular imprisonment had been used in the papal prison of St. Michael in Rome and at Ghent in Belgium. These European models featured cells arranged along the exterior walls of the building housing them, an arrangement now known as "outside cells." Eastern Penitentiary's design borrowed this concept and took it a step further by organizing the cell buildings in a "spoke" plan. According to this plan, cells radiated from a central hub space or rotunda so that an institution's population could be controlled.

This configuration has been used quite extensively in England, France, and other European countries. Figure 47–1 shows the configuration of cell buildings in the Pennsylvania system and the Auburn system (discussed below).

Architecturally, the outside cell configuration is based on flanking cells arranged in a linear plan and facing a common central corridor and another row of cells on the other side. Depending on the number of inmates and floor area constraints, cells are stacked in one or more tiers accessible by stairs at either end of the range. Cell-front design can be open with bars and a barred door, or they can be solid with a panel door. Because each prisoner can touch an exterior building wall in this configuration, the construction details of the wall and any windows it may include become essential to the institution's perimeter security. With the development of modern plumbing systems, outside cell configu-

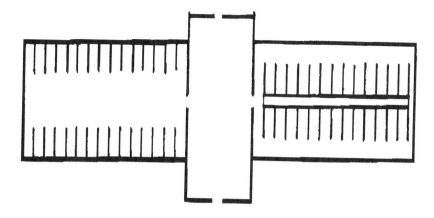

Figure 47–1 Pennsylvania Housing Unit (Left Side) and Auburn/Sing Sing Housing Unit (Right Side), with a Chase

rations now include toilet and lavatory fixtures and (as discussed below) showers. Typically, those fixtures are arranged along the fronts of the cells to permit a full view into the cell and to facilitate maintenance of the mechanical system from the walkway outside the cell.

AUBURN/SING SING

While the Pennsylvania system was introducing its form of linear cell housing, the New York State system opened new prisons at Auburn and Ossining based on another design. In its original form, the Auburn/Sing Sing model featured two back-to-back rows of multitiered cells arranged in a straight, linear plan. A typical cell for an individual prisoner could measure 3 feet 6 inches wide by 7 feet long—approximately 25 square feet—and 7 feet high. (By contrast, today's room standards call for a room 7 to 8 feet wide by 10 feet long—approximately 80 square feet—and 8 feet high.) This housing concept dominated much of U.S. prison and jail design in the nineteenth and early twentieth centuries. Side by side, the cells extend far enough to accommodate the desired number of beds. The number of cells in a row can range from five or six to several dozen. Two cellblocks can be joined at a central space that permits access to both.

Over the decades, with the development of electrical, plumbing, and ventilation systems, the rows of cells were separated a few feet to form a continuous space called a chase for piping and air movement. The chase, which can be entered from either end of the cellblock for maintenance, acts as a spine to serve the toilet and light fixtures at the back of each cell. The piping system in the chase sets a limit on the overall length of the cellblock because of the relationship between a pipe's diameter and the amount of water it can handle. Other than this limit, there are no architectural or construction constraints to the length of a cellblock.

Using this concept, the rows of cells can be stacked in tiers accessible by stairs. There are examples of cellblocks ranging from one to six tiers high. Cellblock geometry places the cells in the middle of the overall cellblock space with cell fronts facing the building's exterior walls. Unlike in the Pennsylvania model, the cells and their occupants do not face each other. The distance from the cell front to the outside wall usually equals or exceeds the length of the cell, allowing for a continuous balcony along the front of the cells on the levels above the ground floor. Because the occupants of the cells cannot reach the walls as long as the cell front is closed, the exterior walls can have windows for light and ventilation without compromising the building's security. Because of their geometry, the Auburn-style cellblocks are also known as "inside cells."

Auburn-style cellblocks were designed to provide a certain number of cells under one roof. In many examples, the longer cellblocks have a crossover corridor midway to allow movement to the other cells without having to walk or run to one end of the building. Gang showers are often located at this same crossover corridor. The building is accessible from one end where it joins a corridor that, in turn, leads to more cellblocks or other components of the institution. Somewhere close to the other end, the building may have another door to the outside to permit entrance into the building by staff in the event of a disturbance. With the more stringent imposition of modern fire and life safety concerns on correctional architecture since the late 1970s, these second doors are more common and are considered emergency exits to allow evacuation. Some old cellblocks have been remodeled to divide them in half and give them built-in areas of refuge.

When supervising in both Auburn- and Pennsylvania-style housing units, officers patrol on the ground floor or the continuous balcony in front of the rows of cells. Officers need to look into each cell during their patrols. The development of gang-locking cell fronts in the early twentieth century permitted the officers to selectively open one or many cell doors at once to let certain inmates out for meals, work, or recreation. The linear configuration and the supervision style it encouraged has led to minimal attention from staff and often contributed to significant neglect and harsh treatment.

Dozens of Auburn-style housing units have been built throughout the United States. This housing concept dominated much of prison and jail design in the nineteenth century. Its features have become so familiar that when most people think of correctional facilities, they think of the inside cell model. There are still several functioning examples of the Auburn housing unit, probably because overcrowded conditions keep the demand for housing so high that replacement

is not economically feasible. But it is interesting to note that many of them have been substantially remodeled and internally subdivided to upgrade their life safety characteristics and convert them into more manageable modules.

The Pennsylvania concept set the pattern for the radiating wing organization in which linear cellblocks were arranged like spokes in a wheel around a central hub space or rotunda. But it is interesting to note that later institutions consisting of combinations of the Pennsylvania and Auburn models arranged in the radial plan have been developed to take advantage of the merits of both (see Figure 47–2). Another site plan arrangement known as the "telephone pole" does much the same thing (see Figure 47–3). In this organization, housing units of different configurations are placed along opposite sides of a central corridor or spine.

The "linear indirect" architectural style was used in American prison and jail institutions in the twentieth century in combination with other housing styles that gave the institution a variety of housing conditions within the same security perimeter.

PANOPTICON

This style of housing unit was created by English architect Jeremy Bentham around 1790. Despite Bentham's English origins, no facilities with this design were ever built in England. The panopticon housing unit consists of two-person cells arranged side by side in a circular plan. A few were built in Virginia, Pennsylvania, and Illinois. Of the three "roundhouses" that once were part of the Illinois State Prison at Stateville, one is still in use. At four tiers high and with its central supervision tower, it must have seemed at one time to be a highly efficient means to house a great number of people under constant supervision. The panopticon is worth studying, despite all its flaws (see Figure 47–4).

In the Stateville panopticon, the cells face each other across a wide circular space with an enclosed officer's observation station at the center. With the cells arranged on the thick masonry

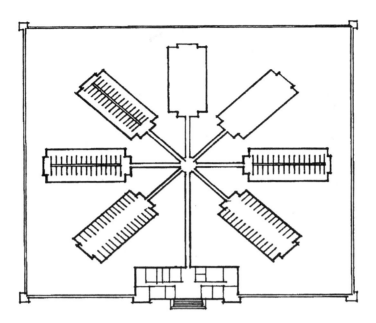

Figure 47–2 Radiating Wing Organization

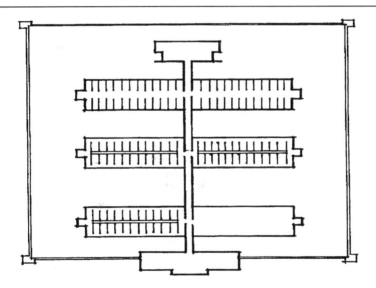

Figure 47–3 Telephone Pole Organization

perimeter walls with narrow windows, if any, this configuration resembles the Pennsylvania concept. The officer station is a two-level tower accessible from the main floor. In one of Bentham's conceptual plans, the circular space was only about 80 feet in diameter. By contrast, the diameter of this space at the Western State Penitentiary at Pittsburgh was over 300 feet.

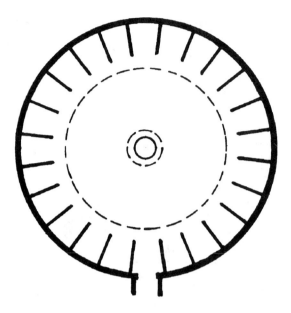

Figure 47–4 Panopticon Housing Unit

Moving around on the ground level is simple. On any of the upper tiers, however, officers must follow the curving, circumferential balcony for some distance to reach a stair. If officers in the observation station need to move quickly from the station to a problem they have seen from within the station, they have a substantial distance to travel.

The panopticon concept includes another unattractive feature that undermines its use. Cell houses are built with concrete or masonry and are furnished with steel bunks and cell fronts for purposes of security and durability. The panopticon has extremely high normal, or ambient, noise levels because of reverberation and echoes within its hard walls. Given the activity in a prison housing unit (e.g., talking, showering, closing doors, doing janitorial work), the ambient noise level in a panopticon at midday is so amplified by its shape that normal conversation sounds like shouting. The effects of these acoustics on occupants is beyond the scope of this chapter, but it takes little effort to imagine what those effects might be.

DIRECT SUPERVISION

One of the most interesting developments in modern correctional facility design occurred when the Federal Correctional Institutions (FCIs) at Pleasanton, CA (1974), and Miami, FL (1975), were opened by the Federal Bureau of Prisons (BOP). Prompted in part by the need to abate the conditions that contributed to a long and deadly disturbance that occurred in the New York State Prison at Attica in 1971, BOP initiated the design of a new style of housing unit that is nearly a square. This significant departure from the linear Auburn and Pennsylvania models features a large, open central indoor recreational or day room space that can be effectively supervised by an officer (see Figure 47–5). Individual cells are organized around this square space. Showers and quiet recreation areas are interspersed among the cells. A correctional officer in the Pleasanton model roams around the unit and can see around the interior space from just about any vantage point. The cells in the housing unit are stacked two high, one level

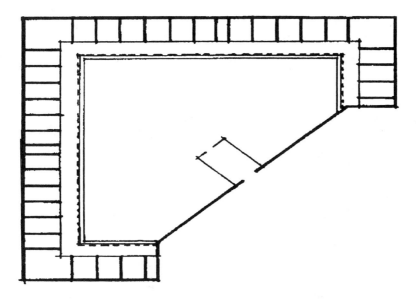

Figure 47–5 Direct Supervision Model

above and one level below the common area. Because the officer on the common floor is within a half-flight of either level of rooms, response to any cell is quicker.

The capacity of the unit was limited to 125 cells, an appropriate number for one or two officers to supervise. The unit, in turn, can be divided in half or quarters by means of sliding doors or temporary partitions. Like its predecessor, the Pennsylvania model, the building envelope (i.e., the exterior walls and the roof) has been detailed to provide the building's perimeter security. The secure envelope means that the interior partitions, doors, hardware, stairs, and other features could be built of lighter materials. This concept, which has become known as the "direct supervision" (and even "new generation") model, encourages a humane atmosphere by facilitating inmate–staff communication as well as security. The models of eighteenth and nineteenth centuries are now called "linear indirect" models.

The exterior shape of this housing unit includes a sloping roof covered with conventional shingles so that persons can be seen on the roof.

Inmate cell windows are quite large and the walls are trimmed with large wood beams. Because more systems from commercial construction (e.g., wooden doors, Sheetrock, vitreous china toilet fixtures) can be used in this concept, it is more economical to build.

FCI Pleasanton, which is now known as FCI Dublin, was designed by BOP to present as "near to normal" an environment as possible within a correctional setting. The same concept was employed by BOP at its three new metropolitan correctional centers (MCCs) in San Diego, Chicago, and New York. These MCCs are high-rises approaching 20 stories or more, and their housing units use the direct supervision model as well. The BOP has continued development of this model, and several states and counties have also adopted it for their new facilities.

ADMINISTRATIVE-MAXIMUM SECURITY

Prison systems have found it necessary to develop high-security institutions to handle groups of inmates who are especially violent. BOP operated the U.S. Penitentiary on Alcatraz Island in the San Francisco Bay for 30 years for very dangerous inmates. Architecturally, Alcatraz was a combination of the Auburn system (with stacked inside cells) and the Pennsylvania system (with rows of cells that face each other across an open corridor or range). It had manually operated gang-locking doors and the central plumbing chase characteristic of the Auburn model. The buildings and support structures around the island were constructed of reinforced concrete. Its capacity ranged from 200 to 250 inmates, each in single cells. The rows of cells were stacked two high, and the main roof over the housing unit was high enough to permit skylights that were well out of the reach of inmates. It also featured a central dining room. Outdoor recreation took place on the south side of the island in a large, open yard enclosed by a tall concrete wall. The institution included industries and some staff housing.

The U.S. Penitentiary at Alcatraz depended on tight operational procedures, traditional gun towers, and the San Francisco Bay for perimeter security. The high-security prison utilized ferryboat service for supplies, including fresh water, and transportation. Operating costs were very high, and the penitentiary was closed in 1963. Its mission moved to the new U.S. Penitentiary at Marion, IL.

Marion included what was called a "control unit" of about 70 cells for inmates within the federal system with dangerous and aggressive behavior, sentence duration, or other administrative conditions that required that they be housed under constant segregation conditions. The unit's design is based on inside cells with a dedicated shower at one end. This shower and a small recreation yard adjacent to the unit can be used by only one inmate at a time. Meals are delivered on trays to each cell, and all movement within the unit is under multiple escort.

High-security institutions were taken to a new level in California in the late 1980s and in Colorado in the 1990s. The California Department of Corrections' Pelican Bay Prison near the Oregon border includes two security housing units (SHUs) totaling 1,056 beds. The SHU is a new model of the administrative-maximum security facility to house management cases, habitual criminals, prison gang members, and the like. In these units, the inmate lives alone in a single cell. Each unit has its own grille-covered recreation yard. The inmate is permitted to use this yard for a short period each day. Doors to each cell are sliding, perforated steel plates with overhead, motor-operated sliding devices operated from a control center. With the exception of escorted, scheduled movements for recreation or other appointments, the inmate never leaves the cell.

The administrative-maximum security institution at the U.S. Penitentiary in Florence, CO, is the current federal edition of the "supermax" facility. As in Marion, the capacity of the Florence, CO, basic module is small. Each unit has 64 cells, each cell is accessible through its own sally port, and each cell includes its own shower as well as toilet and lavatory. Cells are arranged in the outside cell configuration on two levels split at the unit entrance. But a wall down the middle of the unit screens the view of the cells across the corridor. Inmates can use a large outdoor recreation area between units on established schedules.

OTHER DESIGN FACTORS

The housing unit of a prison or jail is the most important element of correctional design. Depending on the capacity of the institution, the housing units typically fill at least half of the land covered by and the construction mass of a correctional facility. The architecture of the inmate housing area has a way of steering the design of the rest of the institution. The other elements, known collectively as the "core," consist of the spaces needed to support the housing units. Space is needed to prepare and serve food, run programs, provide medical services, put out fires, and ensure the institution's security. In many modern institutions, large industrial buildings are included so inmates can manufacture goods or provide services for outside agencies.

A correctional facility is a large, expensive, and complex place to build and to maintain. It costs more to construct prisons than to construct most other types of buildings.

There are other significant operational costs that must be considered in the design of a prison or jail. Correctional facilities are in constant need of maintenance. Their various systems are heavily used each day, and they need to be repaired or replaced frequently. Institution facilities are never truly complete because their changing populations and space needs demand expansion or alteration, which leads to ongoing renovation. And, like all buildings, correctional facilities must face the devastating effects of earthquakes, hurricanes, floods, fire, and other natural disasters.

Prison design tends to adapt itself to new conditions or goals and to use already-existing building options to meet design needs. For instance, rarely is a new technology invented for use in a correctional environment; usually, a new technology is slowly adapted for prison use after first proving itself in some other arena.

CONCLUSION

Over the centuries, prison architecture has always had the same central purpose: to separate convicted offenders from the rest of society. But different forces have influenced how correctional facilities are laid out: social reformers, dismayed at conditions they found in the justice system of their day; correctional science and classification systems, used to identify and separate offender types; management sciences, used to train staff and manage resources; technological advances in construction systems, from thick, heavy concrete walls to precast concrete panels and structural steel; and technological advances in detention hardware and electronic surveillance and control systems. All of these forces have helped prison architecture evolve over the past several centuries.

SUGGESTED READINGS

American Correctional Association. 1983. *Design guide for secure adult correctional facilities.* College Park, MD.

American Correctional Association. 1983. *The American prison: A pictorial history.* College Park, MD.

American Institute of Architects. 1991. *1991–92 architecture for justice exhibit.* Washington, DC.

CHAPTER 48

Accommodating Inmates with Disabilities

Alan Appel

The number of prisoners with disabilities in correctional institutions across the United States is growing steadily. The aging inmate population, the debilitating effects of alcohol and drug abuse, and the injuries sustained because of violence mean that prisons and jails are responsible for a large number of offenders with disabilities.

As the populations of inmates with disabilities have increased, so have the legal requirements established to govern their care. These new standards have had a large impact on the correctional environment.[1]

On July 26, 1990, President George Bush signed the Americans with Disabilities Act (ADA), adding one more federal law to the list of statutes that must be read, analyzed, taught to the prison and jail staff, and enforced. This particular act caused such a commotion and concern among correctional administrators that it prompted almost 7,000 pages of comments and testimony from these administrators as part of the legislative process.

The development of such legislation can be traced back nearly 40 years. The 1960s and early 1970s represented a turbulent period in the United States; Vietnam, the Civil Rights movement, and Watergate were the confrontational issues of the day. It was a time of marches, demonstrations, and a search for nonaggressive, nonviolent methods to persuade people. But the level of violence began to escalate, and the federal government intervened.

THE CIVIL RIGHTS ACT OF 1964

Amidst this backdrop, the Civil Rights Act of 1964 was enacted. This legislation, grounded in the Fourteenth Amendment's guarantee that no state may deny any citizen equal protection under the law, was the precursor of the ADA. The Civil Rights Act prohibited discrimination based on race, color, sex, religion, or national origin in employment, public accommodations, and the provision of state and local government services. This landmark legislation created a framework to protect certain Americans from the biases of others and reinforced the guarantees and protections established for all Americans in the Declaration of Independence and the Constitution.

During this period, correctional institutions across the country also were experiencing struggles and changes. However, as somewhat closed societies, prisons and jails were a little behind the times and fought to prevent, rather than accept, those changes that they could not control.

ARCHITECTURAL BARRIERS ACT OF 1968

During this activist period, many subgroups in the U.S. population sought assistance from the government to ensure them full access to all that the United States had to offer; and the govern-

sions of the Architectural Barriers Act and expand the protections for inmates with disabilities beyond physical barriers. The act sought to prevent discrimination by federal agencies, grantees, and contractors against people with disabilities. For many correctional agencies that received federal grants or funds, either directly or through federal revenue-sharing programs in their state or local governments, the obligations of the ADA are nothing new. The Rehabilitation Act, on which the ADA is directly based, was far-reaching in its protections for the disabled. It required affirmative action programs to assist in the hiring, placement, and advancement of all federal employees with disabilities. The Architectural and Transportation Barrier Compliance Board developed design guidelines for construction and established new standards for buildings. This legislation also had a section that was very effective in that it required all governments or agencies receiving federal grants to ensure that all of their programs, activities, and services were accessible to people with disabilities.

TURBULENCE IN CORRECTIONS

While all of this legislative activity was going on, U.S. prisons and jails were also changing. The number of inmates who belonged to racial minorities was growing, as was the number of women inmates. Riots and disturbances were breaking out in institutions as inmates attempted to empower themselves and exert their newly enforceable rights. Inmate lawsuits were increasing. The courts, in a change of judicial philosophy, were beginning to look carefully at correctional practices and conditions. Increasingly, the courts were finding constitutional flaws to correct.

The demographics of institutional staff began to change. Correctional officials struggled to increase the proportion of staff from minority groups. There was real concern, as the women's rights movement took hold, whether women could, or should, work in men's facilities. Those early women officers, like many of the early non-Caucasian officers, had a difficult time being accepted by other staff, who were mostly

ment acted to satisfy that need. Using the framework of the Civil Rights Act of 1964 for a class of people not specifically included in the protections offered by that act, Congress passed the Architectural Barriers Act of 1968, which requires that all federal facilities and those facilities that received any federal funding be accessible and usable by people with physical disabilities. Again, correctional facilities did not respond positively to this legislation.

THE REHABILITATION ACT OF 1973

In 1973, Congress passed the Rehabilitation Act, which served to both implement the provi-

Caucasian men. Now, nearly 30 percent of officers are non-Caucasian, and 18 percent are women.[5] In time, the percentage of staff with disabilities may be equally high.

As groundbreaking and as far-reaching as the Architectural Barriers Act and the Rehabilitation Act were, they did not solve the problem of discrimination against the disabled. In the late 1980s, two reports issued by the National Council on the Handicapped showed that the disabled were still subjected to discrimination in the important areas of employment, transportation, and public accommodations. Without equal access to these critical functions of our society, the reports implied that the disabled were relegated to inferior status in economic, social, educational, and vocational matters. The members of the council, advocates for the people with disabilities, and members of Congress decided that new legislation was needed: a Civil Rights Act for the disabled.

ADA

The ADA, which President Bush signed on July 26, 1990, recognized that the 43 million Americans with one or more disabilities are a discrete and insular minority and have suffered discrimination, isolation, and political powerlessness. The ADA prohibits discrimination in employment, public services and transportation, public accommodations, and telecommunications services. It is clear what the intent of Congress was in drafting the ADA, as stated in the purpose of the act:

1. to provide a clear and comprehensive national mandate for the elimination of discrimination against individuals with disabilities;

2. to provide clear, strong, consistent, enforceable standards addressing discrimination against individuals with disabilities;

3. to ensure that the Federal Government plays a central role in enforcing the standards established in this Act on behalf of individuals with disabilities; and

4. to invoke the sweep of Congressional authority, including the power to enforce the fourteenth amendment and to regulate commerce, in order to address the major areas of discrimination faced day-to-day by people with disabilities.[6]

To accomplish this purpose, the ADA contains five titles. Titles I and II have a direct impact on the three distinct correctional groups covered by the act. Those groups are staff, inmates, and the public, including visitors (official and inmate visitors) and volunteers. Under the act, "disability," as it refers to an individual, means:

- a physical or mental impairment that substantially limits one or more of the major life activities of an individual;
- a record of such an impairment; or
- being regarded as having such an impairment.[7]

Major life activities include functions such as caring for oneself, performing manual tasks, walking, seeing, hearing, speaking, working, learning, or breathing. Physical impairments include any physiological disorder or condition, cosmetic disfigurement, or anatomical loss affecting one or more of the following body systems: neurological; musculoskeletal; special sense organs; respiratory, including speech organs; cardiovascular; reproductive; digestive; genitourinary; hemic and lymphatic; skin; and endocrine. Mental impairments include any mental or psychological disorder, such as mental retardation, organic brain syndrome, emotional or mental illness, and specific learning disabilities. Of specific importance to corrections, especially in current times, is that infection with the human immunodeficiency virus was included as a protected impairment, as was past alcoholism and drug addiction. Persons currently using illegal drugs are excluded from protection under ADA.

Title I of the ADA concerns discrimination in employment practices. It prohibits employers with 15 or more employees, which should include all but the smallest local jails (which would be covered by the Rehabilitation Act if they receive any federal funds), from discriminating against qualified individuals or workers who are or become disabled. This includes all aspects of employment, including application procedures; the hiring, advancement, or discharge of employees; employee compensation; job training; and other terms, conditions, and privileges of employment. But what constitutes a "qualified individual"? According to the text of the ADA, a "qualified individual with a disability" means an individual with a disability who, with or without reasonable accommodation, can perform the essential functions of the employment position that such individual holds or desires. Pursuant to this legislation, consideration shall be given to the employer's judgment as to what functions of a job are essential, and if the employer has prepared a written description, before advertising or interviewing applicants for the job, this description shall be considered a statement of the essential functions of the job.

This definition then begs another, that of "reasonable accommodation." Again, according to the text, a "reasonable accommodation" may include making existing facilities used by employees readily accessible to and usable by individuals with disabilities. It may also include job restructuring; part-time or modified work schedules; reassignment to a vacant position; acquisition or modification of equipment or devices; appropriate adjustment or modifications of examinations, training materials, or policies; the provision of qualified readers or interpreters; and other similar accommodations for individuals with disabilities.

As a practical matter then, correctional agencies should review each position. It is likely that job descriptions have already been developed

for these positions, because most corrections departments come under some type of civil service or other standard governmental employment structure, but if job descriptions have not been developed, they should be. These job descriptions, and the actual job performances, should be further analyzed to determine the essential, or fundamental, functions of each position. (Not every task in a job description or every task an employee actually does is a fundamental part of the job.) This job analysis must be carried out carefully and with an open mind.

This was clearly seen in the case of *Sharp v. Abate,* 887 F. Supp. 695 (S.D.N.Y. 1995). In this case, the New York City Department of Corrections wanted to fire a group of correctional officers that, because of unspecified physical and emotional disorders, could no longer have contact with inmates. The department argued, in response to the officers' ADA-based lawsuit, that because guarding inmates was an essential function of correctional officers, and to guard inmates, one had to have contact with them, these officers did not meet the definition of qualified individuals under the ADA. The U.S. District Court for the Southern District of New York, however, found otherwise. The court noted that the actual duties of many personnel did not involve guarding inmates: There were staff who worked in the personnel office, staff in the control center, cashiers, staff who covered the entrance and custody desks, as well as staff in the general office and other administrative divisions of the department. The court denied the department's motion to dismiss the suit.

Another common practice of correctional agencies that needs to be reviewed in light of Title I is the preemployment physical and psychological examination procedure. Because such procedures tend to screen out individuals with disabilities, or a class of individuals with disabilities—something the ADA seeks to prohibit—the act permits such preemployment examinations only in certain cases and under certain conditions. These conditions include that the standards the department sets for passing these examinations must be clearly associated with the essential job functions of the position. This is an issue that also came up not many years ago concerning the hiring of women, especially as officers. Requirements about minimum height and weight; running ability; lifting capacity; sight, hearing, and speech thresholds; emotional status; and so on must all relate to a job's essential duties.

The content of the preemployment examinations is important. So is the point in the application process at which they take place. According to the act, these examinations, which must be given to all applicants regardless of disability, must take place after an offer of employment has been made, not before, and prior to the starting date of employment. The offer of employment can, however, be made conditional upon the results of the examinations. Also required under the act is that all data resulting from such physical and psychological exams are to be kept in a separate and confidential medical file and used only in accordance with the requirements of the act.

It is clear that both the spirit and specific intent of Title I is to prevent employment-related discrimination against people with disabilities. But the act does not create an unqualified right to employment, nor does it require a correctional facility to have an affirmative action program to seek out and hire people with disabilities. If applicants or employees cannot perform the essential requirements of a position, with or without reasonable accommodation, they do not have to be hired or retained. Although correctional agencies should make appropriate efforts to accommodate people with disabilities, the ADA does not require an organization to experience "undue hardship" in those efforts. (Undue hardship is defined as an action requiring significant difficulty or expense.) When determining if an accommodation constitutes an undue hardship, the nature and cost of the action is considered in light of the financial resources of the specific agency involved, the number of employees, the effect on expenses and resources, and the impact of the accommodation on the operation of the facility.

Title II of the ADA prohibits discrimination against people with disabilities in public services. Specifically, the title states that no qualified individual with a disability shall, by reason of such disability, be excluded from participation in, or be denied the benefits of, the services, programs, or activities of a public entity or be subject to discrimination by any such entity. This title incorporates a different definition of "qualified individual." A qualified individual with a disability means an individual with a disability who—with or without reasonable modifications to rules, policies, or practices; the removal of architectural, communication, or transportation barriers; or the provision of auxiliary aids and services—meets the essential eligibility requirements for the receipt of services or the participation in programs or activities provided by a public entity.

Title II is applicable to inmates and visitors and involves physical plant conditions as well as access to programs and services. It is often the physical plant issues that most concern correctional administrators because they have the potential for upsetting the other major area over which administrators have little control, their budgets. Although the overall spending for corrections has been steadily increasing because of the dramatic rise in population and related new construction, it should come as no surprise that even these expanded budgets are not sufficient to provide all the facilities and services required to operate correctional institutions. The problem does not seem to be making new facility construction consistent with ADA requirements; it is far less expensive to build in compliance from the start, and new construction usually comes from a government's capital budget and not from a correctional facility's operating budget. Accommodation equipment and physical modifications and renovations to existing facilities, however, can result in tight operating budgets being stretched beyond limits.

To provide guidance to state and local governments concerning what standards must be met, there is the U.S. Architectural and Transportational Barriers Compliance Board. This board created the Americans with Disabilities Accessibility Guidelines (ADAAG). These guidelines apply to all facilities that were newly built or altered since January 26, 1992, providing the alterations required to make the facility fully accessible were not technically infeasible. In pre-1992 facilities that have not been altered or renovated, ADA mandates that the programs and services provided in the facility be made accessible and usable, to the fullest extent possible, by people with disabilities. The act does not require such changes if making programs and services accessible creates an undue burden, either administratively or financially.

CREATING ACCESS

What is involved in making reasonable accommodations to allow for access to facilities and participation in programs and services for inmates and public visitors? The ADAAG created the following requirements (among others):

- To be accessible to someone in a wheelchair, entrance doors must have at least 32-inch-wide clear travel space, open at least 90 degrees, and have a threshold of no more than one-half inch. Passageways must be at least 36 inches wide for a single wheelchair and at least 60 inches for two wheelchairs to pass each other.
- Water fountains must have spouts no higher than 36 inches, and the flow must be across the front of the fountain (there are high-low water fountains on the market that will accommodate both people who use wheelchairs and people who are standing).
- Bathrooms must have accessible toilets and sinks, which means the toilets should be 17 to 19 inches high to facilitate transfer from a wheelchair, have grab bars placed appropriately, and have sinks with rims no higher than 34 inches with at least 29 inches of clearance from the bottom of the sink to the floor.
- In general inmate housing areas, at least 3 percent of cells must be accessible to in-

mates with disabilities, and the cells should not all be in one special area. In special housing areas—such as for protective custody, disciplinary detention, administrative segregation, detoxification, or medical isolation—there must be an additional one accessible cell in each distinct area. Having accessible cells also requires accessible bathroom facilities and showers and accessible travel paths to the cells from all parts of the facility open to these inmates.
- Noncontact visiting areas must have at least 5 percent of the cubicles accessible to both the inmate and staff, with at least 27 to 29 inches of clear knee space, be at least 36 inches wide, and have a counter that extends at least 8 inches from the front partition. Seating in contact visiting areas should be between 17 and 19 inches high to make transfer from the wheelchair easy.

It is clear that there are very specific physical requirements for compliance, far more than this chapter can discuss. Before undertaking any design or renovation project, the corrections administrator should consult with a correctional architect and the government's public property or public works engineer for specific design assistance.

Although we often think of people with disabilities as being those in wheelchairs, one cannot forget that people with visual and hearing impairments are also people with disabilities. There are specific regulations to accommodate these people as well, including large-print signage, Braille instructions and materials, audible alarms for the visually impaired and visual alarms for the hearing impaired, sign language interpretation services, and telecommunications devices for the deaf.

In addition, consideration must be given to making inmate programs accessible. This is not expensive and can often be accomplished by moving the location of a program to an accessible place; providing sign language and Braille assistance; using computers (sometimes with speech synthesizer boards or large-type printers) to open educational programs to all inmates; and providing books on tape in the libraries. Because access to specific programs, such as education, addiction treatment, and vocational training can result in early discharge through good time programs, equal access for qualified inmates to programs becomes a protected liberty interest that is also governed by the ADA.

When ADA compliance is planned at the time that new facilities are constructed, the costs are affordable. In Philadelphia, for example, the estimated cost of making a new 2,000-bed facility fully compliant with ADA was about 8 percent of the total construction cost.[8] The cost of not complying, however, can be staggering.

CONCLUSION

It is clear that prisons and jails can expect to see an increase in their populations of people with disabilities. Because the ADA is an empowering act, institutions also may expect to see an increase in staff, visitors, and volunteers with disabilities as people with disabilities move to join the mainstream of American society. Correctional administrators need to take a proactive approach to accessibility. The ADA is the law, and corrections is a law enforcement function. It is the duty of government and law enforcement to adhere to both the letter and the spirit of the law and to set an example for others to follow. Staff, inmates, and visitors with disabilities will continue to push corrections in the current direction of normalization of its facilities. In much more than a monetary way, compliance with

ADA is the classic case of pay me now or pay me later.

Wardens walk a tightrope trying to balance the real need to control both the behavior and activities of the inmates, staff, and the public who enter the facilities and obey the laws, rules, standards, and procedures that govern their institutions. This balancing act must be accomplished with often less than adequate resources; it is very true that compliance with the law will have a significant impact on an agency's budget.

The ADA presents new challenges and issues for correctional administrators throughout the United States. It is the law. Equally important, making all prison and jail buildings, programs, and activities available to all is the right and fair thing to do.

NOTES

1. A. Appel, "Requirements and Rewards of the Americans with Disabilities Act," *Corrections Today* 57, no. 2 (1995): 84–86.
2. "Disabilities Act Covers State Prisoners, Court Rules," *The Washington Post*, 16 June, 1998.
3. "Disabilities Act Applies Inmates, High Court Says," *Los Angeles Times*, 16 June, 1998.
4. "Disability Act Applies to Prisons," *USA Today*, 16 June, 1998.
5. C. Camp and G. Camp, *The Corrections Yearbook 1995* (South Salem, NY: Criminal Justice Institute, Inc., 1995).
6. *Americans with Disabilities Act, U.S. Code*, Title 42, sec. 12101 et seq. (1990).
7. *Americans with Disabilities Act*, sec. 12101 et seq.
8. Philadelphia Prison System, Philadelphia, PA.

CHAPTER 49

Building New Correctional Facilities

Herbert Bernsen

"If you build it, they will come." This line from the movie *Field of Dreams* can certainly apply to the building of new criminal justice facilities. The construction of jails and prisons is big business. It may indeed be the largest project a county government will ever undertake. Architectural firms from across the country may be making bids. How does an administrator select the best architectural firm? Once the selection has been made, how should the progress of the construction be monitored? How much should correctional staff be involved in the project?

Finding the best architectural firm for a project is obviously very important, but administrators should not believe that the job is then over. Good architects will want the practitioner's input, but it is also critical that the practitioner stay closely involved throughout the project in order to provide input on a timely basis.

Sheriffs, wardens, and correctional directors know about operating jails and prisons but often have little knowledge about building such facilities. This chapter will attempt to guide administrators during architect selection and facility construction.

STANDARDS

The American Correctional Association (ACA) publishes standards for adult local detention facilities (jails) and for prisons. The standards cover a wide range of issues, including security, physical plant, training, recreation, and food service. The ACA Commission on Accreditation will accredit facilities that comply with these standards. Even though adhering to these standards is voluntary, it is advantageous to comply with as many standards as possible to increase the professionalism of staff and operations as well as to prevent litigation. Many states have mandatory jail and prison standards that may be equal to or even more stringent than ACA standards. Is the architect familiar with ACA standards and the standards of the state where construction will occur?

Another set of standards that an architect should be familiar with is the American Standards Testing Materials (ASTM) for detention equipment. There are currently standards published or under development for such materials as locks, glass, hollow metal, walls, sliding door devices, and electronic controls.

It is very important to check that all components of an opening in a security wall being designed or constructed will be secure. The ASTM standards establish a uniform measure of the performance characteristics of these detention components. This allows correctional staff to select materials (for doors, locks, glazing, etc.) that are appropriate for the security level of the wall. Materials that guarantee more security than is needed may be too costly. In regard to glazing, for example, it is very important to know what strength of glazing is necessary to prevent bullets or sledgehammers from penetrating high-security areas such as control centers. Con-

The rate at which prison and jail beds are being constructed in the 1990s is unparalleled in the history of corrections. In 1997, the total costs for prisons were expected to exceed $3.5 billion for the construction of nearly 80,000 new beds. For jails, there were approximately 9,500 beds under construction, at a cost of more than $113 million. Additionally, plans were in the works for an additional 18,000 beds (for which construction had not yet begun) at a cost of $803 million.

The number of prison beds constructed per year remained fairly constant during the 1990s (a high of nearly 125,000 in 1995 and a low of just over 79,000 in 1993), and the average cost remained fairly stable as well. In 1996, on average it cost $80,500 to construct a maximum security bed, and $31,000 for a minimum security bed.

Among jails, the average cost declined substantially between 1990 and 1996 for both new construction and renovation. The average cost per bed for jail system new construction declined from $50,300 in 1990 to $40,600 in 1996, and renovation costs decreased from $30,000 to $22,000.

Source: Data from C. Camp and G. Camp, *Corrections Yearbook 1997,* pp. 66–67, 216–217, © 1997, Criminal Justice Institute, Inc.

AMERICANS WITH DISABILITIES ACT COMPLIANCE

The construction of criminal justice facilities must be in compliance with the American with Disabilities Act (ADA). This will require a certain number of cells for people with disabilities, for example. It will also require program areas to accommodate inmates with disabilities. Even though costs will be added to the project, keep in mind that the ADA provides cost savings as well. If wheelchair accessibility enables an inmate to be incarcerated instead of hospitalized, the costs of hospital charges and an added corrections officer post can be saved. Is the architect knowledgeable about these potential cost savings?

And what about staffing implications? It is important that the owner—the administrator—defines which areas may be staffed by people with disabilities. The architect then needs to explain whether the design can accommodate workers with disabilities.

Design has important implications. For example, staff with disabilities may be able to work in the control center even though it may not be feasible for them to work in a two-level inmate living area.

ARCHITECTS REMAINING ON THE PROJECT

Will the key members of the architectural firm remain on the project until it is finished? This helps maintain continuity and ensure quality. It should be guaranteed in the initial contract between the owner and architectural firm. It is also important to resolve the issue of whether an architect will be on-site during the construction of the project. If an architect were on-site daily, would there be an added cost? This issue should also be clarified up front. An architect on-site daily during construction can be helpful, but this architect needs to be empowered to make decisions for the design team.

versely, those funding the project do not want to pay for the highest-rated secure glazing in nonperimeter areas. It is, therefore, better to work with an architect who is familiar with ASTM standards.

EXPERIENCE

Naturally, it would seem highly desirable for the architect to have had experience in building prisons and jails. But it is important to determine, for example, the architects' actual involvement in past projects. A past project may seem quite similar to the project under design, but the architect may have participated in only an earlier project's master plan, rather than completing the actual design.

An administrator should ask for a list of references from the architect's past projects and contact those references for their comments. Has the architect been involved in projects that have been completed both on time and within budget? If the site for the facility has not yet been selected, does the architect have experience in site selection and site development? What about the maintenance of the building? How are the architectural firm's prior projects holding up? Administrators might contact the person(s) responsible for maintaining the buildings the architect has previously designed.

Has the architect had experience in working with a facilities management team, sometimes referred to as a transition team? If a project is fortunate to have a transition team consisting of dedicated staff responsible for the transition to a new facility, it is critical that they work closely with the architects as well as the construction team. Does the architect welcome this opportunity and see it as beneficial? If not, it could spell problems throughout the project.

The opportunity to visit other similar projects can also prove worthwhile. Proposed innovative designs can be viewed at other locations in which they have been implemented. Inmate visiting venues and procedures can be compared, and designs for food service delivery can be examined. Much can be learned from visiting these sites and learning from other criminal justice professionals. It is great when architects encourage these opportunities to learn from similar projects.

FAST TRACK IMPLICATIONS

Due to budget and time constraints, it is often desirable to build a jail or prison on a "fast track" basis. The faster the facility is built, the sooner construction companies can move on to additional projects. These cost savings can be passed on to the owner.

Jails and prisons are often being built to relieve overcrowded conditions. The facility may also be under a court-ordered consent decree to relieve overcrowding. The faster the facility is built, the sooner the overcrowding and unsafe conditions can be alleviated and the risks of further litigation reduced.

In order to construct a facility quickly, architectural teams must be able to work on various aspects (e.g., footings, walls, building skin) of the building at the same time. Architectural firms must be able to provide more staff to handle all these different aspects simultaneously. Because there are definite advantages for the owner if fast tracking is used, the architectural firm should explain its experience and success in using a fast track method.

There are also drawbacks to fast tracking. If the architect is aware of the potential disadvantages, then the pitfalls can more likely be avoided. The accuracy of the construction documents is very important. Mistakes in the first phases of construction turn into expensive change orders in later phases. The phases of construction must be carefully defined and coordinated in order to avoid the inevitable finger pointing if one contractor completes what another contractor started.

INNOVATIVE DESIGNS AND USE OF MATERIALS

Each criminal justice facility has its own set of challenges. Is the site rural or urban? Will the building be high-rise or low-rise? What security level is needed? How will the facility be operated? Is direct supervision being considered? Will there be a connection to the courts by tunnel or sky bridge? Is the community supportive of the building? What about the durability and availability of the materials being proposed? Are the materials nonproprietary? Governmental agencies require that materials be bid. Nonproprietary materials are needed so that single-source providers are not necessary.

How these questions are resolved may hinge on the architect's knowledge of innovative approaches to design and use of materials. If there is local opposition to the building site, will the principals of the architectural firm join the administrator in making professional, persuasive presentations regarding the design to the community? If a correctional jurisdiction is building a high-rise jail in the middle of a city next to a high-rise office building, is the architect offering any innovative approaches to resolve the sight lines in and out of the building and make the design compatible with its urban surroundings?

JOINT VENTURE

Often a local architectural firm will join with a national firm to bid on a project. This can certainly be advantageous if the national firm has more experience in building criminal justice facilities. The local architect can contribute knowledge about working in the community with the local contractors.

For joint ventures to work, however, roles need to be defined so that the two firms complement each other. Coordination of different disciplines such as mechanical and structural engineering is key. If the two firms have worked successfully together in the past, that is a good sign.

LITIGATION HISTORY AND OUTCOMES

Owners should ask the architects to provide information about any current or past litigation involving their firm's criminal justice projects. It is important to determine if the litigation has resulted from performance by only the architec-

tural firm or is directed at the entire team, including construction managers and owners, for example. If the architectural firm has a history of frequent litigation involving criminal justice projects, even if the litigation does involve the entire team, there are likely to be problems with the methods of operation. The architect also should furnish a history of litigation involving any consulting firms the architect intends to use on the project. If the litigation is significant, it may call into question not only the consulting firm's competence but also its ability to provide critical information in a timely fashion.

PARTNERING

Partnering, a concept becoming prevalent in large-scale building projects, involves a commitment from all the team members (including construction managers, architects, subcontractors, and owners) to work effectively together to achieve a common goal. Partnering often involves preconstruction meetings of all the team members with a facilitator to jointly establish mission statements and, most important, to begin to form trusting relationships.

The owner will ultimately benefit if all the team members on the project are dedicated to working out problems for the benefit of all. There will be problems, of course, on every project. It is always easy to blame the other guy. If trusting relationships exist, team members are apt to work toward win–win solutions rather than resorting to frequent disputes, delays, and possible litigation.

Is the architect aware of the partnering concept? Would the chosen firm be a willing and effective participant in partnering? These are important questions if the owner decides to use partnering in the construction project.

QUALITY CONTROL

What internal mechanisms does the architectural firm employ to ensure quality control? Are there procedures, for example, to carefully scrutinize all drawings or construction documents before they are sent out? If the builders cannot read the documents or if serious flaws exist, it can mean costly delays and possible litigation. What methods will the architect use to solicit information from the owner? Communication is key. The architect needs to spend sufficient time with the owner to obtain not only thorough information regarding the design and features of the building but also feedback. Architects always should verify that they have accurately recorded the information.

What will be the nature and type of progress reports, and how frequently will they be issued? Misinformation can cripple a project. An engineer can prepare a meticulous fire protection plan, but if the fire marshall does not approve it, significant cost overruns and delays could occur as the plan is revised and submitted again.

USE OF CONSULTANTS

It is not uncommon for architectural firms to use consultants for various aspects of a project, such as operational programming and staffing, food service, court services, electronic security, and detention equipment. Owners should not assume that the experience of an architectural firm is based solely on the experience of its in-house staff.

It is important to know up front if the architect plans to use consultants and also to know specifically what their involvement will be. If a consultant will handle programming, for example, will he or she be responsible for actually writing the operational procedures, with the correctional staff's assistance, or will the consultant review the procedures that the staff prepares? Time is money, so the cost of those two options is likely to be considerably different. The owner needs to be aware of these issues to plan resource allocations and control costs.

Coordination is also key. Someone in the architectural firm needs to integrate and coordinate the work of all the consultants on the project. It is also important to commit the key

personnel of the consulting firm to remain with the project until completion.

VALUE ENGINEERING

Value engineering, as the term might imply, does not involve the quality of the engineering or other work on the project. It is a term used to describe a cooperative team effort between the owner, architects, and construction managers or contractors to discover the most cost-effective methods to build a facility. This may involve using different building materials, altering designs, revising construction schedules, or even eliminating certain aspects of the project that seem impractical or too costly. Reducing costs is often the focus, but it should not be the only consideration. Value engineering must also take into account the life-cycle costs. A certain material or piece of equipment may be more expensive up front but may more than pay for itself over the life of the building. Value engineering for the new St. Louis County Justice Center in Missouri, for example, included the decision to use more expensive cooling towers because money would be saved in the long run. Value engineering can be an important tool for keeping a project within budget. An architect should be familiar with value engineering and consider it a valuable tool.

CONCLUSION

These are the basic principles for owners to keep in mind when selecting and working with architects.

1. Owners should make the commitment to be an integral part of the planning team and not let the architect build the facility without the owner's input.
2. Owners should realize the importance of communication and building trusting relationships.
3. Owners should scrutinize the references and experience of the architectural firm,

talking to former clients and reviewing budgets, scheduling, and innovations.

4. Owners should use existing industry and professional standards and evaluate the effectiveness of the architectural firm's internal quality control procedures.

5. Owners should learn from other jurisdictions that have built similar facilities and also from other agencies such as the National Institute of Corrections, which conducts an excellent program entitled Planning of New Institutions.

By following these basic guidelines, owners will find themselves more confident about selecting architects and developing new correctional facilities.

SUGGESTED READINGS

American Correctional Association. 1991. *Standards for adult local detention facilities.* 3d ed. Lanham, MD.

American Correctional Association. 1998. *1998 standards supplement.* Lanham, MD.

American Standards Testing Materials. *American standards testing materials committee F-33 on detention and correctional facilities.* West Conshohocken, PA.

Bernsen, H., and G. Gauger. "ADA's impact, requirements for cell and housing design." *Corrections Today* 57, no. 2: 96–102.

National Institute of Corrections. *Planning of new institutions phase II.* Longmont, CO.

"A partnering primer: How it works, why it works and how to put it to work for you." 1993. *The Corporation Management Journal,* July.

Podular. 1993. *Direct supervision jails information packet.* Longmont, CO: National Institute of Corrections.

PART X

Emergency Preparedness

Aggressive and violent behavior seems to touch every community. Violent criminals are generally placed in penal institutions and often continue their violent behavior. Accordingly, the threat of violence in the prison and jail setting undergirds all operations, procedures, and programs. All policy in a secure correctional facility is designed around the primary need to account for and tightly regulate inmate actions. While most institutions also have an important emphasis on other programs, staff must always be prepared to deal with inmate rebellion. Inmate unrest, physical violence against staff or inmates, and riotous behavior are signs that institutions have failed to control prisoners.

The relaxed routine of any correctional facility can, over time, deteriorate because of many factors. First and foremost, prisons hold a preponderance of violent offenders at the higher security levels where violence is much more likely to occur. Inmates who have always solved their frustrations, anger, disputes, or other problems in the free community in a physical manner will often resort to physical aggressiveness when confined. Stress in a prison or jail is traditionally caused by overcrowding, poor-quality food, perceived injustice, racial tension, or continued staff inattention to detail. When inmates have a cause that unites them, negative behavior often is the result. There are no preventative measures that can consistently guaran-

tee a well-mannered, calm prison community. It therefore becomes imperative that institution administrators are well prepared for any unexpected unrest.

It must also be remembered that many prisoners receive positive reinforcement for their violent behavior. Other inmates respect them. In institutional language, it is good to be viewed as a "stand-up" convict.

Inmate violence against other inmates is expected in even the most secure prison facilities. Aggressive behavior toward staff members is much less expected and, while not uncommon, usually results from isolated problems. Deviant group rebellion is even further from the norm and represents a serious breakdown of control. All three categories of institutional violence are threatening to staff and inmates alike. Staff spend many hours preparing for the calculated or immediate use of force to contain contentious prisoners.

To effectively manage a correctional institution, using force is necessary. Staff are carefully trained to use physical force only when necessary; most jurisdictions believe that an officer's verbal communication skills are often his or her best defense. Physical force is permitted to defend oneself or to prevent harm to property or the well-being of others. The use of lethal force is regulated by an even higher standard and requires a belief that the situation presents imminent danger to the lives of staff or inmates. Judgments about when to use force and how much force to use are very important for correctional personnel to be able to make.

Part X reviews the causes of riots and disturbances, delineates how wardens should prepare for violent situations, and provides insight into and alternatives to the use of force.

LEARNING OBJECTIVES

After studying this section, you should be able to answer the following questions:

1. Why do institutional staff seem to expect violence in the correctional setting?
2. What are several significant causes of institutional unrest?
3. What are the most important things to be accomplished in training prison or jail staff to respond to institutional violence?
4. What are the stages of disturbance management?
5. Why are staff or inmate hostage situations dealt with in a manner different from disturbances that do not involve hostages?
6. What types of power do correctional staff exercise?
7. What civil liability is associated with the use of nonlethal force?

DISCUSSION/REVIEW QUESTIONS

1. Is it possible to curtail violent behavior in the prison or jail setting?
2. What is more threatening to the institution culture—individual violence or collective violence? Is one easier to prevent than the other?
3. What are common signs of tension in the institutional setting?
4. Why are planning and training so critical to emergency response in a prison or jail?
5. Does practicing emergency response tactics lead to tension and unrest in an institution?
6. In a hostage situation, when does negotiation fail?
7. Should a commissioner or warden be directly involved with inmates during a hostage negotiation?
8. What is nonlethal force? What are three examples of nonlethal force?

CHAPTER 50

Causes of Institutional Unrest

John J. Armstrong

Prison riots have existed in the United States since before the Revolutionary War. Their history extends from the first prison riot in 1774 at Newgate Prison in Simsbury, CT, to recent turbulence: Attica, NY (1971); Santa Fe, NM (1980); Atlanta, GA, and Oakdale, LA (1989); and Lucasville, OH (1993). If correctional professionals fail to recognize, understand, and control the causes of unrest, unrest will remain a hallmark of correctional administration.

Author Charles Logan suggests that the mission of a prison is to "keep prisoners in, keep them safe, keep them in line, keep them healthy, and keep them busy—and to do it with fairness, without undue suffering, and as efficiently as possible."[1](p.10) Logan presents eight performance dimensions in which a correctional administrator can assess a facility's performance: security, safety, order, care, activity, justice, conditions, and management (see Exhibit 50–1).

CAUSES OF UNREST

The sources of unrest are as varied as the correctional facilities that have experienced violence. Researchers suggest causes ranging from crowding, insufficient funding, gang activity, and racial and cultural conflict, to changes in policy, poor management practices, insufficient staff training, inadequate facility security, and poor living conditions.

Despite the complexity and diversity of disturbances, the American Correctional Association has narrowed the causes of prison unrest into three general categories: inmates, conditions of confinement, and correctional management. Unrest often involves a failure in more than one category.

Inmates

Felons incarcerated as a consequence of a lack of self-control present special challenges. These men and women often are angry and antisocial and seek immediate gratification when faced with a problem.

Inmate-created unrest does not always spring from a sudden or specific cause. An unhealthy facility climate—born in inmates' perceptions of conditions and festering over time—frequently sparks unrest. Effective staff recognize subtle verbal and nonverbal changes in inmate behavior. If they do not, investigation and control may become after-disturbance efforts.

The presence and influence of gangs also contribute to inmate-created unrest. Gang activity in a prison focuses on dominance and turf control, often along racial or geographic lines. Gang rivalries spawn a climate of tension, violence, and coercion. New gang members will be recruited by force. Nonaligned inmates often arm themselves for protection against gang activities.

Staff control this threat to the well-being of a facility by installing mechanisms to gather intelligence and to identify gang members and leaders. These mechanisms are reviewed regularly to

Exhibit 50–1   Eight Dimensions of Prison Performance Measures

SECURITY
Security procedures
Drug use
Significant incidents
Community exposure
Freedom of movement
Staffing adequacy

SAFETY
Safety of inmates
Safety of staff
Dangerousness of inmates
Safety of environment
Staffing adequacy

ORDER
Inmate misconduct
Perceived control
Strictness of enforcement

CARE
Stress and illness
Health care delivered
Dental care
Counseling
Staffing for programs and services

ACTIVITY
Involvement in and evaluation of:
    work and industry
    education and training
    recreation
    religious services

JUSTICE
Staff fairness
Limited use of force
Grievances, number and type
The grievance process
The discipline process
Legal resources and access
Justice delays

CONDITIONS
Space in living areas
Social density and privacy
Internal freedom of movement
Facilities and maintenance
Sanitation
Noise
Food
Commissary
Visitation
Community access

MANAGEMENT
Job satisfaction
Stress and burn-out
Staff turnover
Staff and management relations
Staff experience
Education
Training
Salary and overtime
Staffing efficiency

Source: Reprinted with permission from Charles A. Logan, "Criminal Justice Performance Measures for Prisons," *Performance Measures for the Criminal Justice System,* p. 34, 1993, Bureau of Justice Statistics.

check that they are performing well and incorporate due process protections. Staff recognize gang-affiliated inmates by their tattoos, association with other known members, personal property, involvement in group activity of a negative nature (assaults, etc.), and by their own admission.

Unrest also results when predators are not separated from particularly vulnerable inmates, such as those who are very young or very old, are weak, or have retardation or disabilities. An effective inmate classification system, in addition to staff who promptly recognize such problems and respond appropriately, undermines this type of threat to the climate.

Conditions of Confinement

Some roots of unrest, which appear inmate created, instead grow in the conditions of confinement. These roots of unrest are related to sanitation, food, idleness, inadequate facility maintenance, cell space, access to medical or mental health care, work, school or addiction programs, or innumerable other service delivery areas.

Crowding has been the most explosive correctional condition in the past decade. Unprecedented prison population growth has plagued jurisdictions throughout the country at a time when public sector funding has slumped as a social priority.

Population growth affects everyone—staff, inmates, and the public. Overcrowding reduces the quality of life in a facility, burdens its physical plant, and increases staff stress. These environmental, physical, and social pressures serve as a seedbed for destructive perceptions that lead to a sense of hopelessness in inmates and staff alike.

Correctional Management

Correctional managers promulgate policies and procedures based on established correctional standards and continually review them against set performance measures. Effective management practices lead to staff success, high employee retention rates, and little or no unrest.

Departmental and facility policy and procedure manuals and post orders supply staff with the organization's mission, values, and expectations; the basis of authority; and an outline of each position's responsibilities. Consistent policies that govern inmate conduct and accountability are the foundation of facility security, order, and safety. In a secure facility, staff and inmates perceive consistency, fairness, and justice as uniform standards applied indiscriminately.

To be effective, disciplinary, grievance, and classification appeal processes must be easily understood by inmates and supported by staff. Appeal process outcomes, fair and uniform in both perception and reality, avoid unrest. By investigating and reviewing incidents, an administrator can evaluate circumstances leading to unrest. The process uncovers predictors of unrest and forms a blueprint for remedial action.

Almost every major prison riot in recent history involved a security breach. To maintain facility security, staff must be able to rigidly control all operational elements.

A unit's operations manual outlines all essential plans, systems, and post orders; proper reporting procedures; practices for issuing and controlling keys, tools, and weapons; techniques for conducting routine and random searches for contraband; methods for conducting urinalysis, inspections, tours, and visiting; and systems for maintaining inmate documentation. Managers also carefully establish the framework in which they communicate with each other, with their subordinates, and with the news media. A clear chain of command with clean lines of authority reduces inmate unrest resulting from mismanaged information or indecisiveness. Established channels of communication to staff and inmates eliminate confusion, misinformation, and destructive rumors.

For example, changes in operating policies disrupt highly structured prison routines and the expectations of inmates and staff. The prudent distribution of information, accompanied by explanation when necessary, lightens the impact of the message. Nevertheless, change—whether in policy, privileges, or living conditions—always heightens tension in a prison. Consequently, timing becomes a paramount concern when implementing change.

Accessible and responsive administrators and staff lead inmates to feel free to communicate and to know that they will receive appropriate and timely feedback. Reasonable questions and concerns are met with reasonable responses.

Staff effectively counter externally driven causes of inmate unrest, such as issues reported in the media, with open and honest communication. Managers also counter externally driven causes by explaining to reporters, legislators, and governmental officials the impact of their messages on corrections. For example, reports of "get tough on crime" proposals often are interpreted by staff and inmates as fact, even before legislation has been introduced.

Managers understand that agency and facility stability results from recruiting quality applicants and maintaining high-quality preservice and inservice training programs. The challenges facing modern corrections also require training in cultural sensitivity.

A social dynamic commonly found in American prisons is staff from predominantly suburban or rural areas supervising urban inmates. Inevitably, most inmates are from major metropolitan areas, and most prisons are located in isolated areas. It is difficult to develop open communication between staff and inmates from such diverse backgrounds.

Staff must be taught to view all offenders the same way, whether the offenders are murderers or drug users, rapists or drunken drivers, black, white, Hispanic, Native American, or Asian. Fairness is the key. Instances of perceived disrespect or injustice involving staff-driven or inmate-driven cultural or racial stereotypes often evolve into a condition resembling a tinderbox waiting for a spark.

ACTIVELY GAUGING THE CLIMATE

Staff in direct contact with offenders are a facility's eyes and ears, its primary resource for identifying unrest indicators. Their evaluation of the inmate population is dynamic and continual. Facility security depends on how effectively these professionals deal with offenders and how the professionals use their training and interpersonal skills to evaluate the institution's climate.

Among all correctional professionals, the correctional officers have the most daily interaction with the largest number of inmates. When the health, safety, and welfare of inmates are preserved, when their lifestyles of criminality are altered, chances are the correctional workers most responsible are not the psychiatrists or social workers, but skilled and concerned correctional officers.

Dedicated and vigilant correctional professionals are the linchpin in the effort to achieve institutional safety and security. Author Richard Keikbusch noted that effective officers possess three indispensable traits: the ability to control, compassion, and unquestionable integrity.[2]

Facility tours are another barometer of facility climate. All employees—including medical and program staff and administrators—conduct area inspections and evaluate trends in incident and disciplinary reports, offender grievances, confiscated contraband, recreational grouping, and commissary activity.

Effective management depends on rumor control, and rumor control depends on rumor identification. Responsive line staff monitor rumors. Disregarding rumors places a prison climate at risk. Most rumors start with a grain of truth; otherwise, they would not be transmitted. Some, however, are propelled by personal issues.

After filtering such information, staff must be empowered to investigate and diffuse a rumor or a consequent condition. (Such empowerment should be tempered by the observance of communication priorities and the chain of command.)

WALKING THE WALK

Managers frequently walk through a facility, not just to be seen, but also to observe, listen, respond, and evaluate. Meeting the correctional mission requires MBWA—management by walking around: "walkin' the walk" and paying attention, interacting with staff and inmates, identifying and addressing problems.

An unannounced or random walk often helps an administrator check on Logan's eight dimensions of performance. All management staff are encouraged to do this. Leadership style and organizational values and expectations are emulated when they are regularly demonstrated by senior management officials; and prison wardens must set the example by daily visits throughout the facility.

The agency commissioner and the facility warden, who hold the most visible positions in corrections, determine whether a department is successful. They ensure public protection; staff safety; and the maintenance of a secure, safe, and humane facility in a climate promoting high standards of professionalism, respect, integrity, dignity, and excellence.

INTERPRETING THE INDICATORS AND ACHIEVING PERFORMANCE

Indicators of unrest and prison performance measures appear dissimilar (see Exhibit 50–2). Yet one set of indicators cannot be assessed without considering the other, and the assessment is crucial to the effective and active management of a prison climate; all such data are linked and, together, provide a valid overview of the insitutional environment.

The mission statement is the foundation for all policy development and decision making. It serves as the benchmark for all operations, as the prime reference and resource for agency and facility administrative directives. When staff apply policies, procedures, and support structures to climate-related problems, they balance their actions against the agency standards and values established in the mission statement.

PREVENTION IS THE KEY

Prevention is an everyday event in a prison—on every shift for every employee. An agency attuned to detecting problems can identify a problem in its early stages and resolve it before it becomes a crisis.

Exhibit 50–2 Predictors of Riots and Disturbances

Separation of inmates by racial or ethnic groups

Purchases of food items at inmate canteens

Transfer requests

Staff requests for sick leave

Inmates gathering with point people facing away from the group

Increase in disciplinary cases

Increase in voluntary lockups

Inmate–employee confrontations

Direct and indirect inmate intimidation of officers

Threats against officers

Inmate sick calls

Inmate violence against other inmates

Increase in number of weapons found in shakedowns

Harsh stares from inmates

Drop in attendance at movies or other popular functions

Unusual and/or subdued actions by inmate groups

Appearance of inflammatory and rebellious materials

Warnings to "friendly" officers to take sick leave or vacation

Employee demands for safety

Staff resignations

Letters and/or phone calls from concerned inmate families demanding protection for inmates

Unusual number of telephone inquiries about facility conditions

Outside agitation by lawyers or activists

Increase in complaints and grievances

Source: Reprinted with permission from *Preventing and Managing Riots & Disturbances,* p. 131, © 1996, American Correctional Association, Lanham, Maryland.

Forestalling unrest requires active monitoring of the prison environment, detection of unrest predictors, investigation of problems, and quick and appropriate resolution. A correctional professional would rather prevent unrest than manage a disturbance, echoing the concept proposed a century ago by American theologian Tryon Edwards: "Preventatives of evil are far better than remedies, cheaper and easier of application, and surer of result."[3(p.516)]

NOTES

1. C. Logan, "Criminal Justice Performance Measures for Prisons," in *Performance Measures for the Criminal Justice System*, ed. J. DiIulio (Washington, DC: U.S. Bureau of Justice Statistics, 1993), 10–57.

2. R. Keikbusch, "Correctional Officer Excellence: What Is It?" *Corrections Managers' Report* 2, no. 5 (1997): 6–14.

3. T. Edwards, *The New Dictionary of Thoughts* (New York: StanBook Inc./Doubleday, 1974), 516.

CHAPTER 51

Preparing for Chaos: Emergency Management

Earnest A. Stepp

Prison and jail riots are the nightmares of institution administrators. Concerns about inmates escaping or taking control of a portion of a penal facility underlie all security operations of correctional institutions. Disturbances are considered a failure of correctional administrators; and are usually isolated events that do not often occur. Yet, a proactive prison warden or superintendent must spend scarce time and human resources to be adequately prepared for this type of failure.

An institution disturbance can be caused by various problems, some of which may be totally outside the control of the prison or jail staff. An emergency situation can occur in an isolated portion of the institution or throughout the facility. Disturbances can range from a passive food or work strike all the way to a massive riot in which prisoners engage in random destruction of property and violent acts against people. Emergencies can spring from a spontaneous reaction of one inmate to a staff member or develop from a highly planned and organized effort by inmates and community supporters outside the prison.

To deal with penal emergencies, there must be an effective and proactive staff that is appropriately aware of and sensitive to the inmate population. The secret of success is preventing critical incidents. Setting that as the goal, one must remember that even the most effective staff cannot always avoid crises. Inmates will always be inmates; they do not want to be where they are.

Given this environment, the staff leaders of an institution must be prepared to respond swiftly and effectively to an inmate-generated crisis. Emergency planning is crucial to successful management of any disturbance, and excellence in prison and jail management mandates that staff be fully prepared for inmate disturbances.

RESPONSE TEAMS

Before correctional administrators can begin to plan for emergencies within their facilities, it is critical that decisions be made regarding the resources that will be dedicated to crisis response. There are several levels of emergency response that correctional institutions can develop: traditional, unarmed disturbance control teams (DCTs), less than lethal intervention options (chemical agents and similar technologies), and the use of deadly force. For the different levels of response, there should be different teams with specific training.

Traditional DCTs

The first level of response is the traditional DCT. DCTs are composed of staff who are usually from all departments or job specialties

Opinions expressed in this chapter are those of the author and do not necessarily represent the opinions of the Federal Bureau of Prisons or the U.S. Department of Justice.

within an institution. The DCTs train in riot control formations; use of defensive equipment such as batons, stun guns, and chemical agents; and control and containment of both large and small groups of inmate rioters. Training for a DCT must be formal and include minimum proficiency standards. Certification in these minimum standards is a must; these standards should include knowledge of agency policy and the use of the equipment mentioned above. DCT members must be knowledgeable about overall institution emergency plans.

Armed DCTs

While traditional DCTs should be viewed as the primary emergency response team for incidents that require containment and control, a second level of response should provide institution managers with an option for dealing with more difficult scenarios. This escalation of managed response involves a specially trained team that can respond with deadly force when necessary. The use of an armed DCT may be necessary if the emergency situation escalates to the point where staff or inmate lives are in imminent danger. When sending an armed DCT into a situation, management accepts that lethal force may be used.

Tactical Teams

Tactical teams are the most highly trained and skilled emergency response staff. These teams—similar to traditional special weapons and tactics, found in most police departments—are usually known as correctional emergency response teams or special operations response teams. Tactical teams must be trained in advanced skills such as barricade breaching, hostage rescue, and precision marksmanship with pistols, rifles, and assault rifles.

Regardless of how teams are selected, all teams have certain qualities that must be the same. All must be composed of volunteers, receive special training in specific skills, and be highly trained in departmental policy regarding

the appropriate use of force techniques. Staff selected for emergency squads should be required to pass physical, academic, and psychological screening.

PREPARATION AND PLANNING

There are three critical stages of disturbance management (see Exhibit 51–1). The first stage is preparation and planning. Before anything happens, managers must prepare staff to respond to any number of emergencies. The second stage is active management of the disturbance or incident, or implementation of emergency plans. The third stage involves recovery from a serious incident. By thoroughly preparing and planning for disturbance management (stage one), administrators ensure that stages two and three will go more smoothly.

The first step in preparing an effective emergency response for a correctional setting is establishing a system of emergency response that includes DCTs, armed DCTs, and tactical teams. Experts in areas such as hostage negotiation and crisis management command are very important. It is especially important to understand the concept of an emergency response system. Each element of the response system is dependent on the others and functions best when used in conjunction with the others. An effective training program should emphasize that each element is an integral part of a system approach. Each crisis situation will be unique, and all emergency plans must allow enough flexibility to permit a variety of responses.

Exhibit 51–1 Three Stages of Disturbance Management

1. Planning and training (before the event)
2. Active management of the disturbance (during the event)
3. Aftermath and recovery (after the event)

Contingency plans should define the responsibility of staff from various departments in an emergency. Plans must be developed through cooperative means, using the collective experience of all staff. If plans are written by only "security" staff, they may make assumptions about duties of staff from other departments that turn out to be unrealistic when tested, or worse, when needed during an actual incident. Plans should be developed by "think tank," or committee. In this way, everyone agrees ahead of time, and planning assumptions are realistic.

There are general elements that should be clearly covered in all emergency plans.

- Communication of the alarm. Once an emergency situation is identified, all prison and jail staff must be trained on how to notify personnel of the situation.
- Securing the scene. In order to prevent the situation from escalating, it is critical to contain the crisis by locking the area or building.
- Command. All plans should specify who is responsible for an immediate emergency response before senior staff members arrive.
- Notification and call-back procedures. Emergency situations must be swiftly and effectively communicated to the institution's chief executive officer. A process for the timely and urgent recall of staff to the institution should be in place.
- Establishment of a command center. The location of a command center must be clearly established. It should be in a secure portion of the facility, and it should be appropriately equipped.
- Assessment of the situation. It is important to have intelligence that is accurate and current. Information must flow to the command center in a timely manner.
- Preparing emergency teams. Dress out and brief the institution emergency squads so they are ready for action.
- Notify external law enforcement and request assistance if necessary.

- Prepare options for emergency resolution. Consider all available resources and review all contingencies. Appropriate equipment should be prepared and placed with emergency teams.

As indicated in the list above, most correctional institutions will require assistance from outside law enforcement sources during very difficult situations, especially those that last several days. Managers must ensure that institution contingency plans include cooperative contingency plans with outside agencies. These plans may be as simple as assistance with traffic control and institution access, or as complicated as using outside tactical resources in a hostage rescue attempt. Regardless of the level of assistance, agreeing upon terms and limits of assistance in advance reduces confusion and delays. The middle of a major disturbance or incident is not the time to hold philosophical debates about what should be done or who has the expertise or resources to accomplish a given goal.

Cooperative contingency plans should be signed by the outside agency representative and the institution's warden. Only when this approach is taken is role definition achieved. Once these plans are signed and practiced, an institution liaison officer should be assigned to coordinate the combined effort.

An integral part of emergency response that is sometimes overlooked is the command center. When this element of emergency management is taken for granted, problems occur at the onset and are resolved only over time. A preestablished command center structure with a clearly defined chain of command (spelled out in contingency plans) is vital. Staff who are properly trained in their role, and what each particular command center job entails, will limit the amount of time spent recovering from confusion. In the beginning of any incident, there will be mistakes. The beginning is the most critical time, because there is often an early window of opportunity to resolve the incident. An effective, well-rehearsed plan limits confusion over decision making, emergency management goals, and

Exhibit 51–2   Important Aspects of Emergency Planning

- Plan for communication at all levels, including sharing intelligence.
- Ensure use-of-force guidelines are clearly defined.
- Plan for the worst-case scenario.
- Know what each emergency response team can do well—senior staff must monitor training routinely.

Exhibit 51–3   Training Staff for Decision Making during a Crisis

- Managers should establish clearly defined objectives ahead of time.
- Managers should develop a crisis management plan—decisions down the road need to conform to the plan to ensure an acceptable solution.
- Staff should not make decisions in a vacuum but include others in the process.
- Staff should weigh all decisions against the preestablished plan.
  - Is the contemplated action really necessary?
  - Is the risk necessary and warranted?
  - Is the action legal and ethical?

the agency's philosophy of crisis management. Exhibit 51–2 lists important aspects of emergency planning.

Training and Mock Exercises

The preparation and planning stage also includes training, which must include all key staff. Not all staff will be available and respond during an emergency. Managers must ensure that cross-training of department heads includes assistant department heads and first-level supervisors. Cross-training can affect the overall outcome of any incident, particularly in the command center area. Staff will be much more effective and valuable if they can perform multiple and varied roles during a crisis.

For a plan to succeed, all staff must be prepared to respond to an emergency situation. Managers must evaluate plans and analyze mock emergencies, determining what plan they want to test and how much of that plan they want to evaluate. Many times, an emergency plan test can be accomplished with little or no disruption of normal institution operations. Major exercises that involve all staff and outside agencies probably should be conducted at least annually. Smaller, internal training exercises for institution staff should occur throughout the year on a regular, yet unannounced, basis. Exhibit 51–3 lists some issues that should be covered when training team members to make decisions in a crisis.

To properly test an emergency plan, it is important to take several steps in advance.

- Identify those staff who are to respond and those who will be used as role players. Not all staff will be available to respond in a real emergency. Ensure that training is accomplished with that in mind.
- Preestablish monitors to oversee and evaluate the training exercise. Staff with experience can watch the exercise from differing perspectives and offer valuable suggestions for management.
- Provide a method of terminating the mock exercise should a real incident occur. The test scenario should include a code word or signal that all staff are aware of. If the signal or code is used, the exercise stops immediately and actual emergency response measures can be implemented.
- Arrange for an immediate evaluation or critique of the exercise by all staff immediately upon conclusion. An immediate after-action review provides invaluable feedback from the scenario participants. The review should ask how useful and realistic the emergency plan was. Staff offering a cri-

tique should be asked to identify all problems they noted during the exercise; small problems during an exercise can become life-threatening ones during an actual incident. The evaluation should assess the swiftness of organization of emergency teams, the effectiveness of intelligence gathering and communication, and the competence of usage of emergency equipment. An evaluation should also note whether all emergency procedures were followed.

An important aspect of crisis management is knowing what emergency management teams can and cannot do. Training with the teams is the best means of gaining this knowledge. It is equally important to know what other agencies may be available for assistance and what their capabilities are. Practice scenarios will provide this information to proactive managers.

From a legal standpoint, it may be important to have prearranged agreements with other jurisdictions that can be implemented on short notice. If the senior staff of other agencies do not know what they legitimately can or cannot do, the aftermath of an institution disturbance could be very focused on the authorities who approved the emergency response. The existence of a well-developed "memorandum of agreement" in advance will delineate what personnel from other agencies can legitimately be asked to do during a crisis. For instance, if a state prison staffer is asked to staff a perimeter post of a county jail facility, it is imperative to know if this state employee has the legal authority to use lethal force during an emergency situation.

Tactical Options in a Correctional Setting

Tactical plans are important. When and how will tactical assault teams be used? A standard tactical plan will not be incident specific but based on the agency philosophy and goals. This tactical plan will use a set of preestablished critical factors based on management philosophy to lead into an incident-specific operations plan. Even if a standard plan does not exist, all tactical plans must be based on the particular agency's philosophy and policy and must always be flexible. Management must retain maneuverability.

During emergency response team and plan development, planning for worst-case scenarios is critical. Management must prepare for incidents in which a tactical team may have to intervene in a hostage barricade situation and use deadly force.

As mentioned above, there are three options in every situation: negotiation, the option involving the least amount of force, is the preferred option when time permits; DCTs using less than lethal options such as chemical agents and distraction devices; and the use of deadly force through intervention by a tactical team.

It is interesting to examine these options and determine if any of them can or should stand on its own. In the final analysis, these three force options always are dependent on each other. Emergency management is one structure. These force options are really just parts of the overall structure and will only work properly when used together. Negotiations cannot succeed without tactical options. Tactical options, whether they involve deadly force or less than lethal technologies, cannot be completely successful without negotiations. All teams must trust and cooperate with each other. One tier is not more important than any other. Success for one is success for the entire emergency management team.

It is almost impossible to plan a specific response to each potential crisis situation, especially when tactical teams are involved. However, managers can plan how all areas of an institution will be accessed in an emergency. Preplanned breach points and means of entry will provide a greater opportunity for a safe and successful resolution of an incident. Preestablished breaching plans should include the following:

- Identification of a staging area. It is important to have primary and secondary staging sites for tactical teams. These sites should not be visible to inmates, media, or the public.

- Plan of the approach. Primary and secondary approaches that conceal a team and allow it to reach the objective quickly are desired.
- Preparation for entry. Planning a primary and secondary point of entry into all buildings should be done well in advance of a crisis.
- Knowledge of physical hardware at entry points. Every building inside the secure perimeter of a penal facility should have blueprints that identify all tunnels, hatches, doors, windows, and locking devices. The tensile strength of each access point must be known prior to an emergency.
- Identification of method of entry. The means of opening or removing by force each entry point must be planned in advance. All possible methods should be identified: key rings, cutting tools, torches, saws, and explosives.
- Assignment of primary entry teams. Staff should certainly be selected for this type of work and have regular practice time before being placed in a real situation. Teams will need to be properly equipped and trained with chemical agents, distraction devices, stinger grenades, stun weapons, batons, restraints, and lethal weapons.

Adjustments to preapproved plans will be made based on each situation.

A very important part of emergency preparedness is ensuring that the use-of-force guidelines are clear for all staff members. All involved in an institution crisis must know agency regulations for the use of force—for instance, precisely what threat must be present before lethal weaponry can be authorized. They should also know what less than lethal options are available (see Exhibit 51–4).

Exhibit 51–4 Less than Lethal Options (Graduated Use of Force)

- Handheld chemical agent weapons and agents
- Handheld and hand-delivered distraction devices
- Less than lethal munition for 37-mm, 40-mm, and 12-gauge systems—long and short range
  - Wooden baton round
  - Rubber pellet round
  - 60-caliber rubber round for 12-gauge

CONCLUSION

In today's climate of younger offenders and longer sentences, the potential for violent encounters is on the rise. Institution managers must be prepared to deal with situations quickly and decisively. Emergency preparedness has taken on an entirely different character. No longer can it be put off for later or not funded properly.

Emergency preparedness should be a firm priority in prison and jail management to ensure a safe and orderly institution. Staff will recognize a commitment to emergency preparedness as a statement of support and caring for them. Inmates will also recognize that an institution is prepared for crises. Most will appreciate the safe and orderly environment that results from being prepared for emergencies.

SUGGESTED READINGS

American Correctional Association. 1996. *Preventing and managing riots and disturbances: Correspondence course.* Lanham, MD.

Arnold, J. 1980. *Holocaust at New Mexico State Penitentiary.* Lubbock, TX: C.F. Boone.

DiIulio, J. 1987. *Governing prisons.* New York: The Free Press.

CHAPTER 52

Hostage Situations in Correctional Facilities

Gothriel Lafleur, Louis Stender, and Jim Lyons

The safety, security, and orderly operation of a correctional facility can be severely interrupted by inmate disturbances. Such events are particularly threatening and stressful when they involve the taking of hostages. The potential for major disturbances, including hostage situations, exists at any time in any facility, regardless of whether the facility houses maximum or minimum custody inmates. As the official commission investigating the Attica uprising warned, "Attica is every prison, and every prison is Attica."[1(p.xii)] Via television and other media, millions of people experienced the dramatic unfolding of events at New Mexico, Oakdale (Louisiana), and Atlanta. Because of the types of people they detain and their conditions of confinement (often perceived as less than pleasant), correctional facilities are vulnerable to hostage-taking events.

Proactive strategies—effective administrative attention to institution operations, with staff attuned to inmate climate and unrest—can significantly reduce the potential for major crises. Even a small event, however, can result in a prison riot and a hostage situation. When faced with such a situation, administrators must be prepared to respond. It is critical to have a coordinated plan to address the incident. The way in which prison administrators prepare for and handle this type of crisis can make the difference between a small-scale disturbance and a full-fledged riot.[2]

USE FORCE OR NEGOTIATE

Thomas Strentz offers four options for responding to a hostage incident.[3] Each option has its place in strategic planning and preparation, and each has benefits and drawbacks.

First, an assault of the location can produce a rapid conclusion. It poses significant risk, however, to hostages, the tactical team, and the captors; hostages are most likely to be harmed during the initial phase of a disturbance. Statistics will confirm that more individuals are injured when use of force is employed than when negotiation tactics can be utilized.[4] Certain hostage takers may leave no option but a straightforward tactical response if homicidal or threatening actions have occurred or are expected.

Second, selected sniper fire is another option. If hostages have been harmed or are in serious danger, sniper fire could end the situation quickly. Use of a sniper may be considered if members of the tactical team are in imminent danger. But hostage takers have been known to switch clothes with hostages, and the incorrect person could be shot. The size and complexity of the disturbance are factors to consider; riotous situations of large magnitude may not be easily resolved by selective lethal force by designated marksmen. Sniper fire is generally not considered an initial option.

Third, use of chemical agents may force a hostage taker out of the area, allowing for hostage escape or rescue. But chemical agents may not reliably produce the desired effect and could be harmful to the hostages' health. Chemicals usually have been used for diversion or a supporting element, occuring at the same time that a tactical assault is initiated.

The fourth option is to contain and negotiate. This process is proven to save lives. The success rate of negotiations is very high when communication has been isolated and the captor speaks only with the negotiator. If the captor is allowed to speak with friends, family, members of the media, and others, the situation has the potential to regress quickly.

PURPOSE AND THEORY OF HOSTAGE NEGOTIATION

The basic purposes for negotiating during a hostage incident are to preserve life and regain control of the correctional facility and the inmates. First and foremost, there is a need to negotiate because of the value of human life.[5] McMains and Mullins have prioritized negotiators' objectives in correctional facilities: Negotiators attempt to save the lives of hostages, citizens (if involved), prison staff, and hostage takers, in that order. The authors further state that prison staff should negotiate to regain control of the prison environment and prevent escape, minimize casualties, apprehend the hostage takers, and recover property, in that order of priority.[6]

The negotiation process takes time. The passage of time helps decrease stress levels, increase rationality, allow development of rapport and trust and clarification of communication, exhaust the hostage taker, and increase the probability that hostages will be released unharmed. With more time, important intelligence can be gathered, tactical teams can prepare, and command personnel can organize. Captors' expectations will drop, and hostages will have more chances to escape. The Stockholm Syndrome is a psychological development whereby people taken hostage and their captors begin to identify with each other. This helps decrease the likeli-

hood that hostages will be harmed. In a prison setting, correctional officers are the likely hostages, and negotiators are coworkers or friends. The Stockholm Syndrome, at the start of a hostage incident in prison, will often already be in effect, or it may never develop. If the syndrome is in effect, hostages are often relatively safe and will be cared for by the captors. If the syndrome is not present, hostages may be in great danger, and negotiating efforts will focus on keeping hostages alive.[7] Whether or not the syndrome is in effect, the seemingly uneventful passage of time can be a benefit.

Though negotiation is the preferred method to resolve a hostage situation, negotiation may not be a viable alternative in some cases. The Federal Bureau of Investigation (FBI) has pinpointed characteristics that an incident must have to be negotiable: The hostage taker must want to live, threat of force by authorities has to be present, the hostage taker must have demands, and the negotiator must be viewed as one who can hurt or help the captor. There needs to be time to negotiate and a reliable channel of communication between captor and negotiator. The location and communication of the incident must be contained; it is important that all communication be channeled to and through the negotiator. If there is more than one captor, the negotiator must be able to deal with the captor who is the decision maker. If all of these characteristics are not present, negotiation becomes a less viable option, and hostages are in more danger.

STRUCTURE AND ROLE OF RESPONSE TEAMS

At the onset of any hostage situation, a command post should be established in a quiet area between the inner and outer perimeters that have been established by the tactical team. The on-scene commander (OSC) will direct all activities from this site. Large numbers of people will be involved in the incident, so an effective process of communication is imperative. The FBI recommends that an OSC be situated in the command post with a few advisors in the roles of second in command, negotiation team leader, and special weapons and tactics (SWAT) team leader (see Figure 52–1).

The second in command supervises interaction with the media, legal representatives, public officials, or other entities. This person organizes all incoming information to present to the commander. The negotiation team leader briefs the commander on the negotiation process, intelligence gathered, and the hostage takers' current mental status or information obtained from others such as a psychological consultant. The SWAT team leader informs the commander about the position and readiness of his or her team members and the feasibility and likelihood of success for various assault options. The commander should inform the negotiation team leader of any action that is planned. Actions taken without the negotiator's knowledge will make it difficult for the negotiator to provide a cover story to the hostage takers and maintain the trust of the captor. Should negotiations prove unsuccessful, the negotiator can confirm the hostage taker's location or otherwise

provide distraction at the time of any planned assault.

It is not possible to have a negotiating posture without tactical support and containment. Boltz and Leak used the following phrase to illustrate the working relationship of the hostage negotiations and tactical teams: "Negotiators are the velvet glove over the iron fist."[8] Tactical and negotiation teams must share information and intelligence.[9] Both teams gather intelligence (e.g., hostages harmed, medical needs, weapons involved, mental stability of hostage taker) invaluable to the other team, and strategies are altered based on this information.

A negotiation team must gather intelligence, formulate tactics to defuse an incident, communicate with hostage takers, record intelligence, keep record of negotiations, and coordinate with the commander and tactical team. FBI guidelines suggest the team be composed of a supervisor, a primary and secondary negotiator, an intelligence gatherer, and a mental health consultant. The team members need to know and be able to function in a variety of roles. Members

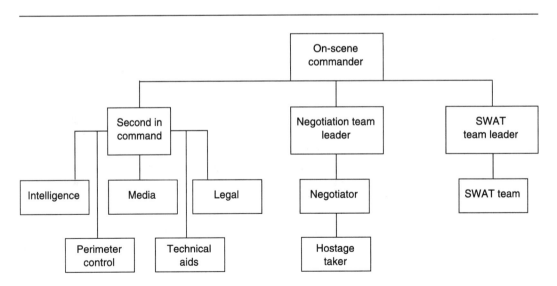

Figure 52–1 Recommended Lines of Communication—Hostage Negotiation. *Source:* Reprinted from G. Fuselier, "Lines of Communication," *FBI Law Enforcement Bulletin,* March 1961, Federal Bureau of Investigation.

may initially all be intelligence gatherers, until specific roles are established in an incident. Teamwork requires several skills that must be developed systematically.

Team members should be nonmanagers and nonuniform staff. They should have a minimum of one year of correctional experience and be carefully selected and trained in negotiation.[10] The FBI requires negotiators to complete the FBI's Basic Hostage/Crisis Negotiations course, a 40-hour training program that is available to correctional and law enforcement personnel. A premium is generally placed on the training of tactical teams. Administrators should place no less emphasis on the training provided to their negotiation team.

Fuselier suggests several personality characteristics that negotiators should have. They should be emotionally mature, good at listening and interviewing, able to make logical arguments, and persuasive. They should be "streetwise," experienced, able to communicate with people from all walks of life. Candidates must be able to accept responsibility for the negotiation, yet understand that a key principle of negotiation is that the authority of the decision maker is removed from the scene. They should be able to cope with uncertainty, be flexible, and be totally committed to the negotiation approach. Lastly, individuals need to understand that if negotiations do not go well, they may have to help plan and support an assault.[11]

Prison hostage situations usually become sieges. Because the hostages are often employees of the facility, it is advisable to establish (prior to the incident) a victims' assistance team. When a situation occurs, this team should notify hostages' families and provide an area for them to gather. The victims' assistance team should provide emotional support to the families, disseminate information and intelligence on the hostage situation, and shield family members from the news media.[12] This team may be used to provide emotional debriefing to the released hostages.

NEGOTIATION STRATEGIES

The goals of the hostage negotiation are to open communication lines, reduce stress and tension, build rapport, obtain intelligence, stall for time, allow hostage takers to express emotion and ventilate, and establish a problem-solving atmosphere. Inmate demands most often involve complaints about living conditions or unfairness; concessions can be made in these areas. The following principles are to be inviolate: No hostage should be exchanged for release or reduction in sentence for any inmate, no weapons should be supplied to hostage takers, no intoxicating substances should be exchanged for the release of hostages, and no hostage should be exchanged for a different hostage.

Prison negotiators need to be concerned about minimizing property damage. Prison hostage takers often take over and destroy the very settings needed to maintain the inmate population. Before beginning any negotiation, the negotiators should ensure the hostage takers are contained. Tactical teams should, to the extent possible, minimize the area occupied by the hostage takers.

In a riot, it is impossible to negotiate. It may be necessary to assault if the situation does not stabilize.[13] It may also be preferable to assault before leaders begin to emerge. The courts have ruled that using force to quell a riot is not unlawful unless the assault team acts maliciously and sadistically for the purpose of causing harm.[14]

Hostage takers are generally categorized in three main groups: the mentally unstable (e.g., the suicidal, the paranoids, the antisocial), the criminals (e.g., robbers, murderers, rapists, gang members, those whose escape attempts failed), and the crusaders (e.g., white supremacists, militant Muslim groups, terrorists, religious fanatics). Negotiation team members should become familiar with inmate types and be trained to communicate effectively with those of each type. A peaceful resolution for everyone involved is the goal for the negotiator, regardless of the situation.

RETURN BACK TO NORMAL OPERATIONS

Administrators need to plan and systematically implement steps to return the facility to normal operations at the conclusion of any disturbance. Especially following hostage situations, tension among inmates and staff may be high. Resolution of an incident may produce a tendency to believe the worst is over and to reduce attention to important concerns. But the following issues should be addressed after any disturbance:

- Short-term responsibilities should include searching for contraband, securing inmates, assessing damages, counting inmates, providing medical care to hostages and inmates, and collecting evidence for future prosecutions.
- Medium-term efforts should include providing continued support and counseling to employees in coping with their experiences, repairing damage to facilities, working toward normalization of institutional operations, and undertaking a thorough investigation of the causes of the crisis, and an evaluation of how it was handled. Actions such as publicly recognizing the sacrifice made by hostages and expressing appreciation for exemplary action by staff may help reintegrate the corrections community.
- Long-term solutions include developing policy reflecting what was learned from the disturbance. Institutions may discover better ways to forecast problems, improve the flow of information, fix previously unrecognized problems, improve relationships with other agencies, boost morale, and meet challenges.

TRAINING, TRAINING, TRAINING

It does little good to have an institution disturbance control plan unless staff and supervisors have been trained to activate it. Administrators should give training a high priority. For a coordinated response to be successful, people in each component need to understand clearly the functions of people in other components. To enhance cooperation, negotiators and personnel from tactical teams should train together regularly.[15] Command and supervisory personnel must be trained in the nature of a negotiable incident so they can make informed decisions.

To protect themselves from liability, administrators should develop policies and procedures that cite required training, as well as records that show who was trained during what period of time. It is important to be able to prove in court, if necessary, that officers received training. All staff members should receive training in disturbance control and hostage incidents, including realistic simulations of incidents. Many states have centralized training academies that should coordinate with institution training needs. The way in which corrections administrators prepare for and handle a disturbance can make the difference between a peaceful resolution and a true disaster.

NOTES

1. *The Official Report of the New York Commission on Attica* (New York: Bantam Books, 1972), xii.
2. R. Boin and V. Dunne, "Prison Riots as Organizational Failures: A Managerial Perspective," *Prison Journal,* 35, no. 3 (1995): 357–379.
3. T. Strentz, "Law Enforcement Policies and Ego Defense of the Hostage," *FBI Law Enforcement Bulletin* 48, no. 4 (1979): 1–12.
4. H. Schlossberg, "Psychiatric Principles of Negotiations," *The U.S. Negotiator,* Spring 1996.
5. R. Prince and A. Prince, "Hostage Negotiating," *Police Product News,* March 1995.
6. M. McMains and W. Mullins, *Crisis Negotiations: Managing Critical Incidents and Hostage Situations in Law Enforcement and Corrections* (Cincinnati: Anderson Publishing, 1996), 290.
7. McMains and Mullins, *Crisis Negotiations: Managing Critical Incidents and Hostage Situations in Law Enforcement and Corrections,* 286.
8. F. Boltz and G. Leak, "Negotiations from Munich to Atlanta," *The U.S. Negotiator,* Spring 1996.

9. R. Loudin and G. Leak, "Command and Control during Crisis Incidents," *The U.S. Negotiator,* Spring 1996.

10. American Correctional Association, *Standards for Adult Correctional Institutions,* 2d ed. (College Park, MD: 1981). Standard #2-4094.

11. G. Fuselier, "What Every Negotiator Would Like His Chief To Know," *FBI Law Enforcement Bulletin* 55, no. 3 (March 1986): 12–15.

12. P. Miller et al., "Lesson Learned: The Oakdale/Atlanta Riots—Interviews with BOP Wardens Johnson and Petrovsky," *Corrections Today* 50 (1988): 16–18.

13. A. Saenz and T. Reeves, "Riot Aftermath: New Mexico's Experience Teaches Valuable Lessons," *Corrections Today* 51 (1989): 66–70.

14. *Whitley v. Albers,* 106 Sup. Ct. 1078 (1986).

15. B. Wind, "A Guide to Crisis Negotiations," *FBI Law Enforcement Bulletin,* October 1995, 1–7.

CHAPTER **53**

The Use of Force in Correctional Institutions

John R. Hepburn, Marie L. Griffin, and Thomas V. Schade

Correctional institutions are extremely coercive organizations in which all activities are carried out in an environment of uncertainty. In both jails and prisons, where staff are usually unarmed and always outnumbered by the population of resistant prisoners, the ability of staff to control the prisoners is a matter of major importance. For the most part, staff rely on their legitimate power; that is, prisoners accept that staff have the authority to give reasonable instructions related to inmates' daily activities.[1] Of all the types of power, legitimate power results in gaining compliance by the largest number of prisoners, over the widest scope of prisoner activities, and over the greatest amount of time and effort devoted to those activities.

Coercive power, in contrast, is most effective when it is always available but seldom used. In prisons and jails, coercive power is an ever-present resource that can be mobilized to provide the force necessary to support legitimate power. Lethal force is a rarely used option that represents the extreme end of the continuum. Lethal weapons are issued routinely only to those who guard the perimeter of an institution. Few, if any, officers working within the population are armed with lethal weapons unless they are responding to an internal disturbance. Nonlethal force is used much more often than lethal force; officers routinely rely on direct physical contact with prisoners to maintain control and security. For the most part, this use of force involves only some form of hands-on contact with the prisoners, but such nonlethal weapons as stun devices and chemical sprays are becoming more prevalent within jails and prisons.[2]

INCIDENCE OF THE USE OF FORCE

It is generally known that deadly force is rarely used and that nonlethal force is frequently used, but there are few studies that provide data about how often the different types of force are used. Each institution keeps its own records of the "use of force" incidents that occur, but totaling these incidents across institutions or making comparisons between institutions is difficult, if not impossible. Institution policies have different definitions of "force," different requirements about when incidents involving force should be reported, and different specifications about the type and completeness of such reports.

In 1993, the American Correctional Association conducted a national survey of the use of force in 325 prison facilities, representing 49 state correctional systems and the Federal Bureau of Prisons.[3] The number of incidents during the 12 months before the survey ranged from 0 in 17 facilities to 200 or more in 8 facilities (with a high of 652 in 1 facility). Most facilities fell between these extremes, however, with somewhere between 7 and 90 incidents reported. Overall, there were a reported mean of 70 and median of 34 incidents per facility. In general, the incidence of the use of force is greater within larger facilities and within maximum security facilities.

Lethal force is most likely to be used against escaping inmates and to control group disturbances, whereas nonlethal force is most likely to be used when officers become involved in inmate-on-inmate fights or when an inmate refuses to comply with lawful orders.[4] Most incidents of nonlethal force are spontaneous, use only hands-on force, occur in housing units, and involve only one inmate. Although lethal force is designed to have deadly consequences, nonlethal force rarely results in injuries to either officer or inmate. Most inmate injuries and nearly all officer injuries from nonlethal force are minor abrasions or scrapes.

THE USE AND EFFECTIVENESS OF NONLETHAL WEAPONS

Both the American Correctional Association's 1993 national survey of 325 state and federal prisons and the 1993 survey by the Institute for Law and Justice of 154 jails and 62 prisons reach quite similar findings with regard to the availability of nonlethal weapons in correctional facilities. These reports indicate that nonlethal weapons are present in most facilities, although prisons are more likely than jails to have nonlethal weapons. Chemical irritants and batons (or some type of impact weapon) were available for use in nearly all the prisons studied, but in only about half of the jails. Less than lethal projectile guns were available in nearly half the prisons and less than 20 percent of the jails, and a stun device was available in approximately one-third of both the prisons and the jails.[5,6]

Not all officers are routinely equipped with these weapons, however. Instead, these weapons are more likely to be stored in a central arsenal or distributed only to certain, perhaps supervisory, staff. As a result, many jails and prisons report that the weapons were not used during the preceding year. Even in those facilities in which these weapons had been used at least once during the past year, only the chemical irritants were used an average of 10 or more times.

Asked about the effectiveness of these nonlethal weapons, prison and jail administrators rated the less than lethal projectile gun as most effective, but all the weapons were thought effective. Compared with batons and other nonlethal weapons, less than lethal projectile guns, chemical irritants, and stun devices were viewed by jail and prison administrators as the most effective in both subduing inmates and ensuring officer safety.[7] Among the chemical irritants, oleoresin capsicum (also referred to as pepper spray) is considered the most effective alternative to the use of hands-on techniques, batons, and other conventional force.[8]

LETHAL FORCE AND CIVIL LIABILITY

Different standards are used to judge the civil liability of the use of lethal force by police and correctional officers. For police, the appropriate use of lethal force is judged in terms of the Fourth Amendment's prohibitions against unreasonable seizure.[9] The standard is defined by the Supreme Court's 1985 decision of *Tennessee v. Garner,* which specifies that deadly force is only appropriate to seize a fleeing suspect when, under the totality of the circumstances, "the officer has probable cause to believe that the suspect poses a significant threat of death or serious physical injury to the officer or others."[10]

In contrast, civil liability for correctional officers is defined in terms of the Eighth Amendment, which provides that "Excessive bail shall not be required, nor excessive fines imposed nor cruel and unusual punishments inflicted."[11] Although the cruel and unusual punishment clause is an explicit "intention to limit the power of those entrusted with the criminal law function of government,"[12] it protects against only those actions that are "repugnant to the conscience of mankind."[13]

As a result, correctional officers have more latitude than police officers in the use of force. First, the courts begin with the assumption (often false) that all escaping prisoners are dangerous, so evidence of a threat is not required to justify the use of lethal force. Second, warning shots and shooting to maim cannot be justified by current standards that govern police (if the situation permits less than deadly force, then deadly force should not be used) but can be justified, and may even be preferred by the courts, in correctional settings. Warning shots may be more safely used when prisons are separated from the neighboring populace by open fields, and disabling force is preferred to deadly force.[14]

Finally, the courts have established that only the unnecessary and wanton infliction of pain constitutes cruel and unusual punishment as forbidden by the Eighth Amendment.[15] In *Whitley*

v. Albers, a case involving an officer who shot an inmate during a disturbance, the Supreme Court concluded that "whether the particular measure undertaken inflicted unnecessary and wanton pain and suffering ultimately turns on whether force was applied in a good faith effort to maintain or restore discipline or maliciously and sadistically for the very purpose of causing harm."[16]

NONLETHAL FORCE AND CIVIL LIABILITY

Correctional officers may use force within a correctional institution in defense of self or oth-

Correctional Officers' Actions Deemed Not Excessive

The Fourth Circuit U.S. Appellate Court has ruled that injuries sustained by an inmate while correctional officers were attempting to control an institutional disturbance were not constitutionally significant. In the case of *Stanley v. Hejirika* (134 F. 3d 629 [4th Cir. 1998]), the federal court ruled that the State of Maryland prison staff exercised reason and appropriate procedures in dealing with an "angry, highly charged, threatening, resisting, and kicking" inmate.

The case, decided on January 21, 1998, stemmed from the use of a prison extraction team attempting to remove ringleaders from their cells during an institution disturbance. Steven Stanley, a prisoner well known for his disruptive and dangerous behavior, was first on the staff list for removal from his cell. He was described as uncooperative by staff, and he threatened to stab one of the staff members. Stanley was encouraging other inmates to continue the riot. Institution authorities videotaped the incident, and the tape showed the prisoner resisting staff. Officers attempted to subdue Stanley by pushing him against a wall, taking him to the floor, and placing him in restraint equipment. Stanley's resultant injuries consisted of bruises on his arms, jaw, and back and a loose tooth.

A magistrate judge originally found that staff had crossed the *de minimis* threshold for excessive force, but the appeals court overruled the magistrate upon appeal by the state.

The appellate court declared itself "struck by the rational reaction and measured response of the correctional officers to Stanley's resistance and threats." The court found that staff did not act maliciously or sadistically. The opinion further added that the prisoner "could not have expected treatment on the same level as if he were in a civilized conference with the warden." The judicial decision also stated that "the Supreme Court has instructed that 'not every push or shove, even if it may later seem unnecessary in the peace of a judge's chambers, violates a prisoner's Constitutional rights.' "

ers, to enforce prisoner rules and regulations, to prevent a crime from occuring, and to prevent escape. In all cases, the degree of force used must be shown to have been reasonable under the totality of the circumstances known at that time. A successful claim of excessive force must demonstrate that, either intentionally or through gross negligence or recklessness, officers used excessive force that inflicted bodily harm under circumstances when officers knew or should have known that it was an unnecessary and wanton infliction of pain.[17] Force applied in a good faith effort to maintain discipline is not excessive; a successful plaintiff must prove that the force was applied maliciously and sadistically to cause harm.

A recent summation of court decisions resulting from allegations of excessive force involving nonlethal weapons concludes that litigation is most likely under one of four conditions.[18] As already discussed, one grouping consists of those cases that assert that an officer reacted improperly to an inmate, either in overreacting to a resistant inmate or in using or threatening to use force against a nonresistant inmate. The use, or continued use, of a nonlethal weapon is examined in terms of the officer's reasonable belief that such force was necessary.

A second condition of alleged excessive force involves the negligent use of nonlethal weapons contrary to the manufacturer's recommendations. This implies carelessness, not wanton harm, and is judged against the standards of use expected of any trained officer.

A third issue is the failure to provide timely medical aid to an inmate who has been injured. In *Estelle v. Gamble,* the Court ruled that there must be a "deliberate indifference" to the inmate's medical needs and not simply an inadvertent failure to provide medical care.[19] Indifference implies culpability whenever a reasonable person would have known that medical aid was needed. Further, the deliberate indifference must result in substantial harm to the inmate.[20]

Finally, legal liability for any misuse of a nonlethal weapon may extend to supervisors or administrators. Supervisors may be liable whenever it can be established that they (1) failed to intervene at the scene to prevent an officer's excessive use of force, (2) assigned an officer to a duty or issued to the officer a weapon that he or she was not trained to use, or (3) failed to investigate or discipline an officer who was known to have misused nonlethal weapons. Administrators who fail to provide training or to establish clear policies regarding the proper and appropriate uses of lethal and nonlethal weapons also may be liable.[21]

POLICIES AND TRAINING

Both the National Sheriffs Association and the National Association of Chiefs of Police have recommended a few basic actions that agencies can take to reduce their legal liability for excessive force claims. Miller offers a similar, but more detailed, set of recommendations.[22] Further, model policies have been drafted by the American Correctional Association and the Commission on Accreditation of Law Enforcement Agencies. At a minimum, each agency should have a written use of force policy, use of force training, and systematic institutional review of all incidents in which force is used.

Use of Force Policy

One recommendation is to create, and then to periodically review, written policies regarding the appropriate application of force. The use of force policy should clarify the levels of force that are appropriate for various situations that arise, always calling for the use of the minimum force needed. In many cases, the levels of force are portrayed as a continuum, with higher levels of force being used in response to a higher threat or level of resistance from inmates. These policies also should include reporting requirements, review procedures, and a statement of disciplinary actions that may result from the excessive use of force. Finally, the policy must include a clear statement pertaining to medical aid and medical review following the use of force.

If nonlethal weapons are available, the policy should indicate which weapons are authorized for use, which officers are authorized to carry or to use such weapons, and when and how officers will be trained to use such weapons. The policy also will have to include a statement that locates the weapons on the continuum of force (is a chemical spray less severe than, more severe than, or the same severity as the use of "hands-on" contact with an inmate?); gives specific directions or limitations for their use (e.g., stun devices may not be applied to the head or the genitals, and batons are not to be applied to the head or the neck); and defines any situations in which, or persons (e.g., pregnant women, older persons, or persons who are mentally ill) against whom, nonlethal weapons are not to be used.

The use of lethal weapons also must be included in any use of force policy. These policies are likely to be tailored to the individual needs of each correctional facility. The Federal Bureau of Prisons, for instance, stipulates that deadly force may be used to prevent escapes from secure facilities or to stop an inmate whose actions present imminent danger to others. Moreover, firearms are not generally to be used in a minimum security institution; they may be used to prevent an escape from a minimum security institution only when specifically authorized by a warden.[23]

In addition, deadly force policies should clarify expectations with regard to such related matters as the use of warning shots and shooting to maim; both practices are preferred by some jurisdictions and prohibited by others. Indeed, Nebraska, Texas, and some other states have policies that explicitly state that disciplinary actions may be taken against officers who fail to use deadly force to prevent an escape.

Use of Force Training

Another recommendation is that agencies should provide all officers with entry-level and inservice training in the use of force. Training should include a review of all institutional policies pertaining to the use of force as well as some general guidelines about the officer's civil liability when using force. Also, the training should include technical information and physical train-

ing regarding the proper use for each authorized force technique or weapon, whether handholds, physical restraints, or such nonlethal weapons as stun devices and chemical irritants. Trainees also should receive basic information about rendering temporary medical assistance to those who may be harmed by the use of force, especially by chemical irritants. Finally, the training should acquaint officers with a large number and variety of situations through role-playing activities that require them to exercise discretion along the entire use of force continuum. It is important to train for deescalation of force[24] and to emphasize that verbal communication skills are the preferred means of inmate control.

Systematic Institutional Review of All Incidents in Which Force Is Used

Lastly, agencies are urged to develop and maintain a process by which all instances of the use of force are systematically recorded and reviewed.[25] All incidents of any physical contact with an inmate, regardless of whether they result in an injury, should be recorded and reviewed, as should all incidents in which an inmate is threatened with a lethal or nonlethal weapon. Systematic and formal review will help to identify problem areas and problem inmates within the institution, officers who are doing well, and officers who may need further training or formal sanction. Unacceptable behaviors by officers or supervisors must be addressed and, if appropriate, sanctioned according to a set of written disciplinary guidelines.

UTILITY AND COSTS: THE NEED FOR RESEARCH

Use of force policies, practices, and training vary widely across correctional institutions. There is no single standard or model that fits all institutions. For that matter, there is no consensus about what is defined as use of force or what is an appropriate response to a given situation. Systematic data on use of force incidents are almost nonexistent. The state of current knowledge about the use of force in corrections is best illustrated by the fact that these simple questions remain unanswered: (1) How often, and in what contexts, is lethal force used annually? Nonlethal force? (2) What types of inmates and officers are involved, and what situational factors are present, in use of force incidents? (3) How many inmates, and how many staff, are injured annually as a result of lethal and nonlethal force incidents, and what is the extent of their injuries? Despite the fact that the use of force is a common and expected occurrence in correctional settings, little is known about its utility and its costs.

Utility

The question of utility revolves around the issue of what type or level of force is most useful in maintaining safety and control. Today, the focus is on the utility of nonlethal weapons in corrections. The Science and Technology Division of the National Institute of Justice is supporting many efforts to examine the usefulness of chemical irritants, electronic stun devices, intense pulsating lights, sticky foam, capture nets, projectile launchers, stun grenades, and other less than lethal weapons in prisons and jails. The limited data available suggest that nonlethal weapons can be used effectively in corrections,[26] but more research is needed to discern which weapons are effective and which weapons are ineffective (or worse, counterproductive) for specific situations or settings. Should such nonlethal weapons as chemical irritants and handheld stun devices be issued to all officers? If so, will the presence or threat of a nonlethal weapon calm or exacerbate the situation? Will the use of a nonlethal weapon be more effective than conventional hands-on force in gaining control over the inmate and in reducing injuries to the inmate and officer involved in the incident?

Costs

The use of force involves many potential costs. One is the direct financial cost associated with injuries that occur to inmates or officers in the application of force. For inmates, these direct costs are represented by the medical treatment received; for officers, these costs include medical treatment, workers' compensation claims, and lost work days. Indirect financial costs to the institution accrue in the form of the time and dollars spent to process inmate grievances and to respond to civil lawsuits alleging excessive force. In addition, Miller raises the possibility that, in cases of serious injury to inmates, civil liability might be extended by the courts to the point of holding culpable both those agencies that do not make nonlethal weapons available to their officers and those officers who do not use nonlethal weapons when they are available.[27]

The use of force also has emotional costs for those who use force, especially deadly force. Law enforcement agencies routinely require some level of counseling following shooting incidents. How (if at all) does the use of force, especially deadly force, by correctional officers lead to feelings of guilt, remorse, or despair that affect an officer's quality of work and interpersonal relationships with family and friends? Unfortunately, these questions remain largely unanswered.

CONCLUSION

Available data on the incidence of the use of lethal and nonlethal force in correctional institutions suggest a wide disparity within and among federal, state, and local jurisdictions. It is generally agreed, however, that lethal force is restricted to use against escaping inmates and in response to group disturbances, while nonlethal force generally is applied to individual inmates as a means of control. Nonlethal weapons most commonly used in prisons and jails are chemical irritants and batons. Less than lethal projectile guns and stun devices are available in about one-third of all correctional institutions and, together with chemical irritants, are generally considered to be most effective in controlling inmate behavior.

Issues of civil liability revolve around both lethal and nonlethal force. Although given more latitude than the police in resorting to lethal force, correctional officers are held to the cruel and unusual punishment prohibition contained in the Eighth Amendment to the Constitution as interpreted by several federal courts. Appropriate nonlethal force must generally meet the tests of reasonableness, nonnegligence, timely medical aid for injuries resulting from the use of force, provisions for adequate training, and the existence of clear policies regarding the use of force.

To avoid liability for claims of excessive force, agencies should have a written policy on the use of lethal and nonlethal force. Such a policy should establish a continuum of force available to correctional officers and associate the levels of force with the levels of inmate resistance or threat. Training in the use of hands-on techniques for control of inmates, as well as lethal and nonlethal weapons, should be mandatory and regularly updated. A process of supervisory review is also helpful.

Issues surrounding the utility and costs of the use of force by correctional officers remain largely unresolved. The level of force and type of weapon best suited to a particular incident remains the subject of continuing debate. Injuries to both inmates and correctional officers and the economic impact of medical treatment, processing inmate grievances, and civil lawsuits must be seen as real costs likely to be incurred when even reasonable, nonexcessive force is used.

NOTES

1. J. Hepburn, "The Exercise of Power in Coercive Organizations: A Study of Prison Guards," *Criminology* 23, no. 1 (1985): 145–164.
2. P. Henry et al., "Use of Force in America's Prisons: An Overview of Current Research," *Corrections Today* 56 (1994): 108–114.
3. Henry, "Use of Force in America's Prisons: An Overview of Current Research," 17.
4. J. Senese, Summary Report: Institutional Use of Force Reports (Paper presented at the American Correctional Association Open Symposium on Use of Force, Orlando, FL, 1994), 6–7.
5. P. Henry, "The 1993 National Survey on the Use of Force: Incidents and Procedures in Corrections Institutions," Unpublished report prepared for the American Correctional Association under the *Prison Setting Field Evaluation Project* (Alexandria, VA: 1994), 27.
6. Institute for Law and Justice, "Less Than Lethal Force Technologies in Law Enforcement and Correctional Agencies" (National Institute of Justice, Alexandria, VA, National Institute of Justice, photocopy), 1993, 3–12.
7. Institute Study, p. 13–16.
8. J. Onnen, *Oleoresin Capsicum: Executive Brief* (Alexandria, VA: International Association of Police Chiefs, 1993).
9. B. Roberts, "Legal Issues in Use-of-Force Claims," *Police Chief* 59, no. 2 (1992): 16–29.
10. *Teneessee v. Garner,* 471 U.S. 1 (1985).
11. U.S. Constitution, amend. 8.
12. *Ingraham v. Wright,* 430 U.S. 651, 664 (1977).
13. *Hudson v. McMillian,* 503 U.S. 1, 10 (1992).
14. J. Walker, "Police and Correctional Use of Force: Legal and Policy Standards and Implications," *Crime and Delinquency* 42, no. 1 (1996): 144–156.
15. *Wilson v. Seiter,* 501 U.S. 294, 298 (1991).
16. *Whitley v. Albers,* 475 U.S. 312 (1986).
17. *McRorie v. Enomoto,* 633 F. 2d 780, 784 (9th Cir. 1986).
18. Institute for Law and Justice, "Less Than Lethal Force Technologies in Law Enforcement and Correctional Agencies," 5-17–5-18.
19. *Estelle v. Gamble,* 429 U.S. 97 (1976).
20. *May v. Enomoto,* 633 F. 2d 164 (9th Cir. 1980).
21. D. Daane and J. Hendricks, "Liability for Failure To Adequately Train," *Police Chief* 58, no. 11 (1991): 26–29.
22. N. Miller, "Less-Than-Lethal Force Weaponry: Law Enforcement and Correctional Agency Civil Liability for the Use of Excessive Force," *Creighton Law Review* 28, no. 3 (1995): 733–794.
23. Federal Bureau of Prisons Program Statement 558.12, "Firearms and Badges," 1996, p. 6.
24. J. Nicoletti, "Training for De-Escalation of Force," *Police Chief* 57, no. 7 (1990): 37–39.
25. D. Lyons, "Preventive Measures Cut Physical Force Suits," *Corrections Today* 52 (1990): 216–224.
26. Institute for Law and Justice, "Less Than Lethal Force Technologies in Law Enforcement and Correctional Agencies," 3–17.
27. Miller, "Less-Than-Lethal Force Weaponry: Law Enforcement and Correctional Agency Civil Law Liability for the Use of Excessive Force," 767.

CHAPTER 54

Working with the Media

Judith Simon Garrett

The public's fascination with crime and criminals does not stop when an offender is hauled off to jail or prison; the curiosity and interest continues into the institutions. Accordingly, reporters frequently produce stories about inmates and the prisons in which they are housed. Unfortunately for prison and jail administrators, the stories are usually centered around the plight of the inmates; the anger and disgust over the crime committed has been replaced with sympathy for the life that inmates must lead behind bars. On other occasions, the stories focus on the violence and corruption reputed to pervade prison life.

While portraying prisons as unpleasant places may deter some potential criminals, these visions rarely provide an accurate description of what goes on behind institution walls and fences. Media stories often fail to mention the many positive things that transpire in institutions and they distort the motives and actions of staff.

Prison and jail administrators must provide media representatives and the public with a more accurate, positive picture of what goes on inside their institutions.

It is very likely that at some time a prison administrator or chief executive officer will have

to respond to a news media request to interview an inmate or do a story about some aspect of his or her institution's operations. Such a request may involve making an inmate available in the visiting room for 30 minutes, allowing a reporter to shadow a staff member for a week, or anything in between. Therefore, a written policy regarding the handling of media requests would be very helpful. Such policy should recognize that while the media do not have the right to enter a correctional institution for the purpose of completing a story, and inmates do not have the right to unlimited or unrestricted access to media representatives, all reasonable media requests should be given appropriate consideration because media coverage can keep the public better informed about the institution.

MEDIA ACCESS—A CONTENTIOUS ISSUE

How much access should the media have to prison and jail operations? Some correctional agencies permit representatives of print and electronic media into their facilities upon request. Other agencies believe such contact with inmates can be disruptive and a threat to the orderly running of the institution.

In 1974, in a case entitled *Pell v. Procunier,* the Supreme Court upheld the California Department of Corrections' prohibition on face-to-face interviews between individual inmates and representatives of the news media.[1] The Court

Opinions expressed in this chapter are those of the author and do not necessarily represent the opinions of the Federal Bureau of Prisons or the U.S. Department of Justice.

<table>
<tr><td>

The Value of Media Training

Doctors, lawyers, politicians, corporation chief executive officers, prison wardens, and many others are increasingly enrolling in media training programs offered by pubic relations experts. Such programs are intended to even the playing field somewhat; reporters have substantial advantages over the people they interview: they ask the questions, edit the answers, and frame the story. Through media training, the students will learn how to communicate their message most effectively and concisely, even when facing a difficult interview. The training sessions tend to focus on three areas, all of which affect the speakers' credibility, in the following order: body language, tone of voice, and choice of words.

While there are many "tips" to be learned from media training (such as not to cross one's arms over the chest because it gives the appearance of defensiveness), the most valuable aspects of the training may be that it forces the student to think in advance about the potential pitfalls of an interview and how best to avoid them. In short, if nothing else, media training students learn that everyone must prepare in advance for a media interview, including giving careful thought to the types of questions to be asked and the best possible ways to respond in order to communicate the desired message.[2]

</td></tr>
</table>

concluded that this restriction was permissible because inmates had other avenues of communicating: They could correspond with the media and be visited by family and friends. Thus, prisoners had adequate means of expressing their concerns about their conditions of confinement. Further, journalists were permitted tours of the prisons and could ask inmates questions while visiting.

At the same time the Court decided *Procunier,* it decided another media access case, this one involving the Federal Bureau of Prisons. In this case, entitled *Saxbe v. Washington Post,*[3] the Court ruled that the First Amendment does not provide the press a constitutional right of access to information that is not generally available to the public.[4] The Court upheld the Bureau of Prisons' rationale that giving individual inmates access to the media would create undue attention for specific inmates who may already be notorious (the "big wheel" theory), potentially causing tension among inmates or between inmates and prison personnel. Even though the Bureau of Prisons won this legal battle, the agency does permit media representatives to interview individual inmates under clearly identified policy parameters and on terms set by the agency.

On occasions, state legislatures have stepped in to try to require departments of corrections to alter their policies to ensure that the media is granted appropriate access to prison facilities. In one state, the legislature passed a bill that would have reversed an agency policy that prohibited members of news agencies from securing interviews with particular inmates.

IMPORTANT CONSIDERATIONS BEFORE APPROVING MEDIA INTERVIEWS

Many correctional jurisdictions believe it is important to permit representatives of the media into institutions to interview specific prisoners. In these situations, there are significant questions that should be asked and evaluated before granting approval.

Who Is Making the Request?

- Does this person have press credentials, such as affiliation with a local or national newspaper that circulates among the general public, television, or radio station whose primary purpose is to report the news; magazine that is sold by newsstands or mailed to the general public; or book publisher?

- Does this person have a relationship with the inmate he or she wishes to interview, with the victim of a crime, or with a member of the staff?
- Does this person have a known agenda that is likely to substantially color the reporting?

What Is the Purpose of the Intended Story?

- Is the inmate who is the focus of the story particularly well known (or notorious)? Was his or her case of substantial media interest before and during the trial phase?
- Is the author hoping to garner sympathy or support for a particular inmate's case?
- Is the author hoping to encourage a public outcry against the treatment of one or many prisoners held at the facility?
- Are prison operations being targeted as being corrupt or excessively harsh?

What Will Be the Demands on Staff?

- How many people will be interviewed and for how long?
- How many people will be entering the prison in order to complete the story (e.g., are there camera people)?
- For how long will the media representative(s) be in the institution?

What Will Be the Effect on Prison Operations, Including Security?

- To what extent will the media representative(s) disrupt daily operations? Will scheduled activities be prevented from taking place?
- How are the inmates likely to react to the presence of the media representative(s) and to the completed story?
- How are people (including other members of the media) likely to react to the completed story? Are they likely to demand changes to prison operations or make additional media requests?
- To what extent will pictures that are taken provide members of the public or inmates with information that could be used to fashion escape or plan other disruptive activities?

There are no right or wrong answers to the above questions, nor should the answer to any one question necessarily mandate a particular conclusion. But consideration of these questions will help make the administrator aware of the many possible ramifications of granting or denying media requests.

The administrator's foremost responsibility, at all times, is to maintain the safe and orderly operation of the prison facility. At times, fulfilling this responsibility will conflict with granting a media request, in which case the media representative must be made to accept, if not understand, the reason that the request has been denied. For example, permitting extensive filming of staff training, of prison perimeter fencing, and of control room operations could create security concerns. Allowing substantial or sustained media coverage of a particular inmate has the potential to create difficulties for the inmate (who may become the target of jealousy and anger from other inmates) and for prison administrators (when the inmate decides he or she has special status and therefore should not be treated like other inmates).

In cases where the media request can be accommodated with minimal disruption and little chance of a threat to the safe and secure operation of the prison, it may make sense to grant the request. It should always be assumed that denying a media request will give rise to accusations that the institution is attempting to hide something or that the prison administration is silencing the inmate in order to protect itself, an elected official, or some other government representative.

In general, the more restrictive the access policy is, the more a correctional agency stands at risk of angering the public, representatives of the media, and elected representatives. Severe restrictions on access prevent correctional staff from gaining the public's confidence and support. In the face of the public pressure to rehabilitate criminals and use tax funds wisely, it is important that prison and jail administrators be held accountable for their stewardship of public funds. "Put simply, for the public to accurately and effectively hold corrections officials accountable, it must be better informed on correctional issues."[5(p.47)] The best means of disseminating information is welcoming outsiders into the closed environment of the prison or jail.

Finally, administrators should be cautious not to routinely grant media requests made from one source and deny requests made from another. Doing this would give rise to a perception of favoritism that could create a variety of problems.

The accreditation process of the American Correctional Association requires that a prison or jail facility have a written policy that provides for reasonable access between inmates and media representatives, subject only to limitations necessary to maintain good order and security, as well as to protect an inmate's privacy.[6]

An institution's written policy regarding access by the media should include a variety of key provisions, including the following:

- All media requests should be in written form and should include an acknowledgment by the requestor of a familiarity with institution rules and regulations and an agreement to comply with such rules.
- The news representatives must make reasonable attempts to verify all allegations leveled against inmates, staff, or the institution, and the institutions will be provided an opportunity, prior to publishing the story, to respond to allegations.
- The media representative must make appointments to visit the institution.
- Inmates may not receive compensation for interviews with the media.
- The request for an interview with news media representatives may originate with the representatives or with an inmate; an inmate's request or consent to be interviewed will be in writing.
- The administrator should approve or disapprove media requests in a timely fashion, and all denials shall be provided in writing based on a variety of factors, including the inmate's medical or mental condition, a threat to the health or safety of the interviewer, a threat to the safety and good order of the institution, a threat to the safety of the inmate, or a court order forbidding news interviews.

When the prison or jail accommodates a media request, it is the responsibility of the institution's liaison or spokesperson to work with the author or producer to learn as much as possible about what the story will say and to try and minimize distortions of prison operations. The staff member responsible for managing the media request should be appropriately screened and trained to avoid contentious relationships with media representatives and defensiveness (or the appearance of defensiveness).

Ideally, the appointed staff member will successfully shape the response to the media request by providing effective "sound bites" or "sockos" to ensure the most positive portrayal of the institution and its staff. Additionally, the parameters of the media's access to inmates, staff, and the institution should be made clear at the outset to avoid any confusion. Finally, the media representative must be made aware of the right to privacy that all inmates and staff enjoy and the institution's responsibility to protect this right.

There are occasions when newsworthy events occur at a correctional institution and the administrators or chief executive officers should contact the news media. Examples of such events include escapes, disturbances, and deaths of inmates. When such events occur, administrators should provide to the media information that is considered public, such as an inmate's name, register number, age, race, conviction and sentencing data, and general institution information such as the unit where the inmate was housed, his or her work assignment, and so on. Similarly, information about staff that is generally considered public includes position title, job assignment, number of years of service, and previous duty stations. Any incident that has the potential to give rise to criminal prosecutions should be discussed only in the most general terms and to the extent possible, upon the advice of legal counsel. As a general rule, it is wise to provide few details at the outset, at least until all relevant facts have been established to a substantial degree of certainty.

It is possible that media representatives will request access to write or produce a story about a positive aspect of prison operations. On a rare occasion, the media will become interested in a particular program or aspect of prison operations, such as a program to permit women inmates to care for their young children inside prison. It is more likely to be the case that the prison or jail administrator will have to actively solicit media support for worthy programs. The chief executive officer or administrator might occasionally invite representatives of the news media to visit the institution and observe particular programs or operations. It would be inappropriate to extend such invitations on a regular basis because it might give the impression that administrators were more concerned with attracting media attention than with operating the facility.

Another means of obtaining positive media coverage is through members of the community. Garnering support in the community for prison programs and operations is generally an effective strategy to gain positive media coverage. Many prisons administrators create a community relations board comprising senior prison staff and members of the community, including representatives from local businesses, elected officials, and others. Through this board, potential conflicts (such as expansion of the prison or a change in the security level) between the prison and the community can often be avoided by facilitating factual discussions rather than emotionally charged debates. Such debates are often played out in the media, and thus it is important to expend considerable resources to avoid conflict at the outset. Additionally, community relations boards often give rise to partnerships between the community and the prison that effectively serve the interests of all participants. For example, prison inmates can assist the community by building homes for underprivileged families or building toys for needy children from scrap materials. The community benefits through free labor, the inmates benefit from the satisfaction gained from helping others, and the prison staff benefit because inmate idleness tends to breed unrest.

CONCLUSION

Granting media representatives access to correctional institutions, including their staff and inmates, is a sensitive matter that must be carefully considered and should be managed by experienced personnel. The focus of media coverage will undoubtedly vary; there will be opportunities for positive exposure for the institution and the community, and thus it is essential to maintain positive relationships with representatives of the media.

Clearly, the media play a significant role in shaping public opinion. Correctional administrators must think of communication specialists as information messengers. Through media representatives, administrators can convey a sense of the difficult and complex responsibilities of working in and managing correctional institutions.

NOTES

1. *Pell v. Procunier,* 417 U.S. 817 (1974).
2. P. Farhi, "Beat the Press," *The Washington Post Magazine,* 7 June, 1998, pp. 1–4.
3. *Saxbe v. Washington Post,* 417 U.S. 843 (1974).
4. C. Cripe, *Legal Aspects of Corrections Management* (Gaithersburg, MD: Aspen Publishers, Inc., 1997), 117–119.
5. C. Turnbo, "News at Eleven: Correctional Accountability and the Media," *Federal Prisons Journal* 3, no. 3 (1994): 47.
6. American Correctional Association, *Foundation/Core Standards for Adult Correctional Institutions* (Washington, DC: St. Mary's Press, 1989).

PART XI

Community Relations

In the past, prisons have been built in isolated, rural locations—out of sight and out of mind. But this is no longer true today. Many older facilities that once were located miles from residential communities have found cities gradually expanding, moving closer to the institutions' grounds. New institutions are deliberately located reasonably close to population centers to improve their ability to recruit staff, to increase the availability of service providers and contractors, and to make it easier for family members to visit with their confined loved ones. Correctional institutions are now commonly found within or close to the city limits of metropolitan areas.

With institutions so close to the community, correctional administrators must be sensitive to their neighbors. "Partnership" has become recognized as an integral part of the successful management of a prison or jail. Senior institution leaders increase the public's acceptance of the facility by regularly purchasing goods and services locally, offering tours of the institution, involving minimum security inmates in community service projects, and fostering a strong volunteer program in which citizens become involved with inside programs that affect the well-being of prisoners. Volunteers may work as education tutors, religious discussion coordinators, and leaders for current event discussion groups. Citizens also are called upon to serve on a detention facility's community relations board, an important liaison with the local community.

Many academics and correctional practitioners routinely call upon institution leaders to take a stand on issues that affect them and attempt to influence public opinion. Public opinion is extremely hard to shape, but it can change; current research clearly shows the mood and beliefs of citizens regarding public safety and institution management will shift over time. Whereas the public was much more supportive of rehabilitation 30 years ago, today's opinion polls show that people favor long sentences to keep criminals off the streets.

Even though people currently believe in punishment by incarceration, they still support some positive activities for prisoners while they are confined. Current polls show the public is likely to support training, counseling, drug treatment, and education. Experienced penal administrators know that local public opinion can be influenced by allowing citizens to tour an institution and see firsthand how the facility operates. Recent National Opinion Surveys on Crime and Justice clearly show that public opinion can be swayed and that citizens are concerned about corrections.

Part XI emphasizes the importance of public perception of the facility, media relations, advocacy groups, and professional association memberships for the senior staff of jails and prisons.

LEARNING OBJECTIVES

After studying this section, you should be able to answer the following questions:

1. How does public opinion change the administration of justice? How does this process of change evolve?
2. How much access should representatives of the news media have to prisons and jails?
3. Does the public's fear of crime create harsher conditions in correctional institutions?
4. Can a warden, superintendent, or sheriff impact the public's perception of what a prison or jail can or should accomplish?
5. What are the objectives of an institution's community relations board?
6. Why should correctional administrators join professional associations?

DISCUSSION/REVIEW QUESTIONS

1. What are five different ways that institutional leaders can affect public opinion on the local level?
2. What are four important factors that should be considered prior to approving an interview between a representative of the news media and an inmate?
3. Why is it important to use specific sound bites or "sockos" when responding to representatives of the electronic media, such as television or radio reporters?
4. What is the real value of a community relations board?
5. How can membership in a professional organization such as the National Sheriffs Association or the American Correctional Association assist a public administrator?
6. Is it easier to establish positive community relations in a small city or in a large metropolis?

CHAPTER 55

Community Relations Boards

Paul McAlister

As society continues to depend upon incarceration to control criminal behavior, it also continues its "love/hate" relationship with correctional institutions.

The presence of a correctional facility within a community has often made its residents fearful. But, beyond the fear, there have also been reactions that suggest that correctional institutions threaten people by reminding them that all things are not peaceful or pleasant in life. They seem to want institutions to be "out of sight and out of mind."

The "hate" element in the relationship is in sharp tension with the "love" of such institutions. Society has become so dependent upon correctional institutions. The incredible growth of the number of prisons has made their invisibility impossible. And yet few people want a correctional facility nearby.

Community relations boards (CRBs) can help a community and an institution live together as neighbors, joint participants in the effort to deal with the reality of criminal behavior. Institutional personnel can become aware of community concerns. The community can learn that those staff members are also a part of the community and share their concerns. Communities can learn to strengthen the effectiveness of those institutions, not just endure their presence.

COMPOSITION OF CRBs

There is no prescribed number of CRB members; some boards consist of a few members, and others have 30 to 40 members. The number should be determined by each facility. Nominations may be sought from appropriate agencies or individuals. Those individuals may be approved by the board, but final selection should be made by the warden. There are several groups of community members who should be represented on a CRB.

- those people most directly affected by the physical presence of the facility (such as immediate neighbors and realtors)
- local officials—police, sheriff, city council, and county commissioners—with whom the institution will want to build relationships
- outreach members who provide a significant link to the rest of the community (educational representatives, clergy, civic groups, charitable organizations, multiethnic organizations, and so on)

OBJECTIVES FOR A BOARD

There are many objectives commonly associated with an institution's CRB. First and foremost, a prison or jail administrator should use the CRB to improve communication with the local community. This will involve the education of the CRB members in all aspects of institution operations so they can serve as a conduit to other citizens. The CRB can help community members recognize staff as community members too and can enhance the facility's program through supporting volunteer programs. The board can also suggest ways that the institution can contribute to the community.

As suggested by author and philosopher John W. Gardner, occasionally the "very nature of the large organization makes it necessary to reach outside for assistance. . . .[Outsiders have] the advantage of operating outside the stultifying forces which hem [the organization] in. [They] can take a fresh view. [They] can speak out. And [they] may be listened to."[1(p.104)] CRB members can provide honest and worthwhile feedback to senior correctional managers.

Since the early 1980s, when CRBs began to develop, their central goal has been to enable the exchange of accurate information between the institution and the community. Honesty is critical to effective institution–community communication. CRB members need to be given accurate information about facility functions and policies and encouraged to ask honest questions. If the institution does not provide honest information, the CRB, and its role will be undermined. Board members must be encouraged to express the concerns of the community openly to the institution.

CRBs can share their insight and experience with other communities where institutions may be built. CRBs can still some of the other community's fears and encourage strong cooperation between the institution and the community.

Board members should be "in the know" regarding institution incidents that would be of public concern. The CRB members can be contacted with accurate information regarding events and can then provide a measure of reassurance and calm to the community. The community may then ask the institution for additional information. The institution must respond honestly to these requests.

CRBs also may help enhance community involvement in institution programs. They may encourage volunteer participation to extend the facility's programming; inmates will realize that there are people other than correctional staff who honestly care about them. CRBs may also provide options for the inmates to be involved, as appropriate, in community service. Through this work, inmates will feel good about contributing something to others. CRBs also help the community recognize staff as community members and contributors.

CONSIDERATIONS TO HELP MEET OBJECTIVES

Institutions should provide CRB members with information about trends, programs of the institution, and the difference between facility policy and government-mandated programs or policies. This education can be provided at regularly scheduled CRB meetings or on specific training days. Because policies change regularly, education must be ongoing.

Each board meeting can include a different aspect of the program and introduce those staff members involved with each program. Possible agenda items include emergency preparedness planning, medical/drug programs, reaction to national trends, changes in the institution's mission, and construction or expansion plans.

Placing the institution's issues in the context of national trends, legal concerns, and expansion pressures, helps enhance CRB members' understanding of local facility's program needs and mandates.

Educating the community also includes working with educational institutions, civic groups, religious groups, and media representatives. Institutions may consider giving tours. Exhibit 55–1 lists some of the pros and cons of opening correctional institutions to the community. With appropriate concern for safety and inmate privacy, tours can be an effective aspect of community education. Each institution should provide an internal list of areas that tours would cover so that tours are consistent and key community concerns are always addressed.

The CRB can look for opportunities to suggest that community members become involved with the institution though volunteer programs. The public often fails to understand that inmates generally return to society. Positive changes in

Exhibit 55–1 Is Openness the Best Policy?

PRO: Taxpayers absolutely have the right to know what is going on behind the walls and fences of their institutions of confinement. Allowing the citizens of our country access to prisons and jails is the fair and reasonable thing to do and is required by law in many jurisdictions. Law-abiding members of American society should be able to visit and receive detailed information about institutional operations and activities, and public officials should see such a process as an important aspect of their community relations effort.

As experts in the field of corrections, public administrators responsible for local, state, and federal lockups should want their neighbors and fellow citizens to know that institutional staff are doing a terrific job on their behalf. The more external constituencies are exposed to our penal institutions, the more they understand the issues and are willing to provide the necessary resources for the safe and secure incarceration of criminals. Citizen volunteers can help extend staff capability in the offering of important programs such as religious discussions, tutoring in education programs, and in many other aspects of service to the facility. Local individuals who serve on advisory boards or CRBs offer varied types of expertise, from business savvy to local law enforcement experience. Neighbors of a confinement facility can present differing points of view that must be considered in the development of new policy or programs that could affect the surrounding community. Further, once neighbors' concerns are addressed, it will be much easier to avoid ill will and confrontation with people not associated with the operation of the facility.

Establishing positive relations with the communities in which prisons and jails are located is critical to daily operations and will pay major divi-

dends in all aspects of institution operations, both within and outside of the facility. Inviting volunteers into the correctional environment is good public policy.

CON: Members of the public really do not belong inside the secure perimeter of a correctional institution, nor should they have a voice in the operation of such a facility. Prison and jail management should be the exclusive domain of those who know and understand the realities of such facilities.

Every time outside visitors enter an institution, there is the chance for the introduction of contraband. This is a serious issue and presents potential danger to those who must work inside and keep order among dangerous prisoners.

Prisoners often seek avenues to voice their displeasure with institutional controls or to profess their innocence. Local, state, and federal facilities have no obligation to provide inmates with the opportunity to express themselves to outsiders. Such complaining offers little value to an institution's public relations, particularly when a prisoner has no obligation to provide a fair and truthful rendition of a situation.

Finally, members of the local community who may serve on a CRB have little knowledge of prisoners, institution operations, or the daily challenges faced by correctional administrators. They certainly cannot be expected to serve in an advisory capacity when they know little of the serious and multifaceted issues dealt with by staff every day. The expertise to operate safe and secure correctional facilities should be vested in those who know the environment and understand the ramifications of poorly conceived decisions and policy.

---

inmate behavior are often inspired by dedicated volunteer efforts. The community has a vested interest in inmates' rehabilitation.

The CRB may help develop programs in which inmates provide the community with needed services. This may be some inmates'

first positive experience of giving to someone else. It can enhance an inmate's self-image and awaken in inmates a desire to contribute further to society. These projects can help warn young people at risk about the costs of criminal behavior, provide help during emergencies, and support charitable activities, such as home repair projects for low-income people.

It is important for prison staff to be respected by the community and for the community members to feel gratitude toward them. Activities that encourage public contact with staff should be encouraged. It is very important to community–institution trust that the staff be seen as having a vested interest in maintaining a quality environment for their families' living.

LOGISTICS

To enhance the CRB's understanding of the institution and its staff, CRB members may be encouraged to attend certain social events. During these events, CRB members can learn from staff about what institution programs need enhancement.

Board members can be invited to certain staff meetings such as a staff recall. At the meetings, CRB members will learn more about institutional goals and needs and report what they learned to the community. Confidentiality is necessary in some aspects of institution operations, but CRB members should feel that the institution is not hiding things that the community should know.

CRB members should help decide on their meeting times. It is not always easy to find a meeting time that works for everyone. Try to inform prospective members of the scheduled time before they are asked to participate. Noon meetings often are preferred, but certain members of the community may have difficulty attending because of employment obligations. Early evening meetings also work well sometimes. Meetings may be monthly, bimonthly, or quarterly. Special meetings can be called if there is a crisis or some decision about which the CRB may be asked to make recommendations.

Because a truly representative CRB is the goal, every effort should be made to make full participation as likely as possible.

It must be said that the CRB is not a policy-making entity but a vehicle for the exchange of information between the institution and the community. The CRB may be called on to make recommendations to assist prison or jail administrators in their efforts. If the administration has good information to work with concerning community perceptions and concerns, decision makers can anticipate community reaction and help community members accept institution decisions.

Board members' terms will be established by each institution in conjunction with actual community members. There is an advantage to allowing some members to serve for a specified period of time: People can participate and yet not commit themselves too far into the future. A two- or three-year term may be appropriate. It is difficult to provide the education necessary to contribute to the function of the CRB if the term is any shorter. In some cases, there are members who are willing to commit to an extended period of service. They can provide expertise that is beneficial to all. It is perhaps best to allow automatic reappointments after terms end (if members want to continue serving). The downside of the extended term is that others who wish to serve are not able to fill a vacated position.

There needs to be a public awareness of the CRB and its members. If the community members do not know who the CRB members are, they cannot learn about the institution or give their opinions about the institution to CRB members. An article in the local paper would help community members learn about the CRB, its role, and its members.

The CRB chair facilitates meetings through handling introductions and welcomes, and following agendas as well as contributing to the building of meeting agendas. Each agenda should be sensitive to developing issues as well as address ongoing information and education issues. The chair should be nominated by the board members, who will decide the chair's term. A term of one year with the possibility of reappointment is common.

Each facility and board may draft its own by-laws. The bylaws will normally be structured by the warden or superintendent with input from members and should spell out details about membership, terms of service, and functions. Issues of security and confidentiality may well be covered in the bylaws.

CONCLUSION

Community relations has become a very important aspect of institutional planning. A CRB can contribute greatly to an institution and its surrounding community. The effectiveness of such boards will be directly impacted by their sense of honest involvement. Perfunctory CRBs are doomed to fail. Institutions will need to provide honest answers to questions generated by CRB members or communicated by the CRB on behalf of community members. The capacity of the CRB to react to incidents or to prevent confusion within the community can be a great help to all. Wardens can use CRB members as sounding boards. CRBs must carry information and understanding from the facility to the community and from the community to the facility. Both directions of this information channel must remain open for CRBs to be effective.

Each local facility, in conjunction with the respective community, will have to use a CRB to fit its specific situation and circumstances; CRB models can be adapted to any circumstances. The growing numbers of people incarcerated and new institutions mean that the issue of community relations will remain very important for many years to come.

Serving upon such boards can be a privilege. CRB members often feel a sense of meaningful investment in the partnership between community and facility and in helping to ensure a safe and effective approach to criminal justice. Members of a CRB have a significant opportunity to contribute to a vital partnership and make a difference in a local community.

NOTE

1. J. Gardner, *Self-Renewal: The Individual and Innovative Society* (New York: Harper and Row, 1963), 104.

SUGGESTED READINGS

Jones, J. 1991. Community relations boards. *Federal Prisons Journal* 2, no. 2: 19–22.

American Correctional Association. 1993. *Helping hands: A handbook for volunteers.* Laurel, MD.

CHAPTER 56

The Value of Association

James A. Gondles, Jr.

The benefits of belonging to an association are as many as there are associations in existence today. Recent survey information shows 7 out of 10 adult Americans are now members of at least one association.[1] Currently in this country, and in many others, there are associations for all of the major areas of business, marketing, education, accounting, law, corrections, medicine, science, and engineering. Associations also exist for very specific groups such as fashion designers, book editors, environmental scientists, twins, and amateur weather observers. As this diversity of association topics demonstrates, many people feel that they benefit from association membership.

The *American Heritage Dictionary* defines "association" as "an organized body of people who have some common interest, activity or purpose; a society." This definition explains the basic reason why one would wish to be a member of an association: to be in the company of others who have a common interest, to be in the society of persons with similar concerns and opinions.

Associations are organized to address the various needs of their constituents. Some groups unite merely to be with people in similar situations, such as lottery winners or twins. Others band together for political reasons, in support of or opposition to proposed laws or changes in their community. Still others meet to better their profession and its reputation. Through membership in these professional associations, individu-

als can band together to ensure that the issues they promote are publicized and gain support. The primary purpose of most professional organizations and associations is to amplify the individual members' voices in ways that members could not do alone. Membership allows individuals to increase their understanding of and influence over situations usually beyond an individual's control.

Professional associations also offer many other benefits, including standards and accreditation, legislative representation, professional development, access to resources and publication, conventions, advertising and marketing opportunities, and group benefits.

STANDARDS AND ACCREDITATION

A good example of an association that offers standards and accreditation is the bar association in many states. A function of these bar associations is to test those who wish to practice law in their jurisdictions. This ensures that a candidate has a predetermined level of knowledge and skills before he or she begins to practice law in that specific legal environment. This type of testing benefits all parties. Individuals being tested are given an indicator of their level of knowledge by an unbiased third party. The individuals in the community who require legal representation are assured that those who have bar approval will have the tools necessary to adequately do their job within that jurisdiction's legal parameters. The jurisdiction will have fewer mistakes and malpractice suits due to incompetence, leading to less waste of valuable court resources.

An association also benefits its members by enhancing the integrity of the profession. Refusing professional credentials to unqualified applicants can decrease their market demand, giving them less opportunity to create a negative industry image.

The example of having to be credentialed by a state bar illustrates the significant responsibility many associations have to their members and the community at large. Associations need to maintain a level of professional standards while constantly evaluating, for their approval and endorsement, new ideas and new practices. In professions where the standards remain similar from year to year, maintaining these criteria for evaluation is easier. In industries such as medicine, where the frontiers and technologies are constantly changing, evaluation and approval of new procedures and techniques are difficult. Evolution must be handled carefully: An association must not deter the process of growth, but at the same time it must be certain that approved practices are based in sound principle and their applications have been proven.

Through the design, implementation, and measurement of compliance to standards, an association can better balance the goals of ensuring the best possible service for the public and providing an environment that promotes its members. Setting up an association-level framework for evaluating new technologies and procedures can reduce the risk of catastrophic error on the part of the individual and diminish safety risks for the community at large. Few people realize that any airplane, boat, elevator, or even Ferris wheel must have passed standards established by associations that ensure the public's health and safety. Having standards is an enormous and resource-consuming task. Too liberal standards will permit risky operating practices with damaging repercussions, while too restrictive standards prevent forward movement and growth.

To keep on top of standards, associations must stay in constant communication with their members. This is the only way to accurately reflect the members' needs and desires and to use the knowledge of the many professionals whom they represent in determining future policy.

By applying accepted policies, members also are able to better focus their use of resources. Individuals need not waste their resources making the same mistakes that their peers have made. This ongoing process of group review and implementation ensures that an association has state-of-the-art guidelines and practices.

This review and approval of generally accepted practices can assist in many different management arenas. These guidelines, forged through the experience of the entire industry, will reduce the liability an organization will assume by trying new approaches and possibly provide background and outcomes on other solutions the organization's peers have experienced. The ability to draw on the experience of the association's many other professionals for guidance is a very powerful tool. Learning from colleagues who have had a particular experience previously is smart. If an organization follows accepted association procedures and finds itself questioned, it has the credibility of the association and its many supporting professionals to rest on, rather than standing alone on its own decision.

LEGISLATIVE REPRESENTATION

As mentioned earlier, associations are sometimes formed for representational purposes. These organizations ensure that they represent the concerns of the members in proposed legislation and public policy. An association can monitor legislation around the clock and alert its members at critical points when their action is most needed. An association's legislative liaison addresses the legislative and government concerns that will affect the members of that organization at the local, state, national, and international levels. For an individual, this sort of activity would be far too resource intensive to undertake, but through the efforts of an appointed liaison, an association can maximize the voting power of all its members. The association presents a strong collective voice that is more likely to be heard than if all members were acting on their own. Associations are also invited as industry representatives to many government-level meetings and focus groups to assist in determining future public policy and law because of their recognized expertise in their fields.

PROFESSIONAL DEVELOPMENT

Individuals and organizations improve their professional development through association membership. In most associations, the diversity of the members' backgrounds provides a much broader view of the industry than individuals could attain on their own. By meeting regularly with other professionals in the field, members are kept abreast of the state of their industries. Members are provided access to a pipeline of new industry techniques and ideas. In industries where the environment rapidly changes, some associations assist professional development through educational opportunities and continuing education requirements. Continuing education requirements can be college credit classes, correspondence courses, personal instruction, or seminars, depending on the industry.

Many groups offer technical assistance in upgrading and enhancing facilities to comply with the standards that the associations maintain. They will generally have lists of registered consultants for services that they cannot provide. Often these consultants work at a member rate well below market value. Other associations promote professional development through the provision of funds. They apply for state and federal grants and contracts to provide otherwise overlooked resources for their members.

ACCESS TO RESOURCES AND PUBLICATIONS

Most associations have some form of publications to get information out to their members.

For example, the American Correctional Association publishes *Corrections Today,* which is distributed exclusively to its members. This is an industry trade journal covering a broad range of correctional topics, including juvenile offenders, architecture and design, and industry best practices. Topics are decided by feedback from members on issues most relevant to their needs.

The American Correctional Association also publishes *On The Line,* a newsletter to keep its members up-to-date on issues as they develop. Additionally, chapter and affiliate leaders are provided with a special newsletter publication to help them in addressing the issues facing them specifically as association managers. The American Correctional Association also provides a variety of professional texts, videos, directories, and other publications for the correctional community. Similarly, other associations provide trade journals, newsletters, research materials, videos, and instructional publications for use by their members.

CONVENTIONS

A function of most associations is the organization and hosting of a conference. Conferences are held from one to several times a year and give members network opportunities, seminars in a variety of disciplines, entertainment, and exhibits from the many vendors offering services to members. These conferences offer members the opportunity to get off site and explore the state of the industry without the distractions of their day-to-day responsibilities. The associations gear their workshops and classes toward the issues that their members are interested in knowing more about. Subjects range from the current legal environment and tax advantages to marketing techniques and management training.

Knowing that the conference attendees will be people with credentials, exhibitors go to great lengths to make their presentations effective and relevant to the prospective customers. They tailor packages to meet the needs of that specific industry, and offerings are sometimes presented that cannot be given under other circumstances.

Members have the opportunity to view the newest and best solutions that the vendors can offer their industry.

ADVERTISING AND MARKETING OPPORTUNITIES

As mentioned in the previous section, most associations circulate publications to their members. This provides members with the ability to read up on services and products that might assist them in their business. Like the convention exhibitors, the advertisers in trade publications know the readers' needs and buying behavior and consequently present their products in a way that is most useful to readers. For example, a software advertiser in an accounting journal might highlight its recent spreadsheet breakthroughs as they apply to month-end financial reporting. Trade journals may also provide a listing of open positions around the country or region. Managers with vacant positions can place advertising knowing that it will reach qualified applicants. Members in search of openings can spend less time searching for positions in their field. Members also submit articles for publication about innovative ideas that can assist their peers. These articles can help members meet publishing requirements that their employers may impose.

Many associations now give their members who may be interested in services and products the opportunity to add their names to mailing lists. These lists allow members to receive proposals from potential vendors of products and services that could be useful in their field.

GROUP BENEFITS

Perhaps one of the most overlooked benefits that associations offer is the power of group buying. Merchants will offer discounted rates based on the projected increase in business they will receive from an association's members. Various associations offer different benefit packages, but some commonly discounted services are hotel

rates, car rentals, amusement park admissions, computer hardware and software packages, professional service usage fees, cellular phone billing, and group health, disability, and life insurance policies. Sometimes the savings is great enough that these items are complimentary once members pay their dues.

Larger associations will often form credit unions to help their members financially. Credit unions allow organizations to give their members more comprehensive banking packages and below-market rates on loans and credit cards. Members may have an easier time with loan approval when they apply for loans through credit unions because lending institutions believe that dealing with professional groups is less risky.

CONCLUSION

Association membership has been proven over time to be of great benefit to individual members, the community, and the related industries. The ability to draw on the combined knowledge of an industry's best and brightest is good for a member's professional development. Association membership allows members to reduce their use of resources, broaden their peer network, expand their career, and amplify their voice in addressing issues that affect their industry.

NOTE

1. American Society of Association Executives, Membership Material (Washington, DC: n.d.).

SUGGESTED READINGS

Norris, D. 1997. Generating value through knowledge sharing. *Association Management*. Washington, DC: American Society of Association Executives.

Romano, G. 1996. Affinity relationships that get results. *Association Management*. Washington, DC: American Society of Association Executives.

Criminal Justice Associations

American Correctional Association
4380 Forbes Boulevard
Lanham, MD 20706-4322
(301) 918-1800

American Jail Association
2053 Day Road, Suite 100
Hagerstown, MD 21740
(301) 790-2941

American Probation and Parole Association
P.O. Box 11910
Lexington, KY 40578
(606) 244-8205

Association of State Correctional Administrators
Spring Hill West
South Salem, NY 10590
(914) 533-2562

Correctional Education Association
4380 Forbes Boulevard
Lanham, MD 20706
(301) 465-1838

Correctional Industries Association
2860 Country Lane
Ellicott City, MD 21042
(410) 465-1838

International Association of Correctional
  Officers
P.O. Box 81826
Lincoln, NE 68501-1826
(402) 464-5931

International Community Corrections
  Association
P.O. Box 1987
LaCrosse, WI 54602
(608) 784-5335

National Association of Blacks in Criminal
  Justice
P.O. Box 19788
Durham, NC 27707
(919) 683-1801

National Council on Crime and Delinquency
685 Market Street, #103
San Francisco, CA 94105
(415) 896-6223

National Juvenile Detention Association
Eastern Kentucky University
301 Perkins Building
Richmond, KY 40475
(606) 622-6259

National Sheriffs Association
1450 Duke Street
Alexandria, VA 22314-3403
 (703) 836-7827

North American Association of Wardens and
 Superintendents
714 Meramac Lane
Nixa, MO 65714
(417) 725-8328

PART XII

Technology and Corrections

As our nation moves into the twenty-first century, the sweep of technology into all aspects of our lives is at once exhilarating and frightening. Employment practices within our prisons and jails seem to be upgraded and reinvented each year, suggesting that the brave new world is just beginning. The mushrooming of "anytime anywhere" communication and information technology has improved how people conduct business, but people's inherent fear of change has made them uncertain. People naturally fear new technologies that they do not fully understand.

New technology in the prison and jail business is always considered suspect by most practitioners for several reasons. First, they resist change to their routine. Second, they consider tried and true methods of operation to be safe and trustworthy. Third, new technology often is associated with cutbacks in the work force, and institution personnel are always at a premium. Accordingly, new techniques or types of equipment are not easily accepted in correctional facilities.

Yet the marketplace is alive with companies presenting new and unusual correctional products and systems. And many of these new items are functional, credible, and potentially effective solutions to old problems. How are correctional administrators to decide which of these often expensive new whiz-bangs are worthwhile? What are the hidden costs of new technologies? If an agency were to adopt one of these new techniques, how would staff accept the new process? Making the new technology work and integrating it into the work force is extremely challenging.

Correctional officials must consider technology to help their staff work more efficiently; such items as new and advanced infrared detectors, heartbeat monitors, fence sensors, electronic tracking systems, and trunked radio links are the basics of tomorrow's operation. If correctional institutions do not embrace technology and new ways of operating, staff will still be pounding away on old typewriters while the rest of the world is speeding down the information highway. Paper files must give way to computer memory. Change must come.

Part XII examines some of the major changes that have affected institution administration and offers a glimpse of future operations. Even the reluctant will be forced to modify how they do business, or they will be left behind.

405

LEARNING OBJECTIVES

After studying this section, you should be able to answer the following questions:

1. Why is technology slow to be accepted in correctional institutions?
2. What information management systems are significant in prisons and jails?
3. What are three barriers to the automation of information management?
4. How can information technology help control prison gangs?
5. What implementation techniques can help technology be accepted?
6. What are five major areas in correctional facilities that can benefit from new technology?

DISCUSSION/REVIEW QUESTIONS

1. What are two obstacles to the implementation of information systems?
2. Why is long-term planning difficult in correctional management, especially in the area of new technology?
3. How can information technology assist in the management of case records in a prison or jail?
4. Can new technology be a detriment to institutional security?

CHAPTER 57

Information Management

Lorraine Fowler

Although computers have become commonplace in the United States, the Information Age has yet to have as widespread an impact on day-to-day operations in corrections as it should. Information technology in most correctional agencies, from small jails to large correctional institutions, usually consists of word processing and isolated, often obsolete, data processing systems that may or may not support accounting and personnel functions. Inmate information, when available, is limited and rarely significant either to those making individual case-level decisions or to upper management's strategic planning.

To effectively deploy information technology, correctional and information managers must overcome two formidable obstacles: (1) lack of judicious planning; and (2) inadequate funding for information technology, which is even more troublesome.

The explosive growth of jail and prison populations across the country has taxed budgets and staff. As a result, most correctional entities are immersed in an intense competition for funding. Funding increases that do occur are generally earmarked for institutional operations and staffing directly involving security issues—expenditures that effective information technology could help to shape and to control. Too often, management fails to recognize that investing in automation can lead to improved operational and logistical efficiency, case-level management, and strategic planning. In fact, inadequate

funding for information technology may be rooted in upper management's resistance to information. This resistance is often a misguided attempt to maintain "control" by glossing over financial and operational accountability. Clearly, the first step toward optimum use of automation is management's firm commitment to information technology and its willingness to make decisions based on empirical data, even when such decisions appear to be politically problematic.

KEY DECISIONS

Decisions are as extraordinarily complex as decision makers. It is true that decisions (well- or ill-informed) are based on judgments (sound or unsound). Further, judgments generally result from information (valid or invalid) based on data (accurate or inaccurate). There are basically three types of decisions for which correctional information should be developed.

Policy Decisions ("What For" at What Costs)

- What is the ratio of the potential human and literal cost to benefit of a particular alternative sanction?
- By what percentage can crime be reduced for every 5 percent to 10 percent increase in the prison population? At what costs?

- In which respects should a correctional system deal differently with juveniles and adults? At what costs?

Policy decisions may generally be framed as benefit/cost decision alternatives.

Program Decisions (What Costs with What Results?)

- What constitutes "treatment"? Which offenders should receive which treatment services?
- What/Which returns do institutional vocational programs yield to the offender? To the institution? To the system? To the state/local community?
- Can a single program have positive client effects in the absence of other programs? (Is training adequate without job development?)

Program decisions usually can be framed as cost/effectiveness decision options.

Operations Decisions (How Can We Do What, Better, at What Costs?)

- How can we transfer offenders within the system more efficiently to ensure secure placement at a given point in time?
- Where and why does who do what to whom? (How many of what kinds of offenders are receiving what level of which services for what results, where, at any given time?) How much does "it"—this process—cost?
- Can results for the offender be achieved more efficiently by the system?

Operations decisions may nearly always be construed as cost/efficiency options. Developing a base for decision making means developing a system that provides not only accurate, timely, specific, and relevant information, but also information pertinent to the type of decision to be made. At top system or institutional levels, few decisions are either tactical or operational.

Administrative levels of decisions concern mandates and missions, political and jurisdictional disputes, policy development and strategic planning, resource finding and keeping. Such information needs are best served by formal information summaries, whether these pertain to population projections and spiraling costs, personnel problems and labor disputes, or offender and institutional profiles and trends. Managers and supervisors, on the other hand, may, depending on their roles and responsibilities, need detailed information to perform the following program and operations functions: statistical operations, accounting, cost finding and rate setting, budgeting, program development, research, monitoring and evaluation, program implementation, and security delivery.

CONDITIONS FOR CHANGE

There are not only types of decisions to be "informed," but "necessary" conditions for change. These conditions must exist at an institution (or agency or unit) before it embarks on developing (or revising) a systematic information base for decision making.

- The institution, motivated by enlightened self-interest, perceives the usefulness of good information for management decisions, especially in regard to operations monitoring, research and evaluation, and resource allocation.
- The funders (legislators and their constituents) and administrators understand that good information requires time, money, and—above all—consistent and long-term support for its use at all decision levels.
- Management and staff alike actually use currently available information to make correctional administration, programs, and operations more effective, efficient, and economical. (This is the most important base requirement.)

Automation in courts and corrections has historically lagged behind the development of computer systems for police and other law enforce-ment agencies. While courts have adapted automated systems to serve management and reporting functions (especially in response to overburdened manual systems and emphasis on "speedy trials"), concern with keeping the judi-cial branch separate from the other branches of government has influenced the willingness of courts to adopt person-case tracking systems.

Correctional information systems have devel-oped even more slowly. It has been suggested that this developmental lag is related to the typi-cal security and control milieu of the prisons and jails; this environment tends to limit institutional support for management systems. Correctional administrators too frequently have believed they must secure fences, bars, and cells rather than secure information. Without critical informa-tion, all else can become useless.

Further, there is a great deal of variability in the level of sophistication of existing automated systems. The simplest systems allow production of summary statistics based upon the automation of manual files; other systems are designed to handle at least some inmate tracking. Some of these differences may be attributed to real differ-ences in the need for complex systems. A low volume or a limited type of activity may not re-quire a complex system. Agencies or institutions typically convert to computers when their manual files grow beyond the capacity to store and to retrieve information. When manual files are first automated, system procedures are often not changed significantly. Not changing proce-dures in such instances, however, can lead to a proliferation of inefficient procedures if prob-lems caused by inadequacies of manual systems are carried over to an automated system. In cases where an organization is firmly committed to in-vesting in good information, an obstacle to ef-fective use of automation, thus, may be poor long-term planning, resulting in inefficient use of information technology funds. An organiza-tion should rethink its processes and products before it automates bad or obsolete ones.

An impediment to sound long-term planning is the high turnover rate in correctional manage-ment. The politically charged nature of correc-tions has led to short tenures and an emphasis on meeting an agency's or an institution's immedi-ate needs. Exacerbating the situation is the high turnover rate among data processors. For those left behind who are responsible for information technology planning, the task of conceiving and nurturing an information technology plan is fur-ther complicated by the dynamic nature of the computer industry. Every year, innovative tech-nology is introduced that is vastly superior to, but often incompatible with, hardware and soft-ware already in place. Trade press, vendors, and consultants trumpet the benefits of the newest technology and predict grim futures for those or-ganizations that cling to systems that become obsolete overnight.

Although information technology profession-als should keep abreast of new developments and overall industry trends, constantly buying the latest state-of-the-art technology without having a long-term information technology plan is a sure prescription for failure. An irresolute approach to information technology planning typically results in a wasteful accumulation of underused computer hardware and software or an atmosphere where software developers are expected to constantly learn new processing methods. Even more critical: So much time, en-ergy, and money are expended keeping up that producing good information for decision mak-ing, the primary purpose of information technol-ogy, is difficult.

CASE STUDY

To understand how information systems are developed and implemented by state correc-tional agencies, it may be helpful to review the experiences of one agency. This case study is based on actual experiences of the South Caro-lina Department of Corrections, which estab-lished a functional, usable program in the early 1970s. It was called the Offender-Based Correc-tional Information System.

The first unusual step in this agency's devel-opment of an information system was to turn outside of the correctional agency to the state's information resource management division for the computer hardware, network, and operating system. The department of corrections then used its own (newly retained) programmers, analysts, and statisticians to tailor the software to meet the needs of the department and to perform ad hoc reporting and advanced statistical analysis. The information system automated key processing functions, including inmate release date calculation, trust fund accounting, and inmate population projection, thereby strengthening management's commitment to investing in appropriate information technology.

Nearly 20 years after it was initially developed, the information system had expanded to handle a wide variety of inmate processing functions, but because of its dated internal structure, it also was approaching its performance limits. Accordingly, the system was redeveloped in the mainframe database environment in 1987, using a proven system and application programming environment. The department of corrections elected to use an environment familiar to staff and already available within the department, thereby reducing the development cycle dramatically, especially compared with starting over with a distributed system in minicomputers. More important, using software that staff were already acquainted with led analysts to remain focused on specific processing requirements and system design. To further ensure user acceptance and confidence, transition to the new system was gradually phased in, and a nightly batch interface between the two systems was developed to facilitate uninterrupted service to users who depended on processing provided by the new system. The existing structure was disabled only after all components had been successfully migrated to the new environment. Thus, the point was not which vendor's software was "better" or "worse," but what was optimal given the resources available (money, expertise, staff).

Presently, the information system described above supports the following functions:

- Intake processing and assessment. The central inmate record is created at time of ad-

mission to the department of corrections. It includes information about an inmate's appearance, court-ordered requirements, criminal history, names of accomplices, aliases, family information, and results from intake interviews and testing (e.g., social, mental, and physical health; and educational background).

- Inmate classification and needs assessment. An objective classification review is conducted on each inmate. An on-line automated system scores relevant inmate data using a classification model arrived at through extensive statistical analysis to determine inmate security classification. The system then recommends a level of custody, depending on the need for specific programs.

- Release eligibility screening. Conviction and sentencing information is entered, and a system of on-line and batch programs apply policy regarding service work, educational, and good behavior credit (sentence completion, parole, work program, supervised furlough, etc.) to project inmate release eligibility. Before an inmate is released or placed in community-based programs, his or her record is systematically reviewed, taking into account detainers, victim notification, and other relevant variables.

- Inmate disciplinary and grievance tracking. All aspects of institutional rules infractions and grievance filing—infraction/complaint, disposition processing, and "results" (e.g., segregation, work assignment, policy revision)—have been automated. Historical information is available through the on-line system.

- Institutional assignment and history. Historical information regarding inmate location, work and educational assignment, and custody is also maintained. The system produces daily count and intake and outtake reports. It also generates rosters by dorm and work unit.

- Inmate transportation. Institutional transfers are scheduled—taking into account inmate transfer order priority, bed availability, and bus scheduling—through a centralized bus "terminal." The system alerts staff to the existence of inmate "separation requirements" before confirming a transportation order.

- Education and program services tracking. An automated system tracks enrollment in educational and program services, including certificates and degrees earned, test scores, and attendance.
- Medical reporting. Basic health care information is collected throughout incarceration. A more comprehensive mental and medical health system is currently being implemented. The goal is to be as "paperless" with this system as is feasible.
- Inmate identification. All inmates and employees are issued identification cards magnetically encoded with personal identification information and imprinted with a digitally stored picture. The system also supports inmate and employee "name search," assorted "sign in/sign out" applications, and various inmate summary reports, including an "escape dossier" complete with photograph.
- Inmate trust fund and canteen. Inmate fund-tracking functions—including payroll, restitution accounting, special funds, and canteen purchases—are supported through the automated system.
- Personnel, payroll, position management, purchasing, accounting, receiving, inventories, payables. All human resource and fiscal subsystems are a function of the offender management base. For example, food service costs per inmate per institution are determined regularly and reported on a monthly basis, within six working days of monthly close so that wardens of similar institutions can compare costs in relation to resources.

Using Information Technology

With more than 1,800 system users and 1,200 terminals and printers connected to a high-speed statewide network, the information processing described above continues to use a venerable IBM mainframe. Over time, wardens' assistants, classification supervisors, education coordinators, and other administrative staff have acquired personal computers to support office automation, mostly as an alternative to electronic typewriters. To ensure compatibility, standards were established regarding the type of personal computer hardware and software to be used. Today, more than a third of the mainframe terminals are personal computers that emulate mainframe terminals. Although this approach is considered low tech in comparison with other open systems now in vogue, this "string and bailing wire" environment delivers rudimentary connectivity without the extraordinary costs per workstation, the system administration burdens, and the security concerns inherent in newer open architectures. Data from the mainframe database are electronically downloaded to personal computers to take advantage of data analysis and reporting tools, combining the best of "old" and "new" worlds.

Additionally, a client/server-based cashless canteen was developed recently using 40 personal computers as point-of-sale stations. Each point-of-sale transaction involves scanning universal product bar codes and a magnetically encoded inmate identification card before updating the product inventory on the personal computer and the inmate account balance on the mainframe. Currently, a personal computer–based executive information system that will provide a user-friendly graphical user interface and access to data from the mainframe database is under development. Such "mixing and matching" requires ingenuity and thought but also enables users to get what they need to do their work in a cost-effective manner.

The example above demonstrates how one correctional agency overcame many of the obstacles to effective use of information technology. Because of the strategy employed and the system's productivity, management remains committed to information technology and depends on the system for case-level decision making as well as operational and strategic planning.

The system was developed through a pragmatic approach to information technology planning that focused on processing functionality and favored evolution over revolution in terms of system development and funding requests/expenditures.

Over the years, staff made steady improvements to a conventional, centralized system to achieve a robust, full-functioning management information system. Existing systems were purposefully not thrown out in favor of the newest technological chic. Future plans call for continued expansion of mainframe-based applications, with increased use of personal computers, local area networks, and external networks. Rather than redevelop existing systems to utilize new hardware technology, information technology specialists will modify the current information systems by improving connectivity and system integration to enable use of new technology. This technologically conservative strategy has been a most successful route that has reaped maximum benefit.

CONCLUSION

Correctional information systems must be very broadly conceived. They must be able to handle information needs in management, operations, and client case tracking as well as program planning, budgeting, and evaluation efforts.

While nearly all decision makers can benefit from systematic, accurate information and information flow, not all people need access to data on everything from monetary appropriations to probation and parole reports. It is not necessary that all people know everything all the time. But some of the people must be able to access some of the information when, and as, they need it to make difficult decisions well.

Information has been used by people and other animals since at least the beginning of recorded history. The sources of information (e.g., basic research under laboratory-type conditions; needs assessments from surveys of citizens, key informants, or professionals; utilization or de-

In April 1998, the President of the United States issued a Memorandum for the Heads of Federal Agencies and Departments regarding the prevalence of inmates illegally receiving federal assistance. Most forms of assistance from the Federal Government are suspended when a person is incarcerated. Accordingly, the Social Security Administration (SSA) and the federal Bureau of Prisons entered into an agreement whereby the Bureau of Prisons provided to the SSA a copy of the federal prisoner database which they can use to compare to their database of recipients. Recognizing that the problem of fraudulent distribution of federal assistance stretches far beyond the Social Security Administration, the President ordered the SSA to make the federal inmate database available to other federal agencies that disburse benefits, and to state and local governments who do the same. Moreover, the President directed the federal agencies to create operational computer systems to conduct automated matches of the inmate database and the recipient database. Without the Bureau of Prisons' automated inmate database this initiative would not have been possible.

Source: Adapted from *Memorandum of Prevention of Prison Inmates Inappropriately Receiving Federal Benefits,* Administration of William J. Clinton, April 25, 1998.

mand data; incidence, prevalence, and trend studies; legislative and policy analyses; fiscal and budgetary documentation; laws, regulatory requirements, and judicial decisions; verbal and nonverbal signs and signals from people) are truly varied. It is important for the sake of survival that senior agency staff attend to sources of information that will help staff to realize their needs and goals.

Management of information is the key to planning an activity, controlling its development, keeping it on course, and measuring its impact. Management information systems have emerged as the principal tool for accomplishing these crucial activities.

SUGGESTED READINGS

Chapman, R. 1976. *The design of management information systems for mental health organizations: A primer.* Rockville, MD: National Institute of Mental Health.

Daft, R., and N. MacIntosh. 1978. A new approach to design and use of management information. *California Management Review* 11, no. 1.

Fowler, L. 1990. Developing information for correctional decision making. In *Proceedings of the One Hundred and Ninth Annual Congress of Corrections.* College Park, MD: American Correctional Association.

Greer, S. 1970. *The logic of social inquiry.* Chicago: Aldine Publishing Co.

Hirshorn, S. 1976. *Introduction to analysis of crime and the criminal justice system.* Washington, DC: Law Enforcement Assistance Administration. Photocopy.

McMullan, P., and J. Ries. 1976. *Evaluation of the accomplishments and impact of the programs of LEAA in the areas of information systems development and statistics services (NCJISS).* Research Triangle Institute.

SEARCH Group, Inc. 1975. *OBSCIS: Offender-Based State Corrections Information System.* Vol. 1.

Sorenson, J., and J. Wipers. 1978. Developing information systems for human service organizations. In *Evaluation of Human Service Programs,* ed. C. Attkisson et al. New York: Academic Press.

U.S. Department of Justice. 1976. *LEAA directory of automated criminal justice information systems.* Vol. 1. Washington, DC: Law Enforcement Assistance Administration.

U.S. National Commission on Law Observance and Enforcement. 1931. *Report on criminal justice.* Washington, DC: Government Printing Office.

Ward, J. et al. 1995. South Carolina's coordinated response to information technology. *Corrections Today* 57, no. 4.

CHAPTER 58

New Technology Behind Bars

Peter M. Carlson

The times they are "a changin'." American society is no longer an island unto itself and has not been for many years. Local and national markets interact around the hemispheres with phenomenal effect on international economies, business marketing strategies have become global in order to survive, and the world's media offer a web of networks that allows inexpensive and instantaneous transmission of video, audio, and data. The changes in our lives have been immense as we are influenced daily by technological advances in our homes, schools, recreation areas, and, especially, workplaces.

This is a new phenomenon in the world of corrections. Prisons and jails have not demonstrated an affinity for change in the past. Correctional institution staff have always been reluctant to accept significant change in how they do business, and staff resistance to change is the leading factor in a long list of impediments to importing technology to the correctional workplace.[1]

And there has been some logic to this disapproval of change. Most staff in the business of institution management have been schooled in a basic belief of "doing the basics well," and some new, ill-conceived practices of the past resulted in security concerns that threatened the well-being of staff and inmates. Law enforcement and correctional personnel greatly value the inherent protection of having other staff "looking after their back."

Unfortunately, new ideas have often been championed as a means of scaling back the numbers of staff involved in the supervision of inmates; technology is too often seen as a replacement for direct inmate care and surveillance. New equipment and facility enhancement are often hyped solely as a means of improving cost efficiencies rather than as a way to help staff work more effectively.

Correctional facilities' primary task is to keep the offender in custody. While there are many other important responsibilities inherent in prison and jail management, one old cliche is very appropriate: You can't treat them if you can't keep them. Given this emphasis on custodial issues, it is relatively easy to understand why correctional administrators and line staff members are loath to cut back on the human element of supervising prisoners.

Most criminal justice agencies are struggling to do their work in the face of burgeoning inmate populations and increasingly stark budgets in support of the daily institution operations. All correctional practitioners have heard the philosophy of "doing more with less." And they do. The single saving grace has been new technology and automated processes that allow staff to cover more ground in an age of dwindling resources. Like it or not, today's leaders in prisons

Opinions expressed in this chapter are those of the author and do not necessarily represent the opinions of the Federal Bureau of Prisons or the U.S. Department of Justice.

and jails must leverage technology to enhance productivity.

As correctional systems have expanded, so have the interest and scrutiny of external constituencies. Corrections-related expenditures have grown exponentially and are often one of the largest expenses in local, state, and federal budgets. Elected representatives in state legislatures, government budget personnel, and representatives of the media have all become extremely interested in prison and jail operations. Specifically, they want to know the logic behind institutional management decisions.

External overview today is intense and demanding. Decisions must be based on hard and realistic facts, and such data must be quantifiable. As John Naisbitt has clearly highlighted, our modern world is largely information based.[2] The implication for the world of prisons and jails is significant. New technology is not just important—it is critical for survival. Today's correctional leaders must overcome the inertia that slows the acceptance of change.

Despite the reticence about new concepts, corrections has undergone as much technological change as any other business or industry in the United States and the world. Daily prison and jail routines are very, very different today even than they were three years ago. The information age is upon everyone.

Many of the new technologies today and in the future will be adapted from applications developed by the National Aeronautics and Space Administration (NASA) and the Department of Defense. The National Institute of Corrections has been working at this adaptation since 1989, and several intergovernmental committees are currently exploring possibilities for applying military technologies to justice administration environments.[3] Many military innovations have proven to be very adaptable to the prison and jail setting: man-barrier wire, infrared night vision technology, and the application of identification verification equipment.

In short, technology is having a major impact on the staid world of prison and jail administration, and the best is yet to come. What are these technological whiz-bangs that are available today? New ways of doing business "inside" are plentiful and cover all aspects of institution management.

INFORMATION TECHNOLOGY

Historically, "information systems" in prisons and jails have simply referred to basic handwritten information that was gathered at the time of a prisoner's initial commitment to a facility: name, offense, sentence, and physical description. In either a central file or on index cards in the deputy warden's office, other internal documents that related to the offender's institutional adjustment accumulated: the individual's disciplinary record and classification materials such as work and housing assignments. Records were often rudimentary and could be retrieved or examined only manually, file by file. Basic statistical data were occasionally prepared (with great effort) and analyzed.

In addition to this dearth of systemic information, the tracking of individual inmates during their confinement was labor-intensive and inefficient. The limited paper systems in use made case management very inmate specific and metatrends or other analysis of big picture needs were often not attempted. Even today, this paper-dependent central file system is often the primary basis for information about a correctional agency's clientele. But technology is making more information available.

Information management systems and the ubiquitous personal computer (PC) have had a huge impact on our lives. The advent of the PC has turned life upside down, both in and out of the locked world of correctional facilities. Today, computers monitor many aspects of institutional life, ranging from tracking actual inmate counts to status reports on open security doors. Computers can even alert staff to unacceptable drops in temperature in remote food freezer lockers. PCs have made typewriters look like relics of ancient clerical practice, and today's support staff do everything from ordering supplies on-line to distributing documents around the institution or the state by the simple touch of a keyboard. Wardens take their first cup of coffee in the morning as they check their PCs for summaries of overnight incidents as well as the new day's appointments. Lieutenants' staff roster changes and lists of every nature are modified by electronic entries. Financial management documentation, food service stores, and property inventories are all stored within megahertz and random access memory.

Modern computer technology has enabled correctional institution staff to easily monitor individual inmates throughout their confinement. Staff at the facility or headquarters office can monitor an individual prisoner's key data, insti-

tutional summary data, or the entire correctional system's collective data with ease.

The availability of information to the public sector has also been enhanced by computers and the Internet. For example, the names of violent inmates soon to be eligible for parole in New York are now available on the Internet, and citizens are free to contact the state division of parole if they wish to comment on an inmate's bid for parole.[4] In another development, several counties in Maryland have developed a toll-free telephone number for those who have been victimized to call in and verify the custody status of prisoners who have attacked them. The computerized service, called VINE (Victim Information

---

Is Public Information EverToo Public?

Criminal records have long been available to the public in most states, but the new availability of information on the Internet is being labeled by some as an invasion of the criminal's right to privacy. Critics of this new electronic access believe there is a large difference between going to a public office for data and accessing information via one's home computer.

"It's going to encourage average people who have no need for the information to go surfing for it," said Barry Steinhardt, director of the Electronic Frontier Foundation, a human rights group that focuses on ethical concerns related to new technology. He believes the large-scale availability of prisoner data raises the concern to a new level that should be an issue to anyone concerned about the invasion of privacy.*

Texas is the first state to publish its criminal records on the Web. A new state law in September 1997 mandated this instant access to criminal records. The new serv-

ice has been received with few complaints.

Many other states have sex offender directories that people can access via their home computers and the Internet. California began this trend with its "sexoffenders.net" in August 1997. The information is intended to permit citizens to conduct background checks on people who may be hired to provide personal services such as yard work, babysitting, or home care.

Privacy advocates express their fear that people may be falsely accused because of mistaken identity and that unscrupulous individuals may use this database to gather personal information about those in the files. A significant amount of personal information can be gathered about anyone using prisoner databases and other publicly available databases.

Source: *Reprinted from ZDNet, June 17, 1998. Copyright © 1998 ZD, Inc.

and Notification Everyday), keeps electronic information on offenders: custody status, bond status, court dates, and so on. Registered victims are given access codes and may call in for current information at their convenience.

In short, information technology has changed our communication and work practices—in all areas—for the better.

PRISONER IDENTIFICATION

In the area of prisoner identification, new processes are being found today that greatly enhance institution security and cost-effectiveness. Mug shots are now taken with digital cameras and stored in computers; photographic images of the inmates are now printed for many operational uses and at a fraction of the cost. Fingerprints are often processed today with on-line systems, and retina imaging and iris scanning equipment are becoming more reliable than fingerprinting. Some facilities have pioneered barcoded wrist bands on inmates, and electronic bracelets may be used within housing or program areas to accurately locate any inmate at any time. It is now possible to inventory, record, and track all inmate personal property using mobile bar-code scanning equipment. While these systems are rather expensive today, they are likely to cost much less in the near future.

Perimeter Security

Perimeter security systems are exceptionally accurate today. Taut wire equipment, closed circuit television (CCTV) motion detector, microwave, infrared, and vibration cable systems have enhanced staff ability to monitor fence lines and other secure areas. While no perimeter systems are 100 percent perfect, they are extremely important to minimize the risk of escape. The probability of detection (sensitivity of the sensor) has historically been a tradeoff against the system's nuisance alert rate (false alarms); each new iteration of perimeter systems has improved on the previous iteration, and all are becoming smarter through advanced digital signal processing.

Today's adaptive sensors can detect moving targets based on size or mass and movement. Unless a target has the minimum alarm characteristics, it will not register as a violation of the zone. While a person or vehicle crossing the zone will be identified, typical sources of false alarms such as small animals, birds, rain, or blowing dirt are not a problem. Perimeter lighting is now electronically measured to ensure full illumination of fence lines and other key areas; some systems use lighting that is greatly increased when the area sensor alerts.

California, Colorado, Missouri, and Alabama have recently installed lethal electric fences that have been exceptionally effective in deterring escape attempts. These fences, as an exception to the rule that technology should not replace personnel, truly do offer the opportunity to cut back on staffing in towers and external mobile patrols. California's Department of Corrections has found that the installation of these fences has facilitated the deactivation of nearly all towers and enabled the administrators to redeploy staff to other important posts. The one drawback of these fences is their propensity to inadvertently kill birds and other wild animals; special netting has been developed that allows the lethal fences to protect the perimeters as well as keep wildlife off the electrical grids.

Entrance Procedures

Perimeter points of ingress and egress, the location of many escape attempts, have been greatly enhanced in some jurisdictions by new technology. Special identification cards with magnetic information in bar codes offer the ability to electronically check staff and visitors into and out of secure institution perimeters. When combined with other systems such as "voice printing" or hand geometry readers, the identification cards significantly improve the security of a jail or prison.

Heartbeat detectors are available now for use in vehicle sally ports. The mobile equipment easily attaches to the side of a car or truck and accurately detects the heartbeat of an intruder who may be hiding in or on the vehicle and attempting an escape.

Inmate visitors may now be quickly screened for metal contraband (razor blades, syringes, guns, knives, explosives) with low-power X-ray screening. Although some complain of this intrusion on one's privacy and the exposure to radiation, neither seems to be a valid complaint. Medical industry representatives note that the very limited microrems are actually less than the exposure to radiation that one would receive sitting in front of a television.

Drug detection screening systems also offer an excellent means of protecting an institution's security envelope from the smuggling of illegal substances. Ion drug detection units on the market offer visitor processing stations the ability to screen and prevent the entrance of those who have the scent or trace of specific illegal narcotics on their clothing or bodies. These systems can be programmed to screen for 30 different narcotics.

Crisis Management

Emergency response equipment has vastly improved in recent years. Nonlethal, or more appropriately, less lethal weapons are now the first level of response in crisis situations. Stun guns, flash bang distraction devices, and gas are much safer for all concerned than traditional shotguns, rifles, and revolvers. Stun belts are in use today that provide a hidden passive restraint for inmates under escort out of the institution. Upon activation, these battery-powered devices deliver an electrical jolt to the subject's body that is guaranteed to lay them down. Laser lights are now available that, when directed at an individual, can cause momentary blindness; if the power is stepped up, these laser lights can physically disorient and stun the subject.

New Construction and Reconstruction

Prefinished concrete modules have become widely accepted in prison and jail design and construction. From a modest 3 percent of the market as recently as 10 years ago, precast concrete cells are now estimated to account for 35 percent of all new inmate housing construction.[5] Using traditional masonry construction means that a project takes longer to build. Modular building has exceptional quality control, and budgets stretch further. It is estimated by designers that correctional jurisdictions can save up to 20 percent on hard dollar costs by using precast modular cells. Finally, these precast technological improvements are expected to last longer and require less maintenance.

CCTV

CCTV has been a great technological addition to staff supervision in all correctional environments. Most secure facilities have used camera supervision to monitor and record inmate visiting rooms to help supervise the areas and help prevent drug or other contraband from entering the institution. Monitoring can be accomplished from remote stations, giving management the ability to add to the duties of some posts. High security penitentiaries have found that cameras in cell houses, dining rooms, recreation areas, and work production zones have significantly cut back on the level of violence. Video recordings have also been very effective in subsequent prosecutions of those inmates who chose to assault others under the eye of the camera. Staff members also appreciate the additional sense of security provided by the presence of the cameras.

Implementation of Technological Change

Generally speaking, for new technology to be fully accepted in the custodial environment, it must be seen as helpful and facilitating staff work, not as an additional burden or a threat to institutional personnel. Rather than replace personal interaction, high-tech products must make tasks easier and more efficient. If our electronic "span of control" is made larger, it also must be made more effective.

Exhibit 58–1   A Strategy for Facilitating New Technology

1. Identify the problem area. Change just for the sake of change is not welcomed nor an asset in the correctional environment. Focus clearly on the operational concern.

2. Determine if the problem is really an issue; is it an impediment to effective operations? Careful analysis is very important in correctional work; the old "tested and tried" procedures are often very important to basic institutional security or operations.

3. Involve technical experts as well as the future "customers" in the planning of the recommended changes. If line staff are expected to use a new process, procedure, or piece of equipment, they must have input into the planning and implementation of new operations.

4. Ensure all impediments to successful implementation are identified in the planning process and that an appropriate strategy is developed for dealing with these derailing elements.

5. Develop measurable outcomes that are expected from the change. Establish timelines for accomplishment.

6. It is often helpful to first consider the use of a pilot project, if possible. See how the new technology works in one area before implementing wholesale change in an institution or system.

7. Provide feedback to the affected staff and seek honest evaluations from personnel using the technology. Modify procedures as necessary to improve the local implementation of new operations.

Staff reluctance to adapt to new procedures creates a significant management issue as institution administrators try to modernize their operations. Careful planning is necessary to effect such changes (see Exhibit 58–1). New York's Department of Corrections, for example, has developed guidelines to help senior administrators integrate technology into their institutions and to help line staff overcome reluctance to accept new items.[6] New York emphasizes that new items must be properly designed and helpful to staff, tailored to local operations, and user friendly. And the development should involve line staff in the initial effort to select and implement the new process or equipment. This final point may be the best point of all: Teamwork in the process represents the key to success.

CONCLUSION

Changes in the administration of confinement facilities have come slowly over the years, but the last decade has brought extraordinary and astonishing new concepts to a very old business.

To meet the demands of the future, correctional leaders will need to seek out new ways of doing this business yet not lose sight of the need to operate safe, secure, and humane correctional programs for those who live and work inside. The continuous pressures of inmate management and staff leadership can be overwhelming. Technology will lighten the load.

NOTES

1. National Institute of Justice, *The Correctional Technology Manual: Locating and Evaluating Correctional Technology* (Washington, DC: forthcoming).

2. J. Naisbitt, *Megatrends: Ten New Directions Transforming Our Lives* (New York: Warner Books, 1982), 11.

3. J. Roberts, "Yesterday and Tomorrow—Prison Technology in 1900 and 2000," *Corrections Today* 57, no. 4 (1995): 114–120.

4. *Corrections Digest,* 14 November, 1997.

5. S. Weirich, "Move Over to Mod," *Corrections Technology and Management* 1, no. 1 (1997).

6. C.J. Werder, ed., *Making Corrections Technology Work for You* (Horsham, PA: LRP Publications, 1997), 8.

PART XIII

Creating the Future

Contemporary correctional administrators face a turbulent world of challenges and seem to be constantly entangled in controversy. The courts continue to pour new felons into the justice administration funnel, many institutions are embarrassingly overcrowded, budgets have become tighter, and state and federal elected representatives want to micromanage the lockups despite never having set foot within the environment. The inmates are more violent and often gang affiliated, institution staff are less experienced, and the public expresses increasingly conservative attitudes toward prisons and convicted felons.

Everyone is quick to critique correctional administrators. Inmates often express their opinions through informal, formal, and legal challenges. Staff and their labor representatives do not hesitate to complain about their conditions and treatment. The courts conduct lawful fact finding in conjunction with complaints voiced by various parties and do not hesitate to rule against the institutional staff. In truth, there are some days when one cannot help but wonder why administrators chose such a profession.

It would be relatively easy to despair in the face of these rapid and dynamic influences on the world of corrections. Yet the professionals in the field continue to rise to the challenge and function effectively in the face of adversity.

How do the legions of correctional workers and leaders keep their spirits up? Interestingly, most wardens and institutional leaders love their work. Surveys consistently report that these professionals believe they are performing a valuable public service, they believe that the silent majority truly appreciates their work, and they believe they make a difference in the quality of life in the United States.

The dilemmas of justice administration all center around the American public's many and diverse expectations of the criminal justice system. Almost all people have strong opinions on crime, the courts, and what should be done with those who are criminally convicted. And one will not hear a clear consensus about what we should do or how we should do it. Even at the cusp of the twenty-first century, the mission of prisons and jails is not only unclear . . . it is confused. Our multiple purposes circle between the desire to rehabilitate, punish, deter, and incapacitate. It is no wonder that our goals seem rather schizophrenic; many believe it is extremely difficult to operate a system that can accomplish all these tasks well.

Others believe a correctional organization can balance all of these goals. Whatever your perspective is, it is absolutely necessary to have a disciplined and controlled institutional environment before any of these intentions can be accomplished. Successful prison and jail leaders clearly understand this basic premise; paying attention to detail and ensuring high-quality operations sets the necessary baseline for the accomplishment of any and all aspects of the multiple missions of confinement.

The future of corrections is threatening—and promising. Part XIII presents chapters on critical issues that promise to test today's status quo: the overwhelming cost of confinement, increasingly longer sentences, privatization, legislative interaction with daily management practice, and how all of these factors influence the growth of prison and jail populations.

Our public administrators in the field of institution management must plan for—and help create—the future of corrections. The safety and security of the American public depend upon it.

LEARNING OBJECTIVES

After studying this section, you should be able to answer the following questions:

1. What are the conflicting missions of corrections? How do these conflicting missions impact the field?
2. How will strategic planning help the world of correctional administration? What elements of strategic planning are critical if the effort is to be meaningful within a justice agency?
3. It is clear that changes in sentencing law affect prisons and jails. Why have these laws changed in the last decade, and why are these trends helpful or harmful to American society?
4. What is the history of private companies in corrections? Why has the private sector's role grown again in the last 15 years?
5. Have public and political interest in how correctional facilities are managed grown in recent years? Is this a positive development?
6. Is it inherently wrong for correctional leaders to involve themselves in political debate when the subject is the institutional domain?
7. What issues do you believe are going to command the attention of the leaders of prisons and jails in the United States in future years?

DISCUSSION/REVIEW QUESTIONS

1. Prison and jail populations are growing exponentially. Do you believe incarceration is the solution to crime in the United States?
2. What leadership skills will be critical within the ranks of correctional leaders in steering their agencies in future years?
3. What is the difference between strategic planning and strategic management?
4. What is the difference between an indeterminate sentence and a mandatory minimum sentence?
5. Are sentencing guidelines more fair and reasonable than simple judicial discretion?
6. What are the pros and cons of privatization in corrections?
7. What does it mean to appropriately "position an agency" to withstand political pressure for change?

CHAPTER 59

The Future of Sentencing

Julius Debro

There has been a massive increase in U.S. jail and prison populations in recent years. In 1985, there were 397 sentenced inmates per 100,000 residents; at the end of 1995, there were 796 sentenced inmates per 100,000.[1] Thus, the proportion of jailed or imprisoned inmates nearly doubled in the last decade. America's incarceration rate of 433 per 100,000 citizens is the highest in the world. The states with the highest incarceration rates are the District of Columbia, Texas, Oklahoma, Louisiana, South Carolina, Arizona, Mississippi, Nevada, Alabama, and Michigan.[2] States with the lowest incarceration rates are Minnesota, North Dakota, Maine, West Virginia, Vermont, Massachusetts, Nebraska, New Hampshire, Utah, and Iowa.[3]

Appropriations for corrections at the state level increased more rapidly than any other expense in recent years. From 1991 to 1997, spending by state correctional agencies increased from $18.1 billion to $28.9 billion; on average, the correctional system absorbed 4.8 percent of the jurisdictions' total budget.[4]

One of the major reasons for the increase in prison population is that sentencing policy has changed both at the state and federal level. Another reason is that the public now views crime as one of the nation's most important issues. Legislators are now demanding stiffer penalties, such as "three strikes you're out," and there are constant revisions of sentencing policy throughout the country.

State courts convicted about 872,000 adults of a felony in 1994. Of these, 71 percent were sentenced to a period of confinement—45 percent to state prisons and 26 percent to local jails. Jail sentences are for short-term confinement (usually for a year or less) in a county or city facility, while prison sentences are for long-term confinement (usually for over a year) in a state facility; 29 percent of convicted felons were given straight probation with no jail or prison time to serve. Felons sentenced to a state prison in 1994 had an average sentence of six years but were likely to serve roughly a third of that sentence— or about two years—before release. The average sentence to local jail was six months. The average probation sentence was just over three years.

Besides being sentenced to incarceration or probation, 41 percent or more of convicted felons also were ordered to pay a fine, pay victim restitution, receive treatment, perform community service, or comply with some other additional penalty. A fine was imposed on at least 21 percent of convicted felons. Table 59–1 gives details about felony sentences imposed by state courts in 1994.

What is the purpose of sentencing, and how should that purpose be served? How has sentencing changed over the years, and have the changes been beneficial or detrimental to society? Finally, what is the future of sentencing?

Table 59–1 Average Maximum Sentence Length Imposed by State Courts in 1994 for Felons

Most Serious Conviction Offense	Sentence (in Months)		
	Prison	Jail	Probation
All offenses	71	6	40
Violent offenses	118	6	45
Property offenses	57	6	42
Drug offenses	61	6	38
Weapons offenses	47	5	32
Other offenses	41	5	36

Note: Means exclude sentences to death or to life in prison. Sentence length data were available for 834,124 incarceration and probation sentences.

Source: Data from *Felony Sentences in State Courts, 1994,* January 1997, Bureau of Justice Statistics, NCJ-163391.

SENTENCING DISPARITY

Historically, the purpose of sentencing in the United States was to punish the offender. But, as early as 1870, when the National Prison Association was formed, rehabilitation became the prison ideal. Decisions about types of punishment were made by the legislature, with judges attempting to follow the will of the legislature but often making decisions based on their review of the law. Judges' decisions quite often depended upon information received from the prosecutor or the probation department. Some judges were harsh to certain kinds of offenders, and others were lenient.[5] There was never any consistency in sentencing throughout the country.

Each session, state legislatures would pass different laws relating to different offenders. Thus, judges were never given clear goals, and they had broad powers to impose sentences.[6]

Quite often, sentences imposed by judges were harsh, discriminatory, and inconsistent. Persons committing the same offense but appearing before a different judge would receive vastly different sentences. The major goals were to deter others from committing crimes, incapacitate those persons who were considered dangerous to the community, and rehabilitate the offending person. These goals were often incompatible with public needs. Prisoners were not deterred by long sentences, and those persons who had been incapacitated for long periods of time were being released much earlier than the public expected. There was no "truth in sentencing." A person who received 150 years would be out in 30 or 40 years—or less. Prisoners were expected to serve approximately one-third of the sentence prior to release, and rehabilitation was not working.

For the last 126 years, Americans have used rehabilitative theory to try to change criminal behavior. Every person was considered capable of change. People believed that through a system of extended sentencing, the individual, if given an opportunity, could change with the assistance of programs designed to act as change agents within the prison. With this concept came the indeterminate sentence that was seen by correctional experts as the only method to bring about changes in offenders' behavior. By the 1960s, every state in the nation had an indeterminate sentencing system.[7] While the system was geared to bring about change in inmates' behavior, over time, it became an instrument for the status quo.

INDETERMINATE SENTENCING

Indeterminate sentencing was a form of sentencing in which the judge sentenced a person to a range of years. The range could be from one year to life, which essentially meant that the defendant had to serve a minimum of one year but could serve his or her entire life in prison. As long as a judge sentenced within a statutory range, there were no rules to govern the amount of time a judge could impose. An administrative board called a parole board generally determined the amount of time a person served in prison. The parole board had its own set of guidelines for decision making, and a person could serve many years in prison without any knowledge of when he or she would be released. Over the years, there were complaints about the indeterminate sentence that lead to an investigation by the U.S. Senate Judiciary Committee. The Senate Judiciary Committee noted that the indeterminate sentence lead to an outdated and unworkable model of rehabilitation. The Judiciary Committee stated:

> Recent studies suggest that this approach has failed, and most sentencing judges as well as the Parole Commission agree that the rehabilitation model is not an appropriate basis for sentencing decisions. We know too little about human behavior to be able to rehabilitate individuals on a routine basis or even to determine accurately whether or when a particular person has been rehabilitated.[8]

This essentially was the death of the indeterminate sentence and of rehabilitation, as we had known it in the past. In addition to concerns regarding rehabilitation, there was no consistency in sentencing; one person could get 5 years for an offense while another person involved in the same crime could get probation. The decision about how much time an individual received did not rest with the judges but with the parole board, and the public had begun to see the system of sentencing as a mockery. Defendants rarely served the amount of time given by the judge. If a sentence were for 12 years, in most cases, the defendant would serve only 4 years.

In 1975, *The Effectiveness of Correctional Treatment* by Douglas Lipton, Robert Martinson, and Judith Wilks was published. This was a study of 231 programs designed for rehabilitation. The report concluded that the evaluation "leads us irrevocably to the conclusion that nothing works, that we haven't the faintest clue about how to rehabilitate offenders and reduce recidivism."[9] This sealed the fate for indeterminate sentencing.

The establishment of the Brown Commission in 1966, with former Governor Pat Brown from California as its chair, to review sentencing practices gave rise to hearings about indeterminate sentencing in 1971.[10] Some four years later, Senator Edward Kennedy introduced a bill to establish sentencing guidelines.[11] Subsequently, bills were introduced in the 95th, 96th, and 97th Congresses.[12-15] In 1984, Congress passed the Sentencing Reform Act that created the United States Sentencing Commission and Federal Sentencing Guidelines. In addition, this legislation abolished parole and indeterminate sentences at the federal level.[16]

SENTENCING GUIDELINES

The major change within sentencing in the last two decades has been a move away from the indeterminate sentence to presumptive–appropriate ranges of sentences within which judges must sentence offenders. These ranges have been established initially by a sentencing commission that is given authority by the legislature to study sentencing practices and recommend guidelines to be followed. Judges can depart from these guidelines, but they must state their reasons for the departures. There do not seem to be any clear-cut rules for departure, and when the judge does depart, there can be an appeal. Most guidelines cover felony cases only, but they do regulate prison commitment and the length of time one spends in prison.

Some states enacted mandatory minimum terms that may override the guidelines, but most did not. Some states also eliminated parole, as recommended by the American Bar Association policy group. Other states moved to descriptive guidelines designed to help judges follow existing sentencing norms more consistently.[17]

The major purpose of the sentencing guidelines generally is to eliminate disparity and move away from rehabilitation as the goal for punishment. The guidelines have also been used in some cases to limit prison population growth by tailoring sentences to prison capacity. For the most part, sentences are based mainly on the severity of the crime and the defendant's prior history.

Sentencing guidelines have gradually been adopted in many states. Minnesota moved to guidelines in 1980; one of its main purposes was to try to control prison overcrowding. The state appointed an independent commission to oversee sentencing. The commission was authorized to take existing prison capacity and other resources into "substantial consideration." When prison populations began to increase nationwide in the 1980s, Minnesota moved to reduce presumptive prison durations, thus reducing the rise of the prison population. Minnesota's prison population increased very slowly in the 1980s. For example, the Minnesota prison population increased only 8 percent between 1980 and 1984, while the nation's prison population rose 41 percent.[18] Between 1984 and 1988, the Minnesota prison population rose 29 percent. Compared with the nation's prison population, which increased about 35 to 41 percent during the 1980s, the Minnesota prison population was still somewhat low.[19]

There were three major causes for the increase in Minnesota: more felony convictions, increased parole violations, and significant increases in sentence length. These changes were caused primarily by the rise in crack cocaine trafficking. The number of parole violations grew because of greater use of intensive supervision and drug testing. Also, the legislature applied pressure on the commission to increase penalties. The legislature changed the primary goal of the commission to that of public safety, thus taking back some of the powers it had delegated to the commission earlier. The legislature indicated that correctional resources and current practices should remain as factors but should not be taken into "substantial" consideration at the time of sentencing. Minnesota also established identical penalties for powdered cocaine and crack cocaine.

The State of Washington passed its sentencing reform bill in 1981, and the guidelines went into effect in 1984. Even though there is a sentencing guidelines commission, the legislature has authority to adopt, amend, or veto the commission's proposals. Essentially, the Washington commission must go before the legislature to recommend changes, and getting changes passed has been very difficult.

Washington was fortunate in the late 1980s because it had prison bed space that it could rent to other states. While other states and the federal government were having overcrowding problems, Washington had approximately 1,000 spare beds. The major reason for excessive capacity was that the state housed its less serious felons in county jails. This was similar to what California had done in the 1970s in its probation subsidy program. Through this program, the state paid counties to keep less serious felons within their county facilities or on probation. While this worked for a short period of time for the State of Washington, pressure from the community pushed prosecutors to request stiffer penalties for certain types of offenders, especially those with drug offenses. Within the last few years, the State of Washington has experienced drastic changes in sentencing policy. Prosecutors have been instrumental in getting drastically increased penalties for drug and drug-related offenses. There have also been increased penalties for sexual offenses, and Washington was the first state to pass a "three strikes you're out" law.

The prison and jail population growth is now out of control in the State of Washington; prisons are operating at 167 percent of capacity. By 1999, the operating bill for corrections is expected to double to a billion dollars.[20]

North Carolina began using presumptive sentencing guidelines in 1995. These guidelines were similar to those in Kansas, Minnesota, Oregon, Pennsylvania, and Washington. Prison sentences are required for nearly all violent felonies, there are more work programs, and restitution is imposed more frequently. Under North Carolina's State Structured Sentencing Act, prisoners serve more time; they serve 100 percent of the minimum sentence imposed, and prison is mandatory for serious violent offenders, but nonviolent offenders with little or no priors can be funneled into community-based programs (intermediate sanctions). North Carolina has established a structured sentencing monitoring system that provides detailed data on all sentenced felons and misdemeanants. These data are constantly being analyzed so that changes can be recommended to the legislature.

The federal government has been using sentencing guidelines since 1987. These guidelines are created and monitored by the United States Sentencing Commission, an independent judicial agency created by the Sentencing Reform Act of 1984. Judge Jose Cabranes of the United States Court of Appeals for the Second Circuit describes guidelines this way: "The Sentencing Guidelines system is a failure—a dismal failure, a fact well known and fully understood by virtually everyone who is associated with the federal justice system."[21(p.2)]

One of the major problems with sentencing has been the problem of racial disparity, especially in the area of drugs. There are claims that prosecutors enforce laws in a way that does injury to African Americans.

National statistics indicate that one out of three African Americans in their twenties is in prison or on probation or parole. A recent article in the *Journal of the American Medical Association* indicated that there is no medical difference

---

As of January 1, 1997, 23 jurisdictions had an exclusively determinate sentencing scheme, 9 had exclusively indeterminate sentencing, and 20 had both. Most of the states that had abolished parole (12) did so in the 1980s and 1990s; only Maine had taken this step earlier, in 1976.

Source: Adapted from C. Camp and G. Camp, *1997 Corrections Yearbook,* pp. 50–51, © 1997, Criminal Justice Institute, Inc.

---

between powder and crack cocaine, yet the sentences are very different. Under federal law, possession of 5 grams of crack cocaine brings a mandatory five-year prison sentence, whereas a person must have 500 grams of cocaine, or nearly a pound, to get the same five-year sentence. Many believe that the 100:1 disparity cannot be explained by anything except racial discriminations.

One of the major purposes of the guidelines was to eliminate racial injustices, but the guidelines have actually increased racial injustice, especially at the federal level. Prosecutors admit that crack dealers are targeted and that most are African Americans. They contend that they are not singling out African American offenders, but it is clear that the laws are being enforced in a way that does injury to African Americans. The harshest penalties are given to offenses that African Americans are most likely to commit. Prosecutors in Los Angeles handled 24 crack cases in 1991, and all of the persons prosecuted were African Americans. Of 6,187 crack cocaine cases filed in Los Angeles County from 1990 to 1992, only 7 involved Caucasians!

Attempts to establish or refute discrimination in criminal justice processes—especially in the courts—have been fraught with methodological difficulties. Sample sizes are generally too small, legal and nonlegal variables are difficult to control, and the problem of generalizing from studies of one court to another makes the research vulnerable to criticism. Different findings will always exist in different courts; thus any charges of discrimination must be attributed to the exercise of discretion at some point from apprehension to sentencing.

The federal guidelines were intended to make the sentencing more predictable and less discretionary. But the system has transferred substantial discretion from judges to prosecutors.

Within the last two decades, many states and the federal government have moved from a system of indeterminate sentencing to a system of determinate sentencing that is based in some cases on guidelines designed to eliminate disparity and provide certainty and fairness to all defendants. What has actually occurred is that we have moved away from trying to understand the individual offender and his or her motivation for committing the crime. The system now places all offenders, regardless of the circumstances, into the same category. Judicial flexibility has been eliminated. In effect, we have given too much power in sentencing to the prosecutors.

THE FUTURE

American judicial systems must shift more in the direction of restorative justice, a new concept of looking at justice that shifts the focus away from the offender and puts it on the victim and the community. Crime is now an act against people in the community and not just against the state. Thus, the criminal has to make his or her peace within the community.

While spending time in prison is important, it is not the only variable that should be considered in sentencing. Plans for restitution are as important, as they involve the victim, the community, and the offender. Mediation programs have been established in countries such as Belgium, Canada, England, France, and Germany as well as the United States. Within this country the use of mediation programs has been primarily restricted to juveniles, but some jurisdictions have considered using such programs for adult offenders as well.

The prediction for the future is that the American system of justice will move gradually toward returning more discretion to judges. It is judges who have the complete historical record of the offender and are in a better position to make sentencing decisions. At one time, federal judges followed the recommendations of probation officers in 95 percent of cases.

CONCLUSION

Elected representatives have assumed a much greater role in sentencing in the last 15 years. They must be willing to review the effectiveness of the legislated sentencing guidelines and seek adjustment where necessary. It is extremely im-

portant that sentencing guidelines at the federal and state levels be routinely reevaluated. Legislative bodies need this feedback, and the credibility of the entire American judicial system is at stake.

NOTES

1. U.S. Department of Justice, Bureau of Justice Statistics, *Correctional Populations in the United States,* 1995.
2. C. Camp and G. Camp, *1997 Corrections Yearbook* (South Salem, NY: Criminal Justice Institute, Inc., 1997), 10.
3. Camp and Camp, *1997 Corrections Yearbook,* 10.
4. Camp and Camp, *1997 Corrections Yearbook,* 71.
5. H. Jacob, *Justice in America: Courts, Lawyers and the Judicial Process* (Boston: Little Brown and Company, 1972), 176–178.
6. L. Katz, *The Justice Imperative: An Introduction to Criminal Justice* (Anderson Publishing Company, 1980), 32.
7. I. Nagel, "Structuring Sentencing Discretion: The New Federal Sentencing Guidelines," *Journal of Criminal Law & Criminology* 80 (1990): 883, 913–939.
8. Nagel, "Structuring Sentencing Discretion: The New Federal Sentencing Guidelines."
9. D. Lipton, R. Martinson, and J. Wilks, *The Effectiveness of Correctional Treatment* (New York: Praeger Publishing, 1975).
10. The National Commission on Reform of Federal Criminal Law (Brown Commission), *Hearings before the Subcommittee on Criminal Laws and Procedures of the Senate Judiciary Committee,* 92d Cong., 1st sess., 1971, ____.
11. 94th Cong., 2d sess., S.R. 2699.
12. 95th Cong., 1st sess., S.R. 1437.
13. 96th Cong., 1st sess., S.R. 1722.
14. 97th Cong., lst sess., S.R. 1630.
15. 97th Cong., 2d sess., S.R. 2572.
16. 98th Cong., 1st sess., S.R. 829.
17. R. Frase, "Prison Population Growing under Minnesota Guidelines," *Overcrowded Times* 4, no. 1 (1993).
18. Frase, "Prison Population Growing under Minnesota Guidelines," *Overcrowded Times.*
19. Frase, "Prison Population Growing under Minnesota Guidelines," *Overcrowded Times.*
20. R. Lieb, "Washington Prison Population Growth out of Control," *Overcorwded Times* 4, no. 1 (1993).
21. J. Cabranes, "Sentencing Guidelines: A Dismal Failure, *New York Law Journal* 227 (1992): 2.

CHAPTER 60

Growth of the Private Sector

Douglas C. McDonald

Whether to turn the management and operation of entire prisons and jails over to private firms has become a hotly contested issue in recent years. Such contracts have existed for some time (with little controversy) in juvenile correctional systems and in low security, community-based adult facilities. Contracting for the provision of more narrowly focused services—health care or food services, for example—also raised few objections. All of this changed in the mid-1980s, however, when a vocal private correctional industry emerged and offered to take over entire correctional facilities and, indeed, entire state systems.

The private correctional industry has grown rapidly during the past decade. Although many still see the issue as "government versus the private sector," a more apt description of current affairs in many jurisdictions is government *and* the private sector. Private facilities are now an established part of the correctional landscape, and the further growth of the industry is likely to be very strong.

PRIVATE CORRECTIONS—REPEATING HISTORY

Private imprisonment is not a new invention of the late twentieth century; privately operated jails were commonplace in England until the nineteenth century.[1–3] In the United States, governments took responsibility for prisons and jails, but in the early nineteenth century, prison wardens began leasing out convicts to work for and to be housed by private businesspeople.[4] These practices here and in England were largely swept away by reform movements in the wake of scandals, but privately operated facilities continued to survive into the recent period at the shallower end of correctional systems: in low security, community-based facilities and in juvenile correctional systems.[5]

Public inattention to private imprisonment evaporated in the mid-1980s. A newly formed private firm offered to take over the entire state prison system in Tennessee and to run it more efficiently—an offer that was considered but ultimately declined. With slightly less notice, a number of small firms began to contract with local governments for private management of jails and with states for low security and some medium security prisons.[6] In many quarters, however, opposition to privatization remains powerful, as does the sense of battlement. For example, a national organization of public correctional employees, the Corrections and Criminal Justice Reform Task Force, declared at its third annual meeting in 1997 that privatization was the "number one threat to our profession in the nation."[7]

The emergence of the private imprisonment industry in the mid-1980s resulted from several factors.[8] Demand for prison and jail beds had been growing steeply for a decade, largely because of tougher sentencing laws and a "war" on drugs; taxpayer rebellions were sweeping the country; state and local governments were slapped with expenditure caps; public debt ceilings were being reached; and voters were declining to approve increases in public debt for prison and jail construction.

Faced with conflicting demands caused by these phenomena, many public administrators welcomed the solution offered by private entrepreneurs. Private firms would build the needed facilities using their own capital and then charge the government a price that would recoup both the capital investment and ongoing operating costs. Governments could pay for these services using funds appropriated for operations, thereby avoiding the need to gain voters' approval of increased public debt.

It looked in the mid-1980s as if the private sector was threatening to take over huge parts of the public correctional industry. This did not happen, but growth of the private correctional industry has still been strong. Between 1986 and 1996, the number of beds in private facilities in operation or under construction increased in this country at an average annual rate of 45 percent. Few of these beds were empty: The occupancy rate of all private adult facilities averaged 96 percent during 1996. In 1987, there were about 3,000 prisoners in such facilities. By 1996, the number had soared to more than 85,000. During the 12 months ending December 31, 1996, the number of prisoners increased 30 percent. By the end of that year, there were 132 prisons and jails in operation, with another 39 under construction or in the planning stages. Seventeen state governments plus the District of Columbia have at least one contract with a private facility within their borders, and some (California, Florida, and Texas) contract for large numbers of facilities. Twelve other states also contract with facilities located in other states; these "exported" prisoners accounted for about 13 percent of all those under custody in private facilities at the close of 1996.[9]

As a result of these trends, growth in the private correctional industry's revenues has been explosive: from about $650 million in 1996 to over $1 billion expected in 1997.[10] By mid-1997,

Wall Street and individual investors were impressed with these growth statistics (see Figure 60–1) and with the apparently bright prospects for future growth (private facilities have only about 3 percent of the "market share" of prisoners in the United States). Stock prices of the four publicly traded firms had consequently been bid up very high, providing these companies with substantial amounts of cash to finance further expansion.

The industry is highly concentrated. By the end of 1996, the Corrections Corporation of America, based in Nashville, held 49 percent of all prisoners in private adult facilities. The Wackenhut Corrections Corporation held 27 percent.[11] Long dominated by a few big players, the industry appears to be experiencing still further consolidation, as well as some diversification. Smaller firms are being acquired by larger ones, and some are developing new capacities—such as drug treatment services—to augment their core capabilities. Firms that have been focusing on the adult correctional market are also moving into juvenile corrections.

Whereas the Corrections Corporation of America offered in 1986 to pay Tennessee $250 million for a 99-year lease on the state's prisons, most private facilities have either been newly constructed or are facilities owned by government and operated under a service contract. Unlike in the United Kingdom, governments here have not generally divested themselves of public properties. In 1997, however, exactly that happened. The District of Columbia sold its correctional treatment facility to the Corrections Corporation of America for $59 million, and the firm will operate it for the district under a 20-year lease-back arrangement. Proposals to do the same were being floated again in Tennessee in 1997, and in Florida as well.

As of mid-1997, the private prison industry seems to have a green light for development. Legislatures and chief executives are increasingly calling upon their correctional departments to consider or begin planning for at least partial privatization. The Violent Crime Control and Law Enforcement Act of 1994 permits fed-

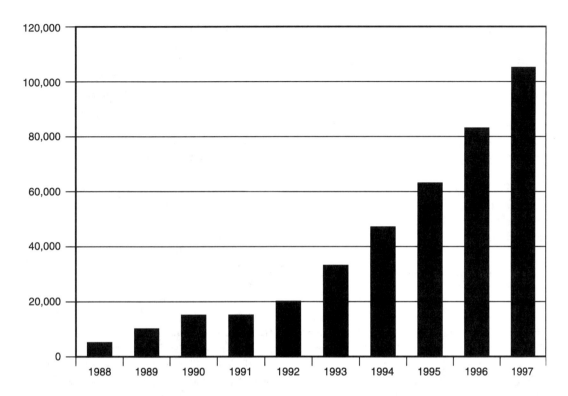

Figure 60–1 Ten-Year Growth in Design Capacity of Secure Adult Correctional Facilities. *Source:* Charles Thomas and Diane Bolinger, *Private Correctional Facility Census: A Year End 1997 Statistical Profile,* Private Corrections Project, Center for Studies in Criminology and Law, University of Florida. Available: web.crim.ufl.edu.

eral funding for prisons to support such privatization efforts. At the federal level, the Government Performance and Results Act of 1993, the Clinger-Cohen Act of 1996, the revised handbook to the Office of Management and Budget Circular A-76, and the Clinton Administration's major management reform initiative—the National Performance Review (NPR)—have all stimulated greater attention to improving government performance. NPR specifically supports privatization as one means of improving effectiveness and efficiency. Although the federal government cannot dictate programmatic preferences of state and local governments, this broad movement to improve government operations and support privatization of services is no doubt very influential beyond

the beltway. Indeed, surveys of state and local governments have found increased use of contracting for a broad range of social services.[12,13]

The effects of this increasing reliance upon private imprisonment have been little studied. Most research attention has been given to whether private facilities are less costly than public ones and, to a lesser extent, whether their services are better or worse. Little systematic research has addressed other questions—such as whether privatization has furthered government objectives other than cost containment, or how the experience of relying upon both government and privately operated facilities has changed (if at all) correctional administrators' approaches to managing imprisonment services. Nor has there been systematic study of what some argue is a new "correctional–industrial" complex, in which a well-financed private correctional industry lobbies for criminal sentencing legislation that expands the supply of prisoners and, by extension, the potential for greater profits. Concerns about such self-interested distortion of penal policy making have been voiced for years,[14] but no studies have sought to determine the extent to which lawmakers are actually swayed by private industry lobbying. The political pressures to pass "get-tough" legislation are already powerful in this country, even without any obviously self-interested lobbying by private correctional firms.

COST COMPARISONS: PUBLIC VERSUS PRIVATE

Studies comparing the cost of private and public facilities have not reported consistent findings. Several reports find private facilities to be less costly. These include Chi's early study of Illinois work release centers,[15] and Logan and McGriff's study of a 350-bed minimum security work camp in Tennessee.[16] (The latter study estimated that contracting was 3 to 8 percent less costly than the public alternative.) The Urban Institute's 1989 study of a private minimum security facility in Kentucky, a similar facility operated directly by the state, and two secure treatment facilities for serious juvenile offenders in Massachusetts—one public and the other private—concluded that government-run facilities were 20 to 28 percent more expensive than private ones.[17] Similarly, a study by the State of Texas[18] estimated that the cost of contracting for four different privately operated prisons was about 15 percent lower than what direct government operation would have cost. A recent study by Archambeault and Dies of two privately operated facilities in Louisiana and one government-operated one concluded that the privately operated facilities were cheaper by 12 to 14 percent over a five-year period.[19]

Still other studies found small or insignificant differences in costs. For example, an early study of the Eckerd Foundation's operation of the Florida School for Boys at Okeechobee found no cost savings attributable to private management compared with the cost of another publicly operated training school.[20] In his study of public and privately operated custodial facilities for juveniles in the United States, Donahue calculated the average cost per resident to be $22,600 in the public facilities and to be $22,845 in the private ones—an insignificant difference.[21] A study by the State of Tennessee compared costs of a private multicustody facility and two state-run medium security prisons and found an insignificant difference.[22]

At least one study found private facilities to be *more* costly than their public counterparts. In a 1985 study, the Pennsylvania General Assembly's Legislative Budget and Finance Committee examined cost data provided by the U.S. Immigration and Naturalization Service (INS) for government-run centers and privately run centers for detaining illegal aliens. The study concluded that the average daily cost per inmate was 17 percent higher in the private facilities.[23] However, another study of INS detention centers[24] estimated that private centers were 7 to 19 percent *less* costly to the government. This was confirmed in yet another study, which found the private facilities to be substantially less costly than INS-operated ones, on average.[25]

Fewer studies have attempted to compare the quality of services delivered. In the Urban Institute's study, the authors reported that "by and large, both staff and inmates gave better ratings to the services and programs at the privately-operated facilities; escape rates were lower, there were fewer disturbances by inmates; and in general, staff and offenders felt more comfortable at the privately-operated ones."[26] Another study by Logan of public and privately operated facilities in New Mexico reported equivocal findings.[27] The State of Tennessee's study found no difference in the level of performance among the privately operated and public facilities studied.[28]

One reason the findings regarding costs are inconsistent is that determining these costs is surprisingly difficult. This has not always been recognized sufficiently by analysts, which explains to some extent the variable findings in the research literature. Accounting practices followed in the public and private sectors differ in significant ways, which frustrates direct comparisons of costs.[29,30] In the private sector, accounting methods have been designed to value all inputs used to produce a good or a service, and most costs are thereby captured. In contrast, public sector accounting systems were designed not to identify costs but to monitor expenditures to ensure that funds are used for their intended purposes. The focus of accounting is therefore on the agency rather than the service being delivered. In many jurisdictions, a number of different agencies and government accounts provide funds or other resources used for correctional institutions; counting only those expenditures by correctional agencies produces an undercount of the true cost of publicly delivered imprisonment. For example, retirement fund contributions for employees in some places are paid not by the correctional agency's funds but from an overhead government account.[31] Other departments may provide medical or psychiatric care, utilities, transportation, or educational services. In nearly all governments, separate accounts are not kept for capital expenditures (as opposed to ongoing operating expenditures), and determining the cost of the capital assets "consumed" during a particular period of service is nearly impossible.

On the private side, other obstacles exist to identifying the costs of contracting. The price charged to governments may not cover all costs, as firms may elect to experience shortfalls in hopes of winning more work in the longer run or may subsidize operations in one place with earnings obtained elsewhere. Still other costs of contracting, not always counted, include the government's expenditures to procure the contracts and to monitor their operations. A fair calculation would include all of the government's costs of contracting, not just payments to contractors.

An additional methodological challenge faced by researchers is that comparable public and private facilities may not exist in the same jurisdiction for study. Consequently, researchers have had to estimate the costs of hypothetical public facilities or have compared costs from other facilities that are not precisely equivalent—which raises doubts about the validity of the inferences drawn.

With respect to costs and savings, students of the evaluation literature have not drawn consistent conclusions. For example, a study by the U.S. General Accounting Office examined five evaluations and reported, "We could not conclude from these studies that privatization of correctional facilities will not save money. However, these studies do not offer substantial evidence that savings have occurred. . . .These studies offer little generalizable guidance for other jurisdictions about what to expect regarding comparative operational costs and quality of service if they were to move toward privatizing correctional facilities."[32] Proponents of privatization, in contrast, read the research literature as showing "still more evidence that operating cost savings in the general range of 10 to 20 percent are typical" and that "evidence from Florida, Louisiana, and the United Kingdom demonstrate that these cost savings are often matched with performance improvements (e.g., few disturbances, few escapes, increased prisoner involvement in work programs, and more programs aimed at reducing recidivism)."[33]

There does not seem to be a universally prevalent cost advantage to public or private entities. Rather, because of various constraints (labor availability, restrictions on employee salary levels, regulatory requirements, government procurement procedures, etc.), private firms may be able to exploit opportunities in specific niches and find ways to deliver services at lower costs. In other places, such opportunities may not exist, and the publicly operated facilities may be less costly, at a given level of service. Some governments are also more sophisticated than others in their contracting practices, which may result in lower relative costs and higher performance by the private firms.

LEGAL AND MORAL ISSUES

Critics have argued that privately operated correctional facilities are of questionable constitutionality, or are improper, regardless of whether they are more cost-efficient. For example, in 1989, the American Bar Association's (ABA's) House of Delegates passed a resolution urging jurisdictions to proceed "with extreme caution in considering possible authorization of contracts with private corporations or other private entities for the operation of prisons or jails."[34] The accompanying report declared that "there can be no doubt that an attempt to delegate total operational responsibility for a prison or jail would raise grave questions of constitutionality under both the federal constitution and the constitutions of the fifty states. The more sweeping the delegation, the more doubtful would be its constitutionality."[35] As I wrote shortly afterwards, however, such warnings were not compelling.[36] No majority opinion of the Supreme Court has been troubled by the delegation doctrine since 1948. For 50 years, the courts have allowed the federal government to delegate broad powers to private actors,[37] and thus at the federal level, "private exercise of federally delegated power is no longer a federal constitutional issue."[38] Nor has delegation by state and local governments been seen as a federal constitutional issue since the 1920s. Not surprisingly, no federal court has found private imprisonment to be unconstitutional, despite the ABA's warning.

Nor are there bans in most state constitutions against private delegation of correctional authorities. Nonetheless, judges in state courts have ruled inconsistently on issues regarding private delegation of state powers. To clarify this, legislatures in several states have passed laws authorizing delegation of correctional authority to private individuals or firms—for example, Colorado, Florida, Massachusetts, Montana, New Mexico, Oklahoma, Tennessee, Texas, and Utah.[39] At least one state legislature (Washington) has passed laws explicitly banning privatization of formerly public functions.

Some critics argue that imprisonment is a core function of government, something that is intrinsically governmental in nature and should not be delegated to private actors.[40] This is no doubt a pervasive belief, but it is only a proposition rather than an established fact. The definition of what constitutes an intrinsically governmental function is being changed. Many policy makers find it entirely appropriate to delegate the *administration* of this function, while maintaining at the same time that the government has the responsibility for ensuring its provision. Accordingly, the courts have ruled that private imprisonment on behalf of government agencies constitutes "state action," and that governments retain the ultimate responsibility for what goes on in them (*Medina v. O'Neill*, 569 F. Supp. 1028 [1984], and *Ancata v. Prison Health Services, Inc.*, 769 F.2d 700, 702 [11th Cir. 1985]). Private facilities are required to comply with the same standards and laws that apply to public ones. They must conform to law and established standards.[41,42]

Still other objections to privatization have been voiced. For example, DiIulio and Robbins argue that the legitimacy of governmental authority in inmates' eyes is weakened by having private (and especially for-profit) corporations administer imprisonment.[43,44] Whether this actually occurs, however, is an empirical question that has not been studied. Moreover, it is reasonable to suspect that inmates' perceptions of legitimacy have more to do with whether the actions of the keepers conform to law and norms of fairness than whether the keepers are public or private employees.

In short, in most states, the question of whether to privatize turns not on matters of constitutionality or statutory law but on matters of policy. And whether one thinks it proper to delegate imprisonment authority to private actors depends ultimately upon the nature of one's fundamental values and principles, as well as consideration of more direct material interests felt by those engaged in delivering correctional services. Given that there is no clear national consensus for or against private delegation of imprisonment services, policy battles in legislative chambers are likely to be pitched ones in the coming years.

A SENSITIVE RELATIONSHIP

The performance of a contractor depends to some extent upon the relationship between the contractor and the government and upon the government's management of the contractor. In at least some jurisdictions, contracting out facility operations has been handled poorly; the government's specification of the services to be delivered has been poorly defined, silent on objectives, and long on procedures to be followed. Even when governments turn to contracting in hopes of reducing costs, they sometimes fail to establish first a benchmark—the costs of direct government operation. Evaluation of bidders' proposals has sometimes emphasized cost over more general value, with the result that "low ballers" have been chosen against the better interests of the government. Monitoring has not always been adequate, despite the federal courts' clear insistence that governments cannot evade responsibility and liability for correctional services by delegating them to private actors. Contracting for both facilities and operations also gives the winning firm an edge on future competitions (because it will then own a facility while others will have to build one) and may reduce competition in the marketplace.

Therefore, rather than focusing on whether existing private facilities are less or more cost-effective than public ones, an important question for public managers is *How can government agencies obtain these results if they elect to seek them?* In contracting, governments have a tool for accomplishing any number of strategic objectives, which may include lower costs or improved correctional services. For example, a government seeking to lower correctional costs while maintaining service quality could establish a cost above which offers would not be entertained, explicit performance standards could be specified in the contract, monitoring systems could be designed to measure compliance with

these standards, and actual costs could be monitored to ensure that targets have not been overrun. Governments can choose to terminate a contract if performance is not satisfactory.

Real life is more complicated and constrained than this simplified model suggests, no doubt. For example, a commonplace observation is that government and businesses differ fundamentally in their purposes: Whereas private firms can be relatively single-minded in their pursuit of revenues or profit, government agencies and programs often serve multiple purposes. This multiplicity of purposes stems, in part, from the genesis of programs in politics. That is, public programs are designed and enacted following a process by which different interests are accommodated. But this does not mean that government programs *must* operate with conflicting (or worse, unstated) missions. These missions can be clarified, and priorities can be established where multiple purposes exist. This creates the possibility of managing to accomplish chosen goals.

CONCLUSION

How these developments will play out will probably depend as much upon politics as upon the merits or faults of private correctional facilities. Because prisons and jails are claiming such a large share of government's budgets (especially at the state levels), pressures for belt tightening will probably continue to be strongly felt. The threat of privatization may encourage public managers to find more efficient ways of delivering correctional services, and organized public employees may succeed in staving off calls for contracting out prison and jail operations. Given the broad interest in relying upon private firms to deliver public responsibilities, however, such calls are likely to continue to be heard.

NOTES

1. A. Crew, *London Prisons of Today and Yesterday* (London: I. Nicholson & Watson, 1933), 50.

2. M.M. Feeley, "The Privatization of Prisons in Historical Perspective," in *Privatization and Its Alternatives,* ed. W. Gormley (Madison, WI: University of Wisconsin Press, 1991), 397.

3. W.S. Holdsworth, *A History of English Law,* Vol. 4, 3d ed. (London: Cambridge University Press, 1922–1924).

4. B. McKelvey, *American Prisons: A History of Good Intentions* (Montclair, NJ: Patterson Smith, 1977).

5. D. McDonald, "Private Penal Institutions," in *Crime and Justice: A Review of Research,* ed. M. Tonry (Chicago: University of Chicago Press, 1992).

6. A. Press, "The Good, the Bad, and the Ugly: Private Prisons in the 1980s," in *Private Prisons and the Public Interest,* ed. D. McDonald (New Brunswick, NJ: Rutgers University Press, 1992).

7. Corrections and Criminal Justice Reform Task Force, *"Report on the 3rd Round Table Conference."*

8. D. McDonald, "Introduction," in *Private Prisons and the Public Interest,* ed. D. McDonald (New Brunswick, NJ: Rutgers University Press, 1990).

9. C. Thomas et al., *Private Adult Correctional Facility Census,* 10th ed. (Gainesville, FL: Center for Studies in Criminology and Law, 1997).

10. N. Xiong, "Private Prisons: A Question of Savings," *The New York Times,* 13 July, 1997.

11. Thomas et al., *Private Adult Correctional Facility Census,* 10th ed.

12. Council of State Governments, *State Trends and Forecasts: Privatization,* Vol. 2, no. 2 (Lexington, KY: 1993).

13. International City/County Management Association, *Municipal Year Book 1994: Alternative Service Delivery in Local Government 1982–1992* (Washington, DC: 1994).

14. K. Schoen, "Private Prison Operators," *The New York Times,* 28 March, 1985.

15. K. Chi, "Private Contractor Work Release Centers: The Illinois Experience," in *Innovations* (Lexington, KY: Council of State Governments, 1982).

16. C. Logan and B. McGriff, "Comparing Costs of Public and Private Prisons: A Case Study," *NIJ Reports,* no. 216 (1989).

17. Urban Institute, *Comparison of Privately and Publicly Operated Corrections Facilities in Kentucky and Massachusetts* (Washington, DC: U.S. Department of Justice, National Institute of Justice, 1989).

18. State of Texas, *Recommendations to the Governor of Texas and Members of the Seventy-Second Legislature* (Austin, TX: Sunset Advisory Commission, 1991).

19. W. Archambeault and D. Dies, Jr., "Cost Effectiveness Comparisons of Private versus Public Prisons in Louisi-

ana: A Comprehensive Analysis of Allen, Avoyelles, and Winn Correctional Centers" (School of Social Work, Louisiana State University, Baton Rouge, LA, 1996), photocopy.

20. A. Brown et al., *Private Sector Operation of a Correctional Institution: A Study of the Jack & Ruth Eckerd Youth Development Center, Okeechobee, Florida* (Washington, DC: U.S. Department of Justice, National Institute of Corrections, 1985).

21. J. Donahue, *The Privatization Decision* (New York: Basic Books, 1990).

22. Tennessee Legislative Fiscal Review Committee, *Cost Comparison of Correctional Centers* (Nashville, TN: 1995).

23. Joint State Government Commission, *Report of the Private Prison Task Force* (Harrisburg, PA: General Assembly of the Commonwealth of Pennsylvania, 1987).

24. D. McDonald, "The Costs of Operating Public and Private Correctional Facilities," in *Private Prisons and the Public Interest,* ed. D. McDonald (New Brunswick, NJ: Rutgers University Press, 1990).

25. D. McDonald, *Contracting for Private Detention Services: The Costs of Private and Government Detention Facilities* (Cambridge, MA: Abt Associates, Inc., forthcoming).

26. Urban Institute, *Comparison of Privately and Publicly Operated Corrections Facilities in Kentucky and Massachusetts.*

27. C. Logan, *Well-Kept: Comparing the Quality of Confinement in a Public and a Private Prison* (Washington, DC: U.S. Department of Justice, National Institute of Justice, 1991).

28. Tennessee Legislative Fiscal Review Committee, *Cost Comparison of Correctional Centers.*

29. McDonald, "Private Penal Institutions."

30. D.C. McDonald, *The Cost of Corrections: In Search of the Bottom Line* (Washington, DC: National Institute of Corrections, 1989).

31. D. McDonald, *The Price of Punishment: Public Spending for Corrections in New York* (Boulder, CO: Westview Press, 1980).

32. U.S. General Accounting Office, *Private and Public Prisons: Studies Comparing Operational Costs and/or Quality of Service* (Washington, DC: 1996).

33. Thomas et al., *Private Adult Correctional Facility Census,* 10th ed.

34. American Bar Association, "Report to the House of Delegates" (Chicago: 1989), photocopy.

35. American Bar Association, "Report to the House of Delegates."

36. D. McDonald, "When Government Fails: Going Private as a Last Resort," in *Private Prisons and the Public In-*

terest, ed. D. McDonald (New Brunswick, NJ: Rutgers University Press, 1990).

37. *Carter v. Carter Coal Company,* 298 U.S. 238 (1936).

38. D. Lawrence, "Private Exercise of Governmental Power," *Indiana Law Journal* 61 (1986).

39. National Criminal Justice Association, *Private Sector Involvement in Financing and Managing Correctional Facilities* (Washington, DC: 1987).

40. I. Robbins, *The Legal Dimensions of Private Incarceration* (Washington, DC: American Bar Association, 1988).

41. C. Logan, *Private Prisons: Pro and Con* (New York: Oxford University Press, 1990).

42. McDonald, "When Government Fails: Going Private as a Last Resort."

43. J. DiIulio, Jr., "The Duty To Govern: A Critical Perspective on the Private Management of Prisons and Jails," in *Private Prisons and the Public Interest,* ed. D. McDonald (New Brunswick, NJ: Rutgers University Press, 1990).

44. I. Robbins, *The Legal Dimensions of Private Incarceration* (Washington, DC: American Bar Association, 1988).

CHAPTER 61

Political Involvement in Penal Operations

Judith Simon Garrett

Although the Uniform Crime Reports data indicate that crime rates have been declining over the past several years, fear of crime remains a primary concern for most Americans. Legislators, eager to be responsive to their constituents, have remained steadfast in their "tough on crime" (and "war on drugs") approach that began in the 1980s. As a result, today there are nearly 1.2 million people in adult prisons in the United States, at a cost of approximately $29 billion per year.[1]

While crime and criminal justice remain largely a state and local issue, the legislative and executive branches of the federal government attempt to influence state and local laws and policies through grants and other means. Congress and the president can more directly influence federal law through statutes, regulation, and executive orders. Elected representatives and those seeking election also do not hesitate to use public forums and the media to express their increasingly conservative views about crime and criminal justice administration.

___

Opinions expressed in this chapter are those of the author and do not necessarily represent the opinions of the Federal Bureau of Prisons or the U.S. Department of Justice.

POLITICAL INTEREST IN PRISON OPERATIONS

As a result of their desire to influence criminal justice policy and demonstrate their commitment to being tough on crime, over the past couple of decades federal and state legislators have taken unprecedented steps toward micromanaging correctional operations. The combination of enacting longer sentences and placing new restrictions on early release mechanisms (such as limiting or abolishing parole and good time) has been directly responsible for the tremendous increase in prison and jail populations across the country. At the same time, legislators have forced correctional officials to reduce or eliminate many programs and recreation opportunities in an attempt to create "no-frills" correctional institutions, in part in hopes that the more harsh environment will increase the deterrent effect of prisons. Such restrictions are also a result of the perception that nothing works to rehabilitate prisoners. For example, the Federal Bureau of Prisons has been prohibited from repairing, replacing, or purchasing new weightlifting equipment and musical instruments. Other legislation that was proposed required inmates to work 50 hours per week or be confined to their cells (for 23 hours per day) if they were not medically able to work. Until recently, federal

One of the most important principles underpinning our democratic form of government in this country are the three distinct branches of government and the checks and balances each branch exercises over the others. For example, the legislative branch (in the federal government) has four duties: legislation, appropriations, confirmation, and oversight. The legislative branch controls the executive branch (including the department of corrections, or in the federal context, the Department of Justice and Federal Bureau of Prisons). On the other hand, the judicial branch oversees the actions of the legislative branch (by ruling on the legality of enacted legislation).

The legislative branch exercises its oversight authority in a variety of ways, including formal hearings, institution visits, letters, and phone calls. Additionally, a variety of vehicles may be used to address various issues; that is, specific direct questions may be posed regarding policies and/or practices, or an issue raised by a constituent (such as the relative of an inmate) may provide the opportunity to review the department of corrections' operations.

All executive branch agencies seek to avoid formal hearings on their programs and operations, because such hearings can be extremely time-consuming and can give rise to serious changes in policies and practices. Executive agencies also seek to avoid the enactment of specific legislation that substantially limits their discretion. One of the best ways to achieve both objectives is to foster positive relationships with congresspeople and their staff members. This is best done by being responsive to requests for information (providing complete and accurate information) and by attempting to educate the congresspeople and their staff members about the myriad issues facing departments of corrections. These issues include the difficulties of ensuring inmate, staff, and public safety while also providing humane living conditions and opportunities for self-improvement.

prison officials were prohibited from distributing to inmates any commercially published material that contained nudity or sexually explicit pictures. This legislation was ruled unconstitutional by a federal court.[2] These examples typify recent legislation and the results of the effort to limit programs in prisons and jails.

It is unfortunate that most lawmakers have little or no direct knowledge of prison operations. Many would benefit substantially from an educational tour, even of a single correctional institution. Most corrections managers would disagree with the legislators' view that prison programs (including recreation opportunities) and modest amenities such as television rooms are frills that make prisons less of a deterrent. According to most correctional managers, these programs and amenities can be instrumental in ensuring an inmate's successful reintegration into the community following release from prison.

Institution recreational opportunities should allow inmates the opportunity to release some of the anxiety and stress that is inherent in prison life and help create an environment with less tension for the staff and inmates. Research has found that prison programs help offenders to reintegrate successfully into the community through lower rates of recidivism and higher rates of employment, which supports correctional professionals' belief that institutional programs (e.g., education, vocational training, prison industries, substance abuse treatment) are essential to effective correctional settings. Nearly all prison administrators agree that making prisoners' lives unnecessarily uncomfortable and unpleasant does little more than make the jobs of staff, particularly correctional officers, more difficult.

Some correctional managers are proponents of the spartan prison existence and help foster the misconception described above; they invite legislators to mandate that all prisons be operated in a spartan manner. Sheriff Joe Arapaio from Maricopa County, AZ, is a classic example of this philosophy; he requires some inmates to sleep in tents and, if they are sex offenders, to wear pink underwear. In contrast, most correctional administrators believe that prisons should be decent places in which to live and should offer reasonable program and recreation opportunities that provide self-improvement activities, offer a safe and healthy environment, and properly control inmate behavior. Institution operations should not seek to embarrass prisoners or create unnecessary resentment.

CORRECTIONAL ADMINISTRATORS IMPLEMENT—NOT ESTABLISH— GOVERNMENT LAWS

Whatever the personal views of prison administrators regarding the wisdom of laws enacted by the legislature (or regulations promulgated by the executive branch), it is their responsibility to implement such laws in a timely and an effective manner and with the least disruption to the institution's operation. It is difficult and dangerous to withdraw privileges or programs from prisoners once these privileges and programs have been given to them; such withdrawals must be carefully planned and implemented. It is the administrators' responsibility to communicate with inmates (through staff–inmate interaction, posted memos, and any other means) and emphasize that the change in practice must be accepted by everyone—prisoners and staff alike.

The prisoners must be made to understand that misbehaving in response to the planned change will result in swift and certain punishment and will not forestall the intended implementation.

Institution administrators should not become involved in the political process. As experts in corrections, professional administrators are sometimes called upon to share such expertise and facilitate the consideration of proposed changes in the law. While senior institution staff should always welcome the opportunity to educate lawmakers, they must be cautious not to give the appearance that they are trying to influence the legislative process.

According to Peter M. Carlson, regional director, the Federal Bureau of Prisons has long believed it is imperative to demonstrate the realities of institutional management by opening prison doors to all who wish to educate themselves. Federal wardens are encouraged to and frequently do invite congresspeople to visit their prisons during congressional recesses.[3] Many congresspeople and, more frequently, their staff, take advantage of such opportunities and find the experience interesting and enlightening.

Institution chief executive officers should be seen as impartial, professional administrators who have a responsibility to fairly implement legislation and executive orders. This concept was best presented years ago by Woodrow Wilson, the twenty-eighth president of the United States. He was an exceptional teacher, historian, and public administrator who was known as the first scholar to advocate studying the operations of government. His 1887 essay "The Study of Administration"[4] presented the philosophy of the progressive movement, created by reformers unhappy with the spoils system. Under the spoils system, employees of government agencies were fired each time a new political party was elected. Political patrons of the party in office were brought in, and the entire direction of the government entity was subject to major change. Federal patronage had a particularly large influence on government operations. The progressive movement lobbied to establish a professional civil service that would be neutral on political issues. Over time, the system of political spoils was abolished at the federal level, except for a limited number of high-level positions such as cabinet heads and select senior members of their staff.

This is the critical reason for government administrators to avoid the strife of politics. As Wilson stated many years ago, the field of administration is a field of business and must be removed from the arena of political rhetoric. Professional administrators in all areas of government must focus on the impartial governance of their agencies; legislators establish policy, and administrators implement their decisions. Public administration is the systematic and detailed execution of public law.

POLITICAL AND SOCIETAL CHANGES IMPACT PENAL FACILITIES

Political winds change over time, sometimes quite rapidly, causing dramatic shifts in prison operations. During the 1970s, prison wardens would proudly show their college campus prisons and well-funded vocational training programs. Today, the public expects prison and jail environments to be more harsh and punishing. At different times, all aspects of the reasons for confinement (punishment, rehabilitation, general deterrence, and specific deterrence) will be emphasized. Prison administrators must accept these changes and not become publicly or emotionally invested in any particular political approach. Administrators are not precluded from holding their own personal and professional views regarding the most appropriate manner in which to operate a prison, but as civil servants all staff are expected to fulfill the requirements of the law as set forth by their legislative bodies.

The public is best served by prison and jail leaders who effectively implement policy established by elected officials. The legislators' newfound interest in the administration of justice is significant and should be considered a positive development.

In a text on prison management, Richard McGee, California's venerable correctional administrator from 1944 to 1967, postulated that

officials should fight political pressure.[5] He strongly advised penal leaders to avoid the outside turmoil and maintain a tightly organized and operated environment inside the institutions. Rather than joining in on the political dialogue external to the agency, his advice was to focus on making prisons and jails as safe, manageable, and humane as possible. He affirmed, however, the need to make institution operations accessible to external players who have great influence in the political dialogue so they can understand the facts of life behind bars.

CONCLUSION

Correctional managers today must work in a public and politicized environment where attention and change are demanded. As people become more and more dissatisfied with crime and violence in the community, they express their anger to those running for elected office. As individuals are placed in public office, they express the frustration of their constituency by venting their emotions on the prisoners in today's penal institutions. This is often perceived by correctional administrators as undue interference with daily operations by those who know very little about the delicate balance maintained by correctional officials inside prisons and jails.

Senior staff of American prisons and jails must exert leadership behind the fences and in the world beyond. It is not appropriate for civil servants to lobby or otherwise directly seek to influence elected representatives of the people; it is, however, acceptable and desired for those who are experts in managing prisons and jails to educate the judicial and legislative branches of government. Correctional systems will not adapt well to today's turbulent external pressures unless they successfully manage these sources of influence. Leaders must comprehend the political context and appropriately position their agencies to withstand the political winds of change.

The leaders of successful correctional agencies are those who are capable of cultivating the critical outside support necessary to deal with the individuals who are intent on wholesale change of the institution regimen. Outside support is necessary in the local, state, and national communities and is generally composed of the media, the judiciary, and the popularly elected legislative bodies. The image of corrections is very much in the hands of chief executive officers of facilities and heads of correctional agencies. Effective leaders in these roles will gather support for their work by being responsive to their constituencies and bringing them inside to show them the realities of institutional responsibilities.

As public administrators, the leaders of institutional operations must be responsive to those who pay the bills and operate according to one of the important principles on which our country was established: the rule of law.

NOTES

1. C. Camp and G. Camp, *The Corrections Yearbook 1997* (South Salem, NY: Criminal Justice Institute, Inc., 1997), 3, 71.

2. *Amatel v. Reno* 96-2774, United States District Court for the District of Columbia, August 12, 1997.

3. P.M. Carlson, interview by author, Washington, DC, 11 January, 1998.

4. W. Wilson, "The Study of Administration," in *Basic Literature of American Public Administration, 1787–1950,* ed. F.C. Mosher (New York: Holmes and Meier, 1981).

5. R. McGee, *Prisons and Politics* (Lexington, MA: Lexington Books, 1981).

CHAPTER 62

Creating the Future:
Strategic Positioning in Corrections

Ronald J. Stupak

In an interview for the *Federal Prisons Journal* in 1989, the statement was made that strategic planning could begin to take hold in the Federal Bureau of Prisons.

There are five reasons I am convinced strategic planning will work in the Bureau. One, when I went out in the field, I saw people who are "cosmopolitans," who are moving up through the system and one day will end up at headquarters or as wardens; and the "locals," who will stay at Lewisburg or wherever they are. The locals and the cosmopolitans have tremendous respect for each other. In many organizations, the high flyers going through the system and the locals treat each other as enemies. But in the Bureau, I saw a camaraderie that I haven't experienced in other organizations, where there are first-class and second-class citizens.

Second, whether you go to the Central Office or Milan, Michigan, there is a fundamental belief in some of the core values and cultural anchors of the Bureau of Prisons; for example, in the correctional officer, in the family, in integrity, in hard work. That said to me that you can build on a strong foundation of agreement on guiding principles.

Third, bright people—not just intellectual, but street smart—knew things were changing. Some of them weren't pleased with the fact that they were going to have to change, but they were savvy enough to know that change was the name of the game.

Fourth, people wanted to learn. Lousy organizations or organizations that don't feel good about themselves are afraid of strangers with insights. When I went out in the field, people gave me the benefit of the doubt. They said, "Help us develop a system, and then we'll see whether it's going to work." When I find learners in an organization, that's a sign of the future health of the institution.

Finally, when I went to the Central Office, almost everyone in headquarters had been "down in the trenches." This leadership group was not going to bring in a consultant to do their work for them, or craft big, useless books of strategic plans that lay on the shelf.

These people said, "We have to make it meaningful for the people in the trenches," and they knew that because they'd been there.[1]

In essence, there was a realistic, integrated base for strategic planning on which to build; namely, (1) respect for each other, (2) guiding principles, (3) willingness to change, (4) learning potential, and (5) committed leaders.

While agencies will never have a crystal ball, it is very clear that strategic planning has become significant for performance-based management in corrections. The use of staff at all levels of the prison or jail organization in the planning process can, will, and must pay major dividends for the prison or jail administrators. And yet, there is no one best way to handle strategic planning in corrections. There must be a clear understanding of what the culture, context, and conflicts are in specific correctional institutions so that any generic model, design, or framework is adapted, adjusted, and retrofitted to the environmental realities of each institution.

No matter how strategic planning happens, there is absolutely no question that it must be done in this age of cost containment, cutback management, reengineering, and privatization. In 1995, four respected corrections professionals each listed what they saw as the major issues facing correctional professionals as they surge forward to the year 2000. Only strategic planning was on all their lists.[2]

To make fundamental quality decisions and trade-offs in productive organizations in the next 10 years, administrators will need to do strategic planning. They also will need to be courageous enough to do the focused priority setting required to actively position their systems or institutions as recognized high performers for the future. In this current "re-inventing government" environment, "let's do more with less" does not work. Results-oriented organizations know that in the 1990s "more with less" is a cop-out for avoiding tough choices in this age of cost containment, cut-back management, and market-driven competition. "Less with less" or "less with more" are now the critical frameworks for effective performance. Sadly, correctional organizations' great affluence of the past encouraged administrators to carry the "more with more" axiom to the point of fiscal and managerial dis-

locations. The affluence discouraged the management discipline, leadership capabilities, performance skills, and creative strategic design and implementation required to manage organizations efficiently, economically, and effectively in the constrained fiscal frameworks of the 1990s. As J. Michael Quinlan, former director of the Federal Bureau of Prisons, said, "Growth for the sake of growth is the etiology of the cancer cell, and that means organizational death. There is only one kind of growth that is sustainable, and that is quality growth based on tough choices, measured outcomes, and cost-benefit trade-offs."[3]

THE PUBLIC SECTOR AND STRATEGIC PLANNING

Until recently, there were loud protests that strategic planning, quality improvement, and re-engineering would not work in the public sector. However, fiscal constraints, taxpayer anger, and the demise of public sector monopolies demand the fiscal discipline, managerial skills, leadership capabilities, performance measurements, strategic design, employee empowerment, and competitive techniques required to make corrections more effective and productive in the market-driven framework of the 1990s and beyond.

LEADERSHIP RESPONSIBILITIES

Strategic positioning challenges can lead to either an overwhelming, uncontrollable wave of disaster or an opportunity for proactively repositioning corrections with a more specific strategic focus. Leadership in corrections needs to reject the deadly viruses of reactive fear, intellectual rigidity, and professional isolation in their earliest stages and replace them with healthy, proactive alternatives. The creative capabilities of correctional leaders must be developed. Vision, direction, and courage are now the essential leadership skills.

Leadership must serve as the galvanizing and integrating force, providing coherent direction and meaning to correctional employees, criminal justice stakeholders, and the other branches of government. Only through vision will those in corrections be able to tolerate the current climate of change. This leadership requires new perspectives anchored in intuition, an ability to make corrections dynamic and meaningful, and attention to diversity concerns. What is needed is strategic leadership based on intuitive, managerial, and behavioral skills as well as integrity, trust, and fiscal responsibility. A servant leadership model infused with a strong strain of the transformational leadership attributes and quality improvement foundations should become the norm for correctional leaders as rigid, macho, authoritarian leadership becomes a style of the past.

MAKING STRATEGIC CHOICES

Clearly, this is a fortuitous time for prison and jail leaders at all levels to come together and take action. It is a time for correctional professionals to get out there, tell their stories, build strategic coalitions, and invent creative agendas for corrections before others on the outside do it for them. It is time to put corrections ahead of the power curve instead of behind it. It is time to ask, "How do we want to position corrections for the future?" That's the essence of strategic positioning—development is never over; it just keeps going. But if correctional leaders build on solid foundations, they can continue to make strategic choices competently and productively for the future.

A STRATEGIC DESIGN FOR IMPROVING CORRECTIONAL LEADERSHIP

Most correctional systems, whether at the national, state, or local levels, have had strong hierarchical traditions with well-defined roles, procedures, and personnel functions. Correctional leaders have tended to employ certain tried and true methods of operation because they have worked successfully in the past. But with an ever more demanding citizenry, a fiscally constrained environment, and a quest for quality improvement throughout the public sector, the limits of

ingrained, inflexible, out-of-date methods of operation have become too apparent. Correctional leaders cannot drive into the future with their eyes fixed on the rearview mirror.

It is important that any strategic design to improve leadership in corrections reflect the extent of cultural and process changes taking place, in addition to identifying and providing process, behavioral, and technological skills critical to the development of correctional leaders and the achievement of goals based on respect for the law and the dignity of all individuals. The design cannot be limited to skill or information content but must be viewed as part of the organizational, cultural change processes of corrections.

All change efforts need to be planned concurrent with critical events occurring in the change process. All implementation and training efforts need to be part of and reinforced by a comprehensive strategic education endeavor so that corrections can leverage the multidimensional and intersecting sources of information channels.

The strategic scope demanded of correctional facilities undergoing quality improvement efforts requires that training and follow-up occur in several interdependent stages. The following strategic action agenda is offered both as a conceptual road map and a set of practical guidelines anchored in five critical change management actions: (1) contextualizing the strategic changes within a set of guiding principles, (2) clarifying the new standards of performance, (3) developing binding agreements from both individuals and work teams, (4) obtaining personal commitments from the employees "on the front lines," and (5) involving the employees actively in the strategic change process.

Developing a Strategic Action Agenda

Strategy

Sessions need to be held that develop realistic strategic visions, followed by sessions that communicate the new strategies to all participants involved in the change process.

- the what and why of change
- the vision and why it is important
- what to expect and when to expect it
- what is strategic positioning and why we are involved in it
- the change process: its stages and reassurances that what participants are experiencing is normal
- principles of strategic positioning, change management, and quality improvement that are critical to the rule of law and correctional performance standards

Values

Programs must be developed that explain and facilitate the integration of the new values among correctional leaders.

- how the new values mesh with and clarify the traditional values in the criminal justice system
- what must happen to hierarchies of power based on control and credentials under conditions of more horizontal team leadership requirements
- roles and responsibilities of corrections leaders
- team-building efforts that encourage collaboration
- application training: the use of strategic planning in specific correctional institutions as real case studies of change projects in relation to leadership anchors, integrated systems, and quality measurements

Core Skills

Core skills cut across organizational process boundaries and are critical to the successful achievement of functional areas and goals. Module topics include

- communication skills
- effective meetings
- group problem solving
- influencing others—media and image projection

- approaches to improving inmate processes
- team leadership skills for high performance
- conflict management and resolution skills
- intrapersonal and interpersonal skills based on self-awareness assessments

Leadership/Management Development

Creating and developing the next generation of leaders by building new leadership competencies, styles, and experiences for individuals. Module topics include

- joint process and functional leadership training—how those in corrections must work together to find opportunities and overcome possible roadblocks
- coaching and mentoring skills
- negotiating skills
- resistance management skills
- team and matrix management skills
- shared power and decision making

Self-Employment Skills

Issues and development of the rank-and-file correctional officers are addressed here. Specific programs would identify coping skills and behavioral requirements as well as developmental opportunities, especially for long-term correctional employees. Module topics include

- how to function individually within a quality framework
- what this new leadership design means for the rank-and-file correctional officer
- how to make a difference in the new scheme of quality improvement
- what opportunities this new leadership design present to correctional employees
- techniques for managing the stress of change
- time management
- organizational culture and awareness training

The overall design will culminate in systems reorientation, leadership development, and implementation actions leading to long-term self-sufficiency, organizational learning, and a solid foundation for productivity and high performance. See Appendix 62–A for an exercise in strategic planning.

CONCLUSION

Clearly, the strategic positioning challenges, opportunities, and realities identified in this chapter are currently being considered by many systems. They are capable of becoming either an overwhelming, uncontrollable wave of disaster or an opportunity for proactively centering corrections at a level of high-performing strategic management. Unequivocally, it is believed that this conceptual, definitional effort along with the suggested strategic action agenda will galvanize the leadership in corrections to reject the deadly viruses of reactive fear and intellectual rigidity in their embryonic stages and replace them with healthy, proactive alternatives. Correctional leaders must be creative. Taking the initiative to reshape an organization to ensure a competitive, vibrant, healthy, fiscally rigorous, and humane decision-making environment is the ultimate challenge to correctional leaders in the 1990s and beyond.

NOTES

1. D. Green, "Taking Charge of the Future: Strategic Action for Quality Growth in the Bureau of Prisons," *Federal Prisons Journal* 1, no. 2 (1989): 11–16.
2. Special Insert, "Practitioner's Corner—Corrections Trends for the Twenty-First Century," *Corrections Alert* 2, no. 6 (1995).
3. J. Michael Quinlan, interview by author, Washington, DC, June 23, 1998.

SUGGESTED READINGS

Alvarez, K., and R. Stupak. 1993. An analytical essay and annotated compendium on organizational theory," *International Review of Modern Sociology* 23, no. 2: 59–82.
Gavin, F., and R. Stupak. 1996. State courts: Establishing a leadership agenda. *The Public Manager* 25, no. 3: 24–31.
Seiter, R., and R. Stupak. 1991. A way to tie corrections and education together. *Corrections Today* 53, no. 7: 158–160.
Stupak, R. 1989. Organizational effectiveness: Back to the future. *The Bureaucrat* 18, no. 3: 41–44.
Stupak, R. 1996. Strategic leadership in the courts. *Court Review* 33, no. 2: 13–16.
Vance, N., and R. Stupak. 1997. Organizational culture and the placement of pretrial agencies in the criminal justice system. *The Justice System Journal* 19, no. 1.

Strategic Planning Design

GETTING STARTED

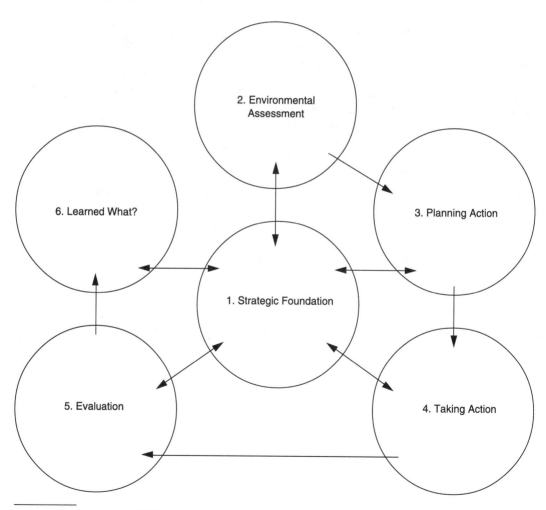

As shown in the previous graphic, the essential steps in a top-level strategic design include

1. Strategic foundation. This must be the anchor for all other steps in the process. Every step in the process must further the underlying assumptions defined and stated in this foundation. Thus, all arrows leading from circle 1 go in two directions.
2. Environmental assessment. This is no more than analyzing the problems, forces, alliances, and supports, that must be dealt with to accomplish the strategic purpose.
3. Planning action. This is the stage in which leaders consider all the possible ways to accomplish their purposes.

4. Taking action. This is the "choosing among options stage." Leaders choose one path to follow. They need to know what resources are required to pursue the option.
5. Evaluation. Leaders should take measurements (qualitative and quantitative) as they move toward the goal. They choose (a) criteria for measurements, (b) time checks or milestone checks, (c) techniques to use, and (d) data to collect for later reference and even "final" evaluation.
6. Learned what? Because strategic planning is ongoing, leaders must sit down and ask what they learned so that they can make adjustments as they plan the next stage of their strategic efforts.

ACTION PLANNING STEPS

1. Goal definition

Each program needs to define its goals within the larger overall strategic goals and purposes. (What?)

2. Techniques/methods for accomplishment

A clear operational set of techniques must be spelled out for accomplishing the goals. (How?)

3. Resource realities:
   • Resources available
   • People needed
   • Competitors
   • Alternate resource possibilities

A realistic assessment must be made of the resources available, the people on line, and what other groups are competitors or interested in what will be accomplished. Are there resource alternatives? (Who? Materials?)

4. Timetable for completion of subtasks

A clear schedule and agenda must be committed to so that it is met and the leadership can hold program managers accountable and responsible. (When?)

5. Measurements of success or failure

Project managers must be able to measure their successes as specifically as possible and be held accountable; if it is not working, the program must be reversed or junked. (Is it working?)

6. Evaluation techniques

A "final evaluation" of the project must be set, and it must be the "brutal choice point" for continuing. (Should the program continue?)

7. Where to next?

After the "final evaluation," leaders will need to find out where they want to go next with this project. (Build on it, fold it, or harvest from it? Or start something new and different?)

Glossary

Accreditation: The process of review and certification by the American Correctional Association (ACA), the National Commission on Correctional Health Care (NCCHC), and the Joint Commission for the Accreditation of Healthcare Organizations (Joint Commission). The ACA, NCCHC, and Joint Commission promulgate standards for accreditation and rate correctional and health care facilities against these standards.

Acquired Immune Deficiency Syndrome (AIDS): An infectious disease that renders the body's system of immunity virtually unable to destroy invading disease or other illness.

Administrative Detention: A confinement status in which the inmate is separated from the institution's general population. This special housing is used to protect an inmate from other inmates, to provide additional security for an inmate who may be a security risk, to house a prisoner who may be pending investigation for a violation of facility regulations, or to separate an inmate who may be pending classification or transfer.

Admission and Orientation (A&O): The initial phase of confinement in which a prisoner is given an overview of institutional operations, rules, program availability, and other general data. Some correctional agencies provide A&O in reception centers and then transfer inmates to another facility; others have a separate A&O housing unit within each facil-

ity and then place the prisoner in a general housing unit upon completion of the program.

Adult Basic Education (ABE): An educational program designed to assist students who are basically illiterate. This program is designed to teach fundamental reading, writing, and mathematics skills.

Affirmative Action Program: A management program designed to ensure the fair recruitment and promotion of women and minorities throughout the organization.

American Correctional Association (ACA): An organization of professional correctional staff who are employed in adult and juvenile prisons and jails as well as probation and parole staff.

Americans with Disabilities Act (ADA): A law passed by Congress in 1990 that establishes specific requirements of accessibility and employability for those with qualifying disabilities. Correctional facilities are regulated by this act.

Appeal: A process by which an individual may request a higher-level review of a decision. This can describe a legal examination of a court decision or a request for reassessment of an administrative decision in the institutional setting.

Appellant: The individual who requests an appeal.

Architectural Barriers Act: A federal law passed in 1968 that requires all federal buildings, or facilities that received any federal funding, to be accessible and usable by anyone with physical disabilities.

Associate Wardens/Assistant Wardens/Assistant Superintentents: Senior institution staff who serve as the primary assistants to the chief executive officer or warden. These administrators are responsible for the management of specific prison or jail divisions.

Auburn System: An early approach or philosophy of confinement in the United States that began at the New York State Prison in Auburn, NY. This penal system emphasized congregate work, silence, and punitive discipline.

Authoritarian Model: An organizational management structure in which power and legitimate authority are consolidated in one person or a few members of an agency's hierarchy.

Bail: A financial guarantee pledged by an individual or his or her family that the person arrested and in custody will, if temporarily released, return for a scheduled court appointment. If the subject does not appear as pledged, the bail is forfeited.

Bill of Rights: The first 10 amendments to the U.S. Constitution.

Bivens Case: In the prison context, litigation in federal court that alleges a civil rights violation by federal correctional officials. This class of litigation was named after a case decided by the Supreme Court and permits a legal challenge that is equivalent to lawsuits authorized under *U.S. Code,* vol. 42, sec. 1983, brought by state inmates for alleged violations of their civil rights by state prison employees.

Body Cavity Searches: Security checks or searches of body orifices such as the mouth, vagina, and anus.

Boot Camps: An alternative correctional program designed for first-time offenders and intended to be used in lieu of prison confinement. This relatively short-term program is structured like the military's boot camps. It emphasizes extensive discipline and intensive program involvement.

Boundary Spanning: A management concept that emphasizes one's ability to work productively across traditional bureaucratic lines of an organization and to develop ties with other organizations, both governmental and private, that affect the agency's work environment and mission.

Bridewell: A term for jails (or gaols) in Great Britain in the sixteenth century. They were intended to detain people until they could pay debts or had a trial.

Bureaucratic Model: An organizational management structure that is formal, hierarchical, and steeped in required process. The structure has a system of supervision and communication that flows from top to bottom.

Calculated Use of Force: The physical response of staff to a controlled situation in which the inmate does not represent an imminent threat to him- or herself or others (example: an inmate in a locked cell threatening to destroy property). In this situation, staff can attempt to peacefully resolve the situation without the use of force. If force becomes necessary, an organized and fully trained team can be used and the entire situation videotaped for later review.

Callout: An appointment schedule published daily in a correctional institution that staff members use to arrange activity for inmates. An example would be a callout from an inmate's normal work routine for a meeting with a staff physician.

Canteen: *See* Commissary.

Capital Expenses: Money spent over a predetermined amount for major items in the institution such as equipment, furniture, and machinery.

Capital Improvement Expenses: Money spent for new construction of prison or jail facilities or for the maintenance of existing facilities.

Capital Offense: An offense punishable by the death penalty.

Capital Punishment: A criminal sanction of the death penalty.

Case Management: The oversight of a prisoner's classification, programming, and release preparation.

Cell Blocks: Inmate housing units in the prison environment. A block is generally one housing unit with many individual or group cells.

Census: An informal accounting of inmates in the correctional setting. At an unscheduled time, the institution is "locked down" (all doors are locked). Staff check all prisoners in the area and write incident reports for all who are found in an area where they should not be.

Chain of Command: The hierarchical structure of management control in an organization.

Chief Executive Officer (CEO): The head of an organization. In the correctional context, the CEO is called a warden or superintendent.

Civil Rights Act: Federal legislation passed in 1964 that prohibited personnel or operational decisions based on race, color, sex, religion, or national origin. Affected areas include employment, public accommodations, and the provision of state or local government services.

Class Action Suits: Lawsuits that allow a person or a group of individuals to bring litigation against an individual or organization on behalf of all those similarly situated.

Classification: The process (within a correctional facility) of sorting or classifying inmates so that they go to the appropriately secure prison, with the necessary custodial supervision. This process also involves the approval of prisoner work assignments, program planning, and release planning. Reclassification occurs at scheduled intervals throughout the offender's confinement as he or she makes progress.

Classification Committee: A group of institutional staff members who make up a central committee charged with the responsibility for inmate classification.

Commissary: A store within a correctional institution where inmates may purchase items such as snack foods, personal hygiene items, and other sundries.

Community Relations Board: A committee of representatives of the local city closest to a correctional facility that volunteer to serve as an advisory team for the institutional management staff. The board is a liaison with the community.

Compelling Government Interest: A legal term that specifies a significant government requirement that is critical to the mission of the agency involved. In the correctional context, this term generally refers to the security and good order of the facility.

Concurrent Sentence: A sentence that is imposed by the court and served at the same time as another sentence.

Conditional Release: Release from a correctional facility in which the sentencing authority maintains a form of supervision over the releasee; if the specified conditions of release are violated, the individual is returned to the institution to complete the term that otherwise would have been served in the community. An example of a conditional release is parole.

Conditions of Release: The requirements of the correctional system that supervise a prisoner's conditional release. Typical conditions include prohibitions against violations of the law and restrictions that affect travel, association, and work.

Congregate System: The philosophy of prison operation that developed at the New York State Prison at Auburn and involved housing prisoners in isolation but permitting them to work together during the day in silence.

Congregate Work: The practice of allowing prisoners to work together.

Conjugal Visiting: Visiting privileges for inmates in some jurisdictions that allow for total privacy for the inmate and his or her visitor(s). Such visits allow for emotional and sexual intimacy without staff supervision.

Consecutive Sentence: A sentence that is imposed by the court to be served after another sentence is completed.

Consent Decree: A judicial order that ratifies an agreement made between two or more parties in a legal dispute. This process is commonly used to resolve litigation between inmates, the correctional jurisdiction, and other interested parties.

Contact Visiting: Visiting privileges for inmates that permit casual contact between the prisoner and his or her family or friends. Minimal physical contact, such as a greeting kiss and hand holding, is permitted under the supervision of staff members.

Contempt of Court: A legal finding that an individual or an agency has purposefully hindered a court after a judge has ruled in a case. A court can sanction an individual or a correctional jurisdiction with fines or imprisonment.

Contigency Plan: *See* Emergency Plan.

Contraband: An unauthorized item in a prison or jail. Contraband can be defined as dangerous (for example, a weapon) or as nuisance (for example, too many articles of clothing).

Convict: A prisoner or one convicted of violating the law and sentenced to a period of confinement.

Corporal Punishment: Any form of physical punishment.

Correctional Emergency Response Team (CERT): *See* Special Operations Response Team (SORT).

Count: An institutional procedure in a prison or jail that involves staff physically counting the inmates. Counts are scheduled throughout the day but can also be called spontaneously by a senior administrator. All routine activity stops during an institution count until the control center indicates the count is correct and all inmates are appropriately accounted for.

Court Order: A judicial decision.

Cross-Gender Supervision: The practice of allowing staff of the opposite gender to supervise inmates.

Crual and Unusual Punishment: A term to denote institutional practice or conditions that are considered to be significantly harsh and fall below constitutional standards.

Deliberate Indifference: A legal term used in prison litigation to identify official conduct that ignored a threat to an inmate's safety or well-being.

Detainee: An individual confined in pretrial, unconvicted status.

Detainer: A legal "hold" or warrant placed against an individual already confined that signifies that another jurisdiction seeks to take the prisoner into its custody once the person is released from his or her current detention.

Determinate Sentence: A judicial sanction for a specific amount of time (for example, a sentence to confinement for a period of five years).

Deterrence: A philosophy or goal of a judicial sentence. The imposition of a sanction of confinement is intended to specifically prevent the law violator from reoffending. Knowledge that an individual has been sanctioned for the offense may generally deter others from committing the offense.

Diagnostic and Statistical Manual IV (DSM-IV): A system of classification for those who suffer from mental illness. This document is published and updated by the American Psychiatric Association.

Discharge: A release from correctional supervision; the term can refer to a release from parole supervision or from confinement.

Disciplinary Report: A formal, written report that documents a prisoner's infraction of an institutional regulation. This report is investigated. If found to have merit, the report is forwarded to a disciplinary committee for a formal hearing. The committee or disciplinary hearing officer may impose an appropriate sanction if the report is found credible.

Disciplinary Segregation: The inmate housing in a correctional institution that is used for punishment. Placement in this status is the result of a formal disciplinary hearing and is for a specific period of time. While in this special housing unit, an inmate receives minimal privileges.

Disturbance Control Team (DCT): A riot control team of highly trained staff members who are fully equipped to respond to institutional disturbances.

Due Process: A legal term that refers to an individual's constitutional right to certain procedures and processes. The Fifth and Fourteenth Amendments to the U.S. Constitution are those generally cited in support of a prisoner's due process rights.

Eighth Amendment: This constitutional amendment precludes excessive bail, excessive fines, and cruel and unusual punishment. The latter is often cited in correctional litigation.

Electrified Fences: Perimeter fences of a correctional institution that use electricity to deter inmates from escape. Some electrified fences may be set to stun while others may be set to electrocute inmates attempting to escape. These fences are used in lieu of perimeter towers with staff in them.

Emergency Plan: A written document that specifies how staff are to respond to emergencies in the institutional setting. Contingency planning is generally required for crises of all types, including riots, hostages, food or work boycotts, natural disasters, and external assaults on the correctional facility.

Equal Employment Opportunity (EEO): A management program designed to ensure that fair and unbiased treatment in work opportunities is extended to all employees regardless of their race, gender, age, or ethnicity.

Escape: An unauthorized departure of a lawfully confined individual from custody.

Excessive Force: A term used to describe force used above and beyond that which is necessary to control a situation.

Execution: The process of carrying out an order of the court. This term also refers to the implementation of the death penalty.

Executive Clemency: An official pardon by the governor of a state or the president of the United States.

Executive Management Team: The senior management staff of a correctional institution that is generally composed of the warden and associate wardens responsible for specific operational divisions of the facility.

Ex-Offender: An offender who is no longer under the jurisdiction of a criminal justice agency.

Federal Bureau of Prisons: A component of the U.S. Department of Justice, this federal agency is responsible for the confinement of those offenders sentenced for violation of federal laws and the operation of all federal correctional facilities across the United States.

Felony: A criminal offense that is punishable by the death penalty or confinement of a year or more in a state prison.

Fifth Amendment: An amendment to the U.S. Constitution that protects individuals from being deprived of life, liberty, or property without due process.

Fine: A financial penalty imposed by a court on a convicted individual.

First Amendment: An amendment to the U.S. Constitution that precludes certain restrictions on the press and an individual's right to free speech and freedom of religion.

Fourth Amendment: An amendment to the U.S. Constitution that protects an individual from unreasonable government search and seizure of person or property.

Furlough: An authorized release from prison or jail for a short duration. Furloughs can be escorted or unescorted. They may be approved for emergency, educational, social, or pre-release purposes.

Gang Locking System: Mechanical or electrical locking systems that enable a staff member to remotely open or close all of the cell doors, individually or collectively, on one range of cells.

Gang/Security Threat Group: A group of individuals who have a formal or informal organization intended for the purpose of criminal activity or other acts of intimidation and violence in support of their nefarious goals. The control of street or prison gangs is a critical element in the successful management of a correctional facility.

Gaol: Early form of a jail in England.

Gender Bias: Discrimination against an individual because of his or her gender.

General Equivalency Diploma (GED): A high school diploma earned by the successful completion of a battery of tests that demonstrate knowledge of reading, writing, and mathematical concepts.

Good Time: A statutory award that reduces the length of time an inmate must serve on a sentence of confinement. This incentive is given to prisoners if their behavior is meritorious.

Government by Proxy: A term that refers to the growing partnerships between government and private enterprise. Many public sector programs are operated in part, and some completely, by nonprofit and for-profit organizations.

Grievance: A formal grievance, in the labor–management context, is a dispute between an employee labor organization and the employer.

Habeas Corpus: A legal process that allows a prisoner to seek relief from a court for allegations of illegal conditions of confinement.

Habitual Offenders: Inmates sentenced to harsher sanctions because of their prior record. These repeat offenders are subject to greater penalties in many jurisdictions because of their repetitive involvement in specific crimes identified by state or federal legislation.

Halfway House: Community corrections facilities intended to permit prisoners to spend the last few months of confinement in a transitional program located near their home. This process is designed to allow an inmate to "decompress" from the rigid and controlled environment of a correctional facility yet have restrictions and supervision during this critical period of preparing for release.

Hands-Off Doctrine: The attitude of the courts prior to the 1960s in response to the filing of inmate litigation regarding the alleged conditions of confinement within correctional institutions. The prevailing philosophy was that the judicial system had neither the institutional management expertise nor the authority to define the constitutional rights of prisoners.

Hawes-Cooper Act: Federal legislation created in 1922 that was designed to restrict the transportation of prison-made goods from one state to another.

High-Mast Lighting: The lighting system for prisons and jails for the outside of buildings; these bright lights are generally elevated over 100 feet above the facility's compound and perimeter fence or wall.

Hooch: *See* Pruno.

Hostage Negotiation Team (HNT): Highly trained team of staff who are called upon to resolve hostage situations in the correctional environment.

House Arrest/Home Confinement: A sanction or status of confinement that restricts an individual to his or her home or residence; the individual may be permitted to depart the specified area for a specific purpose such as work. This status can be regulated by telephonic checks or by electronic monitoring.

Hulks: Abandoned ships used for the confinement of prisoners in England during the 1700s.

Imam: A religious leader in the Muslim religion.

Immediate Use of Force: The instant physical force applied by staff when a prisoner acts out with little or no advanced warning.

Incapacitation: A philosophy or goal of correctional confinement that seeks to prevent crime by placing the offender in a position where he or she cannot violate the law.

Incarceration: Confinement in a correctional facility.

Incentive Award: An honor presented to personnel to express appreciation for exceptional performance and to motivate the continuation of such behavior.

Incident Report: A written record of inmate misbehavior. When an inmate violates institutional rules, the behavior is documented with a formal write-up and referred for investigation and a formal disciplinary hearing.

Incompetent: A legal term used for individuals who are unable to comprehend the nature of judicial proceedings against them and who lack the capacity to assist an attorney with their defense.

Indeterminate Sentence: A judicial sanction for an unspecified amount of time (for example, a sentence to confinement for a period of 15 years to life, with the actual release date decided by a paroling authority).

Index Crimes: The Federal Bureau of Investigation's annual Uniform Crime Report that provides statistical measurement of specific criminal activity. The indexed crimes are limited to homicide and non-negligent manslaughter, rape, robbery, aggravated assault, burglary, larceny, car theft, and arson.

Informant: An individual who provides information against another person.

Informed Consent: The concurrence of a patient for medical or mental health care. All treatment, as well as the absence of treatment, offers the possibility of benefit and risk; patients must be given a full explanation of the ramifications of care and grant their approval.

Injunction: A judicial order that requires the defendants in litigation to cease an identified activity that is directly connected to the court case in question.

Inmate Code: A term used to describe the solidarity between confined prisoners. These unwritten rules reflect the values of inmates at a specific institution.

Inmate Disruptive Group (IDG): *See* Security Threat Groups.

Inmate Grievance System: The formal institutional inmate complaint system allowing a prisoner to file a written request for review and redress of a concern. Most such remedy systems have a two- or three-step system that permits grievances to be reviewed by the warden and appeals of this decision to a headquarters office.

Insane: A legal term defining an individual's mental state. Insanity generally is used to identify a person who does not have a firm grasp on reality and cannot be held responsible for his or her criminal activity at the time it took place.

In-Service Training: Agency training for employees that is intended to enhance staff knowledge, skill, and job performance.

Inside Cell: A physical design of a prison or jail housing unit in which cells are built back to back along a center plumbing chase of the cell house. Cells are not aligned on an outside wall of the building.

Institutional Culture: Organizational beliefs that establish shared values about staff, inmates, and interaction between the two groups within a prison or jail environment.

Intelligence: Pertinent information overtly and covertly gathered that provides the basis for inmate management decisions.

Intensive Confinement Center: *See* Boot Camps.

Intermediate Sanctions: An alternative punishment considered less severe than a sentence to prison or jail confinement but more severe than probation. Examples of intermediate sanctions are short-term placement in a halfway house or home confinement.

Intermittent Sentence: A sanction that is interrupted by intervals of liberty. An example of an intermittent sentence would be a sentence to weekend confinement in the local jail.

Interstate Compact: A legal contract between state jurisdictions and the federal government that enables each participating jurisdiction to transfer confined inmates or paroled inmates from one area to another. While the state with original custody maintains legal authority for custody, the state with the subject provides supervision.

Just Desserts: A phrase that refers to the philosophy of retribution as a goal for the criminal justice system. Offenders receive their proper punishment when they are given an appropriate sanction.

Justice Model: A philosophy for justice administration that reflects the intent to appropriately punish the transgressions of an offender. This model emphasizes the societal desire to punish one who has been found guilty.

Labor–Management Relations (LMR): The formal relationship between the organized labor force of an institution, if unionized, and management. If the line (nonsupervisory) staff have organized and formed a union, the process of collective bargaining is regulated by federal law, and formal rules of negotiation are required for specific work-related areas.

Law Enforcement Assistance Administration (LEAA): A federal agency established by the Omnibus Crime and Safe Streets Act of 1968. This agency provided funding to federal, state, and local authorities for technical assistance and the development of new programs in corrections. It also offered scholarships for students interested in the field of correctional administration. LEAA was dismantled by Congress in 1982.

Lease System: Often found in the South during the nineteenth century, this program allowed prison administrators to lease inmates to outside businesses or agricultural work.

Leg Irons: Metal restraints that connect and restrict an individual's ankles. These restraints are usually a chain similar to handcuffs.

Less Than Lethal Weapons: Weapons that are intended to assist staff in controlling prisoners who are violent or riotous. Examples of these items are batons, mace and other chemical aerosols, flash-bang stun grenades, and electrical stun devices. While any of these have the potential to be life threatening, if applied properly they do not inflict permanent injury.

Lex Talionis: A term that means an eye for an eye and refers to retribution for a crime that has been inflicted upon a victim. It limits the punishment to a sanction equal to the damage originally done.

Liberty Interest: A legal reference to an institutional process that affects a prisoner and is of such importance that it can potentially alter an individual's release date or freedom. If a staff decision (for example, the forfeiture of a parole date due to inmate misconduct) can impact an inmate's release, then the subject must be protected with specific procedural requirements (for example, written advance notice of a disciplinary hearing and the right of an inmate to call witnesses).

Line Staff: The nonsupervisory correctional personnel who directly provide supervision and support services for the inmate population.

Literacy Program: The educational program designed to teach remedial reading and writing skills to those who cannot meet basic testing standards.

Lockdown: The process of securing all prisoners in their cells for an extended period of time. An institution is generally locked down during emergencies and times of extreme inmate tension.

Lockstep: A term describing the controlled, single-file marching of prisoners in which prisoners are required to move in unison with one arm extended forward and resting on the shoulder of the next convict and talking is not permitted.

Lockup: A temporary holding facility used by police and sheriff departments to detain arrestees pending transfer to a more permanent facility (i.e., jail) or release.

Malingering: Faking symptoms of an illness.

Management by Walking Around: A philosophy and practice of organizational management that requires involvement by senior administrators in "walking and talking" daily throughout the correctional facility so that they know what is going on in the facility.

Mandatory Release: A form of prison or jail release after a prisoner has served two-thirds of his or her term. The prisoner completes the rest of the sentence under the supervision of a parole officer. Violations of regulations or new arrests can cause the status to be revoked and the individual returned to confinement to serve the remainder of the sentence.

Mandatory Sentences: A judicial sentence required by statute to specify the amount of time to be served. The intent of lawmakers in establishing such sentencing was to limit the court's discretion in sentencing; these statutes often do not allow probation or parole.

Manslaughter: A lesser degree of homicide. Voluntary manslaughter describes the killing of another intentionally but after being provoked. Involuntary manslaughter is used to describe an unintentional killing that is caused by inexcusable negligence.

Mash: *See* Pruno.

Medical Model: The philosophy of prison management associated with the goals of rehabilitation. This model presumes staff can identify the factors that led a prisoner to a life of crime and offer institutional programs to repair these personal deficiencies.

Mentoring: A formal or informal process of developing staff for future assignments and to help them adjust to new roles and responsibilities in the prison or jail environment.

Methadone: A synthetic prescription narcotic used to the detoxify individuals addicted to illegal substances.

Minnesota Multiphasic Personality Inventory (MMPI): A psychological diagnostic test.

Misconduct Codes: A list of disciplinary offenses that are subject to punishment in a prison or jail.

Misdemeanor: An offense considered less serious than a felony and punishable by sanctions up to the imposition of jail confinement for relatively minimal periods of time, usually less than one year.

Mobile Patrols: Armed institutional perimeter security vehicles.

Mule: One who carries narcotics or other contraband for another person or group.

National Institute of Corrections (NIC): A division of the Federal Bureau of Prisons that provides financial and technical assistance to local, state, and federal correctional agencies. NIC is responsible for the operation of the National Academy of Corrections.

Needs Assessment: An evaluation that ascertains the requirements of an individual or a group of individuals. In the context of inmate classification, a survey of an inmate's personal needs permits valid program planning for the individual.

NIMBY: An acronym that means "not in my backyard." This expression is often used to describe not wanting a new correctional facility built in one's own neighborhood.

Offender: An individual convicted of a criminal offense.

Organized Crime (OC): A term that is used to reference the traditional Italian mafia crime families. Organized crime can also refer to any sophisticated criminal activity of a gang involved in illegal acts.

Outside Cells: A physical design of prison or jail housing in which cells are placed along the inside of an external wall of a cell house building. These cells generally have barred windows or polycarbonate windows that are not breakable.

Overtime Pay: Premium salary paid for work beyond a normal 40-hour work week.

Paramilitary Organization: A term used to describe an organization or agency management style if it is hierarchical and similar to the military's. Most correctional agencies are organized in this manner.

Parole: A conditional release from confinement prior to the expiration of a sentence. The parolee must abide by specific rules or be returned to an institution to complete service of the sentence.

Parolee: An individual who has been conditionally released from a correctional institution and is subject to parole supervision.

Parole Guidelines: Scoring matrix that establishes general guidelines that determine when an offender is eligible for parole consideration. The points accumulated in scoring are generally related to the offense characteristics as well as the personal history of the applicant.

Participative Model: An organizational management structure that is democratic by nature. All personnel are expected to join in decision making. Individual participation is critically important to the process.

Penal System: A correctional system.

Penitence: Regret for one's misdeeds. Encouraging a prisoner to feel penitence or remorse, and to have a subsequent desire for reformation is an important goal of American correctional systems.

Penitentiary: A prison.

Pennsylvania System: An early approach or philosophy of confinement in the United States that was developed by the Quakers in Philadelphia, PA. This experiment established separate, isolated housing for each prisoner, required silence and penitence, and permitted each inmate to read only the Bible. When work was permitted, it was simply piecework accomplished in the prisoner's own cell.

Pepper Spray: A chemical agent used to control inmates who are acting out. Pepper spray (oleoresin capsicum) is a nonlethal gas.

Per Capita Cost: The cost per day of institutional operations. This cost can be expressed as a daily cost for specific items such as food, medical, or maintenance expenses or for the general cost of confinement for each prisoner.

Perimeter Security: The fence line or wall that surrounds a correctional facility. It is usually enhanced by razor wire, electronic detection systems, and armed staff.

Personal Recognizance: A court release, as if on bail, on an individual's personal promise to return to court at an appointed time. This status does not require a financial pledge to guarantee his or her presence.

Personality Disorder: A psychological diagnosis that describes an individual who has developed a pattern of behavior that greatly impairs his or her ability to relate to and care for others, functions poorly in society (as demonstrated by law violations), is impulsive, and is often aggressive toward others. The most common personality disorder in the criminal justice environment is the antisocial personality.

Plea: A defendant's formal response in court to criminal charges.

Podular Housing Units: Jail or prison housing units designed for direct supervision of prisoners. Staff are not isolated behind security glass or bars but supervise by moving among the inmates.

Postconviction Relief: A judicial determination supportive of a prisoner's petition for release or a reduction of sentence. Inmates may seek this court action in appeal of their conviction or sentence as well as challenge an action of the correctional agency and staff.

Premium Pay: A special salary bonus paid by some jurisdictions for work hours on the evening or early morning shifts, or for working a Sunday schedule. Overtime pay is also considered in this category.

Presentence Investigation: A report prepared by a probation or parole officer at the request of the court. This document provides a relatively brief summary of the crime and the personal history of the convicted offender. The document is intended to provide background for a judge after a defendant is found guilty and before the individual is sentenced. The report is often used by prison and jail authorities once the prisoner is incarcerated.

Preservice Training: Introductory training for new employees of a correctional agency intended to establish the agency philosophy of operation as well as teach staff specific techniques. Many correctional agencies have central training academies for the development of their new staff.

Pretrial Detainees: Individuals detained by court authority while waiting for trial or other court proceedings. These detainees are usually held in jail facilities and not mixed with sentenced offenders.

Prison Litigation Reform Act (PLRA): A 1995 federal law that, among other things, limits the ability of inmates to file lawsuits by requiring the payment of full filing fees. This legislation also requires inmates to exhaust all institution administrative remedies before filing.

Prisoner: An inmate in official custody of a prison or jail facility or under the direct supervision of a correctional or law enforcement official.

Prisoner Movement: A reform crusade that occurred during the 1960s within and outside U.S. correctional institutions. Many inmates and citizens within society pressed for more rights for the confined. As a result, there were many changes in routine institution operations and the overall philosophy of institutional management.

Prisoner Rights Groups: Citizens outside the correctional institutions who pressure prison and jail managers to liberalize rules and regulations within the facilities. These groups also support legal challenges that would increase recognition of the constitutional rights of those confined.

Prisonization: The process of acculturation in which a prisoner takes on the beliefs and customs of other inmates in the institution.

Privatization: The performance of government functions by private, for-profit firms. In corrections, there has been a growing trend to turn over specific responsibilities such as food service or medical service to the private sector, and entire facilities are now run by private correctional agencies.

Probation: A form of conditional freedom granted as a sanction by the court in lieu of a sentence to confinement. The convicted offender is supervised by a probation officer and is subject to specific restrictions; violating these rules can result in a probation violation and the invocation of a sentence of incarceration.

Probation Officer: An employee of a probation agency whose primary responsibility is the supervision of a caseload of probationers.

Pro Se: The legal process of acting as one's own attorney.

Prosecutor: An attorney in the employ of the government and assigned to initiate and pursue criminal proceedings against individuals charged with violations of criminal law.

Protective Custody (PC): An administrative detention status in a jail or prison that requires the separation of an inmate from the general population. PC status is assigned if an inmate is threatened by or scared of other prisoners.

Pruno: Homemade alcohol usually made by mixing fruit, yeast, sugar, and/or grains. The natural fermentation creates this intoxicating home brew.

Psychopath: A psychiatric term that refers to the psychopathic personality. Psychopaths are dangerous, emotionally unstable individuals with no moral sense of right and wrong.

Psychosis: A mental disorder in which the patient's thought process is extremely disordered.

Psychotropic Medication: Prescription medication for the mentally ill.

Public Defender: An attorney employed by a government agency who is responsible for the representation of criminal defendants who are unable to pay for private counsel.

Qualified Immunity: A legal term defining the exemption of government employees from lawsuit damages if the plaintiff cannot prove the employee intended to violate the plaintiff's constitutional rights. Wardens and senior administrators are often exempted from lawsuits based on their nonpersonal involvement in the alleged wrong being litigated.

Qur'An: Also know as the Koran, this is the religious text and holy book for those of the Muslim religion.

Rap Sheet: An individual's arrest record.

Rated Capacity: The number of inmates that the correctional institution is designed to accommodate. This capacity figure is based upon the staffing levels, square footage of the housing areas, and the size of the support and program space within the facility.

Reasonable Accommodation: A term that references the requirement of federal law for employers to make existing facilities accessible and usable by individuals with disabilities.

Reasonable Force: The amount of force deemed necessary to control an inmate in a specific situation.

Reasonable Suspicion: A set of circumstances or facts that establishes a reasonable person's belief that criminal activity may be taking place.

Receiving & Discharge (R&D): The section of a jail or prison that is responsible for the reception of new or transferred prisoners and the release of those offenders who have satisfied the legal obligation of their sentence to confinement.

Reception and Diagnostic Center: Correctional institutions that are operated by some agencies that serve as the intake facility for the assessment, classification, and orientation of new prisoners. The inmates are subsequently transferred to a prison or jail for which they are appropriately classified.

Recidivism: The repeating of criminal behavior that results in new arrests, convictions, or the return to confinement.

Recidivist: An offender who has repeated his or her pattern of criminal involvement.

Reformation: A philosophy of justice administration that believes an offender can be reformed by incarceration or other rehabilitation activities.

Reformatory: A correctional institution designed for younger, first-time offenders who are considered able to be rehabilitated and trained.

Rehabilitation: The process of restoring an offender to a legal and law-abiding lifestyle.

Reintegration: The transitional process of returning a prisoner to his or her home community, generally through a halfway house or other community program designed to support the individual during the transition from the structured life of confinement to the freedom of the community.

Release: The legal and authorized process of departure from confinement.

Religious Freedom Restoration Act (RFRA): A federal law that established certain minimum standards for the expression of one's religious beliefs. RFRA had a major impact on correctional institutions for a period of time, although it was subsequently ruled unconstitutional by the Supreme Court.

Residential Treatment Center: A halfway house or other community residential center designed to assist with the reintegration of a prisoner to society. It can also serve as an alternative sanction to prison and function as a halfway-in house.

Restitution: A judicial sanction that requires a convicted offender to pay the victim or the local community as recompense for the illegal act committed. This payment can be in the form of money or mandated time of service to others.

Restorative Justice: A new concept of defining the function and philosophy of the criminal justice system that focuses less on the offender and more on the victim. It concentrates on assisting those who have been seriously affected by crime.

Retribution: A correctional philosophy that emphasizes the punishment of someone convicted of a crime.

Revocation: The act of taking something previously given. In the prison setting, this usually refers to the cancellation of parole or mandatory release status.

Road Gangs: Prison or jail inmates assigned to work on outside crews that maintain roads, parks, or other government property. Some crews are made up of minimum security trustees, while others are made up of higher security prisoners supervised by armed correctional staff.

Road Prisons: Correctional institutions, generally located in the South, whose prisoners were generally used for agricultural work, road maintenance, and other assignments outside the prison grounds.

Sally Ports: Entrances to correctional institutions. Sally ports, both vehicular and pedestrian, have two gates that are never opened at the same time. This security feature prevents a prisoner from escaping through a gate when it is open.

Scalar Principle: A principle of management that describes the vertical organization of command within an organization. This principle describes the difference of responsibilities between various levels within a correctional organization (for example, the difference between serving as a lieutenant and as a correctional officer).

Seclusion: Separate administrative housing for inmates who are mentally ill. They are housed in this very controlled environment only if they have demonstrated an intent to harm or actually harmed themselves or others or if they are so mentally ill that they cannot function on their own.

Section 1983: A federal statute, *U.S. Code,* vol. 42, sec. 1983, that authorizes litigation in federal court for claims of violations of an individual's civil rights by state agents. This is the equivalent of lawsuits permitted against federal agents as authorized by the U.S. Supreme Court in *Bivens v. Six Unknown Narcotics Agents.*

Security Threat Groups: Prison or street gangs who have banded together in the correctional environment and represent a threat to the welfare, safety, and good order of the institution, staff, or inmates.

Segregation: Separate security cells in the special housing unit (SHU) that are intended as a sanction for the punishment of inmates who have been found guilty of violation of institution rules.

Self-Help Groups: Institutional groups for inmates that are intended as a positive activity. Staff members serve as sponsors for these groups. Examples include Toastmaster Clubs, Jaycees, cultural awareness groups, and current events discussion meetings.

Self-Mutilation: Injuries that are self-inflicted.

Self-Surrender: The status of a sentenced offender who has been granted permission of the court to turn him- or herself in to a designated correctional institution on a specific time and date for service of sentence.

Sentence: The sanction or punishment for a crime that has been imposed by a court.

Sentencing Disparity: The difference of sentences given by the courts for similar crimes. When judges are given a range of sentencing options, disparity will occur because different judges will have different sentencing philosophies.

Sentencing Guidelines: A set of guidelines that establish the sentencing options for a court. The matrix of guidelines establishes the range of options based on the characteristics of the offense and the personal history of the convicted offender.

Separate System: The philosophy of prison operation that developed in Pennsylvania at the Walnut Street Jail and Eastern Penitentiary. It required convicts to be housed apart from others in individual cells. They were forbidden to communicate with each other, occasionally were given piecework to perform in their cells, and were expected to reflect on their misdeeds (be penitent).

Shadow Board: A security device in a correctional institution designed to assist staff in the control and accountability of tools. This process requires that the outline of the tool is drawn on the board so the absence of a tool is readily noticed. Tools are checked out to only one person at a time, and this individual must hang a name tag (tool chit) on the board.

Shakedown: The search of an inmate or a place in a prison or jail. These searches are conducted frequently and spontaneously to assist in the control of contraband.

Shock Confinement: *See* Boot Camps.

Sick Call: An institutional process by which inmates who are ill visit the medical clinic to seek health care.

Silent System: A philosophy of prison management that required inmates to remain silent and not communicate with each other. This was intended to prevent prisoners from corrupting each other, punish them for their past misdeeds, and enhance staff control of the population.

Simsbury Mine: The earliest prison developed in the United States was located in the Simsbury Mine in Connecticut. It soon closed because the conditions were so wretched that there were several disturbances.

Snitch: *See* Informant.

Solitary Confinement: A disciplinary sanction used to control unruly prisoners. Few correctional institutions today have the facilities available to truly place an inmate in segregated housing by him- or herself.

Span of Control: The public administration concept that defines the effective limitation of how many staff can be directly supervised by one person.

Special Diets: Specific food requirements for medical or religious needs.

Special Masters: Representatives appointed by the court to oversee correctional institutions that are or have been involved in conditions of confinement litigation. These individuals gather information and monitor operations within the prison or jail.

Special Needs Offenders: Inmates with unusual requirements or unique disabilities. This term is often used to identify the special institutional support necessary for inmates with physical disabilities, those who are mentally or medically ill, and older inmates.

Special Operations Response Team (SORT): Emergency tactical team trained for highly volatile prison or jail crisis situations. These teams are well trained in tactics and weaponry, coordinate closely with hostage negotiation teams, and are called upon to resolve extremely difficult institutional situations.

Special Weapons Assault Team (SWAT): The tactical team used by community law enforcement for unusual crisis situations.

Strategic Planning: The process of preparing for the future by anticipating the issues and problems that will be faced several years in the future. Effective strategic planning is accomplished by involving staff in the planning process at all levels of the organization.

Strip Search: A full search of a prisoner or institution visitor that requires all clothing to be removed and all areas of the body searched.

Subpoena: A court order that mandates the appearance of an individual in a specific court at an appointed time. This document is used to ensure witnesses are in court for judicial proceedings.

Summary Judgment: A ruling by the court based on the presentation of facts without the need for a trial.

Ashurst-Sumners Act: A federal law that prohibits the interstate transportation of prison-made goods.

Superintendent: *See* Warden.

Therapeutic Community: A residential program (for example, drug treatment) designed around a treatment program geared to clients with similar problems. The process is intended to shape individual behavior to be socially acceptable. The communities are often very structured, with well-enforced rules, and many use self-governance.

Three Strikes Laws: These enhanced sentencing sanctions (often life sentences) have been enacted by legislators for offenders who have been convicted of felony criminal acts for the third time. These statutes are often used for those who have committed criminal acts.

Ticket of Leave: An early form of parole or conditional release.

Time Served: A court decision to sentence a convicted individual to the time already spent in confinement. The term also refers to the amount of time an inmate has been confined on his or her sentence.

Tort: A civil wrong; an injury or breach of duty to the person or property of another. Whereas crimes are offenses against society, torts are civil injuries to private persons and may be litigated in civil court proceedings.

Total Institutions: A term describing an institution in which large numbers of individuals live, work, and recreate together in a highly supervised and scheduled manner in a confined environment. This term refers to correctional facilities, mental institutions, military institutions, and many hospitals.

Totality of Conditions: The sum or aggregate of institutional conditions that, when considered as a whole, may violate the prohibition against "cruel and unusual" punishment as specified in the Eighth Amendment of the U.S. Constitution.

Transfer: The movement of a prisoner from one institution to another.

Transportation: A British criminal sanction in which offenders were punished by banishment from England to the New World. Once transportation to America was stopped, the destination was changed to Australia.

Trusty: A minimum security inmate who is assigned to work outside the secure perimeter of a correctional institution, or one who is given more responsibilities within the facility.

Turnkey: A work assignment that involves opening and closing a security gate within a correctional institution.

Unfair Labor Practice (ULP): An action, in the labor–management context, that is an alleged abridgement of either party's rights.

Uniform Crime Report: An indexed crime analysis statistical report published by the Federal Bureau of Investigation annually. The crimes that are compared and indexed each year are limited to homicide and non-negligent manslaughter, rape, robbery, aggravated assault, burglary, larceny, car theft, and arson.

Unit Management: A decentralized form of inmate management in which a team of staff from various disciplines are assigned to one housing unit to work exclusively with inmates. The staff offices are located in the unit, and this team is responsible for the case management and oversight of the unit's inmates.

Unity of Command: A principle of management that specifies that each employee of an organization should have only one supervisor.

Universal Precautions: Specific medical procedures for all staff to use when dealing with medical issues, including potential exposure to infectious diseases and bodily fluids.

Urinalysis (UA): A drug screening test that analyzes an individual's urine. This is one of several security procedures used to ensure institutions are as free of drugs as possible.

Value Engineering: A construction term for a cooperative effort among the owner, architects, and construction manager to use the most cost-effective methods in building a new facility.

Visiting Room: The area of a correctional facility designed for friends and family members to visit an inmate.

Voluntary Commitment: Noncompulsory institutionalization for treatment or care that does not require a court order and is the patient's choice.

Walnut Street Jail: A jail facility in Philadelphia, PA, that was modified to become one of the first prison facilities in the United States.

Warden: The chief executive officer of a correctional institution. This individual is responsible for all aspects of inmate and staff management: budget, security, support operations, programs, and personnel.

Warrant: A court order that directs law enforcement or correctional personnel to perform a specific task.

Wergild: The concept of paying compensation to the relatives of a victim of murder. This old practice was developed to prevent blood feuds between families.

Workhouse: England's penal institutions (gaols) that were used for lesser crimes.

Work Release: A correctional program that permits an inmate to leave a correctional facility to work in the community, but the prisoner must return to the prison or jail facility during nonwork hours. This transitional program can help prepare an inmate for his or her eventual release. Similar arrangements are used for school release.

Writ: A court order that specifies an activity that must be performed.

Yard: The recreation area of a prison or jail, usually a large space of several acres with ball fields and leisure-time equipment.

Zimmer Amendment: A federal law passed in 1996 that severely curtails the use of taxpayers' money to support certain types of prison recreation in the Federal Bureau of Prisons. This no-frills legislation prohibits the purchase and replacement of strength-enhancing weight equipment and electronic musical instruments. This legislation has had a very negative effect on institutional recreation programs.

Index

About the Contributors

Judy Anderson

Judy Anderson, MA, is Chief of Institutional Operations for the South Carolina Department of Juvenile Justice, and is responsible for secure institutions, classification, and disciplinary procedures. She formerly worked for the South Caroline Department of Corrections where she served in many capacities throughout her 27 yers, including warden of two institutions, deputy regional direction, and chaor if state classification. She was honored with the American Correctional Association's E.R. Cass Award in 1998, the North American Association of Wardens and Superintendents' Warden of the Year Award in 1990, the South Carolina Correctional Association Distinguished Service Award in 1987, and the South Carolina State Employees Association's Outstanding State Employee Award in 1986.

Ms. Anderson received her bachelors degree from the University of Southern Mississippi and her masters degree from the University of South Carolina. She has also completed the course work for a doctorate degree.

Ron Angelone

Ron Angelone is Director of the Virginia Department of Corrections. During his 30 year career, he has served as Warden in two states as well as Regional Director for the Texas Department of Corrections. In 1985, Mr. Angelone was appointed Assistant Director of the Nevada Department of Prisons. Then, in 1989, the Governor of Nevada appointed him Director. Virginia Governor George Allen appointed Mr. Angelone Director of the Department of Corrections in 1994. In 1998, while presiding over the largest growth of inmate population in the state's history, he was reappointed Director by Virginia Governor Jim Gilmore. Mr. Angelone is also Vice President of the Association of State Correctional Administrators, Chairman of the Adult Corrections Committee of the American Correctional Association (ACA) and an elected member of the ACA General Assembly.

Mr. Angelone received his bachelors degree in Human Relations from Roger Williams College in Bristol, Rhode Island and a masters degree from American International College in Springfield, Massachusetts.

Alan Appel

Alan Appel, M.Ed., is the Director of Inmate Services for the Philadelphia Prison System and is responsible for all programs and professional services for the five facilities that comprise the more than 5,000 inmate Philadelphia System. Mr. Appel began his career in corrections in 1970 as a social worker at the Philadelphia House of Correction. Having held many assignments during his 28 years of service, he was appointed to his current position in 1991.

483

Mr. Appel received his bachelors degree in Business and Law, his masters degree in Counseling Psychology and his post masters certificate in Social Service Administration from Temple University, Philadelphia, Pennsylvania.

John J. Armstrong

John Armstrong, M.S., is the Commissioner of the Connecticut Department of Correction and has served in this executive role since 1995. He has held positions of increasing responsibility in this state agency since 1977. Mr. Armstrong is an active member of the American Correctional Association and is a member of the Executive Committee of the Association of State Correctional Administrators. He teaches as a member of the adjunct faculty at Naugatuck Valley Community College, the University of New Haven, and the Central Connecticut State University.

Commissioner Armstrong has earned a bachelor of science degree and a masters of science degree in criminal justice from the University of New Haven, Connecticut.

James Austin

James Austin, Ph.D., is Executive Vice President for the National Council on Crime and Delinquency (NCCD). Prior to joining NCCD in 1974, Dr. Austin was a correction sociologist for the Illinois Department of Corrections where he was employed at the Stateville and Joliet Correctional Centers. Dr. Austin has directed numerous major projects for the U.S. Department of Justice and many state and local correctional agencies in the areas of jail crowding, prison classification, population projections, and alternatives to incarceration. He has served as an expert witness and/or consultant for a number of jurisdictions on a variety of issues. Dr. Austin has authored numerous publications and has co-authored three books—*The Children of Ishmael: Critical Perspectives on Juvenile Justice* (with Barry Krisberg) (1978); *Reinventing Juvenile Justice* (with Barry Krisberg) (1993); and *Its About Time: America's Imprisonment Binge* (with John Irwin) (1996). In 1991 he was awarded the Peter P. Lejins Research Award by the American Correctional Association.

Dr. Austin received his bachelors degree in sociology from Wheaton College, his masters degree in sociology from DePaul University in Chicago, and his doctorate, also in sociology, from the University of California, at Davis.

Herbert Bernsen

Herbert Bernsen, M.S.W., is the Assistant Director for the St. Louis County Department of Justice Services. He has been with this department of 26 years and has served in a variety of positions including probation/parole officer, intake manager and superintendent of the maximum and medium security jails. Mr. Bernsen is currently on the Board of Directors for the American Jail Associations, Dart (Drug, Alcohol Rehabilitation and Treatment), and Options for Justice which serves offenders with developmental disabilities.

Mr. Bernsen received his bachelor's degree from Cardinal Glennon College in St. Louis and his masters degree in social work from St. Louis University.

Jacob Bliek

Jacob Bliek is the Director of the Bureau of Operations for the Pennsylvania Department of Corrections. Mr. Bliek began his career as a civil engineer in 1984 and has worked in various capacities of engineering for the Pennsylvania Correctional Department until 1993. Since then, Mr. Bliek assumed the responsibility of managing several divisions which support over 40 correctional institutions and community corrections centers. These divisions include: maintenance, constructions, engineering, food services, and safety and environmental protection.

Mr. Bliek received his associate of science in structural engineering from Allegheny County Community College and his bachelors of science from the University of Pittsburgh.

Julie A. Carlson

Julie A. Carlson works in the marketing and advertising field and maintains an academic and research interest in the field of social policy and criminal justice. She has a bachelors degree in Sociology from Emory University, Atlanta, Georgia.

Peter M. Carlson

Peter M. Carlson, DPA, is Regional Director for the Western Region of the Federal Bureau of Prisons, U.S. Department of Justice, and is responsible for all federal prison operations in the ten states across the West. He has served in many positions throughout his thirty years with the Oregon State Penitentiary and the federal prison system, including service as Warden of three separate federal prisons. Dr. Carlson was honored with the Attorney General's Award for Exceptional Leadership in 1995 and the Presidential Distinguished Executive Management Award in 1996.

He received his bachelors degree from Willamette University, Salem, Oregon, and his masters and doctorate in public administration from the University of Southern California.

John Clark

John Clark, M.D., M.Ph., is the Chief Medical Officer for the Los Angeles County Sheriff' Department in Los Angeles, California, with responsibility for more than 500 medical staff members who provide basic medical care to more than 23,000 inmates in nine of the Los Angeles County correctional facilities. Dr. Clark was the sheriff's department's first medical director when he assumed the job in 1985.

Dr. Clark graduated from McHarry Medical College in 1971 and trained in obstetrics and gynecology at the University of Southern California Medical Center and Martin L. King General Hospital. He obtained his master's degree in public health from the University of California, Los Angeles.

Michael B. Cooksey

Michael B. Cooksey, M.A., is Assistant Director of Correctional Programs for the Federal Bureau of Prisons. He is responsible for psychology and chaplaincy services, unit and case management, custody, intelligence, witness security, emergency preparedness, drug abuse programs, sentence computations and mailroom operations. Mr. Cooksey began his career as Tennessee Probation Officer and has served 24 years with the federal prison system. He has served as warden at four federal prisons, including the United States Penitentiary, Marion, Illinois.

Mr. Cooksey received his bachelor's and masters degrees from Middle Tennessee State University.

Clair A. Cripe

Clair A. Cripe, LL.B., is the retired General Counsel of the Federal Bureau of Prisons. He worked as an attorney for the Bureau of Prisons from 1962-1990. During the last 15 of those years (1975-1990) he was the General Counsel. He is the author of the recent text, *Legal Aspects of Corrections Management,* published by Aspen Publishers in 1997. He has also written numerous articles and has lectured on corrections matters at universities and professional meetings.

Dr. Cripe received an A.B. from Oberlin College and an LL.B. (Later J.D.) from Harvard Law School.

Julius Debro

Julius Debro, D. Crim., is the Associate Dean of the Graduate School at the University of Washington. Dr. Debro began his career in probation with Alameda County in Oakland, California. After seven years, he joined the California Department of Corrections at San Quentin, California, where he worked as a counselor for two years. Dr. Debro joined the U.S. Probation Department in San Francisco on a special research project for four years prior to entering the University of California as a doctoral student. He has taught at the University of Maryland, and has chaired the Department of Criminal Justice, Sociology and Public Administration at Atlanta University, Atlanta, Georgia. He has conducted extensive research in the areas of corrections, juvenile delinquency, and police.

Dr. Debro received his bachelors degree from the University of San Francisco, his masters in sociology from San Jose State University, and his doctorate in criminology from the University of California at Berkley.

John J. DiIulio, Jr.

John J. DiIulio, Jr., Ph.D., is a Professor of Politics and Public Affairs at Princeton University. He is the co-author (with James Q. Wilson) of *American Government* (Houghton-Mifflin, 1998), *Improving Government Performance* (Brookings, 1993), and a dozen other books and selected volumes. He directed the Bureau of Justice Statistics project that resulted in Performance Measures in Criminal Justice (BJS, 1992). He is winner of the American Political Science Association's Leonard D. White award in public administration, and of the Association of Public Policy Analysis and Management's David N. Kershaw award for cumulative contributions to the field. He now directs several programs that study and assist faith-based programs for inner-city youths.

Tom Fewell

Tom Fewell, M.A. is the chaplain at the Allen Correctional Center in Kinder, Louisiana and is responsible for providing religious services to the inmates at this institution. Chaplain Fewell formerly worked for the Texas Department of Corrections at the Huntsville prison and for the Florida Department of Correction. Chaplain Fewell began his work in corrections in 1972 at the Federal Medical Center in Fort Worth, Texas as a volunteer. Prior to that he served as a Cap-

tain in the Marine Corps and completed a tour of duty in Vietnam.

Chaplain Fewell received his bachelors degree from Louisiana College and his masters degree from the Southwestern Seminary in Fort Worth, Texas. He has also completed course work towards for a doctorate degree at the New Orleans Baptist Theological Institute.

Mark S. Fleisher

Mark S. Fleisher, Ph.D., is an associate professor of criminal justice sciences at Illinois State University. He worked for the Federal Bureau of Prisons as Special Assistant to the Regional Director in the Western and North Central Regions. He has published numerous articles and book chapters on youth gangs and prison management and is the author of three books:

Warehousing Violence (Sage, 1989); the award-winning *Beggars and Thieves: Lives of Urban Street Criminals* (U Wisconsin Press, 1995); and *Dead Ends: Gang Girls and the Boys They Know* (U Wisconsin Press, 1998). He has conducted training sessions for the National Institute of Corrections and the Department of Justice's Corrections Program Office on the management of and programming for gang members. He is an evaluator on a national youth gang intervention project funded by the Office of Juvenile Justice and Delinquency Prevention, and is a member of the advisory board of the Gang Crime Prevention Center, Office of the Attorney General, State of Illinois.

Lorraine Fowler

Lorraine Fowler, Ph.D., is the Director of Resource and Information Management for South Carolina Department of Corrections. She has directed offender, budgeting and accounting, and human resources data processing and statistical operations for the South Carolina Department of Corrections for the past fifteen years. These operations include an extensive network encompassing over 33 institutions, over $300,000,000 in operating funds, variable capital funds, 3,000 internal users, and intensive quality-management, cost-based analyses of SCDC programs and services (in house and contracted). In January, 1990, she received the first Peter P. Lejins award ever given by the American Correctional Association for her "significant research and advisory contributions to the field of corrections" and "using her exceptional analytical and research skills to create progressive" corrections initiatives. Dr. Fowler is known for her "leading edge" achievements in classification and prediction, telecommunications and information systems, and cost-benefit/cost effectiveness analyses of public and private services. She is a longtime contributor to "Drugs and Crime," "Intermediate Sanctions," "Classification," "Sentencing Guidelines," information technology and fiscal accountability innovations via the National Institute of Justice, the National Institute of Corrections, the American Correctional Association, and as an expert witness for the U.S. Department of Justice.

Dr. Fowler earned her A.B.magna, from Radcliffe College, her graduate certificate in Business Administration from Harvard University; her M.S.W. (Madison) and Ph.D. (Milwaukee), from the University of Wisconsin.

Jeffery W. Frazier

Jeffery W. Frazier, CJM, has 18 years in corrections, both at the state and local levels, and is currently employed as the Superintendent of the Northern Neck Regional Jail, a 280-bed facility with 73 staff. He currently is serving as the vice-president/president elect of the Virginia Association of Regional Jails and is a member of numerous boards and committees throughout the State of Virginia. Mr. Frazier is the recipient of many awards, the last of which was from the United States Department of Justice for his assistance in solving several homicides in the Richmond, Virginia area. He served in the U.S. Army from 1978-1981 and has served for the past 10 years in the Virginia Air National Guard; he is a veteran of Desert Storm.

Mr. Frazier received his bachelors degree in Business Administration from Strayer College where he graduated cum laude. Mr. Frazier was one of the first in the nation to receive certification as a jail manager through the Jail Manager Certification Commission on November 14, 1997 and is the recipient of the 1998 American Jail Association "Correctional Administrator of the Year" Award. Mr. Frazier is certified as a General and Firearms Instructor through the Virginia Department of Criminal Justice Services and is a member of the International Who's Who of Professional Management, the Society for Human Resource Management, the American Jail Association, and the Veterans of Foreign Wars.

Judith Simon Garrett

Judith Simon Garrett, J.D., is the Executive Assistant to the Assistant Director for Information Policy and Public Affairs, at the Federal Bureau of Prisons. Ms. Garrett joined the Federal Bureau of Prisons' Office of General Counsel in 1991 as a Department of Justice Honors Attorney, after graduating from law school and completing a clerkship with the Honorable Thomas Penfield Jackson, Judge on the United States District Court for the District of Columbia. While in the Office of the General Counsel, Ms. Garrett worked in the Legislative and Correctional Issues Branch on a variety of issues including the cost of incarceration, the Religious Freedom Restoration Act, and implementation of the Violent Crime Control and Law Enforcement Act of 1994.

Ms. Garrett received her bachelors degree from the University of Wisconsin, Madison and her juris doctorate from Washington University, St. Louis Missouri.

Robert S. George

Robert S. George, FAIA, is an architect in private practice in San Bruno, California. He joined the Federal Bureau of Prisons in 1974 as a staff architect in the Office of Facilities Development and Operations In Washington, DC. He served as Regional Architect and as Regional Facilities Administrator in the Bureau's Western Regional Office from 1977 until 1984 when he returned to private practice. In 1988 he opened his own office where he continues his involvement in correctional architecture.

Mr. George received his bachelor of architecture degree from the University of California, Berkeley. He was elevated to the College of Fellows of the American Institute of Architects in 1988.

James A. Gondles, Jr.

James Gondles is the Director of the American Correctional Association. He has previously served as Sheriff of Arlington County, Virginia, and as a Deputy Sheriff in Arlington County.

He has served as President of the American Jail Association and as a member of the Delegate Assembly and Board of Directors of the American Correctional Association.

Mr. Gondles a graduate of Oklahoma City University where he received a bachelors degree in political science.

Angela Gover

Angela Gover is a Ph.D. student in the Department of Criminology and Criminal Justice at the University of Maryland. Her research interest areas include juvenile delinquency, correctional issues and family violence.

She earned her bachelors degree in criminal justice at New Mexico State University, and masters degree at the University of Maryland.

Marie L. Griffin

Marie L. Griffin, Ph.D., is an Assistant Professor of the Administration of Justice at Arizona State University West. A specialist in corrections, she recently concluded studies on professionalism among correctional officers, the impact of the conditions of confinement on recidivism among jail offenders, and the effect of organizational climate on the use of force by officers.

Dr. Griffin received her bachelors degree from Santa Clara University in Santa Clara, California, and her doctorate in justice studies from Arizona State University.

Kenneth C. Haas

Kenneth C. Haas, Ph.D., is a political scientist who is a Professor in the Department of Sociology and Criminal Justice at the University of Delaware. He has won the University's Excellence-in-Teaching Award three times. He specializes in constitutional law with an emphasis on corrections law and the law of capital punishment. His articles have been published in law reviews, social science journals, and scholarly books. He is co-editor of *Challenging Capital Punishment* (1988) and *The Dilemmas of Corrections* (1995).

John R. Hepburn

John R. Hepburn, Ph.D., is a Professor of Justice Studies at Arizona State University. He has conducted research on a variety of jail and prison issues over the past 30 years, including inmate grievance resolution procedures, prison management and control, the work environment of correctional officers, and the use of force by officers.

Dr. Hepburn received his bachelors degree from Butler University in Indianapolis, Indiana, his masters degree from the University of Kentucky, and his doctorate degree in sociology from the University of Iowa.

James A. Inciardi

James A. Inciardi, Ph.D., is Director of the Center for Drug and Alcohol Studies at the University of Delaware; Professor in the Department of Sociology and Criminal Justice at Delaware; Adjunct Professor in the Department of Epidemiology and Public Health at the University of Miami School of Medicine; a Distinguished Professor at the State University of Rio de Janeiro; and a Guest Professor in the Department of Psychiatry at the Federal University of Rio Grande do Sul in Porto Alegre, Brazil. Professor Inciardi has published 45 books and over 220 articles and chapters in the areas of substance abuse, criminology, criminal justice, history, folklore, public policy, AIDS, medicine, and law.

Dr. Inciardi earned his Ph.D. at New York University.

Gilbert L. Ingram

Gilbert L. Ingram, Ph.D., is a criminal justice consultant and adjunct faculty member on the Political Science and Criminal Justice Department at the University of South Alabama, Mobile, Alabama. He is also a licensed psychologist in the State of Georgia. Dr. Ingram retired after 35 years of federal service, including over 30 years with the Federal Bureau of Prisons. His experiences included serving as warden at 2 federal prisons, Assistant Director of Correctional Programs for the agency, and Regional Director in the Mid-Atlantic and Southeast Regions. He has received the Presidential Meritorious Service Award in 1990, the Attorney General's Dedicated Service Award in 1991, and the Department of Justice Distinguished Service Medal in 1995.

Dr. Ingram received his bachelors, masters and doctoral degrees in clinical and counseling psychology from the University of Maryland.

Michael H. Jaime

Michael H. Jaime, M.P.A., is the Chief of Labor Relations for the California Department of Corrections. He is responsible for the administration of the labor relations program in 33 institutions, 4 parole regions and various headquarters locations throughout the State of California. Mr. Jaime has served in California Civil Service for 28 years. Positions he has held include staff budget analyst in the California Department of Finance and labor relations experience in three

state departments. Mr. Jaime is a graduate of the California Department of Corrections Leadership Institute at California State University, Chico.

Mr. Jaime received his bachelors degree in social work and masters in public administration from the California State University, Sacramento.

H. David Jenkins

H. David Jenkins, Ph.D., is the Maryland Division of Correction's Educational Liaison for service provided by the Maryland State Department of Education, a position he has held since 1979 when educations programs were transferred from the Division of Correction to the Department of Education. He began his career in corrections in 1973 as a manager of a major department-wide research and planning project. He is a member of the Correctional Education Association, the American Correctional Association, the European Prison Education Association and the Maryland Association for Adult, Community and Continuing Education. He serves on the State Use Industries' Advisory Committee and the State Advisory Committee for Adult and Continuing Education.

Dr. Jenkins holds bachelors and masters degrees from Florida State University, a doctorate from the University of Maryland, and a certificate of advanced study in education from Johns Hopkins University.

Lavinia Johnson

Lavinia Johnson , CFP, is the Training Development Coordinator, Food Service Specialty for the Virginia Department of Corrections' Academy for Staff Development. Ms. Johnson is a former National President for the Academy of Correctional Food Service Administrators.

Sally C. Johnson

Sally Johnson, M.D., is a Captain in the United States Public Health Service and is assigned to the Federal Bureau of Prisons' Federal

Medical Center in Butner, North Carolina. She serves as Associate Warden for Health Services, providing administrative oversight to the medical and psychiatric programs. She is actively involved in forensic psychiatry, serving as an expert witness to the Federal courts and is director of an accredited forensic training program jointly sponsored by the Bureau of Prisons and Duke University.

Dr. Johnson received her undergraduate degree from Pennsylvania State University, her doctor of medicine from Jefferson Medical College in Philadelphia, Pennsylvania, and completed her psychiatry training at Duke University Medical Center. She is board certified in psychiatry and forensic psychiatry.

Harold L. Kahler

Harold L. Kahler began his career in corrections as an Education Specialist with the Virginia Department of Corrections. Mr. Kahler joined the Federal Bureau of Prisons in 1971. He has served in many positions with the federal system including a stint with the National Institute of Corrections (NIC) in which he served as Director of the Outreach Department of the NIC's Academy. Mr. Kahler retired from the Federal Bureau of Prisons in 1991. At the time of his retirement, he was an Assistant Director of the Bureau's Management and Specialty Training Center. Since his retirement, he has taught criminal justice courses at the Community College of Aurora (Colorado).

Mr. Kahler received his bachelors degree from Howard Payne University, Brownwood, Texas, and his masters in education from the University of Virginia.

J.C. Keeney

J.C. Keeney, M.A., is currently the Warden of Arizona State Prisons, Phoenix West, a private prison in Phoenix, Arizona. Mr. Keeney began his career in Oregon in 1960 as a recreation officer. Mr. Keeney retired as superintendent of the Oregon State Penitentiary in 1986. Mr.

Keeney spent 10 years in the Arizona Department of Corrections, 9 years of which were spent as Assistant Director of Adult Institutions. He has held his current position for one year.

Mr. Keeney received his bachelors degree in education from the College of Idaho and his masters in education from Western Oregon State College, Monmouth, Oregon.

Ken Kerle

Ken Kerle, Ph.D., is the Editor of *American Jails* magazine, a publication of the American Jail Association, and has served in this role since 1986. He has worked as a jail consultant over the years and is a specialist in detention operations. Dr. Kerle is the author of *American Jails: Looking To The Future,* a text published in 1998.

He has his Ph.D. and a masters degree from American University in Government and Political Science respectively, and a bachelors degree from Washburn University in Political Science.

Gothriel "Fred" LaFleur

Fred LaFleur, M.A., has served as Commissioner of Minnesota's Department of Corrections since 1976. Commissioner LaFleur has 21 years of state experience. Prior to his appointment, Commissioner LaFleur served as warden of the Minnesota Correctional Facility-Lino Lakes for 7 years. In 1971 Commissioner LaFleur became a planning specialist for the Governor's Commission on Crime Prevention and Control. He started with the Minnesota Department of Corrections in 1973 and has held a number of positions in the agency including correctional officer, halfway house director, community corrections subsidy director and warden.

Commissioner LaFleur is a graduate of Bethune-Cookman College in Florida and did his graduate work at Mankato State University and the University of Minnesota-Duluth.

Robert B. Levinson

Robert B. Levinson, Ph.D., began his career in corrections over 40 years ago as a psychology intern. In addition to changes in roles, responsibilities and recompense, Dr. Levinson has worked as a full-time employee or a consultant for municipal, county, state and federal agencies, and for both private profit and non-profit companies. His longest period of employment was with the Federal Bureau of Prisons, from which he retired as Deputy Assistant Director for Inmate Programs after 22 years of service. For the past 15 years, Dr. Levinson has been an independent consultant working with the American Correctional Association as its special projects manager. In addition to psychology and mental health issues, Dr. Levinson has focused on such corrections areas as: treatment for drug dependency, objective classification (both external and internal), and unit management. Recent government-funded projects which he has led or been involved as a researcher include: privatization, the use of technology in corrections, prison gangs, community based programs for juveniles, and under 18-year-old inmates in adult prisons.

Jim Lyons

Jim Lyons has been employed with the Minnesota Department of Corrections for nearly 20 years. He has worked in medium, close, and maximum custody facilities in a variety of positions. He has served as a behavior analyst, case manager, due process supervisor, and corrections programs director. Jim is curently the assistant to the warden at the medium cusody facility in Faribault, Minnesota.

Jim is a graduate of St. Cloud University.

Doris MacKenzie

Doris MacKenzie, Ph.D., is a professor in the Department of Criminology and Criminal Justice at the University of Maryland. Prior to this position, she was on the faculty of the Louisiana State University where she was honored as a "Researcher of Distinction," and was awarded a Visiting Scientist position at the National Institute of Justice. As a Visiting Scientist, she provided expertise to federal, state, and local jurisdictions on shock incarceration, correctional policy, intermediate sanctions, research methodology, experimental design, statistical analyses, and evaluation techniques. As an expert in criminal justice, Dr. MacKenzie has consulted with State and local jurisdictions and has testified before U.S. Senate and House Committees. Her research has focused on such topics as examining inmate adjustment to prison, the impact of intermediate sanctions on recidivism, methods of predicting prison populations and studies of boot camps in prisons. She has directed nine research projects and is currently Director of National Institute of Justice sponsored grants to study probationer compliance with conditions of supervision and substance abuse treatment using cognitive behavior therapy.

Dr. MacKenzie earned her doctorate from Pennsylvania State University.

Jess Maghan

Jess Maghan, Ph.D., is Director of the Center for Research in Law and Justice and Associate Professor of Criminal Justice at the University of Illinois at Chicago. He has served as an executive in corrections and in law enforcement at the municipal, state, and national levels including: Commissioner for Training, New York City Department of Corrections; Director of Training of the New York City Police Department; Administrator of Correctional Law Programs of the American Correctional Association; Superintendent of the Illinois Correction Academy; and Director of Training for the Louisiana Department of Corrections. Dr. Maghan is a recipient of the Illinois Academy of Criminology - Hans W. Mattick Award for Outstanding Contributions in Criminal Justice Research.

Dr. Maghan received his doctoral degree in criminal justice from The Graduate Center—City University of New York.

Paul McAlister

Paul McAlister, D.Min., is a Professor of Theology, Missions, and Social Ethics at the Minnesota Bible College in Rochester, Minnesota, and has served in this teaching role for twenty-six years. He has been actively involved in community work with the Mayo Clinic and the Federal Bureau of Prisons for many years. He is currently serving on a contract basis in the area of restorative justice planning with the Minnesota Department of Corrections.

Dr. McAlister received his Masters of Divinity from Lincoln Christian Seminary, Lincoln, Illinois, and his Doctorate of Ministry from Bethel Theological Seminary, St. Paul, Minnesota.

Duane C. McBride

Duane C. McBride, Ph.D., is a sociologist and currently serves as Professor and Chair of the Behavioral Sciences Department at Andrews University, Administrative Director of the Institute for the Prevention of Addictions at Andrews and an Adjunct Professor in the Department of Epidemiology and Public Health at the University of Miami School of Medicine.

He has been involved in substance abuse research for over twenty years and has published over 60 articles, monographs, and books in the areas of substance use, treatment program evaluation and AIDS risk behaviors. Dr. McBride also chairs a grant review committee for the National Institute on Drug Abuse (NIDA) and is a frequent special reviewer for NIDA and other federal institutes. Currently he is the Co-Principle Investigator for the Center for Health Services Research at the School of Medicine University of Miami.

Dr. McBride earned a Ph.D. in sociology (deviant behavior) at the University of Kentucky.

Douglas C. McDonald

Douglas C. McDonald, Ph.D., is a Senior Associate at ABT Associates Inc., a policy research organization headquartered in Cambridge, MA. He has directed research projects on a variety of criminal justice topics and has published widely. His professional interests include research on correctional privatization, public finance of corrections, correctional health care, criminal sentencing policies and practices, and substance abuse treatment—especially in prisons and jails. Before coming to ABT Associates in 1981, Dr. McDonald conducted research on sentencing reforms at the Vera Institute of Justice in New York City.

Dr. McDonald received his Ph.D. in sociology from Columbia University, and his bachelors degree from Columbia College.

James A. Meko

James A. Meko, M.A., is an Instructor in Criminal Justice at Gannon University, Erie, Pennsylvania. He served in Viet Nam as a Captain in the U. S. Army and was awarded the Bronze Star in 1971. He retired from the Federal Bureau of Prisons in 1996, after 25 years service. He was Executive Assistant to the Director, Senior Deputy Assistant Director, Chief of Staff Training as well as warden at two federal facilities. In 1996 he received the Bureau's Meritorious Service Medal.

Mr. Meko received his bachelors degree from Gannon University and his masters degree from the University of Notre Dame.

Andora Moss

Andora (Andie) Moss, M.S.Ed., is a Corrections Program Specialist with the National Institute of Corrections, a part of the U.S. Department of Justice, Federal Bureau of Prisons. She has been responsible for the development of technical assistance and training in the areas of staff-offender relations and has worked extensively with correctional agencies in the areas of staff sexual misconduct and institutional culture. Ms. Moss has also served as Chairperson of the Interdivisional Initiative on Women Offenders, Project Manager for the Executive Women's Training Program, and has been responsible for the technical assistance activities provided by the Prisons Division of the Institute. Before joining the Institute, Ms. Moss was the Assistant

Deputy Commissioner of Operations for the Georgia Department of Corrections.

Richard S. Peterson

Richard S. Peterson, M.S.W., is a retired Assistant Director for Adult Correctional Institutions for the State of Oregon. He continues to consult in matters relating to juvenile and adult corrections, both locally and in other states. His professional experience included assignments as State Director of Juvenile Parole, Superintendent of State and Juvenile Institutions, and Superintendent of the Oregon State Correctional Institution. Mr. Peterson has carried out assignments as Director of Juvenile Corrections, State of Oregon, and Interim Director for Adult Corrections, State of Oregon. Mr. Peterson is past president of Oregon Corrections Association. He has been an auditor/consultant for the Commission on Accreditation in Corrections, having consulted in several western states and for the Federal Bureau of Prisons.

Mr. Peterson received his bachelors degree from Lewis and Clark College in Portland, Oregon, and a masters degree in social work from Portland State College.

Beverly Pierce

Beverly Pierce is Associate Warden at the Federal Correctional Institution, Terminal Island, California. She has served in many financial management positions throughout her eighteen years with the federal prison system, including service as controller at two institutions and Western Regional Comptroller.

J. Michael Quinlan

J. Michael Quinlan, J.D., is a 28-year veteran of the corrections field and a former Director of the Federal Bureau of Prisons (1987-1992). Involved in the private corrections industry for the last six years, Mr. Quinlan spent 22 years with the Federal Bureau of Prisons, where in addition to heading the agency as Director, he held posi-

tions as a prison camp superintendent, facility warden and deputy director.

Mr. Quinlan received a masters of law degree from George Washington University, a juris doctorate from Fordham University, and a bachelors degree in history from Fairfield University.

Richard H. Rison

Richard H. Rison, D.P.A., is a retired federal prison warden. Dr. Rison served as warden of five federal prisons in his 35 years in the correctional field. Two of the correctional facilities were major federal medical centers for both male and female inmates. Currently Dr. Rison is serving the private sector in the design and activation of Alternative Opportunity Educational Programs for "at-risk" public school students.

Dr. Rison received his bachelors degree in social work from California State University, Long Beach, a masters degree in public administration from the University of Southern California, a masters degree in Education from Bowling Green University, and a doctorate in public administration from the University of Southern California.

James E. Rivers

James E. Rivers, Ph.D., is Deputy Director of the Comprehensive Drug Research Center at the University of Miami School of Medicine and a Research Associate Professor in both the Department of Sociology and the Department of Epidemiology and Public Health at Miami. Dr. Rivers has research, teaching and administrative policy experience in a broad range of substance abuse areas, including multiagency management information systems and performance evaluation, communitywide prevention and treatment needs assessment, and evaluation studies in the areas of drug abuse treatment and HIV/AIDS prevention/intervention. In recent years he has been Director of the Metropolitan Dade County (Florida) Office of Substance Abuse Control ("drug czar") and Loaned Executive to the Law Enforcement, Courts and Corrections Task

Force of the Miami Coalition for a Safe and Drug Free Community.

Dr. Rivers earned his Ph.D. in sociology at the University of Kentucky.

Thomas P. Roth

Thomas P. Roth, is the warden for the Illinois Department of Corrections, at the Dixon Correctional Center, the largest medium security prison in Illinois. As warden, Mr. Roth oversees a 2,200 bed multidisciplined facility that includes general population male inmates, general population female inmates, developmentally disabled/mentally handicapped male inmates, and severely mentally disabled male inmates. He has served in many positions throughout his nineteen years with the Illinois Department of Corrections including service as warden at three different institutions. Mr. Roth has served as a certified auditor from the American Correctional Association (ACA) since 1980, and has also served as a committee member for the ACA Adult Correctional Institutions Committee.

Mr. Roth received a bachelors degree in sociology from Millikin University and a masters of criminal justice administration from Michigan State University.

Thomas V. Schade

Thomas V. Schade, Ph.D., is the Associate Professor in the College of Public Programs at Arizona State University and a member of the faculty in the School of Justice Studies. His most recent research has focused on the use of force by police and suspects, culminating in a six-city study funded by the National Institute of Justice. Professor Schade has been a consultant to the Arizona Department of Corrections, the Maricopa County Juvenile Court and numerous other law enforcement agencies.

Dr. Schade received his bachelors degree from Hope College in Holland, Michigan and his masters and doctoral degrees in sociology from Western Michigan University in Kalamazoo, Michigan.

Steve Schwalb

Steve Schwalb is Assistant Director, Industries, Education and Vocational Training for the Federal Bureau of Prisons. He also serves as the Chief Operating Officer of Federal Prison Industries, a government owned corporation within the Bureau of Prisons which employs inmates providing goods and services to federal government agencies. Mr. Schwalb began his career in 1973 and has served in a variety of positions, including Warden of a federal prison and Director of the King County Department of Adult Detention in Seattle.

Mr. Schwalb received his bachelors degree in Personnel Management and Labor Relations from the University of Washington.

David Schwartz

David Schwartz, D.Min., has been Religious Services Administrator for the Ohio Department of Rehabilitation and Correction since 1984. Dr. Schwartz began his career in corrections as chaplain at the Lebanon Correctional Institution in 1975. He was certified as a supervisor with the Association for Clinical Pastoral Education (ACPE) in 1974 and established an ACPE Center at Lebanon Correctional Institution during his ministry.

Dr. Schwartz received his bachelors degree from Eastern Baptist College, masters of divinity from Moravian Theological Seminary, and doctorate of ministry from Andover Newton Theological School. He has also done clinical pastoral education programs at Westboro State Hospital, Boston City Hospital, Zion's Reformed Church, Grafton State Hospital, Bethesda North Hospital, and Children's Hospital. He has been ordained since 1973.

James F. Short, Jr.

James F. Short, Jr., Ph.D., is Professor Emeritus of Sociology at Washington State University. His latest book is *Poverty, Ethnicity, and*

Violent Crime (Westview, 1997). A former Editor of the *American Sociological Review,* and Associate Editor of the *Annual Review of Sociology,* he has served as President of the Pacific and American Sociological Associations and the American Society of Criminology. He is a Fellow of the American Society of Criminology's Edwin H. Sutherland Award.

Sam S. Souryal

Sam S. Souryal, Ph.D., is a Professor of Criminal Justice Ethics at the Criminal Justice Center–Sam Houston State University, in Huntsville, Texas. As a former police officer and manager, he taught police and management courses and published *Police Administration and Management* (West 1977) and *Police Organization and Administration* (1995). He later developed a special interest in management ethics, particularly in correctional settings. In 1992, Professor Souryal published *Ethics in Criminal Justice: In Search of the Truth* (Anderson). In recent years he has been a regular presenter on correctional ethics at meetings of the American Correctional Association (ACA) and a lecturer on ethics in probation and parole. Most recently, Dr. Souryal has been featured in ACA's video-based training course, "ethics in corrections." Dr. Souryal has traveled extensively in both the middle east and the far east, most recently as a guest lecturer in Beijing, the People's Republic of China.

Dr. Souryal earned a bachelors degree in education from The American University in Cairo, Egypt, a masters in public administration from the University of New York, Albany, and a doctorate in political science from the University of Utah.

Richard L. Stalder

Richard L. Stalder, M.A., was appointed Secretary of the Louisiana Department of Public Safety and Corrections in January 1992, by former Governor Edwin W. Edwards. Secretary Stalder was reappointed to the position in April 1996 by Governor M.J. "Mike" Foster, Jr. Secretary Stalder began his career with the Department of Public Safety and Corrections in 1971 as a correctional officer and has served as superintendent and warden of major juvenile and adult facilities, and well as holding other management roles. As Secretary, Mr. Stalder has led all components of the department achieve accreditation by the American Correctional Association (11 adult facilities, 4 juvenile facilities, and the Adult and Juvenile Divisions of Probation and Prole). Additionally, he has forged a productive partnership between state and local criminal justice systems that has resulted in the development of uniform "basic jail guidelines" under which 95 local facilities are now certified. Secretary Stalder is an active member of many professional organizations including the Association of State Correctional Administrators and the American Correctional Association (ACA). 1994, he was elected to a 6-year term on the Commission on Accreditation for Corrections. In 1996, he was selected by the membership of ACA to serve as president-elect. He also participated in ACA through active membership on the Standards Committee, and the Constitution and By-Law Committee.

Secretary Stalder received bachelors and masters degrees from Louisiana State University.

Louis Stender

Louis Stender has worked for the Minnesota Department of Corrections for nearly 24 years. He began his career in 1974 as a corrections officer at Stillwater Prison. He has a wide range of corrections experience, having worked all custody levels at five different locations. In 1982, Mr. Stender helped open the state's maximum security prison in Oak Park Heights. For the past 9 years he has worked at the Faribault Corrections Facility where he now serves as warden. He co-chairs the Department of Corrections' committees on institution programs and inmate community transition issues. He is actively involved in community diversity issues and partnership collaborations.

Mr. Stender is a graduate of Augsburg College in Minneapolis, Minnesota.

Ernest A. Stepp

Ernest A. (Tony) Stepp is the warden of the administrative component of the Federal Correctional Complex in Coleman, Florida. Mr. Stepp began his career in corrections as a correctional officer at the United States Penitentiary in Terre Haute, Indiana, in 1978. Throughout his career he has held positions of increasing responsibility including Correctional Services Administrator for the Bureau of Prisons' Western Region and Chief of the Emergency Preparedness Branch in the Bureau's Central Office. Mr. Stepp was the on-site commander for the Bureau of Prisons' response forces to the civil riots in Los Angeles in 1992.

Mr. Stepp received his bachelors degree in criminal justice from Indiana State University.

Ronlad J. Stupak

Ronald J. Stupak, Ph.D., Executive Vice President and Principal of EMCO, L.L.C., was the Dean of the Center for Effective Organizational Leadership and Distinguished Faculty Research Scholar of Management at Mount Vernon College. Prior to that, he was tenured professor of organizational behavior in the School of Public Administration, University of Southern California, an executive, a line manager, and a public servant. As a federal executive, earlier in his career, he helped to establish The Federal Executive Institute. Dr. Stupak is a prolific author, having published more than 175 books and articles. His areas of expertise include national security policy, organizational development, leadership analysis, executive coaching, strategic management, and the courts. Dr. Stupak received the Outstanding Teaching Award at the University of Southern California; in 1994, he served as Distinguished Scholar-in-Residence for the National Center for State Courts; in 1996, he received the Warren Burger Award, and in

1997 he was made a charter member of the Warren Burger Society.

Dr. Stupak received his bachelor's degree (Summa Cum Laude) from Moravian College and his M.A. and Ph.D. from The Ohio State University.

Gaylene J. Styve

Gaylene J. Styve is a Ph.D. student in the Department of Criminology and Criminal Justice at the University of Maryland. Her research interest areas include juvenile delinquency, juvenile corrections and treatment, and psychological correlates of crime.

Ms. Styve earned her bachelors degree in psychology at the University of Manitoba, Canada, and masters degree at the University of Maryland.

Anthony P. Travisono

Anthony Travisono, M.S.W., is a faculty member of the Graduate Extension Education Program at Salve Regina University in Newport, Rhode Island. From 1974 to 1991, Mr. Travisono served as executive director of the American Correctional Association (ACA), and now serves as executive director emeritus of the ACA. Throughout his correctional career spanning more than 50 years he served the State of Rhode Island as Superintendent of the Training School, Director of Social Welfare, Mental Health, Retardation and Hospitals and later as Director of Corrections. He has participated in innovative correctional practices in both adult and juvenile programs. His career has taken him though all phases of practice in jails, probation, parole, halfway houses, foster care, training schools, and adult correctional institutions. In 1983, Mr. Travisono was editor-in-chief of *The American Prison from the Beginning,* and in 1995 he and Mary Q. Hawkes co-authored *Building a Voice: The American Correctional Association, 125 Years of History.* Mr. Travisono serves on the board of trustees of Correctional Properties Trust and is on the Advisory Commission for the Rhode Island Department of Corrections Women's program, the Rhode Island Salvation Army Adult Rehabilitation Center advisory board, the board of directors for Women in Transition, and the board of directors for New Time (a men's community corrections program).

Mr. Travisono earned a bachelors degree from Brown University and a Masters in Social Work from Boston University. In 1991 he was awarded the Boston University Alumni Association Award for outstanding contributions to social work.

Tessa Unwin

Tessa Unwin is the Public Affairs Liaison for the Ohio State Department of Rehabilitation and Correction. She has served in the public information department for 16 years. Previously, Ms. Unwin worked as a producer in public radio.

Ms. Unwin received her bachelors degree in journalism from the Ohio State University.

Ashbel T. (A.T.) Wall, II

Ashbel T. (A.T.) Wall, II, J.D., is Assistant Director of Administration for the Rhode Island Department of Corrections. In this capacity he is responsible for the central management of departmental operations. His career began in 1976 as a probation officer. He has served in the capacity of Assistant Director since 1987.

Mr. Wall received a bachelors degree from Yale University in 1975 and a juris doctorate from Yale Law School in 1980.

Arthur Wallenstein

Arthur Wallenstein, M.A., is the Director of Adult Detention for King County, Seattle, Washington and is responsible for overall institutional operations for this large county jail system. Prior to this assignment he served as War-

den and Director of Adult Corrections in Bucks County, Pennsylvania. He has also served as Assistant Warden at Stateville Correctional Center in Joliet, Illinois. He is an adjunct instructor in the Society and Justice Program at the University of Washington.

Mr. Wallenstein has a bachelors of science degree from Georgetown University and a masters degree from the University of Pennsylvania. He was awarded the American Jail Association Manager of the Year citation and was appointed by United States Attorney General Janet Reno as a member of the Advisory Board of the National Institute of Corrections in 1994.

David A. Ward

David A. Ward, Ph.D., is Professor of Sociology at the University of Minnesota, Minneapolis. He is the principal investigator of a study on the effects of long-term confinement in the nations first super-maximum custody penitentiary, Alcatraz. He served as a consultant to the Committee on the Judiciary, U.S. House of Representatives, on Alcatraz, and the federal prison at Marion, Illinois. Books on each of these special federal penitentiaries will be published by the University of California Press.

Professor Ward received his bachelors' degree in economics from Colby College and his Ph.D. in sociology from the University of Illinois. He has been a Fellow in Law and Sociology at Harvard Law School and a Fulbright Scholar.

Reginald A. Wilkinson

Reginald A. Wilkinson, M.A., has served as Director of the Ohio Department of Rehabilitation and Correction since 1991, and President of the American Correctional Association (ACA) from 1995 to 1998. His list of "firsts" include serving as the first superintendent of Ohio's Corrections Training Academy, the first warden at the Dayton Correctional institution, and the first regional director of the prisons in the southern half of the state. In addition to ACA, he is active in many state and national professional organizations. Mr. Wilkinson has served on the faculties at Wilmington College and the University of Cincinnati.

Mr. Wilkinson holds bachelors and masters degrees from The Ohio State University.

Robert L. Wright

Robert L. Wright, M.A., served 35 years in corrections. His 27 year career in Oregon started in 1963 at the Oregon State Penitentiary where he held progressively responsible positions as psychological assistant, counselor, personnel manager, and executive assistant to the warden. From 1969-1972 her served as executive assistant to the corrections administrator. He was assistant superintendent at the Oregon State Correctional Institution from 1972-1983, and superintendent of the Eastern Oregon Correctional Institution from 1984-1990. From 1992-1998, Mr. Wright was the superintendent of the Clallam Bay Corrections Center in Washington State.

Mr. Wright is past president of the Central States Deputy Wardens' Association (1979) and the Auditor for the Commission on Accreditations for Corrections and American Correctional Association. He received his bachelors and masters degrees from Oregon State University.